Personal Insurance

Underwriting and Marketing Practices

Cheryl L. Ferguson, CPCU, AU, AAI
Director of Curriculum
American Institute for CPCU/Insurance Institute of America

First Edition • Seventh Printing

American Institute for Chartered Property Casualty
Underwriters/Insurance Institute of America
720 Providence Road, Suite 100
Malvern, Pennsylvania 19355-3433

Foreword

The American Institute for Chartered Property Casualty Underwriters and the Insurance Institute of America (the Institutes) are not-for-profit organizations committed to meeting the evolving educational needs of the risk management and insurance community. The Institutes strive to provide current, relevant educational programs in formats that meet the needs of risk management and insurance professionals and the organizations that employ them.

The American Institute for CPCU (AICPCU) was founded in 1942 through a collaborative effort between industry professionals and academics, led by faculty members at The Wharton School of the University of Pennsylvania. In 1953, AICPCU coordinated operations with the Insurance Institute of America (IIA), which was founded in 1909 and remains the oldest continuously functioning national organization offering educational programs for the property-casualty insurance sector.

The Insurance Research Council (IRC), founded in 1977, is a division of AICPCU supported by industry members. This not-for-profit research organization examines public policy issues of interest to property-casualty insurers, insurance customers, and the general public. IRC research reports are distributed widely to insurance-related organizations, public policy authorities, and the media.

The Institutes' customer- and solution-focused business model allows us to better serve the risk management and insurance communities. Customer-centricity defines our business philosophy and shapes our priorities. The Institutes' innovation arises from our commitment to finding solutions that meet customer needs and deliver results. Our business process is shaped by our commitment to efficiency, strategy, and responsible asset management.

The Institutes believe that professionalism is grounded in education, experience, and ethical behavior. The Chartered Property Casualty Underwriter (CPCU) professional designation offered by the Institutes is designed to provide a broad understanding of the property-casualty insurance industry. Depending on professional needs, CPCU students may select either a commercial or a personal risk management and insurance focus. The CPCU designation is conferred annually by the AICPCU Board of Trustees.

In addition, the Institutes offer designations and certificate programs in a variety of disciplines, including the following:

- Claims
- Commercial underwriting
- Fidelity and surety bonding
- General insurance
- Insurance accounting and finance
- Insurance information technology
- Insurance production and agency management
- Insurance regulation and compliance

- Management
- Marine insurance
- Personal insurance
- Premium auditing
- Quality insurance services
- Reinsurance
- Risk management
- Surplus lines

You can complete a program leading to a designation, take a single course to fill a knowledge gap, or take multiple courses and programs throughout your career. The practical and technical knowledge gained from Institute courses enhances your qualifications and contributes to your professional growth. Most Institute courses carry college credit recommendations from the American Council on Education. A variety of courses qualify for credits toward certain associate, bachelor's, and master's degrees at several prestigious colleges and universities.

Our Knowledge Resources Department, in conjunction with industry experts and members of the academic community, develops our trusted course and program content, including Institute study materials. These materials provide practical career and performance-enhancing knowledge and skills.

We welcome comments from our students and course leaders. Your feedback helps us continue to improve the quality of our study materials.

Peter L. Miller, CPCU
President and CEO
American Institute for CPCU
Insurance Institute of America

Preface

Personal Insurance: Underwriting and Marketing Practices is a text developed for the Insurance Institute of America's API 28 course of the same name. It is the third of four courses leading to the Associate in Personal Insurance (API) designation awarded by the Institute. The other required texts and courses for the API designation are *Property and Liability Insurance Principles* (the text for INS 21), *Personal Insurance* (INS 22), and *Personal Insurance: Services, Management, and Issues* (API 29).

INS 21 creates a foundation for understanding the property and liability insurance business. INS 22 specifically addresses the contents of personal insurance products. API 28 builds on the knowledge base put in place by these courses in general insurance by providing a practical, hands-on approach to the application of personal risk management and personal insurance coverages in the working environment. Although tailored to the needs of the API program, this text should also prove useful to persons who perform or are responsible for (1) underwriting, (2) production as an agent or broker, (3) customer service, or (4) the management of these functions.

The personal insurance customer is the focal point of this text. The needs and exposures of the customer drive the marketing, underwriting, and coverage selection process. This book first strives to present an overview of the customers' relationship to the insurance industry. Second, this text presents the technical aspects of the personal insurance coverages and policies, and the ways in which they are applied to the personal insurance customers' coverage needs. It addresses in detail the underwriting concerns regarding customers' exposures and related hazards. This book is designed to enhance a personal underwriter's risk selection and decision-making techniques.

Tasks performed within the personal insurance industry are less distinct than they were twenty years ago. The function of underwriting might be performed, at least in part, by a producer at the point of sale. An individual in a company underwriting department might perform marketing tasks in the research and development of new insurance products. This text recognizes that the tasks addressed might be performed in various departments and by personal insurance professionals with many different job titles. A fuller understanding of all of the facets of risk selection, marketing, and customer-service-related tasks enables any individual working within the personal insurance field to better appreciate the activities of and the decisions made by other personal insurance professionals.

Personal Insurance: Underwriting and Marketing Practices includes the work of many reviewers who gave generously of their time and took an active role in reviewing manuscripts. I am deeply indebted to their commitment in assisting with this project. Joseph F. Mangan, CPCU, reviewed the entire manuscript. His help has been invaluable in ensuring the accuracy and completeness of the text.

Many additional individuals reviewed portions of the manuscript within their areas of expertise. These individuals made essential contributions. The level of detail presented in API 28 exists as a result of the input of the following individuals who were willing to share their training and experience:

Deborah Bindeman, CPCU, ARP

Mark Bohac, AIC

Eric Steven Busse, CPCU, SCLA

Howard E. Candage, CPCU

Patricia M. Coleman, CPCU

Susan A. Erney-Skelton, CPCU

W. James Gray

Edward J. Glinski, AU, CIC

Robert D. Gustafson, CPCU

Michael P. Guth, CPCU, AAI

Judy LaFleur, CPCU

Kevin Letcher, CPCU

Jeffrey A. Lewis, CPCU

Ralph J. Monaco, CPCU

James E. Mooney, CPCU, ARM, AMIM

Marlin J. Quick

Allison A. Rhyne, CPCU

Jeanne Snyder, AIS

Patricia C. Sturm, CPCU, CLU, AU

Christine Sullivan, CPCU, AIM

Tracey M. Thibodeau, CPCU

Bruce W. Thomas, CPCU

Richard A. Villarreal, CPCU

Steven Ward

For more information about the Institutes' programs, please call our Customer Service Department at (800) 644-2101, e-mail us at customerservice@cpcuiia.org, or visit our Web site at www.aicpcu.org.

Cheryl L. Ferguson

Contributing Authors

The Insurance Institute of America acknowledges with deep appreciation the help of the following contributing authors:

Lawrence J. Cipov, CPCU, CLU, JD
Staff Associate - Auto General Underwriting
State Farm Insurance Companies

Karen Hamilton, PhD, CPCU, CLU
Director of Curriculum
Insurance Institute of America

Mary Lou Speckheuer, CPCU, AMIM
Marine Agent
Richard M. Marshall Insurance Agency

Christine Sullivan, CPCU, AIM
Director - Education
Allstate Insurance

William W. Wright, CPCU, CLU, MBA
Manager - Underwriting
State Farm Insurance Companies

Contents

Chapter 1

Educational Objectives

1. Describe personal insurance and its importance to: (pp. 1-3 to 1-9)
   - Economy
   - Society
   - Personal insurance customers

2. Describe the compulsory and semicompulsory natures of personal insurance. (pp. 1-9 to 1-13)

3. Explain the importance of the following in personal insurance practice: (pp. 1-13 to 1-15)
   - Professional ethics
   - Technical competence

4. Describe risk management techniques as they apply to loss exposures of individuals and families. (pp. 1-15 to 1-23)

5. Explain how potential loss frequency or severity affects the selection of risk management techniques. (pp. 1-23 to 1-27)

6. Explain the service-related expectations of insurance customers. (pp. 1-27 to 1-31)

7. Explain why many customers think insurance costs too much. (pp. 1-27 to 1-31)

8. Analyze the major concerns about personal insurance raised by consumer advocates. (pp. 1-31 to 1-35)

9. Given a case situation, explain how a personal insurance specialist would apply risk management techniques, professional ethics, and technical competence in advising an individual or family regarding its loss exposures. (Encompasses entire chapter.)

Chapter 1

What Are the Customer's Insurance Needs and Perceptions?

From the customer's perspective, insurance can be one of the great unknowns. Heads of households often buy insurance because they must, for reasons they do not fully understand. The coverage contained in insurance policies is written in language the customer might not understand. Customers usually only sense or assume the benefits of having coverage.

From the customer's perspective, insurance professionals have done little to make policy language more understandable. Each insurance transaction involves the reality of the situation (the facts) and the impression that the customer forms of the transaction (the perception). The combination of facts and perception determines the customer's opinion of the transaction and his or her satisfaction or dissatisfaction. Insurance customers contact and interact with insurer representatives, and the quality of that contact and interaction creates a lasting impression.

Because insurers understand the importance of making a positive impression on their customers, they rely heavily on those insurance representatives who have direct contact with customers to form the image of the insurance industry. Many of those representatives are among the new specialists in personal insurance who work in underwriting, as producers, in customer service, and as technicians.

Insurers realize that every interaction between a specialist and a customer reflects the insurer's commitment to customer service. These specialists in personal insurance therefore create the customer's perception of the industry.

Consequently, to be effective in their jobs, specialists in personal insurance must possess the following:

- High ethical standards. Although this subject is addressed only briefly in this chapter, the ethical standards of insurance professionals should not be taken lightly. Insurance is a contract of utmost good faith. No level of expertise can compensate for the failure to act in good faith.

- Technical competence in recommending and selling coverages and policies to the public. Most of this course deals with the development of technical competence. Specialists must remain technically competent through continued development. This is a task of career-long learning that will continue well after this course is completed. A specialist must have a solid understanding of customer needs and the ability to relate technical competence to those needs.

This chapter addresses the needs and perceptions of insureds and information the specialist can use to match risk management or an insurance product to those needs.

This course addresses functions or activities performed by specialists. The underwriting function is the same whether performed by an underwriter or by another employee who is a technician, customer service representative, or producer. The functions of underwriting, loss evaluation, premium calculation, and customer service are crucial to the insurance industry. These functions affect the profitability and success of large blocks of personal insurance accounts. The employees who perform these functions will be required to accomplish a wide array of tasks and must, therefore, possess a broad range of skills.

Educational Objective 1

Describe personal insurance and its importance to:
- Economy
- Society
- Personal insurance customers

Personal Insurance

Personal insurance refers to the type of insurance purchased by individuals and families. (The other broad category of insurance is commercial insurance.) Life and health insurance purchased by individuals and families is also personal insurance. However, this text deals mainly with issues relating to personal property and liability insurance. The predominant personal insurance products are private

Jargon Alert!

The terms "personal lines" and "personal insurance" are used interchangeably in this course. "Line of insurance" is just another way of saying "type of insurance." The term "line" probably came from the separate lines (blanks) in the Annual Report forms for the various types of insurance. The Annual Report is a form that each insurance company must file with state regulators each year.

passenger automobile insurance and homeowners insurance. Additional personal insurance products are inland marine, dwelling fire, watercraft, miscellaneous vehicles, and umbrella liability.

The bulk of personal lines premiums (over 38 percent of all property-liability insurance premiums) comes from automobile insurance. Homeowners insurance represents about 9 percent of all property-liability insurance premiums. Together, these two products account for almost half of the property and liability premiums in the United States. Exhibit 1-1 furnishes premium comparisons over a five-year period.

Exhibit 1-1
Personal Auto and Homeowners Written Premiums, 1990-1994 (in millions of dollars)

	All	Personal Auto	Percent	Homeowners	Percent
1990	217,825	78,392	35.9%	18,577	8.5%
1991	222,991	82,754	37.1	19,303	8.7
1992	227,500	88,371	38.8	20,477	9.0
1993	241,563	93,375	38.7	21,546	8.9
1994	250,634	96,813	38.6	22,551	9.0

Source: A.M. Best Company, Inc., *Best's Aggregates & Averages*, 1995.

Life insurance and health insurance are sometimes sold by the same producers or organizations that market property and liability insurance. The public regards both of these types of products as personal insurance, but each type of insurance is handled so differently that they are best addressed separately.

Importance of Personal Insurance to the Economy

A **portfolio** is a group of policies with a common characteristic (such as geography, type of coverage, or producer). As a group, policies are analyzed for losses, change in size, and trends. A portfolio is also called a "book of business."

Many insurance companies write large numbers of personal insurance policies so that they can take advantage of the economies of scale (which means reducing the cost of producing policies as more are sold) to process and computerize policy production. Those insurers also find that, as they add more policies to their **portfolios**, the loss experience of those policies becomes more predictable.

Property-liability insurance is big business, and roughly half of the property-liability insurance premium volume involves personal insurance. Premiums for personal insurance policies tend to be smaller than those for commercial insurance policies, but more personal insurance policies than commercial insurance policies are in force.

All personal insurance lines generated over $129 billion in written premiums in 1994. These premiums represented 51 percent of the total written premiums for the entire U.S. insurance industry. Private passenger auto insurance alone accounted for over $88 billion worth of insurance premiums in one recent year. Homeowners insurance accounted for another $20 billion in premiums. Exhibit 1-2 shows the size and growth of property and **casualty** premiums during a recent eleven-year period.

Jargon Alert!

The terms "casualty" and "liability" are synonymous when used to describe a segment of the insurance industry. The property and casualty business is the same as the property and liability business.

Exhibit 1-2
Net Premiums Written, 1984-1994

	Total Net Premiums Written by Property and Casualty Insurance Companies, 1984-1994 (000s omitted)			
Year	Accident and Health	All Other	Total	Annual % Change
1984	$3,836,695	$114,329,616	$118,166,311	+8.4
1985	3,205,359	140,981,061	144,186,420	+22.0
1986	2,929,510	173,622,560	176,552,070	+22.4
1987	3,814,711	189,431,068	193,245,779	+9.5
1988	4,699,179	197,315,519	202,014,698	+4.5
1989	4,579,572	203,808,381	208,387,953	+3.2
1990	4,947,959	212,876,881	217,824,840	+4.5
1991	5,147,169	217,844,019	222,991,188	+2.4
1992	5,383,911	222,116,187	227,500,098	+2.0
1993	6,796,314	234,767,042	241,563,356	+6.2
1994	7,172,314	243,462,198	250,634,512	+3.8

Source: A.M. Best Company, Inc., *Best's Aggregates & Averages*, 1995.

Over 900 insurance companies and tens of thousands of independent producers participate in the personal lines market, which generates hundreds of thousands of jobs throughout the country.

Insurance is a vital segment of the economy. Not only do insurers provide protection for property and income; they also act as **financial intermediaries**.[1]

A **financial intermediary** is an entity that obtains money from one source and redirects it to another. Insurance companies and banks are financial intermediaries.

Banks, savings and loan associations, and insurance companies are all financial intermediaries. They collect relatively small sums of money from each of their clients and pool the money. Intermediaries then lend large sums to, invest large sums in, or pay large claims to other entities. Unfortunately, most consumers do not understand the role of financial-intermediary insurers, which is to provide a service to society by efficiently collecting and distributing capital.[2]

The amounts of capital that insurers collect and distribute are large. In 1994, the property-liability insurance business (commercial and personal lines combined) collected $250.7 billion in premiums, incurred losses exceeding $198 billion, and held $704.6 billion in assets. More than 80.5 percent of these assets, a total of $567 billion, was invested in stocks, bonds, and other investments. Those investments, in turn, helped provide capital for many other business and government activities. Most of insurance company assets were committed to pay for expected losses of policyholders.[3]

Personal insurance generates substantial tax revenue, and the states use a considerable amount of this revenue to provide goods and services unrelated to insurance. During 1994, personal lines premiums generated premium tax revenue of more than $8 billion.

The U.S. insurance industry leads the world in premium volume, as shown in Exhibit 1-3. Over 31 percent of premiums worldwide are generated in the U.S.

Exhibit 1-3
Leading Insurance Countries in 1993 (000,000s omitted)

Rank	Country	Non-life premiums	Life premiums	Total premiums	Total % world premiums
1	United States[1]	$328,892*	$235,621	$564,513	31.31%
2	Japan[2]	116,807	430,553	547,360	30.36
3	Germany[3]	70,177	45,898	116,075	6.44
4	United Kingdom	39,670	71,263	110,832	6.15
5	France	37,706	57,252	94,958	5.27
6	South Korea[2]	8,411	29,838	38,249	2.12
7	Canada[1]	19,096	18,551	35,646	1.98
8	Italy	22,311	9,610	31,921	1.77
9	The Netherlands	12,902	13,731	26,633	1.48
10	Switzerland	8,673	12,817	21,490	1.19

*Includes health insurance premiums written by commercial insurers. (1) Net premiums written. (2) March 31, 1993 to March 31, 1994. (3) Includes new federal states; gross premiums earned.

Source: Swiss Reinsurance Company, May 1995.

Reprinted with permission from *I.I.I. 1996 Fact Book* (New York, NY: Insurance Information Institute, 1995), p. 12.

Importance of Personal Insurance to Society

Personal insurance fulfills social needs and promotes public safety. Without insurance, individuals in a society cannot plan or assume responsibility with certainty.

Fulfilling Social Needs

Insurance serves some of the noblest needs of humankind, although often operating in the background:

- Insurance alone cannot save a life, but it can pay for the medical treatment that could save a life.
- Insurance cannot create families, but it can help keep families together. It can permit a parent to raise the children after the death of a spouse without having to take a job outside the home. It can replace the income of a disabled breadwinner, help send a son or daughter to college, or pay for quality medical and legal care.

- Insurance cannot eliminate liability or prevent lawsuits, but it can protect the owners of homes, automobiles, and businesses from the adverse financial effects of lawsuits.

- Insurance cannot finance the purchase of a home, auto, or business, but it can make facing the risks involved in owning a home, operating an auto, or running a business manageable.

- Insurance cannot prevent property from being damaged or destroyed, but it can replace a dwelling destroyed by windstorm so that a family has an adequate place to live.

Insurance can protect the individual and the family from financial ruin.[4]

Promoting Public Safety

Personal lines insurers promote public safety for everyone, even for those who do not purchase insurance. For example, the insurance industry sponsors organizations such as the following:

- The Highway Loss Data Institute (HLDI) and the Insurance Institute for Highway Safety (IIHS), which conduct studies and publish safety information on a wide variety of transportation-related subjects

- Underwriters Laboratories (UL), which tests consumer products to ensure that they meet fire prevention and safety standards

- The Insurance Research Council, which publishes studies on public policy matters related to insurance, such as trends in auto insurance claim costs, the accuracy of motor vehicle records, and public attitudes about insurance

Importance of Personal Insurance to Personal Insurance Customers

Insurance is beneficial to personal insurance customers in many ways. The payment of covered claims is an obvious benefit when insurance is selected to cover exposures that subsequently result in losses. Other benefits are equally important but less apparent.

Personal insurance touches almost every American's life on a daily basis. The protection afforded by a personal lines policy is only a portion of the picture. Many policyholders go years without filing a claim. The true value of insurance, however, lies in its potential rather than immediate benefits. Although insurance has the potential to restore a customer's financial position, the need to do so might not arise—which makes it difficult for insurance customers to measure the real value of insurance or to measure the differences in quality between insurance carriers.

Many Americans have a negative perception of the insurance industry, largely because they believe that they are paying too much money for too little return. In 1992, the average household had paid over $8,900 in auto insurance premiums over the previous ten years but had filed only a single claim, with that single claim typically resulting in only about $600 in payment.[5] However, the true value of insurance transcends this example. The cost of insurance also buys peace of mind.

Few people can afford a catastrophic loss, although they can budget timed payments in the form of insurance premiums. For most households, the sum of the payment of insurance premiums over its members' lifetime does exceed the sum of any loss recoveries. Yet for the few households that suffer catastrophic losses, the value of payments received can far outweigh the total premium its members pay over an entire lifetime. Customers tend to overlook the reduction of uncertainty provided by personal lines insurance when they receive a bill for an insurance policy, but the reduction of uncertainty about the future is the true value of insurance.

Financial Security

Customers buy insurance because it is required by law, by lenders, or by other circumstances. They also buy insurance so that they will be indemnified for unpredictable losses. Insurance provides stability and financial security.

When looking for financial security, customers approach insurance on both a practical basis and an emotional basis. On a practical basis, they analyze the possible sources of loss, the cost of possible losses, and the cost of insurance to protect against losses that are insurable. However, unlike insurers, which compile large databases, individuals and families cannot predict future losses with much confidence. Therefore, they make some decisions based on the amount of risk they are willing to take, the amount of security they want, and their own estimates regarding the chance of loss.

Peace of Mind

Peace of mind is part of what the insurance industry sells. This is more than a trite sentiment. Because circumstances change and the potential for loss for a family cannot be known, insurance is a basis of security. Few products or services can offer what insurance does: insurance creates a predictable outcome. If an insured's home is destroyed by fire or windstorm, the insured *knows* how his or her insurance will respond to the event. Having security in this one area significantly lightens the burden of financial planning for a family or an individual. As a result, customers can eliminate concerns about their financial future and can increase their concentration and effort on family and work.

Specialists can play a pivotal part in enhancing the benefit of insurance for the customer. They fill the role of educator as well as advisor for insureds. The more that insureds understand about the coverage they purchase, the greater the effect they can have as partners in keeping their coverage current. Many insurance customers distrust insurance companies because they assume that companies will not compensate them if a loss occurs. However, the specialist's taking the time during the insured's initial purchase of coverage to explain the policy provisions will dispel much of this distrust.

The interpersonal skills of specialists are crucial at each point of contact with the customer to establish a relationship that instills confidence and peace of mind. The relationship between a specialist in personal insurance and a customer is really a "partnering" arrangement in which the specialist counsels the customer to help determine and address exposures.

Educational Objective 2

Describe the compulsory and semicompulsory natures of personal insurance.

Meeting Compulsory Insurance Requirements

Compulsory insurance is coverage required to protect the public from a loss exposure in exchange for a privilege. Driving a car is a privilege; in exchange for that privilege, vehicle owners must purchase auto insurance policies (or provide some proof of their ability to pay, such as a bond) to protect the public from the possibility that a negligent operator will injure a **third party**.

The supporters of compulsory auto insurance believe that all drivers have a responsibility to pay for the consequences of their negligence. They also believe that making insurance compulsory will increase the number of financially responsible drivers.

Compulsory insurance is mandated by government regulatory groups. Personal insurance customers normally encounter compulsory insurance requirements in the form of mandatory automobile insurance. In many states, drivers need to purchase automobile insurance so that they can drive their cars.

All states have financial responsibility laws that require drivers to show proof of their ability to pay for third-party losses, up to a specified amount, after an accident, conviction, or judgment. Liability insurance is compulsory in forty-two states and the District of Columbia. In those states, operating a vehicle without obtaining proof of insurance is illegal, regardless of whether an accident has occurred.[6] Appendix 1-A of this text contains information on the enforcement of compulsory auto liability insurance laws for every state.

A **third party** is an entity with certain rights under the terms of an insurance policy as a result of the insured's negligent acts covered by the policy. The insured is the "first party" to the insurance contract. (The insurer is the "second party" to the contract, but the insurer is never referred to as such.)

Customer Perception of Compulsory Insurance

Despite the penalties for driving without auto liability insurance, the percentage of uninsured drivers is still significant—as high as 20 percent of all drivers in some states.[7] Auto liability insurance can be a big expense, and customers can have difficulty visualizing the benefit derived from an insurance policy. The temptation of not insuring is compounded when any of the following are true:

- The insurance is compulsory; therefore, customers resist being forced to purchase coverage they would otherwise not desire.
- Insurance customers see many other vehicle owners violating the regulations.
- Penalties for offenders are waived. (Even when insurance is compulsory, many states waive penalties for a first offense.)

Semicompulsory Insurance

Although some people pay cash for a car, many people borrow part of the money to buy a car. Few people can afford to buy homes with cash, so they must borrow money and use their car or home as collateral for the loan. The bank or the lender will require insurance (such as auto physical damage or homeowners insurance) in case the collateral is damaged or destroyed. In the event of a loss, the lender becomes a party named on the draft or check that the insured collects. The insured must then satisfy the lender by either paying off the loan on the property or restoring the collateral to its original condition (thus restoring its value as collateral) to the satisfaction of the lender. Without agreement of the lending institution, the insured cannot collect the insurance proceeds.

Auto physical damage or homeowners insurance is semicompulsory because it is a condition of the loan required by the lending institution. In reality, no government organization requires the purchase of this insurance; however, customers sometimes confuse this insurance requirement with compulsory insurance. The perception of insurance becomes clouded because of the requirements imposed by lending institutions, which can add to the negative perception caused by regulatory requirements for compulsory auto insurance.

If a total loss occurs to a home or auto with a secured loan, the insurance policy satisfies the loan with the lending institution. Insureds might perceive this loss settlement to mean that they are paying for insurance for nothing, further worsening their perception of insurance.

The key to resolving such misunderstandings is communication with the customer. The personal lines specialist is the focal point in clarifying for the insured the need for an insurance purchase and explaining how a claim will be paid if a mortgagee or lienholder is securing a loan.

The Customer's Point of Contact for Insurance: The Specialist in Personal Insurance

As mentioned earlier, a new specialist is emerging within personal insurance. Specialists in personal insurance are employed by agencies, brokerages, and insurance companies. They might perform many different functions, but their focus is on helping customers do the following:

- Determine and measure their loss exposures.
- Choose among risk management techniques or "tools" to manage the exposures identified.
- Select the most appropriate insurance product (if insurance is the best tool for the job) to treat the exposure (that is, make it acceptable from a financial standpoint). Alternatives to insurance as risk management are discussed later in this chapter.

The specialist's customer service skills help form the customer's impression of an insurance transaction. Important characteristics for specialists to possess include positive professional ethics and strong technical competency.

Specialists also represent insurance companies, agencies, and brokerages. They should consider the goals and missions of those organizations as they assist insurance customers. The responsibilities of specialists to such organizations include the following:

- Settling small claims within the scope of authority granted
- Identifying, evaluating, and selecting risks that fit a company's underwriting criteria
- Generating and carrying out marketing ideas for attracting customers to purchase insurance products

Traditional Versus Changing Roles

The traditional roles of employees working in personal insurance are changing. The change reflects a blend of many separate functions that were once distinct. Computers and communication systems are largely responsible for allowing the merger of many functions. With information instantly accessible from remote areas, the distinction among one employee who advises customers about risk management alternatives, another who determines the underwriting acceptability of potential policyholders, and a third who calculates the premium is not important. Customers and insurance companies are both better served by specialists who can perform many tasks.

What Were the Traditional Roles in Personal Insurance?

Traditionally, the jobs in personal insurance were distinct. Their titles linger in industry vocabulary, but the boundaries dividing traditional jobs are becoming blurred.

Traditionally, the following facts were true:

- Producers initially contacted customers, determined the exposures for the individual or family, recommended the coverage, completed the application, and sent it to underwriters for review.
- Underwriters selected and rejected new applications and periodically reviewed existing policies to make sure that the policies fell within the current underwriting guidelines of the company. Underwriters usually worked from the insurance

company's home office or regional office. They also ordered external reports and gathered other information to help in the decision-making process.

- After a policy was written, customer service representatives (CSRs) maintained the customer's account, answered questions, resolved problems, and made coverage changes. Both agencies and companies employed CSRs.

- Technicians assisted underwriters in screening applications and assisted agents in calculating premium quotations as well as performing other technical tasks associated with the transaction of insurance. As with CSRs, technicians could be found at both agencies and companies.

How Are the Roles Changing?

Personal insurance has been changing rapidly, and new job opportunities are opening to meet the changing marketing methods. Also, organizations are changing to meet customer needs and to create a more streamlined industry.

Automation has had a positive effect on how the insurance industry handles the massive quantities of information needed to track and manage insurance policies. Automation has also made handling large numbers of transactions with clients in a relatively short period of time easier.

The personal insurance industry needs employees who are flexible and who can adapt to the expanding skills required to perform broader jobs. In his book *Future Shock*, Alvin Toffler contends that lifelong learners, the "future shock survivors," will not be people with a superior grasp of facts but those who can learn, unlearn, and relearn effectively, efficiently, and independently.

Many of the traditional personal insurance job titles remain, but the tasks being performed by specialists have already changed in ways such as the following:

- An underwriter today has a much different role than an employee with that title did thirty years ago. Today, underwriters must have analysis and planning skills to interpret and act on trends revealed by computer data. Underwriters now have marketing responsibilities and written premium goals. In many companies, underwriters must also have highly developed interpersonal skills to deal directly with insurance customers and producers. Those skills must include the ability to write and speak concisely, persuasively, and diplomatically.

- Producers today are often required to adjust claims and to perform the initial underwriting selection process. Interpersonal skills are essential to interact with customers and insurance company representatives.

- Underwriters have marketing responsibilities and written premium goals for their territories. Their job now includes determining customer needs, product design, and pricing.

- Most personal lines policy billing has moved out of producers' offices and into insurance company computer systems. Because CSRs respond to customer questions, they must be able to access, read, and interpret the company's computer information screens to provide accurate answers.

- Producers often perform premium calculations themselves. Completing the rating while discussing coverage with the customer is easier and more efficient than seeking assistance from a technician. Computer calculation of premiums simplifies the process.

- Producers have become **front-line underwriters**. They screen customers according to the company's underwriting guidelines. Some producers are granted underwriting authority and responsibility for the policies they write. Others assume responsibility for settling small claims with customers.

- CSRs and technicians have responsibility for premium determination, policy coverage interpretation, initial underwriting, and billing.

> **Jargon Alert!**
>
> The terms "front-line underwriter" and "line underwriter" are often used interchangeably. Such underwriters initially analyze individual applications or existing accounts and make underwriting decisions.

The Specialist as an Advisor

Insurance buyers should be in a position to make informed decisions. Specialists in personal insurance, whether in an insurance company, an agency, or a brokerage, are primary sources of the information that buyers need to make informed decisions.[8]

Skills and Characteristics Required of a Specialist

Although tasks within jobs are changing, some skills and characteristics form the foundation for the specialist's development. Specialists become a pivotal part of the industry. Two important hallmarks of a good specialist are professional ethics and technical competency.

> **Educational Objective 3**
>
> Explain the importance of the following in personal insurance practice:
> - Professional ethics
> - Technical competence

Professional Ethics

Ethics are an individual's basic principles of right and wrong. Moral conduct is the application of ethical principles. Ethics and their application touch almost every business decision.

Insurance professionals are faced with ethical dilemmas on a regular basis. Often people admit to ethical problems in their industry but cannot see ethical problems that they might have themselves or that might exist within their companies or agencies. Consequently, they believe that they and their companies have higher ethical standards than the industry as a whole does. This perception helps to explain the problem people often have in examining their own ethical conflicts. [9]

Cost considerations make verifying each item on every new business application impossible. As a result, insurance companies sometimes accept misleading information as fact. This situation can continue until something happens to correct the information, such as the submission of a claim. Insurance companies rely on the ethical standards of those who represent them as well as on the ethical standards of their customers. An insurance contract is considered to be a contract of "utmost good faith," which means that all parties are assumed to be disclosing all relevant information truthfully and accurately.

Some insurance representatives consider certain types of omissions or misrepresentations unimportant, since the financial effect of any one transgression might be relatively small. In reality, however, the cumulative financial effect on the industry of erroneous, misleading risk information is enormous. Insurance professionals must weigh the long-term advantages of ethical behavior versus short-term rewards and elect professional ethics.[10]

Fiduciaries are persons or corporations having a duty to act primarily for another's benefit.

Both those who supply and those who receive risk and underwriting information are obligated to behave ethically; they are acting as **fiduciaries**.

Ethics and legality are often confused, but they are distinctly different. Ethics concerns people's relationships with one another: How should they treat others? What responsibility do they have to others? Legality concerns laws that protect society. Unfortunately, many immoral and unethical acts are legal.[11]

Although ethical principles are taught, ethical practices are usually behavior learned through observation. In business and in personal life, people learn their standards and values from observing what others do, not what they say. When the principles that a person has learned are inconsistent with the practices he or she has observed, answers to the following questions can help to determine whether an action is ethical:

- Is it legal? Am I obeying the law or company policy? (This is just the first step in determining whether an action is ethical; as mentioned previously, some legal acts are unethical.)

- Is it balanced? Is it fair, or will I win everything at the expense of someone else?

- How will it make me feel about myself? How would I feel if my family learned of my decision? How would I feel if my decision were announced on the evening news?

- How would I feel if someone did the same thing to me?

One of the greatest challenges to ethical behavior is excessive competition, which creates a focus on the "bottom line" rather than on business ethics. A compromise of ethics might be encouraged if a company's focus is solely on profit goals. If an employer measures an employee's performance by results (insurance sales volume, files underwritten, or claims processed) without giving equal consideration to how ethical the means are in achieving those results, the employer can generate a corporate culture that accepts ethical ambiguity.

Technical Competence

Technical competence is a fundamental requirement of any professional. Many of those who use the term "professional" try, often self-servingly, to reserve professional status for themselves and for members of a limited number of occupations. Yet the opposite is true: "professional" describes a limited number of individuals in many occupations.[12] Think of your own experience in your company. Who consistently does a *high-quality* job? Whom do you go to when you *really* need the right answer? You probably rely on a handful of coworkers to perform their jobs above and beyond their job descriptions. These are professionals who are dedicated to their customers and the quality of the services they provide. Professionalism is not the exclusive property of people who are in the traditional professions or occupations. Professionals can be found at supermarkets, bank teller windows, construction sites, as well as in insurance companies and agencies.

Some people might be highly competent without much formal education. However, no person can be competent without mastering the skills that his or her occupation requires. In addition, every competent person who deserves the label "professional" is deeply committed to high standards of professional ethics.[13]

Unless professionals maintain and improve their competence, it might be lost more easily than it was acquired. If specialists in personal insurance have gaps in their knowledge, they cannot provide information to customers with complete confidence. If, for example, a specialist is unfamiliar with many aspects of personal inland marine coverage, that specialist might recommend only coverage in the area in which he or she has expertise. Having technical information gaps can eventually erode one's self-confidence. After insurance professionals gain information and technical competence, they continually maintain information and technical development, or the gaps can return. In the fast-paced personal insurance environment, becoming outdated is easy. Staying current requires effort.

More and more jobs have a high "mental content."[14] They require better educated, more highly skilled, and more flexible employees to perform the work. Forty-four states now require insurance producers to maintain continuing education for license renewal, with more states likely to adopt such standards. That requirement reflects the need for knowledgeable professionals who maintain their technical skill levels.

One of the benefits of working in a business that is changing rapidly is the array of opportunities that present themselves in the midst of change. With basic technical competence, a specialist's job can grow as the insurance industry changes.

Educational Objective 4

Describe risk management techniques as they apply to loss exposures of individuals and families.

Using Risk Management to Address Customers' Needs

All individuals face loss exposures of one sort or another. When specialists identify the loss exposures faced by their customers and recommend methods to make these exposures tolerable, they often overlook risk management techniques other than insurance. This occurs because the acceptable tool to treat these exposures is often assumed to be insurance, but other effective techniques can be used to transfer or treat risk. Specialists must understand the methods used to transfer and treat loss exposures, including but not limited to insurance. The technical counseling that a specialist provides must include such methods. Counseling provides an excellent opportunity for specialists to give technical advice and expertise that adds to the customer's understanding of effective insurance selection.

Customers place tremendous faith in the technical ability of insurance specialists and the quality of the advice they receive. Clearly specialists need to be technically skilled to justify that faith. An opportunity also exists to educate during the insurance transaction.[15]

Because customers rely so heavily on specialists, specialists can help customers use a rational decision-making process to improve the quality of their decisions. Rational decision making attempts to apply the best risk management option, using correct assumptions and specific criteria.[16] The following section describes a decision-making process for purchasing personal insurance, introducing risk management techniques, and using insurance as part of the process.

The Risk Management Process

Insurance is not the only risk management option. If a customer asks a producer or a customer service representative for advice and the advice does not include a discussion of the risk management techniques (discussed below) available, the customer might never be aware that these alternatives exist. Specialists immediately eliminate some risk management techniques from consideration because many techniques simply do not meet a specific household's needs. However, some risk management techniques can be used in combination with insurance to reduce premiums, to reduce the chance of a loss, or to reduce the financial consequences of loss. Not all exposures can be treated by insurance. For some exposures, knowing which risk management techniques to use other than insurance becomes vital to the customer's best interests.

Communicating with the customer is imperative. The customer must be given all necessary information concerning possible results that could stem from a risk management technique. For example, a customer who decides to retain a large deductible should be helped to understand what his or her participation will be if a loss occurs. The specialist's advice should be informative and educational. Specialists should make customers aware of any alternatives and allow them to make informed decisions regardless of which techniques they use.

Examining Risk Management Techniques

Risk management techniques seek to eliminate, control, reduce, or finance loss exposures. These techniques, which include personal insurance, avoidance, loss control, noninsurance contracts, and retention, are introduced in INS 21. The following discussion addresses specific ways in which risk management can be applied to an individual's or a family's exposures.

Personal Insurance as a Risk Management Technique

Insurance is a form of risk transfer: The economic results of a loss are transferred by a contract to an insurance company. Although insurance is only one of several broad techniques used in risk management, it is almost always an important component of a personal risk management program.

Retention

Retention is simply keeping the financial consequences of a loss exposure. If an exposure has not been avoided and has not been transferred through insurance or a noninsurance contract, it has been retained. Retention can be intentional or unintentional. Unintentional retention might result from an exposure that was not identified until a loss occurred.[17] Specialists should try to help insureds avoid that type of retention.

Households vary in their ability to retain loss exposures. An affluent family can retain large amounts of exposure in the form of deductibles. Families with limited financial resources commonly have relatively modest deductibles.

Determining the size of a deductible for property coverage is a primary retention decision. For older automobiles and watercraft, a family might decide not to purchase physical damage insurance but to retain the entire exposure.[18] In some cases, when coverage is unavailable, no choice other than retention of the exposure might exist.

Avoidance

Exposure avoidance takes place when a household decides either not to incur a loss exposure or to eliminate one that already exists. (By definition, avoidance reduces to zero the probability of loss from the avoided exposure.) Avoidance is often difficult to accomplish. Parents might decide, for example, that the teenager in their family will not have a car, but they might have a hard time guaranteeing that the teenager does not drive *any* autos. Thus, the auto liability exposure for that teenager has not been avoided.

Examples of avoidance include the following:

- An individual can avoid the possibility of losing a $10,000 diamond necklace by not owning one.

- A family can avoid a liability exposure from selling home-grown produce by not selling it.
- A person living in a densely populated metropolitan area can avoid automobile losses by choosing not to own an automobile.

Generally, unless a loss exposure is avoided, it should be treated. Most personal risk management is concerned with loss control, insurance, and retention.

Loss Control

Several types of loss control exist, including loss prevention, loss reduction, separation, and duplication. In general, they are all used in attempts to reduce the frequency, severity, or consequences of losses. However, they do not eliminate the existence of a loss exposure.

Frequency of loss indicates how often a loss occurs or is expected to occur.

Loss Prevention   This technique seeks to lower the probable **frequency of loss** from an exposure. Following are examples of loss prevention:

- Anti-lock braking systems in automobiles are devices designed to prevent a vehicle from skidding and striking an object, a person, or another vehicle when its brakes are suddenly applied.
- A deadbolt lock on a door is designed to prevent a thief from entering a home.

Anti-lock braking systems and deadbolt locks are designed to reduce the frequency of losses, so they are examples of loss prevention. Many personal loss prevention measures are obvious. For example, placing a six-foot-high fence around a swimming pool is a loss prevention measure. The fence tends to keep the neighborhood children and pets, as well as nondomesticated animals, from entering the pool and drowning. The fence does not eliminate a homeowner's liability if a person or an animal drowns in the pool, but it does reduce the frequency of drowning.

Severity of loss refers to the dollar amount of damage that results or could result from the exposure to loss.

Loss Reduction   This technique seeks to lower the **severity of losses** that occur. Following are examples of loss reduction:

- Air bags in an auto do not stop accidents from happening, but they might reduce the injuries that result.
- A fire extinguisher in a kitchen can reduce the size of a fire, but it cannot prevent one from starting.

Some loss control devices reduce both frequency and severity. A smoke detector can reduce the frequency of losses by sounding a warning before a fire actually ignites. It can also reduce the severity of losses by prompting faster fire extinguishment.

Separation   This technique divides resources or activities to minimize the effect of a single event. Following are examples of separation:

- If a member of a family requires daily medication that must be refrigerated, having a backup plan would be wise. Keeping a spare dose of medicine at a friend's house could prevent a medical emergency if power were lost at the family's home and the medication were unusable.

- Charcoal lighter fluid can be separated from ignition sources by storing it in the basement rather than in the kitchen.

Duplication   This technique relies on backups or spares. Following are examples of duplication:

- If an individual runs an office from the home, he or she should implement a plan to back up business data on a personal computer and store it away from the home.

- If someone needs a china service for eight people, purchasing several spare pieces to store in the attic to replace any broken pieces would be a good idea.

- An individual who depends on eyeglasses might want to keep an extra pair handy in case his or her glasses break.

Noninsurance Contracts

Nearly every adult and nearly every business enter into contractual agreements through which loss exposures are shifted from one party to another, a technique known as noninsurance transfer. An individual is unlikely to shift many exposures to another party. However, auto rental agreements, apartment lease agreements, and equipment rental contracts often contain these transfers, which shift exposures to an individual. A common form of transfer found within a contract is a **hold harmless agreement**, which transfers the financial consequences of loss from one party (who is held harmless) to another party.

Although individual insureds rarely use noninsurance transfers to shift exposures to another party, they often assume exposures when they sign the type of agreement mentioned above. When specialists first meet with applicants for personal insurance, they should inform them of the types of loss exposures that they might assume under a hold harmless agreement. They might also express their willingness to advise their customers about specific exposures assumed under specific contracts before the customers sign them.

> **A hold harmless agreement** is the promise of one party to hold another harmless for any liability arising from an activity.

Combining Risk Management Techniques

Some loss exposures are treated with a single risk management technique. However, risk management techniques should also be considered in combinations such as the following:

- A family that chooses an automobile with air bags (an application of a loss control technique) will probably also purchase insurance to meet compulsory insurance requirements.

- An insured who owns valuable pieces of jewelry might both insure them and store them in a safe-deposit box when they are not being worn (another loss control technique).[19]

Households depend heavily on insurance to treat loss exposures. However, deductibles (a form of retention) help reduce the cost of insurance. Some forms of loss control can be implemented in combination with insurance or retention, such as driver education programs, smoke and burglar alarms, and deadbolt locks on doors.

Choosing Among Risk Management Techniques

Risk management techniques have very practical applications. Exhibit 1-4 illustrates a scenario based on a customer's question regarding an expensive personal computer that her daughter is taking to college. The exhibit contains alternatives for addressing that exposure.

After considering how various risk management techniques might be applied to particular loss exposures, the specialist must next decide what combination of risk management techniques best serves the household's objectives.

Economic Concerns

The most difficult decision for many individuals and families is not whether to buy insurance, but which exposures to insure and which to retain. When insureds purchase unnecessary insurance, they might forgo additional necessary insurance. Many insureds rely on insurance as the only method of financing loss exposures, whether or not the potential for loss is significant. In many cases, insureds are only "exchanging dollars" with the insurers—paying a premium that is equal to the severity of the exposure being transferred.

Households are like businesses in that they operate within a budget and that they probably have goals for the future that involve money, growth, and stability. Businesses often document those goals in a written plan. Family members might express those goals less formally:

- "We want to put the children through college."
- "We want a comfortable retirement."
- "We can't afford a new car now, but we'd like to buy one next fall."

As mentioned earlier, some households are better able to absorb retention than others.

The idea of risk retention might appeal to a young person who has just graduated from high school or college. A recent graduate would probably have few possessions and would consider saving on premium to be highly important. A couple that is nearing retirement might be less willing to retain risk and more inclined to purchase insurance because any financial loss would delay retirement and become a financial challenge. Considering such economic concerns in selecting risk management alternatives is important.

Critical Consequences

Critical consequences are those with the potential of financially impairing a household severely, for a long time. A recent college graduate might furnish an apartment from a relative's attic. If the furniture were

Exhibit 1-4
Risk Management Alternatives

The teenage daughter is taking her computer to school. She will keep it in her dormitory room. The largest exposure is theft of the computer and loss of the documents she is storing on the computer.

The Risk Management Technique	What the Technique Does	Applying the Technique
Personal Insurance	Transfers the financial consequences of a loss through an insurance policy	The family adds an endorsement to its homeowners policy increasing coverage for the computer at the dormitory.
Avoidance	Eliminates, or avoids, the exposure	The daughter does not own a computer. She can use the one in the campus library and save her documents on a backup disc.
Loss Control 1. Loss prevention	1. Lowers the probable frequency of loss	1. The daughter keeps the dormitory room locked at all times. She would lock the computer to the desktop and save the documents on a backup disc.
2. Loss reduction	2. Lowers the severity of losses	2. The parents buy the daughter an inexpensive, used computer. If it is stolen, the loss will not be so severe as it would be with a new one. She can save the documents on a backup disc.
3. Separation	3. Divides resources or activities to minimize the effect of a single loss	3. The daughter backs up the papers she has stored on the computer daily and carries a copy of the disk home on the weekends.
4. Duplication	4. Provides backup or spares	4. The daughter prints two copies of each paper. She keeps one copy and submits the other for grading.
Noninsurance Contract	Transfers the exposures or the financial consequences of the exposures to someone else	This is a difficult alternative for an individual or a family. In this case, the dormitory has probably already used a transfer technique in the lease agreement absolving the college of responsibility for any stolen property.
Retention	Keeps the financial consequences of a loss exposure	The standard homeowners policy provides coverage of up to $1,000 (or 10 percent of the household contents, whichever is greater) for another residence (the dormitory room qualifies). The insured will retain the deductible. The insured might also decide to retain the value of the computer in excess of the $1,000 coverage limit.

lost in a fire, the financial effect would probably be minimal. Accumulating similar furniture at little or no expense would not be difficult. Therefore, this property exposure could probably be retained.

However, if this individual negligently started a grease fire in the kitchen, the consequences could be severe. The landlord and other tenants could bring a lawsuit. The cost of hiring an attorney to help provide a defense in a lawsuit could create financial consequences for years if the individual were held accountable for the fire loss. The individual might never recover financially. Therefore, the liability exposure should probably not be retained.

Affordable Consequences

The cost of risk management techniques should be compared to the possible financial loss that might occur. For example, a fifteen-year-old car would have a low value. If the car were stolen, the loss would be affordable. Is the potential loss a better consequence than the cost of insurance for a vehicle that has a low value?

The choice of loss control methods has financial consequences. What is the cost of changing the locks in a house to deadbolts? Is it more affordable than installing a central-station burglar alarm?

Risk management techniques involve a tradeoff of expense versus reduction in risk. The cost and the benefit should be weighed for each possibility in light of the individual's or family's goals. The specialist in personal insurance should try to manage a family's exposures so that losses are minimal over the long run. Although this ideal outcome is uncertain, specialists have a responsibility to establish a risk management program that strives for the ideal.

Objective and Subjective Decisions

In theory, customers should make insurance decisions objectively, based on economic efficiency, that is, on a desire to minimize the long-term cost of insurance and insured losses, insurance premiums, and loss control measures. In practice, people make subjective decisions based on ideas about their chances of incurring losses. For example, a person buying an auto policy might purchase towing and labor coverage with a $25 limit for $4 in premium, but the same person might not buy a $1 million limit umbrella for a $150 premium. A person can visualize breaking down on the road and needing a tow, but imagining being sued for hundreds of thousands of dollars is difficult.

A specialist should be aware of the distinction between objective decisions (based on facts) and subjective decisions (based on opinions and emotions) and explain how both affect insurance buyers' coverage selections.

Probability, Risk, and Utility

The following are concepts about probability, risk, and utility that influence how people make risk management decisions:

- *Objective probability* is the "long-run relative frequency of an event based on the sum of an infinite number of observations and of no change in the underlying conditions."[20] In other words, it describes how often something will theoretically happen. For example, the likelihood of being killed in one flight in a commercial airliner is approximately 1 in 100,000. This is roughly equivalent to one fatal crash in more than six years of actual time in the air.[21] Thus, flying is a relatively safe method of travel when viewed objectively.

- *Subjective probability* is "the individual's personal estimate of the chance of loss."[22] Many apprehensive airline travelers are more fearful of an airplane flight than of a car ride, despite statistical evidence that riding in a car is more dangerous than riding in a commercial airliner.

- *Subjective risk* is "uncertainty based on a person's mental condition or state of mind."[23] Some people are **risk-averse** and want to minimize risk at all cost. Risk-averse insurance buyers are likely to purchase insurance even when the cost is high relative to loss exposures. In contrast, **risk-takers** are much more willing to deal with the possibility of having an uninsured loss or with the chance that they will be fined for driving without insurance.

- *Utility analysis* recognizes that the value of certain gains (or losses) need not be proportionate to the amount of those gains (or losses). Utility analysis helps explain why people do not purchase insurance based only on mathematical probabilities.[24] Flight insurance is still available at airport counters, even though the objective probability of an insurance claim from a crash is extremely small. People see value in purchasing the coverage, even though the coverage is not a good buy from a statistical standpoint.

Risk-averse people are uncomfortable with assuming the uncertainty and consequences of unknown outcomes. The opposite of being risk-averse is being a **risk-taker**. A risk-taker has a higher degree of comfort with the unknown than someone who is risk-averse.

The Myth of the Completely Rational Person

To some extent, the personal insurance market is based on the assumption that people always make rational decisions when buying insurance. In theory, people evaluate their loss exposures, comparison-shop to determine the cost of various insurance coverages, and make informed choices. In practice, insurance buyers often behave irrationally, because of subjective evaluations of their loss exposures and incomplete information regarding their cost and coverage alternatives rather than because of reasoning. Specialists must recognize that customers are influenced by both rational and irrational factors.

Educational Objective 5

Explain how potential loss frequency or severity affects the selection of risk management techniques.

Selecting the Best Risk Management Techniques

Because many states require auto insurance and because mortgage holders require homeowners insurance, many people consider insurance to be the only practical personal risk management technique. This attitude can lead to the unwise practice of using insurance rather than other risk management techniques merely because it is available. Many complex and interrelated factors must be considered in designing a personal risk management program. The best solution is usually not to purchase all the insurance that is available, but rather to treat all identified exposures with appropriate control and financial techniques, including insurance. In many cases, a number of techniques might be considered appropriate.

Frequency and Severity

To select the appropriate risk management technique for handling a loss exposure, the specialist must consider the potential frequency and severity of the potential loss. Exposures with very low frequency might be so insignificant that they can be disregarded without any great concern. On the other hand, exposures with high potential severity should be *carefully* considered. For example, the expected severity of earthquake losses in Florida is low; therefore, a homeowner in Florida might decide to retain an exposure. On the other hand, given the destruction south of Miami caused by Hurricane Andrew in 1992, a Florida homeowner would be unlikely to retain a windstorm exposure.

Exhibit 1-5 depicts the frequency-severity matrix, a tool that can help a specialist counsel a customer about appropriate risk management techniques for an exposure. The matrix helps specialists do the following:

- Determine the likely frequency and severity of losses for an exposure
- Identify the possible risk management techniques from the available options
- Determine what alternatives make sense for the exposure, the insured, and the circumstance

This matrix serves only as a *preliminary guide*. The specialist in personal insurance must also perform a more detailed analysis. For example, the premium for any coverage must be compared to the severity of the risk. The specialist must also consider the insured's concerns, situation, and goals.

The techniques shown in each frequency-severity block in Exhibit 1-5 are listed from most to least appropriate.

The Severity and Frequency That Can Be Retained   Insureds must determine at what point they can no longer afford to pay for a loss. The decision process is fairly straightforward and can be based on the following questions:

- How bad might a loss be?
- Might the insured afford to absorb the financial consequences of this loss?
- Is the loss likely to occur often? (If "yes," could the insured afford more than one occurrence?)

Exhibit 1-5
The Frequency-Severity Matrix

High severity/high frequency: If the insured wants to teach senior citizens to roller-skate, chances are they could hurt themselves. The recommendation of *avoidance* would be prudent. If avoidance is not possible, losses should be *prevented* (full-body padding) or *reduced* (an ambulance on standby).

Transferring the liability exposure to an insurance company is a good idea, but if no company is willing to accept the risk, *retention* might be the only alternative.

Low severity/high frequency: If the insured owns an older home or auto, frequent repairs might be needed, but they are usually relatively affordable. Periodic preventive maintenance can be performed to *reduce* losses.

Checking for worn auto hoses can *prevent* a breakdown on the highway. The chimney in an older home should be checked for loose and cracked mortar. Maintenance losses cannot be insured, so the other alternative is *retention*.

The Frequency-Severity Matrix		
	High Severity	Low Severity
High Frequency	Avoid Prevent & Reduce Transfer Retain	Prevent Retain
Low Frequency	Prevent & Reduce Transfer	Retain Prevent

High severity/low frequency: These exposures do not occur very often, but their potential consequences can be devastating. The loss of a home in a fire and a large liability lawsuit fall into this category. Smoke detectors and fire extinguishers are commonly used loss *reduction* devices. Neither of these prevents a fire from starting, but both can help to minimize the damage one might cause. Using safe-driving techniques can *prevent* an auto accident and a lawsuit but cannot guarantee that one will never occur. The next best alternative is to *transfer* the risks through an insurance policy.

Low severity/low frequency: These are exposures that do not create losses frequently, and when they do occur, the consequences are not particularly severe. New cars usually do not break down on the road. If they do, towing them to the repair shop is usually inexpensive. If a customer is offered an extended warranty on a toaster, *retaining* this exposure (how bad could the loss be?) and *preventing* a recurrence through maintenance might be the best option.

When the chance of loss and the potential cost of a loss pass the point that the insured can bear without serious financial consequences, insurance makes sense. This is true as long as the cost of insurance bears a reasonable relationship to the exposure and the exposure involves a peril that is not extremely remote. If the chance of loss and the potential cost of a loss are low, then retention might make sense. Following are examples of appropriate retention decisions:

- A customer who has a steady job and a small savings account owns a five-year-old auto. She can probably afford a $250 deductible, perhaps even a $500 deductible. That retention would still be affordable if the insured incurred two or three losses in a year.

- A customer who has an apartment with $20,000 in contents lives in a neighborhood with a security guard and controlled entrances. Break-ins in the neighborhood are rare. The customer has decided that he can retain a $1,000 deductible on the contents of his apartment.

The Cost of the Loss Versus the Cost of Treatment Seeking a technique that offers the greatest benefit for the cost involved in treating exposures is an example of **maximizing behavior**.[25] Purchasing insurance for $4 for a towing and labor exposure when the maximum collectible coverage for a single loss is $25 is not an example of maximizing behavior. Purchasing coverage that will reimburse the insured for a $250 deductible when an auto is rented might not be the best choice if the insurance costs $12 per day. These are loss exposures with low severity and low frequency. The **probable cost** of these exposures is low.

The cost of a possible loss should be compared to the cost of a risk management technique. Relatively low-cost risk management techniques can be effective in addressing loss exposures. Following are examples of low-cost risk management techniques for potentially costly losses:

- A $50 smoke detector can prevent a fire and save lives. This is a good loss control investment.

- A $1 million personal umbrella policy with a $250 retention might cost as little as $150 per year. For many people, paying $150 to transfer a possible loss of hundreds of thousands of dollars to an insurer is good risk management.

Maintaining the Risk Management Program

One important step in the risk management process remains: the maintenance of the risk management program for the client. Putting policies in force, letting them renew, and not checking them until the insured asks for service do not make up a sound risk management program. Specialists must focus on their contribution to their customers' risk management programs, *especially when preparing for a renewal.*

Maximizing behavior seeks a solution that offers the optimum or greatest payoff. It assumes that individuals are rational and consistent and have complete knowledge of their environment and alternatives. With this information, an individual will select the alternative with the greatest payoff.

The **probable cost** is a combination of the potential loss frequency and severity. How often is the loss likely to occur, and how bad might the economic loss be?

Specialists should check with their clients periodically to see whether their exposures have changed. Specialists should also remember that clients might not realize the ramifications of the changes they make as they relate to their insurance program or exposure to loss. Clients might add on to their premises or enter into activities that necessitate changes in their coverage. Specialists should ask questions and follow up with insureds periodically to keep their programs current. Renewal questionnaires are an efficient method of performing this follow-up if they are written effectively and nonthreateningly. Questions that are asked in a way that is direct but positive are likely to prompt a similar response from the insured. For example, a specialist might ask questions such as the following:

- Have you traded cars this year?
- Are there any new drivers in your household?

Educational Objective 6

Explain the service-related expectations of insurance customers.

Educational Objective 7

Explain why many customers think insurance costs too much.

Customer Perceptions and Insurance Service

Customers want prompt, accurate, professional, courteous, friendly service when buying insurance, receiving bills and making payments, making policy changes, and especially when settling claims.

Regardless of why customers buy insurance, they have certain perceptions regarding the service they receive. A specialist can provide a level of service that might fall short of, meet, or exceed a customer's expectations.

Customers cannot always get the coverage they want at the price they are willing to pay. Coverage changes might not always be possible. Claims will not always be paid or paid in full. However, prompt, accurate, professional, courteous, and friendly service is one aspect of the relationship between customers and insurers over which the insurers have continuous control.

Creating Perceptions and Meeting Expectations

Buying insurance is, for customers, not comparable to buying other goods and services. Compare the way insurance is sold with a visit to a large, trendy, and expensive mall in a major financial center.

Malls create an environment through the use of marble and classical music. The comfort and affluent surroundings in the mall create a marketing illusion that drives a customer's emotional, impulsive side.

Insurance sales occur in legal and regulatory environments that create a pervasive illusion of paranoia rather than of comfort. Specialists cannot change those environments, but they must be aware that they work in them. One way that specialists can help to generate more positive perceptions of the industry is to take the time to explain to insureds the meanings of some of the common insurance terms that perhaps have negative connotations. For example, a specialist might explain that a "limit" is actually a level of protection. Similarly, a "deductible" is really a level of retention that reduces the insured's premium. Explanations such as these can both communicate information and make the customer more comfortable with an insurance product.

The customer perceptions that the specialist can influence most directly are those derived from interactions with customers. Two types of customer expectations exist—**inherent expectations** and **spontaneous expectations**. Customer service programs can meet or exceed both of these.

Inherent Expectations

Inherent expectations are those expectations created by the nature of the service or industry. A certain level of service and a certain level of expectation are associated with any product. Inherent expectations can be met or even exceeded. As an example, to encourage customers to purchase its products and attract repeat business, a bookstore established a club and provided customers with a membership card. When a customer purchased a book at the regular price and showed the card, the customer received a second book discounted 25 percent. Most industries dealing in commodities use programs like this to move merchandise and to encourage multiple purchases. Customers have an inherent expectation about how such a club will work; in fact, a customer would probably expect the discount to be applied to the lower priced book. But the bookstore wanted to exceed the customer's inherent expectation, so it gave the discount on the higher-priced book. This is an excellent example of exceeding the customers' inherent expectations.

Examples of inherent expectations in the insurance industry are plentiful. For example, a customer might expect little or no anxiety while filling out an application for a homeowners policy. He or she might expect to obtain an insurance policy in a reasonable amount of time, say, fewer than thirty days, and that claims will be paid on a timely basis without undue difficulty.

Problems arise when insurers fail to set any expectations and then allow the expectations to be set by default. Insurers cannot meet expectations if they are unaware of their existence. When they identify expectations, they must not ignore them. The following scenario illustrates one such missed expectation:

Inherent expectations are customer expectations about a business, industry, or product.

Spontaneous expectations are customer expectations about a particular situation or circumstance.

A customer purchases insurance from a producer. The producer places the business with a company that has a backlog of paperwork and is late in issuing policies. Fifteen days later, the producer receives a call from the customer inquiring about the status of the policy. The producer assures the customer that the policy is in force. On the thirtieth day, the producer receives another call from the customer, and the customer says she has still not received her policy and wants an explanation. The producer explains that the company is back-logged and that the policy has not been issued.

The customer's call at fifteen days indicates the customer's inherent expectation that the policy will be issued in fewer than fifteen days. The company failed to meet that expectation because it was unaware that the customer had it. On the occasion of the second call, the customer has begun to wonder whether the policy has ever been ordered and is forming new expectations. At this point, the customer is thinking, "If it takes this long to get an insurance policy from this company and I'm giving them money, I wonder how long they'll take if I'm trying to collect money." Because the producer ignored the first clue about the customer's inherent expectations, and because the customer interpreted the producer's failure to act on that expectation as poor service, the customer has formed negative perceptions about the producer and the company.

The producer had a few options at the outset to prevent this problem. He could have asked what the customer expects about the timing of the delivery of the policy and then explained to the customer that the company is backed up and will take more than thirty days to issue the policy. Or he simply could have informed the customer about what she could expect the time line to be. Then he could have issued a binder to make the customer more comfortable until receiving her policy.

An Inherent Expectation That Has Been Met

At the sale of a policy, the specialist should discuss the sequence of events that will occur. In that way, the company and the specialist can create and meet a service expectation for the customer relative to the transaction at hand.

An Inherent Expectation That Is Exceeded

A customer purchases a policy from a specialist. The specialist enters the policy information into a computer, which issues the declarations page and the forms on a laser printer in the agency office. The specialist delivers the policy to the client the same day and receives payment. This is an example of exceeding the expectation of the customer because issuing a policy on the spot at the point of sale is not yet customary.

Spontaneous Expectations

Spontaneous expectations occur on the spot. They come to the customer's mind during the transaction and are acted on at the point of sale. Meeting and exceeding these expectations require flexibility. The employees involved in customer contact must have the authority to act on their own spontaneous ideas. As an example, a producer receives a call from a customer who arranged a closing on a house. The notice was short, and the customer's regular insurance contact is on vacation. The customer's spontaneous expectation is that producers will be able to provide immediate service during this unusual circumstance. After collecting the information, the producer agrees to prepare the closing papers for the homeowners and flood insurance. The normal procedure would have been to have the paperwork printed from the computer the following morning and to mail the documents to the bank. The producer prepares the paperwork immediately and drives to the bank to deliver the closing papers to the loan officer. The producer calls the customer back within a few hours to confirm that this portion of the closing was complete.

Specialists are in a position to determine and then exceed their customers' inherent and spontaneous expectations. Every interaction with customers must be managed with care. The goal should be to make a lasting positive impression. Specialists should evaluate the transactions they take part in as a customer would. What is annoying? What is pleasing? Specialists should use their own experience as a customer to guide their efforts in generating positive impressions. Specialists should not only provide added value but should also make certain that the customers recognize it.[26]

Perceptions of Insurance Costs

Many people believe they are paying money for insurance and receiving very little, or nothing, in return. Customers understand the insurance mechanism but to differing degrees. Some customers view only the cost of the policy in relation to claims they have collected and see the disparity between what they pay in premiums and what they receive in claim dollars. Some view insurance as a savings account. This perception can be found in such customer statements as, "I've had insurance with your company for five years, and I've paid $4,000 in premiums. I've only had two losses totaling $3,000, and you want to cancel my coverage!" Insurance, however, involves much more than an exchange of dollars.

Customers at the other end of the spectrum might understand the mechanism of insurance and the financial stability it provides but might still have feelings of discontent from years of paying increasing premiums without making a claim. Specialists must be aware of what they can do to help customers understand what they are receiving for the dollars they spend.

Why Insurance Costs What It Does

Customer perceptions about the cost of insurance are frequently a cause of unfulfilled expectations. Insurance is simply a financial mechanism. An insurance premium is a composite of the expected losses, the expenses to run an insurance organization, and a margin of profit. Of these components, the largest component by far is the expense for losses.

Exhibit 1-6 provides an example of what $1 of premium paid for in 1994.

Exhibit 1-6
How $1.00 of Private Passenger Auto Liability Premiums Is Spent

Loss Incurred	$ .71
Loss Adjustment Expenses	.12
Underwriting Expenses	.22
Total	$1.05

Source: A.M. Best Co., Inc., *Aggregates and Averages 1995*, p. 339.

In this example, insurers paid more in losses and expenses than they received as premium income. Insurance companies invest premiums and gain income from those investments; income from those investments helps to offset unprofitable lines of insurance. If losses and expenses far exceed premiums and investment, an insurer might draw additional funds from surplus to meet expenses. Some lines of insurance might have expenses and losses that are lower than premiums, generating a profit. This profit can be used to offset losses on less profitable lines of insurance, or it can be added to surplus. Insurance companies usually try to economize in their operating expenses in order to become more profitable. Tightening the underwriting guidelines to decrease the frequency or severity of claims is another way to try to increase profit. The subject of profitability and pricing of personal insurance policies is addressed at length in API 29.

So why are insurance premiums high and increasing? In part, the answer is that the losses that insurance must pay for are high and increasing. These losses include the costs paid for auto repairs, hospital bills, home repairs, defense attorneys, and lawsuit settlements.

Educational Objective 8
Analyze the major concerns about personal insurance raised by consumer advocates.

Consumer Advocates' View of Personal Insurance

By understanding the criticisms levied against the insurance industry, specialists can begin to correct problems or misperceptions. Denying that a problem exists does not improve a situation. Following are the opinions of three consumer advocates who discuss the insurance industry.

Insurance—The Invisible Banker

Both insurers and bankers are financial intermediaries. Andrew Tobias contrasts the insurance business with the banking business in his best-selling 1982 book, *The Invisible Bankers*. The following paragraphs are taken from Chapter 1, "The Biggest Game in the World: They just want us to *think* it's boring."

In this reading, Tobias takes a different view of the principle that insurance is a contract involving the exchange of unequal amounts. He writes, "Usually, the premium that is paid by the insured for a particular policy is more than the amounts paid by the insurer to, or on behalf of, the insured because there are no losses. It is the additional factor that the insurer's obligation might be much greater (but only if certain events occur) that makes the transaction a fair trade."[27]

We deposit our money with insurance companies to assure nest eggs for our families if we die, money for a new house if ours burns down, cash to fix the car if ours is a wreck. The insurance companies manage that money until we need it, lending it out to others in the meantime. Insurance companies are thus very much like savings banks—with one crucial difference: the amount of money any one of us might withdraw is based not on what he has deposited by way of premiums, but rather (within strictly defined limits) on what he *needs*. The $700 billion (1981 assets of the U.S. insurance industry) that we have, as a group, saved up through private insurance companies comes to more than $8,500 for each of the nation's 82 million households. Hence, "the invisible bankers."

The analogy to banking is an important one. In both cases, the product is really only money. Banks—and insurance companies—are "financial intermediaries." They collect deposits from people and businesses with extra cash and lend it to people and business (and governments) that need to borrow some. The difference is that with a bank you are entitled to withdraw 100 percent of what you deposit, often with interest. With an insurance company, you and your fellow insureds as a *group* will wind up withdrawing much of what you put in, but just how much any *individual* can draw out depends on his luck. The worse his luck, the more he is allowed to withdraw. This is the deal we make, implicitly, with our fellow depositors, just as, millennia ago, Phoenician shippers agreed to share the hazards of the seas.

But there is a second difference as well. Where a bank is able to safeguard your money, process all your checks, insure your account with the FDIC, pay for all those radio jingles, pay the rent on its building, and so on, at little or no charge to you—living off the investment income your deposit earns—insurance companies are unable to do this. For every dollar we collectively "deposit" with an auto insurer, for example, only 65 cents or so is available for our collective withdrawal. (Some will withdraw much more, many will withdraw nothing, but *on average*, for every dollar Americans pay in auto insurance premiums, 65 or 70 cents gets paid back.) Some bank! Deposit a dollar, withdraw 65 cents. The rest of our dollar, plus the interest the insurance company earns on it, goes to expenses, overhead and profit.

What kind of bank gives back just 65 percent—often less—of what you deposit? Indeed, when you compare the services of a bank and an insurance company, common sense suggests something is out of whack. Think how often you deal with your bank, how many checks it clears for you in the course of a year, how many statements it mails you, loans it discusses with you. . .and then think how much contact you are likely to have with your insurers. Why can one live off the interest on the balance in your checking account, while the other needs to take 35 cents—or more—of each dollar you deposit? Could it be that one is vastly more efficient?

It takes 1.9 million people to staff the insurance industry. Would you say it takes twice as much to run the banks? Five times as many? (After all, they have all those credit applications to analyze, all those security guards to keep on patrol, all those toaster-ovens to give away.) At the end of 1980 there were actually more Americans employed in the insurance industry than in banking. The banks presided over three times as much money, handled vastly more "transactions"—and yet managed to make do with about a quarter of a million fewer people. And without grabbing 20 or 40 or 50 cents of each deposited dollar.[28]

How Much Does the Consumer Know?

In their 1990 book *Winning the Insurance Game*, consumer advocates Ralph Nader and Wesley J. Smith contend that insurance inflicts several forms of pain on consumers who do not know "what is going on." The following excerpt is from Chapter 2 of the book, which goes on to furnish a great deal of useful information designed to help consumers understand insurance. It also points out why consumers need information and advice regarding their options. Informed personal insurance specialists can help meet this consumer need.

> What is insurance and how does the industry operate? Most of us do not really know. More important, we don't really understand how to make insurance work effectively for us. Oh, we complain about the costs of premiums (frequently with justification), but fundamentally, as consumers, too often we just do not know what is going on.
>
> This is a risky state, for while ignorance might be bliss in affairs of the heart, in matters of insurance it's what you do not know that can and often does hurt you. This pain most frequently comes in one of the following forms (and sometimes in all three):
>
> - **The insurance consumer pays more money than necessary for the coverage received.** Many companies charge more than is reasonable for their services. Part of this is the fault of the system, but a great deal of the problems rests with consumers themselves who allow the companies to get away with it because they do not spend the time it takes to find the best deal. Thus, the potential for competition that does still exist is not actualized—to the benefit of the overchargers.
>
> - **The insurance consumer does not understand what is being purchased.** As a result, there might be a duplication of coverage and a resulting overpayment of premiums.
>
> - **Worst of all, the consumer has no understanding of what is *not* being purchased.** This causes dangerous gaps in coverage, leaving the consumer exposed, unprotected, and ripe for the financial fall or even bankruptcy. [29]

The Consumer Viewpoint

Harvey Rosenfield, a consumer advocate, is chairman of Voter Revolt, the California-based citizens' organization for Proposition 103. He is also the author of Proposition 103.

In November 1988, California voters passed Proposition 103 despite extensive opposition by the insurance industry. Among other things, it called for auto insurance rates to be rolled back by 20 percent to below November 1987 levels. It also changed the state's longstanding competitive rating laws to prior-approval laws (both types of laws will be discussed in Chapter 4) and granted an additional 20 percent discount to good drivers, defined as drivers with no more than one conviction for a moving violation. Although the legal effect of Proposition 103 is limited to California, shock waves were felt throughout the entire U.S. property-liability insurance industry when this bill was passed because of the potential for similar propositions appearing across the country.

The following material is an excerpt from a much longer article, "Proposition 103: The Consumer's Viewpoint," published in the 1991 publication of the CPCU Society, *The Impact of Consumer Activism on the Insurance Industry*. Much of Mr. Rosenfield's article deals specifically with Proposition 103 and its effects, but the excerpted material below deals mainly with general consumer issues relating to insurance.

> Unlike virtually every other private industry in the United States, the insurance industry's relationship with the consumer is often an involuntary one. At the very least, insurance is a matter of economic survival for businesses, homeowners, municipal entities, and other consumers. And in many states, motorists are compelled to become consumers of insurance by law.
>
> This crucial distinction is the basis for understanding the consumer viewpoint toward insurance reform—a viewpoint manifested by Proposition 103 and its progeny across the United States. In a free marketplace, when the relationship between the seller and the buyer become unsatisfactory, buyers have the option of looking elsewhere—or not buying at all. In the insurance system, unhappy consumers do not have the luxury of refusing its purchase. Instead, as in the provision of essential services such as police, fire, water, gas, and telephone, consumers first look to the government to protect them in their contractual relationships with private insurance firms. If that proves unsatisfactory, consumers will ask the government to take a more active role in providing the product they need. . . .
>
> Central to the consumer analysis is the understanding that the insurance industry is no longer strictly a mechanism for risk sharing, as it once was many years ago. Rather, the insurance industry has become a financial institution devoted primarily to maximizing profits; premiums are simply the funds used to fuel the profit engine.
>
> Rates, in turn, are a function of conditions in the financial marketplace. Indeed, the industry has it own "cycle": in times of high interest

rates, insurer investments produce an excellent return. Under such conditions, the industry reduces rates and frequently underwrites poor risks to attract capital for investments.

When interest rates are low and investment yields are correspondingly reduced, the industry increases insurance premiums to maintain high profits and offset the results of imprudent business judgments. The rate "crises" of the last two decades correspond exactly to the troughs in this financial cycle.

The recognition of the insurance industry as merely another form of profit-oriented financial institution illuminated a profound contradiction in the industry's fundamental purpose and responsibility. Though insurers are in the business of compensating for loss, as profit-making ventures they have nothing to gain—in fact they have a great deal to lose if accidents or claims decrease.

Put another way, insurers operate on a "cost-plus" basis: accident costs are passed through to consumers, along with very considerable markup for profit and profit hidden in the form of bloated overhead, surplus and reserves. Thus, the more accidents and claims, the more justification for higher rates, which in turn, means more funds for investment and hence higher profits. The present system of insurance perversely rewards the very events insurance is designed to protect against. . . .[30]

Resolution of the Disparity

A breakdown in communication and understanding between customers and the insurance industry has occurred. Consumer advocates have become a voice echoing the resulting uneasiness. Reviewing the definition of insurance returns focus to the intent of the insurance mechanism. Insurance is three things:

- It is a transfer technique whereby one party—the insured—transfers the chance of financial loss to another party—the insurance company.

- It is a business and, as such, needs to be conducted in a way that provides a reasonable profit for its owners.

- It is a contract between the insured and the insurer that states what financial consequences of loss are transferred and expresses the insurer's promise to pay for those consequences.[31]

Educating consumers and improving communication between consumers and the insurance industry are vital in helping policyholders understand how insurance operates and how insurance can help them meet their needs. This brings the discussion back to the beginning and to the pivotal point between the insurance industry and the consumer: the specialist in personal insurance. Employing specialists who can generate a greater level of understanding and a spirit of partnership will not fix all of the problems with the image of the insurance industry or fill all of the customers' needs, but it will be a start.

Summary

Property and liability insurance accounts for a large segment of the economy, and personal insurance accounts for half of the property and liability insurance industry's premium dollars. The personal insurance industry fulfills social needs, sponsors programs in public safety, and provides financial security and peace of mind to insurance customers. The role of personal insurance becomes clouded in the customer's mind when insurance is made compulsory by state auto regulations or semicompulsory by lending institutions.

Specialists in personal insurance fill a crucial role within the insurance industry by understanding the customers' perceptions of insurance and by providing service as well as education to customers. The roles and requirements of specialists are changing. Therefore, they need to improve their skills and develop characteristics to remain effective. For example, valuing professional ethics and possessing technical competence are vital to the success of a specialist in personal insurance.

Specialists must interpret insureds' financial needs, financial goals, and ability to accept risk. They can apply risk management techniques to fulfill personal insurance customers' individual needs. Insurance is only one of the possible techniques for addressing risk.

Customers carry their service expectations into each insurance transaction. Even if customers do not communicate those expectations, specialists should be aware of the customers' service needs and work to meet or exceed those expectations.

When customers' needs are not met, consumer advocates are often active in expressing customer dissatisfaction. Specialists should be aware of these points of view in order to correct real or perceived problems.

Chapter Notes

1. George Leland Bach, *Economics*, 9th ed. (Englewood Cliffs, NJ: Prentice-Hall, 1977), p. 210.
2. Peter R. Kensicki, Christopher J. Amrhein, Thomas S. Marshall, and Seeman Waranch, *Principles of Insurance Production*, vol. 1, 3d ed. (Malvern, PA: Insurance Institute of America, 1991), pp. 14-16.
3. Insurance Information Institute, *The Fact Book*, 1996 (New York, NY: Insurance Information Institute, 1995), p. 20.
4. Adapted from Ronald C. Horn, *On Professions, Professionals, and Professional Ethics* (Malvern, PA: American Institute for Property and Liability Underwriters, 1978), p. 50.
5. *Consumer Reports*, August 1992, p. 489.
6. Ruth Gastel, "Compulsory Auto Insurance," *Insurance Issues Update*, May 1995, pp. 1-6.
7. Gastel, p. 6.

8. Bruce McEwan, "Rights and Responsibilities: The Consumer Contract," *CPCU Journal*, June 1993, pp. 81-83.

9. Samuel Weese and Egnar Jensen, "Ethics in Life Insurance and Related Financial Services," *Essays on Ethics:* vol. II (Malvern, PA: American Institute for Chartered Property Casualty Underwriters, 1994), pp. 6-9.

10. Richard W. Malus, "Ethical Conduct in Supplying and Receiving Underwriting Information," *Essays on Ethics: vol. II*, pp. 31-33.

11. Carl Ferraris, "Legalistic Versus Ethics-Based Management," *Essays on Ethics*, vol. II, p. 27.

12. Horn, p. 47.

13. Horn, p. 48.

14. Genevieve Reday-Mulvey, "Continuing Training until End of Career: A Key Policy for the Fourth Pillar," *The Geneva Papers on Risk and Insurance*, no. 73, October 1994.

15. CPCU Society's Connecticut Chapter, Research Committee, "Differing Perspectives on Auto Insurance: Consumers, Company Personnel, and Agents," *CPCU Journal*, March 1994, pp. 19-21.

16. George White, Ronald Duska, and Victor Lincoln, *Organizational Behavior in Insurance* (Malvern, PA: Insurance Institute of America, 1992), p. 132.

17. Adapted from Robert Gibbons, George Rejda, and Michael Elliott, *Insurance Perspectives* (Malvern, PA: American Institute for Chartered Property Casualty Underwriters, 1992), pp. 56-57.

18. Adapted from Smith, Trieschmann, Wiening, and Johnson, *Property and Liability Insurance Principles*, 2d ed. (Malvern, PA: Insurance Institute of America, 1994), pp. 160-161.

19. Gibbons, Rejda, and Elliott, p. 58.

20. George E. Rejda, *Principles of Risk Management and Insurance*, 4th ed. (New York, NY: Harper Collins Publishers, 1992), p. 6.

21. A. James Fix and David Daughton, *The Odds Almanac* (New York, NY: Follett Publishing Company, 1980), p. 44.

22. Rejda, p. 6.

23. Rejda, p. 6.

24. Joseph J. Launie, J. Finley Lee, and Norman A. Baglini, *Principles of Property and Liability Underwriting* (Malvern, PA: Insurance Institute of America, 1986), pp. 321-325.

25. Adapted from White, Duska, and Lincoln, p. 133.

26. Howard Candage, "Perceptions and Adding Value," *Delivering Insurance Services—AIS 25 Course Guide* (Malvern, PA: Insurance Institute of America, 1994), pp. 153-155.

27. Smith, Trieschmann, Wiening, and Johnson, p. 171.

28. Andrew Tobias, *The Invisible Bankers* (New York, NY: Linden Press, 1982), pp. 5-6.

29. Ralph Nader and Wesley J. Smith, *Winning the Insurance Game* (New York, NY: Knightsbridge Publishing Company, 1990), pp. 8-9.

30. Harvey Rosenfield, "Proposition 103: The Consumer's Viewpoint," excerpted in "The Impact of Consumer Activism on the Insurance Industry," The Society of CPCU, 1991.

31. Smith, Trieschmann, Wiening, and Johnson, p. 1.

Chapter 2

Educational Objectives

1. Explain how insurers use market segments in the marketing process. (pp. 2-1 to 2-7)

2. Describe how an insurer differentiates its insurance product from competitors' products. (pp. 2-7 to 2-11)

3. Describe the insurance product development process. (pp. 2-11 to 2-13)

4. Explain how an insurer selects a distribution system. (pp. 2-14 to 2-18)

5. Explain how an insurer promotes insurance products. (pp. 2-18 to 2-21)

6. Describe the marketing research process and the sources of information that can be used in the marketing research process. (pp. 2-21 to 2-26)

7. Explain how marketing can be performed in service areas such as sales, underwriting, and claims. (pp. 2-26 to 2-28)

8. Given a marketing case study for a personal insurance company, describe how to identify customer needs, design the product, and distribute the product. (Encompasses entire chapter.)

Chapter 2

How Insurers Market Insurance to Customers

Marketing is the process of identifying customers and their needs and then creating, distributing, promoting, and pricing products or services to meet those needs. Insurers use marketing to develop strategies and plans to obtain and retain customers.

Marketing is not only a department or function within an organization; it is also a management philosophy. Every person in an insurance organization is responsible for understanding the customers' needs and responding to them effectively. Every person should be aware of the organization's marketing approach and his or her role in providing support and customer service to reinforce the company's marketing goals.

To contribute to their companies' ability to succeed, producers, customer service representatives, underwriters, and managers should have a broad knowledge of marketing techniques and trends. They should know who their customers are and, generally, how their customers' needs are changing.

Educational Objective 1

Explain how insurers use market segments in the marketing process.

The Marketing Process

The following items make up the three steps in the marketing process:

1. Identifying who the customers are and what the customers want according to their needs and perceptions
2. Designing products that meet the customers' needs
3. Selecting distribution systems to serve the customers

This marketing process is not unique to insurance marketing. Whether a company sells toothpaste or cotton T-shirts, it must first identify the customers who might purchase its product. The company then designs the product and the product's image to appeal to its customers. Distribution and advertising are tailored to attract the attention of those customers.

Insurance companies follow this marketing process with one difference: insurance companies try to sell to customers who fit certain profiles (described by their underwriting guidelines). Insurance companies want to sell policies, but they also want to be able to select the buyers of those policies. Insurers must market in a way that targets the customers they wish to attract and encourages those customers to apply for coverage so that the insurance company can avoid adverse selection. Consequently, insurance advertising is a highly specialized field.

At the heart of the marketing concept is the customer. The marketing process stresses product development based on studies of customer attitudes and behavior. To deliver insurance to customers, an insurer must first determine who the customer is and what the customer's characteristics are. Customer needs should drive product design and development. Companies that hold the customer as the focus of the marketing process recognize that profit lies in creating, marketing, and selling products and services that satisfy customer needs.

Identifying the Customer

An insurance company could identify the entire population of a state, a region, or the country as its potential customers. However, a single product would probably not meet the needs of all those customers. More frequently, an insurance company evaluates, selects, and groups customers who have similar characteristics.

Understanding the Customer

When using the marketing process, market researchers first develop a profile of potential customers. Market researchers gather, tabulate, and analyze customer profile data, but all employees in decision-making positions should be familiar with customer characteristics. An underwriter or a producer who recognizes customer characteristics will be able to respond more effectively to opportunities to promote company products or correct problems in a way that is consistent with the customers' needs. Examples of groups and group characteristics that are of current interest to insurance marketers are the following:

- *Depression babies* are customers who grew up in the era of the Great Depression. Because these people lived during a period of severe economic instability, they tend to be extremely security-conscious. They fear policy cancellation and look for the security that insurance provides. They want a relationship with a trustworthy insurer that advises them and helps them make insurance decisions. Depression babies tend to rely on formal rather than informal information sources.[1] Insurers who wish to market to depression babies might stress long-term relationships and security.

- *Baby boomers* are a huge population segment of people born between 1946 and 1964. Few market segments have drawn greater attention or inspired more ideas from marketing executives and advertisers than baby boomers.[2] Studies show that this customer group uses convenience products and services more than other customer groups.[3] Consequently, they are willing to use 800 numbers, read insurance contracts, and call insurance commissioners in order to get the best service and coverage for their premiums. In this respect, insurers who wish to market to baby boomers must make their service accessible and present it in a format that helps baby boomers answer their own questions.

- *Nesting adults* are young adults during any time period who are settling into homes and raising families. They are generally new in their careers and homes, so they have little disposable income. Because nesting adults do not have money to waste, they are likely to shop around for coverage and be conservative in insurance purchases. Insurers might present their products as bargain buys to nesting adults. By demonstrating to this group that an insurance product is less expensive than other products, insurance marketers can capture this group's attention. Since customers have varied needs during different stages of their lives, insurers are starting to pay more attention to this group of customers because in time they will attain more financial security and will acquire larger homes and possessions that require additional insurance coverage.

These market groups do not reflect all possible groupings of insureds. There are as many market groups as there are imaginative marketers who group them. These groups are interesting, but they have no value unless they are used to assess product development opportunities. Insurers must transform their products or services to meet changing customer behaviors, tastes, and lifestyles. For example, if the customer is a young family, that family wants low-price, basic coverage, and it will probably purchase that coverage through direct mail if the price is lower than through other distribution channels. On the other hand, if the customer is a retiree, he or she is less likely to be concerned about price and is more likely to seek reassurance that he or she is secure and covered.

Segmenting the Market

Market segmentation is the grouping of customers with similar or related characteristics who can be expected to buy a product or service that satisfies their similar needs.

Of all the possible buyers in the market, on which customers will an insurance company focus? **Market segmentation** enables companies to determine who their customers might be by dividing the marketplace into clearly defined groups based on demographics, geographic location, lifestyle, and other factors, which will be described later. Once market segments have been determined, insurers develop plans to tap the potential of each segment.

Insurance companies use the phrase *target market* to describe a chosen market segment. Once an insurance company divides the population of customers into segments, it *targets*, or focuses on, specific groups for marketing efforts. For example, a company might target local college graduates for auto insurance sales.

Attractive Market Segments

Any market includes more customer groups with specific needs than any one insurer could possibly serve adequately. Therefore, attractive market opportunities exist when competitors do not satisfy customer needs.

Marketing management defines logical market segments. Each marketing segment should meet the following criteria:

- *Accessible*—Segments should be able to be effectively reached and served.

- *Substantial*—Size and purchasing power should suggest potential profitability.

- *Responsive*—Actions taken by the insurer should produce satisfactory results.

A marketing *niche* is a well-defined, often small marketing segment of the population that has specific needs. Niches are especially attractive in marketing because they provide an insurer with the opportunity to develop expertise regarding the customers' special needs. A product can be specifically tailored to meet such customers' needs, and a company or an agency can become an expert within that niche. An insurer is less likely to encounter competition in a niche market than in the open market. An example of niche marketing within insurance is marketing done by producers who specialize in condominiums, mobile homes, or large watercraft.

Creating Segments

Groups of buyers with similar characteristics and therefore similar insurance needs form market segments. By grouping customers with common needs into market segments, marketers gain a degree of **homogeneity**. Whatever basis a company uses to segment its market, the final segment should be prospective customers who are as similar to each other as possible.

Homogeneity describes the similarity among individuals in a market segment as well as the similarity among insureds in the same rating class.

Demographic Segmentation   Demographic segmentation is the division of customer markets based on variables such as income, age, sex, education, stages in the family life cycle (child rearing, middle age, and retirement), and lifestyle. A company that produces music on compact discs would be interested in using this type of segmentation to determine prospective customers for the type of music it produces, because no one style of music appeals to all listeners. An insurer marketing auto insurance might also use this form of segmentation: a young family would be interested in a product that offers a low price, but a professional couple with substantial assets might seek an auto insurance policy that provides high limits and extended service.

Geographic Segmentation   Geographic segmentation divides customers according to the location in which they live. This is the most widely used approach to segmentation. Companies target metropolitan or rural markets or regions with different climates, cultures, and social characteristics. A clothing manufacturer would develop some products that appeal to customers in Alaska and other products that appeal to customers in Texas. An insurer selling homeowners insurance in the northeastern United States might offer a product that provides coverage targeting historic homes, and an insurer selling homeowners insurance in the Southwest might target owners of farms and ranches.

Lifestyle Segmentation   Lifestyle segmentation (also called psychographic segmentation) is the division of customers according to their lifestyles so that their buying behavior can be identified. This method of segmentation focuses on individual consumption patterns, according to the theory that people project a lifestyle and associated habits through the products they consume. In the 1970s, toothpaste companies discovered that many people brush their teeth after they wake up but before they eat breakfast. Although that is an ineffective time for dental care, people had adopted that habit so that their mouths would be fresh at the breakfast table. Toothpaste companies used that marketing information to intensify the flavors of their products and advertise the mouthwash quality of their toothpastes. Insurance companies might use this approach to appeal to a retiree's need for security. For example, product features such as a limited cancellation clause, which restricts policy cancellation for a period of years or for specific events, might appeal to retirees. Lifestyle segments are identified through studies of customer activities (such as hobbies, sports, work, entertainment, and clubs), interests (such as family, home, community, and recreation), and opinions (regarding politics, religion, education, and social issues).

Unique Market Segments in Personal Insurance

As previously noted, identifying customers and their needs is an important first step in the marketing process. **Risk analysis** is a method of determining customer insurance needs, and creating broad market segments is unique to insurance. For an individual or a family, the process of risk analysis might be relatively simple. A brief application might provide the information needed for the analysis.

Insurers often group customers into broad market segments based on their risk analysis of those customers. Insurance companies then set rates and guidelines for those customer segments. An insurer or a producer can also use segments for further marketing refinement, though all

Risk analysis is the process of identifying loss exposures and estimating the potential financial consequences of those losses.

insurers do not sell to all market segments and different insurers will define different boundaries for the same market segment. Exhibit 2-1 is an insurance market segment chart that depicts the broad markets defined by some insurers. A column has been added in which you can identify which market segments your organization uses.

Educational Objective 2
Describe how an insurer differentiates its insurance product from competitors' products.

Designing the Insurance Product

After the customer segment has been profiled and the insurer has determined what market it will target, the product design step begins. Differentiating a product from that of the competition, making it appeal to a specific customer segment, and communicating the product's characteristics and service standards in a persuasive and believable manner are all part of product design.

The Insurance Product

Customers do not always know what they want a product to do, so they often represent their needs in the form of feelings and opinions. People generally have feelings about insurance, but they do not always know how to translate them into insurance product ideas. Marketers should listen carefully to customers' opinions in order to determine those elements that can be used in product design.

Insurance customers often do not fully understand what they are buying, so they have difficulty expressing what they need or want from an insurance product. All products have elements of tangibility and intangibility. In insurance, the tangible product is a legal contract represented by words on paper. Insurance policy packaging, which includes appearance and presentation, is also a tangible aspect of insurance. Other tangible elements of insurance are the physical appearance of the producer's office, the demeanor of the customer service representatives, and the appearance of the insurer's office building.

Insurance products also have elements of intangibility. When customers buy insurance products, they are buying promises, and promises are intangible. An insurer can only create an image that inspires confidence or provides testimony about how it has fulfilled other promises. Although promises are intangible, insurers often find ways in advertising to describe insurance to make it seem more tangible and therefore easier to understand. The message, theme, and content of property and liability insurance marketing communications often personalize the insurance product and represent it tangibly. For instance, the message might be that the insurer is "your partner" with a "blanket of protection."

Exhibit 2-1
Insurance Market Segments by Risk Group

Insurance Market Segments	Description	Your Notes
Standard Risks	Standard risks are average risks. They are comparable to the risks on which the rate has been based for average property and liability exposures. Standard risks are not subject to rate loadings or restrictions because of unacceptable exposures or hazards.*	
Preferred Risks	Preferred risks are considered to be better than standard risks, on which standard rates are determined.*	
Excess and Surplus Markets	Excess and surplus markets provide coverage for unusual or high-risk exposures that are not written by insurers licensed within the state.	
Involuntary Markets/ Residual Markets	Involuntary market mechanisms provide coverage for insureds who cannot qualify for coverage elsewhere. Residual markets (also called shared market mechanisms) comprise various markets outside of the normal agency-company marketing system. Residual markets include government insurance programs and specialty pools.*	

*Thomas E. Green, ed. *Glossary of Insurance Terms*, 5th ed. (Santa Monica, CA: The Merritt Company, 1993).

How Insurers Create Unique Products

Designing a product or service to gain a competitive advantage in a market segment entails pinpointing those customers or market segments with unmet needs. Products that will meet those needs must then be distinguished from the existing competitive products. Once those distinguishing characteristics are identified and communicated to the targeted market segment, a company can position its product for competitive advantage. Positioning is the process of developing and maintaining a distinctive place in the market. Positioning helps a company to establish a clear, positive image of the company itself, its product, its performance, or specific attributes distinct from the competition.

Insurers might differentiate products to meet specific customer needs. The following sections describe ways in which insurers have made their products unique.

Product Specialization

Insurers develop personal insurance policies that meet the insurance needs of many insurance customers. Those policies can be fine-tuned to address the specific loss exposures of a market segment by creating endorsements to modify coverage. Insurers often develop their own endorsements to meet the needs of customers within a targeted segment.

An insurer can pursue a **product specialization** strategy by tailoring one line of insurance in several ways to meet the needs of multiple market segments. Different market segments have different needs, requiring different products and sales strategies. The following examples illustrate this point:

Product specialization in insurance is the tailoring of an otherwise standard policy to meet the needs of a market segment.

- A retiree could need coverage for a golf cart used for transportation within a retirement community. This need could be satisfied by creating an endorsement to be added to a homeowners policy to provide liability and physical damage coverage.

- College students could need a special low-limit, inexpensive tenant homeowners policy or a roommate's policy. This need could be satisfied by providing an HO-4 homeowners policy with underwriting guidelines modified to provide lower coverage limits and allow nonrelatives to be joint policyholders.

- Collectors of memorabilia, antiques, limited edition prints, and so forth, could need specialized fine arts coverage. This need could be satisfied by expanding their homeowners coverage by adding an endorsement that would provide agreed value coverage for antiques and collectibles.

Market Specialization

An insurer could follow a **market specialization** strategy by selling various coverages to one type of market segment. For example, an insurer could serve the multiple-lines needs of homeowners with offices in their homes. The insurer could add business by identifying additional insurance and service needs of the target market and then

Market specialization targets a specific market segment. Multiple lines of insurance products are then targeted to that customer group.

developing products to meet those needs. "Office-in-home" accounts could be targeted for increased computer, personal umbrella liability, business liability, and business auto coverage. Specialized customer service could be provided to answer the unique questions these customers have, which pertain to both personal and commercial insurance.

Price Differentiation

Personal lines insurers often use price to differentiate their products. An insurer that wants to charge a lower price than its competitors must reduce its costs, its profits, or both to a level below those of the competition. It must also comply with the statutory requirement that rates be adequate to allow the insurer both to respond to losses and to generate enough income to remain in business over the long term.

An insurance rate includes components for losses, expenses, and profit. An insurer might justify a rate reduction by reducing any one of those three components. The allowance for losses might be reduced through more restrictive underwriting guidelines. The allowance for expenses might be reduced through expense control measures. Price differentiation might also be achieved by refining rating classes. One rating class might be divided into two subclasses, with a lower rate for members of one subclass and a higher rate for members of the other.

Service Differentiation

Service differentiation has been a key element in the product differentiation strategy for many insurers. Services offered by insurers can be effectively promoted to customers as tangible product improvements. The following are some examples:

- Drive-in claims centers for auto estimates
- Conveniently located producers
- 800 telephone numbers
- Financing terms or installments for premiums
- Annual insurance reviews
- Long-term policyholder recognition (membership recognition such as a premium discount)
- Claims and service centers open twenty-four hours a day

An Insurer's Marketing Personality

Insurance companies have personalities that emerge through the company's characteristics. The following are some examples of ways companies can be characterized:

- A company is willing or unwilling to take risks.
- A company is competitive or is conservative in its policy pricing methods.
- A company targets liability coverages or targets property coverages.

Characteristics are determined by company traditions, the success in past markets, expertise in product lines, and capital/capacity strength. Traditions, goals, and changing forces in an insurance company's environment (such as economy, market cycles, competition, and catastrophic losses) shape the insurance company's personality and its marketing direction. A company that is conservative and successful in writing property coverage might target a preferred or high-valued homeowners market segment. A company that has successfully underwritten classes with above average expected losses might seek new market segments such as owners of high-powered watercraft or ultra-light aircraft.

Educational Objective 3
Describe the insurance product development process.

Product Development Process

Management must decide which insurance products and services will be sold to which markets. There are many product decisions to be made, ranging from what product lines to offer to what coverages, limits, and deductibles will be included in the policy.

Insurers usually follow a process in product development. Exhibit 2-2 shows the steps in the product development process for property and liability products.

Opportunity Assessment

The first step, opportunity assessment, consists of monitoring the marketplace to identify potential opportunities. Monitoring the market consists of several activities. For example, producers might alert insurers when they learn of innovative products offered by competitors. Also, some insurers use producer advisory councils to assess market threats and to obtain suggestions about ways to counter them. New product ideas are often developed based on those suggestions. Producer associations provide their members with information on insurer product development on a state-by-state basis.

The A.M. Best Company publishes a monthly newsletter, "Best's Intelligencer," describing the filings insurers make. In addition to describing new product features, the report gives information on modifications to existing products. "Best's Intelligencer" typically describes programs in terms of the type of policyholder eligible for the program, the rate deviation from filed levels, and the policy endorsements that either expand or restrict coverage.

After new product opportunities have been identified, they can be evaluated against the insurer's objectives. Management must determine whether the insurer's long-term objectives would be served if it were to offer a product rather than wait until the market becomes further developed and the major participants in that market emerge.

Exhibit 2-2
Product Development Process

Major Steps

I. Opportunity Assessment

- Monitor market
- Identify opportunity
- Relate opportunities to business strategy
- Develop specifications
- Secure approval to proceed

II. Development of Contract, Underwriting, and Pricing

- Develop coverage/policy forms
- Develop guidelines for underwriting/claims
- Develop classifications
- Develop pricing structure
- Secure insurer management approval

III. Business Forecast

- Review the forms, underwriting guides, and pricing with profit center management
- Identify requirements for statistics
- Develop business forecast
- Secure insurer management approval

IV. Regulatory Requirements

- File with regulators
- Develop statistical information systems
- Communicate regulatory approval

V. Distribution Requirements

- Develop sales promotional information
- Develop advertising
- Develop sales training
- Plan roll-out strategy

VI. Product Introduction

- Implement sales training and promotion
- Measure/compare results to plan

Development of Contracts, Underwriting, and Pricing

If management decides to continue with product development, the next steps are to develop the policy forms and underwriting guidelines as well as to determine price. Cooperation among various insurer functions—including underwriting, actuarial, claims, reinsurance, premium audit, and loss control—is essential.

Often, those functions create task forces with their own personnel to investigate the implications of new products on the insurer's operations. Each functional representative enhances the product and assists in identifying operational changes necessary to make implementation feasible. For instance, an underwriting representative might create new applications to capture the factors essential in underwriting and pricing the new product. A CSR might identify training needed by the staff who will respond to customers' phone calls.

An important consideration in product development is the ability of the insurer's information system to accommodate the new product. Data processing personnel usually require extensive lead time to determine the effect of a new product on automated system resources. Some relatively simple product innovations might require substantial programming costs.

Business Forecast

The business forecast step establishes a number of benchmarks for evaluating the success of the product, including the following:

- The premium volume expected to be generated
- The number of producers expected to participate
- The expected loss ratio
- The methods to gather data that can be used to analyze product success or failure

This information is sometimes developed from past experience, from the experience of others, or from estimates based on the demand for a product.

Regulatory Requirements

After the profit center management approves the business forecast, the product development process moves to the regulatory step. State regulators usually require notification of new policy forms, rating plans, and policy underwriting rules. In most states, to protect policyholder interests, state regulatory officials must approve changes in existing products and the introduction of new ones.

Distribution Requirements and Product Introduction

After regulatory approval, the insurer determines distribution require-ments. The insurer develops an overall plan for effectively advertising and distributing the new product to the targeted customers. The selection and development of a distribution system is the third step in the marketing process and is discussed in the next section. The insurer develops advertising and promotional material that will attract customer attention. Producers will receive training regarding the new product and its features.

After the product has been distributed, the insurer monitors the results compared to the benchmarks developed in the business forecast. Corrective actions are taken to assist in the distribution and sales of any product that is not performing as planned.

> **Educational Objective 4**
> Explain how an insurer selects a distribution system.

Selecting a Distribution System

A distribution system communicates product information between the seller and buyers (or potential buyers) and distributes the product.

A **distribution system** consists of the necessary people and physical facilities to (1) communicate information between the seller of the product and buyers or potential buyers and (2) move the product between the seller and the buyers. For tangible products, such as automobiles and refrigerators, the distribution system might include extensive and costly physical facilities, such as trucks, terminals, warehouses, and showrooms. Distribution systems for intangible products are more flexible and adaptable because they do not require large investments in physical facilities.

Producers are the sales force in property and liability insurance.

The word **producer** is used to describe a person who sells insurance (that is, who *produces* sales). As will be described later in this chapter, producers might be either employees of the insurer or independent contractors. Insurers meet sales objectives by recruiting, selecting, training, motivating, and rewarding producers.

The major marketing distribution decisions include what type of producers to have, how many producers to have, and where to locate them. In addition, the marketing department might form a profile of an ideal producer so that appropriate recruiting and training can be developed. Then, for example, if a company has targeted retirees as a market segment, the company should train producers on the needs and concerns of that group so that they can provide more effective service.

Customer-Driven Distribution Systems

Increasingly, insurers are selecting distribution systems based on the customers' needs within a target market. Whatever distribution system and services meet the customers' needs drives the system selection. The following examples illustrate a customer-driven distribution system:

- A young family might shop for insurance based on the lowest price. The distribution system that best meets the needs of these customers might involve shopping on the phone using a toll-free number and completing paperwork through the mail. Regarding service, these customers might require a knowledgeable CSR who can respond to specific questions.

- As customers prosper, acquire larger homes, and become involved in more activities, low price might not be the most important consideration in selecting an insurance product. They might decide to expand the scope of coverages purchased. To meet these changing needs, they might select a local producer who acts as an advisor.

An insurer identifies the needs of the targeted customer segment. Those needs drive the distribution system and the customer service provided.

Commonly Used Distribution Systems

Personal lines insurance companies in the United States commonly use the following six distribution systems:

1. Independent producers
2. Exclusive producers
3. Direct writers
4. Direct response
5. Mixed marketing
6. Brokers

Exhibit 2-3 provides a comparative summary of the different distribution systems. INS 21 discusses these systems in detail.

Emerging Distribution Systems

Insurance distribution systems are changing because the insurance market is changing. Insurers are adjusting to the customers' changing needs and use more than one system when necessary or appropriate. For instance, insurers now help customers buy insurance as groups or purchase insurance by phone and through electronics.

Group Sales and Associations

Insureds can affiliate with groups to increase their purchasing power. As a result, insurers are finding that selling to groups creates a new distribution method, which enables the insurer to reach still more markets.

Employers are exploring group property-liability sales, such as personal auto insurance for their employees. The American Association of Retired Persons, the American Automobile Association, customer groups, and clubs now arrange insurance for their members. Such groups give members a price advantage through arrangements negotiated with the insurer providing the coverage. Insurers bid for the blocks of business and the advertising conducted by the member organizations. Selling insurance through groups and trade associations is not unusual in commercial lines and is becoming more common in personal lines.

Sales Through Banks

For the past three decades, banks have shown an interest in entering the insurance market. Consequently, banks are exploring the option of selling insurance through their distribution channels. Insurers are also exploring their options in combining their expertise in insurance with the banks' distribution systems. The following are bank customer groups that could be potential markets for insurers:

- Credit-card holders
- ATM users
- Auto loan borrowers
- Mortgage borrowers
- Investors

Exhibit 2-3
Insurance Distribution Systems

System of Distribution	System Description	Company Employees or Contractors	Compensation	Ownership of Renewals
Independent Agents	Producers can represent many insurers.	Independent contractors.	Flat percentage commission or profit-sharing commission.	Independent producers own the expirations.
Exclusive Agents	Producers can only represent one insurer or a group of related insurers.	Independent contractors.	Commissions (the percentage can differ depending on whether it is new business or renewal).	Insurance company owns the expirations, unless a contract grants the producer limited ownership.
Direct Writers	Producers can represent only their employers.	Employees of insurance company.	Salary, commission, or a combination of the two.	Insurance company owns the expirations.
Direct Response (Mail Order)	Insurance companies offer services through mail, telephone, and advertising.	Company employees provide customer service.	Salary is paid to employees.	Insurance company owns the expirations.
Mixed Marketing	The insurance company uses more than one system.	Both company employees and independent contractors can be used.	Salary, commission, or a combination of the two.	Insurance company owns the expirations.
Brokers	Brokers shop for the best coverage for their clients.	Independent businesses or firms that represent customers.	Commissions from the insurance company.	The broker or the producer who places the policy for the broker generally owns the expirations.

Jargon Alert!

The terms "renewal" and "expiration" are often used interchangeably. Both terms refer to the continuation of the policy at the anniversary. Typically, the company determines which term is used.

Banks have many features that make their distribution systems attractive to insurers. Some of the features are as follows:

- Networks of facilities and CSRs
- Long-term customers
- Extensive technology
- Money management capabilities

Regulatory barriers have prevented banks and insurers from combining, but these prohibitions are under attack at the state and federal levels. The similarity of these industries (both meet the financial needs of individuals through a network of customer-oriented service representatives) causes the potential marketing combination of banks and insurers to be continually revisited.

Telemarketing

Telemarketing is selling directly to customers over the phone. Used properly, telemarketing can be an effective selling tool. Used improperly, telemarketing can be an irritation to potential customers who receive intrusive sales pitches in their homes by phone.

When insurers use telemarketing as a distribution method, they normally do so with caution because of the potential of creating negative impressions with prospective customers. Consequently, telemarketing calls are often limited to very specific questions. Insurance telemarketers might use a call only to obtain the individual's auto policy expiration date or to provide a quotation in response to a questionnaire.

Telemarketers can make a powerful and positive impression if they are knowledgeable about insurance and can effectively describe their insurance products' features. A pleasant voice, a helpful demeanor, patience, and an unflappable personality that can tolerate phone hang-ups are essential characteristics for a telemarketer.

Selling Through Electronics

Insurance companies are exploring technology-based selling using kiosk systems, cable television, Web sites on the Internet, and telecommunication access to the prospective customers. The insurance industry is considering all of the electronic media highways as possible insurance distribution channels. Exhibit 2-4 discusses kiosk sales and their effect on the insurance industry.

Insurance companies are well aware of the constant growth of technology and its potential for communicating with insurance customers. Web sites on the Internet contain computerized insurance advertisements that show a company's logo or an appropriate picture, an introduction to the company, general information about the company, and a menu for accessing needed information.[4]

The customer's insurance Internet experience need not be limited to viewing advertisements, though. Insurance customers can enter Web sites and obtain insurance rates for the county, city, and state in which they live.

Exhibit 2-4
Kiosk Sales

Kiosk Insurance Sales Set to Explode

CHARLOTTE, N.C. By all accounts, the kiosk sales channel for insurance products is about to explode.

With hardware and software technology now capable of providing real-time, face-to-face video conferencing, company after company is looking into simplifying access to potential customers by automating their products sales efforts.

The interactive kiosk system developed by Personal Financial Assistant (PFA) Inc., Charlotte, N.C., which Metropolitan Life has used to market insurance for the past few years, is one of the most technologically advanced on the market.

It permits off-site buyers and insurance producers to see one another on video as they confer in real time.

Agents can run what-if scenarios, send illustrations, and transmit hard-copy applications.

In states where an original signature is not needed, the buyer can sign on a signature pad or sign the application itself and scan it back to the office.

However, in states where original signatures are needed, the kiosks have a slot where applications can be dropped off for later pickup by the agency.

At present, PFA's kiosks can sell annuities, universal life, term, auto, and homeowner's insurance.

Banks have been automating their product sales for a few years now, and recently began working out how to distribute non-traditional products, including insurance, through automated systems.

PFA is working with banks and insurance companies to facilitate sales of insurance products through bank-run kiosks.

Amy S. Friedman, "Kiosk Sales Set to Explode," *National Underwriter,* October 17, 1994, pp. 7, 20.

Educational Objective 5
Explain how an insurer promotes insurance products.

Promoting Insurance Products

Insurers seek ways in which to promote products and reduce or eliminate obstacles to sales. To do this, they must find an effective method of communicating to potential customers and seek answers to the following questions:

- What are the most effective ways to communicate with potential customers?

- What are the obstacles in the communication process?

Communicating With Potential Customers

An insurer must decide how best to communicate with the markets it wishes to serve. Four basic modes of communication with target markets are advertising, sales promotion, publicity, and personal selling. Exhibit 2-5 provides examples of tools for each of the four basic modes of communication. The insurance marketer must choose communication objectives, expenditure levels, messages, media, and measures of effectiveness. An insurer should manage all communications consistently in support of marketing and business objectives.

Insurance marketers establish communication objectives that are designed to elicit customer response. The insurer might want to build customer awareness of the insurer or product, change customer attitudes, or persuade customers to take specific actions.

Exhibit 2-5
Communication Tools in Property and Liability Insurance

Advertising	Sales Promotion	Publicity	Personal Selling
Print and broadcast ads	Giveaway items	Press kits	Sales presentations
Mailings	Fairs and trade shows	Speeches	Sales meetings
Brochures and booklets	Exhibits	Seminars	Telemarketing
Posters and leaflets	Premium financing	Annual reports	
Directories	Entertainment	Charitable donations	
Billboards	Inserts in premium renewal notices	Public relations	
Display signs			
Point-of-purchase displays			
Symbols and logos			

Adapted with permission from Philip Kotler, *Marketing Management: Analysis, Planning and Control* (Englewood Cliffs, NJ: Prentice-Hall, Inc., 1984), p. 603.

After an insurer defines the intended customer response, it can develop messages that attract attention, hold interest, and cause action. The marketing department must decide what to say, how to say it, and who will say it.

Insurers use a communications/media mix that includes both personal and nonpersonal advertising channels. Personal channels involve two or more people communicating directly with each other. In insurance, the producer and the producer's staff communicate regularly with policyholders and potential customers. Nonpersonal advertising channels include newspapers, magazines, radio, television, and billboards.

Establishing an Advertising Budget

Advertising is expensive. Insurers face a dilemma when trying to decide how much advertising is enough to communicate effectively with customers while staying within a reasonable budget. An insurer might set an advertising budget through one of the following methods:

- The *percentage of sales method* limits communication expenses to a percentage of sales volume over a period of time (usually a year). This method assumes that a certain amount of advertising creates a certain amount of sales. For example, an insurer might have discovered through prior experience that $100,000 spent on billboard, newspaper, and radio advertisements generates 5,000 sales averaging $500 apiece. So the total sale of $2,500,000 was created by $100,000, or 4.0 percent of sales. To maintain this level of sales, the company must allocate 4.0 percent of each year's projected sales for advertising.

- The *competitive-party method* maintains a level of spending relative to that spent by certain competitors.

- The *objective and task method* develops communication budgets by defining specific objectives, determining the tasks to be performed, and estimating the costs of performing those tasks. This method is the most detailed, because it relies on knowledge of customer behavior and the amount of advertising required to trigger that behavior.

- The *balanced budget method* is used when the insurer is under pressure to control expenses. This method limits the permissible expenditure on advertising to pre-set amounts.

The effectiveness of marketing communications can be measured in several ways. An insurer might **pilot test** advertising to determine its effectiveness. An insurer might also show proposed advertising to a **focus group** to obtain feedback.

Pre-testing can be used to help design effective messages. Post-testing helps to determine whether the target audience recognizes or recalls the message, how many times the audience saw it, how the audience felt about the message, and what the audience's previous attitudes toward the product and insurer were as well as what their current attitudes are. Sales and customer retention measures might also be useful, especially when the communication objectives are to persuade or remind.

Obstacles in the Communication Process

Insurance companies have the same advertising problems that other industries do. In advertising, the challenge is to get the message across and to get people to believe it.

Insurance companies have some communication problems that are unique to the industry, including the following:

- Insurance is expensive, and in many situations compulsory insurance regulations and lending organizations obligate people to purchase it.

- People do not like to pay for insurance because they cannot see what they are getting.

- People are inclined not to trust insurance companies because they do not understand insurance and because they have heard so many recounts of problems in claim settlements that they tend to view insurance companies as adversaries.

A **pilot test** is a trial of an advertisement or a product to a limited group or a geographic area in order to determine whether the desired results can be achieved.

A **focus group** is a group of potential customers (usually ten to twelve) who meet with a marketer. The marketer solicits their responses to advertisements, products, or potential product changes.

Insurers understand these problems and develop communications and advertising to try to overcome the barriers. However, the barriers are formidable, and insurers have varying opinions about the most effective method for convincing potential customers that insurers are financially strong, provide good service, and treat policyholders equitably if a claim occurs. The following are some insurer opinions about effective insurance advertising:

- The most effective advertisement is word-of-mouth recommendations from current policyholders. Concentration on consistent, positive customer service is the highest priority.

- The goal of newspaper, magazine, and billboard advertising is recognition of the company name or logo. Insurance advertisements should focus on a wide publication of just those names and logos.

- People change insurers most frequently for a lower price, so insurance advertisements should focus on price to attract potential insureds. Service will then be the factor that retains the customer.

Avoiding Marketing Failure

Because the marketing process does not always work as planned, some lessons can be learned from the marketing failures of other industries. The following can serve as a checklist of practices to avoid:

- *Failure to target advertising to defined market segments.* Some companies have effectively segmented the market and conducted extensive research but have failed to focus advertising in those segments and to use the results of research. They have tried to sell a market target product through a mass advertising campaign rather than honing the advertising to the selected segment.

- *Failure to properly match distribution system and target market.* Some distribution systems reach particular buyers better than others do. For example, retirees are unlikely to purchase insurance by phone. A distribution system that features direct contact to provide a sense of security would be a better distribution system for this group.

- *Overemphasis on price as a competitive strategy.* A low price strategy could be attractive to some customers but could hurt a product's image with quality-minded customers. It is sometimes better to differentiate a product by offering a coverage feature or service as well as a competitive price.

- *Inability to carve out a defensible niche.* By pursuing a broad market, some companies invite intense competition. By narrowing the focus of the market, a company automatically limits the competition.[5]

Educational Objective 6

Describe the marketing research process and the sources of information that can be used in the marketing research process.

Marketing Research

Marketing research is the systematic gathering and analyzing of data to assist in making decisions in all three steps of the marketing process. Marketing research cannot guarantee success, but it can improve an insurer's chances of making correct decisions.

Many people view marketing research as a complex process involving computers, models, and statistics. To them, marketing research seems more complicated than it actually is. A marketing research project (even a large, complicated one) is based on a logical, common-sense process. That process generates useful facts and data with or without the use of a computer or complex tools.

Marketing is more of an art than a science. It does not lend itself fully to a scientific method because even the simplest experiment or study involves the difficult-to-analyze human element. Many of the processes or tools that can be used are subjective and are open to subjective interpretation. The best that can be done is to approach marketing research as scientifically as possible. A researcher should strive for objectivity, trying to eliminate preconceptions and bias as much as possible.

The checklist in Exhibit 2-6 displays the major areas of market research. If you are a producer with an idea about targeting newly graduated nurses for a tenant homeowners policy and a personal auto policy, or if you are an underwriter who would like to consider targeting retirement communities for golf cart endorsements to be attached to a homeowners policy, you might use this checklist to complete your initial marketing research. The checklist helps determine customer needs, the size of the target group, the competition, and the general environment that could affect your marketing campaign.

Answering these questions can improve decision making and eliminate obvious problems in a marketing project. For example, a producer who wants to target newly graduated nurses as a market segment might discover in answering these questions that 90 percent of the graduating nurses leave the state as soon as they are certified. The fact that only 10 percent of graduating nurses remain in the state might make this group less attractive to a producer as a target market than other potential target markets.

The checklist can also help to uncover potential risks or latent business opportunities. For example, the underwriter who is considering writing golf cart coverage for retirees might discover during market research that people in this group also need increased limits of coverage for silverware and jewelry. This group could be a target market for personal article floaters.

Sources of Marketing Research Data

Marketing decisions should be based on valid and comprehensive information. Personal insurance producers and underwriters should have

Exhibit 2-6
Initial Market Research Questions

Customers: opinions, attitudes, and behavior

1. How do the customers view the company or agency?

2. What is the demand for the product? Would the product be accepted?

3. What is the customer's preferred delivery method?

4. Do customers have any service preferences?

5. Is price a consideration?

6. Do customers have any product quality considerations?

7. What is the customer's purchase motivation?

8. What promotion or advertising would create the best impression?

Markets: characteristics and trends

1. What are the size, location, composition, geography, and demography of the target group?

2. Are there any opportunities for developing or expanding the target market?

3. Can this target market be used for other products?

Competitors

1. Who are the competitors for this target group?

2. What products or services do they sell?

3. What are the competitors' strategies?

4. How do the competitors advertise and promote their products?

5. How does the competition price its products?

6. What are the competitors' claims and customer relations services?

7. Has the competition been profitable in this target market?

Business environment

1. What are the pertinent economic conditions and trends (national, regional, and local)?

2. What are the pertinent social conditions and trends (such as population, urban/rural, lifestyle, education, health, welfare, and safety)?

3. What are the pertinent political conditions and trends (legislative or regulatory)?

---

a working familiarity with the techniques of gathering information and the sources from which data are compiled. Although marketing research in a large insurance organization is normally the responsibility of a marketing manager or department, a personal insurance specialist should understand how decisions are made and how research is evaluated. In addition, many employees within an insurance organization are asked to provide input for a market research effort. Only by knowing why the information is required, how it is used, and how it fits into the larger scheme of the project can specialists appreciate the need for such data.

Secondary data consist of information gathered for a nonspecific purpose by someone other than the market researcher, from sources within or outside the company.

Primary data refers to original information collected for the specific purpose of the market research project.

The two broad categories of market data are **secondary data** and **primary data**. Research typically begins with secondary data because it is immediately available at little or no cost. Many research questions can be answered at minimal expense from secondary data before the more costly primary research is conducted.

Secondary Data

Secondary data have already been collected inside a company or from external sources. Departments within each company compile huge amounts of information for their own purposes. The following is a list of some of the data that are normally available for internal company reports:

- Financial statements
- Loss histories by line of business
- Policy records (written and retained)
- Claim profiles

Secondary data provide information about population trends, community growth, level of income, developments and changes in lifestyle patterns, and shifts in the importance of various geographic regions.

Sources of externally generated secondary data are virtually limitless. Researchers must pinpoint the information needed in advance and be familiar with the sources that best fulfill their needs. The following are common secondary sources that could be useful:

- Government reports and statistical tabulations
    - *County Business Patterns* (published by U.S. Department of Commerce) provides statistics on the number of businesses by types, employment, payroll data, and state and county.
    - *Census of Population* (U.S. Department of Commerce) provides detailed data on U.S. population by geographic regions, including such demographic breakdowns as sex, marital status, age, education, race, ethnic background, family size, employment, and income levels.
    - *Current Population Reports* (U.S. Department of Commerce) is a regular series of publications that includes interim reports on population estimates, projections, and special analyses of population characteristics.
    - *Statistical Abstract of the United States* (U.S. Department of Commerce) includes statistical tables covering a wide range of subjects, including a variety of demographic data and product and consumer price indexes.
    - *State and Metropolitan Area Data Book* (U.S. Department of Commerce) is a source of statistical information on population, household, income, employment, housing, and finance.
- Private company documents (press releases, product literature, and annual reports)
- Commercial information services (Standard and Poor's and A. C. Nielsen)

- Special reports published by business trade associations
- On-line databases
- Standard reference works (*Reader's Guide to Periodical Literature*)
- Market research agencies

An underwriter who is supporting the marketing of a new golf cart endorsement might want to review external secondary sources to determine the size of the retirement population that is targeted and the location of retirement communities throughout the country. The underwriter would probably seek information about the relative affluence of that group to determine the number who could afford to live in retirement communities (and purchase golf carts). The underwriter might also obtain reports from golf cart manufacturers regarding safety features and sales and historical data. Data regarding the growth of the golfing industry might also be helpful.

Companies often buy market research from an agency or a consultant either because they have a small internal research staff or because they require specialized information or expertise. A company might contract with a database that specializes in compiling general information about industries or demographic trends.

Primary Data

A company cannot truly know who its customers are or how they feel about its products, services, pricing, or advertising by relying on secondary data. Even sales records that provide information about the retention or attrition of policyholders fail to explain the results. Two major sources of primary data can answer questions about specific customer groups and their possible response to advertising: surveys and observations.

Surveying To Collect Primary Data

Personal or face-to-face interviews, telephone surveys, and mail surveys are used to obtain information from targeted groups.

Personal interviews sample a group of individual responses to a series of questions. This method is used to test customer receptivity to a new or modified product or service. Interviews can be conducted door-to-door or in selective locations.

Focus groups, which were discussed previously, are a form of personal interview. Focus groups are usually videotaped for subsequent viewing and analysis. Such groups are useful for identifying original ideas about how products or service can be improved.

Telephone interviews are a popular way of collecting primary research data, especially when the research involves a random sample of the population, when the questions are few, and when face-to-fact contact is not necessary or practical.

Mail surveys involve questionnaires distributed to a target or random audience. A cover letter, instructions, and a self-addressed return envelope are provided. Mail surveys are generally used for relatively large samples and when the information requested can be clearly communicated in writing.

Observing To Collect Primary Data

Observation involves viewing customer habits and behavior either directly or indirectly, sometimes using video cameras. Some marketing researchers believe that observing customer behavior is a more objective method of data collection than is surveying. Watching a customer actually buy a product or use a service provides useful information.

Producers can provide information about customers through direct observation during the purchase process. The following are examples of questions producers might answer regarding customers' insurance purchases:

- Was price or service the key factor when making a purchase?
- What were the important service features sought by the customer?
- Why did the customer leave his or her last insurance company?

Making a Marketing Decision

From a review of the marketing research information presented, it should be apparent that marketing research does not give the answer to marketing questions. The decision-making process for marketing involves forming many hunches and personal beliefs. No amount of research or data can replace the human element in that process. The best result that can be accomplished is to compile information that answers questions about the available market, the trends, and the likelihood of success. Insurers use that information to make decisions about marketing choices that seem to offer the best opportunity for success. All marketing factors can be reduced to statistics and numbers representing the chance of success, but sometimes these statistics and numbers try to quantify so many variables that their validity should be questioned. Statistics cannot prove whether a customer will purchase a new car or a personal articles floater.

Educational Objective 7
Explain how marketing can be performed in service areas such as sales, underwriting, and claims.

Marketing Performed Throughout Insurance Organizations

All divisions and departments within an insurance company perform marketing. Presidents and executive officers communicate the marketing philosophies of the organization to all employees in order to enlist their support in the marketing effort. Incentive systems for employees tie salary increases and bonuses to productivity gains. Employees who understand and adopt the marketing philosophy of the company can recognize and respond to the service needs of customers. They will also be aware of the potential for product improvement that can address customer needs.

Some of the service areas of insurance organizations that employ service and marketing philosophies include the following:

- Counseling and coverage selection (sales)
- Underwriting
- Claim adjusting

Counseling and Coverage Selection (Sales)

The first step in selling is to contact the customer, perhaps several times, and establish rapport. The next step is to determine the customer's needs. Then the producer prepares a proposal to present to the customer. The final step is to close the sale by obtaining the customer's agreement to purchase all or some of the coverages included in the proposal.

Historically, most producers prepared policies themselves, using printed forms the insurers provided. A copy of the policy, called the "daily report" or simply the "daily," was sent to the insurer. In recent years, the trend has been for insurers to prepare the policies and either mail them directly to policyholders or send them to the producer for delivery.

Time-saving processes such as computer-generated policy issuance allow more time for producers to spend with customers. Producers can perform property inspections to better identify hazards and coverage needs. Producers can ask questions to help reveal exposures best addressed by insurance. By saving time on other tasks, producers can better serve their customers and expand a single policy account into a multiple policy account for an entire family.

Underwriting

Underwriters work closely with producers during the review of new applications. The exposures and hazards presented by an applicant might be borderline or unacceptable when compared to underwriting guidelines. An underwriter can provide effective service by discussing the problem with the producer and working with the producer to find an equitable solution that reduces the risk to an acceptable level and provides adequate coverage to the customer.

An underwriter is also in a position to be an effective marketer. An insurer who has targeted residential property policies can be assisted by an underwriter who knows about the special needs of those property owners. For example, an underwriter could request information from the security alarm servicing companies in a certain area and recommend additional credits for homeowners with alarm systems offered by companies providing exemplary service. If silver prices increase suddenly, the underwriter could draft a letter to producers or customers with large silver schedules reminding them of the need to maintain current values so that their coverage limits will be adequate in the event of a loss.

In general, an underwriter who is aware of the insurer's marketing philosophy can find ways to help the insurer meet its marketing objectives.

Claim Adjusting

All producers probably handle claims to some degree for the insurance policies they sell. Since the producer is the policyholder's principal contact with the insurer, insureds naturally contact producers first when claims occur.

In some cases, the producer might simply give the policyholder the telephone number of the claim department and the name of a person to contact. Alternatively, the producer might obtain from the policyholder some basic information about the claim, relay it to the insurer, and arrange for a claim representative to contact the insured.

Insurers often authorize producers to adjust some kinds of claims. Insurers usually grant authorization only for small property claims, generally under $5,000. Claims that are serviced by producers receive fast service because insureds are only dealing with one person. Insureds appreciate the speed and simplicity with which these claims are handled.

Whether handled by the producer or the company claim representative, claims present an opportunity for the specialist in personal insurance to provide excellent service and promote the insurer's marketing goals.

Many personal auto losses involve an insured and a third-party claimant. Claimants can be so positively impressed by service provided in a claim settlement by the third party's insurer that they seek coverage from that insurer. Insureds also discuss claim settlements and service with friends, co-workers, and family. A positive report from a claimant can generate valuable word-of-mouth advertising and new policyholders for an insurer.

Summary

Marketing involves three basic steps:

1. Identifying customers and their needs
2. Designing products to meet the customers' needs
3. Selecting a distribution system to serve the customers and support products

Central to implementing any marketing process is a profile of its targeted customers. Insurance customers, in general, fit the profiles of other customers who are placed in the same demographic groups. Demographic groups are of interest to marketers because those groups have similar product needs. Market researchers gather, tabulate, and analyze customer profile data, but all employees in decision-making positions should be familiar with the latest trends of the demographic groups.

All divisions and departments within an insurance company perform marketing. Presidents and executive officers communicate the organization's marketing philosophies to all employees to enlist their support in the marketing effort. Employees who understand and adopt the company's marketing philosophy can recognize and respond to the service needs of customers and the marketing objectives of their employers.

Chapter Notes

1. Brian Davis and Warren A. French, "Exploring Advertising Usage Segments Among the Aged," *Journal of Advertising Research*, February/March 1989, pp. 22-29.

2. John J. Burnett and Alan J. Bush, "Profiling the Yuppies," *Journal of Advertising Research*, April/May 1986, pp. 27-35.

3. Burnett and Bush, pp. 27-35.

4. David R. Fordham, "Connecting Your Company to the Internet," *Management Accounting*, September 1995, pp. 69-74.

5. Research Institute of America, *Marketing Management* (New York, NY: Research Institute of America, 1984), pp. 16-17.

Chapter 3

Educational Objectives

1. Explain the following terms and their applications: (pp. 3-3 to 3-6)
   - Eligibility versus acceptability
   - Point-of-sale underwriting
   - Underwriting guides
2. Describe the underwriting process. (pp. 3-7 to 3-8 and Exhibit 3-1)
3. Describe the sources of information used in personal lines underwriting, and explain how information is selected in evaluating an application. (pp. 3-8 to 3-15)
4. Explain how an underwriting decision is made, and describe the following aspects of that process: (pp. 3-15 to 3-24)
   - Identifying exposures
   - Identifying and distinguishing among the physical, moral, morale, and legal hazards, and regulatory influence
   - Measuring the exposures
   - Identifying and evaluating the alternatives
   - Selecting the best alternative
5. Explain what must be accomplished to implement underwriting decisions and to monitor the results of those decisions. (pp. 3-24 to 3-27)
6. Contrast individual account underwriting and underwriting by exception. (pp. 3-27 to 3-28)
7. Distinguish between effective and ineffective underwriting research and documentation. (pp. 3-29 to 3-31)
8. Describe the skills needed to make sound underwriting and coverage placement decisions. (Encompasses entire chapter.)
9. Given a case situation, apply the underwriting decision-making process. (Encompasses entire chapter.)

Chapter 3

How Insurers Select Risks

Personal insurance is sometimes referred to as a commodity (a mass-produced product). In some ways, personal insurance production follows the same production pattern as commodity manufacturing; efficiency and cost effectiveness increase as sales increase. Increased sales enable manufacturers to purchase raw materials in larger quantities than they previously could, so the manufacturer's products cost less per unit to produce. The manufacturer then makes better use of its factory by running additional production shifts, and the cost per unit drops even further. As that trend continues, the manufacturer increases its profit on each unit. Insurers also gain efficiencies as their volume of production increases.

Personal insurance differs from commodity manufacturing because of risk selection. The idea that an insurance company might reject an applicant who needs coverage is contrary to the action that would be taken by a manufacturer; commodity manufacturers do not usually reject buyers. But insurance companies pay losses as part of their business. If an insurance company accepted all applicants for coverage, some adverse selection would naturally occur. To counteract adverse selection, insurers try to select applicants who are not likely to have insured losses greater than what the insurers anticipate when calculating coverage rates.

So, if an insurance company's marketing department decides to expand a portfolio of business or expand into a new territory, that department must be cautious. Without risk selection control (such as underwriting guidelines and underwriting processes), the insurer could accept applications that are more likely than anticipated to incur losses.

Underwriting a new account begins when a producer reviews a customer's exposures. Exactly who makes the decision to accept, reject, or modify a risk depends on the company and the marketing system it uses. However, regardless of who makes these decisions, the underwriting decision-making process is the same. This chapter will describe the steps in that process.

Educational Objective 1

Explain the following terms and their applications:
- Eligibility versus acceptability
- Point-of-sale underwriting
- Underwriting guides

How Policies Are Underwritten

The underwriting decision-making process occurs in stages. The process varies by insurance company (the process might even vary within an insurance company by line of business). However, one or more of the following stages of underwriting might occur as a specialist processes an application.

- A producer, agent, or customer service representative who helps the customer complete an application at the point of sale assesses the customer's exposures and compares them to the insurance company's underwriting guidelines. The initial review of an application and the identification of associated risks are referred to by many names, including point-of-sale underwriting, prequalifying, field underwriting, and front-line underwriting.

- A technician in an insurance company screens the application. That screening could include checking for complete information and comparing the information on the application to a broad set of guidelines. The screening might also include a review of the motor vehicle report, credit report, or inspection report. The application is then either processed or referred to an underwriter or manager for further review.

- An underwriter reviews and evaluates the individual applications. In some instances an underwriter might review only those risks that have been referred by a technician.

- Some applications (such as those applications with high-value homes or high liability units) are referred to supervisors and managers for evaluation because factors appearing on the application exceed the underwriters' levels of authority for applications they can accept.

Underwriting is the process of reviewing new applicants' and existing policyholders' risk characteristics and selecting those who match the company's underwriting and rating criteria. Underwriting guidelines

Risk **eligibility** is determined by the rules adopted and filed for use in a state. An eligible risk falls within the broad category of risk that *can* be written on a policy.

A risk must be eligible before it can be acceptable.

Risk **acceptability** is broadly defined by underwriting guidelines published by an insurer for a type of policy.

Underwriting guidelines (also called guides or underwriting policies) are a set of parameters or limitations on the type of risks to be written. Each insurance company establishes guides for each line of business it writes.

help insurers ensure selection of policyholders who fit the insurer's underwriting criteria and who present potentially profitable risks.

Eligibility Versus Acceptability

Most personal lines forms, rates, and rules are filed for approval with state regulatory authorities. Risk **eligibility** is usually determined by the rules (often called manual rules because they originally came from published rating manuals) that apply to each type of coverage. A risk that is ineligible for coverage cannot be written on a policy for which it is ineligible. For example, a truck that is used commercially is not eligible for a personal auto policy. Specialists should have a copy of the eligibility rules to perform the initial screening process.

Risk **acceptability** is generally defined by the **underwriting guidelines** published by an insurance company. These guidelines provide a broad framework of risks normally accepted for coverage. In some states those guidelines must be approved by or filed with regulatory authorities. In the process of field underwriting, a specialist might find many risks that are eligible for coverage based on the insurance company's filing but not acceptable based on the risk's characteristics. An example of an eligible but unacceptable risk for homeowners insurance might be a twenty-year-old single-family residence (eligible) that has a roof in need of replacement (unacceptable).

Point-of-Sale Underwriting

During the initial meeting with a customer, the producer should listen carefully and ask leading questions to elicit information from the customer. The producer must quickly gather and assess information to accomplish the following:

- Identify the customer's exposures
- Determine which risk management alternatives, including insurance, can best address the customer's exposures
- Match the customer's insurance needs to available coverage
- Recommend coverage to help the customer make the appropriate insurance choice
- Compare the customer's exposures to the insurance company's underwriting guidelines

The initial meeting is also an important time to perform point-of-sale underwriting, which requires the producer to screen the exposures presented by the insured and the insured's property for basic underwriting qualifications. This screening includes a review of exposures or hazards that might not be specifically listed in the underwriting guidelines but that are recognizable as problems.

In the past twenty years, insurance companies have relied on and stressed the importance of the initial underwriting of applicants done by producers because of the value provided by that early underwriting.

Following are some benefits provided by point-of-sale underwriting:

- If the customer's exposures are clearly outside the company's guidelines, the producer can explain that to the customer during an initial meeting. Then the customer can pursue other coverage immediately, rather than wait for confirmation or denial of coverage from the insurance company. A negative reaction to denial might be reduced because the customer is not held up from securing other coverage.

- If the producer recognizes that the customer has unique exposures requiring a higher classification and premium charge than that expected by the customer, the producer can inform the customer of the higher premium at the initial meeting. The customer can then decide whether to shop for other coverage or to accept the higher premium. An insurance applicant who has been quoted a premium and receives an unexpected additional bill will probably form a negative impression of the producer and the insurer.

- Having the producer deny an unacceptable application is more efficient than having the application denied later in the underwriting process. Making the decision at the first step in processing the application saves other screening and processing efforts and expenses.

During point-of-sale underwriting, an experienced producer can assess any extraordinary exposures that are not apparent on an application. Any producer who contacts a customer directly gains an impression of the customer. For example, a customer who asks unusual hypothetical questions about claims that might occur could be providing clues about a moral hazard. A customer who mentions excessive past claims might be providing clues about a morale hazard. Although insurance personnel are not usually trained psychologists, they can gather important impressions. The front-line underwriter is probably not in a position to act on such unsubstantiated information, which is best addressed by recommending additional specific reports during the application's review. A credit report, a motor vehicle report, or a claim database report might provide information that would identify any hazards in a more substantial manner.

Underwriting Guidelines

Each company establishes underwriting guidelines for each type of policy written. Guidelines might vary by geographic location. They are provided to producers to help them determine risks that are acceptable to an insurance company. An application that meets all of the criteria in the underwriting guidelines might still be rejected because the guidelines only provide a rough framework. The development of underwriting guidelines as well as pricing is addressed in API 29.

Underwriting Authority

Underwriting guidelines list underwriting criteria of normally acceptable risks along with the maximum limits of coverages underwriters may provide. The amount of insurance underwriting guidelines permit is usually derived from the insurer's overall risk preference, its capacity, and its reinsurance. Sound management dictates that not all specialists be given the highest limits an insurer can accept. For example, an insurer might grant a producer the authority to accept the following:

- Maximum acceptable bodily injury limits: $250,000 per person and $500,000 per occurrence

- Maximum acceptable property damage liability limits: $100,000 per occurrence

- Minimum acceptable driving age: 18

- Maximum acceptable driving violations or accidents: 2 minor violations or 1 minor accident within the prior 3 years

A producer could issue a binder (a temporary contract between the insurer and insured) for an application within the underwriting criteria profile. A producer who completes an application for an insured requesting bodily injury liability limits of $500,000 per person and $1,000,000 per occurrence must obtain authorization from an underwriter for an exception to the underwriting guideline before the application can be bound for coverage.

Levels of Underwriting Authority

The underwriting guidelines represent one level of authority. Underwriters, senior underwriters, underwriting supervisors, and underwriting managers are generally granted progressively higher levels of underwriting authority. Some experienced agency members might also have authority that is broader than the authority in the published guidelines. Such authority limits are established in letters of authority or agency contracts.

In the example given for the underwriting guidelines, a senior underwriter might have authority that is broadened to the following:

- Maximum acceptable bodily injury limits: $1,000,000 per person and $1,000,000 per occurrence

- Maximum acceptable property damage liability limits: $750,000 per occurrence

- Minimum acceptable driving age: 16

- Maximum acceptable driving violations or accidents: 4 violations or 3 minor accidents within the prior 3 years

An underwriting manager's authority might be limited only by the insurer's reinsurance treaties (reinsurance provided on entire policy portfolios).

Underwriters apply experience and judgment in determining which applications exceeding the regular underwriting guidelines (but fall within an underwriter's authority) are still acceptable risks for the company. As the level of underwriting authority increases, the responsibility for accurately applying experience and judgment also increases.

Educational Objective 2
Describe the underwriting process.

Underwriting Practices, Decisions, and Alternatives

Underwriters select policyholders by reviewing applications submitted by a producer. The selection process involves identifying and evaluating exposures, comparing policy coverage to the exposures presented by a risk, and determining whether the premium that would be charged is adequate for the chance of loss assumed. The following section describes the underwriting process.

The Underwriting Process

An underwriter is a detective. The underwriter's objective is to make sure the exposures presented by an applicant fall within the profile of policyholders who have a better-than-average chance of being profitable for the insurer. The insurer's underwriting guidelines help to establish the broad framework of applicants that fit this profile; however, the underwriter must also rely on experience and judgment to identify acceptable applicants. The clues for discovering the loss exposures and hazards can be gathered from the application. When the underwriter has questions that are unanswered by the application, the underwriter will investigate further by seeking additional information. Exhibit 3-1 shows the steps in the underwriting process and the related questions that underwriters must answer in reviewing applications.

Exhibit 3-1
The Underwriting Process and Questions

The Steps	The Questions To Answer
1. Gathering the necessary information	What information is missing from the application?
	What is the most efficient way to obtain the missing information?
2. Making the underwriting decision	What are the exposures? Can the exposures be measured?
	What are the alternatives? What is the best alternative?
3. Implementing the decision and monitoring the results	How are the decisions to be implemented?
	How can the results be monitored?

The underwriter uses the information gathered to make an underwriting decision. Decision making includes an analysis of the information gathered and an evaluation of the possible alternatives. The underwriter uses judgment to select the best available alternative. Once the decision is made, it is implemented and the results are monitored to determine whether that decision continues to be the best one available.

Educational Objective 3

Describe the sources of information used in personal lines underwriting, and explain how information is selected in evaluating an application.

Gathering Information

Underwriters begin to develop a profile of an applicant's loss exposures from clues provided by the application. If a piece of information is missing or incomplete, or if the clues indicate the need for more questions, the underwriter must determine what information is missing.

Restrictions on Information Use

Based on the company's underwriting guidelines for the type of policy, an underwriter's own knowledge and experience, and the information gathered, the underwriter forms a composite picture of the application and uses this broad picture as a guide in decision making. Sometimes, however, regulation forces the underwriter not to use certain parts of the picture to make a decision. The picture is then incomplete, which puts the underwriter at a disadvantage.

Underwriters are presented with large amounts of information that they must analyze during risk selection. The process of analyzing exposures and hazards on individual submissions is a line underwriter's primary task. In the past, personal lines insurers were fairly free to determine what hazards were important and the relative importance of those hazards. Regulators are increasingly challenging that freedom. As a result, underwriters are adjusting to new and changing rules governing risk selection.[1]

Regulations limit some types of information that an underwriter may use or actions that an underwriter may take in making an underwriting decision. An example of a rule restricting underwriting activity is the prohibition of rejecting an application based on cancellation by a prior company. Regulators maintain that an underwriter should make a decision based on the application's merits and not on the decision of a prior insurer. Insurers counter that an underwriter might not be able to discover the reason for the prior company's decision based on available information.

The following is an example:

- Company A cancels a homeowners policy because of a suspicious fire loss.
- The homeowner submits an application for homeowners coverage to Company B. The application does not declare the cancellation or the loss.
- Company B's underwriter questions the insured about the reason for changing insurance companies. The homeowner states that he simply decided to change companies.

- Company B's underwriter calls the Company A underwriter and learns that the policy was canceled by Company A. However, Company A's underwriter will not discuss the policyholder's claims history because that information is confidential.

- Company B's underwriter now knows something is wrong. The insured has not been truthful about a prior cancellation. However, regulation prohibits Company B's underwriter from declining the application based only on the prior cancellation.

- Company B's underwriter must seek other information that will identify the reason for the cancellation. This can be a difficult process.

From a regulatory viewpoint, an applicant should be given a fair review. From an insurer's viewpoint, information is often incomplete or unavailable, forcing decisions to be made contrary to negative indicators or incomplete information.

Information Efficiency

Underwriters collect information from many sources to develop an applicant's profile. Underwriters like to have a great deal of information regarding each applicant's activities, property, and character. However, underwriters must balance the amount of information that can be collected with the expenses involved in gathering and analyzing that information. Premiums for personal lines policies are relatively small compared to premiums for commercial policies; therefore, funds allocated for gathering underwriting information must be spent wisely. For example, a house that is less than two years old probably does not require an inspection, because the inspection would yield little information. The house has not had a chance to age, and an insurer could not judge the insured's ability to maintain the dwelling. However, a house constructed in the 1950s might require an inspection to determine its condition, maintenance needs, or the presence of hazardous materials (such as lead paint and asbestos).

Sources of Information

The underwriter's initial source of information about a customer is the written or electronically recorded application. If more information is needed, the most immediate source is the producer or the applicant. If information must be verified (such as a driving record or the condition of a dwelling), external reports are required. Some underwriters become creative in identifying sources of information.

The Application   The application provides the information necessary to process, rate, and initially underwrite the applicant. Because customers usually sign applications (exceptions are allowed by some insurers for homeowners and dwelling applications), an application becomes the legal record of the applicant's statements. That legal record is important if the insurance company ever challenges the information's accuracy.

An underwriter thoroughly reviews an application for information that conflicts with other information provided or that indicates that more

---

FYI

One of the most notorious underwriting failures occurred during the review of a life insurance application. A university student completed a direct-mail offer by taking out a six-month policy on a sixty-cent guppy for a premium of one dollar. He correctly noted on the application that the insured was a fish. He accurately answered questions regarding the applicant's height (three centimeters) and age (six months). The student received an insurance policy listing himself as a beneficiary. When the guppy died, the student filed a claim. The insurance company paid a $650 out-of-court settlement.

Source: Bruce Fenton and Mark Fowler, *The Best, Worst, & Most Unusual* (New York, NY: Galahad Books, 1994), p. 477.

information is required. Screening and modeling systems are helpful backup tools that consistently check for and bring routine problems to an underwriter's attention. These systems are discussed later in this chapter.

The Producer   Depending on the insurer's marketing system, the initial contact with a customer might be through an insurance producer or a customer service representative. These front-line specialists often have firsthand details of the applicant's exposures and determine the applicant's needs and perceptions. Producers gather additional data or answer questions raised by the application.

Excessive inquiries from underwriters to producers can ruin underwriters' relationships with producers. Every response to an inquiry requires time that a producer could otherwise use to generate sales. An underwriter should consider what information is important and limit inquiries to the producer. All inquiries regarding an application should be made at the same time, if possible.

Consumer Investigation Reports   Several independent reporting services provide information on prospective policyholders. These services provide information from insureds, investigations, or databases. A report might be used to verify either an insured's driving distance to work or a dwelling's occupancy.

Government Databases   Some government databases include information that can be accessed for a fee. Criminal court records (which include convictions) and civil court records (which include lawsuits, tax liens, bankruptcies, and wage garnishments) can be accessed through credit reports, which are discussed next.

Motor vehicle records (MVRs) are examples of reports generated by government databases. MVRs generally provide a history of accidents and traffic violations for the prior three years; however, MVRs vary by state and the severity of infraction. MVRs are obtained from the state department of motor vehicles.

A **credit report** (also called a consumer credit report or a credit bureau report) is a record of an individual's income, debt, and payment history. Insurance companies use the reports to identify an applicant's or insured's financial history.

Credit Reports   Many insurance companies use **credit reports** that contain information about an applicant's financial status, payment record, and employment history. A poor credit history does not automatically mean that an insured will create or exaggerate a loss. However, a homeowner who has financial problems might have problems making needed repairs or performing maintenance to a dwelling if few funds are available, increasing the possibility of a loss. Also, in some situations, a person in financial distress might destroy a residence or an auto to collect on an insurance claim or eliminate a monthly payment. In less extreme situations, someone might exaggerate a legitimate claim to gain additional income.

Other Credit Report Uses: Credit reports also provide several other types of data that are used during the application's review, such as the following:

- The number of dependents in the applicant's or insured's household is often provided. Some personal auto underwriters compare that information to the number of operators and children listed on an application to detect undeclared drivers.

- The applicant's or insured's income is usually provided. Some residential property underwriters compare that information to the monthly payments (also provided) to which the applicant is obligated. That is done to determine the applicant's financial pressures.

- Trends in late payments are listed. That information can help an underwriter identify households that are in a deteriorating or improving financial pattern. Households with all levels of income can experience financial problems. Even high-income households can experience problems in maintaining a lavish lifestyle.

A sample credit report is shown in Exhibit 3-2.

Fair Credit Reporting Act. The Fair Credit Reporting Act (FCRA) requires consumer reporting agencies to adopt reasonable information-gathering procedures. Procedures must be fair and equitable to the consumer, with a rigid regard for the confidentiality, accuracy, relevance, and proper use of such information.

A consumer reporting agency issues a credit report only for legitimate business transactions involving the customer. A business must have an acceptable business reason for obtaining the information in connection with that transaction. The following are the only circumstances under which a credit report is issued:

- A credit transaction involving the customer
- Employment of the customer
- Underwriting insurance involving the customer
- Licensing of the customer

Permission To Order a Credit Report. Whenever credit reports are used as part of an insurance application review, the applicant must give permission to order the report. Language granting permission is usually included as part of the application (near the signature block).

Providing Information When Insurance Is Denied. Whenever insurance is denied wholly or partly because of information contained in an external report, the report user must tell the customer the name and address of the agency making the report. Every credit reporting agency must, on the request and with the proper identification of the customer, clearly and accurately disclose the following information to the customer:

- The nature and substance of all information about the consumer in its files at the time of the request
- The sources of the information included in its files
- The recipients of any credit report on the consumer issued within the prior six-month period

Controversy Surrounding Credit Reports[2]   The use of credit reports has been a source of debate between regulators and insurers. An associate coun-

Exhibit 3-2
Sample Credit Report

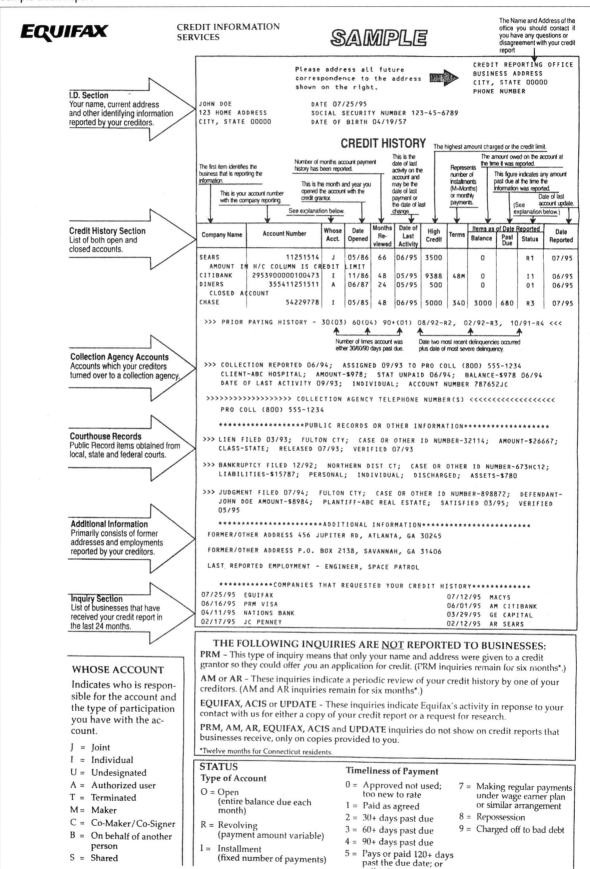

sel with a major insurer made the following statement summarizing the insurance industries' opinion on the use of credit reports, at a 1995 public hearing at the National Association of Insurance Commissioners:

> We have found that financial stability is an extremely powerful predictor of future loss that enables us to write more fairly and accurately than ever before.

At that same meeting, a marketing representative from a company that develops and markets underwriting reporting services added:

> Without question, the analysis we've done tells us that consumer credit management behavior correlates directly to insured risk behavior. Statistically, there are more losses for those people who are less financially responsible as related through their credit reports.

Legislators, regulators, and consumer advocates have criticized the use of financial condition as an underwriting tool as being unfairly discriminatory. Critics of credit report users state that using credit reports is just a way to **redline** and to justify avoidance of poor, inner-city applicants. Critics maintain that credit reports are too often inaccurate. They argue that although credit might relate to homeowners and business losses, it does not relate to auto losses.

Proponents of using credit reports in underwriting state that the positive results gained justify their use. One company reported that in a proprietary study, financially stable policyholders had a loss ratio of 73.6 percent and financially unstable policyholders had a loss ratio of 103.6 percent.

The debate is unresolved, but underwriters continue to seek out credit information and to use it if it proves valid and predictive.

Loss Data   Underwriters usually have access to information about the loss experience of policyholders and producers as well as on an aggregate basis by class, line, and territory. An insured's loss history can be obtained from an insurance company's own records.

Databases of information that combine the loss history of accounts from member companies are also available. Specialists can use those databases to check an applicant's loss history. CLUE (the Comprehensive Loss Underwriting Exchange) is a database that was introduced in 1987 for personal auto insurance. It has since been expanded to include personal property data. Member companies contribute claim information from their loss records. Underwriters from member companies access the data. From those data, underwriters can verify information provided by an applicant or discover losses that have not been declared.

Inspection Reports and Photographs   Insurance company personnel or vendors can perform property inspections. Such inspection reports provide information on the risk's physical condition and the inspector's perception of the property. Inspection reports are usually ordered for residential property according to the underwriter's judgment. A color photo of

Redlining describes a practice underwriters once used of drawing a red line around an area on a map. Applicants within that area would not be accepted solely on the basis of geographical location. The term has been extended to mean any exclusionary practice that judges an applicant based on criteria that cannot be statistically substantiated. Redlining is a prohibited practice.

the property is typically provided. From the photo, an underwriter can view the **housekeeping**, maintenance, roof condition, and other general hazards.

Producers frequently take photographs of autos when an application is filed, in order to record any preexisting damage. Without such a record, an insured could claim that damage occurred after the policy's effective date. For example, hail damage is a notorious problem for auto insurers. After a severe hailstorm, car dealers discount damaged vehicles. An unscrupulous insured could purchase a hail-damaged car, purchase an insurance policy, wait for the next hailstorm, and claim that damage was caused by the storm and occurred after the policy was in force. Photo records reduce that problem.

Special Investigation Reports   If clues found on the application indicate unusual hazards, special investigation reports can be ordered from vendors who prepare specialized reports. For example, a homeowners application that indicates that the applicant has a wood stove might cause the specialist to order a wood stove report to check for appropriate installation, sufficient wall and floor clearances, and proper stovepipes. Similar reports can be ordered to check the following:

- Electrical systems at residences
- Plumbing systems at residences
- Driving distances for personal autos
- Personal auto use
- Additional drivers in the household
- Watercraft inspections

Extended property inspections are also available that can respond to specific questions asked about risks or hazards.

Special reports incur additional expense, so they are normally ordered only for specific concerns identified during the underwriting decision-making process.

The Insurance Services Office (ISO) offers a Geographic Underwriting System (GUS), which can provide information that allows insurers to more accurately rate personal lines policies. GUS can provide the following type of information:

- Driving distances to work
- Name of responding fire station (and distance)
- Public protection classification
- Distance to ocean or nearest body of water

Claim Files   When reviewing existing policies for renewal or when rewriting a prior policy, an underwriter can obtain insights into past losses by reviewing claim files. Claim adjusters frequently develop significant underwriting information during a loss investigation, which includes a first-hand evaluation of the insured and the loss exposures.

An underwriter should review a prior claim with two questions in mind:

- *Could the loss have been prevented?* Does the file indicate that the loss occurred because the insured failed to perform maintenance or take some action that a reasonably prudent person should have taken? Did the insured take an unusual action that resulted in loss and that could have been avoided? For example, assume that a liability loss results when a grandmother drops her infant grand-daughter and injures the child. This is an accident that would probably never occur again, and nothing could have prevented the first occurrence. Having a negative reaction to that loss and cancel-ing the policy would not benefit the insurer. However, a loss that resulted from a leaky roof could reveal that the roof had not been maintained, which raises questions about other maintenance prob-lems and potential future losses. An underwriter might require an inspection of the property or cancel the policy to avoid another loss.

- *Has the insured done anything to prevent a recurrence of the loss?* After a loss has occurred, an insured who wants to reduce losses would probably take practical measures to prevent a recurrence. For example, an insured who has had a home burglary might install deadbolt locks, window locks, and a burglar alarm. An underwriter might question the continuation of a policy insuring a policyholder who has taken no preventive measures.

Educational Objective 4

Explain how an underwriting decision is made, and describe the following aspects of that process:

- Identifying exposures
- Identifying and distinguishing among the physical, moral, morale, and legal hazards, and regulatory influence
- Measuring the exposures
- Identifying and evaluating the alternatives
- Selecting the best alternative

Making the Underwriting Decision

After the information about the applicant's exposures has been gath-ered, a decision must be made as to whether to accept or reject the application. Making that decision involves several steps. First, an underwriter identifies exposures gathered from the application and other sources. The underwriter then determines how severe those exposures are. He or she might also identify hazards that could increase the potential frequency or severity of loss. Then the underwriter con-siders the alternatives available for addressing those exposures. Finally, the underwriter selects the best alternative.

Identifying the Exposures

Fifty years ago, personal lines underwriters were primarily concerned with underwriting against the risk of property loss of a dwelling and its contents by fire or wind. The primary concern regarding loss to autos was collision or liability exposures. Arson, theft, and vandalism were important, but of minor concern. Today, personal lines policies are much broader in coverage. New liability exposures have appeared, and existing ones have become more pronounced, such as lead paint poisoning, radon dangers, and day-care exposures. All of those exposures create an environment of change in which some hazards assume more importance because they have more potential for adversely affecting underwriting results.

One of the underwriter's major responsibilities in reviewing an application on an existing policy is performing an *exposure analysis*, which includes the following:

- Identifying loss exposures (loss exposures are addressed in depth in Chapters 5 through 12 by line of business)
- Identifying hazards that can increase the frequency or severity of a loss
- Measuring the extent of the loss exposures and hazards

Hazards result from a variety of situations and circumstances. During the information-gathering process, the underwriter identifies any hazards associated with the submission that would affect the risk's acceptability. From an underwriting perspective, evaluating the application includes judging whether the hazards are greater than average or uncontrollable by the prospective policyholder.

This section discusses the four categories of hazards: physical, moral, morale, and legal (including regulatory influence).

Physical Hazards Physical hazards are characteristics that can be identified by the senses or measured physically. A decayed tree next to a house, which increases the chance of damage to the house during a windstorm, can be identified in a photograph. Termite damage that increases the possibility of collapse can be identified by physically inspecting beneath the house. A professional electrician can detect an inadequate number of electrical circuits.

Moral Hazards A moral hazard exists when an insured might intentionally cause a loss or exaggerate a loss that has occurred, in order to collect the proceeds of insurance. Potential indicators of a moral hazard are weak financial condition, undesirable associates, and poor moral character.

Weak financial condition can be identified by evaluating credit reports and government or court records involving liens, multiple mortgages, garnishments, and bankruptcies. An insured with a weak financial condition might intentionally cause or exaggerate a loss to obtain needed funds. Although weak financial condition does not always indicate a moral hazard, financial problems are considered by many insurers when identifying and evaluating hazards.

Underwriters might also consider whether an applicant has undesirable associates or poor moral character when identifying and evaluating hazards. That information can be found through criminal records, unethical or illegal practices discovered during a claim settlement, or the individual's reputation in the community (usually known only to local producers).

The underwriting rule of thumb in addressing a moral hazard is as follows: *there is no successful method for underwriting a moral hazard.* An insurance contract is an agreement made in the utmost good faith. If that faith is violated, no agreement can exist.

If, for any reason, the underwriter suspects a moral hazard, the insured might be able to explain the circumstances surrounding the problem to eliminate the concern. For example, a credit report might reflect an accumulation of unpaid medical bills. The applicant might be able to explain that a medical emergency has occurred, and a payment from a medical insurance policy or the resolution of a liability claim has been delayed. Such problems can appear as credit problems even though the situation is only temporary.

Fraud. Of particular concern to underwriters is the moral hazard associated with **fraud**. An estimated 10 percent of property and liability insurance premium dollars are paid out in fraudulent claims—the equivalent of what would be paid for two Hurricane Andrews every year. Fraud affects every insurer in every market. Every insurance policyholder pays several hundred dollars per year in premiums to pay for someone else's fraud.[3]

> **Fraud** is a clear and willful act of obtaining money or value under false pretenses. Insurance claim fraud is a criminal activity in which the claimant deliberately deceives the insurer about the circumstances of a loss.

Insurance fraud has become an acceptable practice for many people. Increasing the list of items taken in a legitimate theft loss, malingering at home after an accident, and exaggerating the value of lost goods are examples of relatively minor fraud. Accident staging (intentionally causing an accident) is a more advanced and creative form of fraud usually perpetrated by professionals.

Organizations have been formed to help the insurance industry in fraud prevention and detection. The following two are of special interest to underwriters:

- In 1992, the National Insurance Crime Bureau (NICB) was formed. The NICB, which is supported by approximately 1,000 property-liability insurers, focuses mainly on organized criminal operations and on fraud rings that do the greatest amount of damage.
- The Coalition Against Insurance Fraud (CAIF) was formed in 1993. Its membership is composed of insurance companies, insurance associations, consumer advocate groups, and other groups from outside the insurance industry. The coalition's primary objectives are to promote legislative reforms and to provide consumer information and research.[4]

> **FYI**
>
> In its first year of operation, NICB's 200 million-record database on vehicles, thefts, and fraudulent claims was used by member companies and its own staff of 500 to assist local, state, and federal law enforcement agencies in bringing 3,537 prosecutorial actions.

Fraud Warning Signs. Although insurers often place much of the responsibility for fraud detection on claim adjusters, the first line of defense against fraud is the producer, who identifies actions of applicants and customers that are red flags for fraud. NICB has compiled a list of red flags, or fraud indicators. Some are warning signs that can appear on the application, and others are warning signs that can appear later in the underwriting process. Indicators of possible fraud are not actual evidence of fraud. The presence of a red flag can raise the level of suspicion, but it does not directly indicate fraud. The specialist must decide when the level of suspicion is sufficient to take other action. Exhibit 3-3 lists indicators of fraud that can be identified at the application stage and during the underwriting process.

Exhibit 3-3
Fraud Indicators (Red Flags)

Possible Fraud Indicators*

- Applicant is an unsolicited new walk-in, not referred by an existing policyholder.

- Applicant walks into producer's office at noon or end of day when producer and staff might be rushed.

- Applicant neither works nor resides near agency.

- Applicant's given address is inconsistent with employment information.

- Applicant gives a post office box as an address.

- Applicant has lived at current address less than six months.

- Applicant has no telephone number or provides a mobile/cellular phone number.

- Applicant cannot provide driver's license or other identification or has a temporary, recently issued, or out-of-state driver's license.

- Applicant wants to pay premium in cash.

- Applicant pays minimum required amount of premium.

- Applicant suggests price is not the object when applying for coverage.

- Applicant's income is not compatible with value of property to be insured.

- Applicant is never available to meet in person and supplies all information by telephone.

- Applicant questions producer closely on claim-handling procedures.

- Applicant is unusually familiar with insurance terms or procedures.

* See Appendix 3-A for an expanded list of NICB fraud indicators.

Dealing With Potential Fraud. Producers, underwriters, and customer service specialists who work directly with customers often get a *feeling that something is wrong* without being able to clearly articulate the problem or identify a reasonable action.

Picture yourself as a producer interviewing a new customer. He rejected collision coverage when he bought his auto policy several months ago, but he is now demanding coverage—immediately. The customer did not call before coming into the agency. The file shows three claims with the agency in the past two years. Your suspicions are aroused, but you lack justification to withhold the coverage. What should you do?

Whenever fraud is suspected, the following actions can be appropriate:

- Ask enough questions to feel comfortable about the risk. Ask for additional information (such as a physical inspection of a vehicle, a copy of a driver's license, or a second appraisal for a ring). An applicant who refuses or does not return to the office poses a possible problem.

- Document the facts: the time of day, the type of payment, and questions asked by the customer. For example: an insured called a producer at 9 a.m. to report an arson fire, and the producer documented the call. Fire investigators, however, did not label the fire as arson until later that afternoon. The insured knew it was an arson because he had set the fire. The documentation in the producer's file was used as part of the evidence for denying the claim.[5]

- Advise the company underwriter or **special investigation unit (SIU)** of the disconcerting facts and ask for advice. In any documentation or communication, stick to the facts and avoid drawing conclusions. Defamatory accusations could be used against a producer and company in litigation if the insured challenges the denial of the claim.

Morale Hazards   A morale hazard exists when an insured is less prudent or careful because of the existence of insurance. A better description might be a "lack of motivation" hazard because it indicates that an insured might be less motivated to prevent or minimize a loss than would be the case if uninsured. An insured who continually fails to lock a car in an urban area or who leaves the keys in the car when it is in the driveway is exhibiting a morale hazard. A series of minor auto accidents might indicate deficient defensive driving. Such an insured might also make the offhand statement in reference to the auto accidents: "That's what insurance is for."

An underwriter who identifies a morale hazard has few viable alternatives. Rejection or cancellation is a primary consideration for personal insurance specialists. Sometimes a substantial deductible might encourage loss control by the insured.

Legal Hazards   A legal hazard is any characteristic of the legal environment that affects an insurer's ability to collect a premium commensurate with the loss exposure. Legal hazards exist in a **litigious** environment, such as that found in the U.S.

Legal hazards also arise when insurance companies are required by case law to provide coverage to losses not intended for coverage under the insurance policy. The following are examples of legal hazards:

- In some states, the courts have ruled that injuries sustained as a result of drive-by shootings are covered under the victim's personal auto policy.

A **special investigation unit (SIU)** is a group within an insurance company (and in some state insurance departments) typically staffed by former law enforcement professionals. The unit applies criminal investigation techniques to determine whether fraud has been committed. If fraud can be proven, the claim might be denied or referred for criminal prosecution.

Litigious means prone to engage in lawsuits. A person who is litigious might seek situations in which to bring a lawsuit in the hope of financial gain.

- A standard homeowners policy excludes losses that result from the loss of electrical power, such as the unintentional defrosting of a freezer. In some states, that exclusion has been determined unreasonable. Case law prevents enforcing the exclusion, so insurers must pay for such losses.

Case law resolves the distinction between intentional and unintentional acts according to the circumstances presented by each individual case. For example, an insured fired a shotgun in the direction of several boys who he thought were stealing his watermelons. One of the boys was killed, and his parents sued the insured. The courts found that although the discharge of the gun by the insured was intentional, the fatal wounding of the boy was accidental. The result was therefore unintentional, and the insurer was liable for the damages.[6]

Regulatory Influence   Regulatory influence (sometimes considered as a type of legal hazard) exists when an insurance company's ability to independently develop and apply underwriting guidelines for new and renewal business is severely constrained. One example is the limitation on the insurer's use of credit information in making underwriting decisions. Another example is the requirement to adhere to ratios regarding the percentage of business that can be nonrenewed within a year; in some states, an insurer is restricted to regulated percentages of policies that can be nonrenewed.

Measuring the Exposures

Exposures and hazards vary in degree of intensity. A photo of a home might reflect some clutter that could be the signal of an owner who displays a lack of pride in ownership. Or a photo could reflect property in severe disrepair that could cause a loss to the insurer, such as decayed trees next to the house, missing shingles, or broken windows. Any measurements of these exposures are subjective. One underwriter might consider a hazard to be critical, while another underwriter might view the same hazard as trivial. Over time, as underwriters learn how losses occur and which hazards are most likely to cause losses, their judgment becomes more consistent.

Some sources (such as MVRs and credit reports) provide quantifiable information. Violations, accidents, and late payments can be counted and compared to underwriting guidelines.

Identifying and Evaluating the Alternatives

After information has been gathered and exposures identified, the underwriter can identify and evaluate the alternatives.

Two alternatives are easily identified: a submission can be accepted or rejected. However, the following additional alternatives that require modifications to increase the acceptability of a submission should also be considered.

Modify the Premium

A submission that is not acceptable at the premium requested might become desirable business if the premium is increased. In personal lines, changing the rate is usually accomplished by changing a policy from a preferred to a standard policy group, or from a standard to a high-risk policy group. The underwriter tries to place the policy within the appropriate underwriting guidelines presented by the policy groups so that an adequate premium is obtained for the exposures presented by an application.

Rate changes can also be accomplished on personal auto policies by using surcharges (charges made for violations or accidents appearing on a driver's MVR). An auto submission that is not eligible for a safe driver rate might qualify for insurance at a surcharged rate.

Modify the Exposure

Physical hazards are often obvious problems that can be corrected to reduce the chance of loss and to make a submission more acceptable. An insured who owns $25,000 worth of jewelry might not present an acceptable theft exposure unless a central station burglar alarm is installed in her home. An insured who owns a powerful sports car might present a liability exposure that is too high, until a teenage driver is excluded from the policy.

For personal lines, little can be done to change risks with obvious moral, morale, or legal hazards or regulatory influences.

Modify the Coverage

An application or policy renewal can be made acceptable by modifying the coverage that the insurer is willing to provide. A century-old home poses many potential problems when it is written on a homeowners policy with replacement cost coverage. The policy insurer might obligate the insurer to replace the hand-carved moldings and banisters and hand-made tiles with similar components that are no longer available or that are inordinately expensive. The cost for the components could be more than the home's market value. However, the submission might be acceptable if the policy were written on a functional replacement cost basis.

Modify the Limit

Underwriting opinions regarding the value of modifying policy limits are mixed. Some underwriters feel that a submission requesting $500,000 in personal auto liability for a car driven by an inexperienced operator can be made more acceptable by reducing the liability limits to $100,000. Other underwriters believe that the risk remains unchanged because the chance of loss is unchanged. If sufficient premium is collected for the increase in coverage, then modifying the limit does not change the risk.

Changing the coverage limits might be more appropriate for property exposures. A dwelling that is underinsured can become a more acceptable risk by increasing the limits of coverage to the amount needed to replace the home. A schedule of guns that is too large for an insurer's underwriting guidelines can be made more acceptable by reducing the size of the schedule.

Modify the Deductible

Increasing the insured's deductible can be effective for eliminating small claims. A large deductible can also increase an insured's interest in loss control because the insured assumes more financial responsibility for future losses.

An underwriter reviewing a personal auto application reflecting two small vandalism losses (which occurred to vehicles at night) in the past three years might find the risk unacceptable unless the other-than-collision (comprehensive) deductible is increased to $500 or $1,000. The larger deductible should be high enough to cover an average vandalism loss. The increase in deductible and the insured's increased participation in any loss might be enough incentive to encourage an insured to seek off-street parking.

Increasing a deductible is not as effective if the losses the underwriter is trying to avoid are potentially large. If the underwriter notes two collision losses on a personal auto application, increasing the collision deductible would probably not be effective. Any future collision claim could be a large loss. The underwriter does not avoid the chance of a future loss by increasing the deductible. Also, the insured is unlikely to improve driving skills simply because a higher collision deductible applies.

Loss Control

Loss control activities can be used alone or with any of the other alternatives previously addressed (with the exception of rejecting the risk). Loss control activities reduce potential loss frequency or severity. In personal insurance, some loss control opportunities are available to enhance a submission. Theft-control devices (deadbolt locks), reduction in liability exposures (a fence around a swimming pool), and maintenance (cleaning the chimney) are all examples of loss control.

Using the auto vandalism example mentioned above, the underwriter might recommend that the insured install a car alarm to prevent more extensive vandalism damage to or theft of the vehicle.

Selecting the Best Alternative

After carefully reviewing the alternatives, the underwriter chooses the best course of action, which is determined by weighing the pros and cons of the information gathered and using judgment.

The underwriter must determine whether to accept the application as submitted, accept it with modifications, or reject it. Although the decision to reject an application is sometimes appropriate, underwriters should be open to viewing a submission as potentially acceptable if modified.

Insurance applications and renewals present a mixture of positive and negative elements. One simple tool for reviewing a risk and selecting an alternative is a plus-and-minus chart like the one shown for a homeowners renewal in Exhibit 3-4. On a blank sheet of paper, the underwriter draws a line down the middle with a "+" on the top of one column and a "−" on the top of the other. The underwriter then lists the application's positive and negative characteristics. Liability exposures, property exposures, special hazards, and aspects of the risk that are better than average must be considered. Often, the process of categorizing and viewing the characteristics helps to make the appropriate decision apparent.

Using the plus-and-minus decision-making tool requires judgment and a measurement of the scale of negatives and positives presented. In the example provided, the overgrown shrubs are a minor issue. The maintenance problems are more troublesome. Moreover, the maintenance problems combined with the late payments on the credit report could indicate an insured who cannot afford the upkeep of the home. The positive factors listed in the example are relatively minor. The underwriter might check the loss history of the personal auto and watercraft policies. If the plus and minus sides are equal, an underwriter still has a difficult decision. Modifications to the minus side might create a more positive risk. In the case shown in Exhibit 3-4, requiring maintenance to the home and trimming the shrubs so they do not cover the windows might be good loss control alternatives. The specialist might also mark this file for a future review of the credit report to determine whether a late payment trend has developed.

Some underwriters keep this type of decision-making tool as documentation in a policy file, which helps any future specialist understand the decisions already made.

Exhibit 3-4
Underwriting Decision-Making Tool (Plus-and-Minus Chart)

+	−
• The house is only five years old (probably with no major mechanical problems)	• Photos of the home show overgrown shrubs in front of the windows, vines on the house, and a broken mailbox (invitations for a thief and housekeeping issues)
• Deadbolt locks are on all doors, and locks are on windows (loss prevention technique)	• Photos show poor exterior maintenance: rotten trim boards, missing guttering, and debris on roof (possible morale hazard)
• Smoke detectors are on each floor (loss reduction technique)	• Credit report reflects some late payments (possible financial problem or moral hazard)
• The applicant has two-year loss-free history with this company	
• This company also writes the insured's personal auto and watercraft policies (supporting business)	

The underwriter should also be familiar with the insurance company's current marketing position. Some insurers do not want to increase the size of a portfolio of accounts. An insurer might even want to reduce the size of a portfolio. Borderline risks might be accepted during periods of growth and rejected when an insurer is reducing policy count. The underwriter can control the increase, decrease, or stability of a portfolio of accounts by deciding which applications fall within the acceptable range.

The Presence of Supporting Business

An individual submission that appears borderline on its own might be acceptable if the rest of the insured's policies are profitable and written with the same company. In **account underwriting**, all of the business from an insured should be reviewed and evaluated before one policy is rejected. For example, a personal auto application might reflect a loss history (two vandalism losses in three years) that is slightly less acceptable than underwriting guidelines (maximum of one vandalism loss in three years). However, the customer might have several other policies with the company that are considered acceptable risks. Consequently, the customer's overall account would probably be acceptable.

Some underwriting rules of thumb that have been adopted in reviewing accounts are as follows:

- A good property risk does not balance a poor liability risk. (A potential loss for a liability risk can be severe. Positive property exposures are not enough to justify the acceptance of a potentially large liability loss.)
- A good personal risk does not balance a poor commercial risk. (The risks under a commercial account are often too large in comparison to a personal lines policy to make the comparison equitable.)

Producer and Underwriter Relationships

Producers make all or part of their living by selling insurance policies. An underwriter's success is often measured by a low loss ratio, which could require him or her to reject some applications submitted by producers. Underwriters and producers sometimes disagree about how to reach their mutual goal: building and maintaining a profitable portfolio of policies.

The relationship between the producer and the underwriter should be based on mutual trust and respect in order to achieve their common goal. Underwriters and producers develop working relationships. Sometimes producers work with underwriters to make marginal applications more acceptable. The underwriter might encourage policy writings from a producer by assisting the producer with a risk that is difficult to place. A successful relationship between the underwriter and producer is characterized by communication, trust, and reasonable give and take.

> **Account underwriting** is the process of evaluating all of the policies written by an insurance company for an insured.

Educational Objective 5
Explain what must be accomplished to implement underwriting decisions and to monitor the results of those decisions.

Implementing the Decision

The following three steps are required to implement an underwriting decision:

- The first step is communicating the decision. The reason for the decision, particularly when the decision was to reject the submission, must be clearly communicated to both the producer and the customer. Communication should be complete and concise. As a practical matter, a risk accepted by the underwriter requires no other communication than policy issuance. If an application is accepted contingent on the implementation of loss control measures (such as installing a central alarm system or repairing a stair railing), the underwriter must mark the file to follow up on the required change. An underwriter normally has only sixty days from the effective date of the application to reject a policy if the required changes are not made. The underwriter must either trust that the changes will be made after the sixty days or require that the changes be accomplished within the sixty days.

- The second step is ensuring that the appropriate documentation, such as binders, worksheets, and filings required by regulation, is properly completed. If the policy is accepted with a modification of the deductible, the coverage, or coverage limits, the file must clearly reflect that the change has been communicated to and accepted by the insured. If that is not done, the insured might later declare that he or she was never notified of the modification.

- The third step is recording policy information for the accounting records, statistical tracking, and policy monitoring. A computer usually performs those reporting functions.

Monitoring the Results

Underwriters should be alert for changes in the loss exposure once the policy has been accepted. Daily monitoring is not feasible, but midterm changes to a policy or a claim during the policy period might trigger the review of a particular risk.

Monitoring also involves an aggregate evaluation of the entire book of business. Underwriters are often assigned a loss ratio goal for each line of business. Results for those lines are compared to the goals. The underwriter then begins to highlight problem areas and possible corrective actions.

The link between individual underwriting decisions and the insurer's profitability is not always clear. Many factors outside the specialist's control make a short-term comparison between risk underwriting and results complicated. The lack of an adequate rate or an unusual number of losses can cause the results on a set of well-selected risks to deteriorate temporarily. Nevertheless, good underwriting decisions contribute in the long run to positive loss ratio results.

Continuation of the Underwriting Process

Underwriting occurs at several times during the policy's life. Periodic reviews are required as property ages or as certain events occur, such as an adolescent's obtaining a driver's license. A claim usually triggers an account review. Negative loss results for a portfolio of accounts might also spur a review of policy information.

Renewal Underwriting

Renewal underwriting is conducted during the policy period before renewal (usually 90 to 120 days before renewal to allow ample time for investigation and a nonrenewal notice, if needed).

The underwriting decision-making process for renewal is similar to new business underwriting but can become more complicated over time. Making a negative underwriting decision on a risk that has been written without loss for several years is difficult. For example, assume that an insurer has written a homeowners policy for ten years without a loss. A photograph ordered during a routine check reveals a roof that is extremely deteriorated. The underwriter knows from experience that the roof can begin to leak at any time. The underwriter issues a letter to advise the insured that the roof must be replaced. The underwriter receives no response and now faces terminating an account with a ten-year, loss-free history.

The renewal underwriting alternatives might also be limited by state regulation, such as a limitation placed on the reasons allowed for nonrenewals.

Midterm Underwriting

Some events occur during a policy term that trigger the underwriting process and a policy review.

Underwriting a Midterm Change

Changes to exposures or hazards can alter the conditions under which the policy was originally accepted. The underwriter must decide whether the changes are significant. Following are examples of changes that would alter exposures or hazards:

- Adding a teenage driver to an auto policy
- Increasing the coverage limit on a homeowners policy by 75 percent
- Adding a business office to the home

Underwriting a Claim

An underwriter should review or screen all claims to determine the following:

- Type of loss
- Hazards involved

- Whether the loss could have been anticipated or prevented
- Actions taken by the insured to prevent a recurrence
- Account history, including other losses that occurred under the policy

The policy files, either electronic or paper, should be set up so that the claim history for a file can be accessed conveniently. Information including the claim date, the amount paid, and a brief description of the loss should be available for review. A working relationship with the claim adjuster is helpful during underwriting. Special reports or letters from the claim adjuster notifying the underwriter of unacceptable risks can trigger action to avoid a future loss. Adjusters work closely with policyholders and have much information about the hazards present and the recommended actions.

Educational Objective 6
Contrast individual account underwriting and underwriting by exception.

Individual Account Underwriting Versus Underwriting by Exception

A company can take several approaches to implementing and monitoring underwriting decisions. These approaches are guided by the company's goals and objectives and the established underwriting policy.

Some personal lines companies use the traditional approach to individual account underwriting, in which each application and file are reviewed according to their own characteristics. Every policy is weighed according to the balance of positive and negative underwriting factors.

Underwriting by exception eliminates most files from the individual underwriting review process. Under this system, computers or support staff process acceptable files and issue cancellation notices for rejected files. Only those applications or files in the middle ground are referred to the underwriter for a decision.

Automation plays a major role in the insurance industry, particularly in policy processing and underwriting. Most companies have automated their personal lines underwriting to some extent. Automation has been used in the areas of screening, modeling, and expert systems in the policy selection process.

Screening

Underwriting by exception is often accomplished by **screening** files so that only those which require decisions are reviewed by underwriters. The screening process is typically accomplished by a **checklist** or **scoring approach**. Acceptable and unacceptable risk characteristics are defined and entered into a checklist or a software program. For example, a roof that is over twenty years old might be coded as unacceptable.

Screening is the process of categorizing applications to allow underwriters to concentrate on those applications that require a decision.

- A **checklist approach** refers to an underwriter only those applications that require underwriting decisions (as determined by a checklist). Obviously acceptable applications are issued as policies and unacceptable applications are canceled.

- **Scoring** is performed by a computer program that assigns a number grade to an application based on the information in the application.

If a scoring system is used, that characteristic might be given a high (meaning poor) score. As information is entered into the computer database from an application, the risk is screened. Risks that fall within an acceptable profile or within an acceptable score are automatically issued as policies. Risks that fall outside an acceptable profile (with a high score) are referred to an underwriter for review.

One of the advantages of using the scoring method is monitoring a portfolio by reviewing the average scores. A book of preferred business in which each risk barely satisfies the preferred criteria can indicate problems that require further investigation. Average scores that deteriorate over time also reflect a change requiring research.

Modeling

Modeling is a method of assisting an underwriter in the decision-making process by identifying hazards and degrees of hazards that are not part of an ideal (or model) risk.

Many insurance companies are beginning to use automated **modeling**, which involves defining the ideal characteristics of a risk as well as the acceptable ranges around the ideal. Modeling can assist underwriters in identifying and evaluating alternative decisions. For example, a company writing homeowners policies might identify the ideal fence around a swimming pool to be a seven-foot privacy fence that is locked from the inside. A seven-foot chain-link fence would be only slightly less desirable. A four-foot chain-link fence would be much less desirable. A four-foot hedge would be unacceptable as a protective device. On-line information is provided to underwriters regarding the acceptable variances from the ideal model and the recommended standards. With the assistance of this information, the underwriter can make a final decision.

Expert Systems

Expert systems are computer software programs that supplement the underwriting decision-making process. The system asks for the information necessary to make an underwriting decision, ensuring that no necessary information is overlooked.

Some companies use **expert systems** to assist underwriters in the decision-making process. Expert systems build on both the screening and modeling processes. If the risk falls outside the acceptable range, the computer presents hypothetical scenarios to the underwriter to help determine what modifications could be made to make the risk more acceptable. The selection process and ultimate decision are still the underwriter's responsibility, but the expert system conducts much of the investigation and analysis of alternatives.

Individual Versus Portfolio Underwriting

An underwriter reviews individual applications and existing policies when he or she gathers necessary information; compares the information to the insurer's underwriting guidelines; and makes the decision to accept, reject, or modify a submission based on each applicant's risk characteristics application.

Retention (also called renewal retention), as it is used here, refers to the percentage of policies renewed at an anniversary. The opposite of retention is attrition. A company might have a 90 percent retention rate for homeowners policies, which means that the attrition rate is 10 percent.

Portfolio or book-of-business underwriting refers to the monitoring approach insurers use in evaluating an entire block of accounts. Premium volume, loss frequency, loss severity, and **retention** are a few of the factors that a specialist analyzes when reviewing a portfolio. Reviewing a portfolio of policies enables a specialist to measure trends over time and determine corrective actions for an entire group of policies. Portfolio underwriting is addressed in API 29.

Educational Objective 7
Distinguish between effective and ineffective underwriting research and documentation.

Research and Documentation

Underwriters conduct research during the decision-making process. The information gathered as a result of this research should be documented so that other specialists handling the file understand the basis for the decision. Effective documentation eliminates the need for duplicating previous effort and provides a history that can be reviewed later. A decision made when the policy was written might have been based on a premise that is no longer valid.

Because each company has its own documentation style, specialists must ensure that their own company's documentation process is thorough. A sample of a documentation form that could be written manually or used as a computer screen for electronic documentation is provided in Exhibit 3-5. This form could be used by a producer, a CSR, a technician, or an underwriter.

Even though company styles and forms differ, some guidelines help to determine when documentation is appropriate and what it should contain.

Effective Research

Effective research is an important element of thorough underwriting. When underwriters review accounts, they must effectively research the exposures and hazards based on the information presented. Effective research means responding to the clues presented by the applications or policies and determining whether the exposures and hazards are acceptable. The following are examples of effective research:

- A dwelling fire application indicates that a home is twenty-five years old. No roof updates have been noted on the application. The specialist orders photos and inspections to verify the roof's condition.

- A personal auto policy lists a classic auto written under a stated amount endorsement. A letter is provided by a local garage stating the estimated value. The specialist requests an appraisal from a second source and the credentials of the second source.

- A homeowners application shows a new home with a wood stove. The specialist requests the name of the licensed contractor who installed the wood stove to verify that it was professionally installed.

The difference between effective and ineffective research is reflected in care taken to investigate exposures and hazards. The underwriter should, of course, investigate obvious clues indicating hazards in order to determine the degree of risk that the insurer would be accepting. If that is not done, the research has been ineffective.

Exhibit 3-5
Sample Documentation Form

DOCUMENTATION WORKSHEET	
POLICY #: HO 1234567	DATE: 12-9-96
INSURED: Chris Watkins	YOUR INITIALS: CF

Check the activity

☑ Insured called	☐ I ordered an MVR
☐ Agent called	☐ I called underwriter
☐ I called the insured	☐ I ordered a credit report
☐ I called producer	☐ I dictated a letter
☐ I ordered an inspection	
☐ Underwriter called	

Information / Documentation

The insured called for a quote to add replacement cost for contents to her homeowners policy. I quoted the additional premium at $39.00 through the end of the policy ($52.00 annually).

The policyholder said she would think about it and call me back.

Action taken

Diary the file for 1-9-97 and call the policyholder.

Effective Documentation

Effective documentation is a component of the policy's history. File documentation should record whatever research was done to effect an underwriting decision. The specialist should record all facts.

Care should be taken to document *facts* found in reports or investigations. *Opinions* regarding the insured should not become part of the file. Insurance files are subject to subpoena in court disputes. A good question to ask when determining what should be included in documentation is, "How could these comments be used in a court of law?"

Document Exceptions

Any action that is an exception to normal underwriting guidelines, but within the specialist's authority, should be documented. An example of such documentation might be a policy that is written for a coverage limit above the standard underwriting guide. The objective is to leave a paper trail that reflects the reason for the exception.

Document Additional Information

Any additional information gathered about an account should be documented for others who handle the file. If a photograph of a residence shows peeling paint, it is not a significant physical hazard, but it can indicate a morale hazard. Assume that during a phone call the producer learns that the insured is waiting for warmer weather to add gutters and paint to the house. If the producer does not document the information, anyone examining the file later will see only the peeling paint in the photo and question the condition of the house again.

Document Phone Conversations

Any phone conversation with an insured that is more than a simple exchange of information should be documented. Even "would this be covered?" phone calls should be noted. Decisions and agreements made with clients must be recorded. If the specialist agrees to write coverage on a policy or deny a request for additional coverage, the documentation could later be the only record. Research and documentation of exceptions, additional information, and phone conversations are primary components of thorough record keeping.

Skills for Underwriting

Many skills are necessary for making sound underwriting decisions. Some of them are technical. However, interpersonal, or "soft," skills are also equally important to an underwriter.

Underwriters must have effective oral and written communication skills. Those skills are crucial because underwriters must be able to explain the rationale for their decisions. Additionally, underwriters must be good listeners and demonstrate flexibility and adaptability as conditions or situations change. Also, underwriters must build relationships with producers, customers, and other company personnel. Often persuasion and influencing skills serve the underwriter well in encouraging application submissions, selling the appropriate coverages, and promoting loss control measures.

Underwriters need strong analytical skills; they must often deduce possible outcomes from factual situations. Underwriters must also be decisive once they review and evaluate alternative outcomes.

Certain technical skills are also essential in making sound underwriting decisions. Knowing market conditions, regulations, industry trends, products, and services is crucial. Underwriters must be thoroughly familiar with their insurance companies' underwriting philosophies as well as their underwriting guidelines. It is essential that the underwriter be able to apply that knowledge in the day-to-day decisions they make about new and existing policies.

Summary

The act of underwriting applications and existing policies is the foundation of the insurance business. Underwriting is a process of selecting eligible and acceptable risks according to published rules and underwriting guidelines.

The process of underwriting includes the following steps:

- Gathering necessary information from the application, investigative reports, databases, and claims files.
- Making the underwriting decision by identifying exposures such as physical, moral, morale, and legal hazards, and regulatory issues. Alternatives can be applied to reduce unacceptable exposures or hazards.
- Implementing the decision and monitoring the results to ensure the profitability of a portfolio of accounts.

Producers, agents, CSRs, underwriters, and underwriting managers perform this underwriting decision-making process. The skills required to carry out the underwriting process require sound application of technical knowledge as well as effective communication and interpersonal skills.

Chapter Notes

1. David Foppert, "Waging the War Against Fraud," *Best's Review*, March 1994, pp. 45-46.
2. L.H., "Credit Reports Draw Fire at NAIC," *National Underwriter*, June 12, 1995, p. 4.
3. Foppert, p. 46.
4. Foppert, p. 102.
5. Roland Stephan, "How Agents Can Help Reduce Insurance Fraud," *SAFECO Agent*, July/August 1994, p. 13.
6. State Farm Fire and Casualty Co. v. Worthington, 405 F .2d 683 (1968).

Chapter 4

Educational Objectives

1. Describe insurance regulation in general with respect to each of the following: (pp. 4-3 to 4-7)
   - Why it is regulated
   - Who regulates it
   - What activities are regulated

2. Explain the major types of insurance regulation, and identify the types applicable in your state as the regulations relate to:
   - Rates, rules, and forms (pp. 4-8 to 4-11)
   - Licensing for agents (pp. 4-23 to 4-25)
   - Continuing education for agents (pp. 4-25 to 4-26)
   - Countersignatures (p. 4-26)
   - Complaints (p. 4-26)
   - Surplus lines (pp. 4-26 to 4-28)

3. Explain the constraints on the use of rating classifications. (p. 4-13)

4. Identify prohibited marketing and underwriting practices in property and liability insurance. (pp. 4-14 to 4-22)

5. Explain the role of state insurance departments in responding to and resolving consumer complaints. (p. 4-26)

6. Explain the purpose of the surplus lines market and how that market is regulated. (pp. 4-26 to 4-28)

7. Explain the role of the NAIC in personal insurance regulation. (pp. 4-28 to 4-30)

8. Describe the need for insurance regulation and the ways in which it benefits customers and society. (Encompasses entire chapter.)

9. Given a case situation, explain how insurance regulation might apply to marketing and underwriting practices. (Encompasses entire chapter.)

Chapter 4

How Personal Insurance Is Regulated

The personal insurance industry began as a means to meet the risk-financing needs of individuals and families, primarily for the risk of fire. As the industry evolved to become a risk-financing source for many of the risks faced by individuals and families, insurance regulation evolved to ensure that, among other things, the personal insurance industry fairly and adequately meets the risk-financing needs of individuals and families.

Insurance specialists encounter regulations in many aspects of their jobs. For example, personal insurance companies and their producers must be licensed in each state in which they sell insurance. Furthermore, most states require producers to continue and update their education with continuing education requirements. Additionally, the products sold by insurance companies and the prices at which they are sold must generally be approved by state insurance departments. The underwriting standards and rules applied by personal insurance companies must also generally be in line with state insurance regulation and, in some states, must be approved by state insurance regulators. Insurance regulation restricts how insurance companies handle premium payments, applications, renewals, cancellations, and any claim settlement activities in which they participate. Finally, the methods that insurance companies use to advertise and promote their services are also subject to insurance regulation.

This chapter first provides a general overview of insurance regulation. It then discusses how insurance regulation applies to the personal insurance industry.

Introduction to Insurance Regulation

Insurance regulation in the United States has evolved along with the insurance industry. As insurance companies have been established and have grown, expanding into new lines and new products and crossing state lines, insurance regulation has been developed and implemented to address problems that have arisen, such as insurer insolvency.

Educational Objective 1

Describe insurance regulation in general with respect to each of the following:

- Why it is regulated
- Who regulates it
- What activities are regulated

Why Insurance Is Regulated

Traditionally, insurance regulation has been considered necessary to achieve two goals:

1. To ensure that insurance companies remain solvent to pay claims when they arise

2. To protect insurance consumers from those in the insurance industry who are unscrupulous

The nature of the "business of insurance" prompted those goals. Insurance is a unique product. Consumers purchase a promise in the form of a contract—insurers promise to pay the covered losses of their insureds after the losses have occurred. However, contracts are often difficult for laypersons to understand. Furthermore, insurance contracts are based on the insurer's promise to pay for the insured's covered losses at some point in the future. Insurance regulation has been developed and implemented to protect consumers by ensuring that insurance products are not defective and will meet consumer needs. Insurance regulation has also been designed and implemented to ensure that insurance companies remain solvent to pay future claims.

The two goals of insurance regulation are not mutually exclusive. For the protection of consumers, insurance companies must remain solvent. When insurance companies become insolvent, insureds can lose prepaid premiums, and claimants might not collect for covered claims. Thus, by ensuring insurance company solvency, insurance regulation also protects insurance consumers.

Who Regulates Insurance— Development of the Dual System

Insurance regulation in the United States is primarily the responsibility of the states. However, the federal government does regulate certain aspects of the insurance industry. This dual system of regulation has evolved over the history of insurance regulation in the United States.

When the insurance industry began in the United States in the 1700s, it was a local product—sold by local individuals through local companies to local insureds. Regulation of insurance activities was the natural domain of the individual states.

Samuel B. Paul v. Commonwealth of Virginia

As the country grew, insurance products began to cross state lines. Questions were raised as to whether the states should retain control of insurance regulation. An 1869 case involved Samuel Paul, who was seeking to become a licensed insurance agent in Virginia. However, Mr. Paul wanted to represent New York insurers that had not fulfilled Virginia's requirements to be allowed to sell insurance in Virginia. The following events occurred:

- Mr. Paul applied for a Virginia agent's license.

- Mr. Paul's application for a license was denied.

- Although unlicensed, he sold insurance in Virginia for the New York companies.

- In ensuing court battles, Mr. Paul claimed that Virginia had no jurisdiction to penalize him since he was engaged in interstate commerce, which only Congress could regulate.

- The U.S. Supreme Court determined in 1869 that insurance was a local contract in the jurisdiction in which it was sold, so it was not interstate commerce.

- Mr. Paul was penalized under Virginia law.

The outcome was the continuation of the state system of insurance regulation.[1]

United States v. South-Eastern Underwriters Association

The states' authority to regulate insurance was again questioned in 1944. By that time, insurance companies were participating in interstate compacts (binding agreements) and associations of insurance companies, agents, and others involved in insurance transactions. These compacts and associations were not publicly supported in the existing **antitrust** environment. One such association, the South-Eastern Underwriters Association (SEUA), was investigated and charged with violations of the **Sherman Act**, which prohibited collusion among businesses to gain monopoly power. The following events occurred:

- The SEUA had used its power to shut nonmembers out of the insurance industry in several Southeastern states, and it did not

Antitrust refers to legislation, such as the **Sherman Act**, that opposes "trusts" (monopolies) or unfair business practices.

deny that it had done so. It did, however, claim that it *could* do so since the insurance industry was not subject to the Sherman Act. According to the SEUA, the insurance industry was subject to regulation by only the individual states under the Paul v. Virginia decision.

- The SEUA case was heard before the U.S. Supreme Court, which disagreed with the SEUA argument.
- The court determined that insurance *was* interstate commerce and was subject to the Sherman Act and other federal legislation.[2]

The result of this legislation would place insurance regulation under federal jurisdiction if the industry did not do something to prevent that from occurring.

The McCarran-Ferguson Act

The insurance industry and state insurance regulators did not agree with the Supreme Court's decision and lobbied Congress to enact legislation that would provide states with the authority to regulate the insurance industry. The McCarran-Ferguson Act, passed by Congress in 1945, provided the states with the authority to regulate the "business of insurance" unless the federal government enacts legislation that specifically addresses the insurance industry. Thus, the states regulate insurance industry activities that relate directly to the insurance product and related services. The federal government regulates those insurance activities for which it has enacted legislation and regulates insurance industry activities that do not directly relate to insurance products and services.[3]

What Insurance Activities Are Regulated

Nearly every activity that insurance companies engage in, as well as insurance industry agents, brokers, adjusters, financiers, and bondsmen, is regulated to some extent. As indicated above, state regulators oversee activities considered to be the "business of insurance," and the federal government regulates activities that are not within the "business of insurance" or that federal legislation has specifically addressed.

Activities Regulated by the States

The activities that constitute the "business of insurance" were not defined in the McCarran-Ferguson Act. Essentially, courts have since defined those activities in cases heard after the McCarran-Ferguson Act was passed. The areas of insurance activity regulated by the states include the following:

- Licensing of insurance companies, producers, and claims adjusters
- Marketing and sales
- Ratemaking activities
- Underwriting activities
- Claims settlement activities
- Treatment of consumers
- Solvency of insurance companies

- Receiverships, rehabilitations, and liquidations
- Mergers and acquisitions
- **Guaranty fund** operations

State-regulated activities that pertain specifically to personal insurance companies are discussed in the next major section of this chapter.

Activities Regulated by the Federal Government

The federal government oversees the operations and activities of insurance companies and other insurance industry participants that are not unique to the insurance business. Those areas include the following:

- Labor relations
- Sale of securities
- Federal taxation
- Employee benefits
- Discrimination against employees
- Employee safety and health

The activities and operations within the insurance industry that relate to those areas listed above fall under the jurisdiction of the federal government. For example, insurance companies with many employees must comply with such legislation as the Occupational Safety and Health Act (OSHA), which requires companies to institute adequate safety and health programs for their employees, and the Employee Retirement Income Security Act (ERISA), which establishes standards for retirement plans maintained by businesses, including insurance companies.

The federal government has also intervened in the "business of insurance" in certain areas by enacting federal legislation that deals specifically with insurance activities. For example, the Product Liability Risk Retention Act of 1981 and the Liability Risk Retention Act of 1986 preempted state laws that had restricted or prohibited the formation of **risk retention groups** (and **purchasing groups** under the latter act). Congress believed that such groups were necessary to address the availability crisis in liability insurance that existed at the time those acts were drafted. According to Congress, state legislation was unable to handle the formation of these groups, so federal action was necessary. Thus, the federal laws were enacted, and, in the area of risk retention groups, those federal laws are primary to any state legislation addressing the same concerns.[4]

State Regulation of Personal Insurance

As previously mentioned, the states are permitted by the federal government, through the McCarran-Ferguson Act, to regulate the "business of insurance." State insurance regulation is the responsibility of

A **guaranty fund** is a system through which claims of insolvent property and liability insurers are paid. Generally, the money in guaranty funds is provided by charges assessed against all insurers in the state.

A **risk retention group** provides limited insurance lines to business organizations that would otherwise have difficulty obtaining such insurance. A **purchasing group** is a group of insurance buyers who purchase liability insurance together.

a state insurance department in each of the fifty states and four jurisdictions of the United States.[5] The state insurance department is often a separate entity within the state government, but in some states it is a division of another state department. For example, in Florida, the state insurance department is part of the State Treasurer's Office. For the purposes of this text, the state office responsible for regulating insurance will be referred to as the state insurance department.

Each state insurance department is directed by an individual usually referred to as the insurance commissioner, although that person might alternately be called the superintendent or director of insurance or have some other title. For example, in Minnesota, the title of the person who directs the insurance department is Commissioner of Commerce. In this text, the person in charge of the state insurance department will be called the insurance commissioner.

The insurance commissioner is the individual charged with regulating the insurance industry in his or her state. However, many of the insurance commissioner's regulatory duties are delegated to various divisions within the insurance department. Personal insurance regulation is part of the regulation for which the insurance commissioner is responsible.

Exhibit 4-1 illustrates an organizational chart for a typical insurance department. The divisions that are shaded indicate those regulatory areas that apply to personal insurance. The remainder of this section describes those areas of personal insurance regulation shown in Exhibit 4-1.

Exhibit 4-1
Organizational Chart for a Typical State Insurance Department

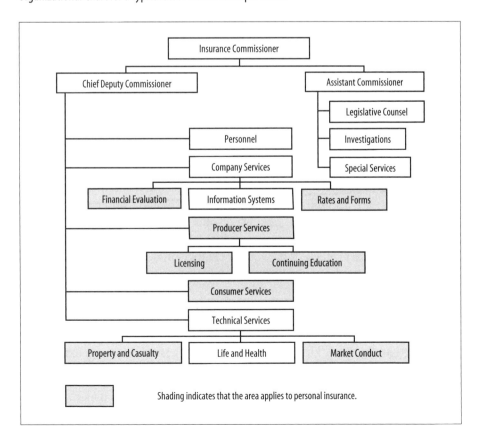

Shading indicates that the area applies to personal insurance.

Regulation by State

Each state regulates the operations of insurers within that state. The rates, licensing, consumer issues, and forms all fall within the method of regulation adopted by that state. The discussions that follow address those methods. First, though, specialists should know how their individual state addresses these issues. Exhibit 4-2 is a partial list of the regulatory methods by state. This information should be obtained for each state in which a specialist operates. The state commissioner's office is one possible source for obtaining this information. Other sources might exist within the specialist's own organization. The addresses and phone numbers for the state insurance commissioners' offices appear as Appendix 4-A to this text.

Regulation of Rates, Rules, and Forms

The policies (or forms) sold by personal insurance companies and the rules used to determine which applicants are eligible for those policies are subject to regulatory requirements and constraints. In most states, personal insurance companies cannot use personal insurance policies before receiving approval to use them from the state insurance department. In addition, in many states, the underwriting guidelines that personal insurance companies use to determine whether applicants are acceptable risks must also be approved before they can be applied by insurers. That type of regulation ensures that insurance consumers are protected.

The rates for which personal insurance policies are sold and the rules used to calculate the prices for particular risks and insureds (called rate rules) are also subject to regulatory requirements and constraints. State insurance regulators review personal insurance rates to ensure that insurance companies remain solvent and that personal insurance consumers are protected. In most states, personal insurance rates must be approved by the state insurance regulators before they can be used.

The process of submitting policies, rules, and rates to state insurance departments is called **filing**. The information required in those various filings, its format, and the time frame within which the filings must be made vary by state. However, four general types of filing laws exist:

- *Prior-approval.* Under a prior-approval filing law, the item subject to the law must be *filed* with the state insurance department and

Exhibit 4-2
Regulation Methods By State

Regulatory Issue	How Your State Addresses This Issue
	Your Notes:
• **State of operation:** For which state is information being obtained? (Copy this exhibit for additional states.)	
• **Forms, underwriting rules, and rate filings:** What are the restrictions on underwriting classifications?	
• **Rates, rules, and forms:** How are rates determined to be fair, adequate, and not excessive in your state?	
• **Rate filings:** What forms must be used in your state to file rates? What types of rating laws apply?	
• **Agent licensing:** What are the qualifications for obtaining an agent's license?	
What types of education and exams are required for obtaining an agent's license? What are the exemptions for licensing exams?	
• **Continuing education (CE) for agents:** What are the CE requirements for agents? How often must they be met? Are there any exemptions to the CE requirements? How is the insurance department notified of CE completion?	
• **Countersignatures:** Are countersignatures for personal property-liability policies required? Are there any exemptions to those countersignature requirements?	
• **Complaints:** How are complaints handled in your state?	
• **Surplus lines:** How are surplus lines policies regulated in your state?	

approved by the department *before* the insurance company submitting the filing can use the item.

- *File-and-use.* A file-and-use filing law requires the insurer to file the item with the state insurance department at a specified period of time before it is used. If the state insurance department does not reject the item within a certain period of time following its filing, the insurer can use the item. The amount of time required to satisfy each timing constraint is specified in the file-and-use law.

- *Use-and-file.* Under a use-and-file filing law, insurers can use the item before it is filed with the state. However, the item must be filed within a specified period of time after its initial use. The state insurance department then has a specified period of time in which to disapprove the item. The time periods are specified in the law.

- *No-filing.* In a state with a no-filing law (sometimes referred to as "open competition"), the item is not required to be filed, nor is the state insurance department's approval required to use the item.

Not all personal lines forms and rates must be filed. Further details of form, rate, and rule filings, including the requirements of different states, are discussed below.

Forms and Form Filings

In most states, personal insurance forms are subject to prior-approval laws. Generally, insurers must file any new or revised forms with state insurance departments and get approval for those forms before they can issue policies with the forms. In addition, applications, jackets, and declarations pages that contain contractual language usually need to be filed and approved before they are sold.

Three states and the District of Columbia have laws that apply to policy forms that are not prior-approval laws. In Missouri, policy forms are subject to use-and-file laws. In Utah and Washington, DC, forms are subject to file-and-use laws. In Colorado, a no-file law applies to policy forms. The remaining states have prior-approval regulation that applies to personal insurance forms.

State insurance departments check filed personal insurance forms to make sure they comply with regulations that concern policy wording, contract clause requirements, and readability. Many states require that certain provisions, such as the following, be included in personal insurance policies:

- Policy cancellation and nonrenewal provisions
- Loss-reporting requirements
- Claims settlement provisions
- Subrogation provisions
- Fraud and dishonesty definition and penalties
- Dispute resolution provisions

In some states, the wording of these clauses is specified.

Most states also have readability requirements for personal insurance forms. These requirements establish a minimum standard based on the Flesch reading ease scale, a system designed to ensure that the personal insurance policies are written at a level that their intended audience will understand. (Reading-ease benchmarks can be established based on other scales as well.) Some states even specify the font size used on forms to ensure that no "fine print" appears in the contracts.

Rates and Rate Filings

Under insurance laws in all states, state insurance regulators must ensure that rates charged by insurers for their insurance products are adequate, not excessive, and not unfairly discriminatory. To achieve these goals, the rates proposed for most personal insurance in most states must be filed with state insurance regulators on a prior-approval basis. However, some states provide exceptions to that requirement.

At least one state has a form of rate regulation that differs from the four types described above. Massachusetts requires that auto insurers use state-made rates for personal auto insurance sold in Massachusetts. State-made rates are, as the name suggests, rates calculated by the state.

Rate filings must typically include information that supports the level of the filed rates, including the following:

- The percentage change in the insurer's statewide average rate
- The insurer's recent loss experience and expenses in the state in which the filing is being made for the coverages for which the rates are being filed
- The actuarial assumptions used in calculating the proposed rates
- The expected loss experience and loss adjustment expenses
- The expense loading data
- Investment income information if investment income is included in the rate calculations
- Sufficient explanatory material for state insurance regulators to understand and evaluate the filing

No typical rate filing format exists. However, rate filings generally include both narrative and exhibited information. An example of a rate filing form is provided in Exhibit 4-3.

Rate filings can be filed electronically in some states. However, most filings continue to be made on paper copies that are mailed or hand-delivered to state insurance departments.

Exhibit 4-3
Example of a Rate Filing Form

NAIC
PROPERTY - CASUALTY FILING TRANSMITTAL FORM

DEPARTMENT USE ONLY
Date Received: _____
Filing No.: _____
Assigned to: _____
Action: _____

1. a) Company name _____ 2. Date _____

    b) Group name/Bureau/Rating organization(s) _____

    Address _____

3. NAIC Group and Co.# _____ *(This is assigned by NAIC for its tracking.)*

4. Federal ID# __ *(the "FEIN")* _____

5. a) Domiciliary state: ____ *(insurer's home state)* _____

    b) State ID# *(state tracking #)* _____

6. Program Title _____

7. Annual Statement lines _____ *(lines of coverage that will be affected on the Annual Statement report)*

    _____

8. Type of Filing: [ ] Personal   [ ] Commercial

    a) Form: [ ] Independent

        [ ] Reference of _____
        (include bureau filing #)

    b) Rule: [ ] Independent

        [ ] Reference of _____
        (include bureau filing #)

        [ ] Deviation *(modification of a prior rule)*

    c) Rate: [ ] Independent

        [ ] Reference of _____
        (include bureau filing #)

        [ ] Deviation *(a modification of a prior rate—such as a discount)*

9. Proposed effective date: _____ *(dates the company targets for implementation)*

    _____

10. Brief description of this filing: _____

    _____

11. Attachments:

    [ ]   Form filing transmittal supplements

    [ ]   Domiciliary filing fee; indicate if retaliatory: _____

    [ ]   Filing fee amount $ _____

    [ ]   Other _____

    _____

12. Name and title of person making this filing _____

13. Phone number _____

14. Insurance company filing # _____

> **Educational Objective 3**
> Explain the constraints on the use of rating classifications.

Rating Classifications

Insurance companies classify similar risks into groups for rating purposes. State insurance regulation limits the types of factors that can be used to classify insureds. To ensure that personal insurance companies abide by state rating classification regulations, insurers include their rating classification plans as part of their rate filing.

Factors on which rating classifications for personal insurance can be based vary by state. For example, Wisconsin does not allow "health condition" as a rating classification factor for auto insurance if an applicant or insured has a valid driver's license. Montana does not allow gender as an auto insurance rating classification factor. The different state limitations are too numerous to mention, but specialists should be aware of the regulatory constraints on rating classifications in states in which they do business.

Modifying Filed Rates

Rating plans often include means to adjust rates for individual risks that are part of a particular class. Adjustments to filed rates based on actual claims experience (experience modifications) are popular in commercial insurance but are seldom used in personal insurance. If experience modifications are to be used, the information about the modifications must be included in any rate filings.

Role of Advisory Organizations

Advisory organizations are often involved in the rate-filing process. In the past, these organizations developed rates for their member companies and filed the rates according to the requests of their members. However, advisory organizations have begun to concentrate on filing prospective **loss costs** rather than final rates because regulation now allows advisory organizations to do so and because companies then file their loadings and modifications. Prospective loss costs are the components of rates that cover the expected losses and loss adjustment expenses.

Once an advisory organization has filed prospective loss costs with state insurance departments, personal insurers using those advisory loss costs to calculate their rates file additional information concerning how they arrived at their final rates based on the filed loss costs. For example, those personal insurance companies will need to file, if required by state law, their expense loading information and supplementary statistics to support the loading.

> **Loss costs** are the expected losses relating to each exposure unit. An insurer can add its own loadings and modifications to establish its rates.

> **Educational Objective 4**
> Identify prohibited marketing and underwriting practices in property and liability insurance.

Market Conduct

A market conduct examination is a review of an insurer's underwriting and ratemaking practices conducted by the state insurance market conduct examiners.

To ensure that personal insurance companies are using the filed policies, rates, underwriting guidelines, and rate rules, state insurance regulators periodically investigate the companies' underwriting and ratemaking practices. These investigations fall under the auspices of **market conduct examinations**, in which the state insurance market conduct examiners closely investigate the market conduct activities of an insurer. Market conduct examinations can also consider marketing and claims settlement activities of personal insurance companies.

The scope of market conduct examinations depends on what the state insurance department conducting the examinations hopes to achieve through the examination. Market conduct examinations of personal insurance companies might be targeted to a specific area of the insurer's operations, such as underwriting or marketing. Market conduct examinations are often targeted at areas about which consumer complaints or other indicators raise concerns. The examinations might also be comprehensive, looking into all aspects of personal insurers' market conduct activities—underwriting, ratemaking, marketing, and claims. Comprehensive market conduct examinations are often done at regular intervals (usually about five years).

Unfair Trade Practices and Claims Settlement Acts

In addition to the concerns addressed above, much market conduct regulation is concerned with unfair trade practices and unfair claims settlement practices acts. Every U.S. jurisdiction but Washington, DC, has a version of an unfair trade practice act that sets out what activities are considered unfair trade practices if committed by insurance companies and insurance industry participants. In most states, those acts define unfair trade practices in three areas: marketing, underwriting, and ratemaking. They might also include definitions of unfair claims practices. However, some states also have a separate unfair claims settlement practices act rather than including claims settlement provisions in the unfair trade practices acts.

Market conduct also concerns state cancellation and nonrenewal laws. These laws restrict an insurance company's ability to decline, cancel, or nonrenew personal insurance policies. The provisions of these laws are discussed separately below, but in many states the provisions are part of the state's unfair trade practices act.

The provisions of states' unfair trade practices acts and unfair claims settlement acts typically incorporate the model Unfair Trade Practices Act and model Unfair Claims Settlement Practices Act of the National Association of Insurance Commissioners (NAIC). The activities relating to personal property-liability insurance and defined by those models as unfair are listed in Exhibit 4-4.

Exhibit 4-4
Unfair Trade Practices and Unfair Claims Settlement Practices

Unfair Trade Practices	Unfair Claims Settlement Practices
Misrepresenting and falsely advertising insurance policies	Misrepresenting relevant facts or policy provisions
Making public or including false information in advertisements, announcements, or statements	Failing to promptly acknowledge pertinent communications concerning claims
Defaming an insurance company	Failing to use reasonable standards for prompt investigation and settlement
Entering into an agreement to boycott, coerce, or intimidate	Not attempting to settle promptly and fairly and in good faith
Making false statements and entries about the financial condition of an insurance company	Compelling suits to recover amounts due by offering substantially less than amounts due
Using stock or advisory board contracts to induce the purchase of insurance	Refusing to pay claims without reasonable investigation
Unfairly discriminating	Failing to affirm or deny a claim within a reasonable time following its investigation
Failing to maintain marketing and performance records	Trying to settle or settling for less than the claimant is entitled to according to written advertising material with or attached to the application
Failing to maintain complaint-handling procedures	
Misrepresenting insurance applications	Trying to settle or settling on the basis of an application materially altered without the knowledge or consent of the insured
Failing to provide claims history	Making claims payments without indicating the coverage
	Unreasonably delaying investigation or settlement by requiring duplicate paperwork
	Failing to promptly explain denied claims or compromises
	Failing to provide the necessary paperwork within a reasonable time
	Failing to adopt and use reasonable standards to ensure that repairs by a required repairer are performed in a workmanlike manner

Sources: National Association of Insurance Commissioners, "Unfair Trade Practices Act," *Model Laws, Regulations and Guidelines*, January 1993, pp. 880-2 to 880-8; and NAIC, "Unfair Claims Settlement Practices Act," *Model Laws, Regulations and Guidelines*, July 1991, pp. 900-2 to 900-3.

Unfair trade practices acts and unfair claims settlement acts usually require that a trend of such unfair practices be evidenced before insurers and producers can be penalized for the violations. So, if an underwriter denies coverage to one applicant solely because of the applicant's home address, the underwriter has probably not committed an unfair trade practice. However, if statistics indicate that the underwriter tends to deny coverage to applicants in a particular neighborhood, the underwriter might be unfairly discriminating and therefore committing an unfair trade practice.

The NAIC model acts concerning unfair trade practices and unfair claims settlement practices recommend that one occurrence of an unfair activity be considered an unfair trade practice or unfair claims settlement practice if it is gross and willful misconduct and if intent to commit the activity can be shown. However, most states have not yet adopted this recommendation.

Unfair Trade Practices in Marketing

As indicated in Exhibit 4-4, several unfair trade practices relate to market activities of personal insurance companies and producers. Misrepresentation or false advertising of insurance policy coverages and provisions is an unfair trade practice. The following activities are considered unfair advertising practices, particularly when such actions induce the purchase, renewal, lapse, or cancellation of insurance policies:[6]

- Misrepresenting benefits, conditions, or terms of insurance policies
- Making misleading statements about or misrepresentations of the financial condition of an insurance company
- Using names for insurance policies that misrepresent their true nature
- Misrepresenting the premium

False announcements, advertising, or statements made to the public; defamation of insurance companies; and misrepresenting insurance application information are also unfair trade practices. Insurance companies and their producers are expected to be honest with consumers about insurance products and other information that might affect consumers' decisions to purchase or renew personal insurance policies. The material in the box below shows an example of an unfair trade practice in advertising and public pronouncements.

An agent regularly tells clients that the homeowners policy he sells is better than any other homeowners policies available because the policy automatically provides "all-risks" coverage on personal property. The agent fails to tell the clients that the broadened coverage is available only through an endorsement that he automatically adds onto any homeowners policies he sells at an extra premium. The agent is committing an unfair trade practice act by misrepresenting policy benefits and provisions.

Another area of unfair trade practices in marketing involves attempts by insurers and producers to gain monopoly power or to restrain the business activities of other insurance industry participants. When marketing insurance products and services, insurers and producers are not to form agreements to gain marketing power through boycott, coercion, or intimidation of other insurers and producers or of consumers. For example, if producers in a certain area agree not to provide insurance through a particular insurer, they are forming an agreement to boycott an insurer, thus committing an unfair trade practice.

Finally, under unfair trade practices acts, insurers are required to maintain marketing records, generally for the current calendar year and for a number of years preceding the current year. The NAIC model recommends that insurers maintain two years worth of data in addition to the current year's data. This information must typically be accessible and retrievable by state insurance regulators for examination.

Unfair Trade Practices in Underwriting and Ratemaking

Many unfair trade practices concern unfair discrimination. The following activities constitute unfair discrimination in personal property and liability insurance under most unfair trade practices acts:[7]

- Refusing to insure or renew, or canceling or limiting insurance coverage based solely on the geographic location of the loss exposure *unless* such a decision is based on sound underwriting and actuarial principles

- Refusing to insure or renew, or canceling or limiting insurance coverage on residential property or personal property contained in the residential property, based solely on the age of the residential property

- Refusing to insure or renew, or canceling or limiting insurance coverage based on the gender, marital status, race, religion, or national origin of the applicant or insured

- Refusing to insure or renew, or canceling, modifying, or limiting insurance coverage solely because the applicant or insured is mentally or physically impaired

- Refusing to insure solely because the applicant has been refused insurance or had his or her insurance canceled by another insurer

The following are examples of unfair discrimination in underwriting and ratemaking:

- An underwriter routinely rejects otherwise acceptable applicants who are over retirement age.

- An insurer uses an applicant's prior rejections for insurance as an underwriting standard. Applicants who might otherwise be acceptable are denied coverage if they have been turned down for coverage by another insurer.

Unfair Claims Settlement Practices

Certain activities that might occur within the claims settlement process are considered unfair to claimants and insurance industry participants.

Insurers, independent adjusters, and producers who commit such actions can be penalized. In essence, the activities listed in Exhibit 4-4 as unfair claims settlement practices are considered unfair because they harm the insured and the claimant. Personal insurers are expected to hold up their end of the personal insurance contracts they sell. This responsibility includes settling claims in a professional and reasonable manner. The following are examples of unfair claims settlement activities:

- After investigating claims, a claim adjuster typically waits two weeks beyond the state-mandated maximum period for settling claims before she will offer to settle. She has discovered that claimants who wait longer are more willing to settle for amounts less than what they are due.

- Another claim adjuster often settles for less than the amount that is due claimants on homeowners claims involving loss of trees and shrubs. Most insureds are not aware of the additional coverage provided for such items, so if insureds do not claim coverage for those items, the adjuster does not include payment for those items in the claims settlement.

Declination, Termination, and Disclosure Laws

> A **declination** occurs when an insurer rejects an application.

As previously discussed, provisions concerning **declination** and **termination** of insurance policies are often included in unfair trade practices acts. However, these provisions are important and are discussed separately in this text.

> A **termination** is a policy cancellation during its term or a policy nonrenewal at the end of its term.

Declination, termination, and disclosure laws describe acceptable reasons for which insurance coverage can be denied or canceled and establish requirements for informing applicants and insureds of denial or cancellation. In all situations involving the declination or termination of personal insurance, the reason must be disclosed to the applicant or insured and notice must be given to the applicant or insured with an explanation of why the insurer is taking such an action and, in the case of termination, stating the effective date of termination. Time requirements are established for those notices.

Allowable Declinations and Terminations

Laws in most states, whether they be declination, termination, and disclosure laws or unfair trade practices acts, establish reasons that are acceptable for declining or terminating personal insurance coverages. The reasons are often noted separately for auto insurance and for other property and liability insurance. Typically, personal insurance companies can cancel an insurance policy in force for less than a certain amount of time (usually sixty days) for any reason. This period is often called the underwriting "window." For nonauto personal insurance policies in force for longer than the window, the following reasons for cancellation or nonrenewal are usually allowed:[8]

- Unpaid premium
- Fraud or material misrepresentation by or with the permission of the named insured

- Willful and reckless acts performed or omissions made by the named insured that increase the insurer's risk

- Substantial increase in risk

- Insured property in violation of local fire, health, safety, building, or construction regulations or ordinances, which substantially increases the insurer's risk

- The insurance commissioner's determination that if the insurer provided insurance, it would be violating a law

- Not paying property taxes for at least two years

Personal insurance companies can typically cancel or nonrenew personal auto policies in force for longer than the window for the following reasons:[9]

- Unpaid premium

- Fraud or material misrepresentation by or with the permission of the named insured

- Failure of the named insured or any driver in the same household to provide a copy of his or her driving record upon the insurer's written request

- Suspension or revocation of the named insured's driver's license or the license of any driver in the same household

- Conviction or forfeiture of bail arising out of or in connection with operating an auto, which could cause suspension or revocation of the license of the named insured or any driver in the same household

- An insured auto that is mechanically defective and that endangers public safety; is used to carry passengers for hire; or is altered during the policy period, which substantially increase the insurer's risk

- The named insured's relocation to a state in which the insurer is not licensed

- The insurance commissioner's determination that if the insurer provided insurance, it would be violating a law

State laws vary from the allowable reasons listed above. For example, New York allows an insurer to nonrenew only 2 percent of the auto policies it has in force each year. But for every two new insurance policies the insurer sells voluntarily, it can nonrenew an additional auto insurance policy above the 2 percent threshold.

In Massachusetts, personal insurance companies cannot deny auto insurance coverage. Insurance must be provided for at least a year, after which insurers can nonrenew only for the reasons listed above.

Declinations and Terminations That Are Not Allowed

Some reasons for declining or terminating coverage are not allowed:

- A declination or termination based solely on race, religion, nationality, ethnic group, age, gender, or marital status of the applicant, named insured, or, for auto insurance, other occupants within the same household

- A declination or termination based solely on lawful occupation or profession of applicant, named insured, or, for auto insurance, other occupants within the same household
- The previous declination or termination of the applicant or named insured from another insurer
- The use of residual market mechanisms by the applicant or named insured
- A declination or termination based solely on the age or location of the insured residence or residence to be insured *unless* based on sound underwriting principles (such as too great a moral hazard)
- The principal location of the insured motor vehicle *unless* based on sound business reasons (such as a vehicle not licensed in the state in which the vehicle is garaged)

Notification Requirements

When policies are canceled or nonrenewed for allowable reasons, personal insurance companies are generally required under state declination, termination, and disclosure provisions to notify the insureds a specified number of days before the policy is effectively terminated. The NAIC recommends that the time periods in Exhibit 4-5 be used.

States vary from these recommendations. For example, Pennsylvania requires fifteen days' notice for cancellation because of nonpayment of premium or because the issuance of the policy was based on material misrepresentations. Florida requires forty-five days' notice for nonrenewal of personal auto policies unless the policy is not renewed because of nonpayment of premium, for which nonrenewal can be without notice.

Exhibit 4-5
NAIC's Recommendations for Number of Days' Written Notice in the Event of Policy Termination

Property insurance	Cancel policy in force ≤ 60 days	14 days' notice
	Cancel policy in force > 60 days	30 days' notice
	Nonrenew	30 days' notice
Auto insurance	Cancel for nonpayment of premium	10 days' notice
	Cancel for other reason	20 days' notice
	Nonrenew	30 days' notice

Sources: National Association of Insurance Commissioners, "Property Insurance Declination, Termination, and Disclosure Model Act," *Model Laws, Regulations and Guidelines,* July 1992, pp. 720-2 to 720-3; and National Association of Insurance Commissioners, "Automobile Insurance Declination, Termination, and Disclosure Model Act," *Model Laws, Regulations and Guidelines,* July 1992, pp. 725-2 to 725-3.

Market Conduct Examination Concerns

In conducting market conduct examinations, regulators look not only for violations of unfair trade practices acts, of unfair claims settlement practices acts, and of declination, termination, and disclosure laws; they also look for compliance with filing laws and other forms of regulation, depending on the functional area of the insurers being examined.

Marketing and Market Conduct Examinations

Market conduct examinations of insurers' marketing activities focus on the insurers' sales and advertising activities. The examinations generally involve reviewing advertising and sales materials to make sure they comply with state regulatory requirements, particularly concerning false, deceptive, and misleading information.

Examiners also review claims complaints indicating that insurers' advertising and sales practices are deceptive. For example, suppose a company has an above-average number of complaints involving claims that were not paid but that insureds and claimants believed should have been covered based on information provided when the policy was purchased. Market conduct examiners might investigate the insurer's advertising and sales activities to determine whether coverage was misrepresented to induce sales.[10]

Underwriting and Market Conduct

Market conduct examinations of underwriting functions typically involve the review of the following underwriting-related activities:[11]

- An insurer's compliance with its stated underwriting guidelines
- The insurer's use of forms filed in accordance with state regulation
- The compliance of the producers involved in the sale of the reviewed insurance policies with state licensing laws
- An insurer's compliance with state cancellation and nonrenewal laws
- An insurer's use of rates filed in accordance with state regulation
- The insurer's application of its stated rate rules
- The insurer's use of proper insurance policies and endorsements

Claims and Market Conduct Examinations

Market conduct examinations of personal insurers' claim activities involve the review of various aspects of the settlement process to determine whether the insurers are complying with unfair claim settlement acts and other regulations pertaining to claim activities and policy provisions. The review might include the following aspects of claims:[12]

- General handling and timeliness of payment
- Settlement valuation procedures
- Amount of subrogation involved in settling claims

- Number of and reasons for claims denied or closed without payment
- Amount of litigation involved in settling claims

Financial Regulation

Personal insurance companies are subject to financial regulation by state insurance departments. Such regulation takes many forms, from limitations placed on investments to financial examination. The emphasis of financial regulation is to ensure the solvency of insurance companies. Financial regulation that affects personal insurers can be divided into four categories:

- Financial reporting
- Solvency monitoring
- Capital adequacy monitoring
- Accreditation

State insurance regulators use financial reporting to gather information about the financial condition of insurance companies to help them monitor the solvency of insurance companies. For that reason, insurance companies must file **annual statements** with state insurance departments in each state in which the companies are licensed to do business. State financial examiners conduct ratio analysis on the data included in annual statements to determine whether companies are in compliance with **statutory accounting** requirements for insurance companies and to measure whether insurers are near or in financial trouble. The ratio analysis helps financial examiners identify those insurers who need to be more closely examined because of solvency concerns of regulators.

Insurance Regulatory Information System

One of the systems that insurance regulators use to detect financial trouble in insurance companies is the **Insurance Regulatory Information System (IRIS)**. This system comprises two phases: (1) the statistical phase, in which ratios are calculated by comparing annual statement data to benchmarks, and (2) the analytical phase, in which, based on the information received during the statistical phase and from other sources (such as consumer complaints), insurers might be slated for financial examinations or might be notified that they need to improve their financial status.

State insurance regulators use financial examinations of insurance companies to detect possible insolvency early enough to prevent the insurers' actual insolvency. As with market conduct examinations, financial examinations might be targeted to a specific area of operations, or they might be comprehensive. Under the laws in most states, insurance companies must undergo a comprehensive (also called full scope) financial examination every three to five years. However, the targeted (or limited scope) financial examinations are increasingly used to assess an insurer's risk of insolvency more effectively and efficiently and to help prevent an insurer's insolvency.

Annual statements are formal financial reports presented to state insurance regulators. They must be prepared for each state in which the insurer is licensed.

Statutory accounting employs a set of rules and procedures for insurance financial reporting. Most other industries use generally accepted accounting principles (GAAP) as a standard. Statutory accounting tends to be more conservative than GAAP accounting.

The **Insurance Regulatory Information System (IRIS)** is an early warning system for the potential financial failure of an insurance company.

Risk-Based Capital

In monitoring capital adequacy, the **risk-based capital** model has been developed to replace the traditional fixed amount of capital. Traditionally, state laws have required that insurers maintain a fixed amount of capital, which was tied to the types of insurance being written. For example, in Arizona, a personal insurer needed a minimum of $600,000 in capital to write property insurance. Risk-based capital requirements relate the amount of capital to more than the line of insurance being written. For example, the ability to collect reinsurance recoverables and the ability to establish reserves that are adequate to cover actual losses are considered in the formula to calculate risk-based capital for insurance companies. Furthermore, risk-based capital laws give state insurance regulators more authority to act when they determine that insurers are financially troubled.

Risk-based capital is a model for developing the amount of capital an insurer must have available. It considers the insurer's assets (and their strengths), credit (including receivables and reinsurance recoverables), and underwriting risks.

Accreditation Program

Under the accreditation program, state insurance departments are certified by the NAIC if they pass a rigorous review of their solvency regulation. The ultimate goal of accreditation is to ensure that all states have at least a minimum standard of solvency regulation.

Just as risk-based capital was developed and implemented to improve solvency regulation, so was the accreditation program. Although the **accreditation program** does not directly affect personal insurance companies, it can indirectly affect them because the financial regulation to which they are subjected as a company can become more rigorous.

The **accreditation program** is a certification program for state insurance departments. The purposes of the accreditation program are (1) to provide consistency of solvency regulations among states and (2) to improve the standards of solvency regulation and financial examinations in all states.

Regulation of Agents and Brokers

Agents and brokers selling personal insurance, collectively referred to as *producers*, are subject to regulation by state insurance departments. Producers must be licensed in all states in which they sell insurance. In addition, forty-three states and Puerto Rico have continuing education requirements that producers must meet in order to maintain their licenses. Furthermore, countersignature laws, described later in this chapter, might apply to sales of insurance by producers in states other than their home states.

Licensing for Agents

Personal insurance producers spend the majority of their time dealing with individuals and families. In doing their jobs, producers are expected to act responsibly and professionally. Licensing of producers *before* they begin dealing with the public is one means of ensuring that personal insurance consumers are protected from unprofessional and unscrupulous producers.

State laws define who is eligible to become an insurance agent or broker. Both residents and nonresidents of a state are eligible to become licensed in that state. However, they must be at least eighteen years of age in most states. Furthermore, nonresidents might be required to show that they are citizens *in good standing* in their home state as well as licensed within that state. For example, Texas requires nonresident applicants for a Texas agent's license to include a Certificate of Good Standing issued by their home state in their application package to the Texas Insurance Department.[13]

The Licensing Process

The producer licensing process typically involves the following steps:

- Enrolling in and successfully completing a pre-licensing course
- Applying for a license
- Registering for and passing a licensing examination

State insurance departments often indicate which pre-licensing programs are acceptable. The information is usually provided to applicants in each state's licensing bulletin or another publication provided by the state insurance departments. Upon successfully completing a pre-licensing program, applicants generally receive a certificate of completion indicating that they have taken and have passed the program.

When applying for an agent's or a broker's license, applicants are usually required to complete a form provided by the state insurance department in each state in which the applicant wants to sell insurance. The application includes general information about the applicant, such as name, address, and age. It also requires educational and insurance industry experience and information concerning prior convictions or pleadings to any misdemeanor or felony. In some states, a photo of the applicant might be required. Included with the application delivered to the state insurance department must be payment for the state's license fee and the certificate of completion of any required pre-licensing course.

Once their applications are filed, applicants must take licensing examinations to ensure their competency in personal property and liability insurance. Licensing examinations are usually held frequently, daily in some states, at approved locations. Licensing examinations are typically divided into two or more sections: one or more sections that deal with coverage issues, and one or more sections that deal with state insurance laws and regulations. For example, a coverage section on homeowners insurance might ask a question about the loss settlement clause or about a particular exclusion, and a section testing knowledge of state laws might ask a question about the state's financial responsibility requirements.

Upon passing their licensing examinations, and if the insurance department approves their applications, applicants are generally issued personal property and liability insurance licenses. If applicants do not pass their licensing examinations, they might be required to retake the entire examination or to retake only those areas they failed. The options depend on the laws in the states in which the examinations were taken.

Licensing Requirement Waivers

In some states and in certain situations, one or more of the licensing requirements might be waived. For example, in Texas, individuals holding the Chartered Property Casualty Underwriter (CPCU) designation or the Certified Insurance Counselor (CIC) designation are not required to enroll in Texas' otherwise mandatory pre-licensing program. Another area of exemptions applies to nonresident license applicants. In some states, nonresident applicants are not required to take the coverage sections of the licensing examinations if they have passed licensing examinations in their home states. However, the nonresident applicants are often required to pass the state law sections of the licensing examinations.

License Renewal

Once a license is received, it must typically be renewed after a specified period of time, which varies by state. Some states, such as Georgia, require agent licenses to be renewed each year. Other states, such as Rhode Island, require agent licenses to be renewed every three years. In most states, as discussed below, proof of continuing education is required to renew personal insurance producers' licenses.

License Revocation

State insurance departments can revoke, suspend, nonrenew, or deny licenses for various reasons, including the following:

- Material or fraudulent misrepresentation on the application
- Violation of insurance laws
- Cheating on the licensing examination
- Conviction of a felony
- Misappropriation of insurance premiums and claim payments

The list is not exhaustive. Furthermore, the reasons allowed for denying or otherwise terminating a license vary by state. Depending on the reasons for termination, producers might also be fined, jailed, or both.

Continuing Education for Agents

Once licensed, personal insurance producers are required to meet continuing education requirements in forty-four states[14] and Puerto Rico to maintain their licenses. Continuing education requirements are a means for ensuring that personal insurance producers keep current on the available personal insurance products and services and any regulation that applies to the services they provide. These requirements help to protect personal insurance consumers by making sure they are informed about new developments that might affect their insurance coverages.

Most states specify their continuing education requirements as a number of hours per a period of time. However, the continuing education requirements for each state and jurisdiction differ. For example,

Nevada requires thirty hours of continuing education every three years, and Arkansas requires sixteen hours every two years.

As with the licensing process, state insurance departments notify producers of those continuing education programs that are approved to fulfill continuing education requirements and the number hours for which they are approved. Approved programs must typically relate directly to insurance.

Countersignature Laws

Most states have countersignature laws that require that all insurance policies sold in the state be signed by at least one licensed agent who is a resident of that state. In some states, that agent must also share in the commission earned.

Educational Objective 5

Explain the role of state insurance departments in responding to and resolving consumer complaints.

Handling Consumer Complaints

State insurance regulators collect data and maintain databases on consumer complaints lodged against insurance companies, agencies, and producers. The complaints are analyzed to determine whether particular insurance companies, agencies, or producers are receiving more complaints than the normal or average amount. When an insurer, agency, or producer is found to have a higher-than-normal complaint ratio, state insurance regulators might begin an investigation into those areas of operation against which most complaints are made. For example, if the complaints about a particular insurer's claims settlement practices are twice their normal level, a problem might exist in the insurer's claim-handling procedures and its claim-settlement process. Therefore, the state insurance department might decide to conduct a targeted market conduct examination of the insurer's claims settlement functions.

State insurance regulators also periodically investigate insurers' methods of handling the complaints they receive from their insureds and claimants. Insurers in most states are expected to maintain records of the complaints they receive and how they are addressed. During market conduct examinations, those complaint records might be investigated to determine whether insurers are meeting state requirements for handling consumer complaints.

Educational Objective 6

Explain the purpose of the surplus lines market and how that market is regulated.

Dealing With Surplus Lines

To this point, this chapter has focused on the standard personal insurance market in which personal insurance is sold by licensed (or admitted) personal insurance companies. In some situations, personal insurance might be sold via **surplus lines** transactions. Surplus lines transactions involve purchases of insurance coverage from nonadmitted insurance companies, often through licensed surplus lines brokers. Nonadmitted insurers are not licensed in the state in which the transaction occurs. However, surplus lines brokers are required to be licensed under special surplus lines licensing requirements.

Purchasing personal insurance coverage through surplus lines transactions is allowed when, after a diligent search of the standard market, the potential insured finds that the desired insurance coverage is not available in the standard market. For example, some homeowners in inner-city neighborhoods or in coastal communities subject to extreme windstorm hazards cannot purchase homeowners coverage through standard personal insurance companies. Those homeowners can seek personal property and liability coverage in the surplus lines market.

With respect to regulation, the surplus lines market differs from the standard market in several areas. Since nonadmitted insurance companies are the providers of surplus lines coverage and they are not licensed in the states in which they sell that coverage, policy forms and insurance rates are not subject to policy and rate regulation. This lack of regulatory control allows such insurers more flexibility in meeting the needs of their insureds. However, the surplus lines transaction itself and surplus lines brokers are more strictly regulated because of the lack of regulatory control over nonadmitted insurers. Also, guaranty funds do not provide protection against insurer insolvency to policyholders of nonadmitted insurers.

Surplus lines brokers must meet licensing requirements that are more stringent than those described previously for standard personal insurance producers. Although these requirements vary by state, they typically include the following:

- Brokers must be bonded.
- Brokers must already be licensed as property and liability agents or brokers.
- In the majority of jurisdictions, brokers must be residents of the state or, in states without the resident status requirement, must maintain an office in the state.

Surplus lines laws also specify requirements that nonadmitted insurance companies must meet before they are eligible to participate in surplus lines transactions, such as the following:

- Minimum capital and surplus levels
- In some states, minimum number of years of operation (a seasoning requirement)

Surplus lines describes any insurance for which there is no licensed insurer within the state. Coverage is written by a nonlicensed insurer. This is done through a surplus lines agent or broker who is licensed to provide this service.

- For alien insurers, minimum asset valuation that must be established as a trust fund in a bank that is a member of the U.S. Federal Reserve System for the benefit of policyholders
- Being licensed in at least one state or jurisdiction as an insurance company

---

Educational Objective 7
Explain the role of the NAIC in personal insurance regulation.

The Role of the National Association of Insurance Commissioners (NAIC) in Personal Insurance Regulation

The National Association of Insurance Commissioners (NAIC) is a professional organization whose members are state insurance commissioners. The NAIC was established in the early 1930s to improve cooperation, communication, and coordination among state insurance commissioners and their staffs. The stated objectives of the NAIC are as follows:

- To promote the public interest through the regulation of insurance and the fair, just, and equitable treatment of insurance consumers and claimants
- To improve reliability of the insurance institution regarding solvency, financial solidity, and guaranty against loss
- To maintain and improve state regulation of insurance in a responsive and efficient manner[15]

NAIC Committees

The NAIC has evolved into a large organization of committees, task forces, and working groups charged with studying the insurance industry and state regulation, determining how the industry can be better regulated to achieve the objectives of the NAIC, and developing regulation to achieve the objectives. The NAIC committee structure is supported by the following three NAIC offices:

1. The Support and Services Office, which provides the majority of the support services required by NAIC members, including maintaining databases and performing research at the request of insurance commissioners
2. The Securities Valuation Office, which focuses on valuing insurance companies' actual and prospective investment vehicles and helping insurance companies to value their investments

3. The Financial Analysis and Government Relations Office, which maintains relations with Congress, deals with international issues, and studies and develops better financial analysis tools

The NAIC has also established the Personal Lines—Property and Casualty Insurance Committee. As the name implies, this committee deals with regulatory concerns in personal property and liability insurance. The recent issues dealt with by this committee include catastrophe insurance and consumer information. Under the Personal Lines—Property and Casualty Insurance Committee are two working groups, established to consider those issues: the Catastrophe Insurance Working Group and the Consumer Information Working Group. These groups are of special interest to personal insurance specialists.

NAIC Catastrophe Insurance Working Group

The Catastrophe Insurance Working Group recently developed a handbook to help state insurance departments deal with catastrophes before, during, and after their occurrence. One of the biggest concerns of state insurance regulators in states that have experienced massive natural catastrophes, such as Hurricane Hugo in South Carolina, Hurricane Andrew in Florida, and the Northridge earthquake in California, was the lack of a body of information on how to deal with such catastrophes. The handbook developed by the working group has been provided to all state insurance departments and not only contains methods used by those states that have experienced catastrophes, but also lists contacts in those state insurance departments who serve as resources. In addition, the working group has recommended establishing a network of insurance department staff members who would be the "catastrophe contact" in each insurance department. Such a network would be useful for coordination and communication in dealing with catastrophes.

NAIC Consumer Information Working Group

The Consumer Information Working Group is responsible for drafting consumer publications on personal lines. The NAIC has released consumer information guides on homeowners insurance and auto insurance, both of which this working group developed. The guides provide descriptions of the insurance coverages, methods of identifying the best coverage, and other information consumers might find useful in purchasing personal insurance. State insurance departments can use these publications or can modify them to fit their particular markets before providing them to state citizens.

The Consumer Information Working Group, as of January 1996, was studying how to get consumers the information they need to make their insurance buying decisions. The Nevada Insurance Department had conducted focus groups with consumers indicating that although the information was available, consumers were not getting it. The working group decided this should be their next principal concern. One of the areas the group plans to explore is the use of the Internet to provide information to consumers.

NAIC Insurance Availability and Affordability Task Force

The NAIC Insurance Availability and Affordability Task Force deals with issues that concern personal property and liability insurance companies, agencies, and producers. The task force, as of January 1996, was continuing its study of the availability and affordability of insurance in urban and rural environments. Allegations of redlining by various consumer groups led to the formation of this task force. Insurance commissioners needed a forum in which to discuss the issues involved in availability and affordability. The task force conducted a study of urban insurance markets and determined that urban residents in poorer neighborhoods have problems purchasing insurance. At the NAIC meetings in 1995, the task force invited organizations that had implemented various solutions to present them to the task force and other interested parties. Given the information received during the presentations, the task force plans to develop its own recommended courses of action to deal with insurance availability and affordability. Those recommendations might include consumer and insurer education, making insurers' underwriting guidelines public information, and further limiting underwriters' ability to decline or terminate personal insurance coverage. The group also plans to monitor improvements in urban and rural insurance availability and affordability.

Summary

The purpose of insurance regulation is to protect consumers and to ensure insurance company solvency. Insurance is regulated under a dual federal and state system. This system has evolved over the past three centuries. The federal government regulates activities that are common to all businesses. State governments regulate activities that are unique to insurance operation.

Of special importance to personal lines producers, underwriters, and customer service representatives are the regulations that involve rate filings, complaints, licensing, continuing education, surplus lines, and countersignatures, and the regulations governing forms and underwriting rules. Specialists should understand what each of these are and how they are addressed within the specialist's state(s) of responsibility. Specialists should find a source for updating this information on a regular basis. Many sources can provide this information. The state insurance commissioners' offices are possible sources; their addresses and phone numbers are provided in Appendix 4-A to this text.

Some marketing, claims, and underwriting practices are prohibited by regulation. Market conduct examinations are a means of discovering prohibited or unfair insurance activities. The NAIC has defined unfair trade and unfair claims settlement practices as claims, marketing, and underwriting activities that fail to protect consumers in insurance dealings.

Insurance companies are subject to financial regulation by state insurance departments. These regulations have the overall goal of ensuring the solvency of insurers.

Agents and brokers are regulated through licensing and continuing education regulation as well as through countersignature laws.

Handling consumer complaints is an important function of state insurance departments. State regulators help consumers resolve problems with insurers. Regulators also maintain records regarding complaints to investigate companies or agencies that are receiving a higher-than-normal complaint ratio.

Surplus lines involve coverages or policies that are not written by an insurer licensed within the state. These policies are regulated through licensed brokers who hold special lines licenses.

The NAIC is a professional organization whose members are state insurance commissioners. The NAIC's objectives are the promotion and protection of the public interest, the solvency of insurance companies, and the maintenance of effective insurance regulation.

Chapter Notes

1. Samuel B. Paul v. Commonwealth of Virginia, S.C., 8 Wall., 168-185 (1869).

2. United States v. South-Eastern Underwriters Association, et al., 322 U.S. 533 (1944).

3. McCarran-Ferguson Act, 15 U.S.C., March 9, 1945.

4. *Interagency Task Force on Product Liability: Final Report*, U.S. Department of Commerce (October 31, 1977) quoted in *Interagency Task Force* at I-20; "House Report No. 197-190 of the Energy and Commerce Committee," quoted in *U.S. Code and Cong. News*, vol. 2, 97th Congr. 1st Sess. (1991), p. 1434.

5. District of Columbia, Guam, Puerto Rico, and the U.S. Virgin Islands.

6. National Association of Insurance Commissioners, "Unfair Trade Practices Act," *Model Laws, Regulations and Guidelines*, January 1993, pp. 880-2 to 880-3.

7. "Unfair Trade Practices Act," *Model Laws, Regulations and Guidelines*, January 1993, pp. 880-4 to 880-5.

8. National Association of Insurance Commissioners, "Property Insurance Declination, Termination, and Disclosure Model Act," *Model Laws, Regulations and Guidelines*, July 1992, pp. 720-3.

9. National Association of Insurance Commissioners, "Automobile Insurance Declination, Termination, and Disclosure Model Act," *Model Laws, Regulations and Guidelines*, July 1992, pp. 725-3.

10. National Association of Insurance Commissioners, *Market Conduct Examiners Handbook*, December 1989, pp. V-6 to V-7.

11. *Market Conduct Examiners Handbook*, December 1989, pp. V-7, V-10.

12. *Market Conduct Examiners Handbook*, December 1989, p. V-11.

13. *Texas Department of Insurance Licensing Information Bulletin*, Insurance Testing Corporation, 1994, p. 1.

14. Arkansas, California, Colorado, Delaware, Florida, Georgia, Idaho, Illinois, Indiana, Iowa, Kansas, Kentucky, Louisiana, Maine, Maryland, Massachusetts, Michigan, Minnesota, Mississippi, Missouri, Montana, Nebraska, Nevada, New Hampshire, New Jersey, New Mexico, New York, North Carolina, North Dakota, Ohio, Oklahoma, Oregon, Pennsylvania, Rhode Island, South Carolina, South Dakota, Tennessee, Texas, Utah, Virginia, Washington, West Virginia, Wisconsin, and Wyoming.

15. National Association of Insurance Commissioners, *Constitution of the National Association of Insurance Commissioners*, as it appeared in the NAIC Summer National Meeting program, June 1995, p. 34.

Chapter 5

Educational Objectives

1. Explain how liability is determined. (pp. 5-3 to 5-5)
2. Distinguish among and illustrate situations giving rise to liability based on the following: (pp. 5-5 to 5-11)
   - Negligence
   - Intentional acts
   - Absolute liability
   - Contractual liability
3. Explain how coverage under a liability policy is determined. (pp. 5-11 to 5-16)
4. Describe an insurer's options when notified of a claim or suit against a policyholder. (pp. 5-16 to 5-18)
5. Explain how each of the following factors might affect the frequency or severity of liability losses: (pp. 5-19 to 5-23)
   - Liability fraud
   - Property ownership
   - Fame
   - Occupation
   - Personal activities
   - Legal environment
6. Describe the liability exposures and hazards associated with the following: (pp. 5-23 to 5-37)
   - Farming
   - Swimming pools
   - Firearms
   - Animals
   - Incidental offices and businesses in the home
   - Child care or elder care in the home
   - Dwellings rented to others
   - Underground storage tanks
   - Other special hazards
7. Given an application or case study for a personal liability risk, demonstrate the ability to analyze the liability exposures and recommend appropriate actions. (Encompasses entire chapter.)

Chapter 5

Personal and Premises Liability: Exposure Analysis and Coverages

Liability exposures for an individual or family can arise from a variety of sources, including personal activities, residence premises, and other property. Lawsuits and insurance claims involve a wide array of accidents, injuries, and alleged misconduct. This chapter focuses on the sources of these liability exposures and the personal liability coverages that apply to them.

Because the causes of potential liability are numerous, addressing *all* sources of personal liability exposures is not practical. Instead, this chapter concentrates on methods for detecting liability exposures when a personal insurance specialist evaluates an application or an existing account. It is important that a producer be able to identify liability exposures to assist a customer in selecting insurance or other risk management techniques for addressing those exposures. It is also important that an underwriter be able to recognize the nature of a liability exposure and the hazards that can increase the likelihood of loss frequency or severity so that those characteristics can be evaluated.

Although *all* personal liability exposures cannot be practically addressed, some personal and premises liability exposures are explored in this chapter because they either commonly occur or are of particular underwriting concern.

The Difference Between Liability and Coverage

Liability and coverage are different concepts that can easily be confused. When claim representatives review a claim, they attempt to answer two initial questions:

1. *Does coverage apply?* Does the insurer have a contractual obligation to the insured to defend and/or pay for the loss? The answer to this question is found in the contract language and its interpretations.

2. *Is the insured liable?* Will the insured be obligated to pay damages to a third-party claimant? That question is answered outside the relationship between the insurer and the insured; insurance policies do not determine whether insureds are liable. The question "What determines liability?" is a question of law.

For an insurance company to pay for a loss, the answer to both questions must be "yes." The following are examples of cases in which these questions were applied:

- *Liable but not covered.* A shopkeeper deliberately shot his niece when he felt his life was in danger. Liability was clearly established for the injuries, but coverage was denied under the homeowners policy because the shooting was an intentional act and the insured intended to cause injury. Because the contract stated that coverage would not apply for intentional acts, no coverage applied in this case, and no claim was paid.[1]

- *Not covered because not liable.* During a severe storm, a large tree on the insured's property fell onto a neighbor's garage, damaging the two autos parked in the garage. The tree was in good condition before the storm. The neighbor submitted a claim against the insured. That type of loss would be covered under a homeowners policy if the insured were negligent. However, no negligence or liability was found, so no coverage applied and no claim was paid.[2]

Educational Objective 1
Explain how liability is determined.

The Law Determines Liability

A liability loss occurs when one party is legally responsible for injury or harm to another party. Common law, statutes, and contract law are the basis for liability claims because they create legal responsibilities. An injured person has a right of recovery from the party who is responsible for the injury if a law or legal principle establishes a relationship that supports a liability claim. Those laws and principles are addressed in INS 21. Exhibit 5-1 reviews the sources of law and their relationship to torts, which are the most frequent source of liability in personal insurance.

Exhibit 5-1
How Liability Originates

Sources of law: There are essentially four sources of law in the United States

Constitutional law
is the supreme law in the United States. All other laws must conform to the U.S. Constitution. Each state also has its own constitution, and all state laws must conform to the state constitution.

Common law
(case law) has evolved in the courts. Case decisions become precedents for similar future cases.

Statutory law
is enacted by legislative bodies at the national, state, and local levels.

Administrative law
is derived from statutory law. Federal, state, and local government agencies have regulatory powers to issue rules and regulations to implement statutory responsibilities.

The above four sources of law develop criminal and civil law, the two broad categories of law.

Criminal Law
Certain kinds of conduct so endanger the public welfare that society enacts laws to punish people for such conduct. Crimes are punishable by fines, imprisonment, or death.

Civil Law
Civil law settles disputes and redresses wrongs against individuals that are not necessarily crimes. Some civil wrongs are also crimes. Civil law protects personal rights and enforces contractual rights. Civil laws are the basis for insurance claims.

Elements of a Liability Loss: A liability loss occurs when one party is legally responsible for injury or harm to another party.

The following are the three elements of a liability loss:
1. One party has a legal basis for a claim against another party.
2. Harm is done to the party making the claim.
3. The parties agree or a court stipulates the form or the amount of the damages owed to the injured party.

Legal Rights of Recovery
From civil law, rights of recovery and claims for liability can be based on torts, contracts, and statutes.

Torts
A tort is a civil wrongful act (other than a crime or a breach of contract).

Contracts
Contract law enables an injured person to seek restitution because the other party to the contract has breached a duty accepted in a contract.

Statutes
Statutory law might extend, restrict, or clarify the rights of injured parties under tort or contract law. In some instances, statutes have preempted tort and contract common law. Such statutes try to ensure adequate compensation for injuries without lengthy court disputes.

Torts
Torts are frequently the basis for insurance claims. Torts fall into three categories.

Negligence
Negligence occurs when a person fails to exercise the appropriate degree of care, causing harm to another person (or legal entity). Most liability claims are based on negligence. Negligence usually involves acting differently from the way a reasonably prudent person would act under similar circumstances.

Intentional Torts
An intentional tort is a deliberate act that causes harm to another person (or legal entity), regardless of whether the harm is intended. (Some intentional torts are also crimes.)

Absolute Liability
In situations involving inherently dangerous activities, tort law gives an injured person a right to damages whether negligence existed or not.

Negligence
A liability judgment based on negligence depends on four elements.

Elements of Negligence
A liability judgment based on negligence requires the following four elements:
1. A duty to the person (or legal entity) who claims harm
2. A breach of that duty
3. Actual harm
4. Harm caused by breach of duty

A liability loss exposure can present substantial possibility of financial loss for an individual. A liability loss exposure can also generate a claim for damages for alleged wrongdoing. Some liability claims result in lawsuits. Even if a lawsuit is groundless, substantial legal expenses might be required to defend against it.

Educational Objective 2

Distinguish among and illustrate situations that give rise to liability based on negligence, intentional acts, absolute liability, and contractual liability.

Principles of Law That Create Rights of Recovery

Liability exists when a party is found legally responsible for injury, harm, or property damage to another. That responsibility can be obvious from the circumstances surrounding the event. When responsibility is not obvious or the parties cannot agree on the extent of the injury or damage, the loss might have to be evaluated by a court to determine whether liability exists and the extent of the restitution owed. An injured party has the right of recovery from the responsible party if there is a principle of law that creates that right.

The following is a brief review of common tort and contractual liability principles that create rights of recovery under personal liability policies.

Torts

Torts are the most common source of liability for an individual or family. A tort is a wrongful act other than a crime or a breach of contract. A tort can result from negligence, intentional acts, or absolute liability.

Negligence

Negligence is the most frequently occurring tort that results in personal liability insurance claims. All insureds are exposed to loss from claims of negligence, so they must use reason and prudence in their actions in order not to cause others to suffer injury or loss. Negligence can result from carelessness, thoughtlessness, forgetfulness, ignorance, or poor judgment. The standard of what is reasonable is measured by what society expects of an individual, not by what the individual considers reasonable. In a negligence case, the judge might compare the actions of an individual to those of a *reasonable person* (also referred to as an *ordinary* or *prudent* person) in the same circumstances. A reasonable person is a fictitious person similar in education, background, and experience to the people in the community.

Injuries caused by dogs are a common source of tort negligence in personal liability insurance. Consider the example of a dog owner who must obey leash and animal confinement laws of the community.

The following four elements must be present to establish negligence:

1. A duty (a legal responsibility) must exist to the person who claims harm. Dog owners must obey leash and animal confinement laws. Laws and regulations specify duties.

2. A breach of the duty must occur. The injured party (the plaintiff) must be able to show that the tortfeasor (the individual who committed the wrongful act) not only had a duty but also breached the duty. For example, a breach of duty probably occurs if an insured allows his dog off the leash during a walk and the dog bites a jogger.

3. An injury must result from the breach of duty. An injury can include property damage, bodily injury, loss of income, humiliation, pain, or suffering. For example, the jogger in the example above might claim damages for medical bills, work loss, scarring, and pain and suffering.

4. Breach of duty must be the **proximate cause** of the harm. The relationship between the breach of duty and the plaintiff's injury must follow from an unbroken chain of events leading to the injury, that is, the breach of duty must be the injury's proximate cause. For example, the relationship between the dog and the jogger's injury is clear. If the insured's dog barks at a neighbor's cat, and the cat injures its owner as a result, the dog might not be the proximate cause of the injury.

> A **proximate cause** is an event that, in a natural and continuous sequence and unbroken by any intervening cause, produces injury or damage.

Intentional Acts

If an act is committed with the objective of injuring another person, the result is an intentional injury or an intentional tort. Intentional injury is excluded under most liability policies because defending and compensating an insured who willfully hurts people or damages their property is not reasonable. The following are types of intentional torts:

*   Battery—Battery is intentional, unpermitted contact with another person. This can include, for example, contact with a person's clothing or the car a person is driving.

*   Assault—Assault is a physical threat of injury to another. The victim must believe that injury is about to occur. Oral threats and insults are not assaults unless they are accompanied by threatening gestures.

*   Mental distress—Liability can result from intentional acts that cause someone severe and extreme mental or emotional distress. Simple anxiety is not grounds for liability. Usually, a serious physical illness resulting from mental distress is necessary to qualify for damages.

*   Defamation—Defamation involves communication of untrue statements that injure another's reputation. These acts can be in the form of libel, which is written defamation, or slander, which is spoken defamation. Both libel and slander must be communicated to someone other than the defamed party.

*   False arrest or detainment—Intentionally restraining another person's freedom of movement can create liability for false

imprisonment. For example, this could occur when a homeowner unjustly detains a salesman because the homeowner suspects the salesman has stolen jewelry from the home.

- Trespass—Trespass occurs when someone wrongfully enters the property of another or fails to remove belongings from another's property when there is an obligation to do so. Trespass to personal property occurs when someone interferes with possessions of another without legal justification to do so.

- Conversion—Conversion is the unlawful taking or use of another's property. The following are examples of conversion:

  - Taking goods or exercising control of property that adversely affects the property owner

  - Depriving the owner of his or her property through an unauthorized transfer of goods

  - Refusing to surrender goods to one who has a right to them

  - Misusing the goods in defiance of the owners

  - Intentionally damaging, destroying, or altering property[3]

Absolute Liability

Absolute liability occurs when a person engages in an activity that is so dangerous that any property damage or injury thereby resulting automatically becomes the liability of the person undertaking the activity. If a person stores dynamite in a tool shed and the dynamite explodes, that individual would be held responsible for any damage to others, regardless of whether the method of storage was negligent.

The same type of liability would be imposed if a family keeps dangerous wild animals fenced in its yard. Any injury caused by the animals would result in liability.

The term strict liability is similar to absolute liability. It is usually applied to products liability. Manufacturers are held liable for injuries caused by releasing unreasonably dangerous products.[4]

Contractual Liability

People who enter into agreements often refine those agreements into contracts. A contract makes the agreement legally enforceable. It spells out the actions that both parties must take and usually answers the questions: where, when, who, what, and how much.

Contractual liability occurs when a person assumes financial responsibility for the liability of another person's tort as part of a contract. Some leases contain clauses that require a tenant to assume liability for some injuries to others for which the landlord might otherwise be responsible. Such clauses are called hold harmless agreements. Other situations that might involve an individual assuming contractual liability include the following:

- Signing an agreement for rented power tools
- Entering an organized bicycle race
- Joining a health club

Contractual liability is the tort liability of another person (or entity) assumed under contract.

Factors That Modify Liability

The principles of loss and an injured party's rights of recovery for injury or property damage might be modified by applicable legal tort doctrines or modifying factors.

Several factors might alter the insured's liability or the extent to which the insured and the insurer must respond. A list of factors that affect the degree of liability is presented in Exhibit 5-2. Some of these factors increase the liability of a tortfeasor, but others eliminate or reduce the liability.

Exhibit 5-2
Liability Modifiers

Modifying Factors	Meaning of the Factors	Example
Act of God	This term describes any accident that is caused by the forces of nature and uncontrolled by the power of man. When a loss is determined to be an act of God, no liability is imposed on any person.	A landowner builds a dam across a stream on his own property. The dam works well for years. Unprecedented heavy rainfall increases the pressure against the dam, which breaks. The water floods a neighbor's property. The unprecedented rainfall is determined to be an act of God, and the dam owner is not liable for the damage caused by the water.
Assumption of Risk	Assumption of risk is defense for an accusation of negligence against an insured. If the plaintiff consents (expressly or impliedly) to release the insured/defendant of responsibility for the chance of injury, the plaintiff assumes the risk, and the defendant is not held responsible.	During a neighborhood softball game, the insured hits a ball into the outfield, hitting Mrs. Jones and breaking her nose. It can be argued that the insured is not negligent because Mrs. Jones assumed the risk of injury by being in the outfield.
Attractive Nuisance	Children do not always understand what can cause them harm. A person who has something on his or her property that could be a danger to a child (such as a swimming pool, a trampoline, or an abandoned building) has a duty to take precautions to prevent injury to children who might be attracted to the item.	An old barn on a farm is no longer used because it is in a state of disrepair. Children are drawn to the barn as a place to play. One child falls through the decaying floor and is injured. The owner is responsible for having an attractive nuisance on the property and not taking reasonably prudent precautions to remove the building or bar entry to the structure.

Modifying Factors	Meaning of the Factors	Example
Charitable Institutions Immunity	A charity is an association that voluntarily assists others. Immunity from liability is granted in some situations (depending on the state). (Charitable immunity is frequently eroded by statute and judicial precedent.)	A charitable hospital collects donations to operate a ward to care for severely burned children. A child dies and the parents sue the hospital. To award the parents would mean depriving other children who require care. (If a $1 million award is made, 100 other children might not be admitted for medical care.) Immunity is granted to protect the charitable effort.
Contributory Negligence	A defendant might use contributory negligence as a defense for an accusation of negligence if the plaintiff failed to act in a way that provided for his or her own protection. If this can be proven, the plaintiff is denied recovery from the defendant.	A defendant blocks part of a public road with a pole. The plaintiff leaves a bar intoxicated and rides his bicycle home. He hits the pole and is thrown to the road. A person riding with reasonable and ordinary care could have seen and avoided the obstruction. The bike rider contributed to his own loss.
Comparative Negligence	Comparative negligence is another defense against the accusation of negligence. Under comparative negligence, both the plaintiff and the insured are found at fault to some degree. Depending on the legal jurisdiction, the insured could be required to compensate the plaintiff for a percentage of the injuries and damage.	In the case described for contributory negligence, the plaintiff was to some degree at fault for leaving an obstruction in the road. The bicycle rider was to some degree at fault for riding a bicycle while intoxicated. The defendant might be required to compensate the plaintiff for the percentage for which he is found to be at fault.
Dangerous Instrumentality	This doctrine applies the principle of absolute liability. A person who possesses, stores, or maintains dangerous instruments (such as dynamite, explosives, weapons, or wild animals) is liable for any injury or damage caused by the instruments.	A property owner keeps dynamite (used to remove stumps) in his barn. The neighborhood children find it and blow up a car. The owner is liable because of ownership of a dangerous instrumentality.
Foreseeability	A reasonable person can imagine behavior that might harm others or damage property and will avoid that type of activity. If a person acts in a way that he or she knows will cause harm, he or she has not acted as a reasonably prudent person and will be found negligent.	A driver riding through a subdivision sees a ball roll across the street. A prudent person would foresee a child following the ball into the road and therefore slow down or stop the vehicle.

Continued on next page.

Modifying Factors	Meaning of the Factors	Example
Governmental Immunity	Political entities cannot be sued for a tort (without their consent). This rule is eroding, and suit is often allowed for government functions that are not proprietary and that could be accomplished by a private entity.	An amusement park is erected on a section of land that has been zoned for commercial use. The neighboring homes lose substantial value because of the noise and traffic. The homeowners are barred from suing the government because zoning is a government function.

However, a person injured in a city swimming pool could sue the city because operating a swimming pool is a function that could be performed by a private entity. |
Gross Negligence	Gross negligence is conduct that is more blameworthy than ordinary negligence. It indicates that exceptional misconduct has occurred. In situations like this, the error is so obvious that a jury might be very generous in its award to a plaintiff in an effort to punish the wrongdoer.	A school bus driver was found to be intoxicated when the driver caused an at-fault auto accident in which fifteen children on the bus were injured. The bus driver, who has been entrusted to care for the children, is negligent for causing an accident and grossly negligent because of intoxication.
Intrafamily Immunity	No lawsuit based on tort liability is allowed between members of a family. A husband cannot sue his wife (and vice versa), and a child cannot sue a parent (and vice versa). The purpose behind this is preservation of the family in the public interest. (The acceptance of this doctrine depends on the local legal jurisdiction.)	A husband injures his wife in an auto accident in which he is found to be at fault. The wife would not be allowed to sue the husband for the resulting loss. This doctrine is eroding. Intrafamily suits are allowed in some jurisdictions.
Joint Tortfeasors	When two or more people cause an accident that results in injury or damage to another, they are joint tortfeasors. They are all responsible for the legal consequences of their acts.	Two cars negligently collide at an intersection, and the impact forces one of the vehicles to strike a house on the corner. Both owners are tortfeasors who are jointly liable for the damage to the house. The homeowner may recover damages from either vehicle owner or from both owners.

Modifying Factors	Meaning of the Factors	Example
Last Clear Chance	Everyone has a responsibility to use care for the safety of others. Individuals are required to prevent injury to others if possible. When a person has the last clear chance to avoid injury to another person or another person's property and fails to do so, he or she will be found negligent.	The insured is waiting in an intersection when the car in front of him stalls. The light turns red, and the insured cannot move from the middle of the intersection. An oncoming car that just got the green light runs into the insured. That driver is negligent because that vehicle had the last clear chance to avoid the accident and did not.
Statute of Limitations	State legislatures have determined that the possibility of litigation must stop at some point in time. Statutes provide for a period of time within which legal action for a liability must be brought. If the suit is not brought within that period, the plaintiff cannot later file a claim.	A state with a statute of limitations of three years would not allow a lawsuit for an injury that occurred five years ago.
Ultrahazardous Operations	This doctrine is similar to the "dangerous instrumentalities" doctrine. A person who engages in abnormally hazardous risks will be held absolutely liable for damage that results.	A property owner uses dynamite to remove an old stump from his yard. The explosion lifts the stump into the air, and it lands on a neighbor's house. The property owner is responsible for the damage to the neighbor's house because blasting is an ultrahazardous operation. The neighbor does not have to prove negligence.

Educational Objective 3

Explain how coverage under a liability policy is determined.

The Insurance Contract Determines Coverage

Many liability claims are groundless or involve situations in which the insured is ultimately not held responsible for paying damages. However, such situations are still liability *losses* for the insurer because of the time and expense involved in resolving them. Every claim requires a response, and many claims can be closed or settled only after substantial legal expenses have been incurred. If litigation is involved, then failure to acknowledge the lawsuit and offer a defense might lead to a **default judgment**. Therefore, even groundless, frivolous, and fraudulent claims in litigation require attention.[5]

A default judgment is a decision found in favor of the plaintiff because the defendant failed to respond to the notification of the suit.

Liability insurance is a promise to the insured from the insurance company: the insurance company agrees to defend the insured against claims of liability and pay resulting liability awards (up to the policy limits). The insurance contract describes the types of events for which liability coverage is provided.

Contract Interpretation

Insurance companies go to great lengths to make policy language clear and to include provisions that are legally required. However, the meaning of policy language is often still debatable when it is applied to a claim situation. In contract interpretation, specific rules apply when the language is unclear. Generally, any ambiguity favors the insured because the insurer has the most knowledge and bargaining power in the transaction and the insured has the least control over the contract content. Exhibit 5-3 provides a brief summary and examples of rules that are used to assist in contract interpretation.

Exhibit 5-3
Rules Used in Insurance Contract Interpretation

The Rule	Its Meaning	Its Effect in Claim Settlement	Example
Contract of Adhesion	A contract of adhesion is prepared by one party with the other party having little alternative other than to accept or reject all the terms. In insurance, the wording of a policy contract is drafted by (or on behalf of) an insurer, and the insured cannot change it.	Because a contract of adhesion creates an unbalanced negotiating situation in favor of the insurer, courts offset the imbalance by ruling any ambiguities or uncertainties in an insurance contract against the insurer.	The insured has a leak in a waterbed, which ruins a hardwood floor. Homeowners policies cover leaks from appliances, but whether a waterbed is an appliance is unclear. Courts have interpreted the meaning of appliance to include waterbeds and therefore allow coverage under homeowners policies.
Utmost Good Faith	The nature of insurance requires complete honesty and disclosure of all relevant facts between parties. All dealings are expected to be ethical. Insureds and insurers have a right to rely on promises and statements made.	If the insured has reason to believe that the insurer has acted in bad faith, the insured may take legal action against the insurance company. The courts have imposed severe penalties on insurers in cases in which bad faith claims have been sustained.	An adjuster offers $5,000 for injuries when a settlement for the policy limit of $100,000 was clearly indicated for an injury. The adjuster was acting in bad faith by trying to settle for an amount that was clearly less than fair.
Reasonable Expectations Doctrine	The courts sometimes use this rule to balance the rights of the insured with those of the insurer. This	When the courts apply this doctrine, the insurance policy is interpreted to provide the protection that the insured	If an insured loses electrical power at his or her insured home (a simple loss of power) and the

The Rule	Its Meaning	Its Effect in Claim Settlement	Example
Reasonable Expectations Doctrine, continued	doctrine is not triggered by an ambiguity in the policy but by what the typical consumer would believe a contract should cover.	might reasonably have expected, even though that expectation is not clearly expressed in or supported by the policy.	food in the kitchen's freezer thaws and spoils, the standard homeowners policy excludes coverage. Some state courts have determined that the loss is covered regardless of the contract language because it is reasonable to expect that type of loss to be covered under a homeowners policy.
Waiver and Estoppel	Waiver is the voluntary relinquishment of a known right. If a right is waived, a party cannot change its position on an issue because the change would be inconsistent with past conduct (there can be no estoppel of a waived right).	Once an insurer establishes a position (through the insurer's actions or words), the insurer might have waived any rights to reverse that action later. The insurer may be estopped from reestablishing those rights.	A claims representative advises a claimant injured in an auto accident caused by an insured to begin car repairs and seek medical treatment. The representative then discovers that the insured's policy has been canceled. The representative's conduct may have waived the insurer's rights; the insurer may be estopped from denying the claim.
Vicarious Liability	An insured might be found liable for actions of another person. This is usually found in employer-employee, principal-agent, partnership, and parent-child relationships.	Even if an insured does not create any harm, he or she might be held responsible for actions of another person.	An employee damages the property of a customer. The customer may hold both the employee and the employer liable. Either or both may be found financially responsible for the damage, even though only the employee's actions caused the damage.
Parol Evidence Rule	A contract is the final explanation of an agreement between two parties. No other prior discussions or notes can normally be introduced to vary the unambiguous terms of a written contract.	All final intentions must appear in a final insurance contract or in any contract.	An agent tells an insured that a day-care operation would be excluded for liability coverage under the homeowners policy. The policy was issued without the excluding endorsement attached. A child is hurt because of the insured's negligence. Because the exclusion was not attached, coverage applies.

Covered Exposures

For liability coverage to apply, a claim must involve an activity covered by the policy. The various forms of liability insurance cover many activities. Some policies cover only one type of activity, such as a watercraft policy. Other policies, such as a homeowners policy, cover many different activities.

Up to this point, this chapter has addressed the sources of liability and the application of the coverage provided by the insurance contract. Specialists in personal insurance must understand the applications of liability and coverage to be able to apply them to the customers' liability exposures.

The producer determines the liability exposures of a customer to suggest appropriate insurance coverage or risk management techniques. To determine the liability coverage needs of an individual or a family, a specialist completes the following four steps:

1. Identifying the liability exposures for the customer based on the customer's activities, real and personal property, automobiles, watercraft, recreational vehicles, hobbies, sports, and other potential exposures (which will be addressed later in this chapter). Producers use applications or lists of questions to help the insured discover exposures that might not readily be recognized.

2. Considering the liability coverage provided by a homeowners policy (or a personal liability policy) and the liability coverage provided by a personal auto policy as the foundation of liability coverage for liability losses. The specialist should identify the covered liability events provided by these two policies. Producers pay particular attention to policy exclusions because most liability policies specify liability coverages by what has *not* been excluded.

3. Comparing the exposures identified in step 1 with the basic covered events found in step 2, and identifying the coverage gaps.

4. Determining the best method for addressing the identified coverage gaps. The following bulleted items provide some examples:

   - Recommending a policy that includes liability coverage for the exposures (such as a watercraft policy if the customer owns a boat or a recreational vehicle policy if the customer owns a motor home).

   - Communicating the coverage gaps to the customer, and identifying loss control measures that can reduce the liability exposures (such as limiting snowmobile use to daylight hours and requiring that all riders wear helmets).

Policy Limits and Other Coverages

Policy limits in liability insurance differ according to the way in which they apply to a loss. The Insurance Institute of America's INS 21 course presents many types of policy limits that might appear on both commercial and personal policies. A discussion of the types of limits and coverages that appear on personal liability policies follows.

Per-Event Limits

Per-event limits are the maximum amount that will be paid for an insured loss. The event might be an accident, an occurrence, or a claim. Following are the types of per-event limits found in personal liability policies:

- Per-accident limits pay up to the policy limits for each covered accident, such as an auto accident.
- Per-occurrence limits pay up to the policy limits for each covered occurrence. An occurrence is an unexpected event that might occur suddenly or over a period of time, such as a water leak that floods a neighbor's basement.
- Per-person limits pay up to the policy limits for each person injured. These limits often appear on personal auto policies.
- Per-claim limits identify the most that will be paid on any claim. For example, even if both a husband and wife are named in a lawsuit for a boating accident, only one limit applies.

Split or Single Limits

Split limits apply separate coverage limits for bodily injury and property damage liability losses. Some split-limit policies show the following:

- A per-person bodily injury liability limit
- A per-accident bodily injury liability limit
- A per-accident property damage liability limit

Split limits are often expressed in a shorthand format. For example, split limits of $250,000 of bodily injury liability per person, $500,000 of bodily injury liability for all people injured, and $100,000 of property damage liability are shown as $250/500/100.

A single limit (also known as a combined single limit) applies a maximum dollar amount to all damage and injury, whether a loss involves liability arising out of one injury, many injuries, property damage, or a combination of damages.

Other Coverages

In addition to the liability coverage limits, personal lines policies usually include supplementary coverages. The following describes the supplemental coverages typically included in a personal liability policy.

Defense Costs   The majority of liability policies provide defense costs. Defense costs are paid in addition to the policy's liability limits. The insurer is not required to pay any stated dollar limit in defending the insured against a claim for covered damages. A typical liability insuring agreement stipulates that the insurer's obligation to defend a claim ends when the amount the insurer pays for damages equals the limit of liability. When the limit of coverage has been exhausted in paying a claim, the duty to defend also ends. The following is an example of this defense provision in an insuring agreement:

> We will pay damages for bodily injury or property damage for which any insured becomes legally responsible because of an auto accident. . . .We will settle or defend, as we consider appropriate, any claim or suit asking for these damages. In addition to our limit of liability, we will pay all defense costs we incur. Our duty to settle or defend ends when our limit of liability for this coverage has been exhausted.

As demonstrated in the defense provision above, the insurer has the exclusive right to control the defense against a claim, which is often a point of contention for insureds who do not feel they are responsible for a loss. A claim representative might decide that a claim should be paid and closed, but the insured might want to continue the battle. The claim representative must make the best possible decision about the claim and the potential financial effect of the claim on all of the insurer's policyholders. This decision might include reducing defense costs by incurring a loss payment.

Supplementary Payments Liability This coverage often provides additional benefits. For example, a typical homeowners policy provides the following (in additional to the coverage limit):

- Premiums on bonds required during a lawsuit's defense
- Reasonable expenses incurred by the insured to assist in investigating or defending a claim or lawsuit

Related Coverages Some policies also provide additional coverages that are not truly *liability* coverage, since no legal liability for damages need exist in order for the coverages to apply. These coverages reduce the need for litigation for minor losses. The following are examples of related coverages provided by an ISO homeowners policy:

- Damage to property of others: $500. This coverage provides replacement cost for damage the insured causes to property of others.
- Medical payments to others: $1,000. Coverage is provided to pay for *necessary* medical expenses that are incurred or medically diagnosed within three years from the date of an accident causing bodily injury.

Educational Objective 4
Describe an insurer's options when notified of a claim or suit against a policyholder.

Defending and Settling Liability Claims

When an insurer is notified of a claim or suit against an insured, it has the following five options:

1. The insurer can accept the claim and agree to pay the damages (up to the policy's limits).
2. The insurer can defend the insured against the allegations of the lawsuit.

3. The insurer can completely disclaim any obligation under the insurance policy on the basis that coverage does not apply. The insurer would neither pay for any liability damages nor defend the insurer against the liability.

4. If liability or coverage (or both) is questionable, the insurer can issue either a **reservation of rights** letter or, less commonly, a **nonwaiver agreement**. If the claim requires research to determine whether liability or coverage exists, the insurer must begin the claim investigation process but reserve its rights to later disclaim coverage under the policy. Without a reservation of rights letter, the insurer might be viewed as admitting coverage and would be estopped from later denying coverage.

5. The insurer can seek a **declaratory judgment** asking the court to establish the parties' rights without actually awarding any relief. This is usually done when the insurer is unsure whether the contract provides coverage.[6]

Defense costs sometimes appear to be nonproductive transactions costs that drive up the cost of insurance without providing monetary benefits. Insurers do not always win the cases they defend. Defense costs are sometimes incurred on claims that could have been settled out of court by paying the amount originally claimed for damages. In reality, insurers sometimes pay small, questionable claims (even those they could probably win) to avoid defense costs or to preclude the possibility of a very large judgment.[7] However, the following can be the benefits of a sound defense:

- A finding of "no liability" could be ruled on behalf of the insured, and the insurer would pay no damages.

- A resulting legal decision in favor of the insured could establish case law and discourage other similar claims. It can send a signal to plaintiffs' attorneys and other potential claimants that the insurer will vigorously defend similar claims. When damages are awarded, the award might be substantially reduced because of evidence introduced through a sound, though costly, defense.

When a trial is involved, the compensable amount of the loss is whatever amount the court decides to award to the plaintiff as damages. The insurer pays the awarded damages on behalf of the insured (up to the policy limits). Neither a judge nor a jury is bound by the applicable insurance policy limit. If a jury awards a judgment in excess of the policy limit, the insured-defendant is responsible for the amount above the policy limits.

Most cases do not go to a formal trial, and the compensable amount of the loss is determined by informal negotiations between the liability insurer's adjuster (or the insurer's attorney) and the claimant (or the claimant's attorney). Generally, both parties try to anticipate what a court would do if presented with the same facts. The insurer naturally wants to minimize the settlement amount, and the plaintiff naturally wants to maximize it. Negotiation is encouraged because both parties are aware of the time and expense of a formal trial. In most types of

A **reservation of rights** letter is a general notice sent to an insured advising that the insurer is proceeding with a claim investigation. However, the investigation does not create an admission of liability. A **nonwaiver agreement** is a document serving the same purpose as the reservation of rights letter; however, it is drafted by counsel specifically for the claim and requires the insured's signature. It is the stronger of the two documents but the more difficult to implement because of the signature requirement.

A **declaratory judgment** is a court ruling on a coverage point within a policy contract or a judgment on a point of law. A declaratory judgment is usually made only when there is a genuine need to resolve such an issue and the claim is substantial enough to warrant the additional effort.

liability insurance, the insured/defendant has no right to prohibit a settlement or to influence its amount when the settlement is within policy limits. For losses that are likely to exceed the policy limits, the insured has a right to his or her own legal counsel to protect the insured's financial interest, usually at the insured's own expense.

The Court System

Issues that courts commonly address in resolving insurance claims involve (1) determining whether insurance coverage applies to a particular claim and (2) determining whether the insured is legally obligated to pay damages for a claim.

Each state has its own court system, which is the system that is most likely to hear an insurance claim case. A federal court system also exists that parallels the state system. The federal court reviews cases that relate to the Constitution, U.S. laws, treaties, controversies between states, and other problems on that scale. Federal courts might also be called on to try cases governed by state law when the plaintiff and defendant are citizens of different states.

A court is usually composed of one or more judges. In certain cases, juries are required to make the decisions. A primary court is the first one to determine the nature of a case and to make a judgment. That court is also called the court of original jurisdiction. If the case is not settled to the satisfaction of either party, the case can be appealed to an appellate court, which exists to review judgments made in primary courts.

Collateral Source Rule

A collateral source is an additional source that might be available to compensate a claimant for a loss. Under the **collateral source rule,** the defendant cannot introduce evidence that shows that the injured party has other sources of compensation for injury.

If an insured is found liable for a loss to a claimant, damages are determined without regard to other sources of benefits or compensation available to the claimant. In an auto accident, the claimant might have coverage available under medical payments or personal injury protection on his or her own personal auto policy. The claimant might also have a major medical policy and a disability income policy that pays for bodily injury expenses. The **collateral source rule** prohibits those other policies from being used as justification for reducing damages. Even if the claimant has such sources of compensation, the insured will (if found liable) owe the claimant the full amount of his or her damage and injury because the court does not allow supporting sources of insurance to be introduced in a trial. They cannot be used to reduce the tortfeasor's responsibility.

The rationale behind the collateral source rule is as follows: A wrongdoer should be fully responsible for the consequences of his or her wrongful act and should not be spared any part of that burden because other benefits are available to the injured party.

The collateral source rule, which permits double (and triple) recovery, is controversial. Not all sources can be used collaterally. In general, an insured cannot collect medical payments coverage or workers compensation benefits in combination with other sources of recovery.

Educational Objective 5

Explain how each of the following factors might affect the frequency or severity of liability losses:
- Liability fraud
- Property ownership
- Fame
- Occupation
- Personal activities
- Legal environment

Factors That Affect Liability Loss Frequency or Severity

Many insurance professionals are often asked to review loss exposures to provide opinions about potential liability exposures. Place yourself in a producer's role and consider how you would respond to the following questions from a customer:

> I'm thinking about building a barn in my backyard and getting a horse. Should I build a fence around the yard? What type of fence is best? Is there anything else I need to do?

You could respond to those questions by using an evaluation method employed by underwriters and claim representatives to determine whether a liability exposure is excessive. You would evaluate the following:

- The nature of the exposure
- Possible injuries that could result from the exposure
- How a jury would view the actions and precautions taken after the fact (to determine whether the insured took the actions that a *reasonably prudent person* would have taken)

Consider how this evaluation could be applied to the following situations:

- The insured installed a swimming pool with only a four-foot-high chain-link fence surrounding it. (Children in the neighborhood are exposed to injury from an attractive nuisance. A reasonably prudent person might have used a taller fence.)
- The insured is raising Rottweiler puppies. The dogs are kept in a kennel in the back yard of a home in a suburban area. (Children or other invitees might be hurt trying to pet the dogs, or the dogs could get loose. A reasonably prudent person might not attempt to raise dogs with an aggressive nature in a confined area or a suburban neighborhood.)
- An insured, tired of trying to evict a tenant on the residence premises through legal means, removes the apartment's front door

to encourage the tenant to leave. (The insured has created a situation exposing the tenant to assault in the unsecured premises, and the tenant's property to theft and damage. A reasonably prudent person might have followed the eviction procedure required by law.)

Measuring potential property loss exposures is often much easier than measuring liability loss exposures and the possible financial consequences that can result. Unlike potential property losses, potential liability losses do not have a measurable maximum possible loss (such as the replacement cost of a building). Confidently predicting the potential amount of a liability loss is difficult because of the following:

- Bodily injury claims might include damages for pain and suffering, which are extremely difficult to measure.
- Property damage liability claims might include loss of use damages, which can exceed the value of the damaged property.
- Jury awards are unpredictable.
- Chance circumstances could lead to extensive bodily injury or property damage.
- A liability claim takes longer to settle than a property claim because of delays in discovering the loss, determining liability, and establishing a settlement.
- Substantial claims can result from the failure of an item with relatively low value.

Identifying a liability exposure requires recognizing those situations that could result in a claim. Some exposures are more significant than others.

When underwriting liability coverage, the underwriter must consider all of the insured's activities, habits, hobbies, and properties to get a broad view of the potential liability exposures. The activities of relatives who reside in the household should also be considered. The following sections address some of the personal and premises liability exposures that are receiving underwriting examination.

Liability Fraud

Fraudulent losses often involve property claims, but liability claims also result from fraudulent losses. According to the National Insurance Crime Bureau, the average American household pays an additional $200 a year in insurance premiums to compensate for all forms of fraudulent claims.

Staged or fabricated losses not only generate large losses for personal lines insurers; these losses also present frustrating dilemmas for claim representatives because they are so difficult to prove (even though the claim representative might believe the loss is fraudulent). The following are some examples of current liability schemes for personal liability coverages:

- *Staged injuries*—Because injured parties are compensated not only for their medical bills but also for pain and suffering, such compensation becomes attractive to those who stage injuries and accidents. Typically, the injured parties seek medical or chiropractic treatment. Some injuries are especially difficult to detect through tangible evidence such as X-rays or CAT scans.

- *Slip and fall*—Slip and fall con artists fake falls and claim the resulting "injuries" to generate income from pain and suffering settlements. Such a fall might occur on the stairs leading to a residence.

Property Ownership

People who are prosperous and have property can become targets for liability losses simply because they are prosperous. However, possessing excessive wealth is not a requirement to become a liability target. A display of property such as expensive vehicles or a large home can create the impression that the owners have more financial resources than is actually the case.

The Residence

Personal lines producers and underwriters should be aware of hazards that could increase the chance of liability losses from people invited onto the premises. Property owners have an active duty to exercise care for an invited visitor's safety. Although a property owner owes no duty to a trespasser (a person who has no right to be on the premises), a property owner does have a duty to use reasonable care for a trespasser's safety after becoming aware of his or her presence on the property. Stairways should be in good repair and free of obstructions such as debris or toys. Swimming pools should be fenced and locked to prevent access by unsupervised children. Trampolines should be in fenced areas and off limits to neighborhood children unless an adult is supervising.

To minimize pollution exposures, fuel tanks at the residence should be periodically checked to ensure that a leak has not caused fuel to seep into the ground.

Homeowners also have a duty of reasonable care to maintain trees on their property. Trees that are not in good condition should be trimmed or removed to prevent dead limbs from being blown onto a neighbor's garage, car, or fence, which could cause damage.

Attitude Toward Premises

Housekeeping and maintenance of the premises are key factors that can increase potential loss frequency or severity. These are hazards underwritten in conjunction with the property portions of the homeowners policies. Conditions that cause concern about property coverage are often also concerns in liability underwriting.

Fame

Fame, by definition, means the loss of anonymity. Fame in our society is usually accompanied by wealth. The rich and famous are often targets of those who desire to acquire both fame and wealth by dishonest means. Indiscretions, whether real or imagined, of those in the limelight can become an opportunity for the greedy to seek their fortune through lawsuit.

Occupation

Personal insurance applications often include questions that ask for the insured's occupation or employment. This information can be used to help identify possible business or premises exposures.

Some home businesses and occupations experience a high frequency of liability claims by their nature. Day-care and child-care services have become extremely risky liability exposures because of the possibility of lawsuits for abuse and sexual molestation.

Insureds can also have liability exposures from professional activities, volunteer work, services as a director or officer without compensation, or ownership in a closely held corporation.

Personal Activities

Personal liability exposures include sports and personal activities and the special hazards associated with those activities. A specialist should be aware of sports, recreational activities, and lifestyles that can create liability exposures.

Sports

The following example is provided to illustrate the liability exposures associated with boating, but liability exposures can be associated with almost any sport:

> A watercraft owner negligently entrusted his boat to someone underage. The boat owner allowed a twelve-year-old to take the owner's catamaran out for the afternoon. The boat collided with another boat, causing injury, and a claim resulted from the owner's negligence in entrusting the boat to a minor.

Another potential liability for watercraft is using alcohol during its operation. Although the rules of the waterways prohibit drinking while operating a boat, violations of those rules are common. Accidents and resultant injuries from hitting swimmers or hitting other boaters are not uncommon when judgment is impaired. In evaluating sport liability exposures, the specialist should consider the following:

- The potential for injury to others
- The potential for negligent entrustment of watercraft and motorized recreational vehicles
- The extent of the insured's training and experience

Host Liquor

Hosts who serve alcoholic beverages to their social guests might be held accountable for injury or damage caused by those guests if they become intoxicated.[8] Hosting a party and providing refreshments seem like a harmless social activity. However, serving alcohol to a guest who has already had too much to drink or allowing an intoxicated guest to drive a car can be the basis for negligence and a liability loss. Again, even if the host is not negligent (perhaps not realizing the guest was intoxicated), the host might still be in a position of having to defend against a suit.

Miscellaneous Personal Activities

The personal activities that can create liability are numerous. Consider the following things that people sometimes do and how they could hurt someone or damage property:

- Allowing a dog to run without a leash
- Teaching neighborhood children how to shoot a BB gun
- Hosting a softball game

Legal Environment

Claim representatives can recount the differences in trial outcomes for insurance court cases by the location of the trial. Insurers consider some locations unfriendly. In such locations, insurance companies prefer to settle claims through negotiation rather than in a courtroom with a history of adverse decisions for insurers.

Insurers have varying ideas about what makes a location unfriendly. The general level of understanding about the financial function of the insurance industry plays a large part. The idea that no one suffers from an inflated claim perpetuates the problem of liberal awards to claimants. Large claims eventually increase premiums. Jury members who are aware of the financial relationship between awards and premiums are more likely to have an objective view of insurance claim awards.

However, when people in a community view a large court award from an insurance company as a lottery in which no one loses, juries are willing to help someone from their own neighborhood achieve financial success.

Educational Objective 6

Describe the liability exposures and hazards associated with farming, swimming pools, firearms, animals, incidental offices and businesses in the home, child care or elder care in the home, dwellings rented to others, underground storage tanks, and other special hazards.

Special Liability Exposures and Hazards

Many individuals and families have a residence and personal auto exposure. When unique exposures are present, the specialist should be aware of the potential hazards associated with those exposures. This section describes special liability exposures and potential hazards.

Farming

Special liability exposures exist for farms to which the public has access. These include farms where customers can pick their own fruit and farms that provide hay rides or other recreation for the public. If hunting is permitted on the farm or if the farm has business operations in addition to the regular farming operation, the specialist should ask for details regarding what happens and when. Any unusual exposure should be questioned.[9]

Swimming Pools

A swimming pool is a classic attractive nuisance for children. The attractive nuisance doctrine is important in residence liability underwriting because attractions often exist at a typical residence. Children are not fully aware of what might harm them, so the burden is placed on the residence owner to anticipate what could attract a child to the premises. The residence owner must create an effective barrier or obstruction to protect children from incurring injury.

A significant liability concern about a swimming pool is the precautions that have been taken to prevent entry by children while the pool is unattended. A pool should be fully surrounded by a fence. A fence that creates a visual barrier provides greater protection than one that allows those outside to see the pool. Many areas have no zoning requirements for fence height, but some communities impose strict requirements. A fence should be tall enough to create a significant obstacle for a child. Suppose a child climbed a four-foot chain-link fence to reach a swimming pool and was injured in the pool. Listen to the possible closing argument that could be made by a plaintiff's attorney before a jury:

> Ladies and gentlemen of the jury, a child can easily climb a four-foot fence, and the children in the neighborhood frequently did so. The owner of the pool knew that the children were climbing the fence. We even have witnesses who heard the owner say "Come over and use the pool whenever you want to!"

> For two dollars more per foot, the owner could have increased the height of the fence from four feet to six feet—creating a much more significant barrier to prevent children from entering an unattended pool and therefore preventing this terrible tragedy.

All liability exposures should be evaluated for their loss potential. If a loss did occur, did the insured do everything that a reasonable person would have done? What arguments could be made against the insured's actions? Effective fencing and locks can make access to the pool more difficult.

An above-ground pool with a stairway that folds up and locks creates an acceptable barrier as long as the pool and railing are high enough to prevent easy entry for a child. The following are additional liability concerns regarding swimming pools:

- Cleanliness and sanitation are essential but can be overlooked during winter months. Injury, sickness, and disease can result from improper pool sanitation. In one case, a child slipped on an algae growth, struck his head on the edge of the pool, and fell, unconscious, into the pool.

- Improper use of chemicals can cause illness. Chemicals can accumulate in pools or hot tubs that are not maintained properly. Pool owners should test and treat the water appropriately.

- Catastrophic claims can result from diving injuries. Neck and spinal injuries can result in settlements that last a lifetime. Supervision around the pool is an important factor in preventing this type of loss. Restricting the use of alcohol is another important precaution.

Hot Tubs and Whirlpools

Hot tubs are usually shallow and are kept covered, so the exposure to a child's drowning in one is generally less significant than a swimming pool exposure. Hot tubs are often equipped with covers that can be locked to prevent unsupervised entry.

Care should be taken to restrict the use of alcohol around and in hot tubs. Hot tubs have become popular because of their relaxing effect. That, compounded with the depressant effect of alcohol, can cause people to fall asleep or become unconscious and slip under the water.

Some heart patients are also restricted from using hot tubs. The hot water raises blood pressure, which can be hazardous to those who have heart-related problems.

Trampolines

Trampolines are another type of attractive nuisance that have recently received media attention. Children who play on a trampoline unattended by adults can land badly, hurting themselves on the metal frame. They can also fall off the trampoline and suffer injury.

Firearms

Several problems can result from the presence of firearms in the home. The most apparent involves children who discover guns and injure themselves or other children. This type of injury is not restricted to small children. When guns are in the house, they should be secured to prevent access.

Hunting also creates a significant exposure. Hunting is a sport that requires expertise and education. Every new hunting season brings newspaper reports of deaths and property damage as a result of mistakes made in target identification.

Good questions to ask when guns are in the household include the following:

- What are the types of guns (rifle, pistol, and so forth)?

FYI

Six thousand mail carriers were bitten by dogs in 1984, prompting the U.S. Postal Service to collect millions of dollars from dog owners for injury and punitive damages. The Postal Service can (and does) interrupt mail deliveries to an individual, or even to a neighborhood, where aggressive dogs are a problem. According to reports by the United States Public Health Service, hundreds of thousands of dog bites occur annually.

Source: William H. Rodda, "Underwriting Update: Killer Dogs," Best's Underwriting Newsletter, October 1985, pp. 1-4.

- How many guns are there?
- How are the guns secured?
- What is the purpose of having the guns?
- If guns are used for hunting, what is the insured's hunting experience?
- Are children in the household?
- Has the insured ever taken a gun safety course?

Animals

Some dog trainers say that any dog will bite under the right circumstances. Even a passive dog becomes aggressive if it believes that it is protecting its territory or owner.

Some dog breeds have achieved notoriety because of their extraordinary aggressiveness. The degree of this exposure varies with the dog's breed and size. A six-pound terrier can inflict less damage than a 100-pound Doberman pinscher.

The method in which a dog was raised can also be a factor in the amount of aggression the dog displays. Many dog attacks that have made headlines involved dogs that were brought into the family as mature animals. The dogs initially exhibited friendly behavior then suddenly turned on a family member. The dogs might actually have been triggered to revert to a prior learned behavior.

A one-bite rule once existed in the court systems. This rule held that a dog owner could not have known that the pet was aggressive until it actually bit someone. From that point on, the owner had knowledge of the behavior and was responsible for any future injury. This rule is no longer valid. Court decisions vary on their assessment of blame for the injuries, but dog owners are usually required to restrain their pets. An owner who allows a dog to run loose is almost certain to be held responsible for any injuries that might occur. Fencing must be adequate to keep the dog in the yard.

If a dog is chained or tied within a yard that a child can easily enter, the dog owner could be held responsible for any injury that occurs on the insured's own property. The dog can be viewed as an attractive nuisance that enticed the child onto the property. If a dog is large enough to harm a child, the yard should be fenced to minimize the chance of injury.

Should a property owner post a sign such as "Beware of Dog" if a large or an aggressive dog is in the yard? Attorneys and claim representatives have mixed opinions about signs:

- A warning sign can protect the property owner. A sign warning a trespasser of the presence of a guard dog can lessen the effect of a suit by an injured trespasser. The property owner's attorney could argue that the trespasser had no right to be on the property and that warning had been posted regarding the possible danger.

- A sign can also be seen as an admission by the property owner that he or she knows the dog is aggressive. This can be used as an argument by a prosecutor on behalf of someone injured by the dog (such as a child who cannot read and climbs the fence).

Generally, a sign is considered to be more beneficial than harmful.

Good questions for the specialist to ask when a dog is present at a residence are as follows:

- What kind of dog is it?
- Is the dog restrained or confined at all times? How?
- Have any incidents of viciousness occurred?
- Have there been any previous claims involving the dog?

If other domestic animals are at the residence, each case should be viewed individually. Zoning and restrictions often eliminate the presence of farm animals in incorporated communities. However, goats, horses, cattle, and various domestic animals are commonly found in the yards of homes outside a city's limits. The following questions can be used to help determine the possible hazards associated with domestic animals:

- Are the animals contained at all times?
- How many animals are there, and what type are they?
- Have the males been neutered? (Large, unneutered male animals are generally too aggressive to keep in a residential area.)
- Have there been any prior losses?
- What is the insured's experience in keeping animals?
- If the animals are for riding, does anyone other than the family have access to them?

If the animals are well-contained, if the number of animals is small, if the males have been neutered, and if neighbors are not allowed to ride the animals, the liability hazard might not increase substantially. An insured with a number of animals might have crossed the line into a farming exposure.

Incidental Offices and Businesses in the Home

Many people supplement their incomes with small businesses they conduct from their homes. Many others have discovered the convenience of running a full- or part-time office from their homes or corresponding with an employer electronically. Home businesses create a wide range of exposures involving people, materials, and equipment to run the business.

Today, full-time work at home is common because computers allow work to be done at a location remote from the main operation. Workers have home computers, printers, and modems. Employers save on office space required for those employees. Employees benefit by being able to live at a remote location without needing to commute to an office.

Work areas might have visitors (including children). Any equipment, such as video equipment, could be an attractive nuisance for a child.

Someone might trip over wires and cables. Electrical apparatus can malfunction, injuring or burning visitors. Both the employee and the employer could be sued.[10]

Basic questions that help determine the liability hazards involved in a home business are as follows:

- What is the type of business?

- Does the insured run it alone or use employees?

- What is the nature of the business clientele? Does the insured ever have customers or suppliers on the premises? If yes, with what frequency? What is the profile of the people who will be in the house (young, professional, maintenance personnel, and so forth)?

- What number of customers might be in the house at one time? Are they always in the presence of the insured, or do they have access throughout the home?

- What is the access between the living portion and the business portion of the residence? (Is the office in a renovated garage with no common access, or must visitors go through the house to reach the office?)

- What possible losses can the business or office cause? Do the number and nature of people who will be on the premises increase the exposure?

- Is the premises free of liability hazards that could injure a person (such as low-hanging branches, uneven sidewalks, obstructed stairways, or cluttered sidewalks and approaches)?

The chance of a liability loss increases as the number of people allowed to be on the premises and to have access to the home increases. The specialist should review the insured's operations, paying attention to what is happening and what could go wrong.

Child Care (or Elder Care) in the Home

A child-care operation has all of the exposures of a business in the home as well as additional hazards. Liability hazards that are present with child care include allegations of injury to the child, as well as potential allegations of physical and sexual abuse. In recent years, the exposures for caring for older citizens have almost equaled the notoriety of child care. Juries tend to be sympathetic regarding injuries to children and the elderly, so much up-front underwriting care is required in reviewing exposures.

The premises should be inspected with an emphasis on conditions that could cause injury.

The following questions can help in discovering child-care-related exposures:

- Are the premises protected to prevent a child from leaving or another person from entering the property? (This would include having an adequate fence around a play yard.)

- How many children are being cared for? What are their ages?

- Is there adequate help for the number of children cared for?

- What type of employment screening is performed on the people who help with the children? Have any of the helpers been involved in a prior loss?

- Has the child-care operation caused any injuries or losses?

- What type of procedures or rules are in place regarding children who are ill and parties who can pick up children at the end of the day?

- Is the day-care facility certified?

The same type of considerations that are important for children are important for older people who need some level of assisted living. In addition, the presence of medical supervision is crucial.

Dwellings Rented to Others

Rental dwellings pose a number of liability exposures for the individual who is a landlord. Exposures include conditions that can harm the tenant as well as conditions the tenant creates that could harm others.

Rental Property Liability

Individuals might own residential rental property, which can be apartments located at the residence premises or rental properties located away from the residence. Units that house up to four families are usually insured through personal lines property and liability policies. Landlords are normally obligated to maintain rental premises in safe condition or inform tenants about known hazardous conditions.[11] However, situations can cause injury to the tenant or to others who enter the premises. A judge or jury might be asked to determine whether the landlord is liable for the injury. The following are examples of liability claims that can arise from the ownership of rental property:

- A tenant advises the landlord that a door is not latching properly. Before repairs are made, a burglar enters the house and assaults the tenant. A claim is brought against the landlord for failure to maintain the apartment in a secure condition after the tenant had advised the landlord of the problem.

- A claim is brought against a landlord because an aggressive dog bites a child entering the rental property. The claim is based on the belief that the landlord knew the tenant had a vicious animal on the premises and did nothing to protect the public from possible harm.

Seasonal Dwellings

In resort areas, dwellings are often rented on a daily, weekly, or monthly basis. Vacationers rent the dwellings to enjoy themselves. Sometimes doing so includes activities on the premises that cause the vacationers harm; for example, intoxicated vacationers might fall down stairs or off decks, injuring themselves. The more frequent the turnover of the temporary residents, the more the problem compounds. The following are factors to consider in reviewing liability exposures for seasonally rented property:

- If the landlord manages the property personally, losses tend to be less than if the landlord were an absentee landlord (living in another state or a significant distance from the rental property). Also, a loss-free record for a landlord is a positive sign.

- If a management company oversees the property (and is also on-site), that is a plus. Any extreme activity at the property might be observed and corrected before injury occurs.

- If the landlord or the property management company uses a selection process that includes references from former clients or uses another method of determining that the property will not be turned over to irresponsible renters, the chances of injury can be reduced.

- If property rental is extended at least to a month-to-month or seasonal basis, the chances of having a more stable rental situation are increased. Rentals over short durations, such as spring breaks, are more likely to be problematic.

Exposures to the Tenant

At common law, tenants are required to inspect property themselves to discover the dangers inherent on the premises. However, statutes, rules, and ordinances in a growing number of states provide that a residential lease includes an implied warranty of habitability. The extent of the warranty depends on the local laws. "Habitable" is defined by law as "suitable for the use contemplated by the parties."[12] A lease might also contain some contractual liability requiring the landlord to inspect, maintain, or repair the property. Misrepresentation of the conditions at a residence can be considered negligence.

If an injury occurs to a tenant or others or if damage occurs to property, asking the following questions would be helpful:

- Did the landlord have a duty to inspect the property (and did the landlord perform that inspection)?

- Did the landlord know that something dangerous was on the premises (and did the landlord notify the tenant about that danger)?

If the landlord did not perform the proper duties and notifications, the prosecuting attorney might have an easy time convincing a jury to compensate the tenant for injuries and to punish the landlord for negligence.

The Landlord's Experience and Loss History

Experience and skill are necessary to screen applicants effectively for occupancy of rental property. Applicants try to impress a prospective landlord positively during the interview process, but people are sometimes less than what they present themselves to be. Property and liability loss history indicates how effectively the landlord selects tenants.

If a property management company is used, its loss history for managed property is also an important factor. Property managers are usually compensated by a percentage of the monthly rent. If a house is not rented, the manager is not paid. This can prompt an unconscientious property manager to ignore sound selection procedures so that the property can be quickly rented. A conscientious manager appreciates the need to adequately screen applicants and to build a long-term clientele.

Assisted/Subsidized Housing

Section 8 housing is a housing assistance program provided by local housing administration offices. A landlord can apply to have rental property accepted under Section 8. If the property is accepted, the housing administration finds a family that qualifies for assistance. The landlord is paid according to the size of the residence and the number of bedrooms. The government mails the check to the landlord at the beginning of each month. The rent is usually a little less than the usual rental rate; however, a landlord who has trouble renting a property can find Section 8 housing to be an attractive arrangement.

The landlord can interview and reject a tenant referred by the housing administration. Handling Section 8 rental property requires special skills to select tenants effectively. The landlord's history and success in handling this type of property should be determined. Physical inspections of the property are a good idea.

From an underwriting standpoint, determining the number of people residing in a Section 8 home is important. Some landlords have discovered that they can get more rent through Section 8 by creating more bedrooms (because that is one of the factors for determining the amount they will receive monthly). Basements might be divided into several small bedrooms with enough bathroom facilities to pass code. The result is that more people live in a home than it was intended to accommodate. Therefore, chances of physical damage to the property and possible injury increase.

Underwriters and producers can expect to see more Section 8 housing in an area that has had a decline in employment, a layoff from a large employer, or the closing of a military facility. Landlords have trouble renting property in such areas, and terminated workers often need financial assistance for housing.

Exposures to Others

A tenant can create liability hazards that others might try to pass along to the landlord. One tenant obtained a pit bull (dog) after moving into a residence. The pit bull attacked and severely injured a neighbor's child, leaving facial scars. The child's parents sued the tenant and the landlord (in an effort to attempt to find the **deep pockets**). The suit

Jargon Alert!

"Deep pockets" is a term used to describe a person or an entity with financial resources that can support a lawsuit.

against the landlord was based on the allegation that the landlord knew the hazardous situation at the property he owned and allowed the condition to continue. In this case, however, the landlord was unaware of the dog's presence but had a difficult time proving that.

With that type of exposure in mind, the landlord could have practiced risk management by specifying tenant limitations. If dogs are not permitted within a rental property (or only dogs up to a certain weight limit are permitted), including that information in a lease or in another written document would be helpful. Other types of limitations that are placed on the property use, such as the following, could also be included:

- The property is to be used only as a single-family residence.
- Any unusual activity that creates pollution is prohibited.
- No business activity is to be conducted.

Consider liability exposures that the tenant might create and how that exposures could harm others (and the landlord).

Hazardous Materials

Hazardous conditions and materials found in residences rented to others have become a substantial liability concern for landlords.

Lead Paint

Lead, which is present everywhere naturally, is a health hazard to people. At high levels of concentration in the body, lead causes death. At low levels, it causes brain dysfunction. The amount of lead in the blood that is considered safe is continually being reduced as the effects of lead are determined. Lead can even cross the placenta during pregnancy and interfere with fetal development. Infants and children are most susceptible to lead poisoning because they ingest it from paint chips and from sucking on toys and fingers covered in dust from lead paint. Its toxicity affects growth and development.

The most difficult, costly, and important form of lead abatement is the removal and proper disposal of lead-based paint from old houses. However, no widespread program to fund or enforce that task currently exists.

In the United States, approximately 2 million children live in homes containing lead paint, and 230,000 of those houses have lead levels that can cause permanent damage.[13] Lead liability lawsuits are expected to result in $3 billion in payouts between 1996 and 2006. Currently, lead paint manufacturers have been successful in defending liability cases for the effects of their product. If this trend continues, much of the payout for lead paint injuries will be made by landlords and public housing authorities. The largest single award to date was $9 million to a child with brain damage as a result of lead poisoning.[14]

Exhibit 5-4 is a map of the United States that shows the concentration of homes that were built before 1940. Lead paint was banned in 1978,

Exhibit 5-4
Percentage of U.S. Residences Constructed Before 1940

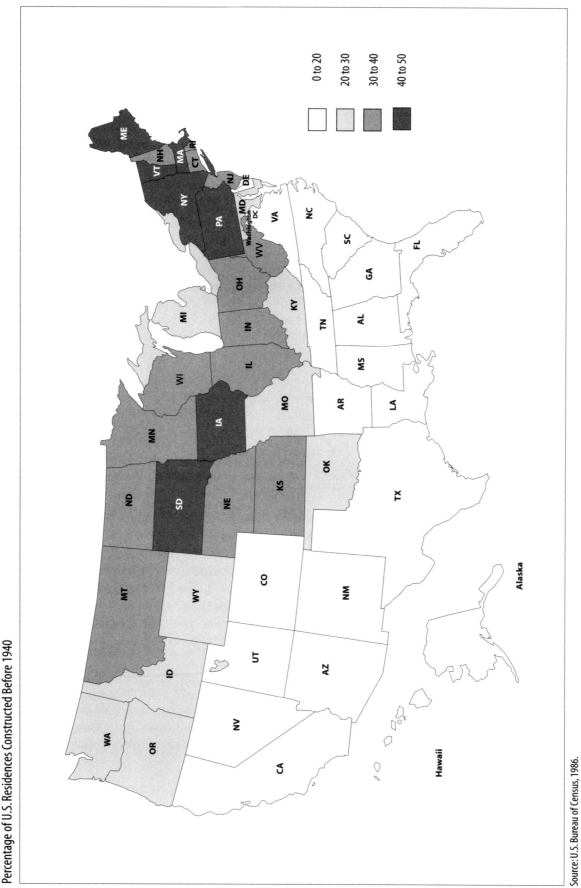

0 to 20
20 to 30
30 to 40
40 to 50

Source: U.S. Bureau of Census, 1986.

but lead paint is still present in many of these old homes and apartments (particularly in cities in the northeastern United States).

In personal lines coverage, the largest liability exposure regarding lead paint occurs in rental dwellings. A landlord who knows that the property has defects is obligated to disclose the existence of that defect.

Typical lead-related liability charges filed against landlords are as follows:

- Failure to inspect and test for the presence of lead-based paint
- Failure to remove lead-based paint
- Failure to warn of the existence of lead-based paint
- Failure to comply with statutes, ordinances, or housing codes concerning maintenance, repair, flaking, or chipping paint and lead-based paint[15]

Property owners currently have no easy way to solve the clean-up problems. The abatement process and disposal are difficult and costly. The Residential Lead-Based Paint Hazard Reduction Act of 1992 provides some grants and loans for eligible applicants. However, eligibility is extremely limited. The grants cover only up to 90 percent of the cost, and the paperwork is extensive.

From an underwriting standpoint, rental properties with lead paint pose a considerable problem. Litigation for victims can take a number of tracks, all of which can be successful.

Asbestos

Asbestos can be present in residences in the form of attic insulation, roof shingles, furnace insulation, and exterior siding. Asbestos becomes a threat when it becomes airborne and is inhaled. The disease asbestosis develops over time. It manifests itself in a number of potentially fatal lung diseases. Asbestos can be removed, but the process is dangerous, expensive, and difficult. One alternative is to seal the material behind a physical barrier so it is not exposed. The underwriting concerns regarding asbestos in rental properties are similar to the concerns surrounding lead paint. A landlord who has neither advised the tenant nor used proper care to protect the tenant can be sued for damages.

Radon

Radon is an odorless radioactive gas that can accumulate within a residence from the soil beneath the house. It was first discovered in 1900 but was not believed to be harmful until the 1960s. Concentrations of the gas pose serious health hazards. Radon ranks second to smoking as the leading cause of lung cancer.

Radon contamination became a major concern in 1984, when it was found in homes in eastern Pennsylvania, northern New Jersey, and New York, all of which areas are along a geological formation known as the Reading Prong. In 1988, the federal government issued a national health advisory that stated, "Millions of homes have elevated radon levels." The government asked people nationwide to test their homes and apartments for radon. According to this advisory, the potential for radon contamination is so widespread that the only people who do not need to test their homes are those living in apartments above the second floor.

The amount of radon gas that enters a building depends on the following:

- How much radon gas (or the parent compounds) is found in the soil beneath the house
- The permeability of the soil
- The faults and fissures (cracks) in the underlying rock
- The openings between the house and the soil

When radon is present, buildings draw the gas through the soil into the interior of a building. The difference between the air pressure outside and the air pressure inside the building (from the rising warm air) sucks the gas inside from the openings, holes, and cracks in the foundation. This suction is much stronger in the winter because of interior heating and closed windows, which is why radon levels are also much higher in the winter than during other seasons.

Radon testing is relatively inexpensive. The solution of what to do when radon is detected involves sealing the foundation openings and increasing the exterior airflow into the house.

The radon exposure becomes a potential liability when a landlord knows that radon is present and does not disclose that to the tenant. Liability can also occur when the landlord has an obligation to test and does not do so.[16]

Heaters

When the price of heating oil rises, people look for alternative and auxiliary methods of heating. Any portable heater can present a fire hazard when it is placed too close to drapes, bed covers, or other flammable items. Kerosene heaters and gas space heaters should be equipped with mechanisms that cut off the fuel if the oxygen is depleted. When a heater is allowed to burn through the night without a control to sense oxygen depletion, resulting carbon monoxide build-up can kill sleeping occupants.

This type of tragedy becomes a liability for the landlord when the landlord supplies the heater to the tenant, or when an inadequate or defective heating source forces the tenant to use an alternative heating source to heat the house.

General Premises Conditions

Insurers often inspect rental property to identify conditions that can cause injury. This is the same general inspection that is performed for physical hazards at the premises. Special attention might also be paid to features of the property that could cause injury or features that do not provide adequate security for the tenant. The following are some features that should be checked in an inspection:

- Safety of exterior stairways and railings
- Condition of porches, decks, and surrounding railings
- Adequacy of functional locks on exterior doors and windows

Underground Storage Tanks

In the 1980s, gasoline stations commonly dug up their paved parking lots, dragged the rusty steel storage tanks from the ground, and replaced them with fiberglass tanks. The process was very expensive but not as expensive as allowing the metal tanks to rust through, which could permit gasoline to escape into the ground and possibly seep into the water table. This same type of exposure can be present with underground fuel oil tanks and gasoline tanks at residences.

The water supply of surrounding properties can become tainted by the presence of even very little gasoline. Homeowners a quarter mile away from a leaky tank can smell gasoline in their basement or detect a foreign taste in their well water.

Eliminating ground pollutants usually means removing the earth until the pollutant is no longer present. The earth can be treated and replaced, but the process is costly. However, once pollution reaches an underground water vein, little can be done to correct the situation.

Homeowners and personal liability policies exclude pollution damage to insureds' property. However, pollution damage is not excluded under the homeowners policies' liability coverage (which can be extended to rental property by endorsement). An umbrella policy usually also provides liability coverage for pollution that is sudden and unexpected. The expectation is that any pollution that occurs from a residence would be minor and accidental.

The following are examples of situations that require underwriting questions about the presence and conditions of underground storage tanks:

- Fuel-oil heating is used.
- The home is a converted country store (which might once have sold gasoline).
- Gasoline is stored in a tank at a farm to supply equipment.
- Gasoline is stored in a tank at a residence (gasoline tanks were sometimes buried in the yards of residential homes during the 1970s oil embargo).

Volunteers and Good Samaritans

Volunteering to help others creates liability exposures. The following case is an illustration. A young medical student stopped at the scene of an auto accident to assist the victim. Because of the victim's crushed throat, he determined that spinal injuries were probable. He also determined from the victim's purple face that he would die before the ambulance arrived if the medical student did not pull him from the vehicle and provide immediate help. While he was dragging the injured man from the vehicle, he realized that he could be causing injuries that would leave the injured man a quadriplegic.

An image flashed through the medical student's mind of the injured man sitting in a courtroom in a wheelchair. He could imagine the attorney addressing the jury as follows:

> This medical student took it upon himself to play God. He took it upon himself to move this gravely injured man, condemning him forever to this wheelchair.

He then also imagined millions of dollars awarded to the injured man by the court and years of hard work lost.

Nevertheless, the medical student successfully resuscitated the injured man. The ambulance driver, however, berated the medical student for his actions and took down his name and address for the reports. The medical student's senior professor advised him that the best course of action would have been to "drive on." Assisting the injured man could have been the end of his career.[17]

Fortunately, the injured man recovered fully, and the medical student graduated from medical school. However, this story demonstrates why people do not become involved as good Samaritans and why some people are reluctant to volunteer their help. Getting involved means taking a chance of causing injury, even if accidental. It also means taking a chance of injuring someone who might retaliate in a courtroom.

People who can do the most good for others are, ironically, the most vulnerable to litigation. From a risk management standpoint, these people need the most counseling about liability protection. From a practical standpoint, they need to be aware of the potential for suit as a result of their actions, and they need increased limits of coverage in case a claim occurs. From an underwriting standpoint, reviewing an insured's civic and political involvement helps in determining the possible exposures to loss.

Summary

For an insurance policy to pay damages for a liability loss, two elements must be present:

1. Coverage, determined by the policy contract
2. Legal liability, determined by a law or regulation outside the policy contract

When an insurer is notified of a claim or suit against an insured, the following options are available:

-   To accept the claim and defend the suit.
-   To disclaim obligations because coverage does not apply.
-   To investigate in order to determine whether the insured is liable and coverage applies (the insurer issues a reservation of rights

letter or a nonwaiver agreement to reserve the insurer's rights until the investigation can be completed).

- To seek a declaratory judgment (usually to answer coverage questions).

The number of sources that can create a potential liability loss for an individual or family is almost unlimited. Torts are the primary source of liability losses covered by personal insurance liability policies. Contractual liability losses are the other source of personal liability, but they are relatively rare. Negligence is the most frequent type of tort covered by personal insurance. For a specialist to help a customer determine what activity might generate a liability loss, the specialist should help the customer evaluate the following:

- Exposures
- Possible injuries that could result from the exposures
- Actions and precautions taken compared to those of a reasonably prudent person

Hazards that increase the frequency or severity of liability losses for personal insurance customers and special hazards associated with farming, swimming pools, trampolines, firearms, animals, offices and businesses in the home, child care or elder care in the home, rental property, underground storage tanks, and other special hazards, require careful review by the specialist.

Chapter Notes

1. Grange Ins. Co. v. Brosseau, 776 P.2d 123 (Wash. 1989).
2. *Homeowners Liability Insurance Law—Questions and Answers Reference Service* (Schaumburg, IL: Property Loss Research Bureau, 1991), pp. 9.1–9.5.
3. Robert I. Mehr and Emerson Cammack, *Principles of Insurance* (Homewood, IL: Richard D. Irwin, 1980), pp. 60–62.
4. Mehr and Cammack, pp. 63–64.
5. Robert J. Gibbons, George E. Rejda, and Michael W. Elliott, *Insurance Perspectives* (Malvern, PA: American Institute for Chartered Property Casualty Underwriters, 1992), pp. 50–52.
6. Eric A. Wiening and Donald S. Malecki, *Insurance Contract Analysis* (Malvern, PA: American Institute for Chartered Property Casualty Underwriters, 1994), pp. 371–373.
7. Wiening and Malecki, pp. 248–253.
8. Karen L. Hamilton and Donald S. Malecki, *Personal Insurance: Property and Liability* (Malvern, PA: American Institute for Chartered Property Casualty Underwriters, 1994), p. 11.
9. G. William Glendenning and Robert B. Holtom, *Personal Lines Underwriting* (Malvern, PA: Insurance Institute of America, 1987), pp. 473–474.
10. William H. Rodda, "Underwriting Update: Insuring the Home Worker," *Best's Underwriting Newsletter*, October 1985, pp. 1–4.

11. James H. Donaldson, *Casualty Claim Practice* (Homewood, IL: Richard D. Irwin, 1984), pp. 68–70.

12. Restatement (Second) of Property §5.4 (1984).

13. Mary Schleevogt and Miles Belgrade. "Lead Poisoning in Children," Working Paper (Cherry Valley, IL: Mutual Reinsurance Bureau, 1991), p. 6.

14. L.H. Otis, "Lead Liability Outlays Could Reach $3 Billion, Insurance Information Institute Warns," *National Underwriter*, May 1995, pp. 1, 47–48.

15. Catherine A. Potthast, "Lead Paint Litigation—an Overview," Working Paper (Baltimore, MD: Smith, Somerville, and Case, 1992), p. 1.

16. Barbara Giles and Carl Giles, *Make Your House Radon Free* (Blue Ridge Summit, PA: Tab Books, Inc., 1990), pp. 22–25.

17. James Dillard, "A Doctor's Dilemma," *Newsweek*, June 12, 1995, p. 12.

Chapter 6

Educational Objectives

1. With regard to driver and vehicle use exposures, explain how each of the elements of the personal auto policy studied in this assignment affects an underwriting decision. (pp. 6-3 to 6-7)

2. Identify and evaluate driver and vehicle use-related exposures that affect the frequency and severity of auto losses. (pp. 6-7 to 6-23)

3. Describe the information needed to make an underwriting decision on a personal auto application, and explain how that information is obtained. (pp. 6-23 to 6-30)

4. Measure the importance of personal auto exposures identified as they relate to potential loss frequency and severity. (pp. 6-30 to 6-31)

5. Explain and evaluate the alternatives available in personal auto coverage implementation. (pp. 6-31 to 6-43)

6. Describe how personal underwriting decisions can be implemented and their results monitored. (pp. 6-43 to 6-44)

7. Evaluate the factors that should be considered when a personal auto liability claim is made. (pp. 6-44 to 6-46)

8. Given a case study involving an application for personal auto liability, analyze the exposures and recommend the appropriate underwriting actions and insurance coverage placement. (Encompasses entire chapter.)

Chapter 6

Personal Auto: Driver and Vehicle Use Exposures

The first line in a newspaper article often reads as follows:

> "The White House announced yesterday. . .," or,
>
> "A car crashed into a house today. . . ."

Just as the White House does not talk, cars usually do not cause accidents. The President has spokespersons, and the person driving the car probably caused the accident. Sometimes a car's mechanical failure, the driver's physical failure (such as a massive stroke), or the roadway's structural failure is the proximate cause of an accident. By far, however, the negligence of at least one driver causes the greatest number of liability and physical damage losses involving vehicles.

This chapter and the next address personal auto exposures, underwriting, and coverages. This chapter addresses drivers and vehicle use, along with concerns related to the personal auto policy. The next chapter reviews vehicles and their characteristics and related physical damage coverages. These topics are separated for discussion purposes only. The auto policy is a unit, and it is underwritten as an entire unit.

Educational Objective 1
With regard to driver and vehicle use exposures, explain how each of the elements of the personal auto policy studied in this assignment affects an underwriting decision.

The Personal Auto Policy

From a practical standpoint, the personal auto policy (PAP) developed by Insurance Services Office forms a standard for personal auto insurance contracts. However, insurance companies offer policies that vary from nonstandard to preferred markets and from monoline to package policies. Therefore, each policy must be reviewed carefully. A single word in a contract could mean the difference between coverage and no coverage.

Although the PAP is designed to address most auto exposures, some types of persons, vehicles, activities, and uses are beyond the scope of the PAP program. In addition, some auto exposures are not eligible for the PAP, and others are not insurable at an affordable price. Such exposures must be identified and alternative insurance methods sought to help insureds protect their assets from the risk of loss because the PAP does not cover them (for example, a family member's vehicles and business use vehicles).

State auto insurance laws vary in many ways (in regard, for example, to how uninsured or underinsured motor vehicles are defined and whether coverage is optional or mandatory). Insurance specialists should be knowledgeable about variations within their states of operation.

As a starting point in reviewing the driver and use exposures for an auto application, the definitions and liability section of the policy require a review with an eye for underwriting and marketing concerns. Some sections have been annotated in Exhibit 6-1, and this chapter will refer to many of the annotations in that exhibit.

Most insurance policies include a section or sections of definitions. The defined terms have a specific meaning within the context of the policy. Whenever an insured charges that a policy is ambiguous, courts usually refer to the definitions section for clarification. If the term is not defined by the policy, the courts consider the term's common usage, referring, if necessary, to dictionary definitions. Not all terms are defined in the policy, and many terms are subject to interpretation. The PAP is one of the most scrutinized and analyzed policy contracts because of the frequency of auto losses, claims, and litigation. In addition, interpretations change over time and across the country. These changes help make careers in insurance challenging.

Exhibit 6-1
PAP Annotations

Definitions

The definition of "you and your" is narrow and limits some coverages. Some companies verify that the vehicle's title and the registration match the name on the policy to prevent coverage gaps.

Note how business is defined. When does a "hobby" become a business? Generally, a business has elements of *continuity* and *profit*. Underwriting guides often help make that determination by specifying:

- A percentage of income
- A dollar limit of income
- A percentage of use

Note that the word "resident" has not been defined. From an *underwriting* standpoint, a family member might be considered a resident if one or more of the following apply:

- Is financially supported by the family (a college student)
- Has the majority of his possessions in the home (a son in military boot camp)
- Has retained the home as a legal residence (a daughter touring Europe)

A producer should be concerned about ensuring that all "residents" are identified to prevent a coverage dispute. It is best to identify and declare all residents.

A. Throughout this policy, "you" and "your" refer to:

1. The "named insured" shown in the Declarations; and
2. The spouse if a resident of the same household.

B. "We," "us" and "our" refer to the Company providing this insurance.

C. For purposes of this policy, a private passenger type auto shall be deemed to be owned by a person if leased:

1. Under a written agreement to that person; and
2. For a continuous period of at least 6 months.

Other words and phrases are defined. They are in quotation marks when used.

D. "Bodily Injury" means bodily harm, sickness or disease, including death that results.

E. "Business" includes trade, profession or occupation.

F. "Family Member" means a person related to you by blood, marriage or adoption who is a resident of your household. This includes a ward or foster child.

G. "Occupying" means in, upon, getting in, on, out or off.

H. "Property Damage" means physical injury to, destruction of or loss of use of tangible property.

I. "Trailer" means a vehicle designed to be pulled by a:

1. Private passenger auto; or
2. Pickup or van.

It also means a farm wagon or farm implement while towed by a vehicle listed in **1.** or **2.** above.

J. "Your covered auto" means:

1. Any vehicle shown in the Declaration.
2. Any of the following types of vehicles on the date you become the owner:

   a. a private passenger auto; or

b. A pickup or van that:

(1) Has a Gross Vehicle Weight of less than 10,000 lbs.; and

(2) Is not used for the delivery or transportation of goods and materials unless such use is:

(a) Incidental to your "business" of installing, maintaining or repairing furnishings or equipment; or

(b) For farming or ranching.

This provision (**J.2.**) applies only if:

a. You acquire the vehicle during the policy period;

b. You ask us to insure it within 30 days after you become the owner; and

c. With respect to a pickup or van, no other insurance policy provides coverage for that vehicle.

If the vehicle you acquire replaces one shown in the Declarations, it will have the same coverage as the vehicle it replaced. You must ask us to insure a replacement vehicle within 30 days only if you wish to add or continue Coverage for Damage to Your Auto.

If the Vehicle you acquire is in addition to any shown in the Declarations, it will have the broadest coverage we now provide for any vehicle shown in the Declarations.

3. Any "trailer" you own.
4. Any auto or "trailer" you do not own while used as a temporary substitute for any other vehicle described in this definition which is out of normal use because of its:

a. Breakdown;   d. Loss; or

b. Repair;   e. Destruction.

c. Servicing;

This provision (**J.4.**) does not apply to Coverage for Damage to Your Auto.

Notice that this is a limitation for "your covered auto" only. However, liability coverage for "you or any family member" is not limited by vehicle size or type. An insured who borrows or rents a moving van or dump truck is provided liability protection.

For a replacement auto (covered for liability only), no "deadline" is specified for reporting the change of autos to the insurer. The replacement auto is covered for liability through expiration of the policy term. The producer should encourage the insured to report a change of auto "promptly." The insured must request the continuation of physical damage coverage within thirty days.

Any temporary substitute vehicle assumes coverage in place of the vehicle that is not operating. This might be a rental or a loan from a neighbor.

Occupying a vehicle does *not* include pushing a stalled auto. However, it might include sitting on the roof or working under the hood, or, as in one case, entering a convertible through the roof.

PART A - LIABILITY COVERAGE

"Damages" that are paid by this policy are not restricted; therefore, punitive damages and non-economic damages (pain and suffering, mental anguish, and loss of consortium) might be compensated by this policy.

The insured is covered for any "accident." However, the word accident is not defined in the contract. This can become another point of legal debate.

The insurance company retains the right to defend and settle "as we consider appropriate." Insurers sometimes settle with the third-party claimants in a way that does not meet the insured's approval.

Notice that "you or any family member" are covered for a blanket of coverage related to "any" auto or trailer. Liability coverage is provided for rented autos and borrowed vehicles (and moving vans).

Anyone who borrows a "covered auto" (with the insured's permission) is also covered by this policy.

Liability coverage is extended to others who might be held responsible for the insured's actions, like an employer if the insured runs an errand on the job.

INSURING AGREEMENT

A. We will pay damages for "bodily injury" or "property damage" for which any "insured" becomes legally responsible because of an auto accident. Damages include prejudgement interest awarded against the "insured." We will settle or defend, as we consider appropriate, any claim or suit asking for these damages. In addition to our limit of liability, we will pay all defense costs we incur. Our duty to settle or defend ends when our limit of liability for this coverage has been exhausted. We have no duty to defend any suit or settle any claim for "bodily injury" or "property damage" not covered under this policy.

B. "Insured" as used in this Part means:

1. You or any "family member" for the ownership, maintenance or use of any auto or "trailer."

2. Any person using "your covered auto."

3. For "your covered auto," any person or organization but only with respect to legal responsibility for acts or omissions of a person for whom coverage is afforded under this Part.

4. For any auto or "trailer," other than "your covered auto," any other person or organization but only with respect to legal responsibility for acts or omissions of you or any "family member" for whom coverage is afforded under this Part. This provision (**B.4.**) applies only if the person or organization does not own or hire the auto or "trailer."

SUPPLEMENTARY PAYMENTS

In addition to our limit of liability, we will pay on behalf of an "insured":

1. Up to $250 for the cost of bail bonds required because of an accident, including related traffic law violations. The accident must result in "bodily injury" or "property damage" covered under this policy.

2. Premiums on appeal bonds and bonds to release attachments in any suit we defend.

3. Interest accruing after a judgment is entered in any suit we defend. Our duty to pay interest ends when we offer to pay that part of the judgment which does not exceed our limit of liability for this coverage.

4. Up to $50 a day for loss of earnings, but not other income, because of attendance at hearings or trials at our request.

5. Other reasonable expenses incurred at our request.

EXCLUSIONS

A. We do not provide Liability Coverage for any "insured":

1. Who intentionally causes "bodily injury" or "property damage."

2. For "property damage" to property owned or being transported by that "insured."

3. For "property damage" to property:

   a. rented to;

   b. used by; or

   c. in the care of;

   that "insured."

   This exclusion (**A.3.**) does not apply to "property damage" to a residence or private garage.

4. For "bodily injury" to an employee of that "insured" during the course of employment. This exclusion (**A.4.**) does not apply to "bodily injury" to a domestic employee unless workers' compensation benefits are required or available for that domestic employee.

5. For the "insured's" liability arising out of the ownership or operation of a vehicle while it is being used as a public or livery conveyance. This exclusion (**A.5.**) does not apply to a share-the-expense car pool.

6. While employed or otherwise engaged in the "business" of:

   a. Selling;   d. Storing; or

   b. Repairing;   e. Parking;

   c. Servicing;

   vehicles designed for use mainly on public highways. This includes road testing and delivery. This exclusion (**A.6.**) does not apply to the ownership, maintenance or use of "your covered auto" by:

   a You;

   b. Any "family member;" or

   c. Any partner, agent or employee of you or any "family member."

Note that the policy does not cover property owned or transported by the insured. Items stolen from the insured's vehicle are usually covered under a homeowners policy.

The liability section of the policy does not provide coverage to other property in the insured's care. One exception is made if the insured collides with a house or garage that he or she rents. This protects the innocent third-party landlord.

Coverage *is* provided for injury to domestic employees as long as they are not eligible for workers compensation benefits.

Be aware of vehicles used for livery (such as an insured who provides sight-seeing tours or transportation for a fee) that fall within this exclusion. Coverage could be denied if an accident occurs during such service.

An "insured" is not covered for liability while using a vehicle without reasonable belief that the "insured" has permission. This is true whether the insured's vehicle is stolen or an insured steals someone else's vehicle and drives it. The term "reasonable belief" becomes debatable. Belief can be established in ways other than explicit permission, such as:

- Permissive use
- Implied permission

Coverage is excluded for the insured's use of a motorcycle or off-road vehicle. For example, an insured would not be covered by this policy if he borrows his neighbor's motorcycle. Such vehicles can be added to the policy through a miscellaneous vehicles endorsement.

7. Maintaining or using any vehicle while that "insured" is employed or otherwise engaged in any "business" (other than farming or ranching) not described in exclusion **A.6.** This exclusion (**A.7.**) does not apply to the maintenance or use of a:

   a. Private passenger auto;

   b. Pickup or van that:

      (1) You own; or

      (2) You do not own while used as a temporary substitute for "your covered auto" which is out of normal use because of its:

         (a) Break-down;
         (b) Repair;
         (c) Servicing;
         (d) Loss; or
         (e) Destruction; or

   c. "Trailer" used with a vehicle described in **a.** or **b.** above.

8. Using a vehicle without a reasonable belief that "insured" is entitled to do so.

9. For "bodily injury" or "property damage" for which the "insured":

   a. Is an insured under a nuclear energy liability policy; or

   b. Would be an insured under a nuclear energy liability policy but for its termination upon exhaustion of its limit of liability.

   A nuclear energy liability policy is a policy issued by any of the following or their successors:

   a. American Nuclear Insurers;

   b. Mutual Atomic Energy Liability Underwriters; or

   c. Nuclear Insurance Association of Canada.

B. We do not provide Liability Coverage for the ownership, maintenance or use of:

1. Any vehicle which:

   a. Has fewer than four wheels; or

   b. Is designed mainly for use off public roads.

   This exclusion (**B.1**) does not apply:

   a. While such vehicle is being used by an "insured" in a medical emergency; or

   b. To any "trailer."

2. Any vehicle, other than "your covered auto," which is:

   a. Owned by you; or

   b. Furnished or available for your regular use.

3. Any vehicle, other than "your covered auto" which is:

   a. Owned by any "family member"; or

   b. Furnished or available for the regular use of any "family member."

   However, this exclusion (**B.3.**) does not apply to you while you are maintaining or "occupying" any vehicle which is:

   a. Owned by a "family member;" or

   b. Furnished or available for the regular use of a "family member".

4. Any vehicle, located inside a facility designed for racing, for the purpose of:

   a. Competing in; or

   b. Practicing or preparing for; any prearranged or organized racing or speed contest.

The policy does not cover vehicles that are owned or regularly available for use by the insured or a family member unless they are added to the policy as insured vehicles. This encourages the insured to declare owned vehicles and prevents the insurer from extending coverage to other vehicles when only one is shown (and one premium is paid) under the policy.

Racing is excluded for liability under this policy. An insured (or family member) who uses the family car at the Saturday night drag strip is not covered by the PAP.

LIMIT OF LIABILITY

A. The limit of liability shown in the Declarations for this coverage is our maximum limit of liability for all damages resulting from any one auto accident. This is the most we will pay regardless of the number of:

1. "Insureds";

2. Claims made;

3. Vehicles or premiums shown in the Declarations; or

4. Vehicles involved in the auto accident.

B. We will apply the limit of liability to provide any separate limits required by law for bodily injury and property damage liability. However, this provision (**B.**) will not change our total limit of liability.

C. No one will be entitled to receive duplicate payments for the same elements of loss under this coverage and:

1. Part B or Part C of this policy; or

2. Any Underinsured Motorist Coverages provided by this policy.

An insured who is driving in another state automatically has limits of liability equal to that state's minimum requirements (if the limits on the insured's policy are lower than that minimum).

An insured who is driving in another state that requires compulsory insurance automatically has that coverage under this policy, whether such coverage was purchased or appears on the policy's declaration page.

OUT OF STATE COVERAGE
If an auto accident to which this policy applies occurs in any state or province other than the one in which "your covered auto" is principally garaged, we will interpret your policy for that accident as follows:

A. If the state or province has:

1. A financial responsibility or similar law specifying limits of liability for "bodily injury" or "property damage" higher than the limit shown in the Declarations, your policy will provide the higher specified limit.

2. A compulsory insurance or similar law requiring a nonresident to maintain insurance whenever the nonresident uses a vehicle in that state or province, your policy will provide at least the required minimum amounts and types of coverage.

B. No one will be entitled to duplicate payments for the same elements of loss.

FINANCIAL RESPONSIBILITY
When this policy is certified as future proof of financial responsibility, this policy shall comply with the law to the extent required.

OTHER INSURANCE
If there is other applicable liability insurance we will pay only our share of the loss. Our share is the proportion that our limit of liability bears to the total of all applicable limits. However, any insurance we provide for a vehicle you do not own shall be excess over any other collectible insurance.

This policy will comply with legal requirements of a state such as minimum liability limits requirements (even if the declarations page reflects a limit lower than the state minimum).

This section explains how coverage will apply if the insured is driving a borrowed or rented auto. The policy on which that auto is written is the "primary" policy. The insured is covered for the use of "any" auto (not otherwise excluded); however, this coverage will be "excess" over that primary policy.

PP 00 01 06 94 — Copyright, Insurance Services Office, Inc., 1994 — Page 4 of 11

Educational Objective 2
Identify and evaluate driver and vehicle use-related exposures that affect the frequency and severity of auto losses.

Driver and Vehicle Use Exposures

Exposures that affect the frequency or severity of auto losses are often the same factors that are used in developing the classifications for auto rating. Classifications used by insurance companies are based on the losses experienced by groups of drivers. By understanding the types and purposes of classification, insurance specialists can help customers understand how classifications are created and how the classifications relate to loss frequency and severity.

Classifying Risks

To begin the process of projecting the loss experience for a class of drivers, an insurer must first determine what constitutes a class. What factor or combination of factors will identify a distinct class so that an insurer can develop an equitable rate? Traditionally, insurers have used several factors.

- Regarding the driver:
  - Age
  - Gender
  - Marital status
  - Driving record
- Regarding vehicle use:
  - Area of operation
  - Miles driven
  - Use classifications

One of the major issues confronting the automobile insurance industry today is the equity of the classifications used. Some states restrict the use of certain traditional factors. For example, Montana does not allow the use of some traffic violations in rating. That state also removes certain types of violations from motor vehicle records if drivers attend a class on traffic safety at a state-sponsored "traffic school." Such practices introduce conflicting ideas regarding the classification process, including the following:

- The only factor that should be considered in determining an individual's rate is the individual's driving record.

- Insurance requires insureds within a class to contribute relatively small amounts of premium. Therefore, every possible relevant fact should be considered for each individual. If, in fact, violations and future accidents correlate, then violations should be considered in this classification. In addition, if insurers are prohibited from underwriting and/or terminating questionable risks (because the motor vehicle record is incomplete), then the insurers' other policyholders could eventually subsidize losses that the company could have avoided.

Evaluating Drivers' Exposures

Drivers constitute the major risk in automobile insurance. The degree of risk is a function of a driver's skill and ability. Assume for a moment that you are an underwriter. Knowing the perils associated with automobile driving and the loss probability within various classes, you analyze the hazards presented by an individual submission and decide to accept the risk, reject the risk, modify the risk, or recommend a reduction of hazards. Within an insurance company's classification and rating structure, and within the bounds of ethical and equitable business conduct, you are to decide where the risk fits, based on all of the operator's personal characteristics and driving ability as demonstrated by past records and habits. These are some of the decisions that must be made as part of the underwriting process.

Insurance and underwriting are based on the ability to discriminate fairly. Fair discrimination involves basing underwriting decisions about individuals on characteristics that determine expected losses. Those characteristics group individuals as part of the classification system used by insurance companies. Insurance specialists must be careful not to **discriminate unfairly**.

Although no one can accurately predict what any one person will do in the future, accurately projecting the ultimate loss potential of large groups of people is possible. The more precise the definitions of a class and the more accurate the statistical records for a class, the more accurate the projection will be.

Unfair discrimination involves applying different underwriting standards to risks that have the same basic characteristics and loss potential.

Age

Some of the dissatisfaction about automobile insurance concerns how insurers spread the cost of accidents over the insured population. Consumers and regulators are challenging many of the traditional rating factors. One of the most distressing aspects of automobile insurance, as far as youthful drivers are concerned, is the difficulty in obtaining adequate coverage and the cost of that coverage when it can be obtained. Because youthful drivers have a greater proportion of accidents than do older drivers, premium rates are considerably higher for youthful drivers than for older drivers. Therefore, most automobile rating systems include age as a **primary rating factor**.

Exhibit 6-2 shows why an insurance company uses age as a factor for projecting future accidents. The exhibit reveals the following:

Many auto rating systems use **primary rating factors** to differentiate the premium by the major classifications of driver and use characteristics. Secondary rating factors refine the premium for selected driver and vehicle use characteristics.

- Drivers under the age of 20 represent only 5.1 percent of all drivers, yet they account for 13.0 percent of all accidents and 11.6 percent of all fatal accidents.

- Extending the numbers to include drivers under the age of 25 increases the total to 14.7 percent of all drivers accounting for 28.0 percent of all accidents and 26.2 percent of all fatal accidents.

Exhibit 6-2
Accidents by Age of Driver, 1994

Age Group	Number of Drivers	% of Total	Drivers in Fatal Accidents	% of Total	Drivers in All Accidents	% of Total
Under 20	8,881,000	5.1	6,100	11.6	2,600,000	13.0
20-24	16,727,000	9.6	7,700	14.6	2,970,000	15.0
25-34	39,684,000	22.7	12,900	24.4	5,130,000	25.5
35-44	38,738,000	22.1	9,900	18.8	4,000,000	20.0
45-54	27,549,000	15.7	6,400	12.1	2,400,000	12.0
55-64	19,140,000	10.9	3,900	7.4	1,340,000	6.7
65-74	16,794,000	9.6	3,100	5.8	970,000	4.9
Over 74	7,616,000	4.3	2,800	5.3	590,000	2.9
Totals	**175,129,000**	**100.0**	**52,800**	**100.0**	**20,000,000**	**100.0**

Source: Used by permission of the National Safety Council, Itasca, Illinois.

Young drivers are involved in motor vehicle crashes at rates that far exceed those of older drivers. Per mile, teenagers are involved in 3.8 times more crashes than older drivers. Per licensed driver, teenagers are involved in 2.2 times more fatal crashes than older licensed drivers.[1]

Countermeasures for dealing with the age and/or experience factors include the following:

- Delaying the age at which young people are licensed to drive
- Limiting youthful driving in hazardous situations
- Encouraging or requiring extended driving practice before licensing

Currently, most countries do not grant drivers' licenses to anyone younger than 17 or 18. Within the United States, licensing regulations vary widely. In several states, teenagers are allowed to hold special restricted licenses at age 14 or 15. A few states allow regular licenses at age 15. In the majority of states, 16 is the minimum licensing age. Only one state, New Jersey, delays licensing until age 17. Delaying licensing until age 17 has been shown to reduce the number of accidents in which teenagers are involved.[2]

Exhibit 6-3 displays the distribution of automobile accidents involving teenagers by time of day. The majority of accidents occur between 9 P.M. and 3 A.M. One way of limiting driving in hazardous situations is a night driving curfew for teenagers. Young drivers, typically 16 and sometimes 17 years of age, are allowed unrestricted daylight and evening driving yet are not allowed to drive during the more hazardous night and late-night time periods. Curfews, whether established statewide or by local ordinance, reduce the frequency of teenage crash injuries.[3] Curfews do not result in the same kind of restriction for young drivers that delaying licensing would, thus making curfews less difficult to implement.

Exhibit 6-3
Distribution of Teenage Motor Vehicle Deaths by Time of Day

Midnight - 3 A.M.	18%
3 A.M. - 6 A.M.	8%
6 A.M. - 9 A.M.	8%
9 A.M. - Noon	6%
Noon - 3 P.M.	10%
3 P.M. - 6 P.M.	16%
6 P.M. - 9 P.M.	15%
9 P.M. - Midnight	19%

Source: Based on analysis of data from the U.S. Department of Transportation's Fatal Accident Reporting System (as compiled by the Insurance Institute for Highway Safety).

Since the physical capabilities of youthful drivers are probably at or near their peak, why do young drivers have more accidents than older drivers? The reasons might include the following:

- Inexperience
- Immaturity

Inexperience

Every state requires some form of driver testing before granting a driver's license to a youthful driver. However, logic dictates that actually practicing an activity many times under varying circumstances gives a person the ability and confidence to react appropriately in different situations. Driver training courses provide some practice, but not as much as can be gained from extended vehicle operation. Experience provides more realistic lessons.

Immaturity

Immaturity is often evidenced by an attitude of supreme self-confidence, perhaps even to the extent of a feeling of invulnerability. Nearly three-quarters of all deaths among school-age youth and young adults are caused by the following:

- Motor vehicle crashes (30 percent)
- Homicide (19 percent)
- Other unintentional injuries (12 percent)
- Suicide (11 percent)

Those results, taken from the 1993 Youth Risk Behavior Surveillance Survey,[4] suggest that many high school students participate in behavior that can increase the likelihood of their deaths. Of the youths surveyed, 19 percent rarely used safety belts when riding in cars or trucks driven by others. During the month preceding the survey, over 35 percent had ridden in a car with a driver who had been drinking alcohol. Maturity is a question not just of age but also of judgment, and judgment usually improves with time and experience.

Most drivers eventually assume an attitude of defensive driving. A realization of fallibility as well as a healthy respect for the following facts contribute to this maturing process:

- That others are on the road
- That a car is limited in what it can be made to do
- That the road, weather, time of day, and physical and mental conditions of drivers all play a part in driving results

Although risky behavior is not the exclusive realm of youth, it does reside more often with youths than it does with older individuals. The producer and the underwriter should consider the following generalizations:

- Much teenage driving is done at night when accidents are more likely to occur.

- Youthful driving is often done in conjunction with social events.
- Youthful drivers are often subject to peer pressure to perform potentially dangerous acts.

Experience has shown that both educational achievement and work history are factors that a producer or underwriter can use to qualify an applicant as potentially one of the better risks, even within a risky class. Underwriters sometimes use the following questions to evaluate individual youthful operators:

- Does the operator do well in school and/or have a job?
- Does the discipline needed for studying and working carry over?

Age alone is not as indicative of future driving results as is the combination of all the driver's characteristics. One of the major conclusions of a recent California Department of Motor Vehicles Study[5] was that teen drivers have the highest accident-involvement and citation rates. As drivers age, their accident-involvement rates decrease through age 69 and then increase slightly. The study further stated that as drivers age, their citation rates decrease.

Good Student Discounts   The good student discount is given to youthful drivers who have good scholastic records. Such drivers are expected to have lower loss involvement than poor students because they are more responsible in general and perhaps spend more time on schoolwork and less time on the road than other youthful drivers.

A good student discount applies to full-time students, sixteen years of age or older, upon certification that the student, for the preceding semester (or comparable period), has met any one of the following qualifications:

- Ranked in the upper 20 percent of his or her class
- Had a B average or higher
- Had a cumulative grade point average of 3.0 or higher
- Was on the dean's list, honor roll, or similar list

Driver Training Discounts   Driver training credit is granted to youthful drivers who have completed an approved driver training course. The rating factor is reduced by five to thirty-five points, depending on the classification factor (the higher the basic factor, the greater the credit granted). Unfortunately, operators who have taken driver training courses do not have a significantly better loss history than those who have not taken the courses. However, encouraging the formal learning process might have a social benefit for insurers because they are encouraging a loss control measure.

The "Graying" Population

Much has been written about the driving record of persons under the age of twenty. However, with the **graying** of America, more attention is now being paid to the driving records of older Americans. Beginning at age fifty-five, some drivers experience a decline in driving skill.

The **graying** of the population refers to the overall aging of the population. The "baby boomers," who were born between 1946 and 1964, form a large percentage of the population. As this group ages, the average age of the population increases.

By age seventy-five, most drivers' skills drop off dramatically. Major problems develop regarding vision (especially at night), hearing, reaction time, and agility. Medication can also affect older drivers. However, the ability to drive and have a license means independence, so the elderly are often reluctant to give up their licenses.

Some have recommended that between the ages of seventy and eighty, drivers should be required to take a driver's test every two to four years. That requirement would allow competent senior citizens to continue to drive and would force the others to surrender their licenses.

Therefore, as part of the process of considering age, an underwriter must also focus on older drivers. According to the U.S. Department of Transportation, in 1993, an estimated 24,522,000 drivers were age sixty-five and older. At the same time, an estimated 25,764,000 drivers were under the age of twenty-five. The unbalanced U-shape of Exhibit 6-4 shows that youthful drivers have a higher number of accidents and fatalities than older drivers do.

Exhibit 6-4
Passenger Vehicle Drivers' Ages in All Reported Crashes and Fatal Crashes, 1990

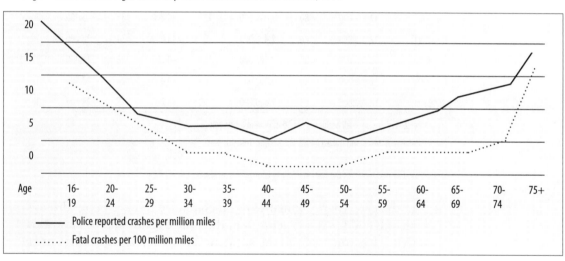

Source: Based on analysis of data from the U.S. Department of Transportation's Fatal Accident Reporting System (as compiled by the Insurance Institute for Highway Safety).

Contrary to the data in Exhibit 6-4, many insurance companies view elderly drivers as customers with an established good driving record with the company and therefore deserving of extra consideration. That viewpoint tempers underwriting judgment about the timing and severity of any underwriting action recommended or taken.

Underwriting is an ongoing process, not a one-time event. The producer is the front-line screener with the responsibility to keep up-to-date on the client. The underwriter not only has the initial responsibility for reviewing the application but also has the responsibility for monitoring the risk and making adjustments as circumstances change. The driving abilities and records of older drivers should be monitored.

Gender

According to the 1993 estimate of the National Safety Council (NSC), men drive 65 percent of the total miles driven each year. They represent about 51 percent of the estimated 175.9 million licensed drivers. Those numbers have held true for many years. Exhibit 6-5 indicates that the rate of accident involvement in all accidents is slightly higher for women but that the rate of involvement in fatal accidents is greater for men. The NSC indicates that at least part of the difference in accident rate might occur because of the time, place, and circumstances of the actual driving. Young male drivers drive more miles in the evening and on the weekends, when the accident rate is higher.

Exhibit 6-5
Gender of Drivers Involved in Accidents 1989-1994

| | Drivers in All Accidents | | | | Drivers in Fatal Accidents | | | |
| | Male | | Female | | Male | | Female | |
Year	Number	Rate*	Number	Rate*	Number	Rate**	Number	Rate**
1989	14,100,000	95	8,700,000	143	47,000	32	14,800	24
1990	12,170,000	80	7,630,000	121	46,800	31	15,400	24
1991	12,070,000	86	7,430,000	97	43,600	31	14,200	19
1992	12,700,000	88	8,100,000	103	40,200	28	13,000	17
1993	12,900,000	87	8,200,000	101	40,400	27	13,500	17
1994	12,400,000	82	7,600,000	90	38,200	25	14,600	17

* Percent of drivers in all accidents per 10 million miles driven

** Percent of drivers in fatal accidents per 1 billion miles driven

Source: Used by permission of the National Safety Council, Itasca, Illinois.

In the past, young, unmarried women tended to have better driving records and fewer accidents than their male counterparts. However, that is less true today as the accident differential is narrowing. Today, young women are driving more than their predecessors and, consequently, are involved in more accidents.

Marital Status

Marital status, which is a factor used in both underwriting and rating, relates directly to stability. From the underwriter's point of view, the effect is strongest at younger ages because marriage tends to raise maturity. Also, young married couples normally spend more time at home than their unmarried contemporaries do. A producer could consider young married couples as the core of a developing book of business, particularly if the producer sells other lines of insurance in addition to auto. The more the couple has to protect, the more mature their actions tend to become.

Driving Record

Driving experience is a crucial component of the insurance specialist's review of a driver. Driving experience is a likely indicator of a driver's future actions and the chance of loss. Most automobile insurers use the *safe-driver rating plan* or a variation thereof, which assumes that a driving record is a valid indicator of the individual's future experience. The experience period comprises the three years immediately preceding the date of the application for the insurance or the inception of the renewal policy. Under the safe-driver rating plan, points are assigned for traffic violations and certain accidents.

Traffic Violations

Most insurers classify violations as major or minor and assign points in relation to the type of violation. The points relate to the rating plans used for calculating premiums. The relative "underwriting weight" that insurers place on each type of driving violation varies by company. The underwriter determines the acceptability of a risk and the appropriate auto **market tier** or plan. The underwriters review traffic violations for the following:

- *Minor violations.* Underwriters generally disregard "nonmoving" violations, such as parking tickets, when reviewing an auto risk. Some moving violations, such as "failure to dim lights," are considered to be of less consequence than others. Even "speeding less than 10 miles per hour over the speed limit" is weighted relatively lightly. "Careless driving" has varying meanings according to the state issuing the violation.

- *Major violations.* Some violations assume felony status and cannot be ignored in an underwriting review. Leaving the scene of a hit-and-run accident and DUI with bodily injury are major violations that often move an auto risk into a high-risk or residual market category.

- *Multiple violations.* Even minor violations assume new meaning when several of them appear within a period of a few years. If a driver is operating a vehicle in a way that frequently attracts the attention of law enforcement officers, it might be just a matter of time before a significant loss results.

- *Date of last occurrence.* Premium surcharges charged by insurance companies can cause enough concern to policyholders that their driving performance improves. Whether an improvement is caused by premium surcharges, experience, or maturation, some drivers do make conscious decisions to drive more safely. An underwriter who observes a significant period of time since the date of the customer's last accident or violation usually considers that to be a factor in the evaluation process.

Accidents

The accuracy of reporting and the type of accidents reported vary significantly among states. Consequently, underwriting is also adapted by state to consider these differences. Chargeable **at-fault** accidents

---

Jargon Alert!

Market tier is a term that is used interchangeably with market plan or market level. It describes the grouping of insureds into preferred, standard, and nonstandard categories for marketing purposes.

FYI

In Fargo, North Dakota, running a stop sign costs drivers a $25 traffic fine *or* a pint of blood. This plan was initiated to help eliminate Fargo's blood shortage.

Jargon Alert!

The expression "at fault" is commonly used to describe an insured's responsibility for causing an auto accident. It is not always accurate. An insured might only have contributed to an accident. The state's rating plan requires the addition of a surcharge to the policy, so the accident is called "at fault" when the insured might be only partially responsible for the event. The opposite of at fault is "not at fault," which is sometimes called "nonchargeable."

must surpass a dollar limit in order to generate a surcharge. Losses that fall below this limit might not appear on a motor vehicle report.

Underwriters review the accidents appearing on a motor vehicle report by looking for the following:

- *Number of occurrences.* Not all accidents result in a surcharge. For example, accidents in which a driver is not at fault generally do not result in a surcharge. However, although not-at-fault accidents generally have no effect on premiums, they are often used as an underwriting selection or retention criterion. If an insured has an inordinate number of accidents, even if that driver is judged not at fault, an underwriter might cancel or nonrenew the policy. Such actions are justified on the basis that those drivers have poorer defensive driving habits than average or that their driving habits result in more accidents. Traffic accidents are relatively uncommon occurrences, and a person who has multiple **nonchargeable** accidents during a short time period might not fit the "normal" driver standard for the class.

- *Type of accident.* Just as traffic violations can be categorized as minor or major, accidents are also labeled minor or major. Backing into a mailbox is not as major as a head-on collision involving two vehicles. Motor vehicle reports do not usually reflect the scale of an accident, so reviewing the claim file or claim database is also required. Opinion regarding the weight to be given to the size of an accident varies. One school of underwriting thought stresses the importance of the resulting dollar loss as an indicator of the accident's severity. A second school of underwriting thought reasons that the size of an accident is largely a matter of chance. Proponents of that opinion believe that the difference between a $5,000 bodily injury loss and a $500,000 bodily injury loss is a matter of point of impact, number of occupants in the other car (and their ages), and the litigiousness of the injured parties.

- *Frequency of accidents.* Frequency of accidents attracts serious underwriting attention. Almost any accident can result in a large dollar loss (given the appropriate circumstances), so even an accumulation of minor losses is weighted heavily.

- *Accident in relationship to driver.* Accidents and violations can indicate a driver with declining reflexes. Accidents such as side-swiping, and traffic violations such as failing to yield, can indicate a vision problem. Such an occurrence becomes a strong indicator of a problem for older drivers. In one case, a driver over the age of seventy-five backed out of a garage with a back door of his auto open. The door was torn off the hinges, and repairs to the car were paid by the insured's collision coverage. When the driver repeated the same accident one month later, the fact that he had a vision or memory deficiency became apparent. The underwriter then had to determine whether coverage could be continued.

Alcohol

Alcohol-impaired driving is a major problem with repercussions not only for **drunk drivers** but also for pedestrians and other drivers.

Jargon Alert!

The term "drunk driving" is frequently used, but it is often inaccurate. This term implies actions taken by a driver who is visibly intoxicated. However, even small amounts of alcohol can impair driving ability.

The probability of having a car crash increases at any blood alcohol concentration (BAC) over zero, as the following demonstrate: [6]

- At a BAC as low as 0.02 percent, alcohol affects driving ability and crash likelihood.

- The probability of a crash begins to increase significantly at 0.05 percent BAC and climbs rapidly after about 0.08 percent.

- Although drivers with BACs at or above 0.10 percent represent only 12 percent of all drinking drivers on weekend nights, 86 percent of the fatally injured drivers who had been drinking had BACs in that range.

- For drivers with BACs above 0.15 percent on weekend nights, the likelihood of being killed in a single-vehicle crash is more than 380 times higher than it is for nondrinking drivers.[7]

Following are some statistics regarding alcohol involvement in auto accidents:

- Crashes involving male drivers are much more likely to be alcohol-related than crashes involving female drivers. Among fatally injured male drivers of passenger cars in 1993, 42 percent had a BAC of 0.10 percent or higher. The percent for women was 23. Alcohol-related crashes are highest for men aged twenty-one to thirty.

- Alcohol-related crashes peak at night and are higher on weekends than on weekdays. Exhibit 6-6 displays the distribution of alcohol-related accidents by time of day. Among passenger-vehicle drivers fatally injured between 9 P.M. and 6 A.M., 60 percent had BACs of 0.10 percent or more. During other hours, the percentage was 21.

- Forty-eight percent of all drivers fatally injured on weekends have BACs of 0.10 percent or more. During the rest of the week, the proportion was 28 percent.[8]

FYI

Alcohol can impair judgment in unusual ways. A traffic violation occurred in Jackson, Mississippi, in 1972. Police flagged down a car that was zigzagging through traffic, only to find out that the driver was blind. He was being directed by the passenger next to him—who was too drunk to drive.

Exhibit 6-6
Fatal Injuries Related to Intoxicated Drivers by Time of Day

Percentage of Fatally Injured Drivers with BACs of 0.10% or Greater by Time of Day	
	Percent
Midnight - 3 A.M.	69
3 A.M. - 6 A.M.	51
6 A.M. - 9 A.M.	10
9 A.M. - Noon	8
Noon - 3 P.M.	14
3 P.M. - 6 P.M.	22
6 P.M. - 9 P.M.	43
9 P.M. - Midnight	55

Source: Based on analysis of data from the U.S. Department of Transportation's Fatal Accident Reporting System (as compiled by the Insurance Institute for Highway Safety).

Other Drug-Related Factors

The role of alcohol as a major contributing factor in motor vehicle crashes is well established. Much less information is available about the contribution of other drugs. Many drugs, both legal and illegal, other than alcohol can impair driving ability, even in moderate amounts, and can increase crash risk. However, drug use among drivers is apparently limited, and insufficient scientific evidence is available about any drug (other than alcohol) to draw conclusions regarding the relationship of drugs to traffic accidents.

According to the National Highway Traffic Safety Administration's 1988 summary report to Congress, the drugs with "the most potential to be serious highway safety hazards" are tranquilizers, sedatives, and hypnotics (for example, barbiturates and marijuana).

Information on drug use by drivers comes primarily from tests on those hospitalized or killed. In most studies, drugs other than alcohol have been found in fewer than 2 percent (more often fewer than 5 percent) of fatally injured or hospitalized passenger car drivers.[9]

SR-22 Filings

In certain situations, owners or operators of motor vehicles are required to provide proof of financial responsibility to state authorities to retain their driving privileges. Most commonly, drivers must provide proof of insurance following an accident or a serious traffic conviction, or after a judgment is entered against them following an accident. In most states, the vehicle owner or operator is not required to file proof of future financial responsibility as long as proof of current insurance coverage is provided. Financial responsibility filings, typically referred to as **SR-22 filings**, are required for some insureds who must certify to the state that they have purchased and continue to maintain auto insurance as required by law. The situations for which an SR-22 filing is required differ by state but might include the following:

* Driving an uninsured vehicle
* Driving under the influence of alcohol or drugs (DUI)
* Having a license suspended because of an accumulation of traffic violations

Insurers file the SR-22 form with the state, certifying that the insured has purchased auto liability insurance with at least the state-mandated minimum limits. When an SR-22 is attached to a policy, the rules for cancellation are restricted and the insurer has additional reporting requirements. An insured is usually required to maintain the SR-22 filing for three years, although not necessarily with the same insurer. The insured can cancel the insurance with one company and replace it with another company's insurance, as long as the insured maintains uninterrupted coverage. The insurance company must notify the state if the company terminates coverage and must indicate the reason.

Many insurers are reluctant to make SR-22 filings. The purpose behind the filing is to provide an absolute guarantee of protection to innocent third-party victims in the future, and as such an insurer's ability to

Jargon Alert!

The term "SR-22" refers to the form number of the document that is required by the department of transportation from an insurance company to confirm that required coverage is in force.

deny claims is restricted. For instance, in some states an insured's failure to provide notice of an accident typically precludes insurance coverage under the auto policy but does not affect coverage under a policy certified by an insurer. Auto policies do provide insurers with recourse against insureds when an insurer pays a claim that it otherwise would not have paid. However, obtaining reimbursement from such a policyholder can be difficult. Also, an insurer is restricted when SR-22 filing is present. For example, some states do not allow a midterm cancellation for nonpayment of premium once an SR-22 has been filed. Therefore, the insurer must be paid in full at policy inception before issuing an SR-22.

Many insurers include a surcharge for processing an SR-22, both to recoup the added underwriting expenses and to compensate the company for the additional risk. Dollar surcharges or percentage surcharges are commonly applied. Proof of financial responsibility is usually required for up to three years, but insurers typically issue certificates every six or twelve months at policy renewal.

Occupation

Occupation is rarely overtly used in evaluating personal auto exposures, but it is sometimes a factor in making an underwriting decision on a particular submission. Occupation sometimes is considered when determining whether a business-use surcharge is appropriate. Self-employed artisans (carpenters, plumbers, electricians, and so forth) often use their vehicles for business to travel to and from job sites, as well as for personal use. Some companies make accommodations for those types of vehicles by rating them as personal autos with a surcharge to reflect the additional exposures. Other companies require such accounts to be submitted under their commercial auto programs.

Certain occupations, such as outside sales, indicate a high volume of miles driven, sometimes in congested or high-accident areas. Real-estate agents often use their personal vehicles to take clients from house to house when selling property, increasing the exposure to loss under their auto insurance policies.

That military employees live on base and college students live on campus could indicate communal living, which creates a tendency to lend a vehicle to friends and roommates. Note from the PART A— LIABILITY COVERAGE of the sample PAP policy (shown in Exhibit 6-1) that the definition of "insured" includes any person using a covered auto (with permission). Auto accidents can result that involve unknown operators who become "insureds" under the policy contract.

Evaluating Vehicle Use Exposures

Driver characteristics are important elements in the evaluation of an auto risk. How the vehicle is used is also an important consideration.

Area of Operation

Population density and density of vehicles on the road are the two most important determinants of loss results among rating territories.

As people and vehicles vie for limited space on the road, accidents are likely to occur. In addition to higher incidences of auto accidents, a higher population density also results in an increase in pedestrian accidents.

Rating territories are based on the losses or risk profiles for given areas. A territory can be a town, a large city, part of a city, a county, or some other geographical subdivision. Boundaries are drawn on the basis of such considerations as population density, traffic conditions, and other factors that affect losses. The premium charged to an individual car owner for collision or liability coverage is directly affected by the number and cost of accidents caused by all drivers who live in the territory. No matter how careful the individual driver might be, if the driver lives in a densely populated area containing many drivers, many accidents, many thefts and much vandalism, and/or poor police enforcement of traffic laws, the driver is statistically more likely to suffer a loss than a driver who lives in a territory with a lower rate of loss. Rates for a territory are also affected by the territory's road conditions and local prices for such things as auto repairs and medical and hospital services.

In addition to population and vehicle density, differences in losses among territories are influenced by the following factors:

- Climate
- Wage rates
- Competition for repairs
- Availability and quality of medical care
- Crime rates

Obviously, no underwriter or producer can know everything about a given risk. However, the amount of miles driven annually (and to some extent weekly) as well as where those miles are mainly driven are factors that can be determined.

For insureds who drive in urban areas, the questions to be asked include the following:

- What is the extent of traffic congestion?
- Have the roads been improved for traffic flow, or is the infrastructure from the 1950s still used?
- Do risks increase during commuting hours (heavy congestion at 7-9 A.M. and 4-6 P.M.)?
- Will the driver be rushing between appointments?
- Will others be riding with the driver?
- What kind of samples or contents will be in the vehicle?

Rural driving usually involves less traffic congestion than city driving, but most rural driving is done at higher speed, so the loss severity and perhaps the chance of loss are greater. Lighting is often poorer in less traveled areas; road signs and traffic control might not be as good as in more populated areas. Rural areas also have exposures from deer (and other animals) crossing the road.

Miles Driven

The type of driving and total mileage driven are important factors in measuring the location risk in private passenger auto insurance. Commuting distances are used in many automobile rating plans to surcharge high-mileage drivers. Critics contend that mileage is difficult to verify because most insurers depend on applicants to self-report mileage, and self-reported mileage is often understated.

When and where miles are driven might be more important than the actual number of miles driven. For instance, an insured who reports a ten-mile, one-way daily drive to work could be driving ten miles of interstate, ten miles of winding country lanes, or ten miles of congested city streets. Additionally, those ten miles might be driven during the peak of rush hour, or the insured might be working the night shift at a convenience store and driving odd hours during periods of little traffic volume.

Insureds often underestimate mileage, but computer technology now exists that allows underwriters to measure driving distances with a high degree of accuracy by comparing home addresses and work addresses. Small insurers unable to establish their own internal information systems of this scope can access such information through statistical services organizations or through other information-retrieval services.

Crossing State Lines

Another factor affecting differences in loss costs among territories is the proximity to another state's borders or travel between states. The PAP contains an "OUT OF STATE COVERAGE" provision that automatically offers the broader of the purchased coverage or the required coverage when an insured travels to another state. For example, the minimum personal injury protection (PIP) limits in Utah are $3,000, and in neighboring Colorado, the minimum limit is $50,000 for medical expenses. Thus, a Utah driver who has purchased $3,000 PIP in Utah enjoys higher limits while driving in Colorado without paying a correspondingly higher premium. An insured who lives in Virginia (a **tort state**) but who works in Maryland (a **no-fault state**), automatically receives PIP coverage every time he or she drives across the state border.

That increased coverage often occurs without the insured's knowledge of the advantage gained during the border crossing. However, some insureds understand the system very well. An applicant who lives in a state with a high mandatory PIP requirement can travel to another state, assume a grandmother's address in that state, and purchase an auto policy. As soon as the new policyholder returns home, his or her coverage automatically increases to include the PIP coverage at no charge. Insurance producers guard against such action by using (1) point-of-sale underwriting to require proof of a residential address or (2) follow-up correspondence and phone calls to the address provided by the applicant.

A **tort state** provides for compensation to a victim of an auto accident through legal remedies.

A **no-fault state** offers policyholders the right to recover financial losses from his or her own insurance, regardless of whose fault caused the accident. This recovery is offered in the form of PIP coverage.

Use Classifications

The vehicle use classifications for personal automobile insurance have standard descriptions. Each category presents underwriting concerns as shown in Exhibit 6-7.

Exhibit 6-7
Underwriting Concerns by Vehicle Use Class

Use Class	Description of the Class	Underwriting Concerns
Pleasure use	The automobile is not used in business and is not customarily driven to work or school more than 3 miles each way. Cars used for car pools and driven less than 15 miles each way are classified as pleasure use, provided they are not used more than 2 days per week in each 5-week period.	This class has a lower rate than commuting classes, so some commuting use is not declared at the time of application. When several adults and several autos are in the household, the chances are fair that some commuting is occurring. Insurance companies frequently perform "telephone checks" and send follow-up questionnaires to try to assure that the appropriate premium is being charged for the exposure.
Drive to work less than 10 miles	The auto is not used in business but is driven to work or school more than 3 miles and less than 10 miles each way.	Some companies use 15 miles as the standard limit for this classification. It might be equally important to consider the type of miles being driven. Driving 10 urban miles is considerably different from driving 10 country miles.
Drive to work more than 10 miles	The car is not used in business but is driven to work or school more than 10 miles each way.	If a person is commuting more than 10 miles to work, the next question is, "How many miles?" During periods of economic downturn, jobs with a considerable commute might be acceptable to a family breadwinner. An hour-long commute to work is not unusual in some parts of the country.
Business use	The car is customarily used in business.	Additional questions should be asked if a vehicle is used in business: • What type of business? • Are customers transported (as in real estate sales)? • Are goods or materials transported? What type? Are there any associated hazards?

Use Class	Description of the Class	Underwriting Concerns
Farm use	The car is principally garaged on a farm or ranch and is not used in any other business and is not driven to school or any other work.	Because the farming class is the lowest rated classification (generally discounted 15 percent from the standard rates), some vehicles appear in this classification that might be questioned. An expensive luxury vehicle (or several) appearing with a farm class might require more questions regarding the farm's nature.

Educational Objective 3

Describe the information needed to make an underwriting decision on a personal auto application and explain how that information is obtained.

The Underwriting Process

The trend in personal lines insurance is toward less scrutiny for individual auto applications by underwriters. The increasing use of automated decision-support systems, sophisticated risk analysis tools, and complex pricing plans has lessened the reliance on the traditional underwriter's individual screening in many companies. However, producers continue to do much underwriting, and a line underwriting function at the company level still exists as well. Submissions must be examined to detect mistakes in the application or to check for completeness. Also, individual submissions might have risk features that were not taken into consideration in the rates charged and that require underwriting attention. Additionally, the underwriter is still required to make modifications to the basic coverage to allow for unusual situations. Each individual submission still requires a great deal of underwriting, but the time available for account review has decreased. Underwriters have less time to devote to each individual submission and must develop decision-making processes that make the best use of time and resources.

Gathering Information

Judgment is always required to determine the quantity of information needed to underwrite an auto policy. All possible reports could be ordered on all applications. However, the cost becomes prohibitive, and all of this information is not always necessary. The application provides clues about the risk, but the information presented might paint an incomplete picture. Additional reports and information should be ordered only to obtain critical information needed for the underwriting decision.

The Application

The application is the starting point in reviewing a risk. Applications vary by company; most companies ask standard questions when insuring a new auto risk. Each piece of information requires review and a logical comparison with other pieces of information. Exhibit 6-8 is a sample application with annotations regarding underwriting judgment as it applies to the information provided.

Other Sources of Information

The application is a foundation for underwriting, but some information must be verified (such as violation and accident records). Gaps in information might appear, and some responses on the application might indicate the need for additional information. Exhibit 6-9 provides examples of responses on an auto application that would require additional research.

After a gap in the information has been identified, the best source with which to fill the gaps must be selected. After the additional information is obtained, it must then be interpreted. Other sources of information follow.

Producer/Applicant Interviews

The primary source of information about the application is the person applying for coverage. The primary source of information about the applicant is the producer. The quality of information depends not only on the application but also on the person who assists the applicant in completing the application. The application itself provides a permanent record of what the applicant said when applying for insurance but does not indicate how the questions were asked. What was the applicant's demeanor? That information can come only from the producer, who is using front-line underwriting skills. Assume that you are the producer developing information about a customer's loss history. You would need to ask a question like, "When was your last accident?" in order to receive an accurate reaction and response. Asking "You haven't had any accidents lately, have you?" could easily prompt a less accurate reaction and response from the client. The information on an application directly reflects the applicant's reliability and integrity, as well as the producer's skill in asking questions. However, even if the producer asks all the proper questions in an unambiguous way, the information could be inaccurate or incomplete. A husband, wife, or parent might not know all the information about a family member's violation record and might innocently give incorrect information. Dishonesty and fraud are also possibilities.

Records and Reports

The sources of underwriting information that are available are relatively limited. The following sections discuss the reports that are widely accessed.

Motor Vehicle Reports (MVRs)   In every line of insurance, the application contains vital information about the applicant. However, in automobile insurance, the application often tells only part of the story and is almost always supplemented and verified by a motor vehicle report, not only on the named insured, but also on all drivers in the household. The MVR is the state's official record and usually contains traffic violation and accident information.

Exhibit 6-10 is a sample MVR, although the actual appearance varies by the computer system used to retrieve the information and by the state of record. Those records usually provide information for the past three years.

State highway departments use various standards to determine which accidents appear on the MVRs:

- Some states include all accidents reported.
- Some states include only accidents reported by the police.
- Some states eliminate reported accidents that fall below a dollar threshold; that involve no injury; or that occur out of state, on Indian reservations, on military bases, or on private property.
- Some states show the accident only if a ticket was issued at the scene.
- Some courts allow the wrongdoer to undergo court supervision or attend driver improvement school, thus keeping the accident off the official record.

Database Subscriptions   One of the most important questions on an auto policy application concerns prior losses. However, MVRs might not be the best way for an insurer to discover information about the applicant's loss history because of the inconsistency of information by state. Some applicants know this. If the applicant chooses to omit information on an application about his or her driving record, an accident could go undetected by the insurer.

Because prior losses are an excellent indicator of future losses, the underwriter must know an applicant's loss history. In fact, involvement in an at-fault accident increases that person's chances of having another at-fault accident within twelve months by 250 percent.

Several vendors have database systems that allow insurance companies to share prior claim information. Those databases include accident history for various time periods and are constructed from information provided by the subscribing companies. Databases provide on-line availability of claim information such as the following:

- The vehicle's driver
- The amount of the claim paid
- Whether a notation of fault is available

Exhibit 6-8
Sample PAP Application

ACORD PERSONAL AUTOMOBILE APPLICATION

Address: Both mailing and residence addresses should be provided. If the insured lives in an area that is within commuting distance to an urban area, location of the commuting area might be an important question.

Garage Address: If the vehicle is garaged at another location, the circumstances and reason should be questioned. If an insured resides at another location, is it in another state that might have mandatory coverages and limits that would be automatically covered by this policy?

Previous Address: Previous address is helpful for investigative purposes. The number and location of moves indicate stability.

Commuting/Use: Some companies ask the employer's name and location to verify distances. If business use is indicated, questions regarding the type of business, distance traveled, and passengers carried might be necessary. If the vehicle is listed as farm use, questions might be necessary to verify the vehicle's qualification for that class.

Name: If more than one name appears, do the individuals jointly own all of the autos indicated? If not, what are the circumstances?

Odometer readings and annual mileage indicate the number of road miles a car is driven. Between 12,000/15,000 is a reasonable average annual mileage.

PRODUCER

CODE: SUBCODE:

AGENCY CUSTOMER ID

APPLICANT'S NAME AND MAILING ADDRESS (Include county & ZIP)

TELEPHONE NUMBER

DATE (MM/DD/YY)

CO/PLAN   POL#:   ACCT#:

EFFECTIVE DATE   EXPIRATION DATE   DIRECT BILL   PAYMENT PLAN

NEW   RNWL   AGENCY BILL

RESIDENCE   CURRENT RESIDENCE IS   OWNED   RENTED

GARAGE LOCATION IF DIFF. FROM ABOVE (Inc. county & ZIP)   VEH #

YRS AT ADDR   CURR   PREV   PREVIOUS ADDRESS (If less than 3 years)

VEHICLE DESCRIPTION/USE   TOTAL NUMBER OF VEHICLES IN HOUSEHOLD:

VEH	YEAR	MAKE, MODEL AND BODY TYPE	VIN/REGISTERED STATE	HP/CC	DATE PURCH	NEW/ USED
1						
2						
3						
4						

VEH	COST NEW	SYMBOL AGE GRP	TERR	MILE 1 WAY WK/SCHL	#DAYS WEEK	USAGE	PERFORM	MULTI- CAR	CAR POOL	GAR- AGED	ODOMETER READING	ANNUAL MILEAGE	GOVERN DRIVER
1													
2													
3													
4													

VEH	PASSIVE SEAT BELT	AIRBAG DRV/BOTH	ANTI-LOCK BRAKES 2/4	ANTI-THEFT DEVICES	CREDITS AND SURCHARGES
1					
2					

VEH	PASSIVE SEAT BELT	AIRBAG DRV/BOTH	ANTI-LOCK BRAKES 2/4	ANTI-THEFT DEVICES	DRIVER USE % (Each veh must = 100%) 1 2 3 4 5 6	CLASS
1						
2						

CREDITS AND SURCHARGES

COVERAGES/PREMIUMS

COVERAGES		LIMITS OF LIABILITY		VEHICLE 1	VEHICLE 2	VEHICLE 3	VEHICLE 4
SINGLE LIMIT LIABILITY		EA ACCIDENT		$	$	$	$
BODILY INJURY		EA PERSON	EA ACCIDENT	$	$	$	$
PROPERTY DAMAGE		EA ACCIDENT	DEDUCTIBLE	$	$	$	$
PERSONAL INJ PROTECTION			DEDUCTIBLE	$	$	$	$
ADDL PERSONAL INJ PROTECTION		TOTAL	$	WORK LOSS	$	MED EXP	$	$	$	$	$
MEDICAL PAYMENTS		EA PERSON		$	$	$	$
UNINSURED	CSL/BI	EA PERSON	EACH ACCIDENT	$	$	$	$
MOTORIST	PD	EA ACCIDENT		$	$	$	$
UNDERINSURED	CSL/BI	EA PERSON	EACH ACCIDENT	$	$	$	$
MOTORIST	PD	EA ACCIDENT		$	$	$	$
COMPREHENSIVE	DED	ACV UNLESS		$	$	$	$
COLLISION	DED	AMOUNT STATED		$	$	$	$
TOWING & LABOR				$	$	$	$
TRANSPORTATION EXPENSES				$	$	$	$
ADDITIONAL COVERAGES/ENDORSEMENTS (Include limit, deductible, premium)		TOTAL PER VEHICLE		$	$	$	$
		ESTIMATED TOTAL		$	DEPOSIT $	BALANCE DUE $	

RESIDENT & DRIVER INFORMATION [List all residents & dependents (licensed or not) and regular operators]

#	NAME	SEX	MAR STAT	RELATION TO APPLICANT	DATE OF BIRTH	OCCUPATION	DATE LIC	STDT >100	GOOD STDT	DRV TRAN	DEFENSIVE DRV DATE	DRIVERS LICENSE # / LICENSED STATE	SOCIAL SECURITY #
1													
2													
3													
4													
5													
6													

ACCIDENTS/CONVICTIONS (Note: Your driving record is verified with the state motor vehicle department)

HAS ANY DRIVER SHOWN ABOVE HAD AN ACCIDENT OR BEEN CONVICTED OF A MOVING VIOLATION WITHIN THE LAST ___ YEARS?   YES   NO   IF YES, INDICATE BELOW

DRV #	DATE OF ACCIDENT/CONVICTION	DESCRIPTION OF ACCIDENT OR CONVICTION	PLACE OF ACCIDENT/CONVICTION	BI OR DEATH YES NO	AMOUNT OF PROPERTY DAMAGE

ACORD 90 (4/92)   PLEASE COMPLETE REVERSE SIDE   © ACORD CORPORATION 1992

Sidebar notes:

All residents and dependents are listed. Children (under driving age) are noted on a diary system. When they reach driving age, the underwriter is alerted to obtain their driver information. All residents are included because they are covered by the policy contract (unless a driver exclusion is attached to the policy).

Accidents and conviction information will probably be verified by an MVR. In reviewing this information, discrepancies should be checked. If tickets and accidents were undeclared, what else might be missing?

Driver information provides information regarding all drivers, ages, dates licensed, occupations, driver training, and "good student" discounts. Information should be compared to the vehicles listed. Family members who are not declared will be covered by the personal auto policy for the operation of the insured's or other vehicles because a family member falls within the definition of an "insured" for liability coverage.

Exhibit 6-9
PAP Application—Finding Missing Information Examples

Information found on an application	Questions the information raises	Finding the missing information
Multiple applicants appear with different last names.	Do all applicants have an insurable interest in all of the vehicles?	The producer and the insured are the best sources for direct questions regarding vehicle ownership. Some companies require a copy of a vehicle registration as confirmation of ownership.
The insured and spouse show occupations, but no commuting use is indicated for the two declared vehicles.	How do the insureds get to work?	Again, direct questions are best. Some producers and companies use local maps to verify distances. Some computer systems are available to assist with driving directions.
The insured is not employed. The insured's date of birth reflects an age that is not within retirement range.	Is this a stable household situation?	Direct questions are helpful. A credit report can help to verify stability and household income.
One driver is shown for the four late-model vehicles.	Why does the insured have four vehicles, and why is there only one driver?	A credit report reflects financial resources to support the vehicles. It might also show the number of dependents in the household, perhaps helping to uncover undeclared operators.

Assume that you are the underwriter using the database information. What could you do with the information you found? As an underwriter, you could do the following:

- Verify the loss data that were given on the application
- Discover other drivers of the vehicle
- Find and charge for undisclosed losses on that vehicle

Other marketplace aids that are available include programs that assist in properly classifying risks, so the correct premium can be charged. These aids include the following:

- Vehicle owner checks using state registration data
- Vehicle identification number (VIN) checks
- Databases that include all licensed drivers by household

Exhibit 6-10
Sample MVR

DRIVER RECORD INFORMATION: PA					DATE: 01/01/XX	

DRIVER'S LICENSE NUMBER:	BIRTH DATE:	SEX:	HEIGHT:	WEIGHT:	ALSO KNOWN AS:
123456789	06/06/30	M	5'09"	165	Russell

ISSUED	EXPIRES:
06/06/96	06/06/2000

NAME: Payne, Russ
LICENSE CLASS: OPERATOR
LIC RESTR: CORRECTIVE LENSES

ORIGINAL ISSUE DATE: 06/06/46
AMOUNT OF HISTORY: OVER 20 YEARS

TYPE	VIOL/SUSP DATE	CONV/REIN DATE	DESCRIPTION
VIOL	08/29/93	11/26/91	UNLAWFUL SPEED-INTERSTATE HWY 79/65 DISPOSITION: GUILTY PTS: 1.5
VIOL	08/23/95	10/13/92	DROVE LEFT OF CENTER DISPOSITION: GUILTY PTS: 2.0
VIOL ACCI	05/12/96 05/12/96	05/24/96 05/24/96	IMPROPER PASSING ACCIDENT 2 VEH/UNITS 1 INJ 0 KILLED PTS: 4.0

To control losses and fraud, insurers are using database services such as the Comprehensive Loss Underwriting Exchange (CLUE), which provides detailed information on all claims associated with an insured and/or vehicle. A recent study found that many claims reported by CLUE reports were not disclosed on insurance applications.[10]

Credit Reports　Many companies use credit reports to show public records about an applicant's financial status, payment record, and employment history. Credit reports also reflect the number of dependents in a household. That information can help in uncovering undeclared members of the household who might be drivers.

Although a credit report would seem to have little relationship to the potential for an auto accident, insurers are identifying a relationship between a poor credit history and a poor driving record. The reason for that relationship is subject to speculation. However, proponents of credit report use in personal auto underwriting believe that these reports reflect a lifestyle that affects both credit and driving.

Using credit reports for automobile insurance underwriting is prohibited in some states unless certain procedural requirements are met. In all states, the Fair Credit Reporting Act requires the subject to grant permission for a credit report to be accessed from his or her records. That permission is usually included as part of the application (near the signature block).

Other Reports　Vendors offer reports and services to insurers to help answer particular questions or to fill special information needs.

The information is often obtained through observation, inquiry of the insured, inquiry of the neighbors, and use of computer databases. The reports are as varied as the vendors that supply them. Following are some examples of information that investigative reports can supply:

- Photos of the vehicles and reports of vehicle condition
- Number of drivers in household
- Vehicle use
- Odometer readings
- Loss history

Making the Underwriting Decision

After all of the relevant information is gathered, a decision must be made about the risk and the placement of coverage.

Identifying the Other Exposures

In addition to the driver and vehicle use exposures addressed previously in this chapter, producers and underwriters should be alert for exposures that extend beyond the "normal" exposures anticipated for a risk. The following four questions can help underwriters evaluate specific risks:

1. Are there any unusual driver exposures?
   - Youthful or elderly operators
   - Driving violations or traffic accidents
2. Are there any unusual usage risks?
   - Commuting long distances or in urban areas
   - Business use
   - Extensive travel outside the state
3. Are there any unique circumstances surrounding the vehicle ownership or the household?
   - Operators who are unknown or undeclared (Note from the PART A—LIABILITY COVERAGE of the sample PAP policy shown in Exhibit 6-1 that the definition of "insured" includes any "family member"—whether or not he or she has been declared on the application.)
   - Financial stresses in the household
   - Children of driving age living at school
4. Are there any past losses that cause concern?
   - Lending a vehicle
   - Accidents involving DUI or single-car accidents

Educational Objective 4

Measure the importance of personal auto exposures identified as they relate to potential loss frequency and severity.

Measuring the Exposures

The risks associated with exposures vary in importance in the underwriting process. Many underwriters have had the experience of opening an MVR or credit report and being thrown back in their chairs by surprise at the extent of accidents, violations, and credit problems. Producers have also experienced a company's overreaction to minor traffic violations. The extent of the exposure can be measured by the following:

- Frequency of a problem
- Duration of time since the last problem
- Information that was not volunteered on the application but discovered through external reports (a potential indicator of an insured who presents a moral hazard)

Severity of losses is informative, but it might not be the best yardstick for measuring losses. Many auto losses can result in either a large or small claim, depending on chance circumstances.

Educational Objective 5

Explain and evaluate the alternatives available in personal auto coverage implementation.

Evaluating the Alternatives

After the information has been gathered, the underwriter must examine the alternatives in coverage placements and risk modification.

Accept or Reject

Accepting a risk might seem to be the easiest course of action. Initialing an application and sending it to the company or to data processing require little effort. However, if the insurance specialist does not carefully review the application, making sure that all appropriate questions are answered, trouble can result. The basic rule is to accept risks whenever possible if they are consistent with established guidelines. However, guidelines are often left deliberately vague to provide flexibility (and related responsibility) for producers and underwriters. The level of individual underwriting authority is largely a matter of the management style in a particular organization, so no right or wrong level of authority can be vested in underwriters or producers.

Probably no risk is universally unacceptable. Almost anyone who is willing to pay the price can obtain auto insurance. However, company underwriting policy must always be respected. If the underwriting guide says that a risk is not acceptable and the underwriter has not been given the authority to make the exception, then any submission that does not meet the underwriting requirements must be declined. Declining a personal auto submission might seem to be the easiest way to avoid losses in the personal auto book of business, but it should be considered the last resort.

Underwriters cannot write new personal auto policies until they consider the state's cancellation and nonrenewal laws. Some states require that all underwriting information be gathered before policy issuance. In those states, when the underwriter issues a policy and then discovers a poor driving record, state law does not allow cancellation.

Rejecting a New Policy   Most states allow an underwriting grace period that extends from new policy issuance to some specified date. That grace period is typically set at sixty days but varies by state. The grace period allows the underwriter time to investigate the insured's risk profile and to verify the facts contained in the application. When the application is made before the expiration of the existing policy, the underwriter has more time to investigate. When coverage is bound immediately, the underwriter must gather whatever information is needed during the underwriting period to make a final determination on the suitability of the submission.

The grace period is often called the "free look period" or the "underwriting window." The insurer puts the business on its books and then takes a free look at the submission to compare it to the underwriting standards. If the underwriter discovers adverse information during that period, the policy can be canceled or modified with little or no restriction. Restrictions still exist on an insurer's right to decline business, though, and each state limits the freedom of insurers to underwrite automobile insurance submissions. For example, declining an insurance application because of the applicant's race is illegal in all states. However, restrictions vary significantly by state, so underwriters must be familiar with the rules in their own assigned territories. Exhibit 6-11 is an excerpt from the NAIC's Model Act regarding terminations or declinations of automobile insurance policies. NAIC produces model legislation as a guide for each state to use, but the actual state legislation enacted often varies significantly from the model. Still, the model illustrates some of the restrictions imposed on auto underwriters by various states.

Another underwriting consideration is the restriction on nonrenewal. Some states limit an insurer's use of nonrenewal powers to only once every year or some other period. Most states limit the acceptable reasons for which a policy can be nonrenewed.

Appropriate Classification

If an application is accepted for coverage, the insurance specialist must take other steps to ensure proper rating for the submission. One important step is to be sure that the correct classification is applied to each driver and vehicle. The insurance specialist should verify the car's use. Is it actually pleasure use, or is the car in fact being driven back and forth to work each day? Are all drivers, whether primary or occasional, identified on the application and rated appropriately? Is the one-way mileage to work four miles or forty miles? Statistics show that cars driven farther to work have a greater chance of being in an accident. The same can be said of vehicles used in business.

Exhibit 6-11
NAIC's Unfair Trade Practices: Prohibited Terminations/Declinations

---

Termination/Declinations: Prohibited Reasons

The declination of an application for, or the termination of, a policy of automobile insurance subject to this Act by an insurer, agent or broker is prohibited if the declination or termination is:

A. Based upon the race, religion, nationality or ethnic group of the applicant or named insured;

B. Based solely upon the lawful occupation or profession of the applicant or named insured, except that this provision shall not apply to an insurer, agent or broker that limits its market to one lawful occupation or profession or to several related lawful occupations or professions;

C. Based upon the principal location of the insured motor vehicle unless such decision is for a business purpose that is not a mere pretext for unfair discrimination;

D. Based upon the age, sex or marital status of an applicant or an insured, except that this subsection shall not prohibit rating differentials based on age, sex or marital status;

E. Based upon the fact that the applicant or named insured previously obtained insurance coverage through a residual market insurance mechanism;

F. Based upon the fact that another insurer previously declined to insure the applicant or terminated an existing policy in that the applicant was the named insured.

Drafting note: While insurers shall not decline an application or terminate a policy simply because of a previous adverse underwriting decision by another insurer, insurers should not be prohibited from inquiring as to the existence of any previous adverse underwriting decision so long as they also inquire as to the reasons given for such decisions. An insurer might decline an application or terminate a policy based on further information as to the reasons for the previous declination, termination or placement in a residual market mechanism.

Unfair Trade Practices Act, NAIC's Model Regulation Service, January 1993.

In addition to use of the car, the classification also depends on the age, sex, and marital status of the operator. Also considered is whether the youthful operator is an occasional driver or a principal driver. In states in which such rating is allowed, the insurance specialist must be sure that the youthful operator class is assigned to the proper car (usually determined by frequency of use). Insurance specialists should ensure that the correct classification is applied in order to generate sufficient premium for the risk assumed. But what happens when the operators of the vehicles are in question? The following are examples of vehicle classification that could be questionable:

*   Dad has a new car he uses in sales, and Mom (who works at home) has an older car for errands. Dad claims that their sixteen-year-old son never drives the new car. In the absence of evidence to the contrary, the benefit of the doubt should go to the customer.

*   A household has three drivers (ages forty-five, forty-two, and sixteen) and three cars. The application says that Dad drives one car to work; Mom drives one car to work; and their son rides the bus to school and is *not* the principal operator of the third car. If the

youthful operator is truly an occasional operator, then the submission should be written as such. However, the insurance specialist must be comfortable regarding the vehicle's actual use and the appropriate premium charge.

Modify the Coverage

Sometimes coverage must be modified so that a risk can be accepted. Coverage can be modified by endorsement. Endorsements can also be added to basic policies to meet an insured's specific needs. They are almost always standard documents, filed with and approved by state regulators.

Over 260 endorsements are currently available to add, modify, or clarify coverage provided by the policy, although fewer than thirty of them are available on a countrywide basis (and only perhaps a dozen or fewer are routinely used). Most states have one or more proprietary, state-specific forms, so over forty versions of a particular endorsement might be available.

Standard Endorsements Endorsements are attached to a standard policy to change the basic terms and conditions common to all insureds. Endorsements are used because a basic contract is written to cover the average driver, but the endorsements are meant for unusual or uncommon situations. Insurers that file forms independently can blend the additional coverage found in endorsements into the basic policy itself, essentially defining such situations as average. Some of the more commonly encountered personal auto endorsements are shown in Exhibit 6-12, along with possible application and underwriting concerns associated with their uses.

Driver Exclusions One modification that can be used is the driver exclusion. With a valid driver exclusion, the insurer is not obligated to pay any claims arising from the operation of the vehicle by an excluded driver. Not all states allow insurers to exclude drivers from coverage, and in some states the judicial system does not allow such exclusions. Driver exclusions are relatively rare with standard and preferred market companies but are rather commonly encountered in nonstandard insurers' underwriting programs because some coverages might still apply, regardless of the exclusion. In one state, the excluded driver is still subject to PIP coverage because the no-fault form makes no allowances for excluding persons from coverage. Some states find the concept of an excluded driver incompatible with mandatory insurance statutes that require coverage for all operators.

If allowed, driver exclusions can modify coverage sufficiently to make an otherwise unacceptable application eligible for a company's personal auto program. The application might include a driver who is a high-risk operator, perhaps a teenage son or daughter who has received several tickets or has been involved in one or more accidents. Without that driver, the submission would be desirable. In such an instance, using a driver exclusion might be appropriate.

Exhibit 6-12
Personal Auto Endorsements for Liability Coverages

ISO form number	Form name	What it does and when to use it	Underwriting concerns and marketing opportunities
PP 03 01	Federal Employees Using Autos in Government Business	This endorsement clarifies the liability coverage applicable when an auto is used for purposes for which federal law governs. It indicates that the United States and its agencies are not included as an "insured."	If this endorsement is required, the circumstances surrounding the vehicle's use should be determined. An insured who uses his or her own vehicle to deliver mail (this often happens in rural areas) might fall into this category. The endorsement does not permit the government to be included as an insured under the contract.
PP 03 06	Extended Non-Owned Coverage for Named Insured	The unendorsed PAP excludes coverage for any vehicle furnished or available for the regular use of a family member unless the vehicle falls within the definition of "your covered auto." When this endorsement is attached, liability coverage is provided for: • Use of a nonowned vehicle as a public or livery conveyance • Pleasure use of commercial vehicles provided for the regular use of an insured	This is not a widely used endorsement. If attached, the circumstances surrounding its use should be determined. This form could extend liability coverage to an insured who delivers pizza in the evening, using the pizza company's delivery auto. An insured with a commercial auto can use this endorsement to extend liability to the family members (if liability is not provided under the commercial auto policy for the family members). The coverage provided is excess over any other collectible insurance.
PP 03 09	Split Liability Limits	This endorsement creates the provisions for "split" limits of coverage rather than single liability limits.	Companies often have preferences for writing either split or combined limits (for bodily injury and property damage liability). The coverages and contracts remain unchanged other than the application of the coverage limits.

Continued on next page.

ISO form number	Form name	What it does and when to use it	Underwriting concerns and marketing opportunities
PP 03 20	Snowmobile Endorsement	This endorsement extends coverage to this special class of vehicles.	The snowmobile endorsement is a useful addition for any family that owns a snowmobile and uses it off the residence premises (use on the residence is covered by the liability coverage of a homeowners policy). Questions should be asked regarding: • Permitted operators • Experience and age of operators • Location of operation
PP 03 21	Mexico Coverage	The personal auto policy covers autos in the U.S., its territories, and Canada. This endorsement extends the policy territory to Mexico *only* for a trip of 10 days or less, within 25 miles of the border *if* the insured injures a U.S. citizen and a suit is brought within the U.S.	A warning at the top of the endorsement cautions that this form does not meet the requirements of the Mexican authorities. Use this endorsement with extreme caution. It has limited coverage and application.
PP 03 22	Named Nonowner Coverage	Liability and Uninsured Motorist coverage is provided for individuals who do not own an auto. Coverage is not extended to a spouse or to family members.	This form is useful for an individual who is provided a company-owned car or uses rented vehicles but does not own a vehicle. Liability coverage would be excess over other collectible coverage, and the insured would be covered if he or she rents or borrows an auto. The coverage provided is excess over any other collectible insurance.
PP 03 23	Miscellaneous-Type Vehicle Endorsement	This endorsement allows coverage to be written on motorcycles, motor homes, dune buggies, and other miscellaneous vehicles.	This form is required to extend coverage to miscellaneous-type vehicles. Underwriting concerns for miscellaneous vehicles will be reviewed in Chapter 12.
PP 03 26	Liability Coverage Exclusion Endorsement	Coverage for bodily injury is excluded for "you" or "family members."	This is often called the "intra-family" lawsuit exclusion. It bars one family member from coverage collection when suing another family member.

ISO form number	Form name	What it does and when to use it	Underwriting concerns and marketing opportunities
PP 03 28	Miscellaneous-Type Vehicle Amendment (Motor Home)	This form is used with PP 03 23 to exclude coverage while a motor home is rented to others.	If a motor home is covered under the personal auto policy, asking questions about renting the motor home to others is a good idea. This endorsement can exclude coverage for that exposure.
PP 03 34	Joint Ownership Coverage	This endorsement extends the definition of "you" and "your" to include autos jointly owned by relatives and unrelated persons who live together.	This is a useful endorsement for unmarried couples or family members (like mother and daughter) who jointly own a vehicle. Underwriting concerns should include: • How is the vehicle titled, and do all applicants have an insurable interest? • If the relationship is cohabitation, is the relationship stable (how long has the vehicle been jointly owned)? Could one party leave with the car and the other party claim a stolen vehicle?

Driver exclusions are modifications that should be used sparingly. How sparingly depends a great deal on the individual state's law. Some states are willing to allow a named insured to exclude anyone from coverage. Those states take the position that the insurance contract is an agreement that is freely entered into to secure insurance at a reasonable price. Other states might not allow the exclusion of "named insured" drivers in the household. Still other states might not allow the exclusion of any drivers whatsoever. In states in which exclusions are allowed, the driver exclusions can be an effective tool for writing or retaining only otherwise desirable business.

Named Nonowner Coverage Endorsement   Another marketing opportunity arises with a driver who does not own a car but still needs auto liability insurance. A policy with a **Named Nonowner Coverage endorsement** provides this type of coverage. The named nonowners coverage is simply an auto liability policy with the following characteristics:

- No auto is listed.
- Coverage is written for liability exposures (medical and uninsured motorists coverages are optional).
- The named nonowner endorsement is attached to the policy.

A **Named Nonowner Coverage endorsement** provides auto liability coverage for a person who does not own an auto. Liability coverage is extended to a vehicle that the insured might rent or borrow, or for a company car. Liability coverage applies in excess over any collectible insurance applying to the vehicle.

- The premium is substantially reduced (usually 50 percent for liability and medical payments coverages).
- The named nonowner coverage provides a driver liability protection when driving any vehicle.

Named nonowner coverage can also be used to cover damages caused by an excluded driver. Although no insurance coverage applies for the excluded driver while operating an insured vehicle, the excluded driver might operate the vehicle, and the vehicle owner's legal liability remains. If the car owner is found to be vicariously liable for the actions of an excluded driver's negligent operation of the vehicle, then the car owner might still be sued but lacks the protection of auto insurance. The named nonowner policy fills that coverage gap.

Liability Coverage Limits Selection   Some underwriters use liability coverage limits to modify auto policy coverage. That practice should be carefully considered. If a risk is acceptable at a $35,000 liability limit, what factor would make it unacceptable for a $50,000 or $300,000 limit? If it is not an acceptable risk, then it is probably not acceptable at any coverage limit.

Modify the Premium

Insurance companies generally modify the insurance policy's price by sorting the risks according to the underwriting guidelines for various auto market plans and by placing the risks within those plans. The premiums vary by plan and by company. Some companies offer only a limited number of the plans described in this section. Other companies might offer all of the described plans and others.

Automobile Insurance Market   There are as many automobile insurance markets as there are companies willing to write the coverage, plus one more per state in the form of an **automobile insurance plan** or some similar state-mandated coverage pool. All states have some sort of residual market mechanism for persons unable to procure insurance in the standard market because of poor loss experience, traffic violations, or other problems.

The following are examples of automobile insurance markets:

- *Personal Auto Voluntary Markets.*   Many insurers have multiple personal auto programs, usually classified as preferred, standard, or nonstandard. Program definitions can differ greatly among insurers. For instance, many nonstandard insurers have introduced "preferred" programs, but those preferred programs are not always comparable to the preferred market programs typical of major insurers. Likewise, the nonstandard program of a preferred market company can have more stringent underwriting standards than the standard program of an insurer specializing in the nonstandard market. Insurance company groups might include one or more preferred, standard, or nonstandard companies that producers use to place business. Underwriters should be aware of differences in their

Automobile insurance plans (also called involuntary, shared, or residual markets) are mechanisms for:

- Ensuring that all drivers have access to insurance
- Equitably distributing the risks that are not written voluntarily by insurers

own programs as well as the programs of competing companies. The following are four typical personal auto voluntary markets:

1. *Preferred Auto Market.* The typical preferred program has lower rates than the other programs, coupled with stricter underwriting standards. Most insurers allow only one violation or conviction (and no accidents) for such a program. Other requirements might involve type of car (no sports cars), age of drivers (all over twenty-five), and use of car (only pleasure use or a short distance to work—no business use). Also, if allowed by law, the insurer might require the support of a homeowners or commercial policy to write the auto policy.

   This market accepts drivers who, according to their loss characteristics, pose the least risk of incurring significant claim cost. Consequently, this group enjoys the lowest rates. A significant portion of this market consists of claim-free drivers who statistically produce good underwriting results. People with the following attributes have the fewest, least costly accidents and allow the company the greatest chance for profitability:

   • They do not smoke.

   • They do not drink.

   • They have no prior accidents or convictions.

   • They are experienced operators.

2. *Standard Auto Market.* Risks that do not qualify for the preferred market are placed in the standard market. This market is the middle market segment and is composed of drivers falling just short of qualifying for preferred treatment, generally because of a prior claim record but also for other reasons, such as certain newly licensed drivers or youthful operators. The standard program rates are generally 15 to 20 percent above the preferred program, but the underwriting rules are less stringent. Many standard programs allow two or three moving violations and even an at-fault accident. Also, there might be allowances for a sports car (if the driver is acceptable) and for business use.

3. *Nonstandard Auto Market.* The nonstandard program is used for high-risk drivers whom insurers might otherwise reject. Still, depending on the insurer's standards and desire for business, even a seemingly poor submission can be written if the price is right. Many things can cause a driver to fall into the high-risk pool. The best course for an underwriter is to listen to the producer and to keep an open mind. If the producer and the underwriter have a good relationship, the underwriter will know that the producer can be trusted, and the producer can feel comfortable discussing such submissions openly and objectively.

Many drivers go through a bad period in which they accrue either tickets or accidents. They might simply be unlucky. The key is to listen to and evaluate the explanation for the high-risk profile. Does it seem plausible? Did the driver get caught in a speed trap? Once might be acceptable, but if a driver gets caught too many times, there is reason for skepticism.

This market segment, sometimes still referred to as "substandard," consists of drivers and vehicles that exhibit higher-than-normal relative loss potential. The premiums for this market segment are consequently high. Insurers that write nonstandard auto policies use independent rate filings to carve profitable niches from the high-risk pool of drivers. The voluntary nonstandard market is said to adversely select against the pool of shared market drivers by picking the "best of the worst" from the potential assigned risks.

4. *Nonadmitted Market.* In addition to the preferred, standard, and nonstandard markets, there is a small surplus lines market for auto insurance made up of those drivers whose coverage is placed with nonadmitted insurers. A nonadmitted insurer is a company that is not licensed by the insurance commissioner of a state to write insurance in that state. Nonadmitted insurers operate much like nonstandard insurers but through the surplus lines market. This market is often limited to physical-damage-only policies, because their liability products might not meet state mandatory insurance or financial responsibility requirements for liability coverage.

- *Involuntary Market.* The involuntary market (also called the residual market, shared market, or automobile insurance plan), remains for those unable to obtain insurance in the voluntary market. Every state has a specific form of residual market, so covering every resident driver of a state is possible. The goal of universal coverage is never reached, but it is still worth trying for.

Insurers often shun involuntary market applications because the pricing structures are inadequate or because the variability of the losses for this set of drivers is too high. The state mandates auto insurance coverage and must therefore make some provision for providing coverage for those drivers who are unable to purchase insurance in the voluntary market.

Drivers often wind up in the shared market because of a lack of prior insurance coverage. Lack of prior insurance might indicate a **high risk** because of a morale hazard. For example, vehicle owners must show proof of insurance to register their vehicles; however, applicants often cancel their policies as soon as practicable after registering their vehicles.

Driving records often force drivers into the shared market, especially during periods of restrictive underwriting. Nonstandard programs try to select the best of these poor drivers; however, premiums charged are often very high. That often results in a driver's electing

---

Jargon Alert!

Applicants and insureds are sometimes referred to as "high-risk," meaning that they have an increased chance of loss because of the hazards present.

to purchase coverage in the involuntary market because the price is lower there than within the nonstandard market. Many involuntary market policies are heavily subsidized by the state government because of regulatory restrictions on pricing, with subsidies being paid by insureds in the voluntary market. The additional costs from the involuntary market are passed along to drivers in the voluntary market through surcharges.

Following are the four basic shared-market structures:

1. *Auto insurance plans (AIPs)*. These are the most common forms of involuntary market mechanism and are used by forty states and the District of Columbia. Under this plan, applicants who are rejected in the voluntary market are randomly assigned to an insurance company operating in the state. That company then issues a policy and is obligated to service the insured just as the company would with a voluntary policy. The rates and forms are uniform for all assigned-risk business in a particular state and are usually developed through the Automobile Insurance Plans Service Office (AIPSO). Insurers absorb any gains or losses from their involuntary business within their overall books of business. Losses are recovered through an increase in the general rate level for voluntary drivers. Under an AIP, insurers are assigned involuntary market drivers based on the insurer's share of business in the voluntary market. Premium volume in the prior calendar year is used as the basis for allocating drivers among insurance companies. Insurers might receive credits for voluntarily insuring certain classes of business, such as youthful drivers.

2. *Limited assignment distribution (LAD)*. Some states have provisions to modify the AIP risk-distribution procedure. The modification is called the limited assignment distribution (LAD). Under the LAD system, small companies that want to be relieved of the administrative burden of servicing private passenger nonfleet AIP assignments can do so by executing agreements whereby the company is exempted from being assigned involuntary market risks for a specified fee. The fee compensates the insurer that eventually services the policy.

3. *Joint underwriting associations (JUAs)*. Under the JUA system, all residual market drivers in a state are assigned to one or more insurance companies that act as servicing insurers. Those companies receive a specified fee for administering the plan and for servicing the involuntary market drivers. The fee, a percentage of written premiums for the policies serviced, pays normal underwriting expenses and some of the loss adjustment expenses associated with high-risk drivers. All auto insurers doing business in that state share losses in proportion to their shares of the voluntary market premiums. The rates are uniform for all servicing insurers.

4. *Reinsurance facilities*. Three states use reinsurance facilities. In this system, each company is required to provide coverage for all applicants, but the company is then allowed to cede

undesirable insureds to a central facility, which is the reinsurance facility. Applicants for insurance might be unaware that they have been ceded to the facility, because they continue to be serviced by the company that wrote the policy. Usually the number of drivers a company can cede to the facility is limited. The limitation restricts the insurer's ability to dump all but the best business, since the profits and losses of the reinsurance facility are shared by all participants in the voluntary market according to market share.

Exhibit 6-13 provides a table of the types of involuntary market mechanisms used by each state.

Exhibit 6-13
Involuntary Market Mechanisms by State

State	Type of Plan	State	Type of Plan
Alabama	AIP	Montana	AIP
Alaska	AIP/LAD	Nebraska	AIP
Arizona	AIP	Nevada	AIP
Arkansas	AIP	New Hampshire	RF
California	AIP	New Jersey	Other
Colorado	AIP	New Mexico	AIP
Connecticut	AIP/LAD	New York	AIP/LAD/Other
Delaware	AIP/LAD	North Carolina	RF
District of Columbia	AIP	North Dakota	AIP
Florida	JUA	Ohio	AIP
Georgia	AIP	Oklahoma	AIP
Hawaii	JUA	Oregon	AIP
Idaho	AIP	Pennsylvania	AIP/LAD
Illinois	AIP/LAD	Rhode Island	AIP
Indiana	AIP	South Carolina	RF
Iowa	AIP/LAD	South Dakota	AIP
Kansas	AIP/LAD	Tennessee	AIP
Kentucky	AIP	Texas	AIP
Louisiana	AIP	Utah	AIP
Maine	AIP/LAD	Vermont	AIP/LAD
Maryland	Other	Virginia	AIP/LAD
Massachusetts	Other	Washington	AIP
Michigan	AIP	West Virginia	AIP
Minnesota	AIP	Wisconsin	AIP
Mississippi	AIP	Wyoming	AIP
Missouri	JUA		

Loss Control Opportunities   Loss control is a difficult option to implement for personal auto exposures (although one case is known of a father who attached a speed control to the accelerator of his teenage son's car, allowing a maximum speed of forty-five m.p.h.). Loss control is often approached through industry and highway control measures to promote vehicle and highway safety and to discourage irresponsible vehicle operation.

The insurance industry encourages responsible and safe driving by offering credits for driver training programs and by offering safe driver discounts. Appropriate surcharges for violations and accidents also discourage unsafe vehicle operation.

Selecting the Best Alternative

The best alternative is the one that applies the appropriate price to the risks presented. To select the best alternative, the insurance specialist must do the following:

- Develop a complete picture of the risk
- Gather missing information and fill gaps in risk data
- Properly price the risk by adhering to the underwriting guidelines and by appropriately classifying the risks

---

Educational Objective 6

Describe how personal auto underwriting decisions can be implemented and their results monitored.

Implementing the Decision and Monitoring the Results

After the underwriting decision is made, the personal auto risk must be implemented first and then monitored for changes. Similarly, the entire portfolio of personal auto policies must be monitored for changes.

Implementing the Decision

Personal auto policies require follow-up to ensure that the driver and vehicle use classification, coverages, and information remain current. Individual risks should be identified for a periodic review of motor vehicle reports, which is normally completed about every three years, although some companies review these records every year. The computerization of MVRs facilitates frequent review. Systems are available to order an MVR, check it against the insured's current policy, and automatically add surcharges for new violations.

Diaries are also established for the following:

- Credit reports that are questionable and require monitoring
- Risks that fall within the fringes of acceptability and are monitored for future development
- Risks that are initially placed in a standard or nonstandard market that might improve and qualify for an improved category and a lower premium

---

Jargon Alert!

Insurance companies use a number of terms to describe the process of marking a file for future review, including:

- "Diary"
- Suspense
- Flag
- Index

- Children in the household who are approaching the age at which they can get drivers' licenses
- Drivers who are not employed at application time and who should be monitored for future employment and commuting use of the vehicle

Any item on the application or a report that is subject to future change should be monitored.

Monitoring the Results

Monitoring personal auto policies usually requires reviewing an entire block of business for loss trends. Little information can be gained from an individual risk. Personal auto insurance forms such a large part of many insurers' portfolios that it deserves attention regarding premium adequacy and loss frequency.

Educational Objective 7

Evaluate the factors that should be considered when a personal auto liability claim is made.

The Claim Review

The adequacy of the information-gathering process often becomes apparent during a claim review. Every insurance company has a method of referring auto claims to underwriters for review. Claims might be marked by an adjuster, technician, or computer for further investigation, or they might be categorized by type of loss. Investigation notes, photos of the accident scene, transcripts of the depositions, and police reports breathe life into what could ordinarily be another statistic. Reviewing claim files is an activity that insurance specialists should seek out as part of their education and development process.

In addition to studying the information provided about the individual auto accident, insurance specialists should review the claim file for the following:

- Indications of the insured's actions that might forecast future behavior (such as level of cooperation with the adjuster, cause of the accident, whether others are allowed to borrow the auto, and unique circumstances surrounding the accident).
- Incomplete information obtained at the time of application. The individual policy data should be corrected. The questions asked on the application and during the underwriting process should also be evaluated to prevent future problems. The following indicate that information was not complete at the time the application was submitted:
    - A teenage child is driving the family car, though no children were mentioned on the auto application.

- A claim report indicates that the insured was driving to work when an accident occurred, but the vehicle was classified as a pleasure-use auto.

Putting Personal Auto Underwriting To Work

Exhibit 6-14 is a checklist of the underwriting process for personal auto policies (driver and use exposures) presented in this chapter.

Exhibit 6-14
The Personal Auto Underwriting Process

The Steps	The Question To Answer	Checklist for the Personal Auto Policy
1. Gather information	What information is missing from the application?	❐ Review the application, checking for inconsistencies ❐ Determine the information gaps and elect the best source of information
	How do you get the missing information?	❐ Select the best source, depending on the information gaps to fill: • Applicant or producer • Motor vehicle report (MVR) • Credit report • Information databases • Other specific investigations
2. Make the underwriting decision	What are the exposures?	❐ Evaluate the exposures based on the driver's: • Age • Sex • Marital status • Driving record ❐ Evaluate the vehicle use exposures based on: • Area of travel • Mileage • Miles driven • Whether business or farm use
	How can you measure the exposure?	❐ Determine the frequency of traffic violations (and the severity, depending on the type of loss) ❐ Determine the time between occurrences

Continued on next page.

The Steps	The Question To Answer	Checklist for the Personal Auto Policy
	What are the underwriting alternatives?	❏ Accept the risk (verify appropriate classifications) ❏ Reject the risk ❏ Modify coverage by attaching: • Standard endorsements • Driver exclusions ❏ Modify price by market selection: • Preferred auto market • Standard auto market • Nonstandard auto market • Nonadmitted auto market
3. Implement the decision and monitor the results	How do you implement the decision?	❏ Issue the policy ❏ Implement the appropriate diary systems to monitor the risk and any changing characteristics
	How will you know whether it worked?	❏ Evaluate the results of the portfolio of business ❏ Evaluate the information in claim reports that could have been identified during the application process

Summary

A personal lines producer or underwriter must be able to review all of the aspects of a personal auto application or existing account to determine what exposures the driver and vehicle present. Once the exposures have been identified, coverage alternatives can be identified and implemented. During this risk review and coverage placement process, the producer or underwriter must be aware of the contract language, so provisions, coverages, and exclusions that alter the application of insurance can be addressed. Understanding the contract provisions will also facilitate the underwriting process. For example, understanding the "OUT OF STATE" provision in the policy contract helps an underwriter determine the coverage implications of a driver who lives in one state and commutes to work in another state.

Factors used to project loss experience include the driver's age, gender, marital status, and driving record. Vehicle operation factors used to project loss experience include the area of operation, mileage driven, and the vehicle use.

The underwriter follows a process in reviewing a personal auto application. The underwriter will first gather information about the risk. The information provided on the application is the primary source of information about the risk. The underwriter verifies or supplements this information by ordering reports such as motor vehicle reports, credit reports, and claims database reports. From this information, the underwriter identifies the loss exposures and the extent of the exposures.

An underwriter then considers the underwriting alternatives. The personal auto market is unique because there are many voluntary and involuntary markets available for coverage placement.

After the underwriter selects an alternative, he or she must implement that decision. If a personal auto policy is written (with or without modification), the underwriter might establish a diary to review the policy at a future date. Policies are reviewed to determine changes in exposures or classification. Personal auto policies are often monitored as a portfolio of accounts so that trends can be evaluated.

Chapter Notes

1. Massie and K.L. Campbell, *Analysis of Accident Rates by Age, Gender, and Time of Day Based on the 1990 Nationwide Personal Transportation Survey (UMTRI-93-7)*, (Ann Arbor, MI: University of Michigan Transportation Research Institute, 1990).

2. A.F. Williams, R.S. Karpf, and P.L. Zador, "Variations in Minimum Licensing Age and Fatal Motor Vehicle Crashes," *American Journal of Public Health*, December 1993, pp. 1401-1402.

3. D.F. Preusser, P.L. Zador, and A.F. Williams, "The Effect of City Curfew Ordinances on Teenage Motor Vehicle Fatalities," *Accident Analysis and Prevention*, January 1993, pp. 641-645.

4. Center for Disease Control and Prevention, *The 1993 Youth Risk Behavior Surveillance Survey* (Arlington, VA: Center for Disease Control and Prevention of the U.S. Government).

5. Michael A. Gebers and Raymond C. Peck, *An Inventory of California Driver Accident Risk Factors* (Sacramento, CA: California Department of Motor Vehicles, 1994), p. 13.

6. Insurance Institute for Highway Safety, *25 Years of Work—1969-1994* (Arlington, VA: Insurance Institute for Highway Safety, 1995), p. 12.

7. Insurance Institute for Highway Safety, *Alcohol: Questions and Answers* (Arlington, VA: Insurance Institute for Highway Safety, 1993).

8. Insurance Institute for Highway Safety, *Highway Safety Facts 1994* (Arlington, VA: Insurance Institute for Highway Safety, 1994).

9. *25 Years of Work—1969-1994*, p. 12.

10. Emmett Vaughan, *Fundamentals of Risk and Insurance* (New York, NY: John Wiley & Sons, 1992), p. 501.

Chapter 7

Educational Objectives

1. With regard to vehicle exposures, explain how each of the elements of the personal auto policy studied in this assignment affects an underwriting decision. (pp. 7-3 to 7-6)

2. Identify and evaluate vehicle-related exposures that influence the frequency and severity of auto losses. (pp. 7-7 to 7-29)

3. Describe what information is needed to make an underwriting decision regarding vehicle-related factors, and explain how that information is obtained. (pp. 7-29 to 7-32)

4. Explain and evaluate the alternatives available in coverage implementation or risk management for auto physical damage exposures. (pp. 7-32 to 7-36)

5. Describe how the results of auto physical damage underwriting decisions can be monitored and evaluated. (p. 7-37)

6. Evaluate the factors that should be considered when underwriting a personal auto physical damage coverage claim. (pp. 7-37 to 7-38)

7. Given a case study containing personal auto physical damage exposures, demonstrate the ability to analyze the exposures and recommend appropriate actions. (Encompasses entire chapter.)

Chapter 7

Vehicles: Exposure Analysis and Coverages

The previous chapter addressed (1) the relationship between drivers, (2) their use of personal autos, (3) related coverages, and (4) the associated chance of loss. This chapter continues analyzing personal auto insurance by discussing vehicle characteristics. From a practical perspective, the producer, CSR, or underwriter reviews an auto application or exposure as a unit. The driver's record, vehicle uses, vehicle exposures, and other related factors are viewed together to determine the applicability of coverage and the acceptability of an application or existing account. An underwriter making a decision about a submission evaluates all of the exposures on the application, develops and selects alternatives, and then makes and implements a decision.

Some of the vehicle characteristics that are discussed in this chapter pertain to occupant safety (safety belts, air bags, and vehicle crush zones). Those characteristics are loss control features that reduce medical payments, personal injury protection, and liability losses. They are reviewed in this chapter under the general grouping of exposures and equipment that relate to vehicles.

The coverages that apply to vehicle physical damage are also reviewed in this chapter with a concentration on provisions that might affect an underwriter's or a producer's decisions.

Educational Objective 1

With regard to vehicle exposures, explain how each of the elements of the personal auto policy studied in this assignment affects an underwriting decision.

The Personal Auto Policy

The personal auto policy (PAP) issued by the Insurance Services Office is the basis for reviewing auto insurance coverages. Chapter 6 presented the liability section of the PAP as a reference for reviewing driver and use exposures. The PAP's physical damage section is supplied in this chapter as a reference. As part of the discussion of exposures that follows, sections of the policy are explained as they relate to the application of coverage.

Auto physical damage coverage originated as a form of inland marine insurance. Coverage was later packaged with liability insurance to better meet the needs of auto owners. Physical damage is a combination of coverages, including collision and other-than-collision (OTC) coverages.

Exhibit 7-1 displays the physical damage section of the PAP with notations about the coverage provided. This policy section identifies coverages and exclusions needed to underwrite an application. Many annotations are referenced throughout the chapter. If you are a producer who is advising a customer of the coverage provided or an underwriter making a decision, the type of coverage that is provided under an auto contract becomes a factor in the advice you provide or the decision you make. For example, consider an applicant who owns a ten-year-old vehicle (valued at $5,000) and who has just installed a $1,000 stereo in that vehicle. At the time of application, you should be able to do the following:

- Assess the stereo type and installation
- Assess the exposure presented by the stereo as an underwriting factor
- Reference pertinent coverages, exclusions, or limitations that might alter or limit coverage
- Advise the applicant about the need for any additional endorsements

Assessing and understanding the contract language are crucial steps in providing advice or making decisions. Policy contracts are a basic tool for any specialist within the roles of production, customer service, and underwriting.

Exhibit 7-1
Physical Damage Section of the Personal Auto Policy

Coverage is triggered by a *direct* and *accidental* loss to the insured's auto or to a nonowned (rented or borrowed) auto. Indirect losses are covered by transportation expense.

The coverage name *other than collision* (OTC) has replaced *comprehensive*.

Glass breakage during a collision may be reimbursed by the collision coverage to prevent the application of two deductibles.

Coverage is provided for non-owned autos. This includes rental and borrowed vehicles with qualifiers:
- **"Other than collision" and/or collision coverage must appear on another vehicle for coverage to apply.**
- **The vehicle must be in the custody of or operated by the insured or a family member.**
- **The vehicle cannot be furnished or available for regular use.**

Although these terms are not defined in the contract, the following definitions are generally applied:
- ***Furnished* means actually provided.**
- ***Available* relates to the control of the auto. Must permission be asked for each use?**
- ***Regular* is governed by the number of occasions and the rate of recurrence.**

PART D - COVERAGE FOR DAMAGE TO YOUR AUTO

INSURING AGREEMENT

A. We will pay for direct and accidental loss to "your covered auto" or any "non-owned auto," including their equipment, minus any applicable deductible shown in the Declarations. If loss to more than one "your covered auto" or "non-owned auto" results from the same "collision", only the highest applicable deductible will apply. We will pay for loss to "your covered auto" caused by:

1. "Other than collision" only if the Declarations indicate the Other Than Collision coverage is provided for that auto.

2. "Collision" only if the Declarations indicate that Collision Coverage is provided for that auto.
   If there is a loss to a "non-owned auto", we will provide the broadest coverage applicable to any "your covered auto" shown in the Declarations.

B. "Collision" means the upset of "your covered auto" or a "non-owned auto" or their impact with another vehicle or object.
   Loss caused by the following is considered other than "collision":

1. Missiles or falling objects;	7. Malicious mischief or vandalism;
2. Fire;	8. Riot or civil commotion;
3. Theft or larceny;	9. Contact with bird or animal; or
4. Explosion or earthquake;	10. Breakage of glass;
5. Windstorm;	
6. Hail, water or flood;	

   If breakage of glass is caused by a "collision", you may elect to have it considered a loss caused by "collision".

C. "Non-owned auto" means:

1. Any private passenger auto, pickup, van or "trailer" not owned by or furnished or available for the regular use of you or any "family member" while in the custody of or being operated by you or any "family member"; or

2. Any auto or "trailer" you do not own while used as a temporary substitute for "your covered auto" which is out of normal use because of its:

   a. Breakdown;   d. Loss; or
   b. Repair;   e. Destruction.
   c. Servicing;

TRANSPORTATION EXPENSES

In addition, we will pay, without application of a deductible, up to $15 per day, to a maximum of $450, for:

1. Temporary transportation expenses incurred by you in the event of a loss to "your covered auto". We will pay for such expenses if the loss is caused by:

---

a. "Other than collision" only if the Declarations indicate that Other Than Collision Coverage is provided for any "your covered auto."

b. "Collision" only if the Declarations indicate that Collision Coverage is provided for that auto.

2. Loss of use expenses for which you become legally responsible in the event of loss to a "non-owned auto." We will pay for loss of use expenses if the loss is caused by:

a. "Other than collision" only if the Declarations indicate that Other Than Collision coverage is provided for any "your covered auto."

b. "Collision" only if the Declarations indicate that Collision Coverage is provided for any "your covered auto."

If the loss is caused by a total theft of "your covered auto" or a "non-owned auto", we will pay only expenses incurred during the period:

1. Beginning 48 hours after the theft; and

2. Ending when "your covered auto" or the "non-owned auto" is returned to use or we pay for its loss.

If the loss is caused by other than theft of a "your covered auto" or a "non-owned auto", we will pay only expenses beginning when the auto is withdrawn from use for more than 24 hours.

Our payment will be limited to that period of time reasonably required to repair or replace the "your covered auto" or the "non-owned auto".

EXCLUSIONS

We will not pay for:

1. Loss to "your covered auto" or any "non-owned auto" which occurs while it is being used as a public livery conveyance. This exclusion (**1.**) does not apply to a share-the-expenses car pool.

2. Damage due and confined to:
   a. Wear and tear;
   b. Freezing;
   c. Mechanical or electrical breakdown or failure; or
   d. Road damage to tires.

This exclusion (**2.**) does not apply if the damage results from the total theft of "your covered auto" or any "non-owned auto"

3. Loss due to or as consequence of:
   a. Radioactive contamination;
   b. Discharge of any nuclear weapon (even if accidental);
   c. War (declared or undeclared);
   d. Civil war;

Transportation expense begins in the first column. It provides up to $15 per day ($450 total) for two types of losses:
1. **Transportation expenses (car rental, bus or taxi fare, etc.) incurred because of a covered loss involving "your covered auto"**
2. **Loss of use expenses incurred because of a covered loss to a non-owned auto (borrowed or rented)**

A 24-hour deductible applies to this coverage (48 hours for a theft). PP 03 02 (Increased Limits Transportation Expense) can be used to increase the coverage limit.

Mechanical and maintenance-type losses are excluded. Flat tires due to road damage are excluded.

Proof of humor in insurance contracts.

Any vehicle that is a temporary substitute for one that is out of service has the broadest coverage applicable to any auto on the declarations page. There are no restrictions regarding drivers as found in item #1 immediately above. There are no restrictions regarding the type of auto that can be used as a substitute.

The policy excludes equipment that reproduces sound, with the following exception:

1. *Permanently* (the interpretation of this word is hotly debated) installed, or

2. Removable from a permanently installed housing, operated solely by the auto's electrical system, and in the auto

The other electronic equipment (sample list provided) is excluded with the following exceptions:

1. Electronics used to operate the vehicle (computers)

2. Equipment permanently installed in the opening of the dash or console normally used for a radio

---

    e.   Insurrection; or

    f.   Rebellion or revolution.

4. Loss to:

    a.   Any electronic equipment designed for the reproduction of sound, including, but not limited to:

        (1) Radios and stereos;

        (2) Tape decks; or

        (3) Compact disc players;

    b.   Any other electronic equipment that receives or transmits audio, visual or data signals, including, but not limited to:

        (1) Citizens band radios;

        (2) Telephones;

        (3) Two-way mobile radios;

        (4) Scanning monitor receivers;

        (5) Television monitor receivers;

        (6) Video cassette recorders;

        (7) Audio cassette recorders; or

        (8) Personal computers;

    c.   Tapes, records, discs, or other media used with equipment described in **a.** or **b.**

This exclusion (**4.**) does not apply to:

    a.   Equipment designed solely for the reproduction of sound and accessories used with such equipment, provided:

        (1) The equipment is permanently installed in "your covered auto" or any "non-owned auto"; or

        (2) The equipment is:

           (a) Removable from a housing unit which is permanently installed in the auto;

          (b) Designed to be solely operated by use of the power from the auto's electrical system; and

          (c) In or upon "your covered auto" or any "non-owned auto";

        at the time of the loss.

    b.   Any other electronic equipment that is:

        (1) Necessary for the normal operation of the auto or the monitoring of the auto's operating system; or

        (2) An integral part of the same unit housing any sound reproducing equipment described in **a.** and permanently installed in the opening of the dash or console of "your covered auto" or any "non-owned auto" normally used by the manufacturer for installation of a radio.

---

5. A total loss to "your covered auto" or any "non-owned auto" due to destruction or confiscation by governmental or civil authorities.

    This exclusion (**5.**) does not apply to the interests of Loss Payees in "your covered auto".

6. Loss to a camper body or "trailer" you own which is not shown in the Declarations. This exclusion (**b.**) does not apply to a camper body or "trailer" you:

    a.   Acquire during the policy period; and

    b.   Ask us to insure within 30 days after you become the owner.

7. Loss to any "non-owned auto" when used by you or any "family member" without a reasonable belief that you or that "family member" are entitled to do so.

8. Loss to:

    a.   Awnings or cabanas; or

    b.   Equipment designed to create additional living facilities.

9. Loss to any equipment designed or used for the detection or location of radar or laser.

10. Loss to any custom furnishings or equipment in or upon any pickup or van. Custom furnishings or equipment include but are not limited to:

    a.   Special carpeting and insulation, furniture or bars;

    b.   Facilities for cooking and sleeping;

    c.   Height-extending roofs; or

    d.   Custom murals, paintings or other decals or graphics.

11. Loss to any "non-owned auto" being maintained or used by any person while employed or otherwise engaged in the "business" of:

    a. Selling;   d. Storing; or

    b. Repairing;   e. Parking;

    c. Servicing;

    vehicles designed for use on public highways.

    This includes road testing and delivery.

12. Loss to any "non-owned auto" being maintained or used by any person while employed or otherwise engaged in any "business" not described in exclusion **11.** This exclusion (**12.**) does not apply to the maintenance or use by you or any "family member" of a "non-owned auto" which is a private passenger auto or "trailer".

13. Loss to "your covered auto" or any "non-owned auto", located inside a facility designed for racing, for the purpose of:

    a.   Competing in; or

    b.   Practicing or preparing for;

    any prearranged or organized racing or speed contest.

A loss due to confiscation can occur by the Drug Enforcement Agency (DEA) as a result of illegal activities or a failure to comply with the Environmental Protection Agency (EPA) or the Department of Transportation (DOT).

Living facilities and equipment are excluded. PP 03 07 (Covered Property Coverage) can be used to buy back coverage for this equipment.

Radar and laser detectors are excluded from the PAP and from the homeowners policy. Neither policy offers buy-back coverage for this equipment.

Continued on next page.

This exclusion was added in 1994. It prevents the rental company from recovering a loss under the insured's policy if state law has enacted legislation precluding the rental car company from holding a renter legally liable for damage to the rented car.

The policy pays the lesser of the following:
1. ACV
2. Replacement cost

The Cost of Repairs (PP 03 08) can be added to provide stated amount coverage.

Vehicle repairs can be made of the parts that are of *like kind and quality* (LKQ). These may be salvage (used) parts, rebuilt parts, or *after-market* parts (made by independent part manufacturing companies).

14. Loss to, or loss of use of, a "non-owned auto" rented by:
  a. You; or
  b. Any "family member";
if a rental vehicle company is precluded from recovering such loss, or loss of use, from you or that "family member," pursuant to the provisions of any applicable rental agreement or state law.

LIMIT OF LIABILITY

A. Our limit of liability for loss will be the lesser of the:
  1. Actual cash value of the stolen or damaged property;
  2. Amount necessary to repair or replace the property with other property of like kind and quality.
However, the most we will pay for loss to any "non-owned auto" which is a trailer is $500.

B. An adjustment for depreciation and physical condition will be made in determining actual cash value in the event of a total loss.

C. If a repair or replacement results in better than like kind or quality, we will not pay for the amount of the betterment.

PAYMENT OF LOSS

We may pay for loss in money or repair or replace the damaged or stolen property. We may, at our expense, return any stolen property to:
  1. You; or
  2. The address shown in this policy.
If we return stolen property we will pay for any damage resulting from the theft. We may keep all or part of the property at an agreed or appraised value.

If we pay for loss in money, our payment will include the applicable sales tax for the damaged or stolen property.

NO BENEFIT TO BAILEE

This insurance shall not directly or indirectly benefit any carrier or other bailee for hire.

OTHER SOURCES OF RECOVERY

If other sources of recovery also cover the loss, we will pay only our share of the loss. Our share is the proportion that our limit of liability bears to the total of all applicable limits. However, any insurance we provide with respect to a "non-owned auto" shall be excess over any other collectible source of recovery including, but not limited to:

1. Any coverage provided by the owner of the "non-owned auto";
2. Any other applicable physical damage insurance;
3. Any other source of recovery applicable to the loss.

APPRAISAL

A. If we and you do not agree on the amount of loss, either may demand an appraisal of the loss. In this event, each party will select a competent appraiser. The two appraisers will select an umpire. The appraisers will state separately the actual cash value and the amount of loss. If they fail to agree, they will submit their differences to the umpire. A decision agreed to by any two will be binding. Each party will:
  1. Pay its chosen appraiser; and
  2. Bear the expenses of the appraisal and umpire equally.

B. We do not waive any of our rights under this policy by agreeing to an appraisal.

If the vehicle is owned, this policy pays on a pro rata basis with any other collectible insurance.

If the vehicles are nonowned, this policy will be excess over any other collectible coverage.

If the insured and adjuster cannot agree on the value of a loss, the appraisal system is provided to reconcile the differences. Use of the appraisal process is common.

The betterment clause was added with this policy edition. Any repair that increases the value of the vehicle will not be reimbursed by the insurer. For example, an insured that owns a ten-year-old vehicle and insists on new replacement parts rather than LKQ might have a repaired vehicle that is better than the original. The insurer will reimburse the value of the LKQ parts, but not new parts.

Educational Objective 2
Identify and evaluate vehicle-related exposures that influence the frequency and severity of auto losses.

Vehicle-Related Loss Exposures

The vehicles listed on an application present physical exposures and hazards that are considered in the underwriting decision. Because the policy contract might or might not insure those exposures, the applicant needs advice to properly protect the values of the vehicles and their accessories. To provide that advice, specialists must review the physical attributes and exposures that each vehicle presents.

Producers and underwriters must be familiar with vehicle-related loss factors for the following reasons:

- To provide discounts for some protective features, the specialist should be familiar with the variations among safety features to determine whether and to what extent discounts should apply.

- To weigh vehicle safety features as an underwriting factor, the specialist must understand what the features are and the extent to which they are effective.

- To discuss vehicle safety features with the customer, the specialist should be aware of appropriate safety recommendations (such as the location of a child safety seat) or the sources for additional safety information that might be appropriate.

- To discuss the exposures or equipment that are not covered by the policy, the specialist should be aware of those limitations and help the customer address those exposures.

A complete evaluation of vehicle physical damage exposures by a specialist is difficult because so many elements must be considered. From a practical standpoint, a producer or underwriter will not perform a complete evaluation of exposures for every vehicle encountered on a personal auto application; the research required to investigate the characteristics and exposures associated with each vehicle is simply not practical. Many companies create underwriting guidelines that incorporate acceptable and unacceptable vehicles or vehicle types, and those guidelines become the basis for the evaluation of many applications. However, a producer or underwriter should possess some basic knowledge about the loss characteristics of the vehicles that are being submitted for coverage. A producer or underwriter should also understand the basis for vehicle restrictions found in underwriting guidelines; without that understanding, it would be difficult to recommend reasonable exceptions to those guidelines. Also, a specialist in personal insurance should be able to evaluate the vehicle-related exposures for those applications or existing accounts that require additional research.

Vehicle Types and Equipment

The automotive marketplace is in a constant state of change. Vehicle manufacturers produce a variety of different models. Personal insurance specialists probably cannot develop in-depth knowledge about even a small segment of the overall class of vehicles encompassed by the terms personal auto and private passenger auto. The struggle to stay current is aggravated because models change every year. Some changes are merely cosmetic; others are substantial. A manufacturer might discontinue a particular model and introduce a new one. Design innovations such as front-wheel drive; four-wheel drive; and full-time, all-wheel drive are found on an increasing number of vehicles each year. Computerized systems are included on a greater percentage of vehicles produced each year. The constantly changing factors make it difficult for personal insurance specialists to perform any kind of knowledgeable and systematic analysis of hazards related to the type of vehicle.

Vehicle Testing and Data Reporting

Insurance companies have difficulty collecting enough information to draw conclusions about vehicle safety systems or the loss results for all makes and models of vehicles. Because of that difficulty, the insurance industry sponsors organizations that perform independent studies regarding driving safety and that promote highway and vehicle safety programs.

The Insurance Institute for Highway Safety (IIHS) is an independent, nonprofit, scientific and educational organization. It is dedicated to reducing losses (deaths, injuries, and property damage) resulting from crashes. IIHS was an instrumental force in the congressional requirement of air bags in all new passenger cars by the 1998 model year. IIHS is supported by numerous national insurance organizations and individual insurance companies. IIHS compiles and publishes information on subjects such as the following:

- Air bag effectiveness
- Highway safety programs
- Comparisons of safety features in new cars
- Safety belt effectiveness

Jargon Alert!

The acronym HLDI is pronounced "hill'-dee."

The Highway Loss Data Institute (HLDI) is a nonprofit, public service organization. It is closely associated with and funded through the Insurance Institute for Highway Safety. HLDI gathers, compiles, and publishes data regarding insurance loss variations among different makes, models, and kinds of vehicles.

Damageability and Cost of Repairs

The auto insurance industry is, of necessity, forced to look back at its experience and identify the extremes—the best and worst experience in areas such as bumper-impact results, damageability, repairability, and likelihood of vehicle theft. Rating symbols assigned to vehicles by ISO are based on the price new of each vehicle, adjusted to reflect the vehicle's physical damage loss experience; therefore, the premium charged for physical damage coverage reflects a vehicle's loss history. The ability to determine the experience of a specific vehicle becomes useful when underwriting by exception. The ability to determine the damageability experience of vehicles is also useful in creating underwriting guidelines.

How Vehicle Results Are Reported

HLDI receives and compiles an enormous amount of loss data and published reports that can give underwriters insight into bodily injury loss and collision loss characteristics of specific vehicles. Exhibit 7-2 is a sample of a HLDI report that summarizes three years of loss results of passenger cars by model year and summarizes collision results by model year.

Exhibit 7-2
Passenger Car Collision Coverage Results by Model Year

Model Year	Total Exposure (insured vehicle years)	Claim Frequency (per 100 insured vehicle years)	Average Loss Payment per Claim	Average Loss Payment per Insured Vehicle Year
1992	9,195,986	7.6	$2,489	$186
1993	5,480,674	8.0	2,578	206
1994	1,316,682	8.0	2,694	216
1992-94	15,993,342	7.9	$2,587	$203

Source: Highway Loss Data Institute.

The last line of Exhibit 7-2 is used as a base against which the results for individual vehicle models can be compared.

Exhibit 7-3 is an abbreviated list of the vehicle models with the best and worst results for 1992-94. The "Result" columns of Exhibit 7-3 are percentages of the base figures provided in Exhibit 7-2. For example, a vehicle with a result of 53 has experienced only 53 percent of the average loss results shown in Exhibit 7-2. A vehicle with a result of 554 has experienced 554 percent of the results. The names of the actual makes and models of the vehicles in Exhibit 7-3 have been substituted with fictitious names for the purposes of this demonstration.

With the information provided in Exhibit 7-3, the following conclusions could be made about the vehicle models from 1992 to 1994:

- The average loss payment varied widely among passenger vehicles with a ten-fold difference between the cars with the lowest and highest average loss payment.

Exhibit 7-3
Collision Highlights—1992-94 Private Passenger Cars

	Best Results				Worst Results			
	Make & Series	Body Style	Size	Result (in %)	Make & Series	Body Style	Size	Result (in %)
Average Loss Payment per Insured Vehicle Year	Basic Van V-1	PV	L	53	Sports Car S-1	SP	M	554
	Luxury Van V-2	PV	L	54	Sports Car S-2	SP	M	372
	Station Wgn W-1	SW	M	55	Luxury Sports L-3	SP	S	324
	Family Car F-1	4DR	M	56	Sports Car S-3	SP	S	386
	Luxury Van V-3	PV	L	56	Sports Car S-4	SP	S	282
Claim Frequency	Luxury Sport L-1	SP	S	56	Family Car F-5	2DR	S	173
	Mid Sport M-1	PV	L	56	Family Car F-6	2DR	S	156
	Luxury Sport L-2	SP	S	64	Sports Car S-5	SP	S	154
	Family Car	F-2	M	64	Sports Car S-6	2DR	S	151
	Luxury Sport L-2	SP	S	65	Sports Car S-7	SP	S	149
Average Loss Payment per Claim	Luxury Van V-4	PV	L	68	Sports Car S-8	SP	M	485
	Basic Van V-5	PV	L	69	Luxury Sport L-4	SP	S	428
	Family Car F-3	4DR	M	69	Sports Car S-9	SP	M	266
	Station Wgn W-2	SW	M	70	Luxury L-6	LX	M	243
	Family Car F-4	2DR	M	72	Sports Car S-10	SP	S	226

Results are relative—100 represents the average for all passenger vehicles.

Body Style: PV-Passenger Van, SW-Station Wagon, 4DR-Four Door, 2DR- Two Door, SP-Sports,
LX-Luxury

Size: S-Small, M-Medium, L-Large

Source: Highway Loss Data Institute.

- Station wagons and passenger vans had the lowest average loss payment.
- Sports cars and luxury cars had the highest average loss payment.
- One sports car (S-8, an aluminum body midsize sports model) experienced average loss payments per claim that were 485 percent of the average.

In summary, from HLDI reports, the actual results for a vehicle can be compared to the average to determine the results for that passenger vehicle. Generalizations can also be made regarding the loss results for certain types and sizes of vehicles.

Protection Afforded to Passengers

Safety features that protect passengers provide loss control for bodily injury. Every new passenger vehicle must meet federal standards that require designs that not only protect people in crashes but that also help drivers avoid crashes in the first place. These standards specify minimum levels of safety performance, but they do not ensure that all cars are equally safe. Automakers decide the extent to which they will exceed the minimums, and some vehicle characteristics are inherently safer than others.

Identifying the *safest* car is impossible, but some cars do have more and better safety features than others. Identifying some of these characteristics is possible. Safety features, performance in crash tests, and on-the-road crash experience are all important vehicle safety factors.

Crashworthiness

The most important safety features are those that reduce the chances of being killed or seriously injured in a crash. This aspect of vehicle design is referred to as **crashworthiness**.

> **Crashworthiness** refers to the vehicle design engineering that reduces or eliminates injury in an auto accident.

How a car's body and structure perform in a crash is no longer an afterthought for auto manufacturers. It is part of the basic engineering design. Exhibit 7-4 shows how engineered crush zones (areas of the vehicle designed to crumple, absorb energy, and reduce injury to occupants) protect the passenger compartment.

Exhibit 7-4
Vehicle Crush Zones

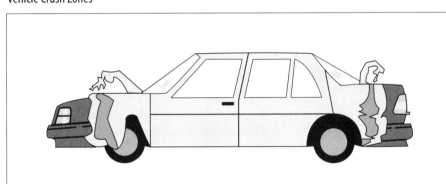

Front and rear crush zones are designed to absorb crash energy and reduce forces reaching the rigid occupant compartment.

Source: Insurance Institute for Highway Safety, September 1995.

Computer modeling allows manufacturers to determine at the design stage how different structures will perform in crashes. Automakers might call these crush zones "safety cages" or "crumple zones." These are structural design features that are basic to modern car crashworthiness. Car bodies used to be built on frames, but now the body itself usually replaces the frame. This **unibody** design includes a strong occupant compartment—the safety cage—with an energy-absorbing structure in the front and rear crush zones. These zones are designed to absorb crash energy in a controlled manner, thereby reducing the forces inside the passenger compartment. The combination of reduced force and little or no distortion of the compartment is key to preventing occupant injuries.

> **Unibody** literally means "one body." Supported by sheet metal, the body of the car acts as its frame. Many current models are constructed as unibodies. Some large passenger cars and full-size trucks still use a conventional frame (chassis) with a car body added on top of the frame.

Vehicle Size

Another design characteristic that plays an important role in occupant protection is vehicle size. The laws of physics dictate that, everything else being equal, the larger the vehicle crush zones, the lower the crash force that reaches the occupant compartment. In crashes, people traveling in small vehicles are at much greater risk of injury than those in large vehicles. In relation to their numbers on the road, small vehicles account for more than twice as many occupant deaths. This relationship can be seen in Exhibit 7-5 for the year 1994.

Some people claim that small cars are easier to maneuver in an emergency (thus less likely to be involved in crashes) and that maneuverability offsets some, or all, of the disadvantages of small-car crashworthiness. This simply is not true. Some small cars might be more maneuverable than some large ones, but they are not less likely to be involved in crashes. The best evidence of this comes from insurance claims data. Another point to consider is that most young people begin by buying small cars. Consequently, a disproportionate number of small autos are driven by drivers who tend to have the most losses. *Claims for crash damage and occupant injuries are more frequent for small cars than for large ones.*[1]

Some argue that the danger of small cars could be minimized if all cars were small, thus reducing the likelihood of mismatches between large and small cars in crashes. However, most deaths in small cars occur in either single-vehicle crashes or collisions with vehicles other than private passenger cars. The death rate in single-vehicle crashes of the smallest cars is more than double the rate of that of the largest cars. So making all cars small would not solve small-car safety problems.

Another assumption regarding bodily injury claims that might seem reasonable is that the worst loss experience occurs within the small-car category with experience progressively improving in the midsize and large-car categories. Data from HLDI validates that assumption.

Personal insurance specialists do not have to be thoroughly familiar with the data, tables, and graphs for all vehicles. However, some generalizations should be noted, especially concerning the relationship between size of vehicle and loss tendencies. Small cars tend to have the worst collision and bodily injury loss experience. Specialists should be familiar with those vehicles that make up the most hazardous of the class. The following are general results reported by the Insurance Institute for Highway Safety:

- Among the ten passenger vehicles with the highest driver death rates, nine are small and one is midsize. Vehicles in this category tend to be small sports cars or two-door cars.

- All ten vehicles with the lowest driver death rates are either large or midsize. They tend to be passenger vans, stations wagons, and large or midsize sedans.

- Many of the single-vehicle crashes causing driver death involve rolling over. These losses tend to involve sports cars or vehicles

Exhibit 7-5
Occupant Deaths by Vehicle Size

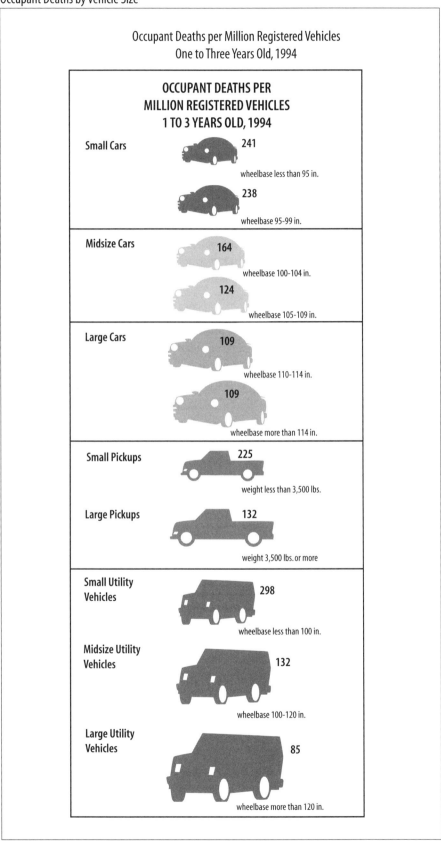

Occupant Deaths per Million Registered Vehicles
One to Three Years Old, 1994

OCCUPANT DEATHS PER
MILLION REGISTERED VEHICLES
1 TO 3 YEARS OLD, 1994

Small Cars — 241 — wheelbase less than 95 in.

238 — wheelbase 95-99 in.

Midsize Cars — 164 — wheelbase 100-104 in.

124 — wheelbase 105-109 in.

Large Cars — 109 — wheelbase 110-114 in.

109 — wheelbase more than 114 in.

Small Pickups — 225 — weight less than 3,500 lbs.

Large Pickups — 132 — weight 3,500 lbs. or more

Small Utility Vehicles — 298 — wheelbase less than 100 in.

Midsize Utility Vehicles — 132 — wheelbase 100-120 in.

Large Utility Vehicles — 85 — wheelbase more than 120 in.

Source: Insurance Institute for Highway Safety, September 1995.

with a high center of gravity.[2] Many sport utility vehicles are more susceptible to rolling over than private passenger vehicles as a group because vehicles with a high center of gravity perform better in off-road use.

Safety Belts (Seat Belts)

> **Jargon Alert!**
>
> Insureds often receive "rate credits" from their insurers when they practice loss control and risk management techniques such as having passive seat belts and childproof door locks. Insurers can adjust the insured's rates to reflect these safety measures.

Safety belts (including lap and shoulder belts) keep the vehicle occupants inside the compartment and prevent or decelerate violent contact with hard interior surfaces. They are also effective in reducing serious injuries and fatalities in severe crashes. When an automobile crash fatality occurs, it is often because the occupant was thrown from the vehicle and was probably not wearing a seat belt at the time of the crash. Seat belts cannot be effective if they are not used. Passive seat belts (activated when a front-seat occupant enters the vehicle and closes the door) are more likely to be used than seat belts that must be buckled manually. Consequently, passive seat belts are often viewed as a more favorable underwriting characteristic. Often, insurers award insureds *rate credits* for having passive seat belts.

Types of Seat Belts

All new passenger vehicles have shoulder belts on inertia reels that allow upper body movement during normal driving but that lock when a vehicle is slowed by hard braking or a crash. Some inertia reels provide additional protection to a passenger by engaging when the shoulder belt is pulled quickly (which might occur during an accident).

In frontal crashes (the most common kind), shoulder belts still allow some forward movement of the upper body because either the webbing on the reel or a loose belt around an occupant pulls tight, and the belt itself stretches slightly. In serious crashes, a belted occupant can move enough to be injured. Two devices can be included in the belting system to reduce this movement:

- *Crash tensioners* tighten belts during the first milliseconds of a crash.
- *Webbing* grabbers clamp the belt just outside the reel.[3]

Seat Belt Laws

Since the 1980s, most states have enacted mandatory seat belt laws designed to increase seat belt usage among adults. These laws (as well as publicity campaigns and law enforcement) have helped to more than triple seat belt usage from around 15 percent in 1984 to just under 50 percent in 1990. The National Highway Traffic Safety Administration estimates that this increase has saved more than 20,000 lives and averted 500,000 serious injuries.[4]

Seat belt laws and their enforcement vary among the states. Enforcement is classified as either primary enforcement (the law can be enforced on its own) or secondary enforcement (the law is enforced only in conjunction with other traffic offenses, such as after being stopped for speeding).

All states have some form of child restraint law that typically requires children under a certain age or size to be buckled in an approved child restraint system or seat belt. The compliance rate, typically over 80 percent for these laws, is much better than for mandatory seat belt laws. However, the application of these laws differs significantly by state. Some states require only seat belt usage for children under age two, and others are more strict. In many instances, children are not required to be belted at all past a certain age, until they become adults and then fall under the mandatory seat belt statutes.

Specialists should be aware of the seat belt laws within their states of responsibility and the enforcement of the laws. Identifying a seat belt violation on a motor vehicle report or in a claim review might indicate a morale hazard.

Air Bags

Even the best seat belt designs and laws cannot prevent all head and chest injuries in serious frontal crashes. **Air bags** help prevent injuries by creating an energy-absorbing cushion between an occupant's upper body and the steering wheel, instrument panel, or windshield. Air bags are a simple device. In moderate and severe frontal crashes, sensors signal inflators to fill the bags with harmless gas. The bags fill within a fraction of a second and begin deflating instantly as they cushion people. Peak inflation occurs in less than 1/20th of a second.

> **Air bags,** also called supplemental restraint systems (SRSs), are loss reduction devices designed to inflate in moderate-to-severe frontal crashes.

Driver deaths in frontal crashes are about 20 percent lower in cars with air bags than in similar cars with belts only. In all kinds of crashes, air bags reduce deaths by about 14 percent in addition to lives already being saved by safety belts.[5]

The Insurance Institute for Highway Safety reported that 91 percent of all 1994 passenger car models were equipped with driver-side air bags. Sixty-three percent had air bags for both drivers and right front-seat passengers.[6] IIHS also reported a 23 percent reduction in deaths in front and front-angle crashes for cars equipped with air bags.[7] As air bag technology advances, significant reductions in crash fatalities and serious injuries are expected.

Instances of serious injury caused by an air bag are rare for adults; the speed and force of air bag inflation might occasionally cause injuries, mostly minor abrasions or bruises. Air bag-induced injuries and deaths result occasionally when children contact bags before full inflation, often because children are not restrained by a seat belt or infants are placed in rear-facing restraints placed in the front passenger seats.

Harmless gasses are used to inflate the bags. Many people mistakenly think the cornstarch or talcum powder used as a lubricant in the bag-folding process is smoke. This powder dissipates rapidly and should not be cause for concern. Personal auto insurance specialists should view air bags as an injury reduction feature.

Side-Impact Protection

Protecting people in side impacts, which account for about 30 percent of all passenger vehicle occupant deaths, involves a different set of considerations than protecting them from frontal crashes does. Many serious injuries occur when the force of a crash drives a door into an occupant. To reduce the likelihood of this, all new passenger vehicles have side-guard beams that can be effective in single-vehicle side impacts with objects like trees and poles. But side-guard beams have not been redesigned to reduce loss due to vehicle-to-vehicle impacts. In 1993, the federal standard was upgraded to include side-impact crash tests for the first time. At least 40 percent of 1996 cars from each automaker must have met these new performance requirements. Many large cars are meeting those standards with few or no design changes. Vans, pickups, and utility vehicles must meet the side-impact-protection standard starting with 1999 models, but some meet it already.

Manufacturers are also developing side air bags to protect drivers and right-front passengers in side-impact crashes. These bags are typically smaller than frontal air bags, and they fully inflate more quickly than frontal bags.[8] The first side-impact air bags to protect drivers and front passengers were introduced in the 1995 Volvo 850.

Head Restraints

In rear-end crashes, seat backs and head restraints can reduce potentially injurious backward movement by occupants. To ensure minimum protection, all passenger vehicles must meet federal seat back strength requirements. To prevent people's heads from being snapped back in relatively minor rear-end crashes, head restraints are required in front seats of all new passenger vehicles. Rear-seat head restraints are not required but are appearing in more and more cars.

All head restraints are not equally effective, as shown in Exhibit 7-6. Some are fixed (not adjustable). Many are not high enough to position behind tall people's heads. They also might be set too far back to provide adequate protection. To keep heads from snapping back in rear-end crashes and causing neck injuries, head restraints must be high enough so that they are directly behind and very close to the backs of people's heads.

In general, fixed head restraints are more effective in reducing injury than adjustable vehicle head restraints. They are more likely to be behind occupants' heads because most people leave the adjustable kind in the down position.[9]

Infant and Child Seats

Children too small to fit adult safety belts should be buckled into specially designed safety seats. When used properly, these offer good crash protection. Infants who cannot sit up should be in rear-facing seats placed in the back seats of vehicles. These child safety seats can pose a safety risk if placed in a front seat with a passenger air bag. In a deployment, an inflating bag could hit the infant seat with enough force to seriously injure a child. In vehicles with no rear seat or in which the rear seat is too small to fit a child safety seat, manufacturers are allowed to install manual cut-off switches for passenger air bags.[10]

Exhibit 7-6
Head Restraint Effectiveness

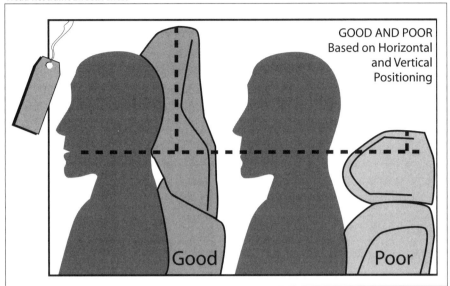

Source: Insurance Institute For Highway Safety, September 1995.

Collision Loss Control Features

The features listed in this section are designed to reduce collisions. A reduction in vehicle collisions would decrease bodily injury and property damage losses.

Anti-Lock Braking Systems (ABS)

Preventing crashes in the first place might seem like a better idea than protecting people during crashes. Manufacturers tout features like traction control and four-wheel drive as safety features. These might improve vehicle performance under certain road conditions, but whether these features actually help prevent crashes is unclear. Drivers might react to the improved vehicle performance by driving more recklessly or by driving in bad weather that might have previously kept them off the road. If these features change driving behavior, the anticipated safety benefits might not materialize.

One of the most touted crash-avoidance features in recent years is the anti-lock braking system (ABS). When a driver hits regular brakes hard, wheels can lock and skidding can occur, causing loss of control and extending stopping distances, especially on wet or slippery roads. An ABS pumps brakes automatically, many times a second, to prevent lockup and to enable a driver to maintain control. An ABS can mean improved braking, but not always. On dry roads, an ABS does not substantially shorten stopping distances compared with conventional brakes.[11]

The National Highway Traffic Safety Administration issued a "Technical Report" in May 1995 on studies of crashes involving vehicles equipped with anti-lock braking systems. The report notes the following findings:

- A significant reduction in nonfatal frontal impacts with another motor vehicle in transport crashes was associated with the presence of an ABS.

- Significant increases in nonfatal impacts with parked vehicles and fixed objects and in nonfatal side impacts with parked vehicles and fixed objects were associated with the presence of an ABS.

- Significant increases in fatal rollover crashes and in fatal side-impacts with parked vehicles and fixed objects were associated with the presence of an ABS.[12]

These study results are consistent with the accident analysis published by the Insurance Institute for Highway Safety in January 1994 and suggest that anti-lock brakes have not completely produced the positive results that were expected.

Why the ABS has not shown expected on-the-road safety benefits is not clear. Perhaps drivers do not know how to use it effectively. Drivers have been trained to brake gently on slippery roads or to pump brakes to avoid a skid. This behavior has to be unlearned with an ABS. The most effective use of the ABS has been called "stomp and steer." ABS activation requires hard and continuous brake pressure.

A federal study reported the effect of ABS at "close to zero." Whether the presence of an ABS is an underwriting plus or minus is still unclear. The ABS might be a plus if the vehicle owner anticipates driving on slick roads.

Daytime Running Lights

Daytime running lights are typically either high-beam headlights operating at reduced intensity or low-beam headlights operating at full or reduced power. The ignition switch activates these lights. These lights, which increase contrast between vehicles and their background to make cars more visible to oncoming drivers, are an inexpensive way to reduce multiple-vehicle daytime crashes.

In Canada and other countries where they are required, daytime running lights have reduced daylight car-to-car crashes. These lights are standard or optional features on many 1996 model cars in the United States.[13]

Vehicle Theft

Theft losses pose a particular problem for personal lines auto insurance specialists because, at first glance, these losses seem as random and unpredictable as any other losses that auto insurance might cover. Two sources of information can help specialists make an informed assessment of the theft peril.

The first source is the data on theft losses compiled by HLDI. HLDI presents tables of the most frequently and least frequently stolen vehicles within a group of model years. The results are compared to the average for the entire year's groups. Why one vehicle becomes a theft target and another vehicle does not is the subject of speculation. Following are some assumptions made about targeted vehicles:

- Their parts can be sold easily (the car is "chopped" and sold as parts rather than as a whole vehicle).

- They can be easily sold. The demand might be in another country, which makes retrieval more difficult.

- They match vehicles that have been totaled and purchased at a salvage auction. The **vehicle identification number (VIN)** plates are then removed from the totaled vehicles and placed on the stolen vehicles. The stolen vehicles then reenter the used car market and are sold.

The second source of theft loss information to consider is the overall theft rate in the community in which the applicant lives or in which the vehicles are garaged. Such data are available from the National Automobile Theft Bureau. Even vehicle types listed by HLDI with the worst theft loss experience might be acceptable if owned by a person who lives in a county that has not had a vehicle theft loss in the last ten years. The same vehicles owned by someone who must park the vehicle on the street each night in an urban community with a vehicle theft rate that is twice the national average represent a much higher risk.

Anti-Theft Devices

Many types of anti-theft devices are available, ranging from simple steering wheel locks to sophisticated passive devices that shut off the fuel supply and the electrical systems when armed or that send radio signals to the local police department when triggered.

Specialists should become familiar with state regulations that require rate discounts to be given for some of these protection features. Careful inquiry might be needed if the driver is operating in a state that requires a discount for anti-theft devices because these features are typically added by vehicle owners rather than included by vehicle manufacturers. Installation by the owner increases concern about the proper installation of the device. The underwriter might request documentation from the anti-theft device installer to verify the exact type of device that has been added to the vehicle. Many alarm systems now include a certificate that the dealer completes to identify the alarm system and verify professional installation.

Devices that lock to steering wheels provide only a limited deterrent to vehicle theft (the thief might choose another vehicle to steal), but they provide no protection from vandalism as the result of a break-in and the theft of the radio or other vehicle components. The weakness of that type of lock is the steering wheel to which it is attached. To protect the driver in the event of an accident, a steering wheel is designed to break. It is made of a small metal rod covered by padding and a decorative cover. A steering wheel looks like a substantial structure, but it can easily be cut with a hacksaw. The steering wheel can then be bent, the lock removed, and the car driven away.

For an alarm system to be effective, the vehicle must have a hood lock that can be released only from inside the vehicle. This lock prevents

A **vehicle identification number** (commonly called the VIN) is the serial number unique to each vehicle. The seventeen-digit number identifies the make, model year, body style, factory, and engine size of a vehicle. The VIN can also be used to identify the symbol used in rating physical damage coverages.

the disabling of the alarm by disconnecting the battery. For premium discounts and credits, alarm systems are placed in the following categories (listed from least to most effective):

- Alarm devices that sound an alarm that can be heard at a distance of at least 300 feet or for a minimum of three minutes
- Active (must be activated) disabling devices that disable the vehicle by making the fuel, ignition, or starting system inoperative
- Passive (occurs automatically—a manual step is not required) disabling devices that disable the vehicle by making the fuel, ignition, or starting system inoperative

Alarms are a deterrent only if the vehicle owner uses them. Some vehicle owners become disillusioned with false alarms that awaken them in the middle of the night. After several disturbed nights, the owner might turn off the alarm.

Active disabling devices require the manual step of enabling the system. The passive disabling devices eliminate the factor of human error and provide the most protection.

Special Vehicle Types and Accessories

Some vehicles and accessories create unique insurance exposures. The variety of these unique exposures is constantly changing. For example, mobile telephones and citizens' band (CB) radios were originally very expensive. Their installation in a vehicle added a unique theft hazard. As these accessories grew in popularity, more manufacturers entered the market, which reduced the cost. These items now produce very little theft exposure because fencing (selling as stolen goods) the items for any value is difficult. Specialists should be aware of the current *popular* accessories and hazards as the environment changes.

Antique and Classic Vehicles

An **antique** auto is a vehicle that is at least twenty-five years old. Vehicles rated as antiques are provided a substantial premium discount, so insurers generally restrict their use to parades and exhibitions.

A **classic** auto is a vehicle that is at least ten years old and has a significantly higher average value than other autos of the same make and model year. A vehicle rated as a classic generally has no use restrictions.

Collectible vehicles have been popular for decades. That popularity has created a market for vehicles that appreciate in value. Specialists need to proceed with more than the usual amount of caution when considering **antique** and **classic** vehicles because of the unique problems associated with these vehicles.

Stated amount is a loss settlement option for auto physical damage coverages. An appraisal is obtained for the vehicle, and the appraised value becomes the basis for rating. Maximum loss settlement is based on the lowest of (1) the stated amount, (2) the ACV, or (3) the amount to repair or replace.

Because antique and classic vehicles are typically insured under a **stated amount** loss settlement option (achieved by attaching endorsement PP 03 08), the value of the vehicle must be established before a policy is issued. If the vehicle has been preserved in its original condition, establishing an acceptable value can usually be accomplished by consulting price guides for old cars, by having the vehicle appraised by a third party agreed to by the vehicle owner and the insurer, or by having the vehicle appraised by someone in the claim department of the insurer who has specialized knowledge of values for old cars.

If antique or classic vehicles are restored to their original condition, the owners expect the cost of restoration to be reflected in the value of the vehicles on a dollar-for-dollar basis. Restoration can be expensive.

If the vehicle requires extensive work to restore it to like-new condition, the vehicle's owner could easily spend more for restoration than the vehicle is worth on the old car market. Specialists should not rely on documentation of purchase price plus documented cost of restoration to establish the current value of such vehicles.

The premiums charged for physical damage coverages are based on the stated amount of the vehicles. If the actual cash value of the vehicle at the time of loss is significantly less than the stated amount, the insurer might pay the stated amount in the event of a total loss (even though the policy states that a total loss will be settled on the lesser of the actual cash value at the time of loss or the stated amount). Even though that is contrary to the policy provisions, the insurer might judge that having insureds pay an additional premium for stated amount coverage and then receive a smaller loss settlement is not reasonable.

Another insurance-related problem unique to antique and classic vehicles is that, over time, they tend to increase in value rather than depreciate. A vehicle insured five years ago for a stated amount of $15,000 might be worth considerably more today. If the insured is not encouraged to periodically review the current market value of the vehicle and adjust the stated amount as needed, the insurer and the insured could disagree about how a **total** loss should be settled on a vehicle that has rapidly appreciated in value. Even though the insurer is relying on policy language specifying that the stated amount is the maximum that will be paid under any circumstances after a total loss has occurred, it is unlikely that an insured would be happy about such a settlement.

> **Jargon Alert!**
>
> The word "total" is often used to describe the severity of an auto loss or the act of damaging a vehicle beyond repair.
>
> A vehicle is a total loss if it has sustained damage which exceeds its actual cash value.

If an insurer fails to use care in establishing an accurate market value of a vehicle when it is insured and agrees to a stated value amount that is considerably above the true market value, another potential problem is created. Should the insured try to sell the vehicle and in the process find that the market value is much less than the insured stated amount, a moral hazard might surface. The insured might be tempted to find a way to total the vehicle in hopes of recovering the full stated amount from the insurer. This is most likely to occur when the owner has invested a great deal of money restoring a vehicle to like-new condition only to learn that the market value of the restored vehicle is less than what was spent on the project. Specialists might review past claims and the insured's credit report when initially underwriting the application to affirm the absence of a moral hazard.

Foreign Vehicles

Foreign vehicles present three unique problems. The first involves vehicles that were manufactured overseas, purchased in the country of origin, and shipped to the United States. Vehicles that are not specifically made for sale in the United States do not usually conform to U.S. safety emissions standards unless modifications are made. The owner is allowed to bring the car into the United States, but the necessary modifications must be made within a specified period of time (usually from

90 to 120 days). If the owner does not provide the government agencies with documentation of the modifications within the applicable time, the vehicle might be seized by the U.S. Customs Department and destroyed. The purchaser of a nonconforming foreign-made vehicle, who is not familiar with the problems involving these vehicles, might be tempted to "sell the vehicle to the insurance company" by creating a total loss rather than pay for safety and emissions modifications or lose the vehicle to the Customs Department without compensation.

The second problem presented by a foreign vehicle manufactured overseas and shipped to the United States (sometimes called a "gray market" auto) is that it often has the same make and model name as a vehicle manufactured in the United States, but is not similar in appearance, and the vehicle identification number (VIN) does not match its U.S. counterpart. These vehicles are costly to repair because the parts that would be used to repair their U.S. counterparts will not fit these vehicles. A photo of a vehicle at the time of application can reveal that the vehicle was made overseas. The specialist can also identify the foreign vehicle by checking the VIN number against the manufacturer's standard codes by using a catalog of the standard codes or using a computer database that performs this function.

The third potential problem for specialists involves foreign-made vehicles that are sold in the United States in extremely low volumes. Either mechanics familiar enough with a particular type of foreign vehicle to do repair work on the vehicle or the repair parts might not be readily available. Repair costs could be unusually high if replacement parts can only be obtained directly from an overseas manufacturer. If the insurer must pay for a rental vehicle while the insured's foreign vehicle is being repaired and repairs are delayed weeks or months, the costs could be substantial. Some insurers place foreign vehicle endorsements on the policies insuring such vehicles. Those endorsements limit payments made for rental vehicles if repairs are delayed for an unusually long time.

Additional Equipment

The PAP identifies the following four types of electronic equipment:

1. Radios and stereos
2. Other electronic equipment
3. Operating equipment
4. Radar and laser detectors

Coverage varies by equipment type. Some equipment presents unique insurance hazards.

Radios and Stereos

The policy covers equipment that reproduces sound (radios, stereos, tape players, and compact disc players) if it is either:

- *Permanently* installed in an insured vehicle

FYI

The rarest production vehicle made was the type 41 Bugatti. In the 1930s, only six hand-assembled Bugattis were made. The vehicles were guaranteed for the life of the owner.

Jargon Alert!

The word "permanent" is not defined in the contract and is a point of debate among insurers. Interpretations of something that is permanent include the following:

- Has wires connecting the equipment to the vehicle
- Requires a tool to accomplish removal
- Was professionally installed
- Was installed using hardware
- Was installed in a radio or console opening

- Removable from a *permanently* installed housing unit in the insured vehicle and operated only from the vehicle's electrical system (a *pull-out* installation allows a stereo component to be easily removed from a vehicle for safe storage)

No dollar limit is provided for electronic equipment, other than the loss settlement provisions (the lesser of the ACV or the cost to repair). If an insured with a vehicle with a $2,500 value installed a $1,000 stereo in the vehicle, the insured would pay a physical damage premium based on a $2,500 value if the insurer has no knowledge of the addition. A stereo of this value is a target theft item. If the stereo were stolen, the insurer would pay the ACV of the stereo plus the repairs for the damage to the vehicle caused by the break-in. For this reason, many insurers are including questions on applications and renewals about the addition of expensive electronic equipment.

Some stereo components can easily be pulled from the housing, unplugged, and stored. The pull-out installation can be a good alternative for an insured who owns an expensive stereo but who lives or works in a high-crime area. The policy states that the component is covered if it is "in or upon" the covered auto. If the insured stores the component in the trunk, coverage continues. If the insured places the component in a briefcase and carries it into the office, coverage is discontinued by the PAP. The personal insurance specialist should caution the insured about this possibility.

Coverage for any tapes, records, disks, or other media is excluded.

Other Electronic Equipment

The PAP groups a second category of covered electronic equipment as equipment that "receives or transmits audio, visual, or data signals." This category includes the following:

- Citizens' band radios
- Telephones
- Two-way mobile radios
- Scanning monitor receivers
- Television monitor receivers
- Videocassette recorders
- Audiocassette recorders
- Personal computers

To be covered, an item must be permanently installed in an opening in the dashboard or the console that is normally used for a radio, which is not possible for all of the equipment listed above. A television or personal computer is an attractive target for a thief. A specialist must consider the location of the vehicle and determine whether coverage can be offered through a coverage-extending endorsement. Risk management alternatives such as alarms or loss control activities (for example, storing items in the trunk when not in use) should be recommended.

Operating Equipment

Vehicle-operating computers and monitors are common in new vehicles. The PAP covers both of those without limitation.

Radar and Laser Detectors

Radar and laser detectors are excluded by the PAP and the homeowners policy. Insurers cannot defend coverage provided to equipment that is designed to assist a driver to speed without detection. Insureds who have a radar or laser detector should be advised of the coverage gap.

Customizing

The PAP excludes living facilities, special furniture, and features (including custom murals, painting, decals, or graphics). The terms *custom*, *furnishing*, and *equipment* are not defined in the policy but are understood to be items that are generally not provided during the original manufacture of a vehicle. Additions and changes made after the vehicle is purchased might be examples of customization. If coverage is excluded, it can often be bought back by endorsement.

Vehicle Age and Condition

Before recommending coverage, specialists must be confident that every vehicle submitted for consideration is in safe operating condition. If the vehicle has any prior damage, that damage must be identified (particularly if the policy is to include physical damage coverage) and evaluated regarding its effect on the safe operation of the vehicle.

Most personal auto insurance applications include areas in which to list the current odometer reading and to briefly describe any existing glass or body damage to the vehicle. However, even when a producer has thoroughly examined a vehicle and meticulously noted any existing damage on the application, the specialist or underwriter, not having seen the vehicle, is at a disadvantage in making informed judgments about the condition of the vehicle. A good working relationship with the producer is necessary if the specialist is to receive enough accurate information to determine whether the condition of a vehicle should weigh as a negative factor in the underwriting process. The importance of the inspection should be emphasized as part of the front-line underwriting process. The importance of a careful inspection increases as the age of the vehicle increases. An inspection helps avoid the following:

- Paying for damage to the vehicle that existed when the application was taken

- Insuring a vehicle that is not in safe operating condition

Several states have enacted regulations that require a pre-insurance vehicle inspection as part of the application process. An inspection form, usually in a format prescribed by the state insurance department, must be completed in detail and submitted with the application. Two color photographs of the vehicle are usually required as well, with the first showing the front and one side of the vehicle, and the second showing the rear and opposite side of the vehicle. A photo might also be required of the safety certification label on the driver-side door jamb taken in a manner that enables the VIN to be read from the photo. Optional equipment included on the vehicle must be noted and existing damage identified on the inspection form. Some state laws require that a copy of the inspection report and photos of the vehicle be included in the claim file for every total loss or be included in the claim file if the claim involves a physical damage loss that exceeds a certain dollar amount, such as $2,000.

Pre-insurance inspection and photo requirements not only help underwriters determine the condition of the vehicle at the time of application; they also deter some forms of insurance fraud. Insurers are not likely to issue a policy on a nonexistent vehicle (sometimes called a "paper vehicle" because it exists only as a forged title) if the applicant must present a vehicle for inspection as part of the application process. Insurers are also less likely to pay for existing damage if the vehicle is photographed and thoroughly inspected and if any existing damage is noted on an inspection form. Some insurers use pre-insurance inspection and photos even though the state does not require them. An inspection program is particularly helpful in a state in which insurance fraud is a conspicuous problem. Exhibit 7-7 is an example of a pre-insurance inspection report form.

The goal for specialists considering vehicle hazards associated with age and condition of the vehicle is to make the best possible assessment of the overall condition of the vehicle from the information available and to determine whether the condition favorably or unfavorably affects the safe operation of the vehicle. For example, suppose an old vehicle has been poorly maintained, as evidenced by exterior physical deterioration worse than the average for vehicles of the same age. The specialist could reasonably assume that the equipment crucial to safe operation, such as tires, brakes, suspension, exhaust system, lights, and turn signals, is in equally poor condition and that the vehicle might be an unacceptably poor insurance risk.

State vehicle inspections can help to ensure proper vehicle maintenance; however, inspections vary widely in quality and scope, and some states do not even have vehicle inspections. A specialist would be able to place confidence in a state vehicle inspection only if it were comprehensive and if the process could not be bypassed.

Vehicles that have been damaged so badly that they become total losses are purchased by an insurer from a claimant during the claim settlement process. These vehicles are then issued a **salvage title** to indicate their status. A salvage title identifies a vehicle that has sustained significant damage. Vehicle owners often buy the car back from the insurance company after the loss has been settled. The vehicle might still be in an operable condition or require minor repairs to become operable. A salvage title should be a good indicator to an underwriter that a vehicle has sustained previous damage. However, a salvage title

A **salvage title** replaces the regular vehicle title when a vehicle has sustained damages which exceed its value.

Exhibit 7-7
Automobile Inspection Report

AUTOMOBILE INSPECTION REPORT

Policy Number

Insured's Name _____ Telephone ( ) _____
            Last   First   Initial

Insured's Address _____
            Number and Street   City   State   ZIP Code

Insurer _____
    (Where Applicable)

VEHICLE INFORMATION

Licence Plate No. _____ State _____ Color _____

Year _____ Make _____ Model _____

Body Style
☐ 2 Door ☐ 4 Door ☐ Station Wagon ☐ Van ☐ Minivan ☐ Truck ☐ Convertible ☐ Hatchback ☐ Motorcycle ☐ Other

Vehicle Identification Number _| 1 | 2 | 3 | 4 | 5 | 6 | 7 | 8 | 9 | 10 | 11 | 12 | 13 | 14 | 15 | 16 | 17 | Mileage _____
(Obtain directly from vehicle)   (Odometer Reading)

ACCESSORIES AND OPTIONAL EQUIPMENT NOT FACTORY INSTALLED: (Check all that apply)

☐ Air Bag(s)   ☐ Power Brakes
☐ Air Conditioning   ☐ Power Steering
☐ Anti-Theft Device   Brand _____   ☐ Power Trunk
                      Model _____   ☐ Radar Detector
☐ Automatic Transmission   ☐ Radio/Stereo
☐ CB Radio   ☐ Rear Window Defogger
☐ Compact Disc Player   ☐ Rear Wiper
☐ Cruise Control   ☐ Tape Deck
☐ Custom Wheels/Tires   ☐ Telephone
☐ Digital Instruments   ☐ Tilt Wheel
☐ Manual Transmission   ☐ Vinyl Top
☐ Mounted Brake Lights   ☐ Other _____
☐ Power Antenna
                                                  _____
                                                  _____

Enter Make and Model, where applicable _____

NOTE: The insured may, at his/her discretion, attach copies of receipts and/or other evidence showing the make and model of any accessories not factory installed.

EXISTING DAMAGE TO THE AUTOMOBILE: (Check for damage or rust)

☐ Front Bumper   ☐ Rear Bumper   ☐ Hood   ☐ Right Rear Glass
☐ Grill   ☐ Trunk/Rear Door   ☐ Roof   ☐ Right Front Glass
☐ Left Front Fender   ☐ Right Rear Quarter Panel ☐ Windshield   ☐ Seats
☐ Left Front Door   ☐ Right Rear Door   ☐ Left Front Glass ☐ Center Console
☐ Left Rear Door   ☐ Right Front Door   ☐ Left Rear Glass   ☐ Floor Covering
☐ Left Rear Quarter Panel ☐ Right Front Fender   ☐ Rear Glass   ☐ Dash Board

Describe items checked above and any other damage _____

THE ABOVE IS A TRUE STATEMENT RECORDING ANY AND ALL EXISTING, VISIBLE DAMAGE, RUST AND/OR MISSING PARTS AS OF THE DATE OF THIS INSPECTION. THE UNDERSIGNED CERTIFIES, UNDER PENALTY OF PERJURY, THAT THIS INSPECTION RECORD IS TRUE AND COMPLETE TO THE BEST OF HIS/HER KNOWLEDGE.

Inspector's Name _____ Inspector's Signature _____

Date _____/_____/_____ Time _____ ☐ AM ☐ PM Location _____

Party Presenting Vehicle for Identification _____

Relationship to Insured _____ Signature _____
                        (Where Applicable)

Date _____/_____/_____ Time _____ ☐ AM ☐ PM Location _____

Photo/VIN explanation section: _____

can be *laundered* (remove the salvage marking from the title record) by selling the vehicle in a state that does not mark the title as a salvage, so it is not always a reliable identification. The vehicle owner could later say that an accident occurred and file another claim for damages. An inspection report and photos of the vehicle at the time of application are among the most effective methods for identifying a vehicle with prior damage and for eliminating this exposure.

Vehicle Location

The underwriting considerations typically associated with location of operation or garaging (traffic congestion, road conditions, and adequacy of traffic controls) might only be available by inspecting the location.

A specialist might not be able to do more than simply form some general impressions about traffic congestion, road conditions, and traffic controls. However, some familiarity with the territories from which risks are submitted is essential to make informed judgments about how these factors affect the acceptability of an auto risk.

Territories used for insurance rating purposes are often large, encompassing both urban and rural driving environments. For example, suppose two otherwise equal applicants from the same rating territory are being considered for comparable coverages on similar vehicles. One drives ninety miles weekly to and from work in a traffic-congested urban area. The other drives thirty miles weekly to and from work in a predominantly rural area. The specialist might conclude that the applicant driving the shorter distance on less congested rural roads is the better risk for the premium dollars charged.

Claiming Behavior by Location

For auto exposures, **claiming behavior** is often measured by the number of bodily injury claims per 100 property damage claims. The differences in claiming behaviors among the states are significant. Exhibit 7-8 shows the number of bodily injury claims per 100 property damage claims for each state.

Not only does claiming behavior vary significantly among states, but significant claiming behavior differences can also exist among major cities (or between urban and rural communities) within the same state. The rate charged for coverage in a territory should support the loss experience in an area.

Differences in claiming behavior numbers are difficult to explain, but they probably have more to do with the aggressiveness of plaintiffs' attorneys and the population's general attitude toward insurance than with the damageability of vehicles or the severity of accidents.

Theft Rates by Location

Specialists should be aware of any areas in which vehicle theft rates are much higher than the average for communities of comparable size

Claiming behavior is the inclination people in a group have for submitting insurance claims.

Exhibit 7-8
Claiming Behavior in the United States (Bodily Injury Claims per 100 Property Damage Claims)

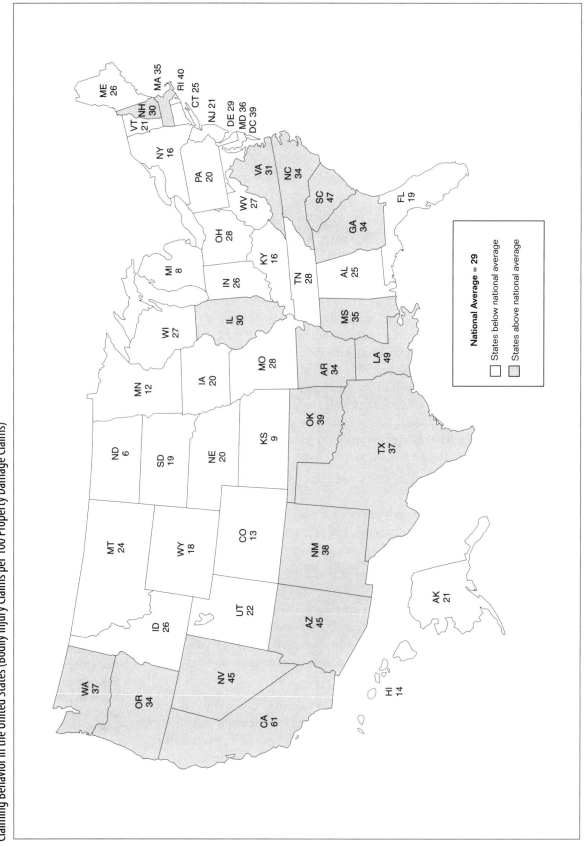

National Average = 29

☐ States below national average
▨ States above national average

within the same state. If an application is submitted on a vehicle that ranks high on the list of most frequently stolen vehicles and if the applicant lives in a community with an excessively high vehicle theft rate, the specialist might need to make further inquiries before making an underwriting decision. The following are appropriate questions:

- Is the vehicle kept in a locked garage overnight or on the street?
- Where is the vehicle parked during the workday?
- Is the vehicle equipped with any anti-theft devices?
- Has the applicant experienced any previous vehicle theft losses?

Too many negative responses to these important questions might mean that some alternatives are needed to limit the insurer's exposure to the theft peril. Available choices might include using a significant deductible on the insured's other-than-collision (comprehensive) coverage, installing an alarm system, or rejecting the application.

Highway Speed Limits

As a conservation measure following the Arab oil embargo of the mid-1970s, the speed limit on all national highways was lowered to fifty-five miles per hour. Until that time, seventy-five to eighty-five miles- per-hour limits had been typical. A byproduct of the lowered speed limit was a reduction in the number of highway deaths, largely attributed to the reduction of the maximum speed limit.

In 1987, the speed limits were allowed to increase to a maximum of sixty-five miles per hour on rural interstate roads, and the number of highway deaths was expected to climb immediately. Although the total number of deaths did increase during this period as states increased their speed limits, the relative number of deaths per mile traveled continued to decline.

Some researchers hypothesize that the increase in the legal speed limits did not have a dramatic effect because drivers had already been ignoring the posted fifty-five mile-per-hour limit. The increase of the speed limit to sixty-five miles per hour merely made legal what many drivers where doing anyway, so the net effect was minimal.

There are a number of reasons to expect that an increase in speed limits would cause an increase in the accident rate and/or the death rate from accidents. At higher speeds, drivers have less time to react to emergency situations and can travel farther before being able to initiate evasive actions. The higher speeds also result in more serious injuries because the amount of energy released in an impact increases exponentially with speed. However, because of improved automotive safety technology (such as air bags, ABS, all-wheel-drive, and crush zones), loss experience might improve despite the higher speed limits.

Educational Objective 3
Describe what information is needed to make an underwriting decision regarding vehicle-related factors and explain how that information is obtained.

Implementing the Underwriting Process

Underwriters who review auto applications scan the driver's characteristics (age and driving record) and characteristics of the vehicle itself, including the location in which it is used and protection afforded to passengers. A teenage student with a small sports car has a package of hazards that are different from those of a fifty-year-old executive with a luxury car or an eighty-year-old retiree with a station wagon. The vehicle and its characteristics become part of the underwriting decision.

Gathering Information

The sources of information for a review of the vehicle exposures are the same as those presented in Chapter 6 for the driver and use exposures. However, in reviewing exposures and hazards involving physical damage to the vehicle, underwriters also look for other key items.

The Application

Applications vary by company, but the information they ask for is relatively standard. The following are items that appear on applications that the specialist or underwriter should consider:

- *Year, make, model, and body type.* Underwriters cannot research every vehicle listed on every application that crosses their desks. However, some key vehicles that have reached HLDI's *worst* list (with 500 times the normal accident rates), such as certain sports vehicles and vehicles that are known to have poor cornering traits (rolling), might be a concern for an underwriter.

- *Garage, location, and parking.* Underwriters might recognize an area that has a high crime history. Parking a vehicle in such an area during the day or overnight would increase exposure to loss. Keeping a stereo or other electronic equipment in the vehicle would be an added hazard. A vehicle parked in a garage overnight or in a secure parking facility could improve the situation.

- *Passive seat belts, air bags, anti-lock brakes, and anti-theft devices.* This chapter has provided a description of these loss control devices and their current effectiveness. Their effects range from neutral to highly effective.

- *Loss payee/lienholder.* The presence of a used-car dealership (often offering auto loans with high interest rates) might indicate a financial problem. A credit report is a good source of information to identify any problem.

- *Car modification or special equipment.* Producers should question any special equipment and its installation. If equipment is noted on the application, the insured might assume that coverage applies; this is often not the case.

- *Existing damage to the vehicle*. The producer should review any existing damage, and photos are very helpful. They could prevent a future claim for past damages.

Credit Reports

Some insurers and underwriters strongly support the value of credit reports. These reports might identify an insured who would destroy a vehicle to eliminate a payment. False theft reports can create an income for insureds. Vehicles are sometimes intentionally damaged in an attempt to justify injury claims.

Poor credit histories have also been linked to poor driving records. Although the reason for this has not been confirmed, many underwriters believe a morale hazard is exhibited in both a failure to make promised payments and careless driving.

Claim Information

Claim files can provide details about the type of prior losses experienced by an insured. This information is available only if the insured has previously been insured by the same company. A claim file reveals the following information about a loss:

- The time of day
- The location
- The number of vehicles involved
- The circumstances surrounding the accident (including photos)

If an underwriter receives a claim notice listing an insured who has had a single car accident that resulted in $500 worth of damage, that information alone might have little meaning. If, upon reviewing the claim file, the underwriter discovers that the insured drove into an irrigation ditch in a field at two o'clock in the morning and the photo of the back bumper displays a sticker that reads "Party Animal," the underwriter might have a different impression.

Claim databases are available to member companies to help identify prior claims with other insurers. Motor vehicle reports might not provide information about all accidents. Other-than-collision losses can only be identified by a database (if they are not declared on the application). An applicant who has four vandalism losses in three years requires additional investigation; if those losses have not been declared on the application, even more review is required.

Making the Underwriting Decision

Sometimes policies are written only for liability coverage or only for physical damage coverage. However, the two are usually written on a single policy. An underwriter reviews the driver and use exposures discussed in Chapter 6 and the vehicle-related exposures to make a decision on the entire risk.

Identifying the Exposures

In reviewing the physical damage exposures, the producer or underwriter looks for positive or negative factors when vehicle, driver, and use characteristics are combined. The following questions might be used during review:

Are there any vehicle-related factors to consider?

- Do the vehicle make and model present any unusual hazards?
- What is the vehicle size (small, medium, or large)?
- What are the safety belt laws in the state? How are those laws enforced?
- Does the vehicle have air bags (driver, passenger, or side)?
- Does the vehicle have an anti-lock braking system? Could an ABS be helpful in this driving area?
- Is this vehicle equipped with daytime running lights?
- Is this a specialty vehicle (antique, classic, or foreign)?
- What are the vehicle's age and condition? Has the vehicle been inspected? Are photos available?

Is there any additional equipment to consider?

- Does the vehicle have a sound-receiving system? If "yes," how has the system been installed?
- Does the vehicle have other electronic equipment (such as televisions, videocassette recorders/players, personal computers, citizens' band radios, or telephones)? If "yes," how has that equipment been installed?

Are there any hazards involving the vehicle location?

- Is this an area known for theft losses?
- Where is the vehicle parked at night?
- Does the vehicle have any anti-theft devices?
- What is the claiming behavior in this area?
- Are the highway speeds enforced?

Are there any apparent moral or morale hazards?

- What information does the insured's credit report reflect?
- Is there a loss history? What are the circumstances of the past losses?
- Does the MVR reflect violations or accidents? Were these accidents or violations omitted from the application?

Educational Objective 4

Explain and evaluate the alternatives available in coverage implementation or risk management for auto physical damage exposures.

Identifying the Alternatives

After the appropriate information has been gathered, the alternatives can be examined. Not all alternatives are practical or available to an underwriter addressing the auto physical damage exposures. This text discusses only those alternatives that are applicable.

Accept or Reject

Policy acceptance and rejection are only two underwriting alternatives. In some states, an underwriter may use a different alternative and accept only the liability coverage and reject the physical damage coverage. An underwriter might accept only the liability portion of the policy if the vehicle presents some unusual characteristic that does not increase the liability exposure. For example, an antique vehicle with an unusually high stated amount value might be outside the company's underwriting guidelines, but the liability exposure is acceptable. This is a relatively unusual alternative because increased vehicle exposures often increase the liability exposures as well.

Modify the Coverage

Most standard endorsements that can be attached to a PAP to modify the physical damage coverage broaden the scope of coverage provided or buy back coverage that has been excluded in the policy. The producer or customer service representative should be familiar with the coverages and exclusions listed in the policy to understand when an endorsement should be recommended to protect an insured's property.

Exhibit 7-9 lists the common endorsements that modify physical damage coverages. Specialists should also become familiar with any state-specific variations of these endorsements.

Modify the Deductible

Modifying the deductible is a practical alternative for an insured or applicant who has experienced a history of relatively small OTC losses. An example might be an insured who has experienced two vandalism losses (paint scrapes probably caused by a key) in a year. If each loss were less than $200, a higher deductible might make the risk acceptable. Requiring a $500 deductible might also encourage the insured to seek another parking area or take other risk reduction measures.

Increasing a deductible as an alternative for collision losses should be approached cautiously. Almost any loss has the potential of being severe. A driver with a history of collision losses (even if those losses are small) has a greater likelihood of having another collision loss, which might be severe. A larger collision deductible will probably not significantly reduce the frequency or severity of collision losses.

Loss Control

Loss control measures for auto physical damage exposures can be highly effective underwriting alternatives. Some, however, are available only

Exhibit 7-9

Personal Auto Endorsements for Physical Damage Coverage

ISO form numbers	Form name	What it does	When to use it and how to underwrite it
PP 03 02	Increased Limits Transportation Expenses Coverage	Transportation expense coverage is provided under the policy contract up to $15 per day and up to a maximum of $450 for: • Temporary transportation expenses incurred as a result of a loss to "your covered auto" • Loss of use expenses incurred because of a loss to a "non-owned" auto (such as a rental) This endorsement increases this coverage to $30 per day up to a $900 maximum.	The transportation expense was expanded in the 1994 Personal Auto Policy revision to provide transportation expense coverage for any covered vehicle involved in a covered loss (previously it only provided coverage for a theft loss). The temporary transportation expenses reimbursed do not require the insured to rent a car (as was the requirement in the older rental reimbursement endorsement). Car rental, bus, taxi, share-the-ride, or similar expenses are reimbursed. The loss of use expenses will compensate an insured involved in an accident when driving a rented auto. The loss of use expenses can be considerable when a rented vehicle is being repaired. This increased limits endorsement is a good feature for: • An insured who has a large vehicle and would not want to rent a smaller auto in the event of a loss • An insured who frequently rents autos and might have a loss of use exposure There are no unique underwriting concerns. The driving records and loss history should be reviewed.
PP 03 03	Towing and Labor Costs Coverage	This endorsement provides coverage (with a limit of $25, $50, or $75) for the labor and towing expenses to move the auto from the place of disablement.	This coverage is inexpensive, but the coverage limit is also low. Insureds might be able to absorb this exposure. Duplication of coverage might exist through an auto club. Underwriting concerns exist when an insured has frequent breakdowns and appears to use the coverage as a substitute for proper vehicle maintenance.
PP 03 05	Loss Payable Clause	This form is attached to the contract when a vehicle is purchased with a loan. This form establishes that physical damage losses are jointly payable to the insured and loss payee. Any notice of cancellation must also be provided to the loss payee.	A specialist should make sure that other-than-collision and collision coverages are provided whenever a loss payee is present. A loss payee that is a used-car dealership can be a signal of an insured who cannot obtain a bank loan. Car dealership interest rates are uncontrolled; they are as high as the market will tolerate. Payments for a car financed through a car dealership are likely to be high. A combination of poor credit and high payments might prompt a loss of the vehicle to relieve the strain. A check of the insured's credit report will reveal the insured's financial strength.
PP 03 07	Covered Property Coverage	The policy excludes coverage for "awnings, or cabanas, or equipment designed to create additional living facilities." This endorsement allows the insured to purchase coverage for these items.	This endorsement would be useful for an insured who has a conversion van with these features added. The specialist should obtain documentation regarding the value of the additions.

ISO form numbers	Form name	What it does	When to use it and how to underwrite it
PP 03 08	Coverage for Damage to Your Auto (Stated Amount Maximum Limit of Liability)	This form establishes a stated amount for physical damage coverage.	The wording on this endorsement requires careful review. An insured who has a classic car would use this endorsement to establish a value (usually from an appraisal) on the vehicle at the time the policy is written. This form does not guarantee that this established value will be paid in the event of a total loss. The endorsement states that the lesser of the following will be paid: • The amount scheduled • The actual cash value • The amount to repair or replace According to the endorsement wording, the insured might pay the premium for the appraised value but actually collect only the actual cash value if a loss occurs. From a practical standpoint, a payment below the amount scheduled is not likely to happen. The result would be an unhappy customer (and probably a court judgment in the insured's favor). The specialist should help the insured in making sure the appraisals are kept current and that the insured value is maintained.
PP 03 13	Coverage for Audio, Visual, & Data Electronic Equipment & Tapes, Records, Discs, & Other Media	The policy excludes coverage for some electronic equipment and all tapes, records, discs, and media. This endorsement allows coverage to be purchased. Coverage for tapes, records, discs, and media is limited to $200.	The specialist should become familiar with the section of the policy that limits the electronic equipment covered. Many items are covered automatically, and other items are subject to company interpretation (see Exhibit 7-1, Page 8 of 11). The insured should be advised of the $200 media limitation (10-15 compact discs would exceed this limit). An extensive stereo system can be a theft target. An alarm system might be required to protect the car from damage (as a thief breaks into the car and extracts the equipment) and the stereo from theft.
PP 03 19	Additional Insured- Lessor	This form is attached to the policy when the vehicle is leased (for six months or longer). A special problem is presented by long-term leases because the title is still held by the lessor. The lessor is exposed to liability claims as a result of ownership of the car. This endorsement addresses this exposure by adding the lessor as a named insured for liability.	An insured who purchases or leases a new vehicle and has a total loss soon might have a loan value that exceeds the ACV. The specialist should caution an insured with a new car or lease about this problem. The Auto Loan/Lease Coverage (PP 03 35) can provide coverage for the difference between the ACV and the outstanding indebtedness on a loan/lease agreement on a new vehicle. There are no unusual underwriting concerns.
PP 03 20	Snowmobile Endorsement	This form broadens eligibility to this class of miscellaneous vehicle. This form provides liability and physical damage coverages.	Underwriting concerns for snowmobiles will be presented in Chapter 12.

Continued on next page.

ISO form numbers	Form name	What it does	When to use it and how to underwrite it
PP 03 23	Miscellaneous Type Vehicle Endorsement	This form broadens eligibility to include motor homes, motorcycles (other similar vehicles), all-terrain vehicles, dune buggies, and golf carts. This form provides liability and physical damage coverages.	Underwriting concerns for miscellaneous-type vehicles will be presented in Chapter 12. Golf carts have become popular methods of on-road transportation in retirement communities.
PP 03 24	Participating Coverage for Damage to Your Auto	This endorsement replaces the standard flat deductible with a 25% deductible (with a $500 maximum) for selected vehicles.	Because a maximum $500 deductible is applied, this endorsement does not create a significant modification. There are no unusual underwriting concerns.
PP 03 28	Miscellaneous Type Vehicle Amendment (Motor Homes)	This form is used specifically for motor homes. It is usually used with PP 03 23.	The insured should be cautioned that coverage is excluded while the motor home is rented or leased to anyone else.
PP 03 35	Auto Loan/Lease Coverage	When this form is attached to a policy, the difference between the ACV value of a total loss and the balance of any outstanding loan or lease amount is paid.	New vehicles depreciate quickly. Insureds who buy or lease a new vehicle and have a total loss within the first two years find they have a loan/lease value that exceeds the ACV of the vehicle. This leaves the insured with an outstanding balance owed and no vehicle. The outstanding balance is often factored into the loan or lease for the next new vehicle the insured acquires. If the insured has another total loss, the problem is compounded. This endorsement is valuable for an insured who has a loan/lease on a new vehicle and has not made a substantial down payment. Underwriting concerns include the insured's financial stability and loss history.

on new autos. For example, an underwriter would not require the installation of an air bag or ABS on an existing vehicle, as an underwriter might require loss control measures for other types of property or liability exposures. Many of the vehicle features addressed in this chapter (such as air bags, ABSs, and anti-theft devices) can reduce the frequency or severity of losses.

Other loss control alternatives might be effective, but compliance cannot be verified. Vehicle occupants should wear safety belts, and vehicles in a high-crime area would have less exposure if they were parked in a garage. Enforcement of these measures is not within an underwriter's control.

Educational Objective 5

Describe how the results of auto physical damage underwriting decisions can be monitored and evaluated.

Monitoring the Underwriting Decision and Evaluating the Results

Implementation of auto physical damage coverage requires the following actions:

- Communication and acknowledgment by the insured of any coverage modifications (such as an increase in deductible)

- Communication to the insured regarding any exposures that the policy might not cover (such as a stereo that the policy language excludes)

- Communication to the insured regarding any recommendations of coverage (such as auto loan/lease coverage for an insured who has a new, expensive auto with a loan)

The physical damage coverage can then be issued with the liability coverage.

The physical damage results are generally monitored based on trends for a portfolio of policies. Collision and OTC losses are monitored for trends. OTC losses are often monitored by the type of loss (such as theft, vandalism, or hail) for patterns in a geographic area.

Educational Objective 6

Evaluate the factors that should be considered when underwriting a personal auto physical damage coverage claim.

The Claim Review Process

Collision and OTC claims usually prompt different types of questions. In a collision loss, an underwriter looks for clues that indicate a pattern that could increase the probability of future losses. Some collision losses are created in an effort to justify fictitious injuries, but this is a relatively unusual occurrence. However, OTC losses more often result from a moral or morale hazard.

Reviewing a Collision Loss

A driver's history is the best indicator of future probable loss. Inexperienced operators or drivers with accident histories are the most likely to have future losses. If two vehicles strike each other on a median, determining which vehicle is at fault is difficult. Two vehicles that simultaneously back into each other in a parking lot are probably equally at fault. A driver with an infrequent history of losses, who is involved in parking lot accidents or losses with both cars showing fault, is not a severe exposure. A driver with a record of repeated accidents is, however, a concern.

An operator who shows less than a normal degree of concern or care creates a morale hazard. The following might indicate a morale hazard:

- Failing to use safety belts
- Driving while intoxicated
- Having single-car accidents
- Having a vehicle record reflecting careless driving violations

A driver who presents a morale hazard is a significant underwriting concern.

Reviewing an Other Than Collision (OTC) Loss

Losses due to acts of nature (windstorm, flood, and hail) generally present little concern for the underwriter. Those losses are resolved by repairs and restorations and present little opportunity for the insured to gain financially. Vandalism losses present concern regarding the location, possible repetition of the loss, and possible morale hazard.

Of greatest concern regarding the OTC coverage are fire and theft losses. With the safety systems present on new vehicles, a fire that occurs without vehicle impact is unusual. In addition, fires rarely begin in the passenger compartments. A fire is unlikely to start in either the engine or passenger compartment without assistance.

Legitimate auto theft losses occur. However, vehicle owners also encourage a few.

The answers to the following questions might be researched from a claim file if a moral hazard is suspected:

- Is anything unusual in the claim report or police report?
- Did the insured leave the keys in the car when it was stolen? (Were other keys on the ring?)
- Where and when did the theft occur?
- Did the theft occur late at night in a "bad" part of town?
- If a fire, did the loss occur on a road normally traveled by the insured?

If a moral hazard is suspected, the underwriter should work in conjunction with the claim department or special investigation unit. The only effective underwriting alternative for an insured with a moral hazard is rejection.

FYI

Some special investigation unit (SIU) members who identify intentional fire losses refer to those losses as friction fires. The cause of the fire is identified as the heat generated by the friction between the monthly payment and the desire for ownership.

Summary

When a specialist reviews an application, the vehicles listed on it present exposures that are considered in the underwriting decision. Each auto presents exposures that the policy contract might or might not insure. The applicant will require advice to properly protect the value of the vehicle and accessories. Each vehicle presents physical attributes or hazards that are pluses or minuses.

Specialists should be familiar with vehicle-related loss factors for the following reasons:

- As insurers, specialists might provide discounts for some protective features. Specialists should be familiar with the variations among safety features to determine whether discounts should apply and to what extent.

- As underwriters, specialists should be able to weigh the safety features as a factor. To accomplish this, they must understand what the features are and the extent to which they are effective.

- As advisors, specialists should be able to discuss vehicle safety features with customers. Safety recommendations (such as the location of a child safety seat) or the sources for additional safety information might be appropriate.

- As advisors, specialists should also be able to discuss the exposures or equipment that the policy does not cover and to help the applicant address those exposures.

Specialists must possess basic knowledge about key characteristics of the vehicles that are being submitted as well as a working knowledge of the area or territory in which the insured vehicles will be garaged and operated.

Collision and OTC claims usually prompt different types of questions. In a collision loss, an underwriter looks for clues that indicate a pattern that would increase the probability of future losses. Some collision losses are created in an effort to justify fictitious injuries, but that is a relatively unusual occurrence. However, OTC losses more often result from a moral or morale hazard.

Chapter Notes

1. Insurance Institute for Highway Safety, *Shopping for a Safer Car, 1996 Models*, September 1995, p. 20.
2. Insurance Institute for Highway Safety, *Status Report*, vol. 30, no. 9 (Arlington, VA: Insurance Institute for Highway Safety, 1995), p. 2.
3. *Shopping for a Safer Car, 1996 Models*, p. 6.
4. *Status Report*, vol. 26, no. 5 (Arlington, VA: Insurance Institute for Highway Safety, May 4, 1991), p. 5.

5. *Shopping for a Safer Car, 1996 Models*, pp. 7-8.

6. *Status Report*, vol. 28, no. 11, p. 10.

7. *Status Report*, vol. 30, no. 3, p. 10.

8. *Shopping for a Safer Car*, p. 9.

9. *Shopping for a Safer Car*, pp. 10-11.

10. *Shopping for a Safer Car*, p. 12.

11. *Shopping for a Safer Car*, p. 13.

12. National Highway Traffic Safety Administration, *An Analysis of the Crash Experience of Passenger Cars Equipped with Anti-lock Braking Systems* (Arlington, VA: National Highway Traffic Safety Administration, May 1995), p. iii.

13. *Shopping for a Safer Car*, p. 15.

Chapter 8

Educational Objectives

1. Describe a personal insurance customer's need for a personal umbrella policy, and evaluate common coverages and variations among personal umbrella policies. (pp. 8-3 to 8-17)

2. Describe what information is needed to make an underwriting decision on an umbrella application, and explain how that information is obtained. (pp. 8-18 to 8-20)

3. Identify the exposures that should be considered in the personal umbrella underwriting decision-making process. (pp. 8-20 to 8-21)

4. Describe the liability exposures for households with residence employees, and explain the underwriting concerns regarding residence employees. (pp. 8-21 to 8-24)

5. Explain and evaluate the alternatives available in coverage implementation or risk management recommendations. (pp. 8-24 to 8-25)

6. Describe how decisions can be implemented and results can be monitored. (pp. 8-25 to 8-26)

7. Given a case study involving an application for a personal umbrella policy, analyze the exposures and recommend appropriate actions. (Encompasses entire chapter.)

Chapter 8

Personal Umbrella: Exposure Analysis and Coverage

Sweeping changes in public attitudes over the past thirty years have significantly affected both the number of lawsuits submitted through insurance companies and the size of their settlements. Newspaper headlines regularly announce shocking multimillion-dollar awards for claims. Some people seem to have a lottery mentality about lawsuits. Those people will seize any opportunity to blame someone else for a loss or an injury if they believe doing so will provide them with a chance to make money. Many liability claims and lawsuits appropriately compensate an injured victim. However, some claims and lawsuits are based on greed rather than need.

Consequently, many insureds need umbrella policies. Thirty years ago, a typical producer would recommend a $1 million umbrella policy for doctors, presidents of corporations, and others with substantial earnings. Those people were most at risk as targets of large lawsuits because of their incomes, possessions, and public stature. Today, many people, such as managers, entrepreneurs, Girl Scout leaders, and day-care operators, also need such limits of coverage, and those who are publicly prominent probably need multimillion-dollar-limit umbrella policies. The chance of being named in a million-dollar lawsuit has increased in possibility because of the following trends in public attitude:

- Insurance companies tend to be viewed as wealth managers with deep pockets.

- Increasingly, people are searching for someone to blame for their injuries and losses, regardless of responsibility.

- The public does not always understand the insurance mechanism. Consequently, the juries do not always recognize the larger consequences of awarding large settlements.

This chapter covers the umbrella policy's structure and coverage, which includes examining the contents of a typical umbrella policy contract. However, the umbrella policy is not a standard policy, so the differences among the umbrella policies offered by different insurance companies are also examined. Finally, the chapter addresses underwriting concerns about the personal liability and personal umbrella coverages.

Educational Objective 1

Describe a personal insurance customer's need for a personal umbrella policy, and evaluate common coverages and variations among personal umbrella policies.

Meeting an Individual Family's Liability Insurance Needs

How much liability coverage is enough? Producers use several rules of thumb to try to answer that common question:

- Three, four, or five times the home's value
- An amount equal to the total of all of the insured's assets
- An affordable amount

That question has no specific answer because it is an attempt to guess how much an insured could possibly be sued for or how much damage someone might allege that an insured caused. No amount is high enough to cover all possibilities. However, the following factors help producers find a reasonable answer:

- Many producers recommend a limit of coverage that is high enough to cover most of the awarded claims in that geographic area. That might be a single auto liability limit of $300,000 and a homeowners liability limit of $100,000. If the insured wants less coverage than the recommendation, the insured must sign a statement indicating that he or she has rejected the recommended limit. Consequently, the insured is forced to think about the potential size of a liability loss. Also, the signed statement provides documentation for the producer if a loss occurs and the insured forgets what has been said. A producer also runs the risk of recommending liability limits that are too low. The producer should help the customer make an informed decision about the limits selected and the consequences of a loss that exceeds the selected limits; however, the producer should remember that the choice is the insured's, not the producer's.

- If a lawsuit goes to court, the insured's lifestyle might influence the jury in the award it grants. An insured who has an extravagant home, high-paying job, and expensive car makes a different impression on the jury members than an hourly worker who lives in an apartment. Because the impression of an insured's lifestyle can influence the dollar damages awarded to a plaintiff, lifestyle can affect the amount of liability coverage that is prudent. The amount and type of insurance that the insured carries cannot usually be entered as evidence in court, so impressions become important.

Public figures and people in professional occupations are the most susceptible to losses for liability and are among those most likely to request umbrella coverage because of the increased number of lawsuits.[1]

Increasing the limits of personal liability coverages or purchasing a personal umbrella policy is still fairly inexpensive for the average person or family. Unusual exposures and high coverage limits cost a little more.

Personal umbrella policies are liability insurance contracts that indemnify third parties because of damage or injuries caused by the insured's negligence. Generally, the umbrella policy coverage "stacks" on top of the underlying policies (such as auto, homeowners, or watercraft). The umbrella policy also fills in the gaps in coverage found in and between the underlying policies.

Reasons for Buying an Umbrella Policy

The first (and obvious) reason for buying an umbrella policy is to obtain coverage limits that are high enough to protect an insured from the risk of a large liability loss. Many losses exceed the coverage limit provided by standard homeowners and personal auto policies. The umbrella policy provides liability limits in increments of $1 million.

Second, the umbrella policy can fill many coverage gaps, with the insured paying only the self-insured retention. The gap for personal injury losses in the **underlying** coverage is the most widely recognized of the gaps covered by the umbrella policy.

In addition to providing indemnification, the umbrella policy covers the legal defense costs involved in protecting the insured.

The terms **underlying** and **primary** are interchangeable when used to refer to the umbrella policy. The terms refer to the policies that provide the first level of coverage for a liability loss. The umbrella policy specifies the type and limits of coverage that the underlying policies must provide. The umbrella policy begins to pay only after the limits of the underlying policy have been exhausted (paid out).

Coverage Gaps and the Umbrella Policy's Response

Finding the gaps between the **primary** coverage and the umbrella policy is difficult. It requires knowledge of the underlying policy coverages and exclusions in comparison to the umbrella policy's coverages and exclusions. The following describes the areas in which the umbrella policy usually broadens coverage and fills gaps to provide liability limits above the insured's retention. Again, not all umbrella policies are alike, so coverages differ by policy.

Personal Injury

Personal injury will be discussed in depth later in this chapter because it is an important coverage provided by the umbrella policy that is not covered by the standard homeowners policy. The personal injury endorsement that can be attached to many homeowners policies does not usually provide the broad range of coverages that the umbrella policy does.

Worldwide Coverage

Many personal umbrella policies provide liability coverage worldwide. The standard personal auto policy extends only to the United States, Canada, U.S. possessions, and ports in between. If the insured has an automobile accident in Mexico, the primary policy does not provide coverage, but many umbrella policies would.

Property in the Insured's Care, Custody, and Control

The umbrella policy provides liability coverage to almost all property in the insured's care. A typical homeowners policy provides coverage up to $500 for damage to the property of others. Liability coverage is provided to property "rented to, occupied by, or used by or in the care of the insured" only for fire, smoke, and explosion. Suppose an insured rents a beach house. While the insured is carrying in the groceries, the top of a bleach bottle comes loose. The insured ruins all of the carpets in the house as the insured tries to find the laundry room ($2,000 damage). The homeowners policy provides $500 coverage. The umbrella policy fills the gap to provide the rest of the liability coverage.

Loss Assessment

If a liability loss occurs on the general premises of a condominium, the loss is paid by the liability coverage on the master condominium policy. However, a loss in excess of a master policy is assessed to the unit owners. The standard condominium unit-owners policy provides $1,000 for the loss assessment. (Additional coverage limits can be purchased by endorsement.) The umbrella policy contains no exclusion for loss assessment, so the umbrella would provide coverage for an assessment in excess of the coverage limit provided by the condominium unit-owners policy.

Liability Assumed Under Contract

The homeowners policy limits coverage for liability assumed under contract to those contracts that relate directly to an insured location or written contracts made before a loss occurs. Under unusual circumstances, the insured might assume liability under a contract that the homeowners policy does not cover. The umbrella policy usually provides coverage for these rare occurrences. Even if the insured is ultimately not found liable, the umbrella would provide for the insured's defense.

Activities as a Director or Officer

If the insured is sued because of service performed in the capacity as an officer or a director for an organization, the homeowners policy would exclude coverage if the loss originated out of the insured's business or occupation, or if the loss involved professional services of the insured. The umbrella policy requires only that the organization served be nonprofit.

Umbrella Policy Coverage

Lloyd's of London introduced umbrella policy insurance in the United States in the 1940s. In the early 1960s, American insurance companies began developing and marketing their own policies. Although coverage is not standard, most personal umbrella policies are similar. The coverage provided by the personal umbrella policy is broad and is designed to cover an individual and a family for personal liability in excess of required **primary insurance** limits. Subject to a retention, the umbrella policy also includes coverage for some exposures not insured by primary policies.

Because personal umbrella policy insurance has no standard form, each company offering this line files its own independently developed form. No two personal umbrella policies are identical. The following sections describe the general provisions of umbrella policy coverage. Differences among contracts are discussed later in this chapter.

Primary insurance refers to the coverage provided by underlying policies.

What Limits Are Required on Primary Insurance Policies?

Umbrella policies are specific about the limits of liability coverage that the insured must maintain for auto, homeowners (or other personal liability coverage), and employers liability insurance (for residence employees). However, those requirements might differ by policy. If the insured owns an aircraft or a watercraft that is added to the umbrella policy by endorsement, underlying limits are indicated for those exposures. Under the umbrella's maintenance of the underlying insurance condition, if the insured fails to maintain the required underlying coverage, the umbrella policy would not drop down to the retention limit if a loss occurred. For example, an umbrella policy requires that the insured carry an underlying limit of $300,000 of liability coverage for automobiles. If, at the time of a serious auto accident, the insured had allowed the auto liability coverage to expire, the umbrella insurer would begin to respond to the loss only after the loss exceeded $300,000. The insured would be responsible for the first $300,000.

Who Is Covered?

Those who are insured under an umbrella policy generally include the following:

- The insured named on the policy.
- A spouse living in the same household as the named insured.
- A family member (a person related to the named insured by blood, marriage, or adoption) who lives in the named insured's household.
- Ordinarily, an umbrella policy also includes other residents of the named insured's household under the age of twenty-one who are in the named insured's care.

Some umbrella policies also insure someone else who uses the named insured's auto or watercraft with permission. If the insured owns animals, other people who have custody of the animals might also be covered under the umbrella policy.

What Type of Liability Is Generally Covered?

The umbrella policy covers damage for **"personal injury"** and "property damage" for which a covered person is found legally responsible. The policy pays up to its limits when the retention (usually $250 to $1,000) or underlying limits have been exhausted in a claim.

In the umbrella policy, the definition of personal injury is much broader than just bodily injury. The definition of bodily injury found in most homeowners and auto policies includes bodily harm and the sickness, disease, and death that can result. The personal injury definition in the umbrella policy is much more generous (and is therefore an important feature of this policy). "Personal injury" includes the following:

Personal injury refers to a group of offenses that includes bodily injury as well as many other offenses specified within the policy language.

- *Sickness.* An illness that results from injury (such as pneumonia).

- *Disease.* A condition related directly to the injury or the resulting treatment (such as a disease carried by a blood transfusion).

- *Shock, mental anguish, and mental injury.* This category can involve the pain and suffering of the injured party. Also, claims filed by bystanders are becoming more common. A bystander claim occurs when someone who was not involved in the injury but who witnessed it claims to have suffered emotional trauma. (Consider the trauma suffered by a grandparent who has witnessed a grandchild's death in an auto accident.)

- *Wrongful detention and false arrest.* If an insured suspects the maid of taking the silverware and refuses to allow her to leave until police arrive, the insured might be accused of wrongfully detaining the maid.

- *Wrongful entry.* Individuals and organizations are entitled to the private enjoyment of their own property. An insured who trespasses onto that property without permission might be accused of wrongful entry. Consider an insured's teenage son who has broken into a rival high school with some friends in the middle of the night. Even though they might not have done any damage, they have wrongfully trespassed.

- *Wrongful eviction.* Leases and laws protect the rights of tenants and landlords. If the insured leases property to a tenant and is offered a generous contract to sell the property, the insured might be persuaded to evict the tenant contrary to a lease agreement or eviction laws.

- *Malicious prosecution.* Money, time, and energy are necessary to defend a lawsuit. It is possible to "punish" someone by suing for a fabricated injury and forcing him or her to mount a defense. What stops this practice from happening is the defendant's ability to file a counterclaim against the plaintiff on the basis of malicious prosecution. Even if the insured has filed a legitimate suit, he or she might still face a countersuit alleging that it was malicious.

- *Humiliation.* This is a catch-all term. Consider an insured who presents a co-worker with a gag gift at an office party. The gift is so tasteless that the recipient and the gift become the talk of the office. The recipient feels that the discussion is the reason that she is not promoted. The result might be a suit based on humiliation.

- *Libel, slander, and defamation of character.* Slander is an injurious spoken statement, and libel is an injurious written statement. Both fall into the category of defamation. The communication must be made to a third party, and the plaintiff must be able to prove the damage that has resulted. The insured can defend against these types of personal injury if he or she can prove that the statements made were the truth. An insured who makes a dinner speech at a civic group's award's banquet might lose some judgment after cocktails. If the insured "roasts" members of the audience in front of some of the community, those members might feel they will suffer in some way as a result.

- *Invasion of right or privacy.* People have the right to be left alone, to enjoy the rights and privileges that are given to them, and to enjoy their property. Invasions of those rights might be a personal injury. The following are examples of invasion of rights or privacy:

  - A newspaper publishes articles about someone without first getting permission (celebrities and politicians do not have the same protection).

  - An insured sends a letter to the editor criticizing the actions of a local doctor.

  - A neighbor dams a stream and denies water to those downstream neighbors who enjoy the water on their property.

The umbrella policy might also include the phrase "other related types of losses" or "including but not limited to" within the definition of personal liability coverages. When such wording is present, any kind of similar personal injury is covered, subject to the policy exclusions.

Intangible losses (for example, the loss of sentimental value) cannot be tangibly appraised.

"Property damage" means physical loss and loss of use caused by the insured to tangible property. The policy does not cover **intangible losses**. Examples of intangible losses that are not covered are sentimental value and depreciation.

The umbrella policy is usually extended over the uninsured/underinsured motorists coverage only in states in which insurers are required by law to offer uninsured/underinsured motorist coverage. Umbrella policies are designed to cover the insured's liability to third parties. They were never intended to provide excess coverage over uninsured/underinsured motorists coverage (which is a first-party coverage). However, some states now require that insurers offer an extension of the umbrella policy over the uninsured/underinsured motorists portions of the underlying auto policy. Statutes and court decisions have required such extensions.[2]

What Is Generally Excluded From Coverage?

Some exposures are generally excluded from umbrella policies, including exposures related to the following:

- Workers compensation
- The insured's property
- Autos and boats owned by family members but not insured by the primary auto or watercraft policies
- Intentional acts
- Aircraft
- Watercraft (exceeding size and horsepower limits)
- Business activities
- Professional liability
- Liability the insureds incur as officers, trustees, and directors
- Discrimination
- Intrafamily suits
- Communicable diseases

Workers Compensation

If the insured is required by state law to provide workers compensation to personal employees, the umbrella policy would exclude coverage. Coverage should be obtained by endorsement to the homeowners policy or through a workers compensation policy that provides that state's specified benefits. That exclusion does *not* eliminate employers liability coverage. This is an important feature of the umbrella policy for those insureds who have employees who do not fall under the workers compensation laws for that state. In other words, the umbrella policy (as well as the homeowners policy) does provide employers liability coverage if the state statutes do not require the insured to provide workers compensation for residence employees.

The Insured's Property

The umbrella policy does *not* pay for the insured's own damaged property. All umbrella policies exclude coverage for property that the insured owns. Some policies also exclude coverage for watercraft and aircraft that are in the insured's care, custody, or control, such as watercraft or aircraft that the insured has rented or borrowed. Such an exclusion can make a big difference to an insured who frequently rents airplanes or borrows a neighbor's boat.

Autos and Boats Owned by Family Members

The umbrella policy covers autos and boats if they are owned or used by the insured or the insured's spouse. Autos and boats that are owned by the insured's family members (or furnished for their regular use) are excluded from coverage. That is an important exclusion, which has the potential for causing problems and confusion. Consider an insured's son who is living in the household but who owns his own car. The umbrella policy does not extend liability coverage to the son while he is using his own vehicle. However, if his mother or father borrows the son's vehicle, coverage is extended to them. This exclusion is similar to an exclusion that is standard in personal auto policies.

Some umbrella policies also exclude coverage for motorcycles, recreational vehicles, racing, and activities that violate the law.

Intentional Acts

Umbrella policies exclude intentional acts that are meant to cause harm or intentional injury. Wording of this exclusion varies among policies and might be written as "acts committed by or at the direction of the insured with intent to cause injury or damage." Other policies use the word "accident" within the insuring agreement to show that only unexpected losses are covered.

Exceptions to the intentional acts exclusion exist because of court precedents even though these exceptions might not be present within contract language. As a result, an insured is protected for the following intentional acts:

- Attempting to prevent or eliminate danger
- Protecting people or property
- Committing assault or battery to save a life[3]

For example, consider an insured driving a car who sees another car coming straight towards her on a narrow city street. The car is weaving in and out of the insured's lane. To the right of the insured on the sidewalk is a newsstand, which the insured quickly notices is unattended. The insured decides to drive onto the sidewalk to avoid a collision that would almost certainly damage both cars and injure both drivers. In the process of driving onto the sidewalk, the insured knocks over a magazine display rack before she can stop her car. Even though the act was intentional, it was committed in an effort to protect people and property and would therefore probably be covered under the insured's umbrella policy.

Aircraft

Aircraft coverage is generally excluded from all personal umbrella policies. However, some companies allow aircraft coverage to be added by endorsement, but an underlying limit of $1 million might be required.

Watercraft

Motorized watercraft are covered if they have very small engines, and sailboats are covered if they are relatively small, roughly within the same size limits listed in the liability section of the homeowners policies. Generally, the watercraft that *are* covered by both the homeowners and umbrella policies include the following:

- Inboard and inboard-outdrive watercraft with fifty horsepower or less

- Sailboats that are twenty-six feet or less in length
- Outboard motorboats with twenty-five horsepower or less

The intention is to automatically provide liability coverage for small watercraft under both homeowners and umbrella policies. Those watercraft are considered within the normal rates for liability coverage. Larger boats can be included by endorsement for an additional premium.

The insured might have a coverage gap if borrowing or renting a boat. Suppose the insured is vacationing and decides to rent a jet ski (an inboard watercraft). The insured has a choice of renting either fifty- or sixty-horsepower jet skis. The homeowners and umbrella policies would provide liability coverage if the insured were to choose the fifty-horsepower ski, but not if the insured were to pick the sixty-horsepower ski.

Business Activities

Businesses activities, business property, and professional services are excluded under the personal umbrella policy. Exceptions are often made for farming activities and private passenger auto use. If the insured has a business auto and her husband drives the auto on a personal errand, the umbrella policy would apply to a loss that occurs.

Many insurers cover business activities and business property on an excess basis for the same exposures covered by the underlying policy. This would include coverage for apartment houses, home offices, and home studios. The specialist should check the definition of "business" in the umbrella policy if the insured has a business enterprise. Normally, automobiles, farms, other premises, and part-time businesses of underage relatives are not included in the definition of "business," so they are covered.

The number of home businesses and part-time enterprises increases when the economy declines. People seek additional income by selling cosmetics and household products or by starting small enterprises. When in doubt about whether an umbrella policy covers a business exposure, the specialist should get an underwriter or underwriting manager's opinion. (Another good idea is to confirm that conversation in writing if the underwriter or manager agrees that coverage is provided.)

Professional Liability

Professional liability is universally excluded from personal umbrella policies. Some insurance companies were once willing to cover professional exposures by endorsement for a large additional premium, but that coverage is now rare. The potential for loss under this exposure is significant. Consider the potential severity of the following professional liability losses:

- A woman with a beauty salon in her home burns a client's scalp with chemicals while giving the client a permanent.
- A CPA who works at home makes a mistake on a client's tax return.

- An attorney who works at home misrepresents a client, causing the client to lose a big case.

Those exposures are too large for the personal umbrella policy and for the rates developed for the "average" individual and family.

Officers, Trustees, and Directors

An insured's actions as an officer, a trustee, or a director of a company or an association are excluded from the personal umbrella policy unless the organization is nonprofit. Umbrella policies provide coverage for the insured's service in this capacity to nonprofit organizations. The exposure for service as a director for a homeowners association, condominium association, or community organization is relatively small. Most lawsuits against officers and directors are for misuse of funds or failure to perform a fiduciary duty. Because the umbrella policy covers only bodily injury, property damage, and personal injury, it already excludes those types of suits.[4]

Discrimination

Discrimination based on race, creed, age, sex, color, or national origin is excluded under most umbrella policies. If an action of the insured is not specifically excluded under the policy, a question arises of whether it is covered under one of the personal injury coverages or whether coverage is eliminated under the business activities exclusion.

Intrafamily Suits

> **Intrafamily suits** are legal actions initiated by one family member against another.

Intrafamily suits are becoming more common under auto and homeowners policies, when permitted by law. Some umbrella policies exclude coverage for suits for injuries between family members. If the exclusion is absent from the policy (in a state in which these suits are permitted), this coverage can be valuable to an insured. For an underwriter, the coverage can be a concern. In this litigious U.S. society, the potential for claims in excess of $1 million could prompt family members to sue each other for damages on the chance that they might win.

Communicable Diseases

Transmission of communicable diseases also appears frequently as an exclusion in the umbrella policy. That exclusion was triggered by a lawsuit for the transmission of genital herpes in 1985.[5] Imagine the effect on homeowners umbrella policies if lawsuits for communicable diseases and hereditary diseases were covered. The costs of losses to property and liability insurers would be astronomical, increasing the cost of homeowners and umbrella coverages as a result.

What Are Other General Policy Provisions of the Umbrella Policy?

The following typical provisions are usually found in a personal umbrella policy.

Legal Defense

The personal umbrella policy provides defense and settlement costs. Those costs are not subtracted from the coverage limit. The costs include expenses for defense counsel, appeal bonds, and reimbursement to the insured for loss of earnings while the case is being settled, and the insured is required to be present. Defense costs are among the major benefits of any liability insurance policy.

Territory

The umbrella policy provides worldwide coverage (some personal umbrella policies limit the coverage territory for automobile liability). However, premiums are based on the rates applicable at the insured's primary residence.

Insured's Duties

If an incident occurs that might be covered by the umbrella policy, the insured must promptly notify the insurance company in writing. The insured must then cooperate with the insurance company in any way necessary to investigate and resolve the possible loss.

How Do Personal Umbrella Policies Vary?

The information that has been provided about personal umbrella policies so far in this chapter reflects a typical policy, but policies vary by company. The specialist should carefully review each policy to determine the applicable coverages, exclusions, and conditions.

Exhibit 8-1 lists some typical differences among policies. A personal umbrella policy should cover as many of the insured's specific exposures as possible.

Exhibit 8-1
Umbrella Policy Contract Differences[6]

Features to check	Where to look	What to look for
❑ Available Coverage Limits	❑ The company's underwriting guidelines and rating manuals	Available limits vary from $1 million to $10 million in $1 million increments.
❑ Self-Insured Retention	❑ The contract definitions of "retained limit" or the declarations page	$250 is a common retention limit for claims that are not covered by underlying policies. Some companies increase this limit to $500 or $1,000.

Continued on next page.

Features to check	Where to look	What to look for
❏ Underlying Insurance	❏ The contract schedule of "required underlying insurance and limits" or "maintenance of insurance"	Large variations in underlying insurance requirements exist among insurers. Comprehensive personal liability or homeowners liability of $100,000 and auto and recreational vehicle limits of $250/500/50,000 (or a $500,000 combined single limit) are typical. The typical underlying limit for a large watercraft is $300,000. Underlying aircraft liability can have a limit as high as $1 million. The provisions in umbrella policies regarding underlying coverage are specific. If the insured fails to carry the required underlying limits, the umbrella policy will pay no more than it would have paid if the underlying limits had been in force. When an insured has higher than minimum underlying limits, the umbrella policy premium is usually reduced.
❏ Company Options	❏ The contract coverage agreements for "Defense Settlement"	When an insured has a liability claim against an underlying policy, the umbrella policy insurer might elect to participate with the insured and the other insurers in the investigation, defense, and settlement. Some companies might also elect to appeal a judgment in excess of the underlying or retained limit. Some companies prefer to be advised of the process in settling the claim to determine the likelihood of involvement of the umbrella policy.
❏ Personal Injury Definition	❏ The contract definition of "Personal Injury"	Policies generally provide a list of offenses that are included within the definition, and this list varies. Some policies insert the exclusion for the transmission of communicable diseases along with the exclusion for any "emotional distress, severe anxiety, or mental anguish" as a result of the disease.
❏ Intentional Acts	❏ The contract exclusions	Some policies exclude all intentional acts. Others make exceptions for intentional acts that protect people or property and prevent or eliminate danger when operating autos or boats.
❏ Insured Person	❏ The contract definitions of "You" and "Your" ❏ The contract definition of "Covered Person" ❏ The contract definition of "Family Member"	"The named insured, spouse, and resident relatives, and other people under the age of 21 who live in the named insured's household in the care of the named insured or a resident relative" is the general definition in many policies. Policies vary in the coverage of permissive users of an auto, a recreational vehicle, or watercraft owned by the insured. Some umbrella policies cover other drivers of the insured's auto to the same extent that the underlying policies provide coverage.

Features to check	Where to look	What to look for
❐ Automobiles and Recreational Vehicles	❐ Check the contract definitions of "Covered Persons" to see whether other vehicle users are covered ❐ The contract definition of "Auto" will define the type of vehicle covered ❐ The contract exclusions of vehicles owned by family members ❐ The contract coverage agreement for any territory limitations	Policies differ widely in this area. Because of the large liability exposure from autos, this is an important section to compare to an insured's exposures. Here are some of the extreme variations in umbrella policies regarding vehicles: "Policy excludes liability for … 'recreational motor vehicles', which are defined as golf carts, snowmobiles, motorcycles, mopeds, dune buggies, all terrain vehicles, or any other similar motorized land vehicles designed for recreational use off public roads and not subject to motor vehicle registration." "Coverage is excluded for motorcycles, motor scooters, motorized bicycles, and mopeds (unless insurance is provided by a listed underlying policy)." "Covered automobile includes private passenger autos, recreational vehicles, trailers, farm tractors, golf carts, snowmobiles, minibikes, trail or dirt bikes, and dune buggies…."
❐ Watercraft	❐ Check the contract definition of "Covered Persons" to see whether other watercraft users are protected ❐ The contract exclusions for watercraft that are not covered ❐ The contract exclusions for watercraft owned by family members ❐ The contract coverage agreements for any territory limitations	Umbrella policies might list the size limitations, or they might specify that coverage applies only if underlying coverage is provided. Some policies exclude liability for boat racing events.
❐ Rates	❐ The company rating guides	No standard rating procedure exists, and premiums vary considerably. Companies usually begin with a basic charge to cover basic residence and other exposures. Additional charges are made for additional residences, autos, watercraft, and other unusual exposures. Credits are usually allowed for underlying limits and retention limits that are higher than those required. Increase factors are applied if more than $1 million of coverage is desired. Umbrella policy rates are generally very low. Cost is relatively small compared to the protection provided.
❐ Underwriting	❐ The company underwriting guides	The largest difference among carriers is in underwriting or risk selection. Some companies aggressively market umbrella policy insurance whether or not they write the underlying coverage. Other companies prefer to write the umbrella policy only if they also write the underlying coverage. This gives them the opportunity to view the exposures presented by the risk.

How Is Umbrella Policy Coverage Coordinated With Other Liability Coverages?

As mentioned previously in this chapter, umbrella policies have stacking features and gap-filling features that broaden other liability coverages. Exhibit 8-2 illustrates the umbrella coverage structure and the relationship of the coverages.

The Stacking Feature

The personal umbrella policy's primary purpose is to protect individuals and families against rare, high-severity liability claims that might exceed the coverage available under a personal auto policy or a homeowners policy. Sold with coverage limits of $1 million or more, personal umbrella policies provide broad excess liability protection. Protection is provided above the liability coverage of other personal liability policies.

The Gap-Filling Feature

Umbrella policies provide coverage that might not be provided by underlying or primary liability policies, such as coverage for claims alleging damage by libel and slander. For those coverages, the umbrella policy drops down to provide coverage over a modest **retention**.[7]

> A **retention** under an umbrella policy acts like a deductible for any loss that is not covered by an underlying policy. The insured is responsible for the retention amount (usually $250–$1,000).

The Drop-Down Feature

A common question asked about umbrella policies is, "How will the umbrella policy respond if, through no fault of the insured's, the required primary coverage is not available when a loss occurs?" This problem occurs most often when the insurer providing the primary coverage becomes insolvent and is unable to respond to the loss. In this situation, some personal umbrella policies will *drop down* and provide coverage over the retention. This has the effect of waiving the requirement to maintain the underlying insurance when the insurer has made a good faith effort to comply with the umbrella policy provision. The umbrella policy then becomes primary liability insurance. Some umbrella policies, on the other hand, will cover only that portion of the loss that exceeds the required limit of primary insurance. Personal insurance specialists should be familiar with the drop-down provisions of the umbrella policies they recommend and should explain these provisions to their clients.

Exhibit 8-2
The Umbrella Coverage Structure

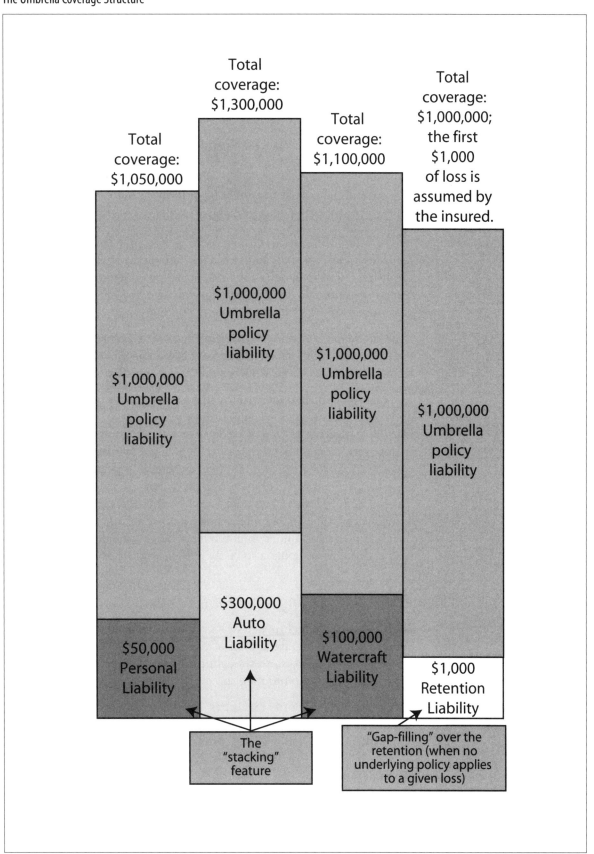

> **Educational Objective 2**
> Describe what information is needed to make an underwriting decision on a personal umbrella application, and explain how that information is obtained.

The Underwriting Process

Underwriting an umbrella policy requires great skill because the underwriter must consider the following:

- The underlying exposures and coverages
- Coverage gaps that the umbrella policy might fill
- The likelihood of a large loss that could exceed the limits of underlying policies

The files for the insured's homeowners, auto, and watercraft policies can be reviewed for much of the risk's primary underwriting. If the insurer does not write the underlying coverage, the umbrella policy underwriter should collect equivalent information.

Exposure identification is challenging because exposures can easily be overlooked. Liability loss exposures are also subject to frequent change. Effective exposure identification should be systematic and continuous.

The umbrella policy underwriter's goal is to obtain a complete picture of the exposures of the residence, personal liability (from the insured's lifestyle and activities), autos, and watercraft. A systematic approach to uncovering exposures should also include uncovering less obvious exposures that the insured might overlook, such as personal injury exposures, recreational vehicles, or activity outside the country. Most investigation is done in conjunction with other lines, particularly the homeowners policy. However, an underwriter cannot overlook a potential exposure to loss under an umbrella policy, so an adequate investigation in this regard should also be done.[8]

Gathering Underwriting Information

An underwriter, a technician, or a producer can be involved in the underwriting process. Regardless of who is involved, however, underwriting follows a consistent thought process and a series of steps, which begin with gathering information.

To systematically identify exposures, an underwriter can use checklists and questionnaires, financial statements, loss analyses, underlying policy file reviews, and personal inspections.

Checklist or Questionnaire

A checklist is a form listing many of the loss exposures faced by individuals and families. A similar form is a fill-in-the-blanks questionnaire that might allow for descriptive information, amounts, or values.

Insurers and insurance groups publish these checklists and question-naires. Many published checklists are limited to loss exposures that can be insured, and they overlook other important exposures that also require treatment. If any are so thorough that they list all conceivable exposures, they are probably too long to be practical. The value of a questionnaire varies in direct proportion to the user's skill. An experienced insurance and risk management professional understands the implications of various items on the checklist and uses the checklist to trigger additional questions or ideas.

Some companies use detailed umbrella applications with questions directed toward the liability exposure. For example, questions are asked about any business activities on the premises, any full-time residence employees, and any watercraft excluded by the underlying policy. Questions should also be asked about any other residence premises because umbrella coverage would extend to them, and a proper rate must be charged.

Financial Statement

Using formal statements to identify exposures has particular appeal to specialists with an accounting or a finance perspective. Each item in an individual's financial statements (such as the balance sheet, income statement, tax return, or budget) and supporting documents are analyzed to determine the loss exposures they reflect. A tax return might show deductions for rental property. The budget could include payments for a boat. Those items should be questioned.

Loss Analysis

Reviewing an insured's loss history to identify the exposures that have already caused losses and to determine what hazards might have contributed to the losses is helpful. For example, a series of losses under an auto policy could indicate a situation that could lead to an umbrella loss. However, loss analysis is only a review of exposures that have already led to an actual loss, many of which might already have been treated. Loss analysis alone does not reveal exposures that have not yet resulted in a mishap.

Underlying Policy Files Review

The same sources of information that are reviewed for other coverages are reviewed for umbrella coverage: the application, motor vehicle records (MVRs), inspection reports, and other policy files. Although most insurers do not require that the underlying policies be written by the same insurer, at least some of them commonly are. In such cases, the other policy files are essential sources of information. If the underlying coverage is written by another insurer, the underwriter must be certain of that company's financial stability. Some insurers require that the underlying insurer be rated B+ or better by A.M. Best Company.

Personal Inspections

Outside inspection reports might be used more often on umbrella policies than on most other policies because of the importance of factors such as financial condition, public exposure, and personal habits. Any hint of possible problems must be examined, because the potential of a large loss is great. Conducting a personal inspection or an on-site visit to help identify loss exposures is wise. Personal inspections often reveal hazards that do not show up on paper. Despite questionnaires and paper investigations, many liability exposures are never revealed until a loss occurs. A careful inspection by the producer might reveal a dangerous playhouse and a trampoline in the backyard that attract the neighborhood children. The cost of individual inspections and loss control activities by the company is often prohibitive compared to the small premium for the coverage. When exposures are indicated, the underwriter uses usual sources to obtain more detail. The producer, the applicant, other files, and inspection reports are all possible sources. [9]

Educational Objective 3

Identify the exposures that should be considered in the personal umbrella underwriting decision-making process.

Making the Underwriting Decision

After the information is gathered, the underwriter must carefully evaluate it in order to determine the best underwriting decision. Underwriting guidelines are an important factor in deciding whether a policy can be written. The umbrella policy might be requested of a company in conjunction with the primary policies, so underwriting the entire account must also be considered.

Identifying the Exposures

Adverse selection is a serious problem in the personal umbrella policy line. Generally, the insureds who want umbrella policy coverage are those with an above-average likelihood of being sued and those who have substantial net worth. Those factors can increase loss frequency and average loss severity. [10]

Potential for Large Liability Losses

Estimating what type of exposure can result in a large liability loss is difficult. If an underwriting investigation reveals a landlord who has lead paint exposures in a rental property, or if an insured purchases a high-powered boat and is teaching friends to water-ski, serious injury and large liability suits are possible. However, the extent of injury in an auto accident can be a matter of chance: the difference between a $10,000 broken leg and a multimillion-dollar paralysis as the result of an accident can be the matter of an extra ten miles per hour of driving speed and the angle of impact. Umbrella policy underwriters view frequent auto accidents negatively (even if the accidents are minor) because each has the potential of being very serious.

Exposures From Gaps in Underlying Policies

The gap-filling benefit of the umbrella policy is minor in relation to the excess coverage limits provided. As previously stated, the most significant gap-filling benefit relates to the personal injury exposure. The possibility of libel or slander is a significant exposure. The possibility of loss increases when the insured or a family member is involved in certain occupations or activities. Occupations that involve the insured's expressing opinions to the public (such as a radio announcer, political leader, or public speaker) or activities that involve the expression of opinion (such as civic leadership or school board membership) can evoke hostility and result in a personal lawsuit.

Educational Objective 4

Describe the liability exposures for households with residence employees, and explain the underwriting concerns regarding residence employees.

Underwriting Concerns Regarding Residence Employees

Many people hire residence employees to do household chores and care for dependents. Although residence employees provide help in caring for the home, the children, the elderly, or the handicapped, residence employees can create liability exposures. They can get hurt while they are working, or they can hurt others.

The Residence Employee Exposures

Individuals and families might be accountable for the injuries sustained by residence employees in the course of their employment. They might also be held **vicariously liable** for the actions of the residence employees who harm others.[11]

Vicarious liability exists when one party is held liable for the actions of another.

Under workers compensation laws, injured employees receive benefits regardless of fault. In return, workers compensation benefits are the sole remedy for employees. Suits against employers are generally barred.

The basic intent of these laws is to guarantee that employees be protected against loss of wages and medical expenses from injuries sustained in the course of and arising out of their employment, regardless of their own carelessness or that of fellow workers. Beyond this common intent, the provisions differ among the states. Most states exclude some types of employees, and the benefits vary widely.

An insured who is required to provide workers compensation insurance (by state law) for residence employees is exposed to the requirements imposed by those laws. An insured who is *not* required to provide workers compensation insurance for residence employees is exposed to the risk of a liability lawsuit if an employee is injured during the course of employment.

Coverage for Residence Employees

The standard homeowners, auto, and umbrella policies provide liability coverage for the insured when employees are performing their jobs within their authority. For example, an insured who employs a maid or a gardener is protected for liability incurred by that employee.

Homeowners, auto, and umbrella policies exclude coverage for bodily injury losses to any personnel, including residence employees, if the insured has a policy providing workers compensation benefits for the injury *or* if the insured is *required* by state law to provide workers compensation benefits. Having knowledge of the provisions regarding residence employees is important when advising insureds of their coverage needs.

However, bodily injury liability coverage *is included* under the homeowners, auto, and umbrella policies for employment situations in which the state law *does not* require the insured to carry workers compensation coverage. For example, if an occasional babysitter or cleaning person is injured on the job, the liability and medical payments portion of the homeowners policy might apply. Coverage is subject to policy limits.

Underwriting Residence Employee Exposures

A factor to consider in analyzing employee exposures at a home is whether the workers are employees or independent contractors. If the insured is having a roof replaced or the plumbing fixed, what type of worker is performing the job? Liability coverage might be provided by the homeowner and umbrella policies for employees, as long as the homeowner has no obligation to provide workers compensation coverage. A contractor is normally responsible for providing workers compensation to the contractor's own employees. If a roofer falls through the roof of an insured's house, could the roofer successfully claim that the insured was negligent in not informing him that the timbers below the roof were rotten? If the roofer is successful, will the homeowners or umbrella policies respond?

The following definitions of and distinction between contractors and employees are important for answering those questions:

* *Contractors.* Contractors use their own work methods and usually set their own hours. They retain the right to employ and direct the action of their own workers. They have the right to control the method of doing the work. Contractors usually use their own tools. They also represent themselves as contractors.

* *Employees.* Employees are governed by the employer in the hours worked and the method of performing the work. An employer generally furnishes the tools required to perform the job.[12]

Insureds do not have any workers compensation responsibility for contractors. A **certificate of insurance** is useful in ensuring that contractors meet their own legal requirements. Certificates of insurance can be obtained from contractors who perform work at the insured's premises.

A **certificate of insurance** is a document that provides information about the liability and workers compensation insurance for a commercial venture.

From a practical standpoint, a certificate would probably be requested from a contractor only when extensive work (such as a roof replacement or room addition) or continuous work (such as cleaning services) was being performed. A contractor can obtain a certificate of insurance from the contractor's insurance producer. There is no cost to the contractor for a certificate. The certificate provides information regarding the insurance coverage (workers compensation, general liability, and auto liability) in force for the contractor. The certificate includes the insurance companies issuing the coverage, policy numbers, effective dates, and limits of coverage.

A certificate of insurance might help the insured in at least two ways, as illustrated by the following examples:

1. If an employee of the contractor is hurt on the premises, the workers compensation coverage reimburses the employee for the injuries. This reduces the possibility that the employee will seek compensation from the insured's liability coverages.

2. If a neighbor's child enters the insured's premises that are being remodeled and is injured by power equipment left by the contractor, the liability coverage purchased by the contractor might provide coverage based on the contractor's negligence.

Responsibilities of the Employee   The underwriting considerations for the employers' liability exposure are essentially the same as for workers compensation exposures. What are the job duties, equipment used, and safety conditions?

Safety Hazards   Underwriters can do little about safety hazards. Personal insurance premiums are generally too small to allow engineering service on personal accounts. The underwriter's primary concerns should be the general attitude of the insured toward safety and general premises hazards. Although very difficult to measure, safety hazards can often be estimated from reports on other lines of coverage, such as auto insurance and the property portion of the homeowners policy. The greatest loss exposure from employers' liability will probably come from residence employees who experience back injury caused by lifting.[13]

Underwriting Alternatives   Since an employer's liability coverage is part of the umbrella policy, the underwriting alternatives are limited. If an extreme hazard exists, the underwriter does not have the option of declining, eliminating, or canceling that coverage alone. If an adequate premium cannot be charged, the underwriter should evaluate the entire policy. If the balance of the policy does not support the added exposure, then the entire policy should be terminated unless the insured purchases a separate workers compensation or employers' liability policy.

Increasing Use of Residence Employees   A number of factors are causing an increased use of residence employees:

• Dual-income families create a need for help in caring for children.

- Greater affluence in professional dual-income families creates the demand for help in cleaning, domestic chores, and yard care.
- The aging of the population is causing an increase in the need for workers who provide in-home nursing care and assisted living arrangements for the elderly.

Educational Objective 5

Explain and evaluate the alternatives available in coverage implementation or risk management recommendations.

Identifying Underwriting Alternatives

The underwriter has a few alternatives when evaluating risks. They include the following:

- Accepting or rejecting the risk
- Modifying the coverage
- Modifying the retention
- Suggesting loss control measures

Accept or Reject the Risk

Frequently, an umbrella policy can only be accepted or rejected because of the strict adherence to the underwriting guidelines by many companies. However, in some situations, modification can be an effective alternative.

Modify the Coverage

Modifying umbrella policy coverage is often not appropriate. An extreme watercraft exposure might be avoided under the umbrella policy by not offering an endorsement for that exposure. Altering the limit of coverage is not useful when the coverage limit is several million dollars. If a risk is not acceptable for $5 million, $1 million in coverage will probably not make the risk more acceptable.

Modify the Retention

Modifying the retention has some limited application. If a risk is unacceptable because of an activity of an insured (for example, the insured's son rents and races motocross dirtbikes, creating an exposure to other bike racers), the risk can be made more attractive if the insured purchases liability coverage for that exposure or if the customer is willing to assume a $10,000 retention limit.

An insured who purchases a sports car might fall outside the underwriting guidelines. Increasing the underlying auto liability limits to $500,000 might make the risk more acceptable by increasing the coverage provided by the primary policy and reducing the chance of the umbrella policy responding to a loss.

Loss Control

Some loss control suggestions are possible. For example, if an inspection report indicates a trampoline in the yard, the risk could be made more acceptable by adding adequate fencing or removing the trampoline.

Selecting the Best Alternative

Because the potential loss exposure is large in comparison to premium received, any underwriting alternative other than acceptance or rejection should be reviewed closely. The alternative selected should be effective in treating the exposure that would otherwise make the risk unacceptable.

Educational Objective 6
Describe how decisions can be implemented and results can be monitored.

Implementing the Decision and Monitoring the Results

Because liability exposures change fairly frequently and the umbrella policy encompasses a large variety of the exposures for a household, effectively implementing coverage and monitoring the results are crucial.

Implementing coverage entails only submitting an application for coverage. If the insured has agreed to reduce any risks through loss control measures, a target date for completion should be established. Depending on the complexity of the loss control measure, the policy's effective date might be delayed until the measure is implemented. The following examples illustrate this point:

- If a swimming pool lacks a surrounding fence, the risk might be unacceptable until the fence is added.
- If a swimming pool has a four-foot surrounding fence, the risk might be acceptable as long as the insured agrees to upgrade the fence to seven feet within sixty days.

A system should also be established to track the primary policies and losses that occur on those policies. A small loss could provide important information regarding the umbrella policy coverage.

Questionnaires at renewal can help identify additional or changed exposures.

On an individual policy basis, an umbrella policy has all-or-nothing results. If a loss that is covered by the umbrella policy occurs, the loss is large in comparison to the premium collected. Monitoring the results of umbrella policies in a portfolio to identify the overall results over time, to find trends, and to determine premium adequacy is more effective than monitoring the individual accounts.

Applying Personal Umbrella Underwriting

Exhibit 8-3 is a checklist of the underwriting process for personal umbrella policies based on the information presented in this chapter.

Exhibit 8-3

The Personal Umbrella Policy Underwriting Process: A Checklist

The steps	Questions to answer	Checklist for the personal umbrella policy
1. Gather information	What information is missing?	☐ Review the underlying coverages and companies. ☐ Consider possible coverage gaps that the umbrella policy might fill. ☐ Identify the potential for large liability loss.
	How do I get the missing information?	☐ Use a checklist or questionnaire. ☐ Review financial statements. ☐ Perform a loss analysis. ☐ Review underlying policy files. ☐ Perform a physical inspection of real property.
2. Make the underwriting decision	What are the exposures?	☐ Identify potential large losses. ☐ Identify exposures from gaps in underlying policies. ☐ Check for residence employees.
	How can I measure the exposures? What are the alternatives? What is the best alternative?	☐ Identify obvious exposures. ☐ Rely on the underwriting guidelines. ☐ Accept or reject. ☐ Change the coverage by not offering extending endorsements. ☐ Increase the required underlying limit for primary coverage or increase the retention limit. ☐ Require loss control actions. ☐ Recommend certificates of insurance. ☐ Select the alternative that is effective in reducing the potential liability losses.
3. Implement the decision and monitor the results	How do I make this happen?	☐ Monitor the completion of any loss control agreements. ☐ Track primary policies and losses on those policies.
	How will I know if it worked?	☐ Evaluate the portfolio of umbrella policies.

Summary

Personal umbrella policies provide liability coverage that stacks on top of the liability coverage provided by the insured's homeowners, auto, watercraft, and other underlying policies. Umbrella liability provides coverage in increments of $1 million. High liability limits are recommended for many insureds because of the increased number and size of lawsuits.

The umbrella policy also fills gaps in coverage (over a retention) in the underlying policies. Typical coverage gaps filled by the umbrella are personal injury; worldwide coverage; property in the insured's care, custody, and control; loss assessment; liability assumed under contract; and activities as an officer or a director for a nonprofit organization.

Coverages provided vary because the contracts are not standard. A specialist who writes an umbrella policy should become familiar with the coverages, conditions, exclusions, and general provisions of the contract. Specialists should compare the insured's specific exposures to the umbrella policy. The umbrella policy should be free of exclusions that leave potential liability risks uninsured. A checklist is provided in this chapter to help compare policy contract differences.

Underwriting personal umbrella policies requires gathering information about liability exposures. Checklists, questionnaires, financial statements, a loss analysis review of underlying policies, and personal inspections are helpful for gathering information. Underwriting guidelines are an important factor in underwriting decision making. The potential for large losses, gaps in underlying policies, and the presence of residence employees are also factors in decision making.

Alternatives in the underwriting process are limited. In appropriate situations, increased retention or loss control can make a risk more acceptable. Personal umbrella policies are usually evaluated on a portfolio basis.

Chapter Notes

1. G. William Glendenning and Robert B. Holtom, *Personal Lines Underwriting* (Malvern, PA: Insurance Institute of America, 1992), pp. 473–474.

2. The National Underwriter Company, *FC&S Bulletins: Companies and Coverages*, "Personal Umbrella Policy Liability Insurance" (Cincinnati, OH: The National Underwriter Company, 1991), p. Z-4.

3. The National Underwriter Company, p. Z-5.

4. The National Underwriter Company, p. Z-8.

5. The National Underwriter Company, pp. Zam 1-2, Zfi 1-2, Zme 1-2, Zna 1-2.

6. The National Underwriter Company, "Packages: Personal," *FC&S Bulletins: Companies and Coverages* (Cincinnati, OH: The National Underwriter Co., 1993), pp. Z-1 to Z-8.

7. Glendenning and Holtom, pp. 473–474.

8. Glendenning and Holtom, pp. 466–467.

9. Robert J. Gibbons, George E. Rejda, and Michael W. Elliott, *Insurance Perspectives* (Malvern, PA: American Institute for Chartered Property Casualty Underwriters, 1992), pp. 53–55.

10. Glendenning and Holtom, p. 476.

11. Karen L. Hamilton and Donald S. Malecki, *Personal Insurance: Property and Liability* (Malvern, PA: American Institute for Chartered Property Casualty Underwriters, 1994), p. 9.

12. James H. Donaldson, *Casualty Claim Practice* (Homewood, IL: Richard D. Irwin, Inc., 1984), pp. 223–225.

13. Glendenning and Holtom, pp. 476–484.

Chapter 9

Educational Objectives

1. Identify and describe the major perils insured by residential property policies, their associated hazards, and the underwriting considerations of each peril. (pp. 9-3 to 9-17 and Appendix 9-A)

2. Describe the information needed to make an underwriting decision for a residential risk, and explain how that information is obtained. (pp. 9-17 to 9-20)

3. Identify and describe the exposures and hazards to consider in the residential property underwriting process. (pp. 9-20 to 9-34)

4. Explain and evaluate the alternatives available in implementing residential property coverage or risk management recommendations. (pp. 9-34 to 9-37)

5. Explain the special underwriting considerations associated with residential property concerning the following: (pp. 9-37 to 9-45)
   - Seasonal occupancy or daily unoccupancy
   - Flood exposure
   - High earthquake frequency areas
   - Coastal areas with severe windstorm exposure
   - High-crime exposure areas
   - Areas susceptible to brush fires

6. Describe the underwriting considerations associated with residential property concerning the following: (pp. 9-45 to 9-48)
   - Rights granted to mortgagees by residential property policies
   - Number and type of mortgagees

7. Identify and evaluate any underwriting special hazards involving loss of use coverages. (pp. 9-48 to 9-49)

8. Given a case study involving an application for a residential property and personal property/contents, analyze the exposures and recommend appropriate actions and coverages. (Encompasses entire chapter.)

Chapter 9

Residential Property: Exposures, Hazards, and Coverage

Residential property insurance is a challenging and diverse area of personal insurance. Residential property insurance underwriting is challenging because the personal lines producer or underwriter must combine knowledge of construction, human nature, and natural perils with policy contract information to analyze the exposures and hazards presented by a risk and to select the appropriate coverage.

The primary differences among the various residential property insurance policies are the number and variety of perils insured against, the type of property covered and excluded, and the loss settlement options. Most homeowners and dwelling property policies cover common perils. Once a specialist understands the common perils and the underwriting considerations for those perils, he or she can apply that knowledge to all of the residential property policies that include such perils.

This chapter begins with a review of the perils commonly covered by residential policies and the underwriting considerations associated with those perils. Exposures and hazards associated with residential risks are then addressed in detail. The final sections of the chapter introduce underwriting concerns associated with special hazards, the rights of mortgagees and underwriting loss of use coverages.

Educational Objective 1

Identify and describe the major perils insured by residential property policies, their associated hazards, and the underwriting considerations of each peril.

Perils Insured by Residential Property Policies

Residential policies group coverages into a variety of contracts. Specialists should be familiar with the perils insured by residential policies in order to recommend appropriate insurance protection and underwrite effectively. Exhibit 9-1 contains a coverage profile for the **HO-3**, which is a frequently used coverage contract. Profiles of all of the homeowners and dwelling policies are provided in Appendix 9-A of this text.

Notes have been included with each policy form to point out the policy's special limitations and applications from an underwriting and marketing standpoint.

The policies that indicate "**all-risks**" coverage provide much broader coverage than those showing "named perils" coverage. "All-risks" forms cover all losses except those specifically excluded in the contract. Underwriters should be aware of the kinds of unusual events that can fall within the scope of "all-risks" coverage. The following losses would be covered under an "all-risks" dwelling or homeowners form but not under a named-perils form:[1]

- The insured takes a hot pan off the stove and sets it on the counter, damaging the counter.
- A bucket of paint is spilled on an oak floor, causing permanent damage.
- A bottle of bleach is dropped on a linoleum floor, bleaching out the color.
- A deer enters a home, causing considerable damage.
- An insured sprays mosquitoes in the bedroom at night without turning on the light. In the morning he discovers that the spray can contained red lacquer, not insecticide.

Jargon Alert!

The ISO homeowners form referred to as "HO-3" is actually form number HO 00 03. The shorter name is used more frequently for all forms.

Jargon Alert!

Insurance professionals usually avoid the term "all-risks" in describing coverages to the public. The term is confusing to customers because some perils are excluded, so the coverage is instead described as "special perils." However, the term "all-risks" is still commonly used within the industry.

Residential Perils, Hazards, and Underwriting

Exhibit 9-1 and Appendix 9-A provide a framework for analyzing residential property perils in the different policies. When a specialist reviews an application, an existing policy, or a claim, the specialist must understand the special considerations for the perils common to most residential property policies. The specialist must also be aware of common hazards that increase the likelihood of those perils.

Exhibit 9-1
Residential Policy Coverage Profile—HO-3

Form	Coverage & Limits	Additional Coverages	Property Items Covered/Limited/Excluded	Building Perils Covered	Contents Perils Covered	Buildings and Contents Exclusions

HO-3 Special Form	A - Dwelling replacement cost
	
	B - Other structures 10% of A
	
	C - Personal Property 50% of A
	
	D - Loss of Use 20% of A
		Debris removal: Additional 5% available. $500 for trees that damage property.
		
		Reasonable repairs: Included in limits.
		
		Trees, shrubs, plants: Limited perils (not including wind/hail). $500 per item and 5% coverage limit.
		
		Fire department service charge: $500.
		
		Property removed: 30 days.
		
		Credit card, fund transfer card, forgery, counterfeit money: $500.
		
		Loss assessment: $1,000.
		
		Collapse: Limited perils excluding earthquake.
		
		Glass or safety glazing: Covers breakage.
		
		Landlord furnishings: $2,500 at residence.
		
		Ordinance or law: 10% of Coverage A.
			• Worldwide contents coverage
			• Limited contents
			  $200 - money
			  $1,000 - documents
			  $1,000 - watercraft
			  $1,000 - trailers
			  $1,000 - jewelry (theft)
			  $2,000 - firearms (theft)
			  $2,500 - silverware (theft)
			  $2,500 - business property
			  $250 - business property (off premises)
			  $1,000 - electronic equipment in vehicle
			• Excluded contents:
			  - Items covered elsewhere
			  - Animals
			  - Motor vehicles
			  - Aircraft
			  - Property of tenants
			  - Property in rented apartment
			  - Rented property
			  - Business data
			  - Credit cards, ATM cards
				"All-risks" except:
				• Collapse
				• Freezing of plumbing in vacant, unattended buildings
				• Theft of construction materials
				• Vandalism to building vacant for 30 days
				• Damage by wear, tear, deterioration, birds, vermin, rodents, insects, and animals owned or kept by insured (water damage as a result of any of these exclusions is covered)
					• Fire
					• Lightning
					• Windstorm
					• Hail
					• Explosion
					• Riot
					• Aircraft
					• Vehicles
					• Smoke
					• Vandalism
					• Theft
					• Falling objects
					• Weight of ice, snow, or sleet
					• Accidental discharge of water
					• Sudden loss from a water system
					• Freezing
					• Power surge
					• Volcanic eruption
						• Ordinance or law
						• Earthquake
						• Flood
						• Power failure
						• Neglect
						• War
						• Nuclear hazard
						• Intentional loss
						
						Direct loss by:
						• Weather conditions
						• Acts of government body or group
						• Faulty planning, zoning, workmanship, materials, or maintenance

HO-3 Notes:

• This is the most widely used of the homeowners forms. Mortgage companies often require this coverage (or the equivalent) for their collateral property.

• Building perils are "all-risks." The contents perils are "named perils."

• Building values must be written to at least 80% of replacement cost to receive replacement cost coverage. If the coverage on the policy falls below 80%, building losses will be settled according to a formula (similar to coinsurance) or actual cash value (whichever is higher).

• Contents losses are settled on an actual-cash-value basis.

Fire

A peril central to residential property insurance contracts is fire. Every year, fire is responsible for more losses than any other residence peril, with the exception of the largest hurricanes. A residential fire occurs every seventy seconds in the United States. Residential fires accounted for over 73 percent of the total fires in the United States and 63 percent of the total dollar losses in 1994. The total dollar losses from residential fire were over $4.3 billion in 1994.[2]

The major causes of fire loss in residences have been related to arson (suspected incendiary), carelessness on the part of the resident, or some type of mechanical failure or malfunction. The chart in Exhibit 9-2 lists the causes of residential fire losses.

Exhibit 9-2
Causes of Reported Residential Fires

Causes of Reported Fires, 1993				
	Residential			
Cause	Fires	Deaths	Injuries	$ Loss
Suspected incendiary	11.0%	13.0%	9.0%	14.0
Children playing	4.0	7.0	11.0	4.0
Smoking	5.0	16.0	10.0	5.0
Heating	15.0	10.0	9.0	10.0
Cooking	20.0	7.0	22.0	7.0
Electrical wiring	8.0	6.0	7.0	11.0
Appliances	6.0	2.0	5.0	4.0
Open flame	5.0	3.0	5.0	5.0
Other heat, spark	1.2	0.6	1.2	0.9
Other equipment	1.1	1.2	0.9	1.5
Natural causes	1.8	0.2	0.6	3.0
Exposure	3.0	0.7	0.5	10.0
Unknown	18.0	33.0	19.0	25.0

NOTE: Columns of figures might not add up to 100 percent because of the effects of rounding.

Source: U.S. Fire Administration; National Fire Incident Reporting System.

Arson

The information in Exhibit 9-2 indicates that **arson** is the leading cause of dollar losses by fire in residential properties.

Arson is the criminal act of burning or attempting to burn property.

Property producers and underwriters should watch for clues to arson or situations that foretell a probability of fraud or arson. A risk might exhibit one or more of these clues but have no increased chance of loss. The following clues simply suggest the need to ask additional questions:

- *New Business.* A request for coverage made by an applicant located 100 miles from the producer is subject to scrutiny. Insurance submissions through a producer normally follow a pattern.

An unusual location or an unusual submission demands more questions.

Surveys by insurance companies of total losses have indicated that one-third to one-half of their total losses have come from property that the company has insured for less than one year. Arson fires are likely to be total. New business is more likely to incur arson losses than seasoned business that has been with the company for several years. A specialist should ask, "Why was the business transferred? Is it the result of good and aggressive marketing, or does the insured have a reason for leaving the previous insurer?"

- *Increase in Amount of Insurance (Existing Policy).* When the insured shows a sudden interest in coverage sufficiency or in replacement cost insurance, questions on the part of specialists are justified. Specialists should be on the alert if the insured does not exhibit a normal interest in the cost of the additional coverage or if an insured insists on paying the premium immediately. The insured might be trying to ensure that the premium is paid and that insurance is in effect before the insured has an intentional loss.

- *Vacancy.* A vacant residence costs someone money every month it remains empty. This mounting financial pressure could tempt the owner to burn the property just to relieve the burden. Vacant property is also an attractive target for vagrants and an attractive nuisance to children.

- *Delinquent Taxes.* Delinquent tax payments usually indicate a lack of current assets—a poor cash situation. Delinquent taxes are also a sign of financial pressure that could tempt the owner to burn the property.

- *Avoiding the Use of Mail.* Sending fraudulent information through the U.S. postal system constitutes mail fraud, which is a federal offense with potentially severe penalties. An insured who mails an application or claim notice with knowledge that the documents contain false information is committing mail fraud. Arsonists have been convicted in several cases of using the mail to defraud insurers. An insured who is planning a fraudulent loss might avoid using the mail, delivering information or premium in person or by messenger. This activity becomes especially apparent when an insured travels significant distances to hand deliver documents.

- *Absence of Financial Information.* Applicants might be reluctant to share their financial situations or be averse to giving permission to an insurance company to obtain their credit reports. However, an insurer that provides thousands of dollars of insurance coverage has as much need for financial information as a banker who is considering making a loan. An applicant who refuses to reveal his or her financial condition could have reason, such as the intention to commit arson, to conceal the facts.

- *A Small Loss in the First Year.* Insurance companies have discovered a pattern in property policies that experience large losses relatively early in the history of the account. Often, these policies have already had one small loss. An insured who is contemplating a total fire loss might test the insurer's claim system with a small loss. This early encounter with the insurance company claim department gives the insured an idea of the type of documentation, receipts, and procedures that the insurer expects. This information helps the insured prepare for the procedure required for a larger loss.

Carelessness as a Fire Hazard

Exhibit 9-2 indicates a number of reported fires apparently stemming from carelessness or a morale hazard: cooking, smoking, and children playing. Cooking is the most frequent cause of residential fires. The human elements in these fire losses make hazards difficult for the specialist to evaluate. The following clues might point to an excessive morale hazard, which could result in a careless fire loss:

- Poor housekeeping and maintenance of the premises (identified by a photograph of the exterior of the structure) might reveal a lack of proper care of the property. This lack of care might be present on the inside of the home as well as on the outside.
- Financial difficulty might indicate the inability to maintain the property.

Fires that result from the malfunction of a heating system or faulty electrical wiring will be discussed later in this chapter.

Lightning

Lightning, the natural discharge of static electricity, starts more than 20,000 fires and kills more than 200 people in the United States each year. Although most atmospheric electricity is dissipated harmlessly within the clouds, lightning strikes somewhere on the earth about 100 times each second. Exhibit 9-3 provides information about the number of thunderstorms that occur in the United States.

Lightning tends to search for the best conductor of electricity in its route to the ground. Because air is a poor conductor, lightning searches for a better one, such as a tall building or a tall tree. Some buildings become repeat targets for a lightning strike because of their location and surroundings. Homes located on hills and elevated above their surroundings are also prone to lightning strike. Lightning can also enter a house by means other than a direct strike. Lightning can hit utility poles and follow the utility wires into the house. It can also follow telephone lines and television antennas into a house.

Lightning cannot be stopped, but methods exist for providing protection to homes that are prone to this risk.

Lightning Rods

A lightning rod conducts lightning from the highest point of a structure to the ground. Lightning rods extend a few feet above a structure's highest point. An invisible tent of protection is created from the top of the rods downward at a 45 degree angle, in order to intercept lightning. A continuous metal cable runs from the rods to the ground, and a net

Exhibit 9-3
Mean Annual Number of Days of Thunderstorms

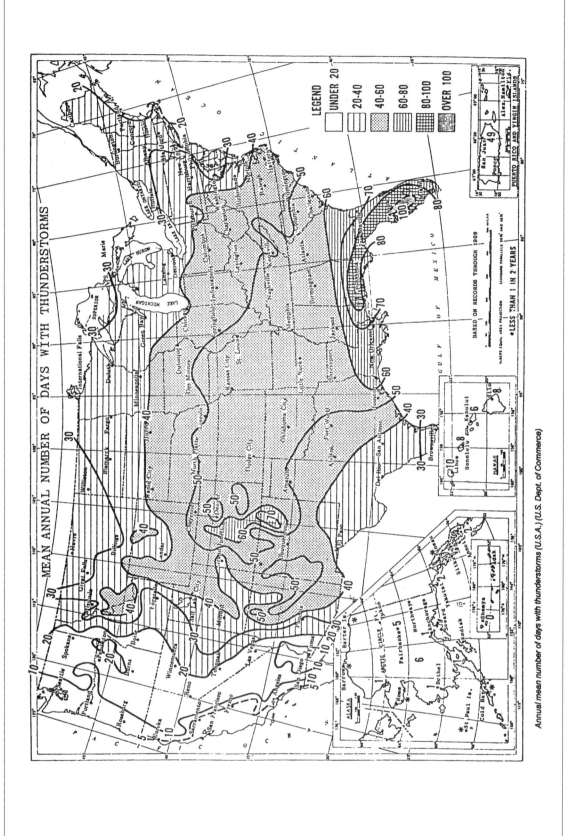

of wires is buried deep enough to ensure connection to moist ground. A lightning strike would be discharged through this ground wire.

In the past, lightning rods were believed to attract lightning. Current thinking is that the opposite is true: positive electrons from a cloud and negative electrons from the earth send out "feelers." When these feelers dissipate through the lightning rods and grounded cable, a charge does not build up, and the chances of an actual lightning strike are reduced.

The popularity of lightning rods as loss control devices and the belief in their usefulness by underwriters vary. One example of lightning rod use involves the Washington Monument in Washington, D.C. The stone at the top of the monument was being chipped from hits by lightning. It is now capped with metal to accept the electrical charge and wired with a cable that carries the charge to the ground.

Surge Protectors

Surge protectors are electrical circuit breakers that can minimize the effects of some lightning strikes. Surge protectors guard computers, stereos, and other expensive electronic equipment from uneven electrical flow. These protectors are not a fail-safe guard against damage by lightning. A direct or nearby lightning strike may generate too much voltage for a surge protector to be effective. Surge protectors do, however, protect property from lower level electrical surges.

> **Surge protectors** are electrical circuit breakers that are plugged into outlets; electronic devices are then plugged into the surge protector outlets.

Satellite Antennas and Electronics

Satellite antennas are especially susceptible to losses by lightning and require additional attention. They are usually set in the ground or bolted to a concrete pad, so they are normally considered to be "other structures." Therefore, satellite antennas are automatically covered by homeowners and dwelling policies. The satellite dish collects the transmission pulses from space satellites and directs them to the horn that is suspended above the middle of the dish.

Lightning is a substantial threat to the electronic horn and tuner attached to the antenna. If the dish is hit by lightning, nothing can be done to save the horn. The horn is connected by cable to the tuning mechanism that decodes the signal in the house. The tuning mechanism is a costly set of electronics that should be protected by surge protectors to stop the current surge from also destroying the expensive tuning mechanism. Even these devices might not be effective against a direct lightning strike.

Theft

Theft is a covered peril under all homeowners policies (but is not covered by any of the unendorsed dwelling policies). The theft peril deserves underwriting attention because it is so easily committed in today's mobile world. Electronic equipment, jewelry, and appliances can easily be stolen and quickly converted to cash by a thief. Insureds should take reasonable precautions to protect property from theft; an insured's failure to protect property might indicate a potential morale hazard. A theft loss is difficult to validate or refute because there is no injured third party and no partially destroyed property to examine; therefore, potential moral hazards should also be considered when underwriting theft exposures.

The following factors alter the probability of a theft loss:

- Concentration of valuable contents
- Property location
- Building occupancy
- Protective measures

Concentration of Valuable Contents

The obvious presence of valuable items increases the chance that a thief will be attracted to a home. Examples are valuable vehicles in the driveway and a display of personal affluence. A $500,000 home displaying Tiffany lamps in the windows, a twenty-six-foot speedboat in the yard, and an $80,000 motor home has more potential for a theft than a conservative home in an average subdivision.

Property Location

Police protection varies by property location. The degree of police protection affects both the likelihood of theft and the chances of apprehension if a theft is committed.

Neighborhoods that are near highway access are targeted more frequently for thefts and provide better exit routes for thieves. Some subdivisions, apartments, and condominiums have private security services that deter thieves.

Building Occupancy

Daily unoccupancy is a term used by underwriters to describe the hazards associated with homes that are unoccupied during the day.

Daily unoccupancy increases the likelihood of theft. Many underwriters become concerned when asked to insure residences that are unoccupied during the day. A house in an isolated location is more susceptible to theft than a house in a location in which neighbors are likely to notice and report suspicious activities.

Protective Measures

Underwriters make recommendations to insureds about protective measures. Security systems are an obvious deterrent to loss. Double-cylinder deadbolt locks make homes more difficult for burglars to enter and exit. (A double-cylinder lock requires a key to operate the lock from the inside or the outside.) Common-sense protective measures include locking all doors and windows not in use and keeping bicycles and other personal property locked in a garage. Homes temporarily unoccupied when residents are vacationing also require the precautions of hiring someone to mow the grass, notifying the neighbors of the vacation schedule, and having mail and newspaper delivery stopped.

Home alarm systems have become an affordable means of protecting residences against theft. The degree of protection these systems provide varies. Professionally installed alarm systems connected to a central station provide an effective means of alerting police to investigate a possible break-in. Locks and alarm systems are discussed in detail in Chapter 10.

Windstorm and Hail

The windstorm peril covers losses caused by the force of wind and by objects moved or carried by the wind. If a tree is blown down, any resulting damage to the residence is considered to be caused by wind. Direct wind damage (such as shingles blown off a roof) is also covered by this peril. Some courts have defined windstorm as wind of sufficient velocity to damage property in a reasonable state of repair; others have defined windstorm by specifying velocity (such as fifty-five miles per hour).

In some states, windstorm and hail are the most frequent cause of loss under residential policies. All the residential property forms that cover wind and hail on a named-perils basis limit the interior and contents coverage. Damage from rain, snow, sand, or dust is not covered unless the direct force of wind or hail first creates an opening in the roof or wall.

Hurricanes

Dwellings in every state are susceptible to windstorm and hail, but the states on the Gulf Coast and parts of the Eastern seaboard are subject to **hurricanes** and tropical storms. These events cause widespread damage when they approach a shoreline or cross land masses. Few natural events can approach the destructive power of a hurricane. The National Weather Service uses the Saffir/Simpson scale (shown in Exhibit 9-4) to classify hurricanes and assess potential wind damage. The scale has categories ranging from 1 to 5. Category 1 begins with hurricanes that either have sustained wind speeds of at least seventy-five miles per hour or have a storm surge of tidal waters four to five feet above normal. Category 5 applies to storms with maximum sustained winds of one hundred fifty-five miles per hour or more. These levels indicate the relative damage a hurricane would do to a coastal area if it were to strike without change in size or strength.

A windstorm becomes a **hurricane** when its winds exceed speeds of seventy-four miles per hour.

Companies generally limit the amount of windstorm exposure they have in areas with a strong possibility of tornadoes or hurricanes. Insurers that write property coverage in these areas watch their geographic spread of risk to make sure that a large storm could not affect all their insureds. Appropriate **catastrophe reinsurance** is another important safeguard in limiting windstorm exposure and maintaining a profitable book of business over time.

Catastrophe reinsurance (also called "catastrophe cover") is a special form of reinsurance that protects insurers against the adverse effects of catastrophes and limits the insurer's total loss from a catastrophe to a predetermined amount.

Hurricane paths have some uniformity, even though each storm is unique. Hurricanes can be penetrating storms that strike the coastline at approximately right angles and move directly inland. Once the eye of the hurricane is over land, the hurricane quickly decreases in intensity. A raking storm that parallels the coast without moving inland can maintain its intensity for a long time if the eye remains over the ocean.

Exhibit 9-4
Saffir/Simpson Hurricane Scale

Scale No.	Wind (mph)	Surge (feet)	Damage
1	74-95	4-5	Damage primarily to shrubbery, trees, foliage, and unanchored mobile homes. No real damage to other structures. Some damage to poorly constructed signs. Also possible: inundation of low-lying coastal roads, minor damage to piers, tearing from moorage of some small craft in exposed anchorage.
2	96-110	6-8	Considerable damage to shrubbery and tree foliage, some trees blown down, major damage to exposed mobile homes. Extensive damage to poorly constructed signs. Some damage to roofing materials of buildings. Also possible: coastal roads and low-lying escape routes inland cut by rising water 2 to 4 hours before arrival of hurricane center; considerable damage to piers; marinas flooded; small craft in unprotected anchorages torn from moorings; evacuation of some shoreline residences and low-lying areas required.
3	111-130	9-12	Foliage torn from trees, large trees blown down. Practically all poorly constructed signs blown down. Some damage to roofing materials of buildings; some window and door damage. Some structural damage to small buildings. Mobile homes destroyed. Also possible: serious flooding at coast and many smaller structures near coast destroyed; larger structures near coast damaged by battering waves and floating debris; low-lying escape routes inland coast cut by rising water 3 to 5 hours before hurricane center arrives. Flat terrain 5 feet or less above sea level flooded inland 8 miles or more. Evacuation of low-lying residences within several blocks of shoreline possibly required.
4	131-155	13-18	Shrubs and trees blown down, all signs down. Extensive damage to roofing materials, windows, and doors. Complete failure of roofs on many small residences. Complete destruction of mobile homes. Also possible: flat terrain 10 feet or less above sea level flooded inland as far as 6 miles; major damage to lower floors of structures near shore caused by flooding and battering by waves and floating debris; low-lying escape routes inland cut by rising water 3 to 5 hours before hurricane center arrives; major erosion of beaches; massive evacuation of all residences within 500 yards of shore possibly required, and all single-story residences on low ground within 2 miles of shore.
5	over 155	over 18	Shrubs and trees blown down, considerable damage to roofs of buildings; all signs down. Very severe and extensive damage to windows and doors. Complete failure of roofs on many residences and industrial buildings. Extensive shattering of glass in windows and doors. Some complete building failures. Small buildings overturned or blown away. Complete destruction of mobile homes. Also possible: major damage to lower floors of all structures less than 15 feet above sea level within 500 yards of shore; low-lying escape routes inland cut by rising water 3 to 5 hours before hurricane center arrives; massive evacuation of residential areas on low ground within 5 to 10 miles of shore probably required.

Adapted from Paul J. Herbert and Glen Taylor, "Hurricane Experience Levels of Coastal County Populations—Texas to Maine" (Washington: U.S. Department of Commerce, National Oceanic and Atmospheric Administration, National Weather Service), 1992.

Tornadoes

Tornadoes occur in all parts of the United States, with a high incidence in the Midwest, Southwest, South Central, and Southeastern states.

Tornadoes can cause almost as much damage as hurricanes, though they are smaller in diameter. Tornado winds usually attain speeds in excess of 200 miles per hour. Although the effect of tornadoes is usually restricted to a narrow path, these storms generate wind speeds capable of demolishing all of the property in their paths. The twirling winds create a partial vacuum that draws up dust and debris when it comes in contact with the ground. The dust and wind create a dark funnel. The Oklahoma Turnpike has signs that read "Do not drive into smoke," since that is what a tornado resembles.

The destructive power of a tornado is tremendous. The destruction comes partly from the high velocity of winds and also from the sudden drop in atmospheric pressure caused when the vortex (center) passes over a building. The near vacuum in the vortex surrounding buildings causes them to explode from the higher pressure within.

A direct hit by a tornado can result in substantial damage to almost any structure. The methods of underwriting tornadoes are limited. Insurers generally underwrite their exposure to tornado losses by monitoring the number and coverage limits of risks they insure in tornado-prone areas. Insurers might limit their exposures in these areas or increase their reinsurance limits.

Hail

Destructive hail falls almost exclusively during violent storms. Individual hailstones have attained a diameter of more than five inches and have weighed over one-and-one-half pounds. Damage from hail can be severe for home windows and fragile structures such as greenhouses. Hail can also damage roofs and siding. Aluminum siding and roofing materials are particularly susceptible to such damage.

Susceptibility to Windstorm Damage

Some construction designs are more susceptible to windstorm than others. Roofs with a slope of more than 30 degrees have an area of positive pressure on the windward slope (the side facing the wind) and a partial vacuum on the leeward slope (the side sheltered from the wind). The forces acting on the roof can be similar to the forces acting on an airplane wing; lift is created, which can remove the roof surface and in extreme cases the roof itself. Overhanging eaves can provide air pockets or air traps increasing the potential pressure buildup, and perhaps causing the roof to lift.

In hurricane-prone states, hurricane straps are being added to new building construction. These steel straps attach the structural support beams to the foundation to provide an extra measure of stability against strong winds. The straps also act as metal connectors that anchor rafters to the structural members in order to provide more stability to the roof. The straps help to hold the structure to the foundation and the roof to the structure in strong winds.

Roof Coverings

Roof materials of all types are susceptible to wind damage from direct wind force. Even tile and slate roofs sustain damage as the wind creates a prolonged rattle, breaking the securing nails and cracking the tiles and slates. The protective natures of roofing materials will be addressed later in this chapter.

Mobile Homes

Insurers generally require insureds to secure mobile homes with tie-downs, which are metal straps anchored in the ground by augers or in cement and which attach to the support frame or pass over the top of the home. These straps provide stability in strong winds and help prevent the mobile home from being blown over.

Smoke

Agricultural smudging usually occurs in the spring in areas near orchards. If a late frost threatens the fruit buds or blossoms, oil-burning smudge pots are burned at night around the trees. A dark oily cloud covers the trees to prevent the frost from killing the buds. If this cloud is blown into a neighborhood of houses, damage could result.

The smoke peril was incorporated into the residential property policies primarily to cover sudden "smudge" losses from oil-heating furnaces. Those furnaces sometimes backfire and send clouds of smoke swirling through a house, covering walls, floors, and contents with a thin coating of black, oily smudge. Over several years of operation, even good oil burners can deposit a slight smudge throughout a house. The smudge accumulation is not intended to be covered, so the words "sudden and accidental" are included in the policies with this named-perils coverage.

Coverage for the smoke peril has become more liberal under the homeowners policies. Almost any source of smoke damage is covered, except for **agricultural smudging** and industrial operations.

Explosion

Explosion is not always easy to define, and most courts hold that explosion means what the average person reasonably thinks it means. Explosion generally has the following four characteristics:

1. It is sudden and violent.
2. It tears objects apart.
3. It generates a loud noise.
4. It fragments exploding objects.

In cases of controversy, these four characteristics are applied in order to determine whether the occurrence was actually an explosion as opposed to a collapse or rupture.[3]

An explosion loss rarely occurs to residential property. Examples of losses covered under the explosion peril include explosion from gas accumulation and damage caused by a gunshot.

Vandalism or Malicious Mischief

Vandalism or malicious mischief is normally included in all the residential property policies, but it is optional under the Dwelling Property

Basic Form-DP-1. Coverage is usually suspended under all policy forms after a thirty-day period of vacancy because a vacant dwelling is much more susceptible to this peril.

Most insureds and properties are good risks regarding the vandalism peril. Vacant homes, homes under construction, geographically isolated homes, and homes in deteriorating neighborhoods are the exceptions.

Water Damage

The interior water damage peril is covered by the "all-risks" coverages provided by the residential property policies. The water damage coverage provided by "named perils" coverages (such as the contents perils provided by the HO-3 or the dwelling coverage provided by the HO-2 or DP-2) is described as "accidental discharge or overflow of water or steam from within a plumbing, heating, air conditioning, or automatic fire protective sprinkler system, or from within a household appliance."

A separate "named peril" provides coverage for "sudden and accidental tearing apart, cracking, burning, or bulging of a steam or hot water heating system, air conditioning system, or an appliance for heating water."

Exterior water damage, such as flood and surface water, is excluded from all residential property policies.

A common water damage claim results from a leak or overflow from an appliance such as a clothes washer, a dishwasher, or a hot water tank. Some courts are now interpreting "appliance" to include waterbeds, which means that leaks from waterbeds can be added to the covered perils.[4] Such leaks and overflows can ruin floors and floor coverings.

Water pipes in plumbing systems are another common source for water damage. Since these pipes are usually hidden within walls, severe damage can result. Rust or freezing are common causes of pipe rupture. Under most policies, the cost to repair or replace broken plumbing is excluded, but the cost of tearing out and replacing the parts of the building to perform the repairs is covered.

Showers are an additional potential source of loss. A shower pan is a heavy plastic liner that is laid in place before tile is cemented to form the floor and walls of a shower. Leaks in the shower pan can go undiscovered for months because of the hidden nature and inaccessibility of the structure below the shower.

Residential property policies must be reviewed carefully to determine whether water damage coverage is provided or excluded. Damage from continuous or repeated seepage was once excluded under homeowners policies. This exclusion is being eliminated in more current policy versions. Coverage usually applies unless an insured takes no action to save and preserve the property once the water damage becomes visible.[5]

Coverage has also been granted under the additional coverage "collapse," if hidden decay as a result of water damage becomes that severe.

Appliance Malfunction

Appliance malfunctions can happen at any time, and there is no effective means of underwriting against this type of loss. The severity of the damage increases if the home is unoccupied for long periods (such as for a seasonal or secondary home) and the leak is not quickly detected.

Plumbing and Heating Systems

Pipes and fixtures are usually not replaced until they begin to cause problems. Consequently, dwellings often incur water damage at some time. Older homes are more susceptible to this type of damage because of deterioration of the older plumbing systems.

Exposed pipes, plumbing that is not adequately insulated, and dwellings that are left without adequate heat are at risk for freezing. Examples include dwellings that have exposed foundations and hot tubs on exterior decks. Insulation and precautions can be used to reduce the chance of freezing pipes. One underwriting alternative is to offer a policy that excludes loss from freezing (such as the DP-1 basic form or HO-1 basic form).

Carelessness as a Water Damage Hazard

Momentary distraction or lack of judgment is another cause of water damage. Permitting the bathtub to overflow or leaving a puppy to entertain himself in a laundry room in reach of the washing machine hoses can cause serious problems. The only underwriting action that is practical for this type of exposure is a review of the insured's loss history. An underwriter can use an insured's loss history to judge the insured's level of care.

Vehicles

Little preventive underwriting can be done regarding the peril of vehicle damage. However, if the evidence shows that property has been damaged by a vehicle, further investigation is in order. If the structure is located so that vehicle damage can be expected (such as on a narrow alley, next to a drive-in restaurant, or at the bottom of a steep hill), some type of protective device should be required. A guard rail or posts set in concrete could be enough to prevent a loss. Another underwriting alternative is to require a substantial deductible. Coverage for vehicles excludes damage caused by a vehicle driven by a resident of the property.

Other Types of Damage

Other types of damage involve those caused by the following:

- Weight of ice, snow, or sleet
- Sudden and accidental damage from artificially generated electrical currents
- Ice damming

Weight of Ice, Snow, or Sleet

The weight of ice, snow, or sleet can damage a building and its contents. Patio roofs and flat-roofed portions of buildings are particularly vulnerable. The exposure is greater in areas subject to heavy snowfalls. Whether a loss occurs depends largely on the design and the condition of the building. If a loss is possible, the practical underwriting alternative is to decline the application or offer a more limited policy form (such as the DP-1 basic form or HO-1 basic form).

Sudden and Accidental Damage From Artificially Generated Electrical Currents

Residences rarely experience damage from electrical power surges because of electrical supply system safeguards. On rare occasions, homes do experience extreme power surges that can produce fires. Such surges can usually be prevented only by eliminating a problem from the power source provided by the electrical service.

Ice Damming

A phenomenon known as ice damming has become an important cause of losses when writing "all-risks" coverage in areas subject to severe winter weather. When snow covers a roof, heat escaping from the building melts snow closest to the roof surface. Water (from the melted snow) flows down the roof and refreezes when it reaches the eaves or the edge of the roof, creating a dam made of ice. The ice dam blocks water from more melting snow and prevents draining. A pool of water accumulates and is drawn into the building through vents along the roof's edge and through spaces between the shingles. Extensive water damage to the interior of the building is a common result.

Losses from ice damming can be prevented by installing an impervious membrane called an ice shield at the edge of the roof below the roof covering. Adequate insulation in the attic to stop the heat from collecting in the attic space can help prevent the ice dam hazard. A house in an area in which heavy freezing occurs should have insulation with an **"R" value** of thirty-eight to prevent this problem. Adequate ventilation at the attic eaves and roof edge can allow air flow to dissipate the heat build-up and the resulting ice dam problems.

"R" value stands for the resistance to heat transfer. The higher the value, the better the resistance and insulation.

Educational Objective 2
Describe the information needed to make an underwriting decision for a residential risk, and explain how that information is obtained.

The Underwriting Process

Once the basic perils that apply to most residential insurance policies and their related underwriting concerns are understood, individual risks can be analyzed. Underwriting considerations and concerns related to specific risks will be identified as part of the information-gathering and exposure identification process.

Gathering Information

The purpose in obtaining information about a residential risk is to develop a composite picture of the property as well as of the owner (and the occupant, if the property is rented). Once that picture is complete, the underwriter can determine whether the risk is acceptable and eligible according to the company guidelines and the policy form requested.

Some sources of information, such as the application, are standard. Others are needed only if the characteristics of the risk are unclear or incomplete.

The Application

The producer must complete an application for every policy. Applications can be written documents or electronic records of initial responses to questions. Most residential applications require the same general information, which can be classified as personal, property, and risk information. Even the most complete applications cannot anticipate every situation. If the applications were extensive enough to include all possible exposures and hazards, they would be too long to be practical. The number of questions that an insured can be expected to answer is limited.

The questions on a residential property application are also limited because the average premium is relatively small, even when compared to auto insurance. This decreases the time and effort that the producer and company can spend placing the coverage. Also, most applicants for homeowners and dwelling policies are acceptable without the need for policy modification or additional information.

The Producer

In addition to providing the information asked for on the application, the producer is the front-line source of answers to other specific questions. The questions can result from unusual circumstances involving the applicant or property. Completion of information might be required if responses are missing from the application or if responses require further details.

Frequently, the producer knows the insured and is a source of additional information. Because the insured's maintenance and care of a home are a primary underwriting concern, the producer's knowledge of the insured can be very important.

Some companies require that the producer inspect and photograph the risk to develop firsthand information for an underwriting recommendation. Companies rely heavily on the producer's knowledge of the area and the value of the types of residences in the area.

External Reports

A number of reports can be ordered from external sources; however, ordering every report for every application is not practical. The premiums on the homeowners and dwelling policies are not large enough to warrant significant expense, and requesting certain reports is impractical. For example, a physical inspection and photo of a newly constructed house in a subdivision will not reveal anything unique about the insured or the property's maintenance.

Much of the underwriting occurs during the initial sixty-day window. For any external report to be useful, it must be ordered, delivered, and evaluated before the end of those sixty days. Turnaround time becomes important in selecting report vendors and establishing office procedures to order and review reports within the sixty-day window.

Reports are also ordered to help review selected renewals. The review might be required on a periodic basis or as a result of claims. This type of review of a property renewal should begin at least 120 days before the renewal date to allow sufficient time to obtain external reports and to take nonrenewal actions by the deadline (if a nonrenewal is recommended).

Inspection Reports

Sometimes the condition of the property is questionable. The application might indicate old property or an unknown neighborhood. A photo provided by the applicant might not provide sufficient information, or it might be taken at an unusual camera angle that eliminates a view of the roof or part of the dwelling. An inspection can verify the property's condition.

Some insurance companies assign specific staff to complete inspection reports. Inspection reports can also be ordered from vendors who provide these services for a fee. Several types of reports are available. They range from a comprehensive report with information about the applicant and property to a simple set of color photos of the house from two angles.

The dwelling photos are extremely helpful. They can provide more information about the construction, condition, and housekeeping than a written description can. They can also provide an impression of the surrounding neighborhood and the building's value.

Specialty supplemental reports can be requested in addition to basic inspection reports. These supplemental reports can supply information about the home's electrical or heating system. They are helpful when the underwriter has special questions regarding system maintenance or installation.

Credit Reports

Credit reports are frequently ordered by residential property underwriters because of the extensive information they can provide and because poor credit history and financial problems have been linked so closely to property losses.

Builder Verification

If a specialist is insuring buildings under construction or if business in a particular area is growing rapidly, the builder's reputation is an important factor in evaluating the risk. Contractors of all types are drawn to areas of rapid growth. Also, after a natural disaster, such as a hurricane, nonlicensed contractors flood the areas for the quick cash available from repairs. Criminals with outstanding arrest warrants follow the disaster scenes because they can get jobs for cash without having to reveal their Social Security numbers and take the chance of being caught. Some contractors might have less than desirable hiring practices for employees and subcontractors. Contractors might not be licensed or carry liability insurance for any negligent acts that are performed.

A contractor's failure to perform acceptable work can result in a loss for the insured and a loss for the residential policy covering that property. If the loss is caused by a contractor's negligence, subrogation against the contractor is possible, but collection is unlikely if the contractor does not carry liability insurance.

Specialists can contact local consumer reporting organizations and state agencies to identify any past complaints about a contractor and to obtain the status of a contractor's license. These organizations and agencies include the following:

- Better business bureaus
- Chambers of commerce
- Home builders associations
- Contractors of America associations
- State residential home builders commissions
- State licensing agencies
- State departments of consumer affairs

Educational Objective 3
Identify and describe the exposures and hazards to consider in the residential property underwriting process.

Making the Underwriting Decision

After the application and reports have been gathered, the underwriter continues the underwriting process. A decision must be made based on the exposures and hazards identified.

Identifying and Measuring Exposures and Hazards

From the information gathered, the underwriter reviews the data to identify exposures and related hazards. During exposure identification, the underwriter also measures exposure severity. This measurement is usually a subjective judgment based on the gathered information.

The Named Insured

Many losses are caused by human error. Determining as much information as possible about the insured's personal characteristics is important. Glimpses of irresponsibility, instability, and immaturity can be gained through inspection reports, investigation of previous claims, and credit histories.

Valuable questions to ask about the insured include the following:

- Is this a new insured for the producer, or is this individual known from past business dealings? A producer's knowledge of an applicant is a positive sign. A new, unknown applicant might not indicate anything negative but would raise the question, "Why is the applicant changing insurance companies?" or "Has the applicant had insurance before?"

- Has the insurer ever insured this individual before? Can prior coverage be determined through a computer database or written records? If not, the insurer might be insuring someone prone to losses. Additionally, applicants who are rejected for coverage can find ways of obtaining temporary coverage by reapplying for coverage. They have protection until inspections and underwriting research are performed on their properties and the insurer issues a cancellation notice.

- What is the applicant's prior address? If the applicant has lived at the current address for three years or less, a prior address should be obtained to help verify the credit report.

A recent prior address might also indicate the presence of additional risk. Has the applicant made a major move from one part of the country to another? What is the reason for this major change? Underwriters become familiar with the economic growth of the territories they handle and the transient nature of the residents of these territories. Some areas have a regular influx of people from other states under normal circumstances. Has the applicant moved to accept a new job, or is the applicant hoping to find a job in the new area? Is the applicant now self-employed in this new location? Has the applicant ever done the type of work that he or she is now taking on as an entrepreneur?

Applicants arriving from other countries might not have accessible prior credit information. Questions about occupation and employment are helpful.

Joint Ownership If property is owned jointly by a married couple, underwriters tend to pose fewer questions than if property is owned by two unmarried adults who live together. An underwriter is looking for factors that can cause a greater-than-normal chance of loss. Following are some appropriate questions:

- Who is the actual owner of the property? If both names appear on the policy, does this mean that both parties co-own the **real property**, the **personal property**, or both of these? If the title of a home is in both names, both parties have an insurable interest, and both

Real property refers to land and all structures permanently attached to the land. **Personal property** refers to property other than real property.

should appear as "named insureds" on the declaration page. This becomes difficult in a tenant homeowners situation. If roommates each own their own personal possessions but are jointly covered by a single insurance contract, how will the company settle the loss in a contents claim? Will one check be issued for the total loss, with the policyholders working out the details? Or is it better to issue a policy to each roommate?

- Are the individuals in a stable household situation? Could the relationship end with one party leaving with the contents? Might the second party then claim a theft loss from an unknown thief? How long have these individuals shared ownership? An answer indicating a long period of time could indicate a stable future.

- Asking questions about adults who live together requires prudence. A natural question to ask is, "What is the relationship between the individuals?" However, if the underwriter asks questions about the individuals' relationship and later decides to reject the application or nonrenew the policy (regardless of the reason), could the underwriter face legal action simply because the questions were asked? Could an argument be supported that the reason for the rejection was discrimination because of gender, marital status, or lifestyle? Will the underwriter be able to prove that the questions asked were the same questions that are asked of all applicants, or could the applicants argue that they were subjected to unfair discrimination?

Occupation   A standard underwriting practice is to compare an applicant's salary with the value of the property. If an hourly worker has purchased a home that would normally require a six-figure salary to support, the underwriter should ask questions regarding additional sources of revenue. If the applicant is unemployed, the underwriter should ask whether the applicant is seeking work or whether other financial support is available.

Prior Home Ownership   Unlike cars, homes do not come with manuals. If the homeowner has never lived in a house with a fireplace, the homeowner might not know how to use the flue or how to properly stack logs in the fireplace to prevent the burning wood from rolling out into the room. Chimneys must be cleaned, roofs and foundations must be periodically checked, furnaces must be maintained annually, and kerosene heaters should not be placed against drapes or bed linens. New homeowners might not realize that a Formica kitchen counter is not designed to tolerate the heat from a pot that has just been taken off the stove. Improper home care and maintenance can generate losses covered by a residential property policy. If the applicant did not learn to care for a home while growing up or through prior home ownership, the applicant might gain that experience through experiencing a loss.

Appendix 9-B of this text provides a checklist showing an appropriate homeowner maintenance schedule.

Financial Strength   Credit reports provide a snapshot of the applicant's financial stability and strength. Homeowners with financial problems might be financially pressured to help their situations by exaggerating the size of claims or creating losses to generate income. A homeowner who is pressed to the breaking point might even consider arson to eliminate a financial burden. An estimated 11 percent of all residential fires are the result of arson.[6]

An applicant with ethical intentions can be financially stressed by the demands of home ownership. The cost of home maintenance and repairs increased 22.8 percent between 1985 and 1994.[7] Financial stress might mean that the applicant cannot replace the roof or clean the chimney when this periodic home maintenance is required. The result might be a claim.

The Property Location, Protection, and Construction

In addition to the insured or applicant's characteristics, the property location, protection, and construction are also crucial factors in writing profitable business. Poor property characteristics can create losses for even the most conscientious insured.

Address and Location On a homeowners application, the first item to review is the property address as compared to the mailing address. If the two addresses are different, the specialist should determine the reason. In rural areas, mailing addresses often appear as rural routes and post office box numbers. If the address does not reflect an exact location, the specific description and legal location should become part of the policy file. This legal description might include a lot and block number or a tax map identification code. The description should also include directions to the property, so that an inspector can observe the physical aspects of the property.

Specialists should watch for dwelling descriptions and values that might differ from the usual dwellings in that area. The differences could indicate that the home replacement value is exaggerated.

The location might also indicate the degree of police and fire protection, isolation, and susceptibility to perils such as flood, windstorm, earthquake, hurricane, brush fire, vandalism, and theft.

A large number of applications from one area over a short period of time might also indicate a problem. Other companies might be reducing the number of policies they write in that area. Inspecting the neighborhood and gathering some information regarding the community could eliminate concerns about the new policies. From a positive viewpoint, this could be an area that a producer targeted for marketing efforts.

Public Protection Classes The public protection class, also called a National Board Class, is a number from 1 to 10 that refers to the public protection facilities in a geographic area. The classes reflect the quality of public fire protection, road conditions, and water pressure levels and availability. The classes heavily emphasize fire protection and safety control. Lower numbers reflect better facilities and protection, as shown by the following:

- A Protection Class 10 has no fire protection (or very low protection).

- A Protection Class 9 has little fire protection and no hydrants within 1,000 feet of the property. Both 9 and 10 classes are considered unprotected classes.

- Some protection class directories show divided classes (for example, 5/9 or 6/9). This means that the lower class is allowed if a hydrant is within 1,000 feet of the residence, but the higher class is to be used if the nearest hydrant is over 1,000 feet from the residence.

Specialists should become familiar with the protection classes and residential areas within the territories they cover. Some outlying areas require property owners to purchase annual contracts to maintain fire protection services provided by neighboring towns. Without the contract, the fire department will not respond in case of a fire. Maintenance of these contracts is imperative. Insureds' files are diaried for a copy of the annual renewal. Failure to renew a fire contract generally changes the protection class to a 10.

Types of Construction Construction is an important factor when analyzing the resistance to damage from perils. Although many construction classes are applied to commercial structures, four basic construction classes are usually applied to residential property. However, most rating manuals group residential property under two broad classifications: masonry or frame. The following are the types of construction descriptions normally used for residences:

- *Frame.* Exterior and interior walls, partitions, floors, and roofs are wood or other combustible material. If a dwelling is partially brick or brick veneer, the building is considered frame if in addition the exterior is over one-third wood.

- *Masonry.* Exterior walls are made of noncombustible materials. Interior walls, partitions, floors, and roofs are made of wood or combustible material. A masonry-veneered dwelling is usually rated as masonry, although it is not truly a masonry construction.

- *Fire-Resistive.* A fire-resistive building is composed of masonry or steel and masonry fire-resistive partitions, a concrete floor, and a tile roof (or similar noncombustible material). If no other rating classifications apply, the building is rated as masonry with an appropriate credit.

- *Noncombustible.* All exterior walls and roofs are made of metal or steel (or other noncombustible materials). The building is rated as masonry with an appropriate credit if no other classifications apply.

- *Townhouse and Rowhouse Construction.* Special attention is required in reviewing the construction of townhouses and rowhouses in writing homeowners coverage. Individual units can be written under standard homeowners contracts. However, standard homeowners rating rules (as provided by the Insurance Services Office) are based on the number of units between fire walls. Those fire walls must be made of one of the following:

- Six inches of reinforced concrete
- Eight inches of masonry
- Material documented and laboratory tested to withstand a minimum two-hour fire

The fire walls must rise to the roof or pierce it. The fire walls must also extend to the exterior of the building or pierce the exterior walls. Many townhouses or rowhouse units have fire walls that were constructed in compliance with local building and fire codes but not in compliance with the Insurance Services Office guidelines.

Older Homes

Older dwellings might have outdated and possibly hazardous features unless renovations have been performed. Physical deterioration and lack of maintenance can also identify a morale hazard.

No uniform underwriting rules apply to the review of older dwellings. However, some systems in older dwellings, such as electric, plumbing, and heating, require attention.

Electrical System   Breakers or fuses are adequate if they have kept pace with the power requirements of the household and any large electrical additions to the house, such as window air-conditioning units, dryers, and electric stoves. If the house is over twenty-five years old, the specialist should ask for the date of the last update or inspection by a licensed electrician.

Plumbing System   Undetected slow leaks can cause a slow decay of the supporting frame structure and, in extreme cases, cause collapse. An inspection of the basement or crawl space under the house should be performed annually to check for wet wood and termites.

Interior Fixtures and Building Materials   Old homes could contain **plaster on lath** walls, wide-board floors, carved hardwood banisters, wood moldings, slate roofs, and hand-painted ceramic tiles. If the residence is written on a replacement-cost basis and the insured has a loss, the insured can insist that these items be replaced as they were before the loss. If the house is in a "historic district," the homeowner might be required to have the house restored.

Plaster on lath is a wall-covering method that was used before drywall. Narrow strips of wood (lath) were nailed to the wall supports with small spaces between the strips. Wet plaster was smoothed over these to create a wall surface.

Asbestos and lead paint are common in old homes. Asbestos was used in insulation, siding, roofing, and carpet until it was determined that its presence was unhealthy. Lead paint was popular from the 1930s to the 1960s. Removing asbestos or lead paint from a building is costly and must be done by professionals. Those materials present a debris removal problem if a house is partially destroyed.

Functional Replacement Cost and Reproduction Cost   Many homeowners insurers offer valuation options tailored to the needs of the owners of older homes. Although the names given these options vary from company to company, the options fall into two general classes: *functional replacement cost* and *reproduction cost*. Functional replacement cost covers the cost of repairing or replacing structural elements with materials and techniques in use today, for example, a plaster-on-lath wall would be replaced with wallboard. The HO-8 and DP-8 forms offer this type of replacement cost. This functional replacement valuation can reduce the amount of insurance needed to provide adequate coverage while still offering the insured full reimbursement for any loss.

Reproduction cost policies are written by some insurers as a specialty insurance policy. Reproduction cost applies to the needs of people who own historic homes. Local codes often require the owner to restore damaged property as nearly as possible to its original condition. This can be an expensive proposition for a home that includes architectural features that are no longer readily available. With valuation based on reproduction cost, the insurer agrees to replace damaged or destroyed property with the nearest obtainable kind and quality. A successful reproduction cost program depends on the development of the specialized claims service these properties require and the identification of a viable market for this specialty insurance policy.

Ordinance or Law   Older homes have materials used in construction that have been replaced in new construction with better, safer materials. For example, aluminum wiring is replaced by copper wiring, and lead pipes are replaced with PVC or copper pipes. If a residence is partially destroyed, zoning in the area might require home repairs that are consistent with the current ordinance or law. It is unlikely that an applicant or insured would be aware of this loss exposure. A producer who is familiar with local building requirements can help insureds identify the extent of their exposure.

Some current ISO homeowner policy forms provide ordinance or law coverage up to an additional 10 percent of Coverage A. Additional limits can be purchased by endorsement. Contracts should be reviewed carefully to identify available ordinance or law coverage.

Dwelling Values

Maintaining insurance-to-value is one of the most important considerations in a residential property policy. Many property policies encourage maintaining an adequate value on the dwelling to replace it in the event of loss by offering replacement cost coverage (versus actual cash value) if the amount of coverage shown on the policy for the dwelling is at least 80 percent of the actual cost to replace the dwelling at the time of the loss. However, most losses are partial rather than total. Knowing this, an insured might want to carry only a fraction of the dwelling value on the insurance policy.

The insured has the ultimate responsibility for maintaining an adequate coverage limit for a dwelling. Obviously, it is in the insured's best interest to keep insurance limits at a pace with the replacement cost of the house. Adequate coverage is crucial in providing protection against a total loss. Following are tools that help the insured maintain adequate coverage limits.

Value Increase at Renewal   Insurance companies help policyholders keep pace with replacement costs by increasing the dwelling coverage limits by a percentage at each renewal. Companies determine that percentage by studying construction cost trends for the geographical area. This across-the-board increase helps maintain an adequate replacement cost but does not always reflect an accurate coverage limit for an individual residence.

Inflation Guard Endorsements   These standard endorsements require the insured to select an annual percentage by which policy coverages are increased during the policy year. The increase applies pro rata during the policy period.

Replacement or Repair Cost Protection   This unique endorsement, also called guaranteed replacement cost, increases the dwelling coverage limit to include replacement or repair cost even if that amount is greater than the coverage limit appearing on the policy declaration.

Overinsured Homes   Being overinsured means having a higher coverage limit on a property than the property is worth, which creates a concern. The two underwriting schools of thought about overinsurance are as follows:

1. Overinsurance creates a moral hazard. The insured might be prompted to create an intentional loss if financial gain is possible.
2. An insurance policy cannot create a moral hazard if one does not already exist. Overinsurance, by itself, cannot change the moral fiber of the individual.

Business in the Home

The existence of an incidental business in the home can present both positive and negative underwriting factors, depending on the location within the home, the type of business, and other considerations involving the business operation.

An important consideration is whether the activities constitute a business or a hobby. At what point does an insured actually have a business rather than a hobby? As a general underwriting rule of thumb, an activity is considered a business when two elements are present:

* Continuity
* The expectation of monetary gain

Regardless of whether property and liability coverage for the business (1) is provided under a separate policy, (2) is provided by an endorsement attached to the homeowners policy, or (3) is retained by the insured, basic underwriting questions regarding the business operation should be asked.

What Type of Business Is It?   Are additional property and liability hazards present in the home because of the type of business? For example, are ignition sources, flammable chemicals, customers, or products for consumption present?

Do Employees Work in the Home? If employees are in the home, how many are there? Are they in professional or nonprofessional occupations? What supervision or control does the insured have over the employees and their location in the residence?

What Are the Customer Characteristics? The insured might have customers meet him or her at the house. If so, how often do customers visit the property? Are customers entering the premises only by invitation and one at a time? Are the customers adults or children? Are they professional or nonprofessional? Are the customers always in the presence of the insured while in the house?

What Is the Access Between the Dwelling's Living and Business Portions? Is the business in a section of the house that does not have immediate access to the living area, or is the living area combined with or open to the business area?

Do Increased Hazards Exist in the Dwelling? The materials and equipment present in the residence could increase or change the hazards. Although a computer terminal would probably not increase property or liability hazards, the presence of industrial sewing machines or manufacturing equipment and flammable chemicals could increase both types of hazards. Ceramic kilns generate thousands of degrees of heat and require special insulation for safety.

Having a business in the home can be an underwriting plus. The insured is home during the day, which can be a deterrent to theft, vandalism, or a loss that might begin during the daytime.

Heating System Type and Maintenance

All heating systems and chimneys require attention from insureds to reduce the chance of a fire loss. Systems that burn oil, wood, or gas need annual professional maintenance. This includes chimney cleaning and furnace cleaning or checkup. Carbon monoxide leakage from a heating unit can be deadly. Electrical heating systems might require a checkup only every two to five years. Filters for the electrical heating systems should be changed several times during the year, depending on dust accumulation.

Chimney Construction and Maintenance Chimney fires can result from improper installation of the chimney or its liner and from creosote accumulation. Creosote is a black, tar-like substance that forms as a result of incomplete fuel combustion. It sticks to all chimney surfaces and is combustible. Creosote develops when a fire is burned at low temperatures or when a chimney pipe passes through cool air. It develops faster when soft woods or woods that are not dry are burning. Ideally, the creosote condenses into liquid and runs back down into the fireplace or wood stove to be burned. The creosote can also form a more solid substance and stick to the chimney. If creosote is allowed to accumulate, a very hot fire can ignite it and cause a chimney fire.

The following are types of chimneys found in residences:

- *Class A masonry, flue-lined chimney.* A chimney that is lined with a 5/8"-thick tile liner, a stainless steel chimney liner, or a porcelain-coated steel chimney liner creates a nonporous tunnel for smoke. These liners are inserted in the brick or stone chimney. They are effective in reducing hazards because they can be cleaned thoroughly.

- *Metal prefabricated chimney.* A metal chimney pipe leads from the fireplace or wood stove. Care must be taken to ensure that the pipe used and the thimble that carries the pipe through combustible walls are adequate.

- *Unlined chimney.* An unlined chimney is made of brick and mortar and has no lining. Coal and wood stoves are not usually vented into an unlined chimney for safety reasons. The potential for a fire is great because the uneven surfaces of the brick and mortar can easily collect creosote. An unlined chimney also deteriorates faster than a lined chimney, causing possible cracks that allow sparks and gasses to escape into the structure.

Damage from a chimney fire can range from none to major. If the chimney has a liner and the creosote buildup is not severe, the accumulation might simply burn off with no resulting damage. The homeowner might not even know that a chimney fire is occurring until a neighbor calls to advise that flames are appearing from the top of the chimney. However, the liner can crack or break as a result of the fire and require replacement or repair. If the chimney is unlined, chinks in the mortar can allow heat and sparks to escape into the house and ignite adjacent combustibles. The worst case is a fire that spreads to the house, which can cause a major or total loss.

Fire department extinguishment of a chimney fire can be almost as bad as the fire itself. It requires running a hose up the chimney and spraying water into the fire. Water and debris are washed into the house.

Insureds should schedule regular stove and chimney inspections. A weekly inspection is recommended for air-tight stoves. A monthly inspection should be performed if a wood burner is frequently used. A cleaning is recommended at least annually.

Wood Stoves   Alternate heating sources become more popular whenever the cost of heating oil and electricity increases. They remain important to many families as supplemental heat sources.

A wood stove should be approved by Underwriters Laboratories or another nationally recognized testing laboratory. The heavier the construction of the stove, the longer it will last. Cast iron is preferred. Lighter metals, such as sheet metal, warp under high heat. A professional should install the stove.

In reviewing wood stoves, underwriters should check the following:

- *Clearances and shielding.* Usually, a minimum of thirty-six inches of clear space should separate the stove and any combustible walls. The distance can be reduced by installing a **radiation shield**

A **radiation shield** protects combustible surfaces from the heat generated by a wood stove.

between the stove and the combustible surfaces. Spaces between the shield and wall should allow the air to circulate freely. A shield made of stove board or steel plate twenty-four gauge or thicker should be placed on the floor. The shield should extend eighteen inches beyond the point at which ashes are removed. The ceiling should also have either a clearance of eighteen inches or installed shielding.

- *Chimney connector.* The vent pipe used to connect the stove to the chimney should be at least twenty-six gauge. Thicker gauges resist corrosion longer and need to be replaced less frequently. A **thimble** must be used to pass the pipe through combustible walls and partitions.

A **thimble** is a double-walled pipe that allows a chimney pipe to pass through a combustible wall without a heat contact.

The connector pipes should be installed so that an upper pipe section fits inside a lower section. This ensures that creosote buildup inside the pipe stays inside and flows down the inside surface. The pipe sections should be connected with a least three sheet metal screws per point. A fire in the chimney causes vibrations, and poorly fastened piping could fall.

A damper should be installed in the connector pipe. The pipe connections to a masonry chimney must be cemented to the chimney, or a thimble must be connected to the chimney. The pipe should be tightly inserted into the thimble without cementing. If the vent pipe passes directly through the roof, a factory-built Underwriters Laboratories-listed or other approved chimney must be used.

Vacant Dwellings

Under standard residential property policies, vandalism and glass breakage are automatically excluded if a dwelling is vacant (unoccupied and empty) for thirty days or more. Vacant dwellings become targets for vagrants and malicious mischief, increasing the fire risk. The circumstances regarding the vacancy need to be reviewed. Is the house for sale? What are the current market conditions for house sales?

Roof Conditions and Construction

The purpose of a roof is to protect a dwelling from loss by wind, water, and fire. Location, proximity to a forest fire hazard, windstorm exposure, maintenance, and age should be considered in underwriting the roof covering of a residence. Exhibit 9-5 provides descriptions of some roof coverings and special considerations for each.

Other general factors to consider in reviewing the roof from personal inspection or photos are missing shingles, cracked or sagging eaves, separated or missing flashing, cracks or indentations in the roof's surface, rotted fascia boards (horizontal boards just below the eaves), and unevenness in the roof line.

Exhibit 9-5
Roof Coverings and Their Underwriting Considerations

Architectural Shingles	These are composition material shingles that are thicker than standard shingles. They create interesting texture patterns on the roof and are usually found in high-value homes. Such shingles usually have warranties for up to thirty years. However, installation began in the 1980s, so actual results are not yet known.
Asphalt or Composition Shingles	These shingles have a life expectancy of about twenty years. Their useful life might be shorter in hot climates because the shingles deteriorate faster than in cooler climates. If they are not replaced when they have deteriorated, they constitute an underwriting concern because of susceptibility to loss from wind and water damage. A shingle roof can suffer a great deal of damage during a hailstorm. Only a new shingle roof can withstand a substantial hailstorm. Shingles have weight designations. In many areas, the recommended type is the 235-pound shingle. This is the weight of a square of shingles, which is the number needed to cover 100 square feet. Other shingles might be 300-pound shingles, which simply indicates a thicker, heavier material. A shingle roof that has come to the end of its useful life can be identified by a grainy appearance and/or curling of the edges.
Built-up	This is a flat roof (or a roof with a slight grade) with built-up layers of hot tar and gravel. These roofs provide good protection from fire, but they are subject to water leaks unless the layer of tar and waterproofing seal is constantly maintained.
Fiberglass Shingles	These shingles are reported to have a useful life of twenty-five to thirty years. This time period might be shortened in hot climates because of accelerated deterioration. Fiberglass shingles are similar to asphalt shingles in appearance and in protection against the elements.
Metal	Even if these roofs do not last the dwelling's lifetime, they last close to it. Maintenance for roofs includes painting when the galvanizing begins to wear off and sealing the joints and valleys with roofing cement if they begin to separate. Metal roofs (of various alloys) are becoming more popular in high-value homes because they can suit so many architectural needs and because they are so durable. They provide good protection from weather and fire.
Rolled	This is asphalt-roll roofing that is spread on the roof in overlapping layers and nailed in place. It has a useful life of five to ten years. It provides moderately effective protection from windstorm.
Selvage Edge	This is rolled roofing that has been tarred down on the seams. It has a useful life of ten years. It provides moderately effective weather protection.
Slate	This type of roof was once considered sturdy enough to last for the lifetime of the dwelling because the material is made of slabs of stone. Normal maintenance requires some replacement of the slates and flashing (the metal strip along the edge of the roof that provides water protection) because of natural deterioration of the nails holding the tiles in place. Violent and extended storms can cause extensive damage to these roofs if the stones are rattled for a prolonged period. The nails and the stone surrounding the holes drilled in the stone break, causing the slates to drop from the roof. It is difficult to find either qualified roofers and replacement stones (roofing slate is now quarried in Italy, Wales, and the U.S. in limited quantities) or highly specialized artisans.

Continued on next page.

Tile Roof	These interlocking ceramic tiles have also been called "lifetime roofs" that only require replacement of broken tiles. During the installation, the roofers must punch out the nail holes formed in the ceramic and properly secure the tiles to the roof. Shortcuts that had been taken in the installation process were uncovered in Florida after Hurricane Andrew, when it was discovered that tiles blown from roofs still had the nail holes intact. The installers had glued the tiles in place, which proved to be an ineffective installation technique.
Wood Shingle	Wood shingles can last twenty years with proper maintenance. Maintenance includes applying chemicals to prolong the life of the roof. The shingles must be treated to maintain their fire-protective quality. The period of time between treatments depends on the type of shingle and the chemicals used; treatment might occur annually or every three to five years. Wood shingles are as effective as composition shingles for weather protection, but they lose their fire-protective properties if not properly maintained. Wood roofs that have lost their fire-protective properties can become hazardous for a home with a wood stove or a home in an area susceptible to forest fires.

Electrical Systems

The electrical system in a residence usually receives only a cursory underwriting review. Electrical equipment that is improperly installed, maintained, or used is a fire hazard. A handyman might be inclined to add to or alter the original installation without realizing the limits to the size and types of wires. Temporary fixes can be hazardous.

Detailed information concerning a dwelling's electrical system is usually not available without ordering a special electrical inspection report. However, a physical inspection can help a specialist determine whether electrical risk of fire for that particular dwelling might be higher than average.

Electricity is carried from the fuse or circuit breaker through the wiring to appliances. A circuit has a maximum capacity stated in watts, and the size (thickness or gauge) of the wire determines the circuit's capacity. A #12 wire limits the capacity of a circuit to 2,400 watts. A #14 wire limits the capacity of a circuit to 1,800 watts. Problems are created when there are not enough circuits for the requirements of the appliances on those circuits. The table in Exhibit 9-6 illustrates the wattage requirements of some household appliances.

If the appliances are loaded (and operated simultaneously) on a circuit in excess of the maximum wattage that the circuit can carry, the fuse or circuit breaker disconnects the circuit. A dwelling should have a sufficient number of circuits to provide adequate electricity for all appliances and outlets.

Fuses and Circuit Breakers A fuse or circuit breaker protects the circuit from an overload and overheating by breaking the flow of electricity through the wire if the circuit's capacity is exceeded. The rated capacity of a fuse or circuit breaker should never exceed the rated capacity of the wire in the circuit. If higher-rated fuses or circuit breakers are

Exhibit 9-6
Wattage Requirements of Household Appliances

Air conditioner	1,600	Hair dryer	1,000
Blender	350	Iron	1,000
Broiler	400	Radio	100
Coffee maker	900	Refrigerator	240
Fryer	1,500	Television	330
Dishwasher	1,120	Toaster	1,146
Dryer	4,900	Vacuum cleaner	650
Electric blanket	175	Water heater	2,600
Freezer	340	Waffle iron	1,116

found (or a penny or piece of aluminum foil is inserted in the place of a fuse), the underwriter should recommend immediate correction.

Circuits   The average dwelling should have a minimum of sixteen to twenty circuits to handle appliances and utilities. If the house has electric heat, additional circuits are required. Older dwellings that have not been rewired in the past thirty years should be checked for an adequate number of circuits. The presence of a **knob-and-tube** circuit indicates a very old electrical system that should be professionally inspected.

A **knob-and-tube** circuit can be identified by glass insulators nailed to roof and ceiling joists in the attic with wire strung between the knobs. The exposed or insulated wire is subject to damage by rodents and other objects that come into contact with it.

Wiring Alloy   Aluminum wiring costs less than copper, so it is sometimes used by do-it-yourselfers and in some low-budget construction. Aluminum wire corrodes when it comes into contact with switches and connectors made of other metals. This corrosion is a poor conductor. The corrosion accumulates and creates a resistance that overheats and can eventually start a fire. Copper is currently the preferred construction material. New alloys are appearing on the market that contain aluminum and that have superior powers of conduction. These alloys do not exhibit corrosion problems and should not be confused with the inferior aluminum wire.

Workmanship   Electrical failures and fires result from inadequate wire size, poor workmanship, or poor wiring installation. For example, stapling through a wire can cause a short circuit and a fire. All electrical work should be performed by a licensed electrical contractor.

Housekeeping

Attention to housekeeping can usually be evaluated only from the exterior. The underwriter rarely obtains a report regarding the residence's interior unless the inspection is extensive, the producer conducts a personal inspection, or an adjuster visits the property after a loss. If waste, litter, appliances, and nonoperational vehicles are in the yard, can the care and maintenance of the residence's interior be substantially different? Although these things by themselves do not pose a property hazard, they might create a liability hazard, and they do cause concern about a morale hazard. Is any better care being given to the maintenance of the chimney? Does the kitchen contain fire hazards from grease accumulation on the stove and in the range hood? Is a slow leak in the bathroom being ignored? If so, the situation requires further research.

Educational Objective 4

Explain and evaluate the alternatives available in implementing residential property coverage or risk management recommendations.

Identifying and Evaluating the Alternatives

Many underwriting alternatives are available for insuring residential property. The key to evaluating the alternatives is to understand the coverages provided by the policy forms and to be creative in exploring the alternatives.

The underwriter is not restricted to simply accepting or rejecting an application or nonrenewing an existing policy. Other alternatives should be explored.

Modify the Coverage

If the residence has an unacceptable exposure, coverage can be modified by offering a different policy form to remove or lessen the exposure. The following are examples:

- A dwelling with an open foundation written on a homeowners policy has a high exposure to losses from the freezing and breaking of the exposed pipes under the dwelling. A basic fire policy could be written, providing named-perils coverage without coverage for losses caused by freezing.

- An oceanfront house with a substantial windstorm exposure could be written with an endorsement excluding wind exposure.

Modify the Deductible

A risk that generated a number of small losses could be made acceptable by increasing the deductible. The following are examples:

- During the initial review of a homeowners application, the specialist notes that the house has a carport rather than a garage. The photo of the house shows that bicycles and a lawnmower are stored under the carport. The carport does not pose a hazard other than a potential theft loss for unprotected property left under the carport. The specialist requires at least a $500 deductible to cover the value of unprotected property.

- A dwelling had two losses in four years. One loss was $500 to repair an air conditioner struck by lightning, and the second loss was $1,000 to repair the roof after a hailstorm. Those losses were not within the insured's control or preventability. A higher deductible could make the risk more acceptable.

Modify the Premium

Modifying the premium on a residential insurance policy is not done as frequently as in commercial lines, but it is possible. The key is to write business that is average or better for any rate classification. If a risk is submitted for a preferred homeowners market but the risk is below the qualifications for that market, it belongs in another market. The standard product line could be the best alternative for this property. The premium is higher in the standard market to reflect the increase in exposure because of the risk characteristics. The following is an example:

> An insurer's underwriting guide requires that a homeowners risk be loss-free for five years for acceptance into a preferred homeowners market. An application indicates that the insured had a minor kitchen fire three years earlier. The standard homeowners market might be more appropriate and reflect a premium in line with the exposures.

Modify the Limits

Suggesting lower coverage limits is common for a residential property policy, but other useful and viable alternatives are possible. For example:

- An old house is submitted for a replacement cost policy. Investigation reveals that this house is in a historic district. The house has many features that would be difficult to replace, such as a slate roof and hand-carved banisters and moldings. Offering a policy that is based on the market value of the house and functional replacement of any damage might make the risk acceptable (such as the HO-8 or DP-8).
- High limits are requested for a small dwelling constructed in a resort area. The limit probably reflects the purchase price and the mortgage value rather than the replacement cost of the structure. Explaining the "replacement" features of the policy and helping the insured determine a fair replacement value make more sense for the applicant and insurer than high limits do.

Modify the Exposure

This option has several possibilities. If the exposures are unacceptable, eliminating the exposures might be possible. The following provide examples of improvements that could be required of the property owner:

- Cleaning up or repairing the dwelling as a condition of accepting the application
- Verifying that chimney maintenance and cleaning have been completed

- Installing a central station alarm system as a condition of the policy renewal
- Insulating exposed pipes to reduce the chances of a freeze loss

The problem with the risk modification alternative is the participation by the insured. If the specialist requires repairs or a chimney cleaning as a condition of writing or renewing a policy, will the insured voluntarily continue this maintenance without prompting?

Implementing the Decision and Monitoring the Results

The final steps in the underwriting process are implementing the decision and monitoring the results. Underwriting decisions must be made several times during the life of a policy. Monitoring ensures that the desired outcomes are achieved and corrective actions are taken.

Implementing the Decision

Residential property underwriters usually face underwriting decisions at three events during the life of a policy: (1) the initial review of the application, (2) review after a claim, and (3) review during a re-underwriting process or at renewal. The review after a claim is the most challenging. At this point, conditions from those existing at the time of application and policy issuance have changed. All claims should be screened or reviewed to determine the following:

- Any hazards related to the loss
- Preventability of the loss
- Actions by the insured to prevent any future losses of the same type
- The history of the account, along with other losses incurred under the policy

A loss is not an underwriting error. If losses did not occur, no one would buy a policy, and the insurance industry would not exist. However, any change in the conditions of the risk and account history warrant careful review.

Monitoring the Results

Specialists typically view the size of the losses and the number of loss occurrences differently. The size, or severity, of a loss is largely a matter of chance. The size of a fire loss depends on the delay in detecting the ignition, the time of day the fire started, and the traffic conditions that might delay the fire department's response. However, large losses often capture the attention of the specialists simply because of their size.

The number of losses and their frequency are important in underwriting residential property claims. The frequency is often more controllable than the severity.

The following is an underwriting rule of thumb used to review the loss results for a book of business. As with every general rule, it is a place to begin uncovering a problem but is not necessarily applicable to every situation:

- A loss ratio problem caused by frequent losses is the result of inadequate underwriting.
- A loss ratio problem caused by a few large losses is the result of an inadequate premium for the exposures or a book of business that is too small to have credible results.

Educational Objective 5

Explain the special underwriting considerations associated with residential property concerning the following:

- Seasonal occupancy or daily unoccupancy
- Flood exposure
- High earthquake frequency areas
- Coastal areas with severe windstorm exposure
- High crime exposure areas
- Areas susceptible to brush fires

Special Underwriting Concerns and Underwriting Alternatives

Some properties present special underwriting concerns because of their location or occupancy. These properties have potential hazards that the underwriter must consider, not only regarding the individual risk but also regarding the entire book of business. An entire book of business that is susceptible to brush fires or earthquakes could create a perilous economic situation for an insurer.

Rental Property

When reviewing rental property, whether it is owned by a business or an individual, the specialist should ask the following questions:

- Are the landlords familiar with the business side of renting residences? Do they screen tenants, maintain the buildings, perform periodic inspections, and deal with difficult tenants? What has the landlord's loss experience been?
- How often does the owner or representative see the dwelling? If the owner is living 1,500 miles away, who is in the vicinity to look after the condition of the dwelling? As a rule of thumb, someone who can make decisions about maintenance and the tenant's care of the property should evaluate a dwelling's condition from the outside once a month. Has the owner hired a rental agency to

perform collections and repairs? Could the dwelling become vacant and go into severe disrepair for an extended period of time without anyone's knowing?

- If a rental group owns a number of dwellings in one location (such as a whole subdivision), what are the characteristics of this rental group? Are the dwellings intended for those in transient occupations? Is this a better-than-average rental area? Is the subdivision leased as a government rent-sponsored project for those with low incomes (often referred to as Section 8 housing)?

Seasonal Occupancy and Daily Unoccupancy

Seasonal rentals are dwellings or condominiums rented on a weekly, monthly, or seasonal basis. The actual rental of the dwelling might be controlled by the insured or by a rental agency.

Hazards develop in the off-season when the dwellings are unoccupied. The unoccupied dwellings can be damaged by vandalism or by temperature changes. If the dwelling is not checked regularly, pipes can freeze. Even if the heat is maintained to prevent a freeze, a loss of power can undermine that precaution. To compound the problem, the resulting water damage might not be discovered for a long time.

The following are good questions to ask when insuring a seasonal dwelling:

- What is the duration of the property lease?
- Is a rental agent on-site?
- Is this rental unit in an area with security (such as a resort area)?
- What is the insured's experience in renting this type of dwelling?
- Have any losses occurred involving this unit?

Many houses are unoccupied during the day because many couples work, and many residences are owned by single, working adults. Nevertheless, an insured can do much to prevent losses. Security alarm systems deter break-ins during the day. Deadbolts and window locks are not foolproof, but they can delay a burglar long enough to attract attention. Some neighborhoods are targeted more frequently. Easy access to a community from a highway and the absence of a car in the driveway encourage prospective vandals and thieves. Cul-de-sacs provide privacy that many thieves find attractive.

Flood Exposure

Floods can be caused by exceptionally heavy rainfall, rapidly melting snow and ice, or overflowing or breaking dams or levees. Losses frequently include injury, death, and substantial property damage. Flood insurance is a target for adverse selection. The demand for flood insurance comes from people living in river-basin areas and lowlands. They are likely to have flood losses at some point, and they seek coverage.

National Flood Insurance Program

Homeowners and dwelling policies exclude damage caused by flood, surface water, wave, tidal water, and overflow of a body of water. Flood coverage is available through policies issued by the National Flood Insurance Program, which is a part of the Federal Insurance Administration. The federal government shares in the flood exposure and the cost of insurance for many insureds. Eligibility for this coverage depends on whether the community qualifies for participation in the flood program by adopting regulations governing land use in flood-prone areas.

In the 1980s, the National Flood Insurance Program expanded its marketing efforts to reach more property owners in flood-prone areas. Private insurance companies issue policies for the government under a program called "Write Your Own," or WYO. Private companies market and issue the policies for a fee. The balance of the premiums goes into the government pool of dollars to pay claims. These WYO companies bear none of the risk because all losses are paid by the government. All WYO companies issue policies providing the same coverage and charging the same premium (with some variations in servicing fees). Companies compete in the areas of service and marketing. One hundred sixty-nine WYOs write this coverage, which amounts to 86 percent of flood policies.[8]

Other Flood Coverage

Some flood coverage can be obtained for residential contents through inland marine policies or inland marine-style schedules attached as endorsements to homeowners policies. The coverage is broad enough under these forms to encompass flood losses for covered items. Some mobile-home insurers also issue flood insurance as an additional optional coverage.

Areas With High Earthquake Frequency

Between 400 and 500 earthquakes occur in the United States in a typical year. Only a few cause any kind of structural damage.

Earthquake underwriting is difficult, since so many geographic regions have significant exposures. However, underwriters can control their total earthquake writings to protect against a catastrophic loss. The underwriting analysis of earthquakes considers three major areas: (1) location within a geologically determined earthquake zone, (2) soil conditions, and (3) building design, construction techniques, and materials.[9]

Location

The earthquakes that occur in California and western Nevada make up 90 percent of all earthquakes in the United States. However, the New Madrid, Missouri, quake of 1811 was the strongest ever recorded. The United State Office of Science and Technology charts seismic risks for each area. The country is divided into four zones, designated

Exhibit 9-7
Earthquake Zones in the United States

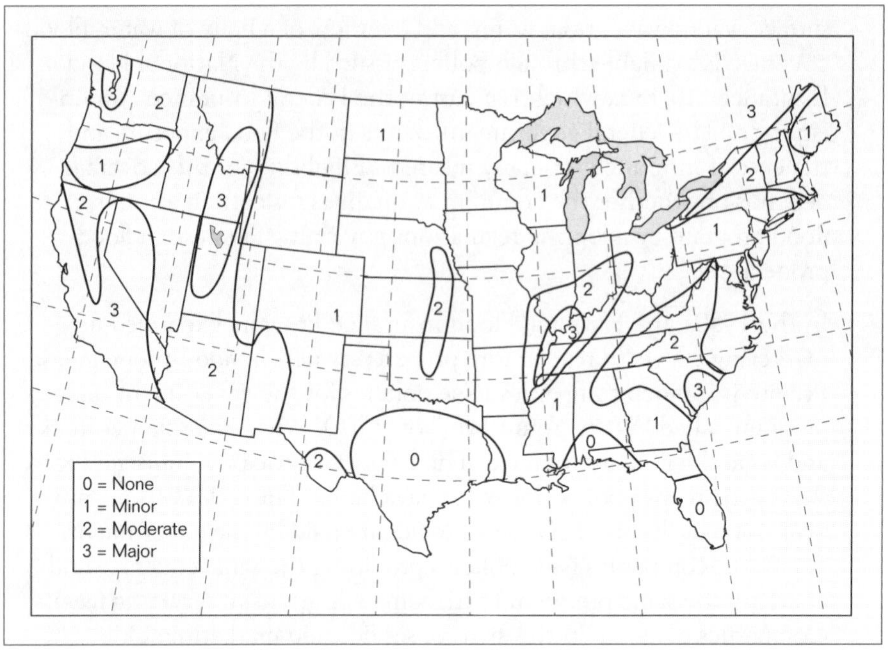

Reprinted from National Oceanic and Atmospheric Administration and National Ocean Survey, Seismic Risk Studies in the United States (Washington, DC: U.S. Department of Commerce).

from 0 to 3. Earthquake risk is almost nonexistent in Zone 0. In Zone 1, minor damage from earthquakes can occur. Zone 2 is exposed to moderate damage. Zone 3 represents an area of significant damage potential. Exhibit 9-7 provides the location of those zones.

Soil Conditions

Since earthquake waves travel at small amplitudes in bedrock, structures built on bedrock or supported on pilings driven into bedrock are less susceptible to earthquake damage than are other structures built on less secure foundations. **Consolidated soil** of long standing (thousands of years), such as limestone and some clay, withstands earthquakes better than **unconsolidated soil** such as sand, gravel, and silt. Filled land, common in many large cities, represents a particularly hazardous type of unconsolidated soil from the standpoint of earthquake. Unconsolidated filled land can **liquefy** during an earthquake, becoming so unstable that it acts like a liquid. This was evident in the 1985 earthquake in Mexico City. Underlying soil that had once been a lake bed intensified the damage.

> Consolidated soil such as clay and limestone has aged for thousands of years to become a solid base for construction. **Unconsolidated soil** such as gravel and sand might include areas that have been filled in to create building sites. Unconsolidated soil might **liquefy** (act like a liquid) during an earthquake.

Building Design, Construction, and Materials

Normal construction places weight on vertical structures that support the building. Most earthquakes cause horizontal stress that weight-bearing columns and walls might not have been designed to bear. Walls can move out from under the floors and roofs that they are supporting, causing collapse. An earthquake-resistant building has all its structural members tied securely together so that the entire building moves horizontally as a single unit when subjected to earthquake forces.

Unreinforced masonry is particularly susceptible to earthquake damage. A masonry building is rigid and subject to structural failure during earth movement. A frame building is relatively flexible and gives way during earth movement, often sustaining relatively minor damage such as cracked plaster. Brick or stone veneer and tile roofs often sustain earthquake damage.

Underwriting Alternatives Regarding Earthquakes

Insurers writing a large volume of earthquake coverage should periodically check the total exposure in each geographic area to estimate the probable maximum loss. If the probable maximum loss is too large for the insurer, writings might be restricted, or more excess (catastrophe) reinsurance can be purchased, if possible. Adverse selection in known earthquake areas can be a problem.

The insurance industry is concerned about the possibility of an unmanageable catastrophe exposure regarding earthquake. The New Madrid fault runs through seven major cities in the central United States. A sizable quake from that fault could shake the financial foundation of insurers that write earthquake coverage. Possible alternatives to the earthquake coverage problem are the basis for much industry discussion.

Coastal Areas With Severe Windstorm Exposure

The costliest and most intense hurricanes in the United States are concentrated in the Southeastern and Gulf Coast states. However, hurricanes occasionally strike the Northeastern states. From 1900 to 1991, an average of two major hurricanes made landfall every three years somewhere along the U.S. Gulf or the Atlantic Coast.

Hurricane Patterns

The charts in Appendix 9-C of this text display the major U.S. hurricanes (category 3 or greater) by decade. These charts illustrate the normal pattern of hurricane activity in the country from 1900 to 1960.

From 1960 to 1979, the number and intensity of hurricanes making landfall decreased sharply, compared to hurricane occurrences during the prior century. Only 75 percent of the expected number of hurricanes struck the United States during those years. Those storms that did strike were of much lower intensity than expected. Consequently, many house buyers and builders were attracted to the coastline. Forty-five million residents have moved to the Eastern Atlantic coast during the past twenty-five years. Areas most susceptible to storm loss are becoming increasingly populated.

Hurricanes resumed their frequency and intensity in 1989. The residential coverage concern is that continued coastal growth and inflation will almost certainly result in large property losses.

FYI

In 1964, the director of the weather bureau in Formosa predicted that Hurricane Gloria would bypass the island. The next day it hit with full force. As a result, two hundred thirty-nine people died. The director was arrested and charged with negligent forecasting.

Building Codes

Adequate building codes and their effective enforcement have the potential to limit losses from hurricanes to manageable levels. Studies have demonstrated, however, that most code enforcement officials and home builders are not aware of the construction techniques needed to comply with current wind provisions in building codes. Hurricane Andrew demonstrated that well-designed building codes alone are not sufficient. South Florida, which had the most stringent wind code provisions in the United States, sustained substantial damage because homes were not constructed in compliance with building code provisions. Public officials and home builders simply do not know enough about wind-resistive construction. In an effort to improve code compliance and assist underwriters in evaluating codes and enforcement, ISO introduced the Building Code Effectiveness Grading Schedule (BCEGS) in 1995. Developed in cooperation with the Insurance Institute for Property Loss Reduction, BCEGS assigns each community a grading similar to the public protection classifications.[10]

Beach Plans

Insurance programs referred to as beach or windstorm plans were developed in the 1960s and 1970s in states along the Gulf of Mexico and the Atlantic Ocean to provide windstorm coverage for coastal properties. The purpose of those plans was to assure an adequate market for the coverage and a fair method of distributing coverage responsibility among insurers. The plans restrict eligibility to coastal areas. In a typical state (such as Florida, South Carolina, or Texas), an insurer deletes the windstorm coverage from a coastal homeowners or dwelling policy by endorsement. The insured then purchases a windstorm policy from the state association. In other states (such as Mississippi and North Carolina), standard fire and extended coverage are also available through the plans. Other states (including Alabama and Louisiana) provide fire, extended coverage, and vandalism and malicious mischief coverage. Losses incurred by the association are proportioned to all the insurers writing property business in that state. Some states allow credits to insurers voluntarily writing coverage in exposed areas. All of the plans have underwriting restrictions and provide limited coverage.

Monitoring Hurricane Exposure

Monitoring the concentration of an entire book of property business within known vulnerable hurricane areas and purchasing adequate reinsurance are effective methods of minimizing loss for an insurer. Some loss control measures can be implemented in order for individual structures to minimize loss; however, many companies seek a spread of risk so that no single loss will affect all of their property risks.

High Crime Exposure Areas

Declining a risk simply because of location is not acceptable underwriting practice. Years ago, underwriters would hang a large map on the wall and draw a red line around those areas that were not going to be written. This practice of "redlining" is no longer acceptable or legal.

However, areas that are known to have a high instance of crime pose potential increased hazards from fire and vandalism. Security systems and alarms on the building should be investigated. A policy covering reduced perils is marginally effective, because the fire peril is still covered by all standard forms.

Another problem surfaces in high crime areas. The market values of the houses decrease as the crime levels increase. Eventually, their owners cannot sell homes for reasonable prices. The market price might not even cover the outstanding mortgage. Consequently, arson might become an attractive option. The warning signs for arson described previously in this chapter apply to all property but are especially important to consider when previewing properties in high crime areas. Of course, the presence of one of those signs does not necessarily indicate the need for further research.

Federal Crime Insurance Program

The Housing and Urban Development Act of 1970 established the Federal Crime Insurance Program. Through this program, the federal government provides insurance coverage to encourage a resolution of problems in availability and affordability of coverage. The act authorizes the secretary of HUD to make insurance available "at affordable rates" in any state in which a need exists.

Policies are issued and serviced by servicing companies under contract with the Federal Insurance Agency (FIA). These servicing companies market, underwrite, and service policies. Premiums are credited to and losses are paid from the National Insurance Development Fund.

Residence crime coverage under the Federal Crime Insurance Program is available to any individual property owner who agrees to do the following:

- Allow inspection of the premises
- Report all covered events to authorities, even if no claim is filed
- Maintain protective devices required by HUD

Exterior doors must have deadbolt or self-locking deadlatch locks that cannot be opened by prying or turning a knob. Sliding doors and windows must have locks. Residential risks can obtain from $1,000 to $10,000 in coverage, with limits of $100 on money, $500 on securities, and $500 on jewelry, furs, antiques, fine arts, and coin and stamp collections. Coverage is provided for burglary and robbery (as defined in the contract) and damage to premises caused by an actual or attempted burglary or robbery.

The FIA rates areas according to three classes: low, average, or high-crime areas, with one rate applying to each.

FAIR Plans

The Federal Crime Insurance Program encourages private insurers to write coverage by offering reinsurance for losses caused by riot and civil unrest. For insurers to be eligible to purchase the reinsurance, participation in a FAIR (Fair Access to Insurance Requirements) plan, established within each state, is required. One of the requirements of a FAIR plan is that rates for standard insureds under the program be no higher than rates for insureds in the voluntary market.

The goal of FAIR plans is to enlarge the market for basic property insurance in a way that is equitable among insurers writing that coverage in a state and to make basic property insurance available to all property owners. The FAIR plans are not meant to replace normal channels of insurance.

FAIR plans have three principal elements:

1. Procedures for inspecting property
2. A facility in each state for placing coverage with participating insurers
3. A joint reinsurance association for distributing losses equitably

A homeowner in an urban area interested in obtaining coverage typically applies to an insurance placement facility. This facility is composed of all property insurers operating in the state. The facility can inspect the property (and the insured can review the inspection). The facility must then decide whether the risk is acceptable, unacceptable, or conditionally acceptable subject to improvements. The neighborhood and conditions of the surrounding building are not acceptable criteria for rejecting a risk.

Areas Susceptible to Brush Fire or Forest Fire

The nature of forest fires varies. They can burn from the ground to the treetops and destroy everything in their path. They can be a brush fire, which is a low-range fire that burns only the underbrush and dead, dry trees.

An increasing number of homes are built in or adjacent to private forests or national forests because electrical lines carrying power to these rural areas are becoming more common and prompting more construction. However, the road systems and the fire protection in these new residential areas take time to catch up with the construction. Roads are often narrow, twisting, and unpaved. Pump or tank trucks have difficulty in, or are obstructed from, reaching isolated dwellings. Additionally, isolated houses are increasing in value. Part of the appeal for building medium- to high-value dwellings in forested areas is isolation and solitude.

Underwriting Construction in Fire-Prone Areas

In any rural area, a dwelling's electrical and heating systems should be superior to prevent a fire's ignition. If a fire begins, it is likely to cause a total loss because of the distance firefighters and trucks must travel to the dwelling and the obstacles they encounter.

In forested areas, the exterior condition of the residence and its possible ignition from wind-carried sparks must be considered. The roof is an important feature. If the house has a wood-shingle roof, it must be treated continually to retain its fire-resistive capabilities (annually, every three years, or every five years, depending on the type of roof and chemicals used). Tracking this maintenance requires underwriting follow-up.

Open foundations also create a possible increase in hazards in forested areas. Leaves can collect at the base of the foundation and under the house. A brush fire can be carried directly to the house and to the exposed timber below the foundation. If a fire begins under a house with an open foundation, or because of an ignition source in the house, the open foundation creates a considerable source of oxygen. Consequently, fire loss is likely to be total.

Other Underwriting Questions for Fire-Prone Areas

Questions an underwriter should ask when underwriting a residence with a forest fire potential include the following:

- Are forest firefighting units available in this area?
- Do good access roads exist for tankers and other firefighting units?
- Does the dwelling have a clear space around it that can stop a low brush fire and help firefighters save the dwelling? (A clearing of 100 feet and an additional 100 feet clearance of brush are recommended as a minimum.)
- What are the roof material and the fire-resistive characteristics of that material?
- How many other dwellings is the company insuring that could be affected by a single forest fire?
- Is the property in sight of other residences so that a fire can be detected?
- If no hydrants are available, is a permanent water source available for a pump truck?

Electrically-operated well pumps are not effective if electrical lines are damaged in the fire. A "dry" hydrant is a buried pipe leading from a nearby water source (such as a pond or lake) to an area near the residence. The pump truck can connect to this access pipe for water. Dry hydrants are an underwriting plus as long as the water source does not completely freeze in cold weather.

Educational Objective 6

Describe the underwriting considerations associated with residential property concerning the following:

- Rights granted to mortgagees by residential property policies
- Number and type of mortgagees

Underwriting Considerations Involving Mortgagees

Mortgage agreements usually require the owner to name the mortgagee on the owner's insurance policy. Insurance policies grant rights to mortgagees that are separate and distinct from the owner's rights. The insurer might have to pay a mortgagee even when the coverage is void to the owner. Each residential property policy contains a mortgage clause that defines the rights of the mortgagees, the order of their payment in the event of a loss to the property, and the method and amount of payment.

Rights Granted to Mortgagees

The mortgagee is granted rights of recovery under the policy for the loss of real property even if the insurer denies the insured's claim, as long as the mortgagee does the following:

- Notifies the insurer of a change in ownership or occupancy, or of a substantial change in risk of which the mortgagee is aware
- Pays any premium due under the policy if the insured has neglected to pay
- Submits a sworn statement of loss within sixty days

Situations exist in which an insured might void his or her coverage while the mortgagee's rights for a valid claim (the policy covers the perils) remain valid. The following are examples:

- An insured is found responsible for an intentional fire loss to a dwelling. The insured cannot collect; the mortgagee can.
- The insurer discovers that the insured has intentionally concealed that an auto repair shop is being operated in a garage attached to the house. The welding equipment and solvents ignite a fire. The insured is not covered for the loss. However, the mortgagee is.

If the policy is to be canceled or nonrenewed, the mortgagee must be given at least ten days' notice.

For a partial loss under a residential policy, an insurer usually lists all parties on a claims check or draft. This means payees include any mortgagee listed on the policy, the named insured, and any additional insureds. This is a practical solution to a problem from the insurer's standpoint. Trying to sort out who should be paid and how much would be very difficult. When all names appear on the check, all parties must agree on how the money will be used. All parties can agree on the needed repairs to the property, sign the check, and proceed. Sometimes the situation becomes complicated when mortgagees want to hold funds until they receive evidence of the completed repairs. It might be financially impossible for the insured to complete the repairs until the claim payment is received. A problem occurs if the parties cannot negotiate a workable alternative. The policy's overall objective is for the insurer to pay the claim under the obligations of the policy and for the funds to be used to repair the property. All of those with an insurable interest will then have their assets returned to their prior value.

In a claim payment for a total loss or payment to a mortgagee when the insured is denied payment, the insurance company pays the mortgagee only to the extent of its insurable interest, which is the remaining principal on the mortgage (plus any accrued interest).

Number and Type of Mortgagees

One-third of all houses purchased by first-time owners are bought with the financial assistance of a relative. Relatives might appear as mortgagees on the policy, or they might provide a loan or gift to assist with a down payment. The appearance on an application of the name of a mortgagee who is an individual rather than a financial institution might indicate that the buyer could not obtain a loan and has made private arrangements with a family member, a friend, or the previous owner. Having an individual mortgagee does not necessarily mean that a problem exists, but it does prompt additional questions.

Along with the financial conditions of the applicant, the specialist might request permission from the individual who is a mortgagee in order to order a credit report. The underwriter can determine whether the mortgagee is in a strong enough financial situation to withstand a financial hardship (loss of a job or illness) without placing pressure on the applicant to refinance the loan or pay the loan early. Even though the legal documents between the parties might not require the applicant to do this, the applicant might feel an obligation. This becomes an insurance problem only if the pressure is so great that a loss results to eliminate the problem.

If several mortgages appear on the policy, the specialist should ask additional questions to determine the reason and any associated increase in risk. A financial problem is one of the first things that comes to mind, but this is not always the case. As the values of dwellings increase, owners are finding that second and third mortgages can better assist them in obtaining the financing needed, rather than taking all of the needed capital under one large mortgage. A credit report can help identify any financial difficulty.

Contract of Sale

Creativity in financing houses, dwellings, and commercial buildings seems to run in cycles and follows an increase in building values and an increase in interest rates. To avoid the high interest rates charged by loan institutions, some people choose to leave the original mortgage in place and purchase a house through a contract arrangement with the original owner. This leaves the original owner in the mortgagee's records as the owner, and the original owner is still shown on the deed. The rights of the occupant (the new owner) are created by a contract established with the prior owner. The contract is called a contract of sale or purchase agreement contract and usually stipulates that the new owner will make the mortgage payments on the existing mortgage. When the interest rates for available mortgages decline to a given point, the new owner proceeds with purchasing and closing on the property.

This arrangement sounds complicated, and it can be. Some underwriting concerns are as follows:

- Who is occupying the property?
- Is the type of occupancy a residence, a rental, or a business?
- Does the occupant have a financial interest in the building (will the occupant take care of it as if it were his or her own)?
- Does an end date appear on the contract, by which time the occupant must close on the sale?

An end date could create financial pressures and make the new residence appear less attractive if the new owner is forced to close at a time of high interest rates. Also, the new owner might be trying to sell a prior residence before closing. Being forced into the ownership of a second house before the first is sold could, but does not necessarily, present a significant problem. Standard rules and guidelines in rating manuals make provisions for this form of ownership.

Educational Objective 7
Identify and evaluate any underwriting special hazards involving loss of use coverages.

Special Hazards Affecting Loss of Use

Direct property insurance coverages are relatively easy to visualize because they are tangible and the financial loss that results is apparent. However, related losses of reduced income and extra expenses associated with direct losses are not so straightforward. These indirect losses result from the property owner's inability to use the property or the loss of rental income when the property is uninhabitable for a time.

In general, property must be safe, sanitary, and secure to be habitable or fit to live in as a residence. As soon as property fails to meet one of those criteria and the cause of the loss is covered under the contract, the insured is entitled to the indirect coverage. The safe, sanitary, and secure guideline depends not only on the loss but also on the occupant. If the interior of a house is dusted with soot from a kitchen fire (a covered peril), does it fail to meet the "sanitary" guideline? It might, if one of the occupants has asthma or is a one-month-old baby. It might not fail the guideline if the sole occupant is a healthy adult who works in a quarry as a stone cutter.

The following are two indirect coverages included under residential property policies.

1. Additional living expense. This coverage is available to an occupant and is an extra expense coverage. This pays expenses that are above the insured's normal expenses so that the insured and family can maintain a normal standard of living. This can include the cost of a hotel room, the fees to board a family pet, and the cost to eat at restaurants (above the normal cost of groceries).

2. Fair rental value (rented to others). This is the compensation for loss of rent for that part of a premises (or the whole premises) rented to others, less expenses that do not continue.

Some hazards affecting indirect coverage are of note. The first hazard is in the availability of living quarters after a loss affecting a large area. After Hurricane Hugo hit South Carolina in September 1989, the local apartments and hotel rooms were filled with families whose houses had suffered storm damage. Construction workers, electrical storm teams, and insurance adjusters filled the remaining spaces. Placing a family in temporary housing meant finding the only remaining openings, some of which were in costly hotels. Because much of the area was without electricity for weeks, restaurants did not open quickly. Many meals were obtained through room service. The claim costs for these coverages were astounding.

A second notable hazard associated with these coverages occurs in states that have beach or windstorm plans. Even if the windstorm exposure is eliminated from the residential policy (and a credit is allowed for the eliminated peril), the policy might still cover the indirect loss.

A third hazard of note can be found in the language of the policies: "Payment under (these coverages) will be for the shortest time required to repair or replace the damage or if you permanently relocate, the shortest time required for your household to settle elsewhere." An uncooperative insured might delay the process of resolving the claim. The adjuster might work to bring the loss to an equitable settlement. However, a team effort is required. The longer the process, the higher the payments for this time element coverage.

Summary

Residential property insurance policies take many forms, but the major perils insured by the policies are similar. Profiles of the standard residential policies were provided as Exhibit 9-1 and continue in Appendix 9-A to this book.

The major perils covered in these standard policies are fire, lightning, theft, windstorm and hail, smoke, explosion, vandalism, water damage, and vehicles. Specialists should understand the exposures and hazards related to these major perils before beginning the process of underwriting individual accounts.

The underwriting decision-making process begins with gathering information. The application is the primary source of information. Gaps in the data provided by the application can be filled by asking questions of the producer and obtaining external reports. Inspection reports of the property and credit reports regarding the applicant are two of the primary external reports used by underwriters.

After the information has been gathered, specialists identify and measure (or evaluate) the exposures. This is a complex process in residential underwriting because of the many variables. The individual and the property must be reviewed for exposures and hazards that can lead to a loss from a covered peril. Specialists should also be concerned with those exposures and hazards that would not be covered by a residential insurance policy so that the insured can be advised of them. The insured can then take appropriate risk management steps.

Many alternatives are available in coverage placement. The variety of residential policies allows specialists choices to modify the coverage or rate. Loss control measures to modify the risk are also a key factor. Property inspections often reveal exposures that can be addressed to reduce the chance of loss. Appendix 9-B of this text provides a checklist of regular maintenance to help reduce loss.

Some exposures of special underwriting concern involve residences in areas exposed to catastrophic peril, high-crime areas, and areas susceptible to forest fire. The specialist should be aware of the nature of the exposures and the coverage that is available through alternative sources.

Residential policies provide coverage to mortgagees. The number of mortgagees and the form of ownership should be noted in the underwriting process.

Loss of use is a coverage provided in varying forms in residential policies. Some special exposures can arise from this coverage. The specialist should be aware of the hazards that can increase potential claims for this coverage.

Chapter Notes

1. William G. Glendenning and Robert B. Holtom, *Personal Lines Underwriting* (Malvern, PA: Insurance Institute of America, 1982), pp. 248-249.

2. Insurance Information Institute, *The Fact Book 1996* (New York NY: Insurance Information Institute, 1995), p. 68.

3. Glendenning and Holtom, p. 243.

4. Lichter v. Liberty Mutual Fire Ins. Co., No. 81-9468 (Pa. Cov. Civ. 1984).

5. Insurance Services Office, *Advisory Notice for Homeowners Policy Program, 1991* (New York, NY: Insurance Services Office, September 6, 1990), p. 3.

6. *The Fact Book 1996*, p. 67.

7. *The Fact Book 1996*, p. 50.

8. *The Fact Book 1996*, p. 46.

9. Bernard L. Webb, Connor M. Harrison, and James J. Markham, *Insurance Operations*, vol. I (Malvern, PA: American Institute for Property and Liability Underwriters, 1992), pp. 210-212.

10. Joseph L. Mangan, "Building Code Compliance Gradings: The Underwriter's New Tool," *Best's Underwriting Newsletter*, June 1995, pp. 1-4.

Chapter 10

Educational Objectives

1. Describe the coverage provided by common blanket and scheduled personal inland marine policies and compare that coverage with the personal property coverage provided by homeowners forms. (pp. 10-3 to 10-13)

2. For each of the classes of personal property commonly written on a personal articles floater (PAF), describe the following: (pp. 10-13 to 10-32, and Appendix 10-B)

   • Articles covered by the PAF

   • Information needed to make an underwriting decision

   • Underwriting concerns

3. Describe how underwriting results for personal inland marine risks can be monitored and evaluated. (pp. 10-32 to 10-33)

4. Describe common residential security systems and their protective features. (pp. 10-33 to 10-38)

5. Given a case study involving a personal inland marine risk, analyze the exposures, and recommend appropriate underwriting actions and coverage placements. (Encompasses entire chapter.)

Chapter 10

Personal Inland Marine: Exposure Analysis and Coverages

The personal auto and homeowners policies were created to form packages of coverage that met the needs of most individuals and families. Policy exclusions eliminate the exposures that are commercially uninsurable and the exposures that most families do not encounter. For example, the homeowners policy excludes property damage to and liability coverage for an insured's airplane ownership. Most families do not own airplanes, and to include coverage for them would mean that all homeowners would have to share the burden of losses that occur from that exposure.

Whenever an insured wants to insure an exposure not covered by standard insurance packages, another type of insurance must fill the gap. The following help insureds fill those coverage gaps:

- *Endorsements.* Endorsements can be attached to policies to modify coverage. Many endorsements or forms can be attached to homeowners policies to add, delete, or modify coverage. Some endorsements act as personal inland marine policies that can be attached to the homeowners policy. Because endorsements modify coverage, each should be evaluated by an agent or producer to determine whether appropriate coverage is being provided for the insured. Endorsements also require an underwriting review to determine the risks and hazards involved. Appendix 10-A to this text provides a list of the common forms that can be attached to homeowners policies, with descriptions of modifications to the policy and the associated underwriting concerns.

- *Personal inland marine policies.* These policies are also coverage packages. They insure both ordinary and unique items. Inland marine is a term that dates back to the days of sailing ships, when ocean marine coverage was the most common form of insurance. As the need for insurance for other property grew, the ocean marine policy was modified. The term inland marine was developed to describe items that were not ships. In personal lines insurance, inland marine now primarily means things that are transportable. The most commonly used personal inland marine policy is the personal articles floater, which is discussed later in this chapter.

- *Specialty policies.* There are as many types of specialty policies as there are things to insure. Many specialty policies are actually inland marine policies that have been modified to cover specific types of property exposures. If a homeowner has a prize breeding bull, the homeowner must find a specialty policy to insure against the loss of that animal. Such policies are called *animal mortality policies.* Owning an airplane would also require obtaining a specialty policy to fill the coverage gap. If a homeowners or a standard inland marine policy does not provide coverage, the next likely source of protection is a specialty policy.

Jargon Alert!

Inland marine policies are often called "floaters." They cover things that move around or "float."

Educational Objective 1

Describe the coverage provided by common blanket and scheduled personal inland marine policies and compare that coverage with the personal property coverage provided by homeowners forms.

Common Blanket and Scheduled Personal Inland Marine Policies

Several classes of personal inland marine coverage are listed in the 1976 **Nationwide Marine Definition**. This definition describes the kinds of risks and coverages that can be classified or identified as marine or inland marine risks under state insurance laws.[1] Following are examples of the classes of personal property floaters described in the Nationwide Marine Definition:

- Personal effects floater
- Personal property floater
- Government service floater
- Personal fur floater
- Personal jewelry floater
- Wedding present floaters not exceeding ninety days after the day of the wedding
- Silverware floater

The **Nationwide Marine Definition** describes the kinds of risks and coverages that can be classified under state insurance laws as marine and inland marine insurance.

- Fine arts floater
- Stamp and coin floater
- Musical instruments floater
- Mobile articles, machinery, and equipment floater
- Installment sales and leased property floater
- Live animal floater

Personal inland marine policies cover many kinds of property that the Nationwide Marine Definition does not mention specifically. The definition includes a provision stating that it does not include all of the kinds of risks that can be classified as marine or inland marine. The Nationwide Marine Definition provides a standard for the common inland marine coverages without restricting the coverage that insurers write.

Many of the personal inland marine classes are filed classes. Filed classes include cameras, fine arts, golfer's equipment, musical instruments, personal furs, personal jewelry, silverware, and stamp and coin collections. This means that insurers (or rating bureaus that act on their behalf) are required to file forms and rates with the state regulators. Several classes can be scheduled under a single "all-risks" form called the personal articles floater or can be insured individually under a floater covering only that class, such as a fine arts floater or a musical instruments floater.

Many insurers have programs to insure nonfiled classes of property as personal inland marine. Examples of nonfiled classes of personal inland marine insurance are home computers, recreational vehicles, guns, antique autos, and hobby collections. Usual policy provisions and underwriting practices apply to these nonfiled classes, but insurer use of those provisions and practices varies widely.

The *personal articles floater* is the principal inland marine form for insuring the filed personal inland marine classes. The other two inland marine forms discussed in this chapter are the *personal effects floater* and the *personal property floater*. These policies group together types of property to fill coverage needs.

Personal Articles Floater (PAF)

This policy was introduced in 1953 to allow various classes of property to be insured on a scheduled "all-risks" basis under a single policy instead of under multiple floaters. Today, the personal articles floater is written either as a free-standing policy or as a Scheduled Personal Property Endorsement (HO 04 61) attached to a homeowners policy.

PAF Eligible Classes

The classes of property eligible under the PAF are printed on the first page of the PAF form. Spaces are provided beside each class to show the amount of insurance and premium for that class. Additional kinds of property that the insurer is willing to cover can be listed on the blank lines at the bottom of the form. Below the class descriptions is a space for describing the items of property with the value for each item also listed. The value listed for each item is the amount of insurance (often called the limit of coverage in other lines of insurance) for that item. Exhibit 10-1 is a sample of the personal articles floater.

PAF Covered Property

In addition to the property described and scheduled on the policies, two additional provisions in the form extend coverage to newly acquired property:

- Newly acquired jewelry, furs, cameras, and musical instruments are covered for up to 25 percent of the amount of insurance that applies to that class or $10,000, whichever is less. The property must be of a class that is already insured under the floater. The insured must report the newly acquired property to the insurer within thirty days after acquiring it and pay an additional premium.
- Newly acquired fine arts are covered for their actual cash value, up to a limit of 25 percent of the fine arts scheduled in the policy. The insured must report the new fine arts to the insurer within ninety days and pay an additional premium. The reporting period is longer for fine arts than for newly acquired jewelry, furs, cameras, and musical instruments because additional time is necessary to substantiate values for fine arts.

PAF Covered Perils

The PAF provides an extremely broad "all-risks" coverage. However, the following perils are excluded:

- Wear and tear, deterioration, and inherent vice
- Insects and vermin
- War and nuclear risks

Some classes of property carry their own specific exclusions.

PAF Valuation

With some exceptions, property covered under a personal articles floater is insured for its actual cash value. The valuation clause states that the company will settle a loss for the least of the following four amounts:

1. The property's actual cash value at the time of the loss
2. The cost to reasonably restore the property to its condition immediately before the loss or damage
3. The cost to reasonably replace the property with substantially identical property
4. The applicable amount of insurance

Even if an individual item is specifically scheduled, a company can opt to replace the item with one of similar quality, which is an important underwriting point. The insurer must obtain a complete and accurate

Exhibit 10-1
Personal Articles Floater—First Page

AMOUNTS OF INSURANCE - SCHEDULED PROPERTY

(a) We cover classes of personal property indicated by an amount of insurance.

Class of Personal Property	Amount of Insurance	Premium
1. Jewelry, as scheduled.	$	$
2. Furs and garments trimmed with fur or consisting principally of fur, as scheduled.		
3. Cameras, projection machines, films and related articles of equipment, as listed.		
4. Musical instruments and related articles of equipment, as listed. You agree not to perform with these instruments for pay unless specifically provided under this policy.		
5. Silverware, silver-plated ware, goldware, gold-plated ware and pewterware, but excluding pens, pencils, flasks, smoking implements or jewelry.		
6. Golfer's equipment meaning golf clubs, golf clothing and golf equipment.		
7.a. Fine Arts, as scheduled. This premium is based on your statement that the property insured is located at the following address.		
7.b. For an additional premium, paragraph 5.b. under Perils Insured Against is deleted only for the articles marked with a double asterisk (**) in the schedule below.		
8. Postage Stamps		
9. Rare and Current Coins		

SCHEDULE*

Article	Description	Amount of Insurance*

THE AMOUNTS SHOWN FOR EACH ITEM IN THE SCHEDULE ARE LIMITED BY CONDITION 2 LOSS SETTLEMENT ON PAGE 3 OF THIS ENDORSEMENT.

*Entries may be left blank if shown elsewhere in this policy for this coverage.

description of each scheduled item. An incomplete or inadequate description makes verification of the insured amount difficult, if not impossible. Descriptions (and serial numbers if possible) aid in recovering stolen items. Complete descriptions also allow a company adjuster to exercise the settlement option of replacing an item. A $10,000 diamond ring might be replaced for $5,000 through a jewelry wholesale market.

Fine arts are an exception to the valuation clause. Because of the unique characteristics and condition of items that are rare, historic, or artistic, replacing those items following a loss is difficult or impossible. That is especially true for antiques and one-of-a-kind items. Establishing a value after a loss for such items is difficult, so fine arts are traditionally written on an **agreed value** basis.

Although the policy extends this agreed value settlement basis only to fine arts, insurers can opt to write all property covered under a personal articles floater on an agreed value basis by amending the valuation clause or by substituting the term "agreed value" for the amount scheduled on the policy declarations page. Generally, insurers only amend the valuation clause for jewelry (because jewelry tends to appreciate over time).

Replacement Cost Basis

Personal articles floaters are often issued as Scheduled Personal Property Endorsements (HO 04 61) attached to a homeowners policy. The HO 04 61 contains the same valuation clause as the free-standing PAF. The valuation clause for the PAF was reviewed previously in this chapter. However, the valuation clause of HO 04 61 is amended *if the Personal Property Replacement Cost Endorsement (HO 04 90) is also attached to the homeowners policy.* The HO 04 90 provides replacement cost coverage on property insured under Coverage C of the homeowners policy. The replacement cost extends to property within the classes of jewelry, furs, cameras, musical instruments, silverware, and golfer's equipment that is covered under the Scheduled Personal Property Endorsement attached to the same policy. For a loss to this covered property, the insurer pays the *least* of the following five amounts:

1. Replacement cost at the time of loss without deduction for depreciation
2. The full cost of repairs at the time of loss
3. The limit of liability that applies to Coverage C
4. Any special limit of liability stated in the policy
5. The amount of insurance listed for any scheduled item

The net result when both the HO 04 90 and the HO 04 61 endorsements are attached to a homeowners policy is that the first listed settlement amount option is changed from ACV to replacement cost for property within the classes of jewelry, furs, cameras, musical equipment, silverware, and golfer's equipment.

Fine arts include works of art and items of rarity or historic value.

Agreed value means that in the event of loss or damage to the property, the insurance company agrees to pay the amount of insurance scheduled. The insured and the insurer agree on the value at the time the policy is written.

Pairs, Sets, or Parts

Scheduled items that are part of a pair or set (such as earrings, cuff links, or a **proof set** of coins) are adjusted based on two options. The insurer can either (1) repair or replace any part to restore the pair or set to its value before the loss or (2) pay the difference between actual cash value of the pair or set before and after the loss. For example, an insured owns five commemorative medals. Each is worth $500, and the complete set is worth $5,000. One medal is lost. For $500, the insurance company can replace the lost medal with another like it if the set's full value would be restored by doing so. But, if the lost medal is irreplaceable, the insurance company would be liable for $3,000, that is, the difference between the set's value—$5,000—and the value of the property remaining after the loss—four at $500, for a total of $2,000.[2]

The loss of a portion of **pairs**, **sets**, or **parts** greatly diminishes the value of the remaining portion. For an additional premium, jewelry items in pairs or sets can be insured by an optional provision that agrees to pay the set's full value if the insured surrenders the remaining article(s) to the insurer.

PAF Locations Covered

Except for fine arts, coverage for articles scheduled on the PAF is provided worldwide. Fine arts coverage is restricted to the United States and Canada. ISO general rules allow coverage to be endorsed to exclude coverage outside the territorial limits of the United States and Canada for all categories of covered property.

PAF Blanket Coverage

The alternative to scheduling individual items is to write coverage on a **blanket basis**. When written on a blanket basis, an amount of insurance is provided for the total class of property being insured without specifically describing each item and showing an amount of insurance for each item. Silverware and golfer's equipment are the only filed classes of property that can be written on a blanket basis under the personal articles floater. A limited amount of blanket coverage can be written for the following classes:

- Stamp and coin collections
- Cameras, musical instruments, and fine arts

Blanket Stamp and Coin Collections

The policy can be issued with a limit of up to $1,000 of blanket coverage on unscheduled **numismatic** or **philatelic** property, and a limit of $250 on any one unscheduled stamp or coin or other individual article.

Blanket Cameras, Musical Instruments, and Fine Arts

Blanket coverage can be written up to 10 percent of the amount of scheduled coverage for the individual property class. When coverage is written in that way, a 100 percent coinsurance clause applies to the blanket items. An insured who schedules only $1,000 in camera

---

A **proof set** is a group of coins that are not circulated (they have never been used as "money") and that have the same mint year. They are valuable because they are in mint condition and are part of a set.

Pairs, **sets**, or **parts** are items that increase in value because they are part of a group. The loss of part of the group greatly reduces the value of the items that remain. Consequently, losses are adjusted to take into consideration the economic loss of the whole group.

When written on a **blanket basis**, an amount of insurance is provided for the total class of property being insured.

Numismatic items are paper money and coin collectibles.

Philatelic items are postage stamp collectibles.

equipment when he owns $2,000 worth of equipment will receive 50 percent of the value of lost or damaged camera equipment covered under the blanket limit.

Under most homeowners policies, personal property (Coverage C) excludes coverage for "articles separately described and specifically insured in that or other insurance." That exclusion prevents the unscheduled personal property coverage from being used as an excess coverage for scheduled personal property. However, Coverage C does provide excess coverage on property insured on a blanket basis under the personal articles floater.

When To Write the PAF

This floater, whether written separately or as an attachment to the homeowners policy, is used extensively. Often, it is to an insured's advantage to remove certain property from the unscheduled coverage available under the homeowners policy and to insure it on a scheduled basis, using a personal articles floater. The floater can also fill coverage gaps left by the homeowners policy.

Scheduling property provides the following benefits to the insured:

- No deductible clause applies to scheduled items.
- Increased limits are available on the listed classes of property.
- Loss by flood, surface waters, and subsurface waters is covered.
- Scheduling property changes the perils to an extremely broad "all-risks" basis. The property's vulnerability to loss should be considered. Silverware that is dropped into a garbage disposal is covered if it is listed on a schedule. If silverware were covered only as an unscheduled item under a homeowners policy, the loss would not be covered.
- Scheduling fine arts provides coverage on a valued basis, which eliminates the problem of trying to place a value on a one-of-a-kind item after a loss occurs.

Personal Effects Floater (PEF)

The personal effects floater, also called the "traveler's policy," covers, on an "all-risks" basis, individually owned property carried by tourists and travelers. Typical property covered under the PEF includes clothing, luggage, and toiletries anywhere in the world other than the insured's own home.[3]

The personal effects floater was popular before homeowners policy forms were standardized in the 1970s. Before that standardization, homeowners polices limited coverage on unscheduled personal property away from the residence premises to 10 percent of the regular on-premises limit on unscheduled personal property. An insured who wanted higher amounts of insurance on property taken on trips needed additional coverage. In addition, the personal effects floater provided "all-risks" coverage.

The ISO homeowners forms used today cover unscheduled personal property away from the residence premises for the full policy limit on Coverage C and can be endorsed to include "all-risks" coverage (Special Personal Property Coverage—HO 00 15). Therefore, many insureds who have a homeowners policy are adequately insured for the exposures covered by the personal effects floater. Today, the personal effects floater has limited application.

PEF Covered Property

The property covered by the personal effects floater includes "personal effects usually carried by tourists and travelers, belonging to and used or worn by the named insured, spouse, or unmarried children who permanently reside with the named insured." The policy is not intended to cover property that is not ordinarily carried by travelers. All coverages are provided for a blanket amount. No coinsurance clause applies. The following three provisions help to define the extent of coverage:

1. *Personal effects while on the "premises of the named insured's domicile" are not covered.* This provision can be deleted by endorsement.

2. *Personal effects while in storage are not covered.* This provision has an exception that allows coverage if the property is "at points and places en route during travel." So an insured who is traveling from Boston to Atlanta and who makes a temporary detour to Pittsburgh can leave clothing in storage during the detour. That clothing is covered by the personal effects floater.

3. *Only fire coverage is provided for personal effects in the custody of students while in a fraternity, sorority house, dormitory, or other premises at school or college.* This provision is necessary because of the high risk of loss to property in a communal living environment. The provision does not apply to students who live in private homes or rooming houses not on the premises of the school or college. This provision can be deleted by endorsement.

PEF Exclusions and Limitations

The exclusions and limitations for coverage under the personal effects floater include the following:

- War and nuclear risks.

- Wear and tear, gradual deterioration, insects, vermin, inherent vice, or any damage from being worked on.

- Breakage of articles of a brittle nature unless caused by thieves, fire, or accident to conveyances.

- Theft from an unattended auto, unless the auto is equipped with a fully-enclosed body or compartment and the loss is a direct result of forcible entry. Such a loss is covered for no more than 10 percent of the total amount of the loss or $250, whichever is less. (This limit can be deleted by endorsement.)

- A 10 percent limitation of up to $100 applies to loss to jewelry, watches, silver, gold, platinum, and furs.

PEF Valuation

The PEF will pay the least of the following settlements for a loss to property covered by the policy:

- ACV
- Cost of repairs
- Cost of replacement with a substantially identical article

Losses to pairs, sets, or parts are settled in the same manner as previously described for the PAF policy.

When To Write the PEF

Situations that still make this form useful are as follows:

- Some homeowners policies still have a 10 percent limitation on unscheduled personal property away from the residence premises. If eligible property exceeds that amount, the personal effects floater can provide additional coverage.
- "All-risks" coverage on unscheduled personal property might be unavailable under a particular insurer's homeowners program.
- An individual who no longer has a homeowners policy might need this coverage for travel. (For example, an insured couple sells their home and furniture. Their objective is to spend a year on a world tour. They require coverage for the items they are carrying with them.)

Personal Property Floater (PPF)

The personal property floater was developed in the 1950s to provide "all-risks" coverage for personal property. Before then, fire insurance was the primary means through which individuals could protect their personal property. This floater provided coverage for a much broader set of perils.

The personal property floater lost much of its impact because the homeowners policies were also introduced in the 1950s. The coverage provided by homeowners policies filled the coverage gap that homeowners were seeking for contents. Many companies no longer offer this policy because coverage is so similar to the homeowners coverage for contents. The difference in coverage between the personal property floater and the homeowners contents coverage is that the floater is written on an "all-risks" basis but the homeowners' coverage for contents is usually written on a named perils basis (unless the homeowners policy is endorsed to provide "all-risks").

PPF Covered Property

The personal property floater is designed to cover household contents normally located at the insured's residence, subject to an amount of insurance selected by the insured in the following classes of property:

- Silverware, goldware, and pewterware
- Clothing and rugs

- Musical instruments
- Paintings, sculptures, tapestries, and art objects
- Cameras and photographic equipment
- Guns and golf, hunting, fishing, bowling, and other sports equipment
- Major appliances
- Bedding
- Furniture
- All other personal property
- Building additions and alterations

Contents within the selected classes are insured within a blanket of coverage rather than as scheduled items.

PPF Exclusions

Specifically excluded are the following:

- Live animals, fish, and birds
- Boats, aircraft, trailers, campers, autos, motorcycles, and other motorized vehicles
- Owned property pertaining to any business or profession
- Articles separately described and specifically insured by this or other insurance
- Property regularly located throughout the year at a residence other than the principal residence of the insured

PPF Covered Perils

The personal property floater is "all-risks," except for the following perils:

- War and nuclear loss
- Water damage from flood, surface waters, or water that backs up through sewers
- Loss caused by animals owned or kept by the insured
- Marring or scratching
- Breakage of eyeglasses, glassware, marble, and collectibles (such as statues and figurines)

PPF Valuation

The PPF will pay the least of the following for property covered by the policy:

- ACV
- Cost of repairs
- Cost of replacement with a substantially identical article

Losses to pairs, sets, or parts are settled in the same manner as previously described for the PAF policy.

When To Write the PPF

In some situations, the personal property floater can still be useful, although those situations are rare. Some situations for which the PAF is still useful include the following:

- Coverage is available by endorsement attached to the PPF for property "regularly situated throughout the year" somewhere other than at the residence listed in the policy. An additional premium is charged for the endorsement. The policy could be useful for covering property for a couple taking a trip around the world. If they have sold their home or canceled their lease, they are no longer eligible for a homeowners policy. This floater could provide coverage for contents the couple has stored at a relative's home or in a storage facility. (Negotiation by the producer with an inland marine underwriter is highly probable. The circumstances and security of the property would have to be determined.)

- Customers who are in temporary living arrangements might benefit by having a PPF. For example, an insured just moved to the area from another city and sold her home in her prior location. She is temporarily living in a hotel room until she can locate an apartment or purchase a home. She brought with her many personal items of a valuable or sentimental nature that she did not want to place in storage. This floater could provide temporary coverage. (Again, negotiation with an inland marine underwriter is likely.)

Educational Objective 2

For each of the classes of personal property commonly written on a personal articles floater (PAF), describe the following:

- Articles covered by the PAF
- Information needed to make an underwriting decision
- Underwriting concerns

Underwriting Personal Articles Floater Classes

Inland marine underwriting is especially challenging because it requires diverse knowledge and expertise. An inland marine underwriter must remain knowledgeable about many types of property and their exposures. Of all floaters written for personal property, the personal articles floater or its equivalent attached to the homeowners policy is the most common. The following notes about underwriting concentrate on the classes of property commonly covered by that form.

Jewelry

The class rules in the ISO Personal Inland Marine Manual define jewelry as follows:

...articles of personal adornment composed in whole or in part of silver, gold, platinum or other precious metals and alloys, whether or not containing pearls, jewels, precious or semiprecious stones.

That definition applies to many items as long as the nature or design of the items allows them to be worn for adornment. Therefore, unset jewels, such as loose diamonds, do not qualify for coverage. The ISO definition does allow underwriters to insure certain miscellaneous items such as pens, pencils, flasks, cigarette cases, and similar items that are completely or partially made of a precious metal or alloy. Costume jewelry also qualifies for coverage as long as the items are made partially or completely of a precious metal or alloy.

All jewelry items must be individually scheduled. The personal articles floater does not allow blanket coverage.

Most jewelry losses tend to be total losses. The most common losses are theft, unexplained (or mysterious) disappearance, loss, and the cracking or chipping of a stone. Coverage is extremely broad, and claims commonly involve items forgotten by the side of a sink in a public restroom, lost in the plumbing, accidentally thrown away, or dropped into the garbage disposal. Consequently, the underwriter will investigate the applicant and the applicant's loss experience. Jewelry losses tend to peak just before the Christmas season, which leads cynical underwriters to believe that not all scheduled jewelry claims are really losses.

Underwriting Jewelry

In investigating the applicant, the underwriter reviews the following:

- The applicant's credit history, to identify any financial pressure.

- The loss history, including searching an underwriting/claims database (if available).

- A comparison of the value of the jewelry to the home or salary of the applicant (a $200,000 jewelry schedule and a home valued at $40,000 prompt additional questions).

- The extent of the applicant's travel, which should be determined if the jewelry schedule is extensive. The underwriter should identify the precautions taken to safeguard jewelry while the applicant is traveling and the care taken to protect jewelry left in the home while the applicant is away. The underwriter evaluates the exposure to loss at the applicant's residence with an emphasis on the theft peril and the safeguards the applicant has taken to minimize exposure to theft.

Jewelry Appraisals

Appraisals are used to describe jewelry items and to establish their value. An appraisal is usually required on jewelry items worth $500 or more. Even if an appraisal is not required, a complete and accurate description of the items of jewelry is extremely important. A policy that lists "a one-carat lady's diamond solitaire ring" without any qualifications makes it impossible for a claims adjuster to know for which one of several rings the insured owns the claim is being made.

The values of one-carat diamond rings vary greatly, depending on the quality of the stones. If the adjuster can accurately identify the stone's quality, the adjuster can exercise the loss settlement option of replacing the item rather than pay the face value shown on the schedule. An insurance company working with a jewelry wholesaler can replace diamond jewelry for 50 percent of the retail value. Problems can arise when the insured (after paying an insurance premium based on the retail appraisal) is offered a replacement that costs the insurance company substantially less. An insured who is dissatisfied with the claim's disposition can contest whether replacement with **equivalent property** has been made, but the insured cannot simply reject replacement outright. However, if the adjuster cannot accurately replace the item (perhaps because of an incomplete appraisal or description), the insurer will have no choice but to pay its scheduled value.

> **Equivalent property** refers to articles that are "substantially identical." The replacement feature of the personal articles floater allows an insurance company to settle a loss by providing an item of equivalent property.

A complete description of a piece of jewelry begins with a detailed description of the item and specifies whether the item is designed to be worn by a man, a woman, or either. A detailed appraisal specifies the value of each stone and the type and weight of the metal.

An appraisal also indicates the appraiser's credentials. Many appraisers can act as such by virtue of their professional experience. Other appraisers have studied a prescribed curriculum, passed tests, and gained professional certification from an appraisal association. Appraising is not an exact science. It involves an educated estimate of the value of jewelry. Trained professionals are more likely to determine a value within a close range. The higher the value of an item, the more important the certification of the appraiser becomes. One of the most highly regarded certifications in the jewelry appraisal field is the Graduate Geologist certificate offered by the Gemological Institute of America (GIA). GIA has established standards of measurement and gradation of stones that provide a high degree of appraisal consistency.

Jewelry is the most prevalent item appearing on personal articles floaters, and diamonds appear most frequently as valuable stones. Consequently, the valuation and the evaluation of diamonds is reviewed in some detail. Exhibit 10-2 is a diagram of a diamond, including the descriptive features used in appraisals.

Reviewing Diamonds

GIA has established international standards for gemstone grading, especially for diamonds. All qualified appraisers should know those standards and include them in the description of the items on the appraisal. Exhibit 10-3 provides a list of the standard descriptions used in diamond appraisals. When most or all of the standard descriptions are omitted, the underwriter should question the appraiser's qualifications. Stones of unusual color and/or high clarity are rarely found in a local retail jewelry shop. If one appears on an appraisal, it is worthy of further investigation. Some appraisers upgrade the quality of the diamonds on an appraisal to justify higher retail price or to convince

Exhibit 10-2
Diagram of a Diamond

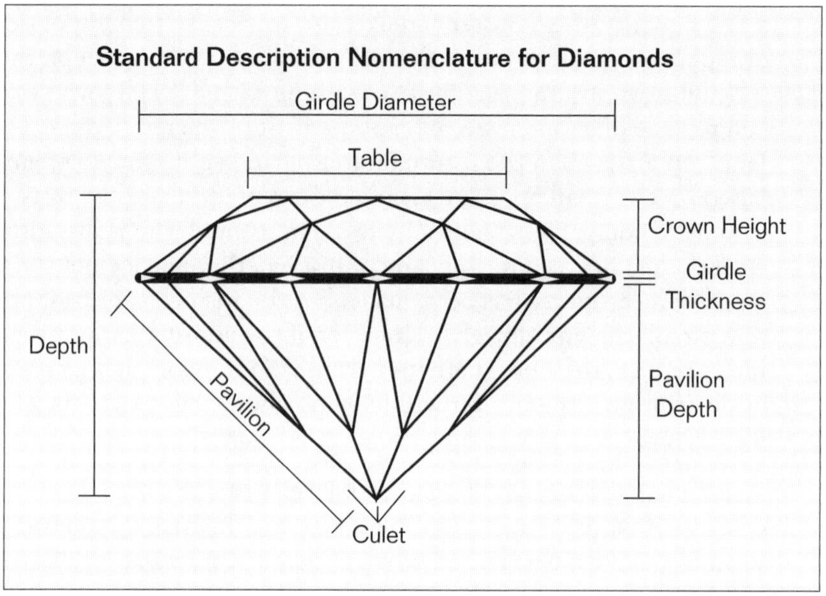

Standard Description Nomenclature for Diamonds

Source: The Gemological Institute of America, 1986.

customers that they are receiving items worth more than the "sale" prices they paid.

Diamond values are based on quality (cut, color, and clarity) and carat weight. In an appraisal, underwriters often talk about the "four C's" of diamonds—cut, color, clarity, and carat weight. As carat weight increases, diamonds become more scarce and more expensive, regardless of stone quality. A one-carat diamond is eleven times more valuable than a one-quarter-carat diamond of equal quality.

Diamonds have an extremely high markup from the wholesale market (which insurance companies can access for replacements) to the retail market.

Metals and Alloys

Each jewelry item is mounted in gold, silver, or platinum, and the value of each mounting is primarily based on the weight of the metal and the workmanship. Gold is measured in karats (k) and pennyweight (dwt) or grams. An appraisal should specify the type of metal and its weight. Because gold is soft and wears away quickly, it is usually used in the form of an alloy.

The following descriptions appear frequently on jewelry appraisals:

- 24 karat gold is pure gold.
- 18 karat gold is 75 percent pure gold (18/24 = 75%).
- 14 karat gold is 58 percent pure gold (14/24 = 58%).
- 20 (dwt) is 1 troy ounce.
- 31 grams is 1 troy ounce.

Exhibit 10-3
Standard Diamond Descriptions

		Diamond Descriptions	
Look for:	*The Measurement*	*What It Means*	*Notes*
CARAT	Carat Point	A carat is a measure of weight. There are 143 carats in an ounce. A point is 1/100 of a carat.	The more expensive pieces of jewelry derive their value primarily from precious stones. Carat weight for diamonds is usually listed on appraisals. The weight of a stone that is mounted in a setting can be estimated by using a formula based on its cut, length, width, and depth. This process is called calibration.
CUT	Round cut	*Old mine cut:* This is an old cut that can be found in antique and heirloom pieces. It has a short pavilion, a short crown, and a large table. *European cut:* This is a cut that was used until about 1950. It has a small table and is very deep. *Round brilliant:* This cut creates a larger table than in the European cut, and the diamond pavilion is a moderate length.	The cut of the stone should be stated on the appraisal. There are some trends in diamond cutting, but they change very slowly.
	Fancy cut	Oval Pear Marquise Emerald Radiant Kite (triangle) Heart Trillion® (triangle) Quadrillion® (box)	The trillion is the registered trademark of L.F. Industries. The quadrillion is the registered trademark of Ambar Diamond.
	Baguette	This cut is similar to an emerald (rectangle) cut, but has fewer facets —generally used as side stones to form a setting for a larger stone.	Many melee stones set close together and flat in a setting are called a pavé.
	Melee	Tiny accent stones	
CLARITY	F-Flawless VVS1-Very, very, slightly included #1 VVS2-Very, very slightly included #2	—No flaws under 10 power magnification —Only one flaw, not larger than a pinhead —Only 2 or 3 flaws not larger than a pinhead	F, VVS1, and VVS2 are very scarce. Usually top commercial grade stones have VS clarity, and average commercial grade have SI clarity.

Continued on next page.

Look for:	The Measurement			What It Means	Notes
CLARITY, continued	VS1-Very slightly included #1 VS2-Very slightly included #2 SI1-Slightly included #1 SI2-Slightly included #2 I1-Imperfect #1 I2-Imperfect #2 I3-Imperfect #3			—Several small flaws, no carbon, not visible —More flaws than VS1 but still not visible —SI1 and SI2: larger flaws than VS2 but still not visible to the naked eye, looking into the table of the diamond —Visible flaws in diamond —More and larger flaws —Many and very large flaws	Jewelers traditionally use the terms "good clarity" and "flaw-less." What they mean is "no flaws visible to the naked eye."

Look for:	GIA grade	OTHER STANDARDS		What It Means	Notes
COLOR		less than 1/2 carat	1/2 carat and more		The Gemological Institute of America (GIA) uses an alphabetical color chart beginning at "D," which is the best, and descending as the diamonds pick up more natural color. This is caused from minerals (iron, copper, etc.), which were in the earth when the diamond crystallized. Other grading standards are sometimes used. Standards are shown in relation to the GIA grading standards.
	D E	Rarest White	River	D, E, F—Are very rare. These are colors that jewelers may call "Blue White," "Fine White," or "Gem Quality."	
	F G H	(Rare White) White	Top Wesselton Wesselton	G, H—Top Commercial Quality; still white.	
	I J K L M	Tinted White	Top Crystal Crystal Top Cape	I, J—Average Commercial Quality, most typical of jewelry store quality, slight yellow hue. K, L and M—Visible color distortion.	If an unfamiliar term is used on an appraisal, the appraiser should be able to explain it in terms that can be related to GIA standards.
	N O P Q	Yellowish	Cape Light Yellow	N-W—Color distortion intensifies.	
	R through W Yellow		Yellow	"Fancies" are rare and valuable diamonds that come in colors. They will appear as pink, green, red, brown, blue, and canary. These should not be confused with the poor-quality "yellow" diamonds. The term "fancy" appears in the appraisal for these stones.	

Adapted from *Diamond Data*, The Gemological Institute of America (GIA) Gem Trade Laboratory, 1986.

Other terms used in describing metal used in jewelry are as follows:

- What is generally considered solid silver is often described as "sterling silver," which legally means 925 parts of silver with 75 parts of copper. Sterling is often stamped with the number "925" or the word "sterling." "Silver plate" is a thin plating of silver over another metal and is much less valuable than sterling silver.

- "German silver" contains no silver and is simply an alloy of nickel, copper, and zinc.

- "Indian silver" contains no silver. It is tin. Indian silver is a term used in some Latin American countries to encourage the purchase of locally made jewelry.

- "Gold filled" and "vermeil" refer to a gold plating that is placed over another metal. "Vermeil" usually means a gold plating over sterling silver.

Because diamonds are usually the most valuable component of a piece of jewelry, the method of mounting should be considered for large stones:

- Platinum is often used to form the prongs that secure a large stone to the ring band. Platinum alloy is a very durable metal (and it has the added feature of a white color, which does not make diamonds seem yellowish, as gold does).

- A diamond's security depends on the number of prongs holding it in place. If four prongs are holding a stone, the breakage of one prong can result in the loss of the stone. Five or more prongs provide more security for the stone.

- "Channel" diamonds are several diamonds set in a groove, which has been set into the ring or other jewelry. The ridge along the groove holds the stones on two sides. A "bezel" setting is a ridge surrounding a single stone. Channel and bezel settings are very secure.

Colored Stones

Colored gemstones (such as sapphires, rubies, and emeralds) can be appraised by cut, clarity, and carat weight in the same way diamonds are; however, more emphasis is placed on color than on the other gemstone qualities. With diamonds, the whiter and clearer, the better. In contrast, with colored stones, richer color is better. The value of colored gemstones is partially based on their transparency or translucency.

No scales can measure color in stones. Some are described using names such as Siberian emeralds or Kanchanaburi sapphires. Color names are also used, such as a cornflower blue sapphire, a pigeon-blood ruby, or a smoky topaz. These names are important in helping to identify jewelry items and values.

Knowing whether a stone has been treated to intensify the color is important. Some processes like irradiation and heat treatments intensify and change the natural color of stones. The changes can be dramatic. Unfortunately, treated stones can later lose their color.

The stone can be treated again, but the color might not reappear. Such treatment is legal and ethical as long as the price being charged for the treated stone reflects that fact. Such treatments can be detected, but the equipment required for detection is expensive. Natural stones are much more valuable. Therefore, the insured should know the merchant, and the merchant should know the wholesaler.

Appraisals for colored stones seldom describe them with technical accuracy, which does not help estimate replacement costs with certainty. Consequently, loss of a colored stone is often settled in cash for the stated coverage limit.

Pearls

An appraisal for pearls should indicate the size and color: white, pink, cream, gold, or black. Pearls can also be irradiated to change their color. Pearls come in the following shapes:

- Cultured pearls and natural pearls are usually round.
- Baroque pearls or mabe pearls have irregular shapes.
- Freshwater pearls are irregular in shape and have bumpy surfaces.
- A half-pearl has a broken surface.

The luster of the pearls should also be noted. The description should include the type of the jewelry item, including its length. Pearls are strung either in uniform size or in graduated sizes.

As a final note regarding jewelry, underwriters are often faced with items of extremely high value. Those items can be insured for a reduced premium if the policy is endorsed to provide that they will be kept in a bank vault or a vault in a nonbank security facility. The insurer must then be given advance notice if the items are to be removed from the vault. The insured pays an additional premium for the time that the articles are out of the vault.

Furs

In the class rules of the ISO Personal Inland Marine Manual, furs are defined as follows: "furs, including imitation furs and fur rugs, and garments trimmed with fur or consisting principally of fur." The intent is to include all furs that have been fashioned into coats, hats, gloves, or garments.

An important peril for furs is theft. Fur garments might be left in an unattended coat room. While the insured is traveling, furs might be left unattended at home. Furs are normally stored during warm weather, which tends to reduce the exposure.

A new covered exposure has recently surfaced for furs—vandalism. Animal rights activists have launched a negative advertisement campaign to dissuade the public from purchasing furs. That campaign has been extended to vandalizing furs worn in public by spray painting the garment and the wearer. The popularity and value of furs have dropped

FYI

The Pearl of Allah is neither round nor especially beautiful, but it has the virtue of weighing over fourteen pounds! Currently valued at $4 million, the pearl is connected with a deadly curse: The first diver who tried to harvest it got his hand trapped in the giant Tridacna clam that produced the pearl. The diver was held under water and drowned.

substantially in the U.S. Many large department stores have discontinued selling furs because of the controversy.

Underwriting Furs

Underwriters tend to pay closer attention to a high-valued, single-item fur. Some companies specify that furs be depreciated 10 to 15 percent per year unless a new appraisal is furnished.

Occupation can be an underwriting factor. Applicants who travel frequently have an increased exposure for those items they take with them and those items left in an unattended home.

Fur Appraisals

The value of furs depends largely on the following three factors:

1. The garment's condition
2. The accuracy of the appraisal of the garment's value
3. The changing popularity of furs and the variability of prices in the garment trade

Despite price fluctuations, the price on the garment's sales slip is usually the best substantiation of value.

Fine Arts

The ISO manual definition of fine arts reads as follows:

> Private collections of paintings, etchings, pictures, tapestries, art glass, windows, and other bona fide works of art (such as valuable rugs, statuary, marbles, bronzes, antique furniture, rare books, antique silver, manuscripts, porcelains, rare glass and bric-a-brac) of rarity, historical value, or artistic merit.

Under the personal articles floater, coverage for fine arts differs from coverage for other property in the following ways:

- Fine arts are covered on a *valued basis*. The amount of insurance appearing on the schedule is the amount that will be paid at the time of the loss.
- Coverage is not provided worldwide. The territory is restricted to the United States and Canada. Coverage is further excluded when the items are on exhibition at fairgrounds and expositions.
- Coverage of up to 25 percent of the amount scheduled for fine arts is provided automatically for ninety days for newly acquired art. However, the extension for new property is only on an *actual cash value* basis.
- The pair, set, and parts clause differs from that provided for other classes of scheduled property. For fine arts that are part of a set, the insurer agrees to pay the full value of the set but then takes possession of any remaining part.
- Covered property must be handled by professional packers if the fine arts are transported.

Actually applying the fine arts definition to evaluate property is difficult. Many objects, such as paintings and sculpture, are clearly fine art. However, other objects fall into categories such as collectors' items, limited editions, and memorabilia. An underwriter can use the following tests to determine whether an item is truly "fine art":

- Does the object have a collector's value because of its rarity, historical significance, or artistic merit? The object must be something that has wide appeal and not solely sentimental value.
- Would the object be classified as a fine art or collectible by a fine arts expert, a dealer, a museum curator, or a member of the American Society of Appraisers (ASA) or the American Appraisal Association (AAA)? International auction associations such as Sotheby's would be considered leading experts in establishing value on unique, highly valued art objects.

Answering those questions is helpful in some situations, but interest in collections and memorabilia creates difficulties. Following are some common dilemmas and suggestions for solutions.

Limited Edition Collectibles

Limited edition collectibles can be part of precious and semiprecious metals, porcelain, or crystal collections. Those objects are generally cast from a mold that is destroyed after a limited number of objects are produced. Their guarantee of value usually comes from the fact that the mold has been destroyed. A defined (limited) number of these objects are available on the market. A person who purchases a limited edition object receives a certificate of authenticity indicating the production number of the particular object and the total number of objects produced. For example, "95/1000" means that the object is number 95 in a series of 1,000.

Memorabilia

The United States is experiencing a nostalgia boom. Objects that are as new as twenty years old are considered collectible. Those objects can be found in numerous catalogs and antique malls. Comic books, Mickey Mouse watches, Coca-Cola trays, baseball cards, and political campaign buttons can be highly valuable. But are they really fine art? Can they be considered "rare" and of "historical value?" The following can be of help in answering those questions:

- *From a Producer's Perspective:*

  Consider the value of the object on the current market and the possible hazards that could damage or destroy it. If it is not covered under the standard homeowners policy, additional protection is needed.

- *From an Underwriter's Perspective:*

  Is it an object of "rarity" with a value that can be determined at the time of loss? Also, what perils can destroy the object? Scheduling an object as a fine art means that it will be insured on an agreed value basis. The insurer will pay that listed value at the time of the object's loss or destruction. Exhibit 10-4 is an illustrative checklist that can be used to help determine whether an object should be scheduled as a fine art.

Homeowners policies already cover many limited edition items and memorabilia. Scheduling simplifies the adjustment of possible future losses and helps determine an appropriate premium for the exposure. The responses to the previous questions can change for objects with probable loss by breakage (such as Depression glass or a Mickey Mouse watch) or loss by spills and cigarette burns (such as antique furniture, baseball cards, and rugs). Under the PAF, coverage is normally excluded for "breakage of art glass windows, glassware, statuary, marble, bric-a-brac, porcelains, and similar fragile articles." However, breakage coverage is provided if it is the result of fire, lightning, explosion, aircraft, collision, windstorm, earthquake, flood, malicious damage or theft, or derailment or overturn of a conveyance. Breakage coverage can be extended to an "all-risks" basis for indicated items on the fine arts schedule. That is done by marking scheduled articles with a double asterisk (**) and charging an additional premium.

Scheduling such objects provides better service from the producer's standpoint: the insured will be better served after a loss. The producer should take care to caution the insured to keep the value of the object listed on the schedule current with its increasing value. The listed value is the maximum that the insured can collect for the scheduled object.

Determining and substantiating the value of the fine arts are probably the hardest part of underwriting fine arts. Once this is done, most fine art schedules are generally nothing more than a residence contents exposure. Exposure evaluation depends largely on the type of property involved and its value. The perils of fire and theft could be the primary consideration for a painting collection. Exposure evaluation would then concentrate primarily on the protection class of the property and any alarm systems or security measures used by the insured. Risks with limited fire protection (such as no fire hydrants or no responding fire department) pose a serious problem. Insureds with highly valued objects scheduled at any one location would be expected to have alarm or security systems to minimize the exposure to theft.

Fine arts collections can be kept by wealthy collectors with property equivalent to that of a museum as well as by individuals who have two or three valuable paintings or antiques that were handed down as heirlooms. As with any inland marine class of property, the applicant's integrity is important to consider. The value of the fine arts coverage would naturally be compared to the value of the applicant's home to determine the relationship. A $150,000 schedule compared to a $60,000 home is unusual and requires investigation.

Occupation is an important factor in underwriting fine arts because the fine arts definition allows coverage only for a "private collection." Art dealers, antique dealers, museum curators, and people with similar occupations pose additional underwriting concerns. For example,

Exhibit 10-4
An Illustrative Checklist for Fine Arts Scheduling

Should this object be scheduled as fine art? Metal 1930s Soft Drink Serving Tray	
Questions to ask:	**Answers:**
1. What are the probable perils that could (within reason) damage or destroy the object?	Fire, theft, windstorm, vandalism.
2. Is this object "rare" and valuable?	Yes. The value can be established in a number of collector catalogs. Dealers can provide an appraisal based on the current value and condition. Ownership and condition would have to be verified.
3. What coverage is now being provided for this object under the homeowners policy (or other policy)?	The homeowners policy already covers the probable perils for unscheduled contents up to the policy limits. There is no limitation for "fine arts." The item will be adjusted on an actual cash value (ACV) basis. If a replacement cost endorsement is attached to the homeowners policy, the item will still be adjusted based on its ACV because it is in the class of "property not eligible" for replacement cost. The ACV for this object is the replacement cost at today's market price. This object has no depreciation because it is appreciating. The insured will have to prove to the adjuster's satisfaction that the insured owns the item and the item's condition. The current value can then be easily established from a collector's catalog.
4. What will the outcome of scheduling be?	• A value will be established for the object, which should simplify adjustment for the insured and the company in the event of loss. • An appropriate premium will be paid for the exposure.

the "newly acquired" provision in the personal articles floater allows an additional 25 percent of the amount of insurance for the fine arts scheduled to apply to newly acquired fine arts for ninety days. If a dealer's newly acquired antique vase is stolen, the dealer might claim it as part of a "private collection" to be insured within the "newly acquired" provision of the PAF rather than declaring it as stock for the store. That problem can be eliminated by endorsing the personal articles floater to delete the "newly acquired property" clause.

Fine Arts Appraisals and Underwriting

Because fine arts are unique and are automatically written on an agreed value basis, value substantiation is important. Most insurers require an appraisal by an expert in that field of art for an object with a value exceeding $1,000. Members of national organizations such as the American Society of Appraisers and the American Appraisal Association are good sources. Local museum curators, members of auction houses specializing in fine arts, and local dealers are also good sources for expert opinions on the value of an object. The artist who provides an appraisal on his or her own work is not a good source.

Fine arts are generally not replaceable, so a detailed description of the property is important to substantiate the value at the time coverage is issued. An appraisal should include the following information:

- Artist
- Type of painting (such as oil on canvas)
- Setting or title of picture
- Style of furniture (such as Chippendale, Queen Anne, or Louis IV)
- Date of origin
- Distinguishing features and marks
- Condition of object

Additional Concerns Regarding Fine Arts

Other concerns about fine arts, such as stolen artwork and reproductions, receive additional mention, as follows.

Stolen Artwork

Auction houses, galleries, and dealers sometimes find themselves unknowingly distributing stolen artwork. Thieves target lesser-known works of famous artists, which have not been photographed and published widely. The International Foundation of Art Research (IFAR) is an organization that catalogs stolen artwork and assists law enforcement agencies internationally in searching for stolen objects. Major certified art appraisers have access to that system. However, art purchased from small, noncertified appraisers and dealers stands a chance of being stolen. If the object is discovered years later, a court battle could result between the current "owner" of a stolen piece of art and its original owner.

Reproductions

The nostalgia interest in American memorabilia has brought with it people who are creating reproductions to help meet the demand for memorabilia. Reproductions are appearing in all areas of American collectibles. For example, pressed glassware from the 1930s (Depression glass) is in high demand, with values that are increasing rapidly.

FYI

There was nothing noticeably strange about two paintings hanging on a wall in an art museum in Gdansk, Poland. That is, until one of the paintings fell off the wall! The original had been replaced by a cheap reproduction from a magazine. Authorities later learned that the second painting had been similarly faked and stolen. The museum's insurance policy covered the theft.

FYI

Vermeer was a famous 17th century Dutch painter. A 20th century painter, Hans van Meegeren, also Dutch, discovered that painting fake Vermeers was more lucrative than painting authentic van Meegerens. Van Meegeren didn't copy existing works, however. Instead, he copied Vermeer's style and created new paintings. His "Vermeers" were hailed by critics as masterpieces and often valued at $250,000 each!

The molds for this glass are being recreated, and new glass is being pressed to look like the old pieces. Reproductions can be valuable, but they are not as valuable as originals. Reproductions should not be mistaken for high-value originals. Experts detect the reproductions by identifying differences in the molds and patterns. A knowledgeable dealer should review any large collection to verify its actual value.

Oriental Rugs

Oriental rugs are popular because they are attractive and a good investment. The term "Oriental" is not accurate, because the majority of rugs with that name come from the Middle East. Oriental rugs are also produced in eastern Europe, Spain, Egypt, Greece, Mexico, and Morocco. Likewise, Native American rugs are placed in the Oriental rug classification. The following information about such rugs should appear in appraisals to identify the rugs' values:

- *Place of origin or pattern*. Tribal names are used to describe the pattern and place of production. For example, Bokhara, Tabriz, and Kasahan name both places and patterns. The patterns can also be described according to the design: willow, gull, prayer rugs, and herati.

- *Condition*. The appraisal should provide comments regarding the condition of the fringe or binding and the rug overall.

- *Age*. Rugs are classified as new (50 years old or less), semi-antique (50 to 100 years old), or antique (over 100 years old).

- *Materials*. Rugs are made of wool, cotton, silk, jute, or animal hair. Silk and lambs wool (kurk wool) rugs are the most valuable.

- *Knots*. Rugs of average quality have 90 to 250 knots per square inch. High-quality rugs have 400 to 700 knots per square inch.

- *Location*. Walking on an Oriental rug improves the condition and appearance of the carpet. Of course, a valuable rug should not be placed in an area in which it can be soiled or damaged. Although rugs can be exposed to spills, care can be taken to reduce that exposure. Underwriting opinions vary regarding displaying carpets. Some underwriters insist that carpets be hung on walls to reduce the possibility of loss. However, hanging a rug can cause it to stretch out of shape unless an elaborate framing device is created to distribute the carpet's weight. Framing would only be used for a carpet of extremely high value. Rolling and stacking rugs for an extended period can cause damage because the foundation fibers warp and break and the pile crushes. Consequently, some insurers insist that valuable carpets be placed on floors but away from main traffic areas.

Silverware

The ISO class rules define silverware as follows:

> Individually owned silverware, silver plateware, goldware, gold-plateware, and pewterware. Silverware includes both "silver plate" and "flatware."

Silverplate, as mentioned in the section in this chapter on jewelry, is an item with a "plating of silver." It can also be "domestic flatware and hollowware of silver or of a silver-plated base metal." Flatware is tableware that is usually formed or cast in a single piece. Tableware need not have any silver content. Common stainless steel flatware, however, would be unlikely to be insured as silverware under a personal articles floater.

Underwriting Silverware

Silverware is similar to jewelry in that it is made of precious metals, but its exposure to loss is much less than that of jewelry. Silverware is generally harder to dispose of than jewelry, so it is relatively easy to underwrite. In the early 1980s, the price of silver skyrocketed from $7 a troy ounce to $55 a troy ounce. Silver became a target for theft, and scheduled values had to be increased substantially to keep pace with the replacement cost values. The price of silver has since stabilized, and so has the underwriting of silver.

The total value of the scheduled silverware normally dictates how much underwriting is required. The location of the residence, fire protection, and security devices or systems are primary underwriting concerns.

Silverware Appraisals

Silverware can be written on a scheduled basis, on a blanket basis, or on a combination basis. Underwriters usually require expensive pieces or sets of silverware to be individually scheduled, allowing blanket coverage for the miscellaneous, lower-valued pieces.

The descriptions on individually scheduled items should include enough detail to readily identify the property for valuation or replacement. They should include the number of pieces, the manufacturer, the type of items, and the individual pattern.

Cameras

Cameras that are limited to nonprofessional use are eligible for coverage under personal articles floaters. The types of property eligible to be insured as cameras are as follows:

- Cameras and projection machines, as well as their equipment
- Movable sound equipment for recording, projecting, and reproducing motion pictures
- Home video cameras and playback recorders, as well as their equipment
- Miscellaneous property such as films, binoculars, telescopes, microscopes, and similar equipment that can be used in conjunction with cameras or photographic equipment when insured with such equipment

Individual items must be scheduled with an appropriate amount of insurance shown for each item. Blanket coverage can be written for miscellaneous items, as long as the amount does not exceed 10 percent of the total amount of scheduled coverage. The blanket coverage amount is used to cover low-valued equipment, such as lens covers, filters, carrying cases, tripods, and film.

Underwriting Cameras

Camera coverage provided by the personal articles floater is intended for cameras with a nonprofessional use; therefore, the first question an underwriter must ask is whether the camera equipment is used professionally. The key to deciding whether a professional exposure exists is whether the insured receives remuneration for the photography.

The primary causes of loss to camera equipment are theft, unexplained disappearance, and breakage. The chance of loss from those perils increases away from the owner's residence. The applicant's travel habits, the value of the equipment normally taken while traveling, and the applicant's loss history are important underwriting factors.

Camera Appraisals

Specific appraisals on individual items are normally not required. Cameras appear in catalogs and can be purchased at any time, so verifying their value is relatively easy. A full description should be obtained for each scheduled item, including the manufacturer, model number, and serial number.

Musical Instruments

Musical instruments are similar to cameras in regard to professional use. However, musical instruments insured under the personal articles floater are subject to a professional warranty stating that "you agree not to perform with these instruments for pay unless specifically provided under this policy." The ISO class rules define "professional" as "a person who teaches or receives remuneration for playing a musical instrument insured during the policy term." The professional warranty can be deleted from the policy by charging a higher rate, which is often done for individuals who play in orchestras or chamber music ensembles and who teach music.

The definition of eligible property includes the following:

> Musical instruments, sheet music, and equipment pertaining to musical instruments when written in connection with musical instruments.

Each instrument must be individually scheduled on the personal articles floater with an amount of coverage. As it is for cameras, blanket coverage is available for musical instruments for up to 10 percent of the total amount insured on scheduled items. That coverage is useful for sheet music, carrying cases, reeds, strings, music stands, and amplifying equipment. The underwriter can increase the 10 percent limit.

Musical Instrument Coverage

The coverage that is provided by the personal articles floater is the same form of "all-risks" coverage provided for other filed classes. A limited form of coverage is available under a "musical instruments floater (limited form)." This coverage can also be triggered under the PAF by adding it as an optional line of coverage at the bottom of the categories of coverage. This coverage excludes unexplained disappearance, breakage of instruments, explosion, and theft from unattended vehicles. The rates for this coverage are about 10 to 15 percent less than for the "all-risks" coverage.

The limited coverage can be useful for a teenager in the household who plays in a rock band. His or her equipment is exposed to possible rough use, frequent transportation in a car or truck, and possible theft from the clubs in which the band performs. The broad form of coverage automatically provided by the personal articles floater (with the additional charge to allow for professional use) might be unacceptable to the underwriter because of the increased exposures, but the limited form might be acceptable.

Underwriting Musical Instruments

The underwriting process is similar when evaluating both cameras and musical instruments. The instrument's type and use should be considered. A grand piano has less theft exposure than a violin. A keyboard with extensive sound amplification equipment indicates that it is being used in a rock group. Musical instruments played in the local school band and instruments used for hobbies are probably the most common exposures that underwriters encounter. Such instruments are subject to fewer losses than other musical instruments because they have relatively low values and because school personnel usually lock music rooms to protect the instruments.

Stamp and Coin Collections

Stamps and coin collections have much in common with fine art objects. Stamps and coins derive their value from their rarity, age, and condition, just as fine arts do. Individuals invest in valuable stamp or coin collections as much as they invest in paintings, antique furniture, and other fine arts. Consequently, underwriting for both types of property is similar. However, coverage for stamps and coins is not on an agreed value basis.

The rules for this class allow coverage only for private collectors, not for dealers or auctioneers. The definition of "postage stamps" and rare and current coins in the personal articles floater allows a broad range of objects to be written in this class.

Postage Stamps

Postage stamps include other stamps (such as government and revenue stamps), related collectibles (envelopes or tokens), and the books and pages the items are mounted on.

Rare and Current Coins

Rare and current coins include the following when owned by or in the custody or control of the insured:

- Medals, paper money, and bank notes
- Tokens of money and other numismatic property
- Coin albums, containers, frames, cards, and display cabinets, if used with the collection

Those descriptions permit not only coins and stamps to be scheduled, but also the property associated with the collections: albums, cabinets, and containers. The definition also allows scheduling of items other than the traditional postage stamps and U.S. coins, such as Christmas seals, subway tokens, and military medals. The definition does not include precious metals in the form of ingots or bullion. Generally, that type of property is accumulated more for investment purposes than for attaining a value as a collector's item. Therefore, ingots and bullion are not usually written under a personal articles floater.

Stamps and coins can be insured on a blanket or scheduled basis or on a combination of the two. Because these collections tend to be made of a large number of small, individual items, large schedules are usual. Individual stamps or coins are not always listed. They are generally grouped or classified and listed with an amount of insurance for each group or class. Grouping decreases the size of the list and is sufficient to identify the items in the collection.

Stamp and Coin Coverage

Some special limitations apply to the coverage provided for stamps and coins. Losses caused by the following are not covered:

- Fading, creasing, denting, scratching, tearing, or thinning
- Transfer of colors, inherent defect, dampness, extremes of temperature, or deterioration
- Any damage from being handled or worked on
- Disappearance of individual stamps, coins, or other articles unless the item can fall into one of two categories:
  1. It has been described and scheduled with a specific amount of insurance.
  2. It has been mounted in a volume, and the page it is attached to has been lost.
- Loss to property in the custody of transportation companies
- Shipments by mail other than registered mail
- Theft from any unattended auto unless being shipped as registered mail
- Loss to property not part of a stamp or coin collection

Coverage can be written on a blanket basis, which requires the equivalent of 100 percent coinsurance. Settlement is limited to market value at the time of the loss, not to exceed $1,000 for any unscheduled coin collection or $250 for any one stamp, coin, or individual article or for any one pair, strip, block, series, sheet cover, frame, or card.

The PAF coverage on newly acquired property requires that additions to a stamp or coin collection be reported to the insurer immediately for coverage to apply.

Underwriting Stamps and Coins

Underwriting stamps and coins focuses on the property's value and its possible exposures to loss. Stamp and coin collectors are generally proud of their collections and exercise a high degree of care to prevent loss or damage to the property, especially when the collections include rare items that are not easily replaceable. Items are typically listed in catalogs, and the collections are frequently kept in a fire-resistive safe to minimize the exposure to theft or fire.

Underwriters should also consider home security features, such as alarm systems, in light of a collection's total value. Collectors often attend stamp or coin exhibitions, which involve exposures away from the residence premises. The underwriter should determine how frequently the insured's collection is exhibited, how the items are being transported, and what safeguards are used while the property is on exhibit.

Stamp and Coin Appraisals

Because individual stamps or coins do not usually involve high values, appraisals are generally not requested to substantiate value. Nationally recognized stamp and coin catalogs published regularly list the values of most stamps and coins based on their condition. Conditions range from "proof" to "not circulated," which indicates purchase directly from the United States Mint or United States Postal Service. The other designations of condition are "good," "fair," and "poor." Most collectors use the catalogs and the condition of the items to estimate the values of their collections. Those estimates are usually adequate for insurance purposes.

Professional appraisals are used to verify the quality and condition of high-value stamps or coins. Some stamp and coin dealers sell items at inflated prices or represent coins as having a better condition than they actually do. A professional appraisal can identify such inflated values.

Golfer's Equipment

The ISO rules list items eligible under golfer's equipment as "individually owned golf clubs, golf clothing, golf equipment and, subject to limitations in the inland marine form, golf balls, and other clothing of the named insured." Any or all of these items can be insured on a blanket basis.

The limitation listed in the form regarding golf balls restricts coverage to loss only by fire and burglary (only when there are marks of forcible entry).

That limitation is proof of humor in insurance policies! Golfballs are normally lost by golfers who drive them into a water hazard or into the woods. The number of balls that golfers lose is legendary, and they often jokingly claim that someone stole their ball. Any policy that would cover a golfer's lost golf balls would truly provide "all-risks" coverage.

Golf Equipment Coverage

The clause for newly acquired property does not apply to golfer's equipment. New items must be reported to the insurer immediately for coverage to apply.

Underwriting Golf Equipment

Golfer's equipment is covered under the contents coverage of the homeowners policy without limitation and includes enough perils to cover most probable losses. A nonprofessional golfer who is active enough in the sport to have invested $1,000 to $3,000 in equipment might want coverage. The purchase price information and appropriate descriptions of the property (including any serial numbers) are usually all that is needed to verify its value.

Educational Objective 3

Describe how underwriting results for personal inland marine risks can be monitored and evaluated.

Monitoring and Evaluating Results for Personal Inland Marine

Underwriters should always monitor and evaluate the results for personal inland marine risks. Doing so helps project future losses and policy changes.

One of the concerns about many of the forms of personal inland marine property is the volatility of the value of collectible items. In the past two decades, the value of silver and gold has fluctuated greatly. A value of collectible gemstones fluctuates with the market and availability. The producer or underwriter should monitor the personal inland marine policies and the schedules placed on homeowners policies to keep values current with the market. If scheduled values fall far below current market values, the insured can lose economically if a loss occurs. Fluctuations also create an underwriting concern if the market value diminishes and the policy is written on an agreed value basis. An unscrupulous insured can create an insurance loss rather than absorb the value lost through the market.

The underwriter should evaluate personal inland marine policies after a claim. Because personal inland marine policies and schedules are unique, many insurers choose to review each claim that occurs involving covered items. The claim file helps determine the loss circumstances. The police report should also provide a consistent list of missing items (if items appear on the insurance claim that do not appear on the police report, further investigation is required). A credit report is a common investigative tool if the loss circumstances are in question. The adjuster handling the loss can provide additional insights into the loss.

The results of personal inland marine coverages should also be reviewed from a portfolio standpoint. Identifying loss trends can be helpful in preventing future losses.

Summary of the Personal Articles Floater Classes

The personal articles floater is the inland marine form that is written most frequently to protect the insured for gaps found in the homeowners policy because of the following:

- Coverage limits
- Limited perils
- Difficulty in valuation of an item after a loss

The table provided as Appendix 10-B to this text summarizes information needed to underwrite the standard filed property classes on the personal articles floater, although unfiled classes can be added and underwritten. The personal property floater and the personal effects floater have had limited use since the introduction of homeowners policies, which fill many of the needs the floaters were intended to address.

Educational Objective 4
Describe common residential security systems and their protective features.

Residential Security Systems

Throughout the review of inland marine exposures and coverages, residential security systems have been mentioned as desirable for insureds who have large collections or highly valued items. A home burglary occurs in the United States every fifteen seconds, for an estimated 2 million burglaries annually. The need for home security for a residence with valuable property is mandatory.

Professional thieves seek the path of least resistance when they select a home for robbery. Target neighborhoods are those that can be accessed easily from major highways and roadways. Homes are selected that require the least amount of time to enter undetected. Thieves prefer homes having the following features:

- Privacy fences or bushes that cover windows or cover the view from the road
- Windows that slide up from the bottom
- A lack of lighting inside or outside (or a spotlight that creates a glare that thieves can hide behind)

Thieves avoid homes with the following loss prevention features:

- Deadbolt locks.
- Alarm systems (they can identify the fake stickers in homes that have no alarm).
- Open view from the street and neighbors.
- Homes lighted inside and outside, if the lighting covers enough of the yard and house to make detection easy. Thieves avoid homes lit on the inside with no covering over the windows.
- Crime watch neighborhoods.

In protecting a house from a break-in, homeowners should consider how they would get into their homes if they lost their keys. If entry requires breaking only one window, entry is easy for a thief (and the thief would be much less reluctant to break a window than the owner).

Assess Security

The underwriter should assess the security the insured uses to protect his or her home. By inspecting doors, windows, and locks, the underwriter can determine whether the home is properly protected.

Doors

Doors are the most obvious barrier to theft. Residences normally have solid wood doors, metal doors, or doors that have glass panels inset into them. When windows are set in the doors or along the side of the door (called sidelights), extra precautions are required. A wire mesh screen can be sandwiched in the glass, or the door should be equipped with a double cylinder deadbolt lock that requires a key to open the door from both sides. Without one of these, access into the home is easy.

Windows

Glass windows require additional physical or electronic protection for safety against burglary. Protective glazing normally used in residences is tempered glass that is five times as resistant to breakage as plate glass. Windows can be in metal frames for added protection. A window lock should be placed so that it cannot be easily accessed through a broken window pane. Windows can be secured with electronic sensors that detect the opening of a window. These sensors are part of the alarm systems that will be discussed later in this chapter.

Locks

Some locks that are commonly installed in residences deter break-ins. Following are descriptions of locks that provide such protection. Pictures of the locks are provided in Exhibit 10-5.

Exhibit 10-5
Common Residential Locks

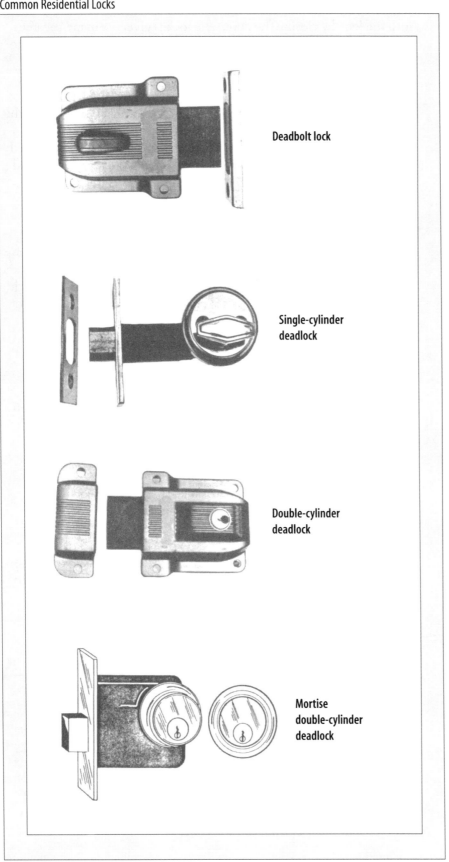

Deadbolt locks

Deadbolt locks usually have a square latch bolt that cannot be pushed into the lock by closing the door. The lock is given its name because once the bolt is extended, it is "dead" and cannot be pushed back into place. Other locks, such as spring locks, have a beveled or rounded edge that allows the striker plate to force the latch bolt into the lock each time the door is closed. This spring action also allows the door to be opened if a credit card or comb is inserted between the door and the jamb. Conversely, the deadbolt requires a key to open and close the latch bolt. The door jamb into which the bolt slides should be secured into the supporting frame by screws so that the door cannot be kicked in and the door jamb broken.

Single-Cylinder Deadlocks

Single-cylinder deadlocks require a key to open from the outside but can be opened with a latch from the inside. They afford no protection from exiting premises through the door after gaining entry by other means. These locks are not preferred where glass is present in or beside the door, since the glass can be broken and the lock can be turned from the inside.

Double-Cylinder Deadlocks

A double-cylinder deadlock requires a key to open or close from either side, making exiting the premises as hard as entering. This is also an effective lock for a door with a glass window or glass sidelights. Even if the window is broken, the burglar cannot reach inside and unlock the door.

Mortise Double-Cylinder Deadlocks

A mortise lock is designed to be installed in a cavity made within a door rather than applied to the door's surface. Mortise double-cylinder deadlocks offer excellent protection if the deadbolt is long enough to prevent prying the door away from the jamb. This lock often appears on aluminum frames, which are easily pried open. The deadbolt should be at least one and one-half inches on such doors to prevent entry.

Alarms

Alarms are recommended when there is property of considerable value in a home. Consideration should be given to the attractiveness of the valuable items to a potential thief. Detection systems can also include alarms that notify a fire department in the event of a fire.

Underwriters Laboratories

An **Underwriters Laboratories (UL)** Certificate is issued for all UL-approved alarm installations. A certificate number, the date installed and certified, and the type and kind of installation are provided whenever an installation of this type is certified.

Premises alarm systems are classified A, B, or C as follows:

- Class A systems must have sufficient staff for two guards to respond to all alarms in an average elapsed time of not more than ten minutes.
- Class B systems must have sufficient staff for one guard to respond to all alarms in an average elapsed time of not more than fifteen minutes.
- Class C systems must have sufficient staff for one guard to respond to all alarms in an average elapsed time of not more than thirty minutes.

Alarms systems are rated 1, 2, or 3 as follows, based on the extent of protection:

- Installation #1 is a system protecting all building openings and vulnerable exterior walls.
- Installation #2 is a system protecting all building openings. It also provides motion detection inside the residence.
- Installation #3 is a system protecting all building openings and provides a web of motion detection sensors that is more extensive than that of #2.

Local Alarms

A **local alarm** is a detection device connected to a bell, siren, or gong on the exterior of the premises. The detection device must be connected to the bell or alarm by a tamper-proof cable. The alarm appliance should be capable of providing an output of at least eighty-five decibels at ten feet to be effective in alerting neighbors. This alarm is not effective for a residence in an isolated area.

> In the event of a break-in, a **local alarm** creates a loud clamor that can be heard only at the premises.

Central Station Alarms

A **central station alarm** is a detection device connected to an alarm-receiving station by leased telephone wires or by home telephone lines with a preemptor that disconnects any telephone call and dials the central station when the alarm is activated. The receiving station is staffed by a security company that dispatches guards and notifies the police when an alarm is received. Protected premises must be within fifteen minutes' traveling time from the central station to be effective.

> In the event of a break-in, a **central station alarm** contacts a security company that responds to the residence and contacts the police.

Underwriters Laboratories certifies alarm companies as well as alarm system components. A UL certified alarm system has to have all UL-listed components installed in accordance with their listings by a certified alarm company. UL inspects installations by certified alarm companies and reviews their response to alarms to make certain they perform up to UL's standards.

Proprietary Alarms

A **proprietary alarm** is like a central station alarm, but the receiving station is usually on the premises and staffed by security guards employed by the premises owner. The guards respond to all alarms.

> In the event of a break-in, a **proprietary alarm** notifies a security guard on the premises, who responds.

Police Connection

A police connection is a detection device connected via telephone or private lines to a local police station. It is sometimes used in combination with a local alarm or proprietary alarm system.

Summary

A producer writing coverage for an individual or family can provide insurance coverage for most of the identified exposures under the homeowners or personal auto policy. Coverage gaps in these two policies might leave an insured's exposures unprotected by insurance. If the customer wants insurance protection, the producer can use the following as tools:

- Endorsements. Many homeowners endorsements are available to tailor an insurance policy to address an applicant's exposures. Attaching an endorsement to a policy is often the most economical method for obtaining needed coverage.

- Personal inland marine policies. These policies (as they are used in personal lines) provide insurance for personal property that is excluded, has limited coverage, or has limited peril protection under other policies.

- Specialty policies. These policies are specifically tailored to meet unique insurance needs.

The following are the three common personal inland marine policies:

1. The personal articles floater (PAF) is the most commonly used inland marine policy. It can be attached to the homeowners policy as an endorsement (HO 04 61) or written as a separate inland marine policy. Coverage is written for classes of property. The underwriting concerns change with each class of property.

2. The personal effects floater (PEF) is designed to protect property carried by travelers. Such property is now covered by a homeowners policy, but the PEF would still be appropriate for an applicant who does not have a homeowners policy or who has unique exposures involving property away from the residence.

3. The personal property floater (PPF) is designed to provide contents coverage for a residence. It became less popular with the introduction of the homeowners policy. However, the PPF is still a useful coverage tool for applicants who do not have homeowners policies or for applicants in temporary living arrangements.

Because the size and value of items insured in residences can become large, home security becomes an important underwriting consideration. Locks and alarm systems are not foolproof, but they can delay or discourage an attempted break-in.

Chapter Notes

1. Roderick McNamara, Robert A. Laurence, and Glenn L. Wood, *Inland Marine Insurance*, vol. II (Malvern, PA: Insurance Institute of America, 1987), pp. 149-162.

2. The National Underwriter Co., *FC&S Bulletins Personal Lines Volume* (Cincinnati, OH: The National Underwriter Co., 1994), p. A-3.

3. *FC&S Bulletins Personal Lines Volume*, pp. Q&A 581.

Chapter 11

Educational Objectives

1. Identify and describe the hazards associated with various types and construction of noncommercial watercraft. (pp. 11-4 to 11-7)

2. Identify exposures and hazards presented by a watercraft risk, and evaluate the importance of those exposures and hazards. (pp. 11-8 to 11-12)

3. Describe the information needed to make an underwriting decision regarding a watercraft exposure, and explain how that information is obtained. (pp. 11-12 to 11-21)

4. Compare the property and liability coverage available under homeowners policies with the coverages available under watercraft policies, and evaluate the alternatives available in coverage implementation. (pp. 11-21 to 11-33)

5. Describe how watercraft policies are monitored and evaluated. (pp. 11-33 to 11-35)

6. Given a case study involving an application for a personal watercraft risk, analyze the exposures and recommend appropriate actions. (Encompasses entire chapter.)

Chapter 11

Watercraft: Exposure Analysis and Coverages

Recreational boating is one of America's favorite leisure activities. Throughout the United States, an estimated twenty million pleasure boats of various sizes, designs, and values are used by people from a variety of backgrounds. The boats are designed for many water activities, including rowing, sailing, power boating (cruising), canoeing, kayaking, water-skiing, living on houseboats, hunting, diving, and fishing.

The increase in boating activity has also increased the number of watercraft-related accidents and the need for watercraft insurance. The boating loss statistical reports published by the Marine Index Bureau Foundation (from a survey of seventeen insurance companies) show that more than 75,000 recreational boating accidents and 12,000 boat-related thefts occurred in 1993. Property damage losses amounted to more than $141 million. According to the United States Coast Guard, more than 3,000 injuries and 1,000 deaths resulted from accidents. Exhibit 11-1 profiles the type of watercraft accidents that are reported to insurers and the size of resulting losses.

The property damage and bodily injury figures in Exhibit 11-1 are low. According to the U.S. Coast Guard, only a small percentage of accidents are actually reported.

Specialists in personal insurance act as advisors in helping customers become aware of the watercraft losses that can occur, the potential financial consequences, and methods for treating those exposures.

Exhibit 11-1
Watercraft Loss Profile

Property Damage for Reportable Accidents by Type of Loss
(Number of Accidents Reported by Type and Dollar Severity)

Type of Loss	Accidents in $ Range						Damage Average ($)	Total Damage ($)
	$2,000 and Under	$2,001–$10,000	$10,001–$50,000	$50,001–$100,000	$100,001–$500,000	$500,001 and Over		
Fire/Explosion	256	192	99	17	9	0	10,412	5,966,076
Collision (NOC)	3,855	1,753	107	2	2	0	2,132	12,192,908
Collision w/Another Vessel	474	174	18	0	0	0	2,099	1,397,934
Collision w/Floating Object	695	329	16	0	0	0	2,061	2,143,440
Collision w/Submerged Object	12,377	5,099	108	1	0	0	1,717	30,193,445
Sinking	1,430	726	119	15	4	0	3,608	8,276,752
Grounding	201	187	30	6	1	1	6,316	2,690,616
Machinery Damage	80	69	24	0	0	0	4,642	803,066
Engine Damage	252	206	6	0	0	0	2,387	1,107,568
Equipment Failure	147	59	9	0	0	0	2,030	436,450
Towing	18	0	0	0	0	0	178	3,204
Capsizing	1,180	734	83	1	0	0	2,703	5,400,594
Swamping/Flooding	187	115	9	0	0	0	2,551	793,361
Hauling/Launching	41	23	0	0	0	0	2,026	129,664
Third-Party Damage (NOC)	74	20	0	0	0	0	1,571	147,674
Bodily Injury	1,094	109	6	0	0	0	1,042	1,259,778
Loss of Life	0	0	1	0	0	0	36,153	36,153
Falls Overboard	0	0	0	0	1	0	107,000	107,000
Falls Within Boat	0	1	0	0	0	0	4,032	4,032
Collision w/Fixed Object	1,406	494	23	0	0	0	1,739	3,344,097
Dismasting	0	3	1	0	0	0	7,135	28,540
Damage (NOC)	411	82	9	0	0	0	1,477	741,454
Ice Damage	203	82	8	0	0	0	2,005	587,465
Not Classified	18,675	7,525	851	38	7	0	2,353	63,535,277
Total	43,056	17,982	1,527	80	24	1	2,255	141,326,548

Source: Marine Index Bureau Foundation, 1993.

> **Educational Objective 1**
> Identify and describe the hazards associated with various types and construction of noncommercial watercraft.

Understanding Watercraft

To write coverage for or underwrite a pleasure boat risk, the specialist must understand basic marine terminology and know the exposures, perils, and coverages relating to watercraft insurance. To seek and market watercraft insurance effectively, insurance specialists need information about available resources for watercraft information.

Watercraft Types and Construction

A boat or a watercraft can be defined as a vessel used for water transportation. Vessel is a very broad term for all watercraft and is used in laws and regulations relating to marine traffic without regard to the size of the watercraft.

In the United States, more than 4,000 different models of recreational boats are available. They range from boats less than sixteen feet long (such as fishing boats used on protected bodies of water) to boats fifty feet or longer (such as power cruisers and sailboats used offshore or in the ocean).

Floatables such as inflatables, canoes, rowboats, kayaks, and rafts usually have no power and are propelled with oars or paddles. However, they might sometimes have small motors. Such watercraft are usually used on small lakes, rivers, and streams.

Runabouts up to about eighteen feet used for fishing, water-skiing, and other recreational activities are powered by outboard motors, inboard motors, or inboard-outdrive motors.

Cruisers from eighteen to sixty feet or longer have living facilities such as berths (beds), heads (toilet facilities), and galleys (kitchens) and are powered by large engines.

Sailboats come in all sizes and designs. A boat might have a single hull, a double hull (a catamaran), or a triple hull (a trimaran). Sailboats might have an auxiliary engine, and large sailboats might have living facilities. A sailboat is considered a yacht when it exceeds twenty-six feet in length and when the owner needs the services of friends or hired crew to navigate or maneuver the boat.

Other classes of boats include houseboats, dinghies (small boats with or without a motor), tenders (used to carry supplies to and from a larger vessel), jet-powered boats, air boats, jet ski boats, and pontoon boats. Exhibit 11-2 illustrates common types of watercraft.

Exhibit 11-2
Types of Boats

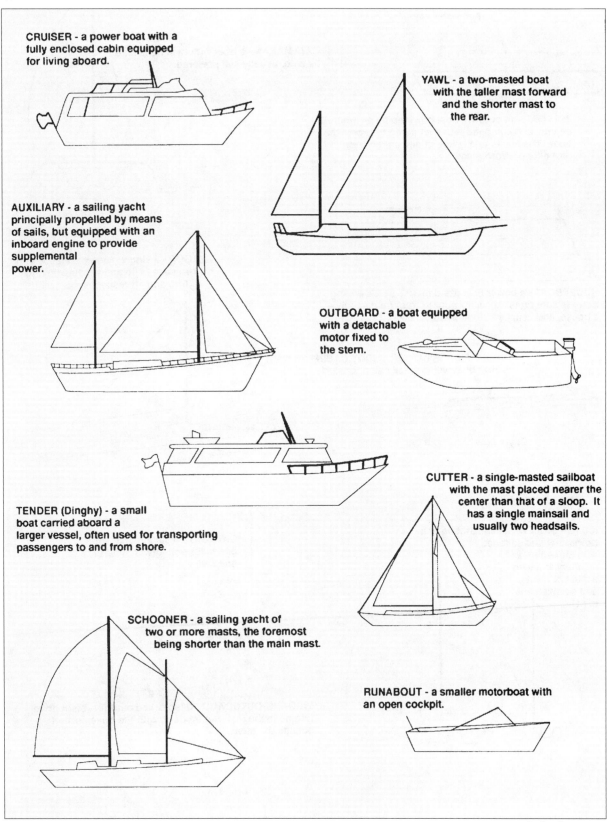

CRUISER - a power boat with a fully enclosed cabin equipped for living aboard.

YAWL - a two-masted boat with the taller mast forward and the shorter mast to the rear.

AUXILIARY - a sailing yacht principally propelled by means of sails, but equipped with an inboard engine to provide supplemental power.

OUTBOARD - a boat equipped with a detachable motor fixed to the stern.

TENDER (Dinghy) - a small boat carried aboard a larger vessel, often used for transporting passengers to and from shore.

CUTTER - a single-masted sailboat with the mast placed nearer the center than that of a sloop. It has a single mainsail and usually two headsails.

SCHOONER - a sailing yacht of two or more masts, the foremost being shorter than the main mast.

RUNABOUT - a smaller motorboat with an open cockpit.

Continued on next page.

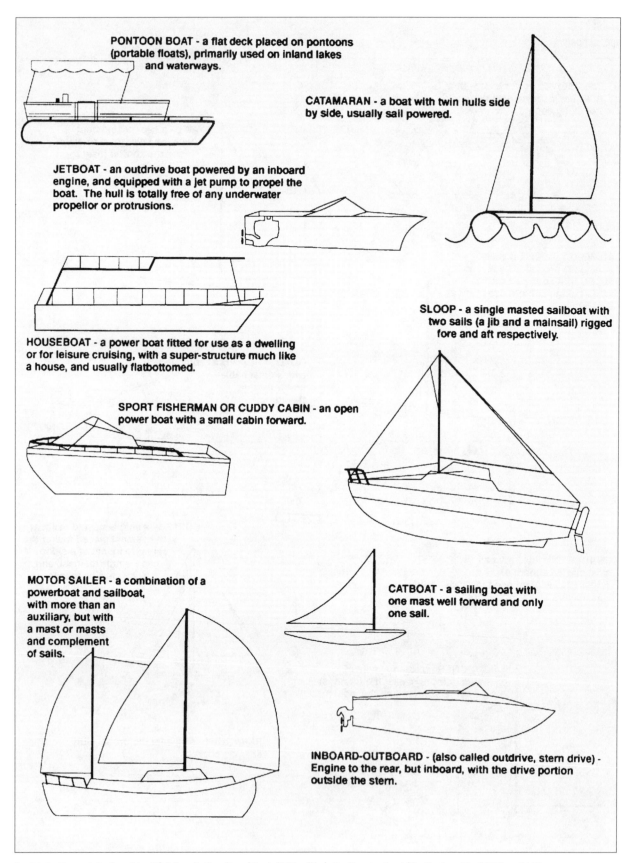

PONTOON BOAT - a flat deck placed on pontoons (portable floats), primarily used on inland lakes and waterways.

CATAMARAN - a boat with twin hulls side by side, usually sail powered.

JETBOAT - an outdrive boat powered by an inboard engine, and equipped with a jet pump to propel the boat. The hull is totally free of any underwater propellor or protrusions.

HOUSEBOAT - a power boat fitted for use as a dwelling or for leisure cruising, with a super-structure much like a house, and usually flatbottomed.

SLOOP - a single masted sailboat with two sails (a jib and a mainsail) rigged fore and aft respectively.

SPORT FISHERMAN OR CUDDY CABIN - an open power boat with a small cabin forward.

MOTOR SAILER - a combination of a powerboat and sailboat, with more than an auxiliary, but with a mast or masts and complement of sails.

CATBOAT - a sailing boat with one mast well forward and only one sail.

INBOARD-OUTBOARD - (also called outdrive, stern drive) - Engine to the rear, but inboard, with the drive portion outside the stern.

Reprinted with permission from Aetna Life & Casualty, Casualty and Surety Division, "Marketing Report—Special Boating Issue," April 1972, pp. 24-25.

The type of boat, size, value, and area of navigation largely determine the exposure to loss.

Customer Built/Unusual Craft

Boats built from kits and boats built by a nonprofessional boat builder usually are insured through specialty or surplus lines markets. These boats require the experience of a watercraft specialist who understands design features and can identify construction problems.

Hull Construction

Pleasure boats are usually constructed of fiberglass, wood, plywood, steel, aluminum, and occasionally ferro-cement (thin cement reinforced with steel mesh). Those materials produce sound, seaworthy vessels.

Wooden boats are more cautiously underwritten than fiberglass boats because dry rot damage (wood decay caused by a fungus) could eventually damage or sink the boat. The cost to repair an old wooden boat is often higher than the cost to repair boats constructed of fiberglass or steel. Often, the insurance rates for boats of wooden construction include a surcharge, especially if the boat is over five years old. Steel construction is subject to rust and corrosion that could weaken the hull. Fiberglass is a porous material, which if not properly maintained might weaken the hull and lead to hull loss.

Hull Design

As stated, a boat can have a single hull, a double hull, or a triple hull. In the past, underwriters had been reluctant to insure multihull boats because of the increased loss exposure; most multihull boats were home-built. If not constructed properly, the multihull boats were susceptible to breaking up or capsizing in heavy weather. Marinas were not equipped to handle the multihull boats because of their bulky size.

Today, more multihull boats are commercially built by reputable builders, and marinas are better equipped to handle them. Consequently, these boats are now underwritten more leniently than they were in the past.

> **FYI**
>
> British Columbia, Canada, holds annual motorized outhouse races on the waters of Cowichan Bay—this is not one of the recognized hull constructions.

Nautical Terminology and Boating Knowledge

Boaters have their own language and terminology, and they like to talk to people who speak their language. For example, a small pleasure boat operator is called a boater. Those who operate large boats are referred to as yachtsmen, skippers, or captains. Traditionally, boats have been referred to as "she" rather than "it."

Nearly every part of the boat has a nautical name: the front is the bow; the back is the stern; the left side is port; and the right side is starboard. Appendix 11-A provides a glossary of basic nautical terms.

Educational Objective 2

Identify exposures and hazards presented by a watercraft risk, and evaluate the importance of those exposures and hazards.

Underwriting Watercraft

When underwriting watercraft, underwriters must concern themselves with watercraft exposures, hazards, and sources of underwriting information that would pertain to each insured.

Watercraft Exposures and Hazards

Watercraft property and liability exposures can be compared to the personal automobile exposures studied in Chapters 6 and 7 of this text. Like an automobile, a boat and its equipment are subject to physical damage loss. A legal liability exposure exists for bodily injury and property damage. Also, a loss exposure exists for medical payments for injury to insureds, passengers, and for guests, and loss against uninsured boaters. The underwriter must evaluate each of those types of loss exposure.

Property Exposures

The property exposure to potential loss includes damage to the following:

- Boats, including hull, deck, and cabin
- Deck hardware
- Motors
- Transmissions
- Propellers
- Cables

Equipment that is a part of the boat's operation is also subject to loss. Examples of watercraft equipment include the following:

- Depth sounders (indicate the water depth)
- Navigation equipment, including compasses, automatic radio direction finders, satellite navigation systems (used to determine the boat's location), radar (used to detect objects), and navigation aids, such as buoys and lights
- Sails
- Electrical equipment not normally removable (for example, water heaters, refrigeration units, heating and air conditioning units, and fresh-water systems)
- Safety equipment (such as fire extinguishers and personal flotation devices required by federal or state regulation)
- Citizens' band and marine band radios

- Small tenders or dinghies (usually limited to those less than twelve feet in length and having less than a ten-horsepower motor)
- Oars and paddles
- Extra fuel tanks

Finally, damage to boat trailers and personal property is a potential loss exposure.

Physical Hazards

Underwriters are concerned about the physical hazards that property is exposed to on land and sea and about perils such as stranding, sinking, collision with a submerged object, fire, lightning, windstorm, explosion, and collision with other boats. Some specific causes of boat property losses are provided by the following examples:

- A boat is beached in a severe storm.
- The line used to secure the boat to the pier breaks, causing the bow (front of the boat) to crash into the pier.
- A boat operator hits a submerged object and damages the propeller, shaft, and hull of the boat.
- A boat fills with rainwater at the pier, causing it to float beneath the dock at low tide and sink as the tide rises.
- Ice punctures a hole in the hull, causing the bow to sink.
- Lightning strikes a boat and burns out the electrical equipment.

The photos in Exhibit 11-3 show the types of physical damage described above.

Liability Exposures

Liability exposures include bodily injury and property damage that might occur while operating the boat on the water, as well as injuries and damage that might occur while navigating or docking or while at a mooring.

Bodily Injury

The liability exposure to loss involves bodily injury and death to passengers, to guests aboard the boat, and to other persons, as illustrated below:

- A sailboat hits a high-power overhead line. The electrical charge is conducted down through the mast (the tall vertical pole that supports the sails) and throughout the metal on the boat, resulting in serious injury or death to those in contact with the metal.
- A boat collides with an oncoming boat, injuring passengers on both boats.
- A speeding motorboat hits a swimmer.
- A gasoline engine explodes, injuring passengers and killing a crew member.
- A guest trips over a loose line on the deck and falls overboard, incurring a head injury.

Exhibit 11-3
Photos of Damaged Watercraft

Sailboat is beached

Boat sinks at pier

Hull puncture causes sinking

Boat fills with rainwater, which causes sinking

Property Damage Liability

The liability exposure to loss involves property damage arising out of the ownership, maintenance, or use of the boat and resulting in losses such as the following:

- Damage is done to another boat as a result of a collision.

- A yacht club pier is damaged as a result of the improper docking of a boat.

- The insured stores paint and turpentine on the boat. A spark from the insured's cigarette ignites the flammable material, setting the boat on fire. The fire spreads and causes extensive damage to the marina and surrounding boats.

- The insured improperly ties his boat to the pier. The lines break, causing his boat to collide with a neighboring boat.

Medical Payments

The medical payments exposure involves bodily injury to the insured and his or her guests and passengers, occurring while in, upon, boarding, or leaving the boat. The following are examples:

- The insured breaks a leg when boarding the boat.
- A child falls and breaks an arm while running around the bow.
- A guest is injured when he loses his footing while getting off the boat.

Uninsured Boaters

The uninsured boaters exposure to bodily injury involves a loss arising out of an accident caused by an uninsured boat owner. Like an uninsured motorist under the personal automobile policy, an uninsured boater is one with no liability insurance or bond to pay for an accident. A hit-and-run boat or one whose insurance company has become insolvent is also included under the uninsured boaters exposure.

Educational Objective 3

Describe what information is needed to make an underwriting decision regarding a watercraft exposure, and explain how that information is obtained.

Underwriting Information

The underwriter analyzes several pieces of underwriting information about the boat's physical characteristics and use. The insurance application has a section regarding the characteristics of the boat's owners and operators and provides the underwriter with the information required for qualifying, classifying, and rating the risk. A typical watercraft application is shown in Exhibit 11-4.

In addition to the application, underwriting information can be obtained from the producer or company representative who inspected the boat and spoke with the boat owner to determine whether the risk meets the company's guidelines. The underwriter and producer might also need to evaluate any moral and morale hazards of the risk.

Finally, a professional survey might be required. The professional surveyor provides expert advice and opinions concerning the value, condition, insurability, and seaworthiness of the boat. A marine surveyor

Exhibit 11-4
Sample Watercraft Application

Watercraft Application

1. Owner _____ Occupation _____ Age _____
2. Address _____ Phone Number _____
3. Number of years' experience operating boats _____ Type/Size of boat(s) _____
4. Previous loss experience _____ Has insurance been declined elsewhere? _____
5. Other operators of this boat _____
6. Their operating experience _____ Their loss experience _____
7. Date purchased by present owner _____ From _____
8. Owner's purchase price $ _____ Present value $ _____ Original cost when new $ _____
9. Is boat free of mortgages or other encumbrances? _____ If not, balance due $ _____
10. Mortgage or encumbrances in favor of _____
11. Boat built in 19 _____ By _____ Where _____
12. Length overall _____ Model or style of hull _____
13. Name of yacht _____ Serial number _____
14. Type: ☐ Runabout ☐ Cruiser ☐ Houseboat ☐ Sailboat ☐ Floatboat ☐ Trawler ☐ Other
15. Material used in hull construction ☐ Sheet plywood ☐ Lap plywood ☐ Lap ☐ Plank ☐ Fiberglass
16. ☐ Steel ☐ Aluminum ☐ Ferro cement ☐ Other _____
17. No. of engines _____ Make of engine(s) _____ Gas _____ Diesel _____ Horsepower _____ (each)
18. Serial nos. _____ Age of engines _____ Maximum speed of boat _____
19. Type of drive unit ☐ Inboard ☐ Inboard/outdrive ☐ Jet Manufactured by _____
20. Description of tender (if any) _____ valued at $ _____ Outboard motor $ _____
21. Type of trailer _____ Mfg. 19 __ by _____ Value $ _____

	Coverage Desired	Premium Quoted
22. Hull and machinery _____	$ _____	$ _____
23. Deductible applied to hull and machinery _	$ _____	$ _____
24. Protection and indemnity _____	$ _____	$ _____
25. Excess medical payments _____	$ _____	$ _____
26. Owned trailer _____	$ _____	$ _____
27. _____	$ _____	$ _____

28. Insurance is wanted from _____ , 19 ____ Noon, until _____ , 19 ____ Noon
29. Waters to be navigated _____
30. Where is boat moored while in commission? _____
31. Boat will be laid up and out of commission from _____ to _____
32. Ashore _____ or afloat? _____ At what yard? _____
33. Is boat transported over land? _____ Number of times per year? _____ Average distance per trip? _____
34. Is boat used solely for private pleasure purposes? _____ Ever chartered? _____
35. Does it ever carry passengers for hire _____ , participate in races _____ , or water-skiing? _____
36. How many portable fire extinguishers? _____ Type and where located _____
37. Are engine and tank spaces protected with built-in fire extinguisher system? _____ Brand _____
38. Type and serial number of ship-to-shore telephone _____ , of radio direction finder, _____
39. Of Fathometer _____ , Equipped with compass? _____
40. Type of fuel used for galley stove _____ , Is woodwork within 18" protected? _____
41. Identify sails by name, kind of fabric, and date purchased _____

It is certified by the applicant that no persons under the age of 16 shall operate any power boat submitted on this application unless accompanied by an adult 21 years of age or over, and under their direct supervision.
The applicant acknowledges that this application does not bind coverages. The applicant is not obligated to accept the insurance, if offered.
The applicant certifies the above information to be true.

Applicant's IRS or Social Security Number _____

Date at _____

_____ , 19 _____

Signature of Applicant _____
Agent or Broker _____
Address _____

The **condition and value survey** establishes the current condition of the hull machinery and equipment and establishes a current market value and replacement value.

The **buyer's survey** examines everything that might be physically wrong with a vessel.

uses one of two types of surveys: a condition and value survey or a buyer's survey. The **condition and value survey** establishes the current condition of the hull machinery and equipment and establishes a current market value and replacement value. The **buyer's survey** is much more thorough because it examines everything that might be wrong with a vessel, such as tears in the curtain, stains on rugs or furniture, and so forth. Generally, the buyer's survey is used to negotiate the price of the boat.

Physical Characteristics of Watercraft

In addition to boat type and hull design, many other physical characteristics are important in underwriting watercraft insurance, including the following:

- *Manufacturer/model of boat.* Underwriters should determine whether the boat was built by a competent manufacturer with a reputation for quality.

- *Length of boat.* The boat's length helps to determine whether the boat should be covered under homeowners or marine insurance. The length in relation to the horsepower is also an underwriting factor. The chance of a collision or other loss is more likely to occur if the motor overpowers the boat.

- *Age of boat.* Underwriters generally prefer boats under five years old. Boats between five and ten years old usually require a professional survey before an underwriter will evaluate the risk for coverage. Virtually all underwriters require a condition and value survey on any boat over ten years old. Generally, older boats are charged higher rates.

- *Type of motor.* The basic types of motors are outboard, inboard, and inboard-outdrive (also called inboard-outboard if the motor is located inside the boat and the drive is mounted outside the boat).

A **knot** is a measurement of speed of watercraft. A knot equals 1.15 miles per hour.

- *Maximum boat speed.* Boat speed is measured in **knots**. High-speed or high-performance boats are usually ineligible for standard insurance and must be insured through specialty markets.

- *Number, make, and horsepower of motor.* The motor should be appropriate for the type of boat. Boat manufacturers publish recommendations for the size and horsepower of motors. Overpowering a boat with a motor for which the boat is not designed creates structural stress on the boat. Overloading the boat with a heavy engine also affects the boat's stability and can throw the boat off balance. Both create a potential loss exposure.

- *Motor/engine fuel.* Most small and medium-sized motorboats are fueled with gasoline. Some motorboats and sailboats are powered by small horsepower diesel engines. Diesel fuel is less explosive than gasoline and presents less of a fire hazard. Diesel engines usually receive reduced insurance rates.

- *Valuation.* Small outboard boats and other small boats are insured for their actual cash value (ACV). Large boats and yachts are usually insured on a replacement cost or agreed value basis.

Generally, sails, protective coverings of fabric and canvas, and batteries are insured for their ACVs. Specialists must gather information about the original cost new, the purchase price, and the cost to replace the property.

Information about the boat's value can be obtained from sales receipts, books publishing manufacturer's prices for new boats, and other books publishing used-boat information. The BUC Research is a three-volume publication available as a new and used boat price guide. Large Boat Appraisal by The National Automobile Dealers Association (N.A.D.A.) is a guide for prices of boats ranging from 26 to 150 feet in length.

Surveyors inspect boats to determine their seaworthiness. They can also estimate the boat's current value.

- *Condition and maintenance*. The boat's condition influences its acceptability for insurance. Boats in poor condition with no maintenance programs are usually unacceptable risks. Poor house-keeping can lead to serious losses. Oily rags, fuel in the bilge (lower part of the boat's hull), and faulty wiring can cause a fire. Gasoline leaks can lead to serious injury or death. Evidence of pride of ownership shows the underwriter that a responsible insured is maintaining and repairing the boat to keep it in insurable condition.

- *Safety equipment*. Federal and state regulations mandate that all boats have certain safety equipment. Such equipment includes personal flotation devices, distress signals, fire extinguishers, ventilation systems, and sound-producing warning devices used in low visibility. State regulations might have additional safety requirements; for example, the Virginia Department of Game and Inland Fisheries establishes the flotation devices that must be worn by water skiers and jet skiers.

  Although federal and state requirements set minimum safety requirements, underwriters look for additional safety equipment such as ship-to-shore telephones, radios, and depth sounders. Insurance rate credit is often given for safety equipment such as automatic fire extinguishers and fume detectors. Exhibit 11-5 is a list of the U.S. Coast Guard minimum equipment requirements. An expanded description of this equipment has been included as Appendix 11-B of this text.

Watercraft Use

A specialist should review watercraft use as well as the location of operation and ports visited, such as the following:

- *Home port*. Underwriters generally prefer that boats not in use be kept in safe and protected locations to reduce their exposure to loss.

- *Waters to be navigated*. The waters in which the boat will be used have a major bearing on underwriting. A small, outboard motor boat being used for fishing on a quiet lake presents far less risk

Exhibit 11-5
U.S. Coast Guard Minimum Equipment Requirements

U.S. Coast Guard Minimum Equipment Requirements				
Equipment	**Boats less than 16 ft.**	**16 to less than 26 ft.**	**26 to less than 40 ft.**	**40 to not more than 65 ft.**
Personal Flotation Devices (PFD Life Jackets) as of April 1993	One approved Type I, II, III, IV, or V PFD for each person on board or being towed on water skis, etc.	One approved Type I, II, III, or V PFD device for each person on board or being towed on water skis, etc. In addition, one throwable Type IV device. Type V Recreational Hybrid PFDs must be worn when the boat is underway. Other Type V PFDs must be approved for the activity in which the boat is being used.		
Fire Extinguishers (Coast Guard Approved)+	At least one B-1 type (see below) Coast Guard-approved hand-portable fire extinguisher. Not required on outboard motorboats less than 26 feet long and not carrying passengers for hire if the construction of such motorboats will not permit the entrapment of explosive or flammable gases or vapors, and if fuel tanks are not permanently installed.		At least two B-1 type approved portable fire extinguishers; OR at least one B-2 type.	At least three B-1 type approved portable fire extinguishers; OR at least one B-1 type PLUS one B-2 type.
Visual Distress Signals	Must carry approved visual distress signals for nighttime use.	Must carry visual distress signals approved for daytime and nighttime use. For pyrotechnic devices (hand-held or aerial red flares, floating or hand-held orange smoke, and launchers for aerial red meteors or parachute flares) a minimum of 3 required, in any combination that totals 3 for daytime and 3 for night use. Three day/night devices will suffice. Devices must be in serviceable condition, dates not expired and stowed accessibly. Exceptions are open sailboats less than 26 feet long and not equipped with propulsion machinery, and manually propelled boats; both required to carry only night signals.		
Bell, Whistle	Every vessel less than 39.4 feet (12 meters) long must carry an efficient sound-producing device.		Every vessel 39.4 feet (12 meters) long, but less than 65.6 feet (20 meters), must carry a whistle and a bell. The whistle must be audible for 1/2 nautical mile. The mouth of the bell must be at least 7.87 inches (200 mm) in diameter.	
Ventilation (Boats built before August 1, 1980)	At least two ventilator ducts fitted with cowls or their equivalent for the purpose of properly and efficiently ventilating the bilges of every closed engine and fuel tank compartment of boats constructed or decked over after April 25, 1940, using gasoline as fuel or other fuels having a flashpoint of 110°F or less.			
Ventilation (Boats built after August 1, 1980)	At least two ventilator ducts for the purpose of efficiently ventilating every closed compartment that contains a gasoline engine and every closed compartment containing a gasoline tank, except those having permanently installed tanks vented outside the boat and containing no unprotected electrical devices. Also, engine compartments containing a gasoline engine with a cranking motor must contain power-operated exhaust.			
Backfire Flame Arrestor	One approved device on each carburetor of all gasoline engines installed after April 25, 1940, except outboard motors. Device must be marked to show compliance with SAE J-1928 or UL 1111 Standards.			

+ When fixed fire-extinguishing system is installed in machinery spaces it will replace one B-1 type portable fire extinguisher.

Coast Guard minimum equipment requirements vary with the size of the boat, type of propulsion, whether operated at night or in periods of reduced visibility, and, in some cases, the body of water on which it is used. Many state requirements go beyond Coast Guard requirements.

Marine Fire Extinguisher Classification				
	Foam	CO_2	Dry Chem.	Halon
Classes	(Gals.)	(Lbs.)	(Lbs.)	
B-1	1.25	4	2	2.5
B-2	2.5	15	10	10
—	—	10	2.5	5

Source: Adapted from BOAT/U.S. Foundation, based on U.S. Coast Guard Requirements.

than a twin-engine 350 horsepower cabin cruiser taken out on the open ocean. The warm waters of the inland lakes of Florida present a lesser hazard than the icy winter waters of the Great Lakes. A storm on the ocean away from any safe harbor presents a far greater hazard for a sailboat than a storm on a small lake where safe refuge is nearby.

- *Port risks*. Boats that are only navigated part of the year have lay-up warranties in their policies indicating a time frame within which they will be out of commission either ashore or afloat. The main reason that a port risk policy would be issued for a yacht is that the vessel is up for sale. Generally, yacht underwriters are reluctant to write port-risk policies because vessel maintenance tends to wane as a result of nonuse or a lack of interest. Owners tend to check their vessels less frequently, and the owner of a vessel up for sale will probably want the underwriter to insure the vessel for a limited amount of time. The chance of the new owner's maintaining yacht insurance with the incumbent insurer is remote at best.

- *Charter*. Boats **chartered** or hired for a fee are excluded from plea-sure watercraft policies. Sometimes the charter exclusion might be eliminated by endorsement, which involves an additional premium charge.

- *Racing*. Except for sailboats, coverage is usually excluded when the boat is used for racing in official speed contests. In theory, sailboats are slower than powerboats and are less likely to cause and receive extensive damage. Sailboat racing is permitted because most yacht clubs sanction weekend racing and participants are more skilled than other boaters, thus reducing the risk of personal injury. These weekend races are often a test of seamanship and sailing skill rather than speed, which is why powerboat races are excluded.

Characteristics of Watercraft Owners and Operators

The insurance application, interviews with the boat owners, and other sources provide information about watercraft owners and operators. The following section describes pertinent information that underwriters need in order to complete the risk evaluation.

Age of the Owners and Operators

Most insurance companies do not want to insure unsupervised, youthful boat operators. Underwriters look for mature, competent insureds capable of operating the boat responsibly.

Boating Experience

Underwriters want to know the number of years the insured has been operating the kind of boat for which the insurance is being written. An inexperienced boat operator might be acceptable if he begins his boating experience with a small outboard motorboat. However, an inexperienced operator of a large power cruiser or sailboat is not a desirable risk from an underwriting viewpoint.

Chartering a boat means renting it. The insured can act as the boat's captain, or the person renting the boat can perform that role.

FYI

Boat racing can prompt unconventional activity. The Todd River, in Alice Springs, Australia, is the site of an annual race in which two-member crews, standing inside bottomless boats and gripping the gunwales, run a foot race along a course mapped out on the dry river bed.

Credit is often given in the rates for completing boating courses, such as the United States Coast Guard Boating Skills and Seamanship course and the United States Power Squadron course.

Loss Experience

The underwriter considers the applicant's loss experience for the past three to five years. If a history of losses exists, the risk might be declined. Usually, rate credit is given for three years of loss-free experience.

Motor Vehicle Records

A boat operator can be compared to an automobile driver. Often, an inexperienced boat operator is unfamiliar with boating operation and safety. The characteristics of boat operators create exposures that should be considered in the underwriting process, just as an underwriter would consider the exposures created by the characteristics of automobile drivers (such as immaturity or inexperience).

A boat operator must be mature, alert, and responsible. How an insured operates an automobile usually reflects how he or she will operate a boat. Boat operators are not required to have a personal boating license, but they are required to know and adhere to the boating laws and regulations in the states in which they boat. Underwriters often look at the operator's motor vehicle record to determine whether he or she might be a good boating risk.

One of the violations that underwriters look for on the motor vehicle report is a record of the insured driving under the influence of alcohol. According to the United States Coast Guard, 50 percent of all boating accidents are related to alcohol. Operating a boat while intoxicated became a federal offense effective January 13, 1988. A pleasure-craft operator with a blood alcohol content (BAC) of .10 percent (.08 percent in some states) or higher is subject to a civil penalty of up to $1,000 or a criminal penalty of up to $5,000 and one year of imprisonment.

Motor vehicle records identifying any excessive speeding, reckless driving violations, or driving under the influence of alcohol are negative underwriting factors. A record of such violations might indicate that the person will operate the boat similarly.

Usually, motor vehicle records are not a factor in underwriting large boats or yachts. For these boats, the main concerns are their speed and the operator's experience in handling large watercraft.

Number of Owners

Multiple owners (other than relatives in the same household) and boats in the name of a partnership or corporation are usually ineligible for personal watercraft insurance because of the increased liability exposure. The increased exposure arises when an at-fault accident occurs and the insured is sued. All owners can be brought into the lawsuit, and the insurer must defend each person named on the policy. Also, each insured could sue the other. Rates do not contemplate that multiple-owner exposure. However, some companies might include multiple owners, partnerships, or corporations for an additional premium charge.

Insureds Living Aboard

Insureds living on their boats might have to pay an additional premium for the live-aboard exposure. Yacht insurance rates normally contemplate that boats are used only occasionally. When an insured lives aboard the boat, there is more activity on the boat. The insured is continually using the boat for cooking, and other household-like purposes such as heating. These additional uses of the boat create additional ignition sources and an increased potential for fire. Other people are also aboard the boat more frequently, creating an increased liability exposure.

Watercraft Moral and Morale Hazards

A moral hazard can arise out of the insured's attitude, financial instability, or lifestyle and can lead to dishonest or fraudulent acts. For example, an owner in financial trouble might sink a boat to collect the insurance, or an insured might intentionally drive a boat aground to finance a new paint job or a new engine.

Also, an insured's poor financial condition might result in negligent care being taken of the boat. Some boats can be expensive to operate; others require constant care and money to keep them from deteriorating.

A morale hazard is usually a major issue in underwriting watercraft. Boating is a recreational sport that people usually pursue in their spare time and with their spare money. Sometimes, an attitude of carelessness can develop, and people might not take as good care of their boats as they do of their other personal possessions.

According to the United States Coast Guard, carelessness is the number-one cause of boating losses. Some examples of losses caused by carelessness are as follows:

- Failing to drain water from the engines in freezing temperatures, causing the engine block to crack
- Storing flammable materials and oily rags in the engine compartment, causing the engine to explode and burn
- Improperly securing lines, causing the boat to crash into the pier during heavy winds
- Allowing a boat to fill with rainwater, resulting in its sinking at the dock

Watercraft Surveys

Professional surveys are usually required before a company will insure boats more than five to ten years old or boats that have experienced a major loss. The surveyor recommends how deficiencies can be corrected to make the risk more acceptable to the underwriter. For example, the surveyor might recommend that additional fire extinguishers be installed in visible and easily accessible areas. The surveyor might recommend that an electric bilge pump (which pumps water out of the boat) be replaced.

As boats age, they require more maintenance. Underwriters generally require a professional survey every three to five years to evaluate

Exhibit 11-6
Watercraft Survey

Report of survey on _____ by _____
                            (Watercraft name and Coast Guard no.)   (Surveyor)

_____ at _____ Ashore ☐   Afloat ☐   on _____
              (Firm)   (Location)   (Date)

Owned by _____ Address _____

When built _____ Where built _____ By whom _____

Length _____ Beam_____ Draft _____ Type of Boat _____

Hull Construction: ☐ Wood   ☐ Steel   ☐ Plywood   ☐ Fiberglass   ☐ Other _____

Advertised or estimated speed of yacht _____ Does propeller extend below keel or skeg? _____

Make of engine _____ Model _____ H.P. _____ Type _____ Age of engine _____

Is engine equipped with backfire arrester? _____ Drip pan under carburetor? _____ Engine serial # _____

Fuel tanks: Location_____Type_____ Material _____

Do overflow and air vents from tanks lead outboard? _____Type of stove_____ Location of tanks _____

How is engine compartment ventilated? _____

Is yacht equipped with built-in fire extinguisher system? _____

Tender, Description _____ Estimated Value _____ Is it powered by outboard motor? _____

	Obscured	Not Applic.	Excellent	Good	Fair	Poor	Very Poor	Recommendation
General overall condition								
Spars, sails, rigging								
Structural strength of hull, frames, etc.								
Bottom								
Topside								
Engines								
Engine spaces								
Bilge spaces								
Cabin spaces								
Ventilation								
Electrical system								
Pumping system								
Fuel system, incl. tanks								
Fire extinguishers								
Galley								
Ground tackle								
Electronic equipment	(List all items separately, showing estimated value, under "Electronic Equipment" on reverse side)							
Maintenance program								
Decks								

Items checked to the right of this line constitute an unsatisfactory report.

the continued insurability of the boat. A sample survey is provided in Exhibit 11-6. That simple survey might be appropriate for a new or a small watercraft. A more complex survey is usually required for larger, older, or more expensive watercraft. Samples of more detailed surveys are included as appendixes to this text. Appendix 11-C of this book is a blank watercraft survey. A completed watercraft survey is shown in Appendix 11-D.

Other methods to determine the boat's condition include the following:

- Questionnaires
- Photographs
- Statements from the insured concerning the boat's maintenance schedule
- The United States Coast Guard Auxiliary's Courtesy Examination (free for boats up to sixty-five feet long)

Educational Objective 4

Compare the property and liability coverage available under homeowners policies with the coverages available under watercraft policies, and evaluate the alternatives available in coverage implementation.

Analyzing Watercraft Coverage

From an underwriting perspective, the specialist should understand the watercraft types, construction, and exposures that have been previously addressed. In applying coverage, horsepower and size often determine the coverage available.

Watercraft insurance has no standard rules, forms, or rates and is usually not subject to state control. Each company might tailor-make coverage according to its own set of underwriting rules and guidelines. However, a few states do require form-and-rate filings for boats of twenty-six feet or less.

Watercraft exposures can be insured in the following five ways:

1. Homeowners policies automatically provide a limited amount of property and liability coverage for certain boats, exposures, and perils.
2. Small outboard motor boats less than sixteen feet in length might be written on an outboard motorboat policy through inland marine departments of property and liability insurance companies.
3. Boats less than twenty-six feet long are usually written on a boatowners insurance policy through an insurer's personal lines department.
4. Boats more than twenty-six feet long are generally referred to as yachts. Yachts are written through the insurer's ocean marine

department or through companies specializing in ocean marine insurance.

5. High-horsepower motorboats and jet skis are usually written through surplus lines companies because their fast speeds make them unacceptable to many insurers.

Watercraft Coverage Provided by the Homeowners Policy

The homeowners policy is often the first place a specialist looks for watercraft coverage placement. Limited coverage is provided for small watercraft, but some important coverage restrictions within the contract should be reviewed carefully. A discussion of those coverages and restrictions follows.

Property Coverage

Exhibit 11-7 is a page of the homeowners contract describing property coverages. Limitations are placed on the value of the watercraft covered. The limitations are noted along with their possible coverage implications.

Watercraft coverage is further limited in the "SECTION I—PERILS INSURED AGAINST" as shown in Exhibit 11-8. This section lists the named perils coverage for personal property.

A watercraft loss will be adjusted on an actual cash value basis unless the replacement cost endorsement has been attached to the policy.

Liability Coverage

Section II of the homeowners policy provides Personal Liability and Medical Payments to Others coverage to some watercraft based on length and engine size. Exhibit 11-9 displays the Section II exclusions from the homeowners policy.

Personal Liability is excluded for "property damage to property rented to, occupied by or in the care of the insured," unless the property damage is caused by fire, smoke, or explosion. Therefore, an insured who negligently crashes a rented jet ski into a power boat, or runs a borrowed sailboat into a dock would not have Personal Liability coverage for damage to the rented jet ski or borrowed sailboat. However, coverage would still be available for the insured's liability to the owner of the damaged powerboat and dock in this example if the insured were operating a covered watercraft.

The "SECTION II—ADDITIONAL COVERAGE" Damage to Property of Others will not pay for property damage arising out of the "ownership, maintenance, or use of. . .watercraft."

An endorsement (WATERCRAFT HO 24 75) is available to extend Section II to watercraft that is not covered because of the size or horsepower of the motors, subject to the general exclusions (racing activities for watercraft other than sailboats are still excluded).

Exhibit 11-7
Watercraft Notations: HO-3 Property Coverages

Section I—Property Coverage

COVERAGE A - Dwelling

We cover:

1. The dwelling on the "residence premises" shown in the Declarations, including structures attached to the dwelling; and

2. Materials and supplies located on or next to the "residence premises" used to construct, alter or repair the dwelling or other structures on the "residence premises."

This coverage does not apply to land, including land on which the dwelling is located.

COVERAGE B - Other Structures

We cover other structures on the "residence premises" set apart from the dwelling by clear space. This includes structures connected to the dwelling by only a fence, utility line, or similar connection.

This coverage does not apply to land, including land on which the other structures are located.

We do not cover other structures:

1. Used in whole or in part for "business"; or

2. Rented or held for rental to any person not a tenant of the dwelling, unless used solely as a private garage.

The limit of liability for this coverage will not be more than 10% of the limit of liability that applies to Coverage A. Use of this coverage does not reduce the Coverage A limit of liability.

COVERAGE C - Personal Property

We cover personal property owned or used by an "insured" while it is anywhere in the world. At your request, we will cover personal property owned by:

1. Others while the property is on the part of the "residence premises" occupied by an "insured";

2. A guest or a "residence employee," while the property is in any residence occupied by an "insured."

Our limit of liability for personal property usually located at an "insured's" residence, other than the "residence premises," is 10% of the limit of liability for Coverage C, or $1,000, whichever is greater. Personal property in a newly acquired principal residence is not subject to this limitation for 30 days from the time you begin to move the property there.

Special Limits of Liability. These limits do not increase the Coverage C limit of liability. The special limit for each numbered category below

is the total limit for each loss for all property in that category.

1. $200 on money, bank notes, bullion, gold other than goldware, silver other than silverware, platinum, coins and medals.

2. $1000 on securities, accounts, deeds, evidences of debt, letters of credit, notes other than bank notes, manuscripts, personal records, passports, tickets and stamps. This dollar limit applies to these categories regardless of the medium (such as paper or computer software) on which the material exists.

    This limit includes the cost to research, replace or restore the information from the lost or damaged material.

3. $1000 on watercraft, including their trailers, furnishings, equipment and outboard engines or motors.

4. $1000 on trailers not used with watercraft.

5. $1000 for loss by theft of jewelry, watches, furs, precious and semi-precious stones.

6. $2000 for loss by theft of firearms.

7. $2500 for loss by theft of silverware, silver-plated ware, goldware, gold-plated ware and pewterware. This includes flatware, hollowware, tea sets, trays and trophies made of or including silver, gold or pewter.

8. $2500 on property, on the "residence premises," used at any time or in any manner for any "business" purpose.

9. $250 on property, away from the "residence premises," used at any time or in any manner for any "business" purpose. However, this limit does not apply to loss to adaptable electronic apparatus as described in Special Limits 10. and 11. below.

10. $1000 for loss to electronic apparatus, while in or upon a motor vehicle or other motorized land conveyance, if the electronic apparatus is equipped to be operated by power from the electrical system of the vehicle or conveyance while retaining its capability of being operated by other sources of power. Electronic apparatus includes:

    a. Accessories or antennas; or

    b. Tapes, wires, records, discs or other media; for use with any electronic apparatus.

> There is a 10% limitation (up to $1,000) for property usually at another residence premises (such as a second home at the beach or lake). This policy only provides $1,000 worth of coverage for watercraft, but this limitation might become important if an insurer has filed its own endorsement allowing an increased limit of coverage for watercraft.

> Only $1,000 coverage is provided for the loss of watercraft. This limit includes all of the engines, equipment, and trailers. There is no standard ISO form to increase this limit. Some insurers have manuscripted and filed endorsements that can be attached to increase the limit. These endorsements should be reviewed individually, especially with regard to the other coverage limitations demonstrated in this contract.

Page 2 of 18   Copyright, Insurance Services Office, Inc., 1990   HO 00 03 04 91

Exhibit 11-8
Watercraft Notations: HO-3 Section I—Perils Insured Against

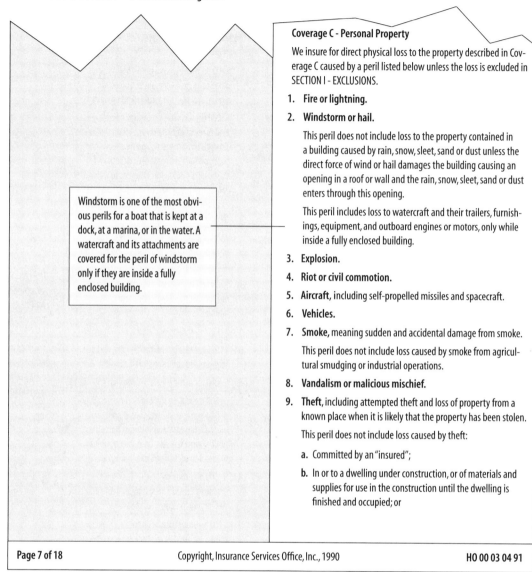

Coverage C - Personal Property

We insure for direct physical loss to the property described in Coverage C caused by a peril listed below unless the loss is excluded in SECTION I - EXCLUSIONS.

1. **Fire or lightning.**

2. **Windstorm or hail.**

   This peril does not include loss to the property contained in a building caused by rain, snow, sleet, sand or dust unless the direct force of wind or hail damages the building causing an opening in a roof or wall and the rain, snow, sleet, sand or dust enters through this opening.

   This peril includes loss to watercraft and their trailers, furnishings, equipment, and outboard engines or motors, only while inside a fully enclosed building.

3. **Explosion.**

4. **Riot or civil commotion.**

5. **Aircraft,** including self-propelled missiles and spacecraft.

6. **Vehicles.**

7. **Smoke,** meaning sudden and accidental damage from smoke.

   This peril does not include loss caused by smoke from agricultural smudging or industrial operations.

8. **Vandalism or malicious mischief.**

9. **Theft,** including attempted theft and loss of property from a known place when it is likely that the property has been stolen.

   This peril does not include loss caused by theft:

   a. Committed by an "insured";

   b. In or to a dwelling under construction, or of materials and supplies for use in the construction until the dwelling is finished and occupied; or

> Windstorm is one of the most obvious perils for a boat that is kept at a dock, at a marina, or in the water. A watercraft and its attachments are covered for the peril of windstorm only if they are inside a fully enclosed building.

Page 7 of 18 — Copyright, Insurance Services Office, Inc., 1990 — HO 00 03 04 91

---

   c. From that part of a "residence premises" rented by an "insured" to other than an "insured."

   This peril does not include loss caused by theft that occurs off the "residence premises" of:

   a. Property while at any other residence owned by, rented to, or occupied by an "insured," except while an "insured" is temporarily living there. Property of a student who is an "insured" is covered while at a residence away from home if the student has been there at any time during the 45 days immediately before the loss;

   b. Watercraft, and their furnishings, equipment and outboard engines or motors; or

   c. Trailers and campers.

> The items that follow are not covered for theft away from the residence premises. Watercraft and attachments are included in this list (b). If the boat is at a dock or on a trailer in a parking lot, no coverage is provided for theft of the boat or items in the boat. Trailers are also subject to this limitation (c).

Page 8 of 18 — Copyright, Insurance Services Office, Inc., 1990 — HO 00 03 04 91

Exhibit 11-9

Watercraft Notations: HO-3 Section II Exclusions

Beyond the ownership or use of a boat, coverage is excluded if insureds entrust an excluded boat to someone. That could occur if an insured lends a boat to a neighbor.

This section is an exception to the Section II Exclusion. Coverage is provided for the watercraft that are described in the remainder of the column.

The insured is covered while using a borrowed or rented inboard or inboard-outdrive of 50 hp or less. An example is a jet ski rented by the insured while on vacation.

If the insured borrows the neighbor's powerboat or jet ski, no horsepower limitation applies for Section II coverage.

Only small-engine outboards are included for coverage. A 25 hp engine is useful for a small fishing boat. These outboards might be owned, rented, or borrowed.

The insured is covered while using a borrowed or rented outboard of any horsepower.

Small-engine watercraft acquired during the policy period are insured if they are declared at the policy inception, reported within 45 days of acquisition, or acquired during the policy period. This extension of coverage ends at policy expiration.

Section II coverages are provided (without limit) for watercraft that is stored. For example, neighborhood children playing in the insured's yard climb onto the powerboat that is trailered and stored there. A child falls from the boat and is injured.

g. Arising out of :

(1) The ownership, maintenance, use, loading or unloading of an excluded watercraft described below;

(2) The entrustment by an "insured" of an excluded watercraft described below to any person; or

(3) Vicarious liability, whether or not statutorily imposed, for the actions of a child or minor using an excluded watercraft described below.

Excluded watercraft are those that are principally designed to be propelled by engine power or electric motor, or are sailing vessels, whether owned by or rented to an "insured." This exclusion does not apply to watercraft:

(1) That are not sailing vessels and are powered by:

(a) Inboard or inboard-outdrive engine or motor power of 50 horsepower or less not owned by an "insured";

(b) Inboard or inboard-outdrive engine or motor power of more than 50 horsepower not owned by or rented to an "insured";

(c) One or more outboard engines or motors with 25 total horsepower or less;

(d) One or more outboard engines or motors with more than 25 total horsepower if the outboard engine or motor is not owned by an "insured";

(e) Outboard engines or motors of more than 25 total horsepower owned by an "insured" if:

(i) You acquire them prior to the policy period; and

(a) You declare them at the policy inception; or

(b) Your intention to insure is reported to us in writing within 45 days after you acquire the outboard engines or motors.

(ii) You acquire them during the policy period.

This coverage applies for the policy period.

(2) That are sailing vessels, with or without auxiliary power:

(a) Less than 26 feet in overall length;

(b) 26 feet or more in overall length, not owned by or rented to an "insured."

(3) That are stored.

Sailboats are limited by length because of additional skill required to sail a boat greater than 26 feet long. The amount of horsepower allowed as auxiliary power is not limited. Section II coverage is provided without limitation if the insured borrows a sailboat.

HO 00 03 04 91	Copyright, Insurance Services Office, Inc., 1990	Page 13 of 18

Wreck removal is a coverage that provides funds to remove the remains of watercraft from the waterways after a loss.

The **United States Longshore and Harbor Workers' Compensation Act** provides essentially the same protection to maritime workers that workers compensation insurance provides to nonmaritime workers.

Homeowners policies do *not* cover some important marine exposures, such as **wreck removal** and the exposures covered by the **United States Longshore and Harbor Workers' Compensation Act**. Those coverages are discussed later in this chapter.

Outboard Motorboat Policy

Traditionally, boats under sixteen feet in length have been insured by outboard motorboat policies covering physical damage to the boat and equipment, including the trailer. A minimum amount of coverage might be provided for property damage to others. Generally, no bodily injury or loss-of-life coverage is provided, because most of these boats are covered for Personal Liability under the homeowners policy. Coverage is provided for named perils or "all-risks" and is usually on an actual cash value basis. Many features contained in boatowners insurance policies addressed later in this chapter apply to the outboard motorboat policy.

Boatowners and Yacht Policies

Generally, most boats are covered under a boatowners policy or a yacht policy, depending on the boat's size and value. Each company has the prerogative to follow its own rules and guidelines for the program into which the boat fits.

Usually, boats under twenty-four to twenty-six feet with outboard motors qualify for boatowners insurance. Sailboats and boats more than twenty-four to twenty-six feet with inboard engines usually qualify for yacht insurance. These coverages are similar to the coverages found in the PAP and include physical damage, bodily injury and property damage liability, medical payments, uninsured boaters, and other optional coverages.

Since boatowners and yacht policies have no standard rules or forms, each company has its own version of the policy. The following are the basic features generally found in most boatowners and yacht policies.

Warranties

Warranties are statements concerning the condition and use of the watercraft to be insured, which are made for the purpose of permitting the underwriter to evaluate a risk. If the statements are found to be false, they could provide a basis for voiding the policy. An **express warranty** is written in the policy. An **implied warranty** is understood rather than written.

Watercraft policies contain express and implied **warranties**. **Express warranties** are printed in the policy. **Implied warranties** apply even though they are not printed in the policy. Warranties appear in marine insurance agreements because the watercraft cannot be observed on the water. Strict compliance with agreements is enforced. Breaching warranties might void the coverage, depending on the severity of the breach.

Pleasure-Use Warranty

The pleasure-use warranty means that the insured will not use the boat for commercial purposes. If the boat is used for charter or transporting persons for a fee, or if it is hired or used for any other purpose in which a fee is charged, it becomes ineligible for personal watercraft insurance.

Some policies also exclude coverage while the watercraft is on exhibition. Watercraft used for other commercial purposes, such as fishing, towing, and hauling cargo, must be written under a commercial watercraft policy.

After the coverage is written, a loss that occurs while the boat is chartered or used for commercial purpose is not covered. Some insurance companies insuring large boats might permit the boat to be covered while chartered. In such cases, a charter endorsement is attached, and additional premium is charged.

Warranty of Seaworthiness

In addition to the pleasure-use warranty in boat and yacht policies written under ocean marine contracts, a warranty of seaworthiness is implied. That means that the insured boat must be in a seaworthy condition. Some policies actually state that the insured must exercise **due diligence** to maintain the boat in a seaworthy condition. If a loss occurs while the boat is not in a seaworthy condition, coverage is void.

Due diligence refers to the level of care that is reasonable, including recognized precautions.

Lay-up Warranty

Some policies require a boat to be laid up and out of commission for a number of months. The rates charged reflect the lay-up periods.

Insurance companies might allow a boat used in warm waters to be navigated year-round. Boats used in cold waters that are subject to the perils of ice damage and strong winter storms must be laid up and out of commission for three to five months out of the year. For example, the lay-up period on the Great Lakes and St. Lawrence River usually extends from November 15 to April 15.

When the boat is subject to a lay-up clause, some companies require that the boat be actually taken out of the water and stored in a safe berth.

Definition of Insured

The definition of the insured typically includes those named on the declarations page, resident relatives of the household, and persons under the age of twenty-one in the insured's care. Other persons or organizations using the boat with the named insured's permission without charge are also covered.

Persons operating marinas, shipyards, sales agencies, charter organization, or similar organizations are not insured. Paid **masters** or **captains** and paid members of a boat crew are also excluded.

The terms **master** and **captain** are used interchangeably. They refer to the person responsible for the navigation, operation, and safety of the watercraft and crew.

Property Covered

The property covered by boatowners and yacht policies usually includes the following:

- In the boatowners policy, the covered property includes the boat described in the policy declarations, including accessories and attached and detached equipment necessary to operate or maintain the boat.

- In the yacht policy, property coverage is referred to as hull coverage. Hull coverage includes the boat described in the policy declarations, including accessories and attached and detached equipment necessary to operate or maintain the boat. Also included are sails; masts; riggings; spars; and fittings for sailboats, dinghies, and other small boats usually carried on deck.

- Boat trailers can be covered if described in the declarations of the boatowners or yacht policies. Some policies automatically include coverage for boat trailers; others show a separate amount applicable to the trailer with an additional premium charge.

- In the boatowners policy, a separate limit might be shown for the motor. In the yacht policy, the amount shown for the boat also includes the value of the motor(s).

Additional Property

The boatowners and yacht policies can include the following additional property coverages:

- Boating equipment, accessories, and other detachable equipment used to operate and maintain the boat owned by others while in the insured's care, custody, and control.

- The insured's and guests' personal property while on the boat, with a limit of $500 to $1,500. The amount can be increased by endorsement.

- Substitute boats up to the limit shown in the policy declarations for the boat, motor, or trailer that has been lost or destroyed, or that is undergoing maintenance, service, or repairs.

- Boats up to twenty-six feet long; and motors and boat trailers that are acquired during the policy period if the new property is reported to the company within a certain time period, usually between fifteen and thirty days after purchase.

Watercraft Deductibles

Small boats are commonly written with a $100 to $250 deductible. Medium to large boats carry a 1 percent deductible of the hull value. The premium can be reduced through higher deductibles (of 2 to 4 percent).

Territory

Boatowners policies usually provide coverage on land, coastal waters, tributaries, inland lakes, and rivers of the United States and Canada. Yacht policies cover watercraft while afloat, ashore, or being transported on a land conveyance in the United States and Canada, including loading and unloading. Some policies require an additional premium to cover the boat's land transportation.

Yacht policies contain a navigation clause on the declarations pages that indicates the waters (navigational area) in which the boat can be used. Most boatowners and yacht policies identify the principal navigation areas as one or more of the following:

- U.S. Atlantic Coast, including Florida
- U.S. Atlantic Coast, excluding Florida
- U.S. Gulf coastal waters
- Chesapeake Bay and tributaries
- U.S. Pacific coastal waters
- Great Lakes and tributaries

If a loss occurs to the boat in waters not listed in the navigation clause, no coverage applies. With prior notice, the insurer might allow the boat to be used outside the navigation area if an endorsement is added and an additional premium is paid.

Some watercraft policies cover boat equipment that is temporarily on land. The coverage amount is usually limited to a small percentage of the amount shown for the hull value on the declarations page.

Perils Covered

Boatowners coverage can be written on either a named perils or an "all-risks" basis. Usually, yacht policies cover "all-risks." The exclusions are generally as follows:

- Wear and tear, gradual deterioration, rust, corrosion, mold, wet or dry rot, marring, denting or scratching, inherent vice, latent or physical defect, insects, animal or marine life, weathering, and dampness of atmosphere.

- Freezing and thawing of ice, unless the insured has taken reasonable care to protect the property. For example, a bubbler (which circulates water) can be installed to keep water from freezing around the boat in icy conditions.

- A mechanical breakdown or faulty manufacturing, unless the loss was caused by fire or explosion.

- Loss that occurs during racing, unless the boat is a sailboat. Some companies eliminate that exclusion with the payment of an additional premium.

- Under some policies, loss caused by electricity other than lightning, unless fire results, and then only for loss caused by the resulting fire.

- Intentional loss caused by an insured.

- War or radioactive contamination.

Liability Coverage

Boatowners liability is usually called **protection and indemnity (P&I)**. Liability or P&I coverage can be compared to bodily injury and property damage liability in the personal auto policy. The insured is covered for damages for bodily injury, loss of life, and property damage for which he or she becomes legally liable through the ownership, maintenance, or use of the insured boat.

Some yacht policies have a collision liability clause, which covers the insured's legal liability as a result of a collision with another boat.

> **Protection and indemnity (P&I)** is a marine coverage that includes bodily injury and property damage liability.

The amount paid under the liability section of the policy is reduced by the amount paid under the collision liability clause. Like the PAP, the liability and P&I coverages include defense costs, claim settlement costs, premiums for bonds, and interest on judgments. Some policies pay up to $50 per day for loss of earnings caused by attending court hearings.

Liability for Wreck Removal

The P&I section of most yacht policies usually covers the insured's legal obligation to remove the boat's wreckage. If the boat is obstructing navigation, the state or federal government places a responsibility on the insured to move it. Costs to raise and remove the boat are included. Some policies also cover bodily injury or property damage resulting from the insured's failure to remove the wreck.

Liability Exclusions

The exclusions commonly found in boatowners and yacht policies are as follows:

- Bodily injury or property damage caused by illegal activity.
- Bodily injury or property damage intentionally caused by an insured.
- Bodily injury covered by the United States Longshore and Harbor Workers' Compensation Act or workers compensation.
- Bodily injury or property damage arising out of transportation of the boat on land. Coverage can be included by paying an additional premium.
- Liability assumed under a contract.
- Liability arising out of water-skiing, parasailing (a type of parachute used in the sport of sailing through the air while being towed by a powerboat), or other airborne or experimental devices. Some policies include liability for water-skiing; others require the payment of an additional premium for this coverage.
- Bodily injury arising out of scuba diving.
- Discharge or escape of pollutants unless it is sudden or accidental. For example, if a fuel tank ruptures as a result of a collision, coverage applies. Some insurers include the cost of cleanup for unintentional oil spills. Fines imposed for oil pollution are not covered.
- Under some policies, punitive damages.
- Under most policies, bodily injury arising out of business pursuits.
- War, insurrection, rebellion, and nuclear perils.

Boatowners and yacht policies do not cover the insured's liability for nonboating activities. For example, no liability coverage exists if the insured's dog bites someone, the insured's child injures another child, or the insured injures someone on the golf course. That lack of liability protection is of special concern for live-aboard insureds who would probably have no protection under a homeowners policy. A boat owner who does not have a homeowners policy must purchase a comprehensive personal liability policy. Further, boat owners need the protection of a personal umbrella policy to cover limits of liability above the limits in their boatowners policy.

Medical Payments Coverage

Medical payments coverage in boatowners and yacht policies is similar to that found in the personal auto policy. Medical payments cover expenses incurred one to three years (depending on the policy) from the date of the injury. Expenses include first aid at the time of the accident; medical, surgical, X-ray, dental, ambulance, hospital, and professional nursing costs; and funeral services.

Medical Payments—Who Is Insured? Medical payments coverage protects the insured, family members, or any occupant while in, upon, boarding, or leaving the insured boat. The following are excluded from medical payments coverage:

- The insured's employees while in the course of employment or while using, maintaining, or repairing the insured's property or doing anything in connection with their work

- Trespassers

- Any person injured in a race or speed test, except in sailboat races

- Anyone covered under any United States Longshore and Harbor Workers' Compensation Act, a workers compensation act, or a nonoccupational disability or occupational disease law

Medical Payments—Coverage Limits The amount shown on the declarations page applies to each person injured as a result of any one accident or series of accidents arising out of the same event. Most policies pay the amount stated on the declarations page regardless of the number of people injured in the same accident.

Other Watercraft Coverages

Other coverages often appear as part of the boatowners or yacht policies.

United States Longshore and Harbor Workers' Compensation Act

Employees engaged in maritime employment who are injured or disabled or who die while working on navigable waters of the United States are entitled to benefits under the United States Longshore and Harbor Workers' Compensation Act and its amendments. The same employees who are injured on land are entitled to compensation under the state workers compensation laws. The following workers are excluded from the United States Longshore and Harbor Workers' Compensation Act:

- Any person engaged by a master to load, unload, or repair any small vessel under eighteen tons net (this equates to a boat approximately thirty feet long).

- A master or crew member of any vessel covered under the Jones Act (an act that controls domestic shipping).

The liability section of the boatowners policy and the P&I section of the yacht policy exclude injury to workers who are covered under any state or federal compensation law or act. Generally, the boatowners and yacht policies include a separate agreement to provide coverage for payments and compensation for which insureds are responsible under the United States Longshore and Harbor Workers' Compensation Act and that arise from the ownership or use of a boat.

Maritime workers who are aboard a boat might suffer injury, disability, or death as a result of their employment. For example, a boat owner employs a maritime worker to load supplies on an eighteen-ton boat. If the worker is injured, he is covered under the United States Longshore and Harbor Workers' Compensation Act. Without that coverage, the insured would have no protection for the responsibility to the injured worker. The chance of a pleasure boat owner hiring such an employee is minimal; therefore, this coverage is provided without an additional premium.

Liability to Paid Crew   Some boatowners and yacht policies providing P&I coverage include the owner's liability for death or injury to paid masters and crew as defined in the Jones Act or under general maritime law. If the yacht employs a master or crew, an additional premium is charged per crew member for that exposure.

Land Transportation   Boatowners and yacht policies can provide hull and liability coverage for land transportation. Coverage applies while the boat is being transported by land conveyance in the continental United States, Canada, or Puerto Rico. Some policies require an endorsement and an additional premium for that coverage.

Personal Effects

Generally, boatowners and yacht policies provide a small amount of coverage for personal property, which can include clothing; scuba and fishing gear; sports equipment; and portable televisions and stereos owned by the named insured, immediate family, and guests. Personal property is covered only while aboard the boat or while being unloaded from the boat. Some policies limit coverage if the boat is laid up for repairs or storage.

Property not covered includes currency, jewelry, furs, china, silver, valuable papers, documents, travelers' checks, antiques, collectibles, computer hardware and software, animals, and photographic equipment.

Personal effects coverage is excess over other insurance. Coverage limits are usually $500 to $1,500 with a $100 deductible.

Boat Trailer

The trailer used for transporting the boat is covered for direct physical loss or damage from any accidental cause. Coverage is provided on a ACV basis. No coverage is provided for wear and tear, gradual deterioration, mechanical or electrical breakdown or failure, corrosion, rust, or inherent vice.

Uninsured Boaters

As in the PAP, coverage is provided for accidental bodily injury incurred if the watercraft is hit by an uninsured owner or operator of another boat who is legally responsible. An uninsured boat is also defined in the policy contract as a hit-and-run boat. Boats owned by government agencies and boats owned or furnished for the insured's regular use are not covered by uninsured boaters insurance.

Commercial Towing and Assistance

If the boat is damaged from an insured peril, the policies generally pay up to $300 for commercial towing to the nearest place at which repairs can be made. Towing includes the delivery of gas, oil, or a battery (excluding the cost of these items) and emergency labor while the boat is on the waterway and away from safe harbor.

Rental Reimbursement

Occasionally, some insurers cover the cost, up to $2,500, to charter or rent a replacement boat similar to the insured boat, if the insured boat is being repaired for covered damage or loss.

Sue and Labor Charges

Coverage might include the reasonable **sue and labor charges** incurred by the insured to prevent damage, injury, or loss of life and to minimize further loss or damage to the boat.

> **Sue and labor charges** are expenses incurred by the insured to take reasonable measures to prevent damage or injury.

Comparing Watercraft Policies

As stated throughout this chapter, except for small boat risks, watercraft insurance is not subject to standard rules and forms. The checklist shown in Exhibit 11-10 can be used as a tool for analyzing the common differences among contracts.

Educational Objective 5
Describe how watercraft policies are monitored and evaluated.

Monitoring and Evaluating Watercraft Policies

Watercraft policies are reviewed as various events trigger the specialist's attention. Some of these events are as follows:

- Watercraft claims are often referred to an underwriter for review. Reviewing a claim requires the same process and questions that are applied in reviewing a new application, with the additional element of an account history to consider. Could the loss have reasonably been prevented through care or maintenance by the insured? What are the circumstances of the loss? Is another loss more likely as a result?

Exhibit 11-10
A Checklist for Watercraft Policy Comparison

Questions to review for each watercraft policy and insurance company the specialist represents.		Company _____ Policy name _____	Company _____ Policy name _____	Company _____ Policy name _____
Navigational Limits	☐ What are the navigational limitations in the policy?			
Property Covered	☐ What is considered boat equipment?			
	☐ What is considered personal effects?			
	☐ Are trailers automatically included?			
	☐ What is the coverage limit for personal effects?			
	☐ Will a loss be settled on an ACV or replacement cost basis?			
	☐ What is the deductible?			
Perils Covered	☐ Is the policy written on a named-perils or "all-risks" basis (and what are the exclusions)?			
	☐ Is land transportation automatically included, or must it be endorsed onto the policy?			
	☐ Is wreck removal covered?			
	☐ Is medical payments coverage provided for the insured, family members, and residents of his or her household?			
	☐ Is uninsured boaters coverage included?			
	☐ Is accidental pollution coverage provided?			

- Watercraft policies are usually diaried for review as boats reach specific ages. As a boat ages, the underwriter selects anniversaries for policy review. A wooden boat might be inspected for proper maintenance and conditioning every two years. A fiberglass boat might be inspected every three years.

Some insurers write watercraft policies as an accommodation to policy-holders who place their homeowners and auto policies with the insurer. These insurers probably have a very small book of watercraft policies.

An insurer that specializes in watercraft policies will have a large book of watercraft policies and will probably monitor those policies according to type of policy and size of watercraft.

Each insurer must review watercraft loss results according to its purpose for writing the accounts. If these policies are written as an accommodation for other lines, the goals and results might be a loss ratio of 100 percent. For a company that writes the accounts as the main line of business, results and profitability are crucial.

Summary

A specialist dealing with personal watercraft must be able to analyze a watercraft submission in order to provide advice to the customer and identify the exposures and hazards. The specialist must then be able to recommend appropriate coverage.

To properly market and underwrite the pleasure boat risk, specialists must understand basic marine terminology and be able to distinguish between the different types of pleasure watercraft. They must also recognize the watercraft exposures, perils, and coverages.

When underwriting watercraft, underwriters must concern themselves with watercraft exposures and hazards and sources of underwriting information that pertain to each insured. Underwriters review information from the following sources in reviewing a watercraft account:

- The application
- The motor vehicle report
- The watercraft survey

Watercraft insurance has no standard rules, forms, or rates and is usually not subject to state control. Each company might tailor-make coverage according to its own set of underwriting rules and guidelines. Watercraft exposures can be insured in the following ways:

- Homeowners policies provide only very limited property coverage and liability coverage for certain boats and exposures.
- Small outboard motor boats less than sixteen feet in length might be written on an outboard motorboat policy through inland marine departments of property and liability insurance companies.
- Boats under twenty-six feet long are usually written on a boatowners insurance policy.
- Boats over twenty-six feet long are generally referred to as yachts. Yachts are written through the insurer's ocean marine department or through companies specializing in ocean marine insurance.
- High-horsepower motorboats and jet skis are usually written through surplus lines companies.

Chapter 12

Educational Objectives

1. List and describe the special exposure and coverage characteristics to consider when underwriting: (pp. 12-3 to 12-19)

   - All-terrain vehicles
   - Antique and classic autos
   - Camping, travel, and utility trailers
   - Customized vans
   - Dune buggies
   - Farm vehicles
   - Golf carts
   - High-value and specialty autos
   - Kit cars
   - Minibikes
   - Mopeds
   - Motorcycles
   - Motor homes
   - Snowmobiles
   - Trail bikes

2. Describe and evaluate special coverages and/or exclusions applicable to recreational or miscellaneous vehicle exposures. (pp. 12-19 to 12-39)

3. Describe the information needed to make an underwriting decision regarding a recreational or miscellaneous vehicle risk, and explain how that information is obtained. (pp. 12-39 to 12-41)

4. Explain and evaluate the alternatives available in implementing coverage for a recreational or miscellaneous vehicle risk. (pp. 12-41 to 12-43)

5. Describe how results of the underwriting decisions regarding recreational and miscellaneous vehicle risks can be monitored and evaluated. (pp. 12-43 to 12-44)

6. Given an application for a recreational or miscellaneous vehicle risk, analyze the exposures and recommend appropriate actions. (Encompasses entire chapter.)

Chapter 12

Other Motor Vehicles: Exposure Analysis and Coverages

Chapters 6 and 7 discussed exposures, hazards, and underwriting of private passenger vehicles. Many other types of specialized vehicles present unique exposures and coverage problems and are subject to particular hazards. The number and variety of these vehicles are expanding with the aging population. Baby boomers have reached a time in their lives when they can afford luxury vehicles, classic cars, touring motorcycles, and all-terrain vehicles (ATVs). Retirees are buying motor homes to explore the country. If retirees live in planned communities, golf carts can meet their local transportation needs. More and more recreational and miscellaneous types of vehicles are finding their way into the garages of American families, and the need for effective insurance coverage for these vehicles is increasing.

The underwriting process for these vehicles should address all of the concerns applicable to drivers when underwriting a private passenger vehicle. In addition, these miscellaneous vehicles create unique exposures based on the type of vehicle being insured and how it is used. Identifying exposures and coverage needs requires additional underwriting information and involves making more decisions.

This chapter will first examine the exposures for the different types of vehicles and then follow with a discussion of coverage. The vehicles described in this chapter can be insured in a number of ways. Some of them are automatically covered by the personal auto policy (PAP). The homeowners policy provides some limited coverage for vehicles that are used on the owner's premises. Other vehicles can be added to the personal auto policy by endorsement or covered by specialty policies. For some vehicles, multiple coverage options are available. Selection of the appropriate coverage is determined by examining the exposures created by the type of vehicle and its use.

Educational Objective 1

List and describe the special exposures and coverage characteristics to consider when underwriting:

- All-terrain vehicles
- Antique and classic autos
- Camping, travel, and utility trailers
- Customized vans
- Dune buggies
- Farm vehicles
- Golf carts
- High-value and specialty autos
- Kit cars
- Minibikes
- Mopeds
- Motorcycles
- Motor homes
- Snowmobiles
- Trail bikes

Underwriting Characteristics of Other Motor Vehicles

Vehicle operators and their driving characteristics are primary underwriting concerns. Accident and traffic violation histories are always principal underwriting criteria. The following sections describe the hazards associated with the special characteristics of each vehicle type and how each vehicle is often used.

All-Terrain Vehicles

All-terrain vehicles (ATVs) are three- or four-wheeled vehicles equipped with balloon tires and designed for off-road use. ATVs can traverse a variety of ground surfaces, including swampy areas, sand, and snow. Such vehicles can usually accommodate the driver and one passenger on saddle seats. The vehicles are usually operated for sport or play, which increases their potential for reckless operation. They usually have a short, narrow wheelbase and handlebar-type steering equipment.

The short, narrow wheelbase of these vehicles makes them particularly susceptible to roll-over and flip-over accidents. The tendency to overturn becomes particularly hazardous because the driver and passengers have virtually no structural protection in the event of such an accident. Since these vehicles are used off-road, often on rough and hilly terrain, the accident potential is greater for them than for private passenger vehicles, as should be the underwriter's concern.

Because ATVs are not subject to registration and inspection, customizing is a common practice among owners of these vehicles, which causes a valuation problem following a loss. Consequently, some insurers write only **stated-value policies** for ATVs.

With vehicles of this type, the underwriter needs to be concerned not only with the past safety record of all drivers but also with the maturity and attitude of the drivers. The safety record of licensed drivers can be determined by checking motor vehicle records. However, the underwriter might have no way of determining whether the unlicensed drivers have responsible, safety-conscious attitudes. Whenever the underwriter determines that an ATV might be operated by a youngster not yet old enough to obtain a driver's license, underwriting concern increases. The overall combination of hazards typically present with an ATV submission makes this one of the least desirable vehicles to underwrite in the miscellaneous private passenger auto category.

Antique and Classic Autos

Antique and classic autos are private passenger vehicles distinguished by limited production, distinctive design features, or quality of workmanship that sets them apart from other vehicles in the private passenger class. Antique vehicles have usually been restored to like-new condition and are not regularly driven on the road. Owners limit their use to exhibitions, parades, and club activities. A vehicle is not eligible for antique status unless it is at least twenty-five years old. Classic autos are more difficult to define with precision. ISO rules define a classic auto as a private passenger auto that is at least ten years old. Classics are usually of special interest to old-car enthusiasts because of limited production, unique design features, or quality of workmanship. A classic auto usually appreciates rather than depreciates if maintained in original condition; replacement parts used for repairs must usually be made with original parts to maintain the vehicle's original condition.

Antique and classic autos are usually insured at a rate considerably below the rates charged for regular private passenger autos. The lower rate is justified, because most insurers will not insure an older vehicle as an antique or classic car unless the vehicle owner agrees to restrict its use to exhibitions, parades, and club activities. Some insurers restrict the use of antique autos to weekend use. These vehicles are generally considered safe risks for liability, medical payments, and uninsured motorists coverage. Antique and classic autos present some concerns about physical damage because of the limited availability of replacement parts, but the restricted use of these vehicles can offset that concern.

A **stated-value policy** is a specialty policy that might be written for vehicles with unusual valuation problems. Because these policies are not standard, each should be reviewed individually. Valuation might be based on an agreed value or stated amount.

Underwriters should be concerned with the garaging facilities provided for antique and classic autos. In most cases, antique or classic car owners protect their cars far better than the average owners of ordinary private passenger cars. Concerns arise whenever an antique or classic vehicle is not provided with indoor garaging because being left outdoors severely increases exposure to weather-related damage and vandalism.

Most insurers provide a PAP with a stated amount endorsement (PP 03 08) on antique and classic vehicles, so the specialist must accurately determine the value of the vehicle at the time it is insured. Obtaining current photos of the vehicle is recommended, and requiring an appraisal from a third party knowledgeable about old car values is simply good business practice. Since the value of antique and classic autos tends to increase over time, the current market value of the insured vehicle should be reviewed periodically, and the value should be adjusted as needed. A stated-value policy might be another coverage option for an antique or classic auto.

Camping, Travel, and Utility Trailers

Most trailers are designed to be pulled behind a private passenger auto, although large travel trailers might be designed with a "gooseneck" hitch for attachment to a **fifth wheel** mounted in the bed of a heavy-duty pickup truck. The expense of the fifth-wheel mounting should be considered in valuing the truck on the PAP. A towing auto must be of sufficient size and power to handle the additional weight, drag, and brake requirements. The trailer's tail and brake lights should be in good working order. Trailer hitches are safest when attached to the frame of the towing vehicle.

A **fifth wheel** is a type of trailer hitch designed for pulling heavy trailers. It resembles a flat metal wheel. The gooseneck hitch from the trailer goes over and connects to the fifth wheel.

Camping Trailers

A camping trailer is a recreational trailer that expands for use as temporary living quarters. When towed behind a private passenger vehicle, the trailer resembles a utility trailer. When in use, the top is raised to provide sleeping quarters and a small dining area for occupants. Plumbing and cooking facilities are not usually included in these trailers.

Camping trailers are relatively light vehicles and usually do not drastically alter the handling characteristics of the vehicle that tows them. However, if a driver has never towed a trailer behind a private passenger auto, even light trailers can present a significant challenge. Towing a trailer creates the following changes in vehicle handling:

- Braking distances are longer.
- A wider turning radius is required.
- Controlling the vehicle on wet, ice-covered, or snow-covered roads becomes more difficult.

Even with a camping trailer, the underwriter should be concerned about the trailer's size and the driver's experience. Geography of the area in which the vehicle will be used might be a concern if the trailer will be towed in hilly or mountainous terrain with winding roads and tight turns. Underwriting is usually not extensive when insuring a camping trailer, particularly when adding a camping trailer to an existing policy for an insured with a good loss history.

Travel Trailers

A travel trailer is constructed of rigid materials and resembles a small mobile home. These trailers can be large (some might be as long as thirty feet) and are equipped with plumbing, cooking, and electrical facilities.

If a trailer being insured is a travel trailer, all of the concerns just mentioned in reference to camping trailers are increased, because travel trailers are typically longer and heavier than camping trailers. The driver's experience with handling such a vehicle is an important factor. An underwriter should be concerned about the towing vehicle's size and power. Is the towing vehicle large enough and powerful enough to handle the travel trailer being towed? Is the hitch attached to the vehicle's frame, or is it merely attached to the rear bumper? Answers to those questions might not be available from the information on the recreational vehicle application. Additional inquiry might be required.

The presence of cooking facilities, heating and air conditioning equipment, and electrical wiring adds hazards that increase with the trailer's age. Requiring photos of the interior of trailers more than ten years old might help the underwriter determine whether a detailed inspection is needed. If both exterior and interior photos are required, a visibly deteriorating exterior and poor housekeeping of the interior might signal a potential morale hazard. Therefore, the interior should be inspected with additional care.

Trailers Used as Living Quarters

An application for a travel trailer that appears to be used as permanent living quarters presents unique underwriting concerns; rates charged for travel trailers normally only anticipate occasional recreational use. Information provided on the application should enable the underwriter to verify that the applicant has other permanent living quarters. Location and protection questions should be asked if a trailer used as temporary living quarters is located away from the insured's residence. A trailer permanently parked near a remote lake or park might be too susceptible to vandalism to be insurable. A trailer used as living quarters by a worker whose job takes him away from home for long periods of time might present increased exposures to vandalism, theft, and fire (from heating and cooking facilities in the trailer).

Trailers Used as Offices

If a travel trailer is used as an office, as a mobile store, or for display purposes, it should not be insured under a recreational vehicle policy. The amount of traffic into and out of the trailer by members of the public creates a potential liability exposure not contemplated by personal lines rates. Commercial coverage should be used for such an exposure.

Trailers Rented to Others

Since travel trailers are fairly expensive, the owner might want to recover some of his or her investment by renting the trailer to others. Insurers differ in their treatment of vehicle rentals. Some simply provide no coverage while the trailer is rented to others. Some do not write insurance for trailers that will be rented. Other insurers allow occasional rentals if insureds notify the insurers in advance and pay an additional premium. The underwriter or producer must know the company's position regarding rentals.

Utility Trailers

Utility trailers come in many designs. Some are designed for hauling specific cargo such as boats, cattle, or horses. Others are simply platforms on wheels for hauling trash or miscellaneous items.

Utility trailers typically present the fewest concerns for underwriters. If trailer size does not cause concern, utility trailers are often insured with little underwriting. The most common concern might be to verify that homemade trailers are safe. A photo is a good way to check that the trailer looks acceptable.

Customized Vans

Private passenger vans have become a popular form of personal transportation. Many such vans are equipped with elaborate customization added by the vehicle manufacturer or by a specialty shop after the vehicle left the manufacturer. Other vans in this category, designed primarily for hauling cargo, have sparsely furnished interiors and limited seating facilities.

The vans discussed in this chapter are private passenger vehicles insured under personal auto policies. Underwriting for these vehicles focuses on the same risk factors that apply to all other autos—driving safety records, age, experience, and vehicle use. These vehicles are discussed separately in this chapter because of a rating problem that was prevalent in the early 1980s. The problem exists today, although to a much lesser degree.

When vans started to become popular as a form of passenger transportation, interiors were relatively plain and the vehicles had few option packages. Manufacturers tended to view them as work vehicles and equipped them accordingly. Specialty shops recognized a trend and began to offer *van conversions*, which turned standard vehicles into luxury passenger vehicles. Vans were often equipped with amenities not available on most luxury automobiles, such as televisions, captain's chairs, state-of-the-art stereo equipment, and food-storage facilities. These conversions added thousands of dollars to the value of the vehicle, making it difficult to accurately establish the vehicle's true value. Van customization reports were developed to help insurers catalogue the options included on a vehicle and to provide a systematic means of determining what the vehicle (with all of its equipment) was worth.

Manufacturers soon followed the trend and began offering passenger vans with a wide array of option packages. Rating these vehicles was much simpler than rating vans converted in specialty shops after manufacture, because underwriters could once again rely on the manufacturer's suggested retail price to rate the vehicle for physical damage coverages. Customized vans are still offered in the automotive marketplace, but they are no longer the difficult rating problem they were in the early 1980s.

Theft of these vehicles might pose a problem in some areas. A large deductible for physical damage coverage might be required to reduce the risk and encourage loss control measures. Underwriters must still be alert to the problem of van conversions and should develop a full listing of optional equipment, with an accurate cost figure for each option, when underwriting a conversion van.

Dune Buggies

Dune buggies are usually small autos that have been stripped down to the engine and bare frame. Some might be equipped with small fiberglass fenders and a **roll bar**. They are usually operated on sand dunes, beaches, and desert terrain but might also be licensed for road use in some states.

A **roll bar** is a device intended to protect vehicle occupants from being crushed if a vehicle overturns. Often made of a heavy metal tube, roll bars should be attached to the vehicle frame and passed over the passenger compartment.

Because dune buggies are vehicles that have been radically modified from their original design, an obvious concern for the underwriter is that most of the safety features built into the vehicle by the manufacturer have been removed. These vehicles are seldom licensed for road use. A photo of the vehicle is particularly helpful to determine the following underwriting factors:

- Existence of a roll bar to protect the occupant during a roll-over or flip-over
- Placement of the gas tank so that is it not exposed to impact

Dune buggies are designed for adventurous operation. Some insurers limit dune buggy writings to existing insureds with proven safety records to help reduce the number of operators who pose extraordinary risk.

Establishing the vehicle's accurate value is difficult. No resources are available to consult, and no large active market exists for these vehicles. The underwriter is often left with settling for a value that seems acceptable. The purchase value or an estimate from a retailer who deals with dune buggies could help.

Farm Vehicles

Pickup trucks and private passenger vehicles used primarily to operate farms and maintain farm premises qualify for farm classification. Flatbed and stake-rack trucks as well as trucks with dual rear wheels might be classified as farm trucks if used in farm operations, but they are typically insured under a commercial policy rather than a personal auto policy.

Some insurers cover farm tractors under an auto liability policy, but they are most commonly insured under a specialty personal lines policy.

Trucks owned by farmers and used to operate farms and maintain farm premises are generally insured at reduced rates, based on the assumption that such vehicles are operated less on public roads than private passenger vehicles are. Reduced rates for farm vehicles are available for both personal and commercial policies. Whether the vehicle should be insured by a personal or commercial policy is usually determined by gross vehicle weight or vehicle load capacity. Often a truck with dual rear wheels is insured as a commercial vehicle regardless of its registered load capacity or gross vehicle weight. The discussion of farm vehicles in this section assumes a four-wheel truck-type vehicle with a load capacity or gross vehicle weight less than the threshold weight, usually 10,000 pounds gross vehicle weight, that separates personal and commercial classifications.

Most insurers acknowledge that nothing inherent in the farm use of a truck makes such use especially hazardous. The underwriter's job in reviewing an application submitted for personal auto insurance at farm class rates is to verify that farm rates apply rather than pleasure or business use personal auto rates. The farm vehicles described in this chapter are private passenger autos by nearly every definition. Farm vehicles are included only because of the special underwriting consideration given to them to verify classification.

Pickup trucks and vans used to operate farms and maintain farm premises are not disqualified for farm use classification simply because they are operated off the farm for personal or pleasure use. The underwriter must decide whether the vehicle's principal use is on the farm. Information provided on the application might not always enable the underwriter to determine principal use. For instance, if the vehicle owner is a farmer who also has a full-time job off the farm, his using a pickup truck to drive to and from work five days a week might disqualify the vehicle for a farm rate even though the vehicle is also used on the farm. Similarly, if a son or daughter regularly drives a truck used on the farm to and from school, farm rates might not apply. Close attention should be given to the driver listed on the application as the principal vehicle operator.

Golf Carts

A golf cart is a small passenger vehicle powered by an electric motor that is run by a battery, or, less frequently, it is powered by a small gasoline engine. Golf carts are low-speed vehicles used mainly on golf courses. In some communities in the Southeast and Southwest, golf carts are licensed for limited use on the roadways of **planned urban developments**.

When the golf cart is used by the owner only on the golf course, the risk of loss is considered to be slight. Premiums for coverage of golf carts under a PAP or recreational vehicle policy are usually modest

A **planned urban development (PUD)** is a preplanned community usually consisting of single and multifamily housing surrounding shops, restaurants, and offices. Motor vehicle use is restricted within a PUD; people there normally walk or ride golf carts.

because of the low risk involved. The only hazards associated with operating golf carts are the possibility of their rolling over if used on hilly golf courses (golf carts have a narrow wheelbase and a fairly high center of gravity) and the possibility of their rolling into a water hazard (a small pond on a golf course).

Golf carts present special hazards when operated on public highways or rights-of-way because of their limited speed capabilities. Except when used on golf courses, the theft potential can be significant.

Underwriting scrutiny varies by company. Some insurers routinely insure golf carts for existing insureds, but other insurers underwrite them carefully because of the roll-over potential and lack of protection for vehicle occupants. If a golf cart is to be operated by youngsters not old enough to be licensed, a conservative underwriting approach might be justified.

High-Value and Specialty Autos

This category mainly consists of expensive sports cars costing more than $100,000 and custom-made cars of very limited production. Also included are hot rods and street rods, which are usually older-model cars that have been modified extensively, often by adding large, powerful engines and by substantially changing the body, frame, and suspension. Very expensive custom paint jobs and extensive chrome accessories are often found on hot rods and street rods.

High-Value Vehicles

High-value imported cars present several problems for underwriters. These vehicles are often sold in relatively low volume in the United States. A Porsche owner in rural Maine might live far from the nearest Porsche dealer. Parts and service for the vehicle could be difficult to obtain. Because of low volume, insurers seldom accumulate enough experience with these vehicles to develop reliable actuarial data to calculate accurate rates. Loss adjustment becomes guess work because claim personnel have few opportunities to develop any expertise with these vehicles. The extremely high value of the vehicle makes theft prevention measures a major concern for the underwriter. If such a vehicle is driven regularly to and from work and parked in an unsecured area during the workday, the vehicle could be susceptible to vandalism or theft. All of these concerns also apply to any high-value, custom-made auto, regardless of where the vehicle was manufactured.

Hot Rods and Street Rods

Although hot rods and street rods are standard or classic cars that have been modified extensively for high speed and fast acceleration, they are still registered and licensed for road use. The extensive nature of the modification these cars have undergone might create safety concerns for the underwriter. Inquiry should be made about the person who modified the vehicle and that person's qualifications. Has the vehicle been thoroughly inspected and certified for safe operation? These vehicles are often finished with expensive paints and lacquers, which could make repairing minor damage extremely expensive. Owners often limit use of these cars to shows, exhibitions, parades, and club activities. The underwriter needs to be particularly concerned about how the vehicle is garaged because of the potential for vandalism, theft, and weather-related damage.

Establishing an accurate value for a hot rod or a street rod poses a problem because the owners typically want to include the cost of the original vehicle plus all parts and labor in the final value. That value is frequently much higher than the market value of the finished vehicle. Finding an impartial expert to appraise the vehicle is often difficult. Many insurers accept these risks only as an accommodation for a valued long-term insured.

Kit Cars

A kit car usually consists of a fiberglass body that can be assembled on the chassis (frame) of a regular production automobile. The body style might resemble a vintage, classic, or antique auto scaled down in size, or it might resemble an exotic sports car. The kit is usually sold to a customer, who then assembles the car. Some kit cars can be purchased already assembled from the manufacturer.

An automobile hobbyist who does not have the funds to invest in a street rod or hot rod might purchase a kit. Assembling the fiberglass body of a kit car on the chassis of a small production-line auto can be a considerable challenge even for a hobbyist with extensive automotive experience. If the owner performed the assembly, the underwriter should be concerned about the condition of the underlying chassis and the quality of the assembly work. In some states, kit cars must undergo thorough inspections before being registered and licensed for road use. If the vehicle has not received such an inspection, an inspection and certification by a qualified mechanic might be a loss control option as well as a valuable source of underwriting information.

If the vehicle is purchased already assembled, the purchase price serves as the current value of the vehicle for rating purposes. If the owner performed the assembly, the vehicle value is normally determined by adding the cost of the kit to the estimated value of the chassis, including a reasonable allowance for the labor involved in assembling the unit. This value should not exceed the cost of a preassembled kit car.

Minibikes

A minibike is a small, low-powered, two-wheeled motorcycle designed for off-road use. Minibikes are usually designed to travel at a top speed of twenty-five miles per hour or less.

Age, experience, and driving attitude (determined by motor vehicle record) are key factors in assessing the risk involved in insuring any motorcycle-type vehicle. Since minibikes are small, low-powered versions of motorcycles and are not licensed for road use, they are often purchased for and ridden by youngsters not yet old enough to be licensed. When the inexperience and immaturity of the vehicle operator are combined with the rough off-road terrain on which these vehicles are often ridden, careful underwriting is mandatory. An added difficulty for underwriters arises from the fact that driving history is not available for unlicensed drivers. An underwriter might be left with no alternative but to evaluate the driving records of the licensed drivers in the household and assume that family members not yet licensed will exhibit similar habits.

Mopeds

Mopeds are light-framed vehicles that more closely resemble a bicycle than a motorcycle. Equipped with a very small engine (two horsepower or less), which is started by pedaling, mopeds can reach speeds of up to thirty-five miles per hour. State laws vary as to how mopeds are treated regarding licensing and registration requirements. They do not normally require licensing and registration to be ridden on public roadways, although this might vary by state. Some states define mopeds in terms of maximum permissible speed (usually twenty or twenty-five miles per hour) or maximum permissible horsepower (usually one or two horsepower). If the capability of the machine exceeds these limits, it must be licensed and operated as a motorcycle.

Regardless of whether they are licensed for road use, mopeds are typically operated on public roadways. With a very small engine and low speed capability, they are not well-suited to operating in traffic. Mopeds usually do not have turn signals or the other required standard features of motorcycles. If licensing is required, safety accessories must usually be added.

Because moped accidents are handled in a manner similar to that of bicycle accidents in many states (no citation is given for a bicycle accident), little reliable statistical data are available to accurately gauge moped accident frequencies. Underwriting done for a moped is similar to the underwriting performed for a motorcycle with emphasis placed on the operator's age, experience, and driving safety record.

Negative underwriting characteristics are often present because of the uncontrolled nature of moped use. Following are some of those negative characteristics:

- Many states do not require a moped to be registered for road use.
- Many states do not require a valid driver's license for operating a moped.
- Drivers might be under the state driving age and unlicensed. An underwriter cannot feasibly verify who is actually operating the moped.

Even if mopeds must be operated only by a licensed driver with a motorcycle license or license endorsement, they present a greater risk than small motorcycles because of their low power and limited speed capability. The underwriter considering a moped application should answer (with as much confidence as possible) the following questions:

- Who will operate the moped?
- How frequently will it be driven?
- Where will it typically be operated?

Coverage is usually obtained under a policy designed for motorcycles or special recreational vehicles policies, which some insurers have developed.

Motorcycles

Most motorcycles are two-wheeled vehicles powered by gasoline engines ranging in size from 250 cubic centimeters to 1,200 cubic centimeters. They are capable of rapid acceleration and very high speeds. Occasionally, a sidecar with a third wheel is attached to a motorcycle to provide space for another passenger. That attachment gives the vehicle additional stability. Motorcycles must be registered and licensed for road use, and a special license or endorsement to a regular driver's license is required to operate the vehicles on public roads.

Motorcycle Types

Motorcycles present a greater risk than private passenger vehicles because of their capability for rapid acceleration and high speeds, and because they present drivers and passengers with virtually no crash protection. Risks vary with the motorcycle's style. Motorcycles are being marketed by distinct demographic categories; different motorcycles have distinctive characteristics, which attract different types of riders. Large touring bikes (or even larger *cruisers*) cost over $15,000, weigh over 1,000 pounds, and have become a status symbol among those in the group aged thirty and older. These big bikes forgo aerodynamic body work to provide comfort.

Touring bikes are built for cross-country adventures and have wide saddles (seats), high handlebars, and more comfortable rider position than other motorcycles. Touring bikers often join groups for socialization, safety, and group travel. One of the largest organizations, the American Motorcycle Association (AMA), sponsors educational courses and legislative activity and provides emergency travel assistance. The AMA encourages safety programs and helmet use. Exhibit 12-1 contains a chart published by the AMA, listing laws and safety requirements by state as well as the available safety programs.

Speed bikes (or sport bikes) are small motorcycles weighing around 500 pounds, which accelerate very quickly and can easily achieve speeds of over 100 miles per hour. These bikes are less likely to attract riders who enjoy touring. Speed bikes are less expensive than touring bikes, so they often attract young riders who seek less expensive (and more exciting) transportation. Extensive vehicle modification might

Exhibit 12-1
Motorcycle Laws By State

AMERICAN MOTORCYCLIST ASSOCIATION

Remember that while other laws vary from state-to-state, all 50 states require a motorcycle operator's license.

The AMA assumes no responsibility for the accuracy of information included in this guide. Every effort has been made to ensure the information is correct at the time of publication.

LEGEND:

- • In effect on designated rural interstate highways
- x required by law
- # available for all eligible applicants
- ■ prohibited to use or possess
- A required if carrying a passenger
- 1 - reflectorization required
- 2 - must have in possession
- 3 - required for novice riders
- 4 - required under age 18
- 5 - required under age 19
- 6 - required under age 21
- 7 - required under age 15 with learner's permit or for one year after obtaining license
- 8 - required for passengers
- 9 - required for instructional permit holders
- 10 - required under age 16
- 11 - required for first-time applicants
- 12 - may waive skills test for successful completion of rider ed
- 13 - may waive knowledge test for successful completion of rider ed
- 14 - required unless equipped with windscreen
- 15 - required unless equipped with windscreen which is 15" or higher above handlebars
- 16 - required at speeds over 35 mph
- 17 - modulating headlight permitted
- 18 - required for vehicles manufactured after 1/1/56
- 19 - required for vehicles manufactured after 4/1/77
- 20 - required for vehicles manufactured during or after 1978
- 21 - required for vehicles manufactured during or after 1980
- 22 - prohibits passengers under age 5
- 23 - prohibits passengers under age 7
- 24 - single earphone only
- 25 - to be used for communication purposes only
- 26 - required by inspection regulations
- 27 - random
- 28 - annual emissions, some areas
- 29 - upon title transfer

MOTORCYCLE LAWS BY STATE (Revised 9/15/95)

State	Safety Helmet	State Funded Rider Ed	Eye Protection	Daytime Use of Headlight	Passenger Seat	Passenger Footrests	Passenger Age Restrictions	Helmet Speakers	Mirror Left (L) Right (R)	Periodic Safety Inspection	Radar Detector	65 mph Speed Limit
Alabama	x	#		17	A	A						•
Alaska	x-4	#-12	x-15	17	A	A			x			•
Arizona	x-4	#-12	x-14	17	A	A			x (L,R)	x-27		
Arkansas	x	#	x	x-17	A	A			x	x		•
California	x	#-6,12	x	x-17,20	A	A		24	x	x-27		•
Colorado	x	#-12	x	17	A	A			x	x-27		•
Connecticut	x-4,9	#-4,12	x-14	x-17,21	A	A			x	x-27		
Delaware	x-1,2,5,9	#-4,12,13	x	17	A	A			x	x		
Florida	x	#-6,12,13	x	x-17	A	A			x	x		•
Georgia	x-1,4	#-12,13	x-14	x-17	A	A			x			
Hawaii	x-4	#	x-14	17	A	A	23	25	x	x		
Idaho	x-4	#-6	x-9	17	A	A						•
Illinois	x-4,9	#-4,12,13	x-4	x-17	A	A			x			•
Indiana	x	#-12		x-17,18	A	A						•
Iowa		#-11,12		x-17,19	A	A						•
Kansas	x-4	#-12	x-14	x-20	A	A			x (L)	x-27		•
Kentucky	x	#-12	x	17	A	A			x	x-28		•
Louisiana	x	#-12	x-14	17	A	A			x (L)	x		•
Maine	x-7	#-11,13	x-14	x	A	A			x	x		•
Maryland	x-1	#-4	x-9,14	17	A	A		24	x (L,R)	x-29		•
Massachusetts	x	#-12	x-14,16	17	A	A		•	x	x-27		
Michigan	x	#-4,12	x-14	17	A	A		24	x	x-27		•
Minnesota	x-4,9	#-4	x-30	x-17	A	A			x			•
Mississippi	x				A	A				x		•
Missouri	x-4	#-12		17	A	A			x			•
Montana	x-4	#-12		x-17	A	A						•
Nebraska	x	#-12,13		17	A	A						•
Nevada	x-4	#-12	x-14	17	A	A			x (L,R)			•
New Hampshire	x-4	#-12	x-14	17	A	A			x	x		•
New Jersey	x-1	#	x-9,14	17	A	A			x	x-27		
New Mexico	x-1,4	#-4,12,13	x-14	x-17	A	A		24	x	x		•
New York	x-1	#-12	x	x-17	A	A			x	x		
North Carolina	x-1,4	#-4,12		17	A	A			x	x		•
North Dakota	x-3,4	#-10	x-14	17	A	A			x			•
Ohio	x-4	#-4	x-14	x-17	A	A			x	x-27		•
Oklahoma	x-4	#		17	A	A			x (L,R)			•
Oregon	x	#-5,12		x-17	A	A			x	x-27		
Pennsylvania	x-3,6,8	#-12,13	x	17	A	A		25	x-19,26	x-27		•
Rhode Island	x-1	#-11,12,13	x		A	A		•	x	x		
South Carolina	x-1,6	#	x-6,14	x-17	A	A			x			•
South Dakota	x-4	#-12,13	x-14	17	A	A			x			•
Tennessee	x	#-12	x-14	x-17	A	A		24	x	x-27		•
Texas	x-4	#-4,12		17	A	A			x	x		•
Utah	x-4	#-12	x-14	17	A	A			x	x		•
Vermont	x-1	#	x-14	17	A	A			x			•
Virginia	x	#-12	x-14	x-17	A	A	22		x (L,R)	x-27		•
Washington	x	#-4	x-14	x-17	A	A			x	x-27		•
West Virginia	x-1	#-12,13	x	x	A	A			x	x	■	
Wisconsin	x-4,9	#-4,12	x-9,15	x-17	A	A			x (L,R)	x-27		•
Wyoming	x-4	#		x-17	A	A			x	x-27		•
District of Columbia	x		x-14	17	A	A			x	x		
Puerto Rico	x		x	x						x	■	•
Canada												

(Remaining information varies by Province.)

indicate to the underwriter that the owner did not purchase the vehicle only to provide an alternate, economical form of transportation.

Motorcycle Accident Profiles

The underwriter must carefully evaluate the age, experience, and driving attitude (from the motor vehicle report) of all potential motorcycle operators. Motorcycle accidents frequently involve operator error. Exhibit 12-2 provides a breakdown of the type and percent of fatal accidents during 1992.

Of the crash types in Exhibit 12-2, running off the road and impact with another vehicle are predominantly the result of errors on the part of the motorcyclist. Both tend to occur more frequently in rural areas and at relatively high speeds. Accidents involving running off the road are often alcohol-related. Review of a motor vehicle record can provide an underwriter with a driver's history of speeding or driving under the influence. These can be helpful indicators of future driving.

Exhibit 12-2
Motorcycle Fatalities—1992

Motorcycle Crash Type	Accident Description	Percent
1. Ran off road	A motorcyclist leaves or strays off the travel lane(s) and overturns or strikes an off-road object (Guardrails, rocks, trees).	41.3
2. Ran traffic control	A vehicle which has a requirement to stop, remain stopped, or yield disregards the requirement and collides with some other vehicle(s).	18.1
3. Oncoming	Vehicles traveling in opposite directions collide.	10.3
4. Left turn oncoming	In the process of making a left turn in front of oncoming traffic, the motorcycle is struck or strikes a vehicle that is coming from the opposite direction and that has the right of way.	8.5
5. Motorcyclist down	A motorcyclist loses control of the vehicle in the roadway and goes down.	7.3
6. Run down	One vehicle "runs down" another vehicle traveling in the same direction, striking it in the road.	3.3
7. Stopped/stopping	A motorcyclist stopped or stopping in a travel lane is hit from the rear.	3.2
8. Road obstacle	A motorcyclist strikes an object in or on the roadway.	2.5
9. Lane change	A vehicle in a travel lane swerves or moves into another same direction travel lane that is already occupied.	1.4
10. Cutoff	A vehicle making a turn, turns in front of a vehicle or into a vehicle traveling in the same direction.	1.2.
11. Other/unknown	Crash types which occur infrequently and miscellaneous crashes	2.4

Reprinted from D.F. Preusser, R.G. Ulmer, and W.A. Leaf, *Accident Analysis and Prevention*, vol. 27, no. 6, Copyright 1995, pp. 845–851, with permission from Elsevier Science Ltd., The Boulevard, Langford Lane, Kidlington OX5 1GB, UK.

Evidence shows that fatally injured motorcycle operators are likely to have alcohol in their blood. In 1992, 48 percent of motorcycle operators killed in crashes tested positive for blood alcohol. By comparison, 29 percent of fatally injured car drivers tested positive for blood alcohol. Alcohol-impaired motorcyclists who are injured in crashes are more likely than nonimpaired motorcyclists to have had prior convictions for speeding, reckless driving, or driving under the influence of alcohol.[1] An underwriter should exercise particular caution in reviewing the motor vehicle report and accident history of the drivers appearing on a motorcycle policy because of the extraordinary increase in hazard caused by the combination of motorcycle operation and alcohol use.

The number of years of experience a person has had with motorcycle riding (or riding a motorcycle of the size currently owned) is another important underwriting factor. New riders are more likely to lose control of a bike than experienced riders are. Conversely, a rider with two or more years' experience has encountered more unusual traffic and travel conditions and is less likely to have an accident. Applications from riders with only motorcycle permits should be reviewed cautiously. Many states issue motorcycle permits without requiring a road or written test specifically for motorcyclists, as long as the driver holds a regular vehicle license.

Motorcycle riders face the same road hazards that vehicle drivers do, but with more serious consequences. Motorcycle impact with a dog or a deer will cause serious injury or fatality to the driver. Helmet use and protective clothing become important safety factors for motorcycle riders. Helmet use will be addressed later in this chapter.

Motorcycle Theft and Vandalism

Motorcycle theft and vandalism are significant problems. This risk is increased with small motorcycles (weighing 500 pounds or less), which can be picked up by several people and loaded into the back of a truck or pushed up a ramp to a waiting truck. However, the possibility of vandalism and theft also still exists for large bikes, and bikes weighing over 1,000 pounds are stolen regularly. Riders who travel with touring groups significantly reduce theft exposures because group members are able to continuously guard members' motorcycles.

Motor Homes

A motor home is a self-propelled vehicle permanently equipped for use as living quarters. Motor homes include plumbing, cooking, and sleeping facilities and might be equipped with heating and air conditioning. They are available in many sizes. Prices can range from $15,000 to $250,000 for an elaborate custom-made unit.

Because of their size, motor homes have handling characteristics that are considerably different from those of private passenger autos. Motor homes have the same size and handling characteristics as trucks; therefore, they can present problems to drivers unfamiliar with their operation. The underwriter should consider the amount of experience the operator has had driving the vehicle being insured or with other motor homes of similar size.

The underwriter should also question whether anything will be towed behind the motor home, such as a boat and trailer or an automobile. Towing an additional unit behind the motor home compounds the handling difficulties and causes control problems if the combined units are operated when roads are slippery.

Motor homes constitute substantial investments for the length of time most are used by the average owner. Many owners are tempted to rent the unit to others when they are not using it themselves. The motor home application should inquire about possible rental to others. The underwriter cannot review all of the use or drivers of the motor home if rental is permitted. The following are some ways in which insurers have chosen to address motor home rentals:

- Underwriting guides exclude motor home rentals.
- Coverage is void if the motor home is rented.
- Rental is permitted if approved by the insurer in advance and an additional premium is paid.

The presence of cooking and heating facilities in a motor home increases the risk of fire damage to the unit. The underwriter might require exterior and interior photos of the motor home to verify the vehicle's overall condition and to better assess the risk of loss from poorly maintained equipment inside the vehicle.

Insurers are sometimes asked to provide motor home coverage for an old bus that has been converted into a motor home. Some insurers refuse to provide coverage for such homemade units, but others might insure them after careful inspection. If such units are accepted, the producer should inspect them thoroughly and take photos of the interior and the exterior of the vehicles. With homemade conversions, the specialist should review not only the quality of conversion work but also the mechanical condition of the bus itself.

Other areas deserving close attention include whether the motor home is used in connection with the insured's business (mobile store or for display purposes) and whether it might be used as permanent living quarters. If either situation exists, the vehicle might not qualify for motor home coverage.

Snowmobiles

Snowmobiles are self-propelled vehicles powered by a gasoline engine and designed for operation on snow-covered terrain. They are propelled by a flexible track located under the rear of the vehicle and steered with handlebars that are attached to skis located on the front of the vehicle. Most snowmobiles can accommodate a driver and one passenger and can reach very high speeds.

Snowmobiles represent a high degree of exposure to loss for the following reasons:

- Inadequate safety features offer little protection for driver or passengers.
- Snow hides many unknown hazards, such as tree stumps, fence wires, gullies, thin ice on lakes and ponds, and potholes, especially at dusk or at night. The majority of snowmobile accidents occur during darker periods (from 4 P.M. to 8 A.M., from November to March). During this time, visibility is reduced, and identifying snow-covered objects is difficult.

- Snowmobiles are often used in races and driven at high speeds.
- The entire vehicle as well as its parts have a high potential of theft.
- Very young operators might drive snowmobiles, because many states do not require a license to operate them.

Acceptability standards are often the same as for private passenger autos, particularly regarding the operators' driving records. Some insurers require that all owned autos be insured by the same insurer to be informed of any driving problems that arise.

The most common hazards associated with snowmobiles are the high speeds that they can reach and the rough off-road terrain on which they are typically operated. Being familiar with operator attitude, driving safety record, and prior experience is crucial to underwriting snowmobiles. The review of accident and violation history for a snowmobile risk is similar to the review done for a private passenger auto risk. The fact that snowmobiles are often driven by young drivers who do not yet have a driver's license creates an additional problem. Attention should be given to the principal driver of each vehicle and to how frequently other members of the insured's household operate the snowmobile.

Snowmobiles that are used for racing competition and high-performance snowmobiles might not be eligible for coverage. The underwriter should be alert to the possibility of their rental to others.

A related exposure is a trailer transporting a snowmobile, which is towed behind an auto. Another exposure to consider is a snowmobile sled, which is a vehicle drawn behind a snowmobile to transport passengers or goods. Underwriters are expected to write such unusual exposures if the snowmobile physical damage coverage is written. An applicant who owns a trailer or sled probably expects coverage to parallel the snowmobile protection, and such equipment is usually written on the same policy. Trailers used to transport snowmobiles are often insured for physical damage coverage on the same policy that insures the snowmobile. Theft of the vehicle and trailer might be a problem in some areas. A large deductible for physical damage coverage might be required to reduce the risk and encourage loss control measures. An additional charge is typically assessed to extend coverage to trailers.

Trail Bikes

A trail bike is a type of motorcycle designed for off-road use. A trail bike is equipped with a rugged suspension system that enables it to be ridden over rough ground at high speeds. If used strictly off-road, trail bikes do not have to be registered for road use. Trail bikes that are not registered for road use are commonly ridden by young drivers not yet licensed. These vehicles are typically driven on rough, challenging terrain. Those two factors mean that the underwriter must carefully examine the attitude of the drivers involved. Close attention should be given to the accident and violation history of all drivers who are licensed.

Since this type of vehicle is commonly used in races and hill-climbing events, underwriters might need to inquire beyond the information provided on the application if they suspect that such activities are occurring. Because trailbikes often involve hazardous operation by young riders, coverage is generally offered only on specialty policies.

As with snowmobiles, carrier trailers might be covered for physical damage under the same policy that insures the trail bike for an additional charge.

Educational Objective 2
Describe and evaluate special coverages and/or exclusions applicable to recreational and miscellaneous vehicles exposures.

Other Motor Vehicle Coverage

A recreational vehicle or specialty vehicle policy is an obvious option for placing coverage for unique vehicles. However, unendorsed homeowners and personal auto policies (PAP) already provide some coverages. Additional coverage can be added to the homeowners and PAP policies by endorsement.

The first step in assisting the insured with coverage placement is to understand the exposures involved. The following questions can help to identify exposures:

- What type of other motor vehicle or recreational vehicle does the insured own?
- Where is the vehicle operated (on the insured's premises, off the premises, on public roads)?
- Is the vehicle subject to motor vehicle registration in the insured's state?
- What is the vehicle's value?
- What coverage such as liability, medical payments, uninsured motorists, or physical damage does the insured require?
- Is there a trailer to tow the vehicle or to be towed by the vehicle?

After those questions are answered, the second step is to review the homeowners and PAP policies and the possible endorsements that can be added to modify the coverage. The information in Exhibit 12-3 provides guidelines to address coverage placement for the exposures. These guidelines will become more apparent as you read the remainder of this section and explore the limitations and exclusions in the standard contracts.

Some vehicles can be covered in more than one way. Many coverage placement decisions will depend on the insurer's underwriting guidelines. A space is left in Exhibit 12-3 for your notes regarding each type of vehicle and the method your company prefers to use in addressing coverage placement.

Exhibit 12-3
Placing Coverage for Other Motor Vehicles

Type of Vehicle	Coverage Options	How does your company prefer to insure this vehicle type?
All-Terrain Vehicles (ATVs)	• The homeowners policy provides liability and physical damage coverage if the vehicle is used to assist the handicapped or to service the premises. • The homeowners policy provides liability coverage if the vehicle is used only on the insured location. • Liability and physical damage can be added to the PAP by adding the Miscellaneous Type Vehicles Endorsement. • A stated value policy can be written through a specialty company (coverage will vary by company).	
Antique and Classic Autos	• The PAP provides liability and physical damage coverages, but the physical damage is based on ACV only. • The physical damage coverage on the PAP can be changed to a stated amount basis by attaching the Coverage for Damage to Your Auto (PP 03 08) endorsement. This form was discussed in Chapter 7. • A stated value policy can be written through a specialty company (coverage will vary by company).	
Camping, Travel, and Utility Trailers	• The PAP covers trailers for liability while they are being towed by an insured vehicle. • The homeowners policy covers trailers for liability while they are not being towed. • The homeowners policy covers physical damage up to $1,000. • Physical damage can be added to the PAP by listing the trailer as an insured vehicle. • Trailers can be added to recreational vehicle policies.	
Customized Vans	• The PAP provides liability and physical damage coverages, but the customizing features and living facilities are excluded for physical damage coverage. • The physical damage coverage for customizing and living facility features can be added to the PAP by attaching the Covered Property Coverage Endorsement (PP 03 07). This form was described in Chapter 7.	
Dune Buggies	• Liability and physical damage can be added to the PAP by adding the Miscellaneous Type Vehicles Endorsement. • Dune buggies can be added to recreational vehicle policies.	

Type of Vehicle	Coverage Options	How does your company prefer to insure this vehicle type?
Farm Vehicles	• The PAP covers farm vehicles without coverage limitation.	
Golf Carts	• The homeowners policy provides liability and physical damage coverage if the vehicle is used to assist the handicapped or to service the premises. • The homeowners policy provides liability coverage when the vehicle is used on the golf course. • Liability and physical damage coverages can be added to the PAP by adding the Miscellaneous Type Vehicles Endorsement. • Golf carts can be added to recreational vehicle policies.	
High-Value and Specialty Autos	• The PAP provides liability and physical damage coverages, but the physical damage coverage is based on ACV only. • The physical damage coverage can be changed to a stated amount basis by attaching the Coverage for Damage to Your Auto (PP 03 08) endorsement. This form was described in Chapter 7.	
Kit Cars	• The PAP provides liability and physical damage coverages, but the physical damage coverage is based on ACV only. • The physical damage coverage can be changed to a stated amount basis by attaching the Coverage for Damage to Your Auto (PP 03 08) endorsement. This form was described in Chapter 7.	
Minibikes	• Minibikes are generally insured under recreational vehicle or specialty policies.	
Mopeds	• Mopeds are generally insured under recreational vehicle or specialty policies.	
Motorcycles	• Liability and physical damage coverage can be added to the PAP by adding the Miscellaneous Type Vehicles Endorsement. • Motorcycles can be insured under specialty policies designed for motorcycles.	
Motor Homes	• Liability and physical damage coverages can be added to the PAP by attaching the Miscellaneous Type Vehicle Endorsement.	

Continued on next page.

Type of Vehicle	Coverage Options	How does your company prefer to insure this vehicle type?
Snowmobiles	• The homeowners policy provides liability and physical damage coverages if the vehicle is used to service the premises. • The homeowners policy provides liability coverage if the vehicle is used only on the insured location. • The homeowners policy can extend liability coverage for off-location use by attaching the Snowmobile Endorsement. • The homeowners policy covers snowmobile trailers for physical damage up to $1,000. • Liability and physical damage coverage can be added to the PAP by attaching the Snowmobile Endorsement.	
Trail Bikes	• Trail bikes are generally insured under recreational vehicle or specialty policies.	

Coverage Provided by a Homeowners Policy

An unendorsed homeowners policy provides some limited coverage for recreational vehicles. This coverage might be adequate for an insured with limited exposures. However, if a specialist relies on these limited coverages when advising an insurance customer, the customer should be thoroughly advised of the limitations.

Homeowners Policy: Section I Coverages for Other Vehicles

Property coverage (Section I) excludes coverage for all motor vehicles. An exception is made for vehicles that are not subject to motor vehicle registration and that are (1) used to service an insured's residence or (2) designed to assist the handicapped. A copy of the applicable pages of a standard homeowners policy is provided in Exhibit 12-4, with notations indicating coverages and exclusions. These exceptions extend coverage to motorized chairs and carts as well as to lawnmowers and similar service equipment. The first of these extensions opens the possibility for coverage to many miscellaneous vehicles. An ATV or snowmobile that an insured uses to check a fence line and pick up trash is a vehicle "used to service an insured's residence" and is therefore covered.

Vehicles that are covered under these definitions have no coverage limitation other than the limit of Coverage C. The Coverage C insured perils provided by the policy apply. Trailers (not used with watercraft) are covered up to $1,000 for the Coverage C insured perils.

Exhibit 12-4
Homeowners Policy: Miscellaneous Vehicle Coverage Notations

COVERAGE A-Dwelling

We cover:

1. The dwelling on the "residence premises" shown in the Declarations, including structures attached to the dwelling; and

2. Materials and supplies located on or next to the "residence premises" used to construct, alter or repair the dwelling or other structures on the "residence premises."

This coverage does not apply to land, including land on which the dwelling is located.

COVERAGE B-Other Structures

We cover other structures on the "residence premises" set apart from the dwelling by clear space. This includes structures connected to the dwelling by only a fence, utility line, or similar connection.

This coverage does not apply to land, including land on which the other structures are located.

We do not cover other structures:

1. Used in whole or in part for "business"; or

2. Rented or held for rental to any person not a tenant of the dwelling, unless used solely as a private garage.

The limit of liability for this coverage will not be more than 10% of the limit of liability that applies to Coverage A. Use of this coverage does not reduce the Coverage A limit of liability.

COVERAGE C-Personal Property

We cover personal property owned or used by an "insured" while it is anywhere in the world. At your request, we will cover personal property owned by:

1. Others while the property is on the part of the "residence premises" occupied by an "insured";

2. A guest or a "residence employee," while the property is in any residence occupied by an "insured."

Our limit of liability for personal property usually located at an "insured's" residence, other than the "residence premises," is 10% of the limit of liability for Coverage C, or $1000, whichever is greater. Personal property in a newly acquired principal residence is not subject to this limitation of the 30 days from the time you begin to move the property there.

Special Limits of Liability. These limits do not increase the Coverage C limit of liability. The special limit for each numbered category below

is the total limit for each loss for all property in that category.

1. $200 on money, bank notes, bullion, gold other than goldware, silver other than silverware, platinum, coins, and medals.

2. $1000 on securities, accounts, deeds, evidences of debt, letters of credit, notes other than bank notes, manuscripts, personal records, passports, tickets and stamps. This dollar limit applies to these categories regardless of the medium (such as paper or computer software) on which the material exists.

   This limit includes the cost to research, replace or restore the information from the lost or damaged material.

3. $1000 on watercraft, including their trailers, furnishings, equipment and outboard engines or motors.

4. $1000 on trailers not used with watercraft.

5. $1000 for loss by theft of jewelry, watches, furs, precious and semi-precious stones.

6. $2000 for loss by theft of firearms.

7. $2500 for loss by theft of silverware, silver-plated ware, goldware, gold-plated ware and pewterware. This includes flatware, hollow-ware, tea sets, trays and trophies made of or including silver, gold or pewter.

8. $2500 on property, on the "residence premises." Used at any time or in any manner for any "business" purpose.

9. $250 on property, away from the "residence premises," used at any time or in any manner for any "business" purpose. However, this limit does not apply to loss to adaptable electronic apparatus as described in Special limits 10. and 11. below.

10. $1000 for loss to electronic apparatus, while in or upon a motor vehicle or other motorized land conveyance, if the electronic apparatus is equipped to be operated by power from the electrical system of the vehicle or conveyance while retaining its capability of being operated by other sources of power. Electronic apparatus includes:

    a. Accessories or antennas; or

    b. Tapes, wires, records, disks or other media; for use with any electronic apparatus.

> Trailers such as those used for snowmobiles and motorcycles are covered up to $1,000. Only Coverage C perils are covered.

> Any vehicle covered by the homeowners policy is covered without territory limit up to the coverage C dollar limit. Coverage is limited to the Coverage C named perils.

HO 00 03 04 91

Continued on next page.

11. $1000 for loss to electronic apparatus, while not in or upon a motor vehicle or other motorized land conveyance, if the electronic apparatus:

   a. Is equipped to be operated by power from the electrical system of the vehicle or conveyance while retaining its capability of being operated by other sources of power;

   b. Is away from the "residence premises"; and

   c. Is used at any time or in any manner for any "business" purpose.

Electronic apparatus includes:

a. Accessories and antennas; or

b. Tapes, wires, records, discs or other media; for use with any electronic apparatus.

Property Not covered. We do not cover:

1. Articles separately described and specifically insured in this or other insurance;

2. Animals, birds, or fish;

3. Motor vehicles or all other motorized land conveyances. This includes:

   a. Their equipment and accessories; or

   b. Electronic apparatus that is designed to be operated solely by use of the power from the electrical system of motor vehicles or all other motorized land conveyances. Electronic apparatus includes:

     (1) Accessories or antennas; or

     (2) Tapes, wires, records, disks or other media; for use with any electronic apparatus.

     The exclusion of property described in **3.a.** and **3.b.** above applies only while the property is in or upon the vehicle or conveyance.

We do cover vehicles or conveyances not subject to motor vehicle registration which are:

   a. Used to service an "insured's" residence; or

   b. Designed for assisting the handicapped;

4. Aircraft and parts. Aircraft means any contrivance used or designed for flight, except model or hobby aircraft not used or designed to carry people or cargo;

5. Property of roomers, boarders and other tenants, except property of roomers and boarders related to an "insured";

6. Property in an apartment regularly rented or held for rental to others by an "insured," except as provided in Additional Coverages **10.**;

7. Property rented or held for rental to others off the "residence premises";

> Property coverage is not provided for motor vehicles unless:
>
> - The vehicle is not subject to registration
> - It is used to service a residence
> - It is used to assist the handicapped
>
> Therefore, a powered wheelchair would be covered, as would a riding lawnmower. An ATV or a snowmobile would also be covered if it is used to service or maintain a residence.

---

8. "Business" data, including such data stored in:

   a. Books of account, drawings or other paper records; or

   b. Electronic data processing tapes, wire, records, disks or other software media;

however, we do cover the cost of blank recording or storage media, and of pre-recorded computer programs available on the retail market; or

9. Credit cards or fund transfer cards except as provided in Additional Coverages **6.**

COVERAGE D-Loss Of Use

The limit of liability for Coverage D is the total limit for all the coverages that follow.

1. If a loss covered under this Section makes that part of the "residence premises" where you reside not fit to live in, we cover, at your choice, either of the following. However, if the "residence premises" is not your principal place of residence, we will not provide the option under paragraph **b.** below.

   a. **Additional Living Expense,** meaning any necessary increase in living expenses incurred by you so that your household can maintain its normal standard of living; or

   b. **Fair Rental Value,** meaning the fair rental value of that part of the "residence premises" where you reside less any expenses that do not continue while the premises is not fit to live in.

Payment under **a.** or **b.** will be for the shortest time required to repair or replace the damage or, if you permanently relocate, the shortest time required for your household to settle elsewhere.

2. If a loss covered under this Section makes that part of the "residence premises" rented to others or held for rental by you not fit to live in, we cover the:

Fair Rental Value, meaning the fair rental value of that part of the "residence premises" rented to others or held for rental by you less any expenses that do not continue while the premises is not fit to live in.

Payment will be for the shortest time required to repair or replace that part of the premises rented or held for rental.

3. If a civil authority prohibits you from use of the "residence premises" as a result of direct damage to neighboring premises by a Peril Insured Against in this policy, we cover the Additional Living Expenses and Fair Rental Value loss as provided under **1.** and **2.** above for no more than two weeks.

Homeowners Policy: Section II Coverages for Other Vehicles

Exhibit 12-5 provides a copy of the Personal Liability and Medical Payments to Others coverage (Section II) of the HO-3 policy. As noted in this exhibit, coverage is excluded for motor vehicles with the following exceptions:

- Trailers that are not being towed are covered. For example, Section II coverage is provided for a camping trailer that has been disconnected from a vehicle.

- Recreational vehicles are covered if they are owned by the insured and used on the insured location. An insured who uses an ATV or a snowmobile on his or her own vacant land is covered if an injury occurs to someone else during that use.

- Insureds are protected when using recreational vehicles they do not own, without limitation to location. Coverage is also provided to an insured's child who rides a neighbor's trail bike (in the neighbor's yard) and causes injury or damage.

- Golf carts are covered while they are on a golf course.

- The handicapped-assisting vehicles and service vehicles covered under Section I are also covered under Section II.

Homeowners Policy: Endorsements for Other Vehicles

Insurers might develop their own endorsements to provide coverage for other vehicles under the homeowners policies. An insurer that is targeting homeowners policy sales to retirees in communities where golf carts are used for local transportation might design an endorsement that extends property damage and liability to golf carts used by the policyholders within the community.

The Snowmobile endorsement shown in Exhibit 12-6 is a standard form that extends coverage under the homeowners policy for these recreational vehicles. This endorsement extends coverage only for Personal Liability and Medical Payments to Others (Section II) provided by the homeowners policy, while the snowmobile is off the insured location.

Coverage Provided by a Personal Auto Policy (PAP)

The unendorsed PAP contains many exclusions for recreational or miscellaneous-type vehicles addressed in this chapter. Excerpts from the contract with notations regarding these vehicles are provided in Exhibit 12-7. (Note that the PAP contract pages shown in this exhibit do not show consecutive policy pages.)

PAP: Liability Coverage for Other Vehicles

Liability coverage provided by the PAP covers *any person using "your covered auto."* However, the word *auto* is not defined in the PAP. This has led to some confusion regarding coverage provided for such recreational vehicles as dune buggies; some courts have viewed such

Exhibit 12-5
Homeowners Policy: Section II Exclusions

Coverage *is excluded* for motor vehicles
- Owned
- Used
- Rented
- Entrusted to others

with exceptions listed below.

Coverage *is provided* for stationary trailers such as travel and camping trailers.

Coverage *is provided* for motorized vehicles not subject to registration if:
- The insured rents or borrows them
- The insured owns them and they are on the insured location (such as an ATV the insured uses only on the premises)

Coverage *is provided* for a golf cart only on a golf course.

Coverage *is provided* for vehicles not subject to registration that are:
- Used to service the residence (such as a lawnmower and an ATV used to check and repair fences)
- Designed to assist the handicapped (such as a motorized wheelchair)
- In storage (such as an antique auto on blocks in the garage)

c. Arising out of the rental or holding for rental of any part of any premises by an "insured." This exclusion does not apply to the rental or holding for rental of an "insured location":

(1) On an occasional basis if used only as a residence;

(2) In part for use only as a residence, unless a single family unit is intended for use by the occupying family to lodge more than two roomers or boarders; or

(3) In part, as an office, school, studio or private garage;

d. Arising out of the rendering of or failure to render professional services;

e. Arising out of a premises:

(1) Owned by an "insured",

(2) Rented to an "insured"; or

(3) Rented to others by an "insured"; that is not an "insured location";

f. Arising out of:

(1) The ownership, maintenance, use, loading or unloading of motor vehicles or all other motorized land conveyances, including trailers, owned or operated by or rented or loaned to an "insured";

(2) The entrustment by an "insured" of a motor vehicle or any other motorized land conveyance to any person; or

(3) Vicarious liability, whether or not statutorily imposed, for the actions of a child or minor using a conveyance excluded in paragraph (1) or (2) above.

This exclusion does not apply to:

(1) A trailer not towed by or carried on a motorized land conveyance.

(2) A motorized land conveyance designed for recreational use off public roads, not subject to motor vehicle registration and:

(a) Not owned by an "insured"; or

(b) Owned by an "insured" and on an "insured location";

(3) A motorized golf cart when used to play golf on a golf course;

(4) A vehicle or conveyance not subject to motor vehicle registration which is:

(a) Used to service an "insured's" residence;

(b) Designed for assisting the handicapped; or

(c) In dead storage on an "insured location";

g. Arising out of:

(1) The ownership, maintenance, use, loading or unloading of an excluded watercraft described below;

(2) The entrustment by an "insured" of an excluded watercraft described below to any person; or

(3) Vicarious liability, whether or not statutorily imposed, for the actions of a child or minor using an excluded watercraft described below.

Excluded watercraft are those that are principally designed to be propelled by engine power or electric motor, or are sailing vessels, whether owned by or rented to an "insured." This exclusion does not apply to watercraft:

(1) That are not sailing vessels and are powered by:

(a) Inboard or inboard-outdrive engine or motor power of 50 horsepower or less not owned by an "insured";

(b) Inboard or inboard-outdrive engine or motor power of more than 50 horsepower not owned by or rented to an "insured";

(c) One or more outboard engines or motors with 25 total horsepower or less;

(d) One or more outboard engines or motors with more than 25 total horsepower if the outboard engine or motor is not owned by an "insured";

(e) Outboard engines or motors of more than 25 total horsepower owned by an "insured" if:

(i) You acquire them prior to the policy period; and

(a) You declare them at policy inception; or

(b) Your intention to insure is reported to us in writing within 45 days after you acquire the outboard engines or motors.

(ii) You acquire them during the policy period.

(2) That are sailing vessels, with or without auxiliary power:

(a) Less than 26 feet in overall length:

(b) 26 feet or more in overall length, not owned by or rented to an "insured."

Exhibit 12-6
Homeowners—Snowmobile Endorsement

POLICY NUMBER:	**HOMEOWNERS** **HO 24 64 12 94**

THIS ENDORSEMENT CHANGES THE POLICY. PLEASE READ IT CAREFULLY.

SNOWMOBILE

SECTION II

For an additional premium, Coverage E-Personal Liability and Coverage F-Medical Payments to Others apply to "bodily injury" or "property damage" arising out of the ownership, maintenance, use, operation, loading or unloading, of a snowmobile, described below, by an "insured," while off an "insured location."

Make or Model*	Serial or Motor Number*
1.	
2.	
3.	

With respect to these snowmobiles, the definition of "insured" includes any person or organization legally responsible for a snowmobile owned by an "insured," but does not include a person or organization using or having custody or possession of the snowmobile without the permission of the owner.

This insurance does not apply:

a. To any snowmobile subject to motor vehicle registration;

b. While any snowmobile is used to carry persons for a charge;

c. While any snowmobile is used for "business" purposes;

d. While any snowmobile is rented to others; or

e. While any snowmobile is being operated in any prearranged or organized race, speed contest or other competition.

*Entries may be left blank if shown elsewhere in this policy for this coverage.

All other provisions of this policy apply.

HO 24 64 12 94	Copyright, Insurance Services Office, Inc., 1994	Page 1 of 1

> This endorsement only extends SECTION II coverage; SECTION I coverage remains unchanged.

> The homeowners policy automatically provides SECTION II coverages on the insured premises. This endorsement provides coverage off the insured premises.

> This coverage will not apply to snowmobiles that are:
> - Subject to registration
> - Hired, rented, or used in business
> - Used in races or contests

recreational vehicles as autos, although others have not. When in doubt regarding coverage, the specialist should err on the side of caution and specifically insure a vehicle under the Miscellaneous Type Vehicle Endorsement or a recreational vehicle policy.

Any trailer the named insured or spouse owns automatically becomes "*your covered auto*" within the PAP; therefore, liability coverage is extended under the PAP to trailers.

Coverage is specifically excluded for the ownership or use of vehicles with fewer than four wheels (such as motorcycles and trail bikes) and vehicles that are designed mainly for use off public roads (such as snowmobiles and ATVs). Coverage is provided if these vehicles are used in a medical emergency.

PAP: Physical Damage Coverage for Other Vehicles

Coverages and exclusions regarding miscellaneous and recreational vehicles are noted in Exhibit 12-8.

Exhibit 12-7
PAP: Miscellaneous Vehicle Liability Coverage Notations

PERSONAL AUTO POLICY
AGREEMENT
In return for payment of the premium and subject to all the terms of this policy, we agree with you as follows:
DEFINITIONS

A. Throughout this policy, "you" and "your" refer to:

 1. The "named insured" shown in the Declarations; and

 2. The spouse if a resident of the same household.

B. "We", "us" and "our" refer to the Company providing this insurance.

C. For purposes of this policy, a private passenger type auto shall be deemed to be owned by a person if leased:

 1. Under a written agreement to that person; and

 2. For a continuous period of a least 6 months.

Other words and phrases are defined. They are in quotation marks when used.

D. "Bodily injury" means bodily harm, sickness or disease, including death that results.

E. "Business" includes trade, profession or occupation.

F. "Family member" means a person related to you by blood, marriage or adoption who is a resident of your household. This includes a ward or foster child.

G. "Occupying" means in, upon, getting in, on, out or off.

H. "Property damage" means physical injury to, destruction of or loss of use of tangible property.

I. "Trailer" means a vehicle designed to be pulled by a:

 1. Private passenger auto; or

 2. Pickup or van.

 It also means a farm wagon or farm implement while towed by a vehicle listed in **1.** or **2.** above.

J. "Your covered auto" means:

 1. Any vehicle shown in the Declarations.

 2. Any of the following types of vehicles on the date you become the owner:

 a. A private passenger auto; or

b. A pickup or van that:

 (1) Has Gross Vehicle Weight of less than 10,000 lbs.; and

 (2) Is not used for the delivery or transportation of goods and materials unless such use is:

 (a) Incidental to your "business" of installing, maintaining or repairing furnishings or equipment; or

 (b) For farming or ranching.

This provision (**J.2.**) applies only if:

 a. You acquire the vehicle during the policy period;

 b. You ask us to insure it within 30 days after you become the owner; and

 c. With respect to a pickup or van no other insurance policy provides coverage for that vehicle.

If the vehicle you acquire replaces one shown in the Declarations, it will have the same coverage as the vehicle it replaced. You must ask us to insure a replacement vehicle within 30 days only if you wish to add or continue Coverage for Damage to Your Auto.

If the vehicle you acquire is in addition to any shown in the Declarations, it will have the broadest coverage we now provide for any vehicle shown in the Declarations.

 3. Any "trailer" you own.

 4. Any auto or "trailer" you do not own while used as a temporary substitute for any other vehicle described in this definition which is out of normal use because of its:

a. Breakdown;	d. Loss; or
b. Repair;	e. Destruction.
c. Servicing;	

This provision (**J.4.**) does not apply to Coverage for Damage to Your Auto.

> The term "auto" has not been defined, which has caused some confusion about miscellaneous vehicles. If any doubt exists, the vehicle should be covered by a Miscellaneous Type Vehicle Endorsement or a recreational vehicle policy.

> Trailers owned by the insured are automatically "covered autos."
>
> Trailers towed by an insured auto automatically assume the liability coverage of the towing vehicle.
>
> Physical damage only applies if it is listed on the declarations page and a premium is charged for other than collision and collision coverages.

PP 00 01 06 94   Copyright, Insurance Services Office, Inc., 1994   Page 1 of 11

PAP: Liability Coverage Exclusions

7. Maintaining or using any vehicle while that "insured" is employed or otherwise engaged in any "business" other than farming or ranching) not described in exclusion **A.6.**

   This exclusion (**A.7.**) does not apply to the maintenance or use of a:

   a. Private passenger auto;

   b. Pickup or van that:

      (1) You own; or

      (2) You do not own while used as a temporary substitute for "your covered auto" which is out of normal use because of its:

         (a) Breakdown;   (d) Loss; or

         (b) Repair;   (e) Destruction; of

         (c) Servicing;

   c. "Trailer" used with a vehicle described in a. or b. above.

8. Using a vehicle without a reasonable belief that that "insured" is entitled to do so.

9. For "bodily injury" or "property damage" for which that "insured":

   a. Is an insured under a nuclear energy liability policy; or

   b. Would be an insured under a nuclear energy liability policy but for its termination upon exhaustion of its limit of liability.

   A nuclear energy liability policy is a policy issued by any of the following or their successors:

   a. American Nuclear Insurers;

   b. Mutual Atomic Energy Liability Underwriters; or

   c. Nuclear Insurance Association of Canada.

B. We do not provide Liability coverage for the ownership, maintenance or use of:

   1. Any vehicle which:

      a. Has fewer than four wheels; or

      b. Is designed mainly for use off public roads. This exclusion (**B.1.**) does not apply:

         a. While such vehicle is being used by an "insured" in a medical emergency; or

      b. To any "trailer".

   2. Any vehicle, other than "your covered auto", which is:

      a. Owned by you; or

      b. Furnished or available for your regular use.

   3. Any vehicle, other than "your covered auto" which is:

      a. Owned by any "family member"; or

      b. Furnished or available for the regular use of any "family member".

      However, this exclusion (**B.3.**) does not apply to you while you are maintaining or "occupying" any vehicle which is:

      a. Owned by a "family member"; or

      b. Furnished or available for the regular use of a "family member".

   4. Any vehicle, located inside a facility designed for racing, for the purpose of:

      a. Competing in; or

      b. Practicing or preparing for;

         any prearranged or organized racing or speed contest.

LIMIT OF LIABILITY

A. The limit of liability shown in the Declarations for this coverage is our maximum limit of liability for all damages resulting from any one auto accident. This is the most we will pay regardless of the number of:

   1. "Insureds";

   2. Claims made;

   3. Vehicles or premiums shown in the Declarations; or

   4. Vehicles involved in the auto accident.

B. We will apply the limit of liability to provide any separate limits required by law for bodily injury and property damage liability. However, this provision (**B.**) will not change our total limit of liability.

C. No one will be entitled to receive duplicate payments for the same elements of loss under this coverage and:

   1. Part B or Part C of this policy; or

   2. Any Underinsured Motorists Coverage provided by this policy.

Liability coverage is excluded for vehicles with fewer than four wheels or designed for off-road use. An exception is made for:

- Use in a medical emergency

- Any trailer (a motorcycle is excluded, but the trailer used to transport the motorcycle is still covered for liability)

Exhibit 12-8

PAP: Miscellaneous Vehicle Physical Damage Coverage Notations

PAP: Part D—Coverage for Damage to Your Auto (Exclusions)

e.   Insurrection; or

f.   Rebellion or revolution.

4.   Loss to:

a.   Any electronic equipment designed for the reproduction of sound, including, but not limited to:

   (1)   Radios and stereos;

   (2)   Tape decks; or

   (3)   Compact disc players;

b.   Any other electronic equipment that receives or
transmits audio, visual or data signals, including, but
not limited to:

   (1)   Citizens band radios;

   (2)   Telephones;

   (3)   Two-way mobile radios;

   (4)   Scanning monitor receivers;

   (5)   Television monitor receivers;

   (6)   Video cassette recorders; or

   (7)   Audio cassette recorders; or

   (8)   Personal computers;

c.   Tapes, records, disks, or other media used with equipment described in **a.** or **b.**; or

d.   Any other accessories used with equipment
described in **a.** or **b.**

This exclusion (**4.**) does not apply to:

a.   Equipment designed solely for the reproduction of
sound and accessories used with such equipment,
provided:

   (1)   The equipment is permanently installed in "your
covered auto" or any "non-owned auto"; or

   (2)   The equipment is:

      (a)   Removable from a housing unit which is
permanently installed in the auto;

      (b)   Designed to be solely operated by use of the
power from the auto's electrical system; and

      (c)   In or upon "your covered auto" or any "non-
owned auto";

         at the time of the loss.

b.   Any other electronic equipment that is:

   (1)   Necessary for the normal operation of the
auto or the monitoring of the auto's operating
systems; or

   (2)   An integral part of the same unit housing any
sound reproducing equipment described in **a.**
and permanently installed in the opening of
the dash or console of "your covered auto" or
any "non-owned auto" normally used by the
manufacturer for installation of a radio.

5.   A total loss to "your covered auto" or any "non-owned
auto" due to destruction or confiscation by governmental or civil authorities.

   This exclusion (**5.**) does not apply to the interests of Loss
Payees in "your covered auto".

6.   Loss to a camper body or "trailer" you own which is not
shown in the Declarations. This exclusion (**6.**) does not
apply to a camper body or "trailer" you:

a.   Acquire during the policy period; and

b.   Ask us to insure within 30 days after you become
the owner.

> Truck campers
> and trailers can be
> covered for physical
> damage under the
> PAP if they are listed
> on the Declaration
> page for coverages.

7.   Loss to any "non-owned auto" when used by you or any
"family member" without a reasonable belief that you
or that "family member" are entitled to do so.

8.   Loss to:

a.   Awnings or cabanas; or

b.   Equipment designed to create additional living
facilities.

> Losses to living
> facilities, awnings, or
> cabanas attached to
> a customized van are
> excluded. Coverage
> can be bought back
> by endorsement.

9.   Loss to equipment designed or used for the detection or
location of radar or laser.

10.   Loss to any custom furnishings or equipment in or upon
any pickup or van. Custom furnishings or equipment
include but are not limited to:

a.   Special carpeting and insulation, furniture or bars;

b.   Facilities for cooking and sleeping;

c.   Height-extending roofs; or

d.   Custom murals, paintings or other decals or
graphics.

> Customizing equip-
> ment for vans and
> pickups is excluded.
> The list provided is
> not limiting; other
> similar items are also
> excluded.

11.   Loss to any "non-owned auto" being maintained or used
by any person while employed or otherwise engaged in
the "business" of:

a.   Selling;   d.   Storing; or

b.   Repairing;   e.   Parking

c.   Servicing;

vehicles designed for use on public highways. This
includes road testing and delivery.

12.   Loss to any "non-owned auto" being maintained or used
by any person while employed or otherwise engaged
in any "business" not described in exclusion **11.** This
exclusion (**12.**) does not apply to the maintenance or
use by you or any "family member" of a "non-owned
auto" which is a private passenger auto or "trailer".

13.   Loss to "your covered auto" or any "non-owned auto",
located inside a facility designed for racing, for the
purpose of:

a.   Competing in; or

b.   Practicing or preparing for; any prearranged or
organized racing or speed contest.

         PP 00 01 06 94

PAP: Part D—Coverage for Damage to Your Auto—continued

14. Loss to, or loss of use of, a "non-owned auto" rented by:

    a. You; or

    b. Any "family member";

        if a rental vehicle company is precluded from recovering such loss or loss of use, from you or that "family member", pursuant to the provisions of any applicable rental agreement or state law.

LIMIT OF LIABILITY

> **Physical Damage Coverage is limited to ACV (or repairs). Any vehicle that might have a value greater than average for its age and type (an antique or a classic) should be changed to stated amount by endorsement.**

A. Our limit of liability for loss will be the lesser of the:

    1. Actual cash value of the stolen or damaged property;

    2. Amount necessary to repair or replace the property with other property of like kind and quality.

    However, the most we will pay for loss to any "non-owned auto" which is a trailer is $500.

B. An adjustment for depreciation and physical condition will be made in determining actual cash value in the event of a total loss.

C. If a repair or replacement results in better than like kind or quality, we will not pay for the amount of the betterment.

PAYMENT OF LOSS

We may pay for loss in money or repair or replace the damaged or stolen property.

We may, at our expense, return any stolen property to:

    1. You; or

    2. The address shown in this policy.

If we return stolen property we will pay for any damage resulting from the theft. We may keep all or part of the property at an agreed or appraised value.

If we pay for loss in money, our payment will include the applicable sales tax of the damaged or stolen property.

NO BENEFIT TO BAILEE

This insurance shall not directly or indirectly benefit any carrier or other bailee for hire.

OTHER SOURCES OF RECOVERY

If other sources of recovery also cover the loss, we will pay only our share of the loss. Our share is the proportion that our limit of liability bears to the total of all applicable limits. However, any insurance we provide with respect to a "non-owned auto" shall be excess over any other collectible source of recovery including, but not limited to:

    1. Any coverage provided by the owner of the "non-owned auto";

    2. Any other applicable physical damage insurance;

    3. Any other source of recovery applicable to the loss.

APPRAISAL

A. If we and you do not agree on the amount of loss, either may demand an appraisal of the loss. In this event, each party will select a competent appraiser. The two appraisers will select an umpire. The appraisers will state separately the actual cash value and the amount of loss. If they fail to agree, they will submit their differences to the umpire. A decision agreed to by any two will be binding. Each party will:

    1. Pay its chosen appraiser; and

    2. Bear the expenses of the appraisal and umpire equally.

B. We do not waive any of our rights under this policy by agreeing to an appraisal.

Part E—Duties After An Accident Or Loss

We have no duty to provide coverage under this policy unless there has been full compliance with the following duties:

A. We must be notified promptly of how, when and where the accident or loss happened. Notice should also include the names and addresses of any injured persons and of any witnesses.

B. A person seeking any coverage must:

    1. Cooperate with us in the investigation, settlement or defense of any claim or suit.

    2. Promptly send us copies of any notices or legal papers received in connection with the accident or loss.

    3. Submit, as often as we reasonably require:

        a. To physical exams by physicians we select. We will pay for these exams.

        b. To examination under oath and subscribe the same.

    4. Authorize us to obtain:

        a. Medical reports; and

        b. Other pertinent records.

    5. Submit a proof of loss when required by us.

C. A person seeking Uninsured Motorists Coverage must also:

    1. Promptly notify the police if a hit-and-run driver is involved.

    2. Promptly send us copies of the legal papers if a suit is brought.

D. A person seeking Coverage for Damage to Your Auto must also:

    1. Take reasonable steps after loss to protect "your covered auto" or any "non-owned auto" and their equipment from further loss. We will pay reasonable expenses incurred to do this.

    2. Promptly notify the police if "your covered auto" or any "non-owned auto" is stolen.

    3. Permit us to inspect and appraise the damaged property before its repair or disposal.

Although there are no specific provisions for physical damage that pertain to miscellaneous vehicles, the following coverage limitations should be noted:

- A camper body or trailer must be noted on the Declarations page with the appropriate physical damage coverages indicated for those coverages to apply.

- Awnings, cabanas, customizing equipment, and equipment that creates additional living facilities are excluded from coverage. This could be an important coverage gap for an insured with a conversion van or a customized van or truck.

- The loss adjustment provided by the PAP is based on ACV. The specialist should be aware of any vehicles that require an alternative settlement basis, such as stated amount.

PAP: Endorsements for Other Vehicles

Standard endorsements can be attached to the PAP to provide coverages to vehicles that are otherwise limited or excluded.

Miscellaneous Type Vehicle Endorsement

Exhibit 12-9 provides an excerpt of the Miscellaneous Type Vehicle Endorsement with notations regarding expanded coverages and form features.

This endorsement is intended to provide coverage for motor homes, motorcycles (and similar vehicles), ATVs, dune buggies, and golf carts. Coverage can be written for liability, medical payments, uninsured motorists, collision, and OTC. This endorsement is helpful in eliminating any doubt regarding the existence of coverage if the policy is ambiguous. For example, an insured who has recently purchased a dune buggy might assume that the vehicle is automatically covered for liability under the PAP because only vehicles with fewer than four wheels are excluded. Some ambiguity exists because the vehicle is designed for use off public roads, but this might not be apparent to the insured. Attaching the Miscellaneous Type Vehicle Endorsement can eliminate any doubt. This endorsement also automatically extends coverage to similar newly acquired miscellaneous vehicles or substitute vehicles.

This endorsement also allows the insured the option of excluding the passenger hazard for a miscellaneous vehicle by noting the exclusion on the Declarations page or the Schedule on the first page of the endorsement. If this option is chosen, the premium is reduced and liability coverage is eliminated for an insured who is liable for injuries to a passenger on the miscellaneous-type vehicle. For example, if the insured were riding a motorcycle with a passenger and had an accident, the insured would face paying liability damages personally. This exclusion should only be implemented with caution; the insured should fully understand the possible exposures.

Use of this endorsement varies greatly, based on the insurer's underwriting guidelines. An insurer might be willing to extend coverage on a golf cart to an insured who has a supporting homeowners policy, but

Exhibit 12-9
PAP: Miscellaneous Type Vehicle Endorsement

POLICY NUMBER

PERSONAL AUTO
PP 03 23 06 94

THIS ENDORSEMENT CHANGES THE POLICY. PLEASE READ IT CAREFULLY.

MISCELLANEOUS TYPE VEHICLE ENDORSEMENT

SCHEDULE

Description and Type of Vehicle	Passenger Hazard Excluded	
1.	Yes ☐	No ☐
2.	Yes ☐	No ☐
3.	Yes ☐	No ☐

Coverage is provided where a premium and a limit of liability is shown for the coverage.

Coverages	Limit of Liability		Premium Veh. 1	Veh. 2	Veh. 3
Liability	$	Each Accident	$		
	$	Each Accident		$	
	$	Each Accident			$
Medical Payments	$	Each Person	$		
	$	Each Person		$	
	$	Each Person			$
Uninsured Motorists	$	Each Accident	$		
	$	Each Accident		$	
	$	Each Accident			$
Collision	$	Less $ Ded.	$		
	$	Less $ Ded.		$	
	$	Less $ Ded.			$
Other Than Collision	$	Less $ Ded.	$		
	$	Less $ Ded.		$	
	$	Less $ Ded.			$
		Total Premium	$		

> A value is shown for each vehicle. Losses are settled based on the lesser of:
> - The amount shown
> - ACV
> - The cost to repair or replace

NOTICE

For the Collision and Other Than Collision Coverages, the amount shown in the Schedule or in the Declarations is not necessarily the amount you will receive at the time of loss or damage for the described property. PLEASE refer to the Limit of Liability provision below.

With respect to the "miscellaneous type vehicles" and coverages described in the Schedule or in the Declarations, the provisions of the policy apply unless modified by this endorsement.

I. DEFINITIONS
The Definitions Section is amended as follows:

A. For the purpose of the coverage provided by this endorsement "miscellaneous type vehicle" means a motor home, motorcycle or other similar type vehicle, all-terrain vehicle, dune buggy or golf cart.

B. The definition of "your covered auto" is replaced by the following
"Your covered auto" means:

1. Any "miscellaneous type vehicle" shown in the Schedule or in the Declarations.

2. Any of the following types of vehicles on the date you become the owner:

  a. A private passenger auto;

  b. A pickup or van that:

    (1) Has a Gross Vehicle Weight of less than 10,000 lbs.; and

    (2) Is not used for the delivery or transportation of goods and materials unless such use is:

      (a) Incidental to your "business" of maintaining or repairing furnishings or equipment; or

> This form extends the PAP to cover:
> - Motor homes
> - Motorcycles (and vehicles similar to motorcycles)
> - ATVs
> - Dune buggies
> - Golf carts

> The PAP's definition of "your covered auto" is modified to fit the description of the miscellaneous vehicle.

Continued on next page.

PAP: Miscellaneous Type Vehicle Endorsement—continued

Newly acquired miscellaneous vehicles are covered if they are like an insured vehicle. For example, if a motorcycle is insured, an additional motorcycle would be covered, but a golf cart would not.

(b) For farming or ranching.

c. Any "miscellaneous type vehicle" of the same type shown in the Schedule or in the Declarations.

This provision applies only if:

a. You acquire the vehicle during the policy period;

b. You ask us to insure it within 30 days after you become the owner; and

c. With respect to a pickup or van, no other insurance policy provides coverage for that vehicle.

If the vehicle you acquire replaces one of the same type shown in the Schedule or in the Declarations, it will have the same coverage as the vehicle it replaced. You must ask us to insure a replacement vehicle within 30 days only if you wish to add or continue Coverage for Damage to Your Auto.

If the vehicle you acquire is in addition to any of the same type shown in the Schedule or in the Declarations, it will have the broadest coverage we now provide for any vehicle of that type shown in the schedule or in the Declarations.

3. Any "trailer".

Temporary substitute autos of any kind are covered. However, there is no coverage for nonowned vehicles other than for temporary substitutes.

4. Any "miscellaneous type vehicle" or auto you do not own while used as a temporary substitute for any other vehicle described in this definition which is out of normal use because of its:

a. Breakdown;

b. Repair;

c. Servicing;

d. Loss; or

e. Destruction

This provision (**4.**) does not apply to Coverage for Damage to Your Auto.

II. PART A - LIABILITY COVERAGE

Part **A** is amended as follows:

A. The definition "insured" is replaced by the following:

"Insured" means:

1. You or any "family member" for the ownership, maintenance or use of "your covered auto".

2. Any person using "your covered auto".

3. For "your covered auto", any person or organization but only with respect to legal responsibility for acts or omissions of a person for whom coverage is afforded under this Part.

B. The Exclusions section is amended as follows:

1. Exclusion **B.1.** is replaced by the following:

We do not provide Liability Coverage for the ownership, maintenance or use of any vehicle which:

a. Has fewer than four wheels; or

b. Is designed mainly for use off public roads.

This exclusion (B.1.) does not apply:

a. While such vehicle is being used by an "insured" in a medical emergency; or

b. To any "trailer"; or

c. To a vehicle having fewer than four wheels if it is insured for Liability Coverage under this endorsement.

The PAP exclusion regarding vehicles with fewer than four wheels is changed when a motorcycle is insured.

2. The following exclusion applies under Section A to any vehicle for which the Schedule or Declarations indicates that the passenger hazard is excluded:

We do not provide Liability Coverage for any "insured" for "bodily injury" to any "insured" while "occupying" the described "miscellaneous type vehicle".

III. PART B - MEDICAL PAYMENTS COVERAGE

Exclusion **1.** of Part **B** is replaced by the following:

We do not provide Medical Payments Coverage for any "insured" for "bodily injury" sustained while "occupying" any motorized vehicle having fewer than four wheels. However, this exclusion (**1.**) does not apply to a motorized vehicle having fewer than four wheels if it is insured for Medical Payments Coverage under this endorsement.

The endorsement provides for a passenger coverage exclusion if a notation is made on the Declarations or Schedule on page 1 of this endorsement.

 PP 03 23 06 94

the insurer might be unwilling to write a motorcycle on the endorsement under any circumstances. Other insurers might be more liberal in writing coverage on miscellaneous-type vehicles for insureds with good loss experience.

The PAP Snowmobile Endorsement

An excerpt of the Snowmobile Endorsement that can be attached to the PAP is provided in Exhibit 12-10.

This endorsement is similar to the Miscellaneous Type Vehicles Endorsement, but it is designed specifically for snowmobiles. Unlike the Snowmobile endorsement, which can be added to the homeowners policy to extend liability coverage only, this endorsement can extend liability, medical payments, uninsured motorists, collision, and other than collision coverages. This endorsement can provide coverage for the trailers that are towed behind snowmobiles, newly acquired snowmobiles, and temporary substitute vehicles.

The endorsement replaces the regular contract language in the PAP, which excludes racing or practice within a facility designed for racing. The new exclusionary language is much broader. Liability and physical damage coverages are excluded during any type of snowmobile "racing or speed contest regardless of whether such contest is prearranged or organized." An insured purchasing this endorsement should be cautioned about this exclusion.

Like the Miscellaneous Type Vehicles Endorsement, the PAP's Snowmobile Endorsement contains a provision allowing for the exclusion of passengers or others being towed (in a trailer or sled). The same caution should be used if this optional exclusion is selected.

Coverage Provided by a Recreational Vehicle Policy or a Specialty Policy

Recreational vehicle policies or specialty policies are not standard, but they tend to be based on the PAP. The following is a discussion of how the PAP is usually modified to create these unique contracts.

Policy Definitions

Policy forms vary significantly among insurers. Definitions are adjusted to address differences between ordinary private passenger autos and the vehicles described in this chapter. The following are some of the definition changes that a specialist might encounter:

- The definition of a recreational vehicle lists the specific vehicle or vehicles covered (such as a 1996 Kawasaki Snowmobile) rather than the type of vehicle (such as snowmobiles).
- The definition of "your covered auto" restricts newly acquired recreational vehicles to the same type that are listed on the Declarations page.
- The definition of "relative" often includes the provision that the relative not own a recreational vehicle of the same type.

Exhibit 12-10
PAP—Snowmobile Endorsement

POLICY NUMBER	PERSONAL AUTO
	PP 03 20 06 94

THIS ENDORSEMENT CHANGES THE POLICY. PLEASE READ IT CAREFULLY.

SNOWMOBILE ENDORSEMENT

SCHEDULE

Description of Snowmobile	Passenger Hazard Excluded	
1.	Yes ☐	No ☐
2.	Yes ☐	No ☐
3.	Yes ☐	No ☐

Coverage is provided where a premium and a limit of liability is shown for the coverage.

Coverages	Limit of Liability		Premium		
			Veh. 1	Veh. 2	Veh. 3
Liability	$	Each Accident	$	$	$
Medical Payments	$	Each Person	$	$	$
Uninsured Motorists	$	Each Accident	$	$	$
Collision	$	Less $ ~~Ded.~~	$		
	$	Less $ Ded.		$	
	$	Less $ Ded.			$
Other Than Collision	$	Less $ Ded.	$		
	$	Less $ Ded.		$	
	$	~~Less $~~ ~~Ded.~~			$
	Total Premium		$		

All PAP-type coverages are available. The snowmobile endorsement available on a homeowners policy provides only liability and medical payments to others.

A value is shown for each vehicle. Losses are settled based on the lesser of:
- *The amount shown*
- *ACV*
- *The cost to repair or replace*

NOTICE

For the Collision and Other Than Collision Coverages, the amount shown in the Schedule or in the Declarations is not necessarily the amount you will receive at the time of loss or damage for the described "snowmobile". PLEASE refer to the Limit of Liability provision below.

With respect to the "snowmobiles" and coverages described in the Schedule or in the Declarations, the provisions of the policy apply unless modified by this endorsement.

This form extends the definition of "auto" and "motor vehicle" to include snowmobiles.

I. DEFINITIONS

The Definitions Section is amended as follows:

A. For the purpose of the coverage provided by this endorsement the terms "auto," "motor vehicle" and "vehicle" are replaced by the term "snowmobile" except for Uninsured Motorists Coverage. In Uninsured Motorists Coverage, the term "uninsured motor vehicle" includes a "snowmobile".

B. The reference to "Declarations" in the Limit of Liability provisions of the policy includes "Schedule".

C. The following definition is added:

"Snowmobile" means:

1. A land motor vehicle which is:

   a. Designed for use mainly on public roads on snow or ice; and

   b. Propelled solely by means of the following or similar mechanical devices:

      (1) Wheels;

      (2) Crawler-type treads; or

      (3) Belts.

PAP: Snowmobile Endorsement—continued

This endorsement can cover trailers towed by snowmobiles.

2. A "trailer" designed for being towed by, but not transporting a vehicle described in **1.** above.

However, "snowmobile" does not include any vehicle which is propelled by airplane type propellers or fans.

D. The term "your covered auto" is replaced by the term "your covered snowmobile". "Your covered snowmobile" means:

1. Any "snowmobile" shown in the Schedule or in the Declarations.

Newly acquired snowmobiles are automatically covered for 30 days during the policy period.

2. Any "snowmobile" on the date you become the owner. This provision applies only if you:

   a. Acquire the "snowmobile" during the policy period; and

   b. Ask us to insure it within 30 days after you become the owner.

Temporary substitute snowmobiles are automatically covered.

3. Any "snowmobile" you do not own while used as a temporary substitute for any other "snowmobile" described in this definition which is out of normal use because of its:

   a. Breakdown;

   b. Repair;

   c. Servicing;

   d. Loss; or

   e. Destruction.

   This provision (**3.**) does not apply to coverage for Damage to Your Auto.

II. PART A - LIABILITY COVERAGE

Part A is amended as follows with respect to a "snowmobile":

A. The definition of "insured" is replaced by the following:

"Insured" means

1. You are any "family member" for the ownership, maintenance or use of any "snowmobile".

2. Any person using "your covered snowmobile".

3. For "your covered snowmobile", any person or organization but only with respect to legal responsibility for acts or omissions of a person for whom coverage is afforded under this Part.

4. For any "snowmobile", other than "your covered snowmobile", any person or organization but only with respect to legal irresponsibility for acts or omissions of you or any "family member" for whom coverage is afforded under this Part. This provision applies only if the person or organization does not own or hire the "snowmobile".

B. The Exclusions Section is amended as follows:

1. Exclusions **A.6.** and **A.7.** are replaced by the following:

   We do not provide Liability Coverage for any "insured" maintaining or using a "snowmobile" in any "business".

2. Exclusion **B.1.** does not apply.

3. Exclusion **B.4.** is replaced by the following:

   a. Operate in; or

   b. While in practice or preparation for;

   Any racing or speed contest regardless of whether such contest is prearranged or organized.

4. The following exclusion is added to Section B:

   We do not provide Liability Coverage for the ownership, maintenance or use of any "snowmobile" while rented or leased to any "insured" or organization other than you.

The racing exclusion under the PAP is limited to racing or preparation inside a facility designed for racing. This snowmobile endorsement excludes *all* racing activities. A similar exclusion appears for physical damage.

5. The following exclusion applies under Section A. to any snowmobile for which the Schedule or Declarations indicates that the passenger hazard is excluded.

   We do not provide Liability Coverage for any "insured" for "bodily injury" to any "insured" while "occupying", or while being towed by, the described "snowmobile".

C. The "Other Insurance" provision is replaced by the following:

OTHER INSURANCE

any insurance we provide shall be excess over any other collectible insurance.

This endorsement provides for a passenger coverage exclusion if a notation is made on the Declaration or Schedule on page 1 of this endorsement.

- The definition of "your covered auto" includes temporary substitute vehicles.
- The definition of "loss" does not include clothes, luggage, and detachable living quarters. Equipment is covered if it is permanently attached or installed and is common to the vehicle's use. Camping gear stored in a trailer would not be covered.

Common Exclusions

Some of the exclusions found in the policies used to cover the types of vehicles included in this chapter are also found in ordinary private passenger policies. Other exclusions are unique to the special policies provided for these vehicles. A list of unique exclusions that might be found on a recreational or specialty policy includes the following:

- No coverage while the insured vehicle is used in racing or speed contests.
- No coverage while the insured vehicle is used in any hill-climbing or jumping contest.
- No coverage if the trailer is used as permanent living quarters.
- No coverage if the insured used the vehicle to carry passengers for a charge.
- No coverage if the vehicle is jointly owned by other than family members, and club ownership might be prohibited.
- Coverage might not apply while the vehicle is rented to others or might apply only if the rental is approved in advance and an additional premium is paid.
- Coverage might not apply to resident relatives unless they are using the vehicle with the permission of the named insured or the named insured's spouse.
- Coverage might not apply in Canada or Mexico. Some policies might provide short-term coverage for operation anywhere in Canada with prior approval and in Mexico for short-term use within fifty miles of the border, again with prior approval. Such approval might include advance payment of an additional premium amount.

FYI

Motorcycle stuntman Evel Knievel is the cousin of John Knievel, Director of Public Affairs for the Federal Highway Traffic Safety Administration. John calls Evel "a bad example." Evel's stunts would be excluded from the PAP and recreational vehicle policies.

The Underwriting Process

The underwriting process for the vehicles described in this chapter is similar to that for personal auto underwriting. The drivers and the vehicle use must be considered. Special characteristics regarding the theft or vandalism exposures for the vehicle should also be considered.

The underwriting process for "other motor vehicles" differs from personal auto underwriting in the following ways:

- Additional exposures presented by the unique type of vehicle should be considered (such as protection provided to the occupants and characteristics of the vehicle that create hazards).

- All operators must be properly identified. Drivers might include unlicensed and youthful operators.
- The loss control measures used (such as helmets and safety courses) must be identified.

These concerns should be addressed in the application and underwriting process.

Educational Objective 3

Describe the information needed to make an underwriting decision regarding a recreational or miscellaneous vehicle risk, and explain how that information is obtained.

Gathering Information

The process begins with the information provided by the application. Additional information might be required for some types of exposures.

Application Differences

Most insurers use their regular private passenger auto applications to write antique and classic autos, farm vehicles, high-value and specialty autos, kit cars (if registered and licensed for road use), motor homes, and vans. Motorcycles are usually written on a regular auto application as well, since many insurers do not consider them recreational vehicles. A special recreational vehicle application is typically used for all-terrain vehicles, camping and travel trailers, dune buggies not licensed for road use, golf carts, minibikes, mopeds, snowmobiles, and trail bikes not licensed for road use.

When insuring high-value and specialty autos, insurers might require photos with the applications to verify the condition of the vehicle. An appraisal might also be required to help establish the value of the vehicle at the time of the application. Photos are also useful when insuring a motor home, particularly if the unit is a converted school bus rather than a unit built by a recognized motor home manufacturer.

The driver section of a recreational vehicle application is usually similar to or the same as the driver section of a regular private passenger auto application, though some questions might be irrelevant because the vehicle is not registered for road use. The specialist should review individual state laws regarding vehicle registration requirements. The vehicle section of the recreational vehicle application is often more extensive than that in a regular auto application because the underwriter needs specific information on the vehicle and how it is used, as well as information about any special equipment installed or attached. Some general items appearing on all applications include the following:

- Year
- Make and model (including the manufacturer)
- Engine size (horsepower rating or cubic centimeter displacement)
- Vehicle identification number (VIN)
- Date purchased (and whether new or used)

- Cost (price new or purchase price, if used; all accessories should be included)
- Prior damage

When the vehicle being insured is a camping or travel trailer, additional information might be required to help the underwriter make a proper risk evaluation. The following is a list of typical questions that should be answered:

- What are the length and width of the vehicle?
- Are passengers ever transported in the trailer?
- Does the applicant maintain other permanent living quarters?
- How many times during the year will the trailer be used as living quarters?
- Is the trailer ever rented or lent to others?
- Where is the trailer kept when not in use?
- Is the trailer used in connection with the applicant's occupation?
- Is the trailer ever used in connection with store, office, or display purpose?

To help develop miscellaneous and recreational vehicle applications, sample applications have been included in Appendix 12-A of this book. These sample applications ask basic underwriting questions. They can be modified and expanded to meet an insurer's underwriting needs.

Identifying the Drivers

Properly identifying recreational vehicle operators is a significant problem in underwriting recreational vehicle exposures. Children under driving age will probably operate family snowmobiles and off-road vehicles even if the children have not been declared on the application. Their driving characteristics cannot be established.

Some insurers use credit reports to identify the number of listed dependents in a household and the number of possible vehicle operators. Applications usually request the number of all operators or members of the household. If an application declares two household members, but the credit report indicates that the insured has three dependents (a total household of four), additional questions should be asked about the names and ages of other family members and their possible operation of the vehicle.

Motor Vehicle Reports

A motor vehicle report is the most important record that can be obtained to forecast the risk involved in the insured's operation of a recreational vehicle. An insured whose driving record indicates a frequency of violations and accidents is likely to operate a recreational vehicle similarly.

Supporting Business

Because of the exposures associated with recreational vehicles, some insurers write the coverage only as an accommodation for existing policyholders. This often simplifies the gathering of underwriting information. The producer or underwriter can gain an impression of the insured's loss history, traffic violations, and responsibility. Although this process is certainly not scientific, the overall picture of the account is helpful.

Making the Underwriting Decision

After a specialist has gathered the information to make a decision, a review of the insurer's underwriting guidelines is important. Some insurers encourage recreational or miscellaneous vehicle exposures, but others might write them only as an accommodation. In identifying and selecting an alternative, the specialist should take care to meet both the insurers' and customers' needs.

Educational Objective 4

Explain and evaluate the alternatives available in implementing coverage for a recreational or miscellaneous vehicle risk.

Identifying the Alternatives

After the information has been gathered, the underwriter has limited options beyond accepting or rejecting a risk. The most effective alternatives involve loss control options; although loss control can be effective, encouraging loss control might be difficult, as explained below.

Accept or Reject

Rejection of coverage might not always be possible. As shown in the PAP and homeowners exhibits in this chapter, some coverage is automatic. The underwriter can, however, add modifying endorsements or issue recreational or specialty policies.

Modify the Coverage

Placing coverage for miscellaneous and recreational vehicles has been addressed previously in this chapter. Because many coverage options are available for these vehicles, the role of the producer, customer service representative, or underwriter in helping the insured match exposures to coverage becomes important. Without that expert assistance, the customer would probably not be able to identify either the coverage automatically provided by the homeowners and PAP policies or the options available for additional coverage.

Modify the Deductible

When the theft or vandalism exposure is high, such as for antique, classic, or high-value automobiles, increasing a deductible can be a viable option. This can encourage greater loss control participation by the insured and perhaps improve the vehicle safeguards.

Loss Control

Some loss control measures that apply to motorcycles and off-road and recreational vehicles are very effective. Wearing helmets and taking safety courses have proven effective in reducing injuries and saving lives.

Helmet Use Many of the recreational vehicles addressed in this chapter are hazardous for operators and occupants because they are not protected in roll-overs or crashes. Two-wheel vehicles, dune buggies, and ATVs provide little protection against injury. The rider's and passenger's unprotected position, the instability of the vehicle, and the diminished visibility of the rider and vehicle compared with that of other road users increase the hazards.

Per mile traveled, a person's chance of death in a motorcycle crash is twenty-two times greater than in an automobile crash.[2] Frontal impacts (usually with cars) are the most common type of motorcycle crash, so the risk of injury is greater for the motorcycle's driver than for its passenger. The outcome of the crash depends on variables such as the type of impact, the surface, the speed of the motorcycle, and the driver's characteristics. Frontal impacts are likely to involve severe, direct impacts and breaking forces that are highly damaging to the face, head, skull, and spine.

Wearing helmets is an effective method of preventing injuries, reducing medical costs, and saving lives. Based on 1991 data, motorcycle helmets reduce the chance of fatal injury by 28-29 percent. Seriously injured motorcyclists who are not wearing helmets at the time of an accident are twice as likely to sustain head injuries as those wearing helmets.[3]

Helmets for motorcyclists are made of fiberglass, fiber-reinforced resin, or polycarbonate and have interior foam padding and webbing that help ensure a proper fit. Motorcycle helmets are designed to cushion and spread the severe forces of deadly blows in crashes. They cover the entire head and cover the face with a removable visor (full-face type) or cover less of the head (three-fourths or one-half helmet). Helmets should fit snugly, and the chin strap should be firmly fastened. The U.S. Department of Transportation has established helmet standards to meet tests to measure strength during impact, strength of the straps and fasteners, appropriate visual field, undiminished hearing acuity, and protection against spinal cord injury. The following groups publish acceptable motorcycle helmet standards:

- The U.S. Department of Transportation
- The American National Standards Institute
- The Snell Memorial Foundation

Wearing protective equipment (boots, gloves, and heavy clothing) for motorcyclists and recreational vehicle users is also important to guard against injury.

States repealing their mandatory helmet use laws have been established to have 20 percent more fatalities than if they had maintained those laws.[4] Underwriters should be aware of the helmet laws and their enforcement in their states. If helmet use is voluntary, the underwriter can ask questions on the application about the driver's and passenger's use of helmets, but even affirmative answers do not assure compliance. Questions about the type of helmets and their certification standards can also be useful in verifying that helmets of the appropriate quality have been purchased.

In addition to performance with regard to motorcycle operation, helmet use has been proven to reduce the risk of death among ATV operators by approximately 42 percent and can reduce the likelihood of head injury in nonfatal incidents by approximately 64 percent.[5] Unfortunately, the only way to verify that ATV operators are wearing helmets is the presence or absence of the helmets after accidents occur.

Safety Courses   Motorcycle rider courses offered by the Motorcycle Safety Foundation provide effective training for beginning, intermediate, and advanced riders. Special schools also use racetracks to provide training at highway speeds within a controlled environment. Applications should ask for information regarding safety courses in which the drivers have participated.

Selecting the Best Alternative

Underwriters have several considerations in deciding which alternative is most effective and which coverage placement option provides the most effective coverage for the insured's exposures. Following are questions to help in this process:

* What are the insured's unique exposures to loss in the use of this vehicle?
* Have the exposures been addressed through the selected coverages and endorsements?
* Does the application meet the underwriting guidelines for the selected coverages and endorsements?
* What are the coverage gaps, and how will they be communicated?

Educational Objective 5
Describe how results of the underwriting decisions regarding recreational and miscellaneous vehicle risks can be monitored and evaluated.

Implementing the Decision and Monitoring the Results

A key consideration in the implementation of coverage is communication with the customer regarding any possible gaps in coverage that the coverage selected has not addressed. Because the potential for serious injury exists with recreational vehicles and motorcycles, information regarding helmet use and safety courses would be appropriate.

Results for these policies are generally monitored at two levels:

- Claims on individual policies are screened or reviewed for concerns regarding inappropriate driver use, hazardous operation, or losses that could have been avoided with appropriate precautions.
- The collective results for a portfolio of recreational vehicle policies are monitored to determine trends.

Summary

Other motor vehicles (also called specialty or miscellaneous vehicles) have exposures that are similar to those for private passenger autos. The vehicle use and the drivers' records are key considerations in underwriting both. These vehicles also have exposures that are unique, based on the type of vehicle and the problems inherent in the design. This chapter explored those unique exposures.

Coverage placement can be complicated because of the variety of sources for coverage. The homeowners and PAP policies automatically cover some exposures. In placing coverage, the specialist should do the following:

- Determine the insured's exposures in the ownership and operation of the specialty vehicle.
- Review the homeowners and PAP policies to determine whether coverage already exists or whether it can be added by an endorsement.
- If coverage is not provided by the homeowners or PAP policies or their endorsements, review available specialty policies for coverage.

Chapter Notes

1. American Medical Association, "Helmets and Preventing Motorcycle- and Bicycle-Related Injuries," *The Journal of the American Medical Association*, Issue Number 19, November 16, 1994, pp. 1535–1538.

2. Insurance Institute for Highway Safety, *Analysis of Fatal Motorcycle Crashes: Crash Typing from FARS Data* (Arlington, VA: Insurance Institute for Highway Safety, 1994), p. 1.

3. American Medical Association, pp. 1535–1538.

4. American Medical Association, pp. 1535–1538.

5. A. Hewitt, D. Solet, and M. Kiely, "Injuries Associated with Use of Snowmobiles—New Hampshire, 1989–1992," *The Journal of the American Medical Association*, February 8, 1995, pp. 448–449 as referencing G.B. Rodgers, "The Effectiveness of Helmets in Reducing All-Terrain Vehicle Injuries and Deaths," *Accident Analysis and Prevention*, 1990, vol. 22, pp. 47–58.

Bibliography

American Medical Association. "Helmets and Preventing Motorcycle- and Bicycle-Related Injuries." *The Journal of the American Medical Association*. Issue no. 19. November 16, 1994, pp. 1535-1538.

"Auto Insurance." *Consumer Reports*. August 1992, p. 489.

Bach, George Leland. *Economics*. 9th ed. Englewood Cliffs, NJ: Prentice-Hall, 1977.

Burnett, John J., and Alan J. Bush. "Profiling the Yuppies." *Journal of Advertising Research*. April/May 1986, pp. 27-35.

Campbell, Massie, and K.L. Campbell. *Analysis of Accident Rates By Age, Gender, and Time of Day Based on the 1990 Nationwide Personal Transportation Survey (UMTRI-93-7)*. Ann Arbor, MI: University of Michigan Transportation Research Institute, 1990.

Candage, Howard. "Perceptions and Adding Value." *Delivering Insurance Services—AIS 25 Course Guide*. Malvern, PA: Insurance Institute of America, 1994.

Center for Disease Control and Prevention. *The 1993 Youth Risk Behavior Surveillance Survey*. Arlington, VA: Center for Disease Control and Prevention of the U.S. Government.

Connecticut Chapter of CPCU Society, Research Committee. "Differing Perspectives on Auto Insurance: Consumers, Company, Personnel and Agents." *CPCU Journal*. March 1994, pp. 19-21.

Davis, Brian, and Warren A. French. "Exploring Advertising Usage, Segments Among the Aged." *Journal of Advertising Research*. February/March 1989, pp. 22-29.

Dillard, James. "A Doctor's Dilemma." *Newsweek*. June 12, 1995, p. 12.

Donaldson, James H. *Casualty Claim Practice*. Homewood, IL: Richard D. Irwin, Inc., 1984.

Ferraris, Carl. "Legalistic Versus Ethics-Based Management." *Essays on Ethics: Vol. II*.

Fix, A. James, and David Daughton. *The Odds Almanac*. New York, NY: Follett Publishing Company, 1980.

Foppert, David, "Waging the War Against Fraud." *Best's Review*. March 1994, pp. 45-46.

Fordham, David R. "Connecting Your Company to the Internet." *Management Accounting*. September 1995, pp. 69-74.

Gastel, Ruth. "Compulsory Auto Insurance." *Insurance Issues Update*. May 1995, pp. 1-6.

Gebers, Michael A., and Raymond C. Peck. *An Inventory of California Driver Accident Risk Factors*. Sacramento, CA: California Department of Motor Vehicles, 1994.

Gibbons, Robert, George Rejda, and Michael Elliott. *Insurance Perspectives*. Malvern, PA: American Institute for Chartered Property Casualty Underwriters, 1992.

Giles, Barbara, and Carl Giles. *Make Your House Radon Free*. Blue Ridge Summit. Tab Books, Inc., 1990.

Glendenning, G. William, and Robert B. Holtom. *Personal Lines Underwriting*. Malvern, PA: Insurance Institute of America, 1992.

Hamilton, Karen L., and Donald S. Malecki. *Personal Insurance: Property and Liability*. Malvern, PA: American Institute for Chartered Property Casualty Underwriters, 1994.

Hewitt, A., D. Solet, and M. Kiely. "Injuries Associated with Use of Snowmobiles—New Hampshire, 1989-1992." *The Journal of the American Medical Association*. February 8, 1995, pp. 448-449. As referenced in G.B. Rodgers, "The Effectiveness of Helmets in Reducing All-Terrain Vehicle Injuries and Deaths. *Accident Analysis and Prevention*. Vol. 22, 1990, pp. 47-58.

Homeowners Liability Insurance Law—Questions and Answers Reference Service. Schaumburg, IL: Property Loss Research Bureau, 1991.

Horn, Ronald C. *On Professions, Professionals, and Professional Ethics*. Malvern, PA: American Institute for Property and Liability Underwriters, 1978.

"House Report No. 197-190 of the Energy and Commerce Committee." Quoted in *U.S. Code and Cong. News*. Vol. 2, 97th Congr. 1st Sess., 1991, p. 1434.

Insurance Information Institute. *The Fact Book 1996*. New York, NY: Insurance Information Institute, 1995.

Insurance Institute for Highway Safety. *Alcohol: Questions and Answers*. Arlington, VA: Insurance Institute for Highway Safety, 1993.

Insurance Institute for Highway Safety. *Analysis of Fatal Motorcycle Crashes: Crash Typing from FARS Data*. Arlington, VA: Insurance Institute for Highway Safety, 1994.

Insurance Institute for Highway Safety. *Highway Safety Facts 1994*. Arlington, VA: Insurance Institute for Highway Safety, 1994.

Insurance Institute for Highway Safety. *Shopping for a Safer Car, 1996 Models*, September 1995, pp. 6, 7-8, 9, 10-11, 12, 13, 15, and 20.

Insurance Institute for Highway Safety. *Status Report*. Vol. 26, no. 5, p. 5; vol. 28, no. 11, p. 10; vol. 30, no. 3, p. 10; vol. 30, no. 9, pp. 2 and 5.

Insurance Institute for Highway Safety. *25 Years of Work—1969-1994*. Arlington, VA: Insurance Institute for Highway Safety, 1995.

Insurance Services Office. *Advisory Notice for Homeowners Policy Program, 1991*. New York, NY: Insurance Services Office, September 6, 1990.

Kensicki, Peter R., Christopher J. Amrhein, Thomas S. Marshall, and Seeman Waranch. *Principles of Insurance Production*. Vol. 1, 3d ed. Malvern, PA: Insurance Institute of America, 1991.

Launie, Joseph J., J. Finley Lee, and Norman A. Baglini. *Principles of Property and Liability Underwriting*, Malvern, PA: Insurance Institute of America, 1986.

Malus, Richard W. "Ethical Conduct in Supplying and Receiving Underwriting Information." *Essays on Ethics: Vol. II*.

Mangan, Joseph L. "Building Code Compliance Gradings: The Underwriter's New Tool." *Best's Underwriting Newsletter*. June 1997, pp. 1-4.

McEwan, Bruce. "Rights and Responsibilities: The Consumer Contract." *CPCU Journal*. June 1993, pp. 81-83.

McNamara, Roderick, Robert A. Laurence, and Glenn L. Wood. *Inland Marine Insurance*. Vol. 2. Malvern, PA: Insurance Institute of America, 1987.

Mehr, Robert I., and Emerson Cammack. *Principles of Insurance*. Homewood, IL: Richard D. Irwin, 1980.

Nader, Ralph, and Wesley J. Smith. *Winning the Insurance Game*. New York, NY: Knightsbridge Publishing Company, 1990.

National Association of Insurance Commissioners. "Automobile Insurance Declination, Termination, and Disclosure Model Act." *Model Laws, Regulations and Guidelines*. July 1992, pp. 725-3.

National Association of Insurance Commissioners. *Constitution of the National Association of Insurance Commissioners* as it appeared in the NAIC Summer National Meeting program. June 1995, p. 34.

National Association of Insurance Commissioners. *Market Conduct Examiners Handbook*. December 1989, pp. V-6 to V-7.

National Association of Insurance Commissioners. "Property Insurance Declination, Termination, and Disclosure Model Act." *Model Laws, Regulations and Guidelines*. July 1992, pp. 720-3.

National Association of Insurance Commissioners. "Unfair Trade Practices Act." *Model Laws, Regulations and Guidelines*. January 1993, pp. 880-2 to 880-3 and 880-4 to 880-5.

National Highway Traffic Safety Administration. *An Analysis of the Crash Experience of Passenger Cars Equipped with Anti-lock Braking Systems*. Arlington, VA: National Highway Traffic Safety Administration, May 1995.

The National Underwriter Co. *FC&S Bulletins Personal Lines Volume*. Cincinnati, OH: The National Underwriter Co., 1987.

The National Underwriter Company. *FC&S Bulletins: Companies and Coverages*. "Personal Umbrella Policy Liability Insurance." Cincinnati, OH: The National Underwriter Company, 1991.

The National Underwriter Company. "Packages: Personal." *FC&S Bulletins: Companies and Coverages*. Cincinnati, OH: The National Underwriter Co., 1993.

Otis, L.H. "Credit Reports Draw Fire at NAIC." *National Underwriter*. June 12, 1995, p. 4.

Potthast, Catherine A. "Lead Paint Litigation—an Overview." Working Paper. Baltimore, MD: Smith, Somerville, and Case, 1992.

Preusser, D.F., P.L. Zador, and A.F. Williams. "The Effect of City Curfew Ordinances on Teenage Motor Vehicle Fatalities." *Accident Analysis and Prevention*. January 1993, pp. 641-645.

Reday-Mulvey, Genevieve. "Continuing Training until End of Career: A Key Policy for the Fourth Pillar." *The Geneva Papers on Risk and Finance*, no. 73, October 1994.

Rejda, George E. *Principles of Risk Management and Insurance*. 4th ed. New York, NY: Harper Collins Publishers, 1992.

Research Institute of America. *Marketing Management*. New York, NY: Research Institute of America, 1984.

Rodda, William H. "Underwriting Update: Insuring the Home Worker." *Best's Underwriting Newsletter*. October 1985, pp. 1-4.

Rosenfield, Harvey. "Proposition 103: The Consumer's Viewpoint." Excerpted in "The Impact of Consumer Activism on the Insurance Industry." Malvern, PA: The Society of CPCU, 1991.

Schleevogt, Mary, and Miles Belgrade. "Lead Poisoning in Children." Working Paper. Cherry Valley, IL: Mutual Reinsurance Bureau, 1991.

Smith, Barry D., James S. Trieschmann, Eric A. Wiening, and Anita W. Johnson. *Property and Liability Insurance Principles*, 2d ed. Malvern, PA: Insurance Institute of America, 1994.

Stephan, Roland. "How Agents Can Help Reduce Insurance Fraud." *SAFECO Agent*. July/August 1994, p. 13.

Tobias, Andrew. *The Invisible Bankers*. New York, NY: Linden Press, 1982.

U.S. Department of Commerce. *Interagency Task Force on Product Liability: Final Report*. U.S. Department of Commerce. October 31, 1977. Quoted in *Interagency Task Force*, p. I-20.

Vaughn, Emmett. *Fundamentals of Risk and Insurance*. New York, NY: John Wiley & Sons, 1992.

Webb, Bernard L., Connor J. Harrison, and James J. Markham. *Insurance Operations*. Vol. 1. Malvern, PA: American Institute for Property and Liability Underwriters, 1992.

Weese, Samuel, and Egnar Jensen. "Ethics in Life Insurance and Related Financial Services. *Essays on Ethics: Vol. II.* Malvern, PA: American Institute for Chartered Property Casualty Underwriters, 1994.

White, George, Ronald Duska, and Victor Lincoln. *Organizational Behavior in Insurance.* Malvern, PA: Insurance Institute of America, 1992.

Wiening, Eric A., and Donald S. Malecki. *Insurance Contract Analysis.* Malvern, PA: American Institute for Chartered Property Casualty Underwriters, 1994.

Williams, A.F., R.S. Karpf, and P.L. Zador. "Variations on Minimum Licensing Age and Fatal Motor Vehicle Crashes." *American Journal of Public Health.* December 1993, pp. 1401-1402.

Index

A

D

M

N

T

U

Glossary

acceptability	Broadly determined by the underwriting guidelines published by an insurer for a type of policy.
account	A person, business, or organization that has purchased insurance.
account underwriting	The process of evaluating all of the policies written by an insurance company for an individual.
accreditation program	A certification program for state insurance departments. The purposes of the accreditation program are (1) to provide consistency of solvency regulations among states and (2) to improve the standards of solvency regulation and financial examinations in all states.
actual cash value (ACV)	The value of property determined by the cost to replace the property, adjusted by subtracting an amount that reflects depreciation.
adverse selection	The increasing likelihood that customers will purchase insurance when the premium is low relative to the risk. Poor underwriting results might occur if too many of the applicants accepted for insurance are those most likely to incur serious loss.
agent	A producer who represents one or more insurance companies.
agreed value (or agreed amount)	The value of property insured under an agreed value provision is the lesser of the following: • The cost to restore the property to its condition before the loss • The amount scheduled The insured and the insurer agree on the value at the time the policy is written.
agricultural smudging	This peril might occur in the spring in areas near orchards. If a late frost threatens the fruit buds or blossoms, oil burning smudge pots are burned at night around the fruit trees. A dark oily cloud covers the trees to prevent the frost from killing the buds. If this cloud is blown into a neighborhood of houses, damage can result.
air bags	Automatic restraint systems that require no action on the part of the vehicle occupants. Driver-side air bags are stored in the hub of the steering wheel, and passenger-side air bags are located inside the instrument panel. Air bags are loss-reduction devices designed to inflate in moderate and severe frontal crashes. The bags form a cushion between occupants and the vehicle interior to reduce the force of impact with hard surfaces. Air bags are also called supplemental restraint systems (SRS).
allegation	A statement by a party regarding the legal action which that party will attempt to prove. This assertion might be unsupported by fact.
"all-risks"	"All-risks" property policies, also called "special" or "open-perils" policies, cover any loss unless it is caused by an excluded peril described in the policy. In an "all-risks" policy, the burden of proof is on the insurer. All losses are covered unless the insurance company can prove that the loss was caused by an excluded peril.
all-terrain vehicle (ATV)	A three- or four-wheeled vehicle equipped with balloon tires and designed for off-road use. ATVs can traverse a variety of ground surfaces, including swampy areas, sand, and snow.

annual statements	Formal financial reports presented to state insurance regulators. They must be prepared for each state in which the insurer is licensed.
anti-lock braking system (ABS)	In a vehicle with a standard braking system, a driver who brakes suddenly can lock the vehicles' wheels and skid, causing loss of control and extending stopping distances. An ABS pumps the brakes automatically (many times a second) to prevent lockup and to enable a driver to maintain control.
antique auto	A vehicle that is at least twenty-five years old. Vehicles rated as antiques are provided a substantial premium discount, so insurers generally restrict use of an antique vehicle to parades and exhibitions.
antitrust	Legislation that opposes unfair business practices.
application	A written request for insurance coverage containing statements made by the applicant.
arson	The criminal act of burning or attempting to burn property.
at-fault	Used to describe an insured's responsibility for causing an auto accident. It is not always accurate. An insured might only have contributed to an accident.
attractive nuisance	A dangerous place, condition, or object that is particularly appealing to children.
attrition	The opposite of retention. The percentage of policies not renewed at their anniversary date is the attrition rate.
auto physical damage coverage	See *physical damage coverage (auto)*.
auto towing and labor coverage	See *towing and labor coverage (auto)*.
automobile insurance plans	Mechanisms for ensuring that all drivers have access to insurance and for equitably distributing the risks that are not written voluntarily by insurers.
avoidance	A risk management technique that eliminates a loss exposure and reduces the chance of loss to zero.
balanced budget method	An insurer might use this method to set an advertising budget. This method limits the permissible expenditure on advertising to pre-set amounts.
bind, bind coverage, binder	An insurance agent is usually authorized by the insurance company to state that certain specified coverage is in force with a specific insurance company as of a particular date and time (or immediately). A binder is a statement that coverage is in force. Its purpose is to provide temporary coverage until an actual insurance policy can be issued. A binder need not be in writing.
blanket	Blanket coverage or blanket limits apply to classes of property. All items within a class are covered for the total limit of coverage for the class.
broker	An insurance producer who is similar to an agent except that, in the legal sense, he or she represents the party seeking insurance.

cancel, cancellation	Stopping coverage during the policy period is cancellation. A policyholder can cancel most policies at any time; state laws often prohibit insurers from canceling policies that have been in force for a certain period of time.
captain	The person responsible for the navigation, operation, and safety of a watercraft and crew. Another term for this role is *master*.
capacity	The comparison of an insurer's written premium to its surplus. An insurer must have adequate capital reserves in the form of surplus to be able to increase the number of policies the insurer writes.
catastrophe	The Property Claims Services Division of the American Insurance Services Group defines catastrophe as an event that causes more than $25 million in insured losses (in constant 1982 dollars) and affects a significant number of policyholders. The threshold used to define a catastrophe occurring before January 1, 1997, was $5 million (in constant 1982 dollars).
catastrophe reinsurance	A special form of reinsurance that protects insurers against the adverse effects of catastrophes and limits the insurer's total loss from a catastrophe to a predetermined amount.
central station alarm	Contacts a security company that responds to the residence and contacts the police.
certificate of insurance	A document that provides information about the liability and workers compensation insurance for a commercial venture.
chartering	A boat is chartered if it is rented for use. The insured can act as the boat's captain, or the person renting the boat from the insured can perform that role.
checklist approach	A method of screening applications. Only those applications that require underwriting decisions are referred to an underwriter. Obviously acceptable applications are issued as policies, and obviously unacceptable applications are canceled. This is also called *underwriting by exception*, and it can be accomplished by a technician who sorts the policies based on a checklist.
claim	A demand by a person or business seeking to recover for a loss. A claim might be made against an individual or against an insurance company.
claim adjuster	The person directly responsible for investigating, evaluating, and settling claims that might be covered by insurance.
claim file	A folder or computer record that is created ("opened") when a claim is made.
claimant	Anyone who presents a claim that might be covered by insurance. For a liability insurance loss, the claimant is a person or business that has suffered a loss and seeks to collect for that loss from an insured. For a property insurance loss, the claimant is the insured who wants the insurance company to pay for repairing or replacing his or her damaged property.
claiming behavior	The inclination that people in a group have for submitting insurance claims.
classic auto	A vehicle that is at least ten years old and has a significantly higher average value than other autos of the same make and model year.

coinsurance	A provision found in many insurance policies that requires the insured to carry an insurance limit equal to at least a specified percentage of the value of the property insured. If the amount of insurance carried is equal to or greater than the required percentage, the insurer will pay covered losses in full (minus any deductible) up to the limit of insurance coverage. If the limit of insurance carried is less than the required percentage, the amount the insurer will pay is calculated by the following formula:

$$\text{Loss payment} =$$

$$[(\text{Limit of insurance carried} / \text{Limit of insurance required}) \times \text{loss}] - \text{deductible}$$

collateral source	Under the collateral source rule, a defendant cannot introduce evidence showing that the injured party has other sources for compensation for injury.
collision	Coverage that applies to the impact of a vehicle with another vehicle or object or the upset (overturn) of the vehicle.
commission	A portion of insurance premiums paid to a producer for his or her sales and service activities.
commodity	A mass-produced, unspecialized product. Wheat and cement are examples of commodities.
competitive-party method	An insurer might use this method to set an advertising budget. This method maintains a level of spending relative to that spent by certain competitors.
compulsory insurance	Mandated by government regulatory groups. Individuals normally encounter compulsory insurance in the form of automobile insurance.
consolidated soil	Soil made from clay and limestone that has aged for thousands of years to become a solid base for construction.
contractual liability	The tort liability of another person (or entity) assumed under contract.
crashworthiness	The vehicle design engineering that reduces or eliminates injury in an auto accident.
credit report	A record of an individual's income, debt, and payment history. Insurance companies use credit reports to identify an applicant's or an insured's financial history.
customer	A person, business, or organization that has purchased insurance.
daily unoccupancy	A term used by underwriters to describe the hazards associated with homes that are unoccupied during the day.
damage	Loss or harm resulting from injury to a person, to property, or to someone's reputation.
damages	Money that the law requires one party to pay another because of loss or injury suffered by the other party.
daytime running lights	High-beam headlights operating at reduced intensity, or low-beam headlights operating at full or reduced power. These lights increase the contrast between vehicles and their background to make cars more visible to oncoming drivers.

declarations, declarations page	The page or pages of an insurance policy containing information, such as the insured's name and address, that the policyholder declared (stated as facts) on the application for insurance.
declaratory judgment	A court ruling on a coverage point within a policy contract or a judgment on a point of law. This judgment is usually sought only when there is a genuine need to resolve such an issue and the claim is substantial enough to warrant the additional effort.
declination	Occurs when an insurer rejects an application.
deductible	A portion of a covered loss that is not paid by insurance. The deductible is subtracted from the amount the insurer would otherwise be obligated to pay.
default judgment	When a party against whom a judgment is sought has failed to answer or defend, that party is in default, and a judgment by default may be entered.
defense costs	Expenses associated with defending a liability claim. Such expenses include wages the defendant loses to prepare for a trial, investigation expenses, witness fees, and premiums for bonds.
definitions	In an insurance policy, provisions that define the words and phrases that have a special meaning when they are used elsewhere in that policy. Words defined in some policies are printed in boldface or enclosed by quotation marks.
demographic segmentation	The division of customer markets based on variables such as income, age, sex, education, stages in the family life cycle (child rearing, middle age, and retirement), and lifestyle.
depreciation	Loss in value of property that develops as items age, wear out, or become obsolete. In a sense, depreciation reflects value that has already been used up.
diary, diary system	A manual or computer system that calls a file to somebody's attention on a specified date (also called *suspense system* or *index system*).
direct marketing system	An insurance marketing system that handles sales by mail or telephone and has no local producers making face-to-face sales.
direct writer	A producer who sells insurance as an employee of one insurance company. The term direct writer is also used to refer to an insurance company that sells insurance directly to insurance buyers through employees.
distribution system	Communicates information between a seller and a buyer (or potential buyers) and distributes the product.
drive-in claims service	A facility for providing repair estimates on damaged cars that are still driveable.
driver training discounts	Applied to personal auto policies for youthful drivers who have completed an approved driver training course.
due diligence	The level of care, prudence, and activity that is reasonable, depending on the circumstances. Someone required to use due diligence must be able to demonstrate that all reasonable and recognized precautions were taken.
duplication	A risk management technique that relies on backups or spares.

eligibility	Risk eligibility is determined by the rules adopted and filed for use in a state. An eligible risk falls within the broad category of risk that can be written on a policy.
endorsement	A document used to amend the coverage in an otherwise complete policy.
equivalent property	Pieces of property of substantially the same economic value.
ethics	An individual's principles of right and wrong. *Moral conduct* is the application of ethical principles.
exclusions	Insurance policy provisions that restrict the broad terms of the insuring agreement by stating some exceptions to coverage—certain activities, loss causes, property, persons, and places—for which the insurer does not provide coverage.
exclusive agent	A self-employed producer who has a contract to sell insurance exclusively for one insurance company (or several related companies).
exposure analysis	A task completed by an underwriter during the review of an application or an existing policy. The task includes the following: • Identifying loss exposures • Identifying associated hazards • Measuring the extent of the loss exposures and hazards
exposures	Exposures, or loss exposures, are situations that could lead to an accidental loss.
express warranty	A warranty written in a policy.
FAIR plans	Fair Access to Insurance Requirements residual market plans provide property insurance for those who cannot obtain coverage in the voluntary market.
fiduciaries	Persons or corporations having a duty to act primarily for another's benefit. The relationship between an insurer and a producer is a fiduciary relationship.
fifth wheel	A type of trailer hitch designed for pulling heavy trailers. It resembles a flat, metal wheel. The gooseneck hitch from the trailer sits over and connects to the fifth wheel.
file-and-use	A filing law that requires the insurer to file rates with the state for a period of time before they are used. If the states do not reject the rates within a stated period, the rates can be used.
filing	The process of submitting information to a state insurance department for approval. The term is often used to describe the completed approval.
financial intermediary	An entity that obtains money from one source and redirects it to another. Insurance companies and banks are financial intermediaries.
fine arts	Include works of art and items of rarity or historic value.
first party	A party is a reference to an entity in a contract. The insured is the first party to an insurance contract.
focus group	A gathering of ten to twelve customers or potential customers who meet with a marketer. The marketer solicits their responses to advertisements, products, or potential product changes.

form	A preprinted document, often several pages long, containing standard wording that makes up the bulk of an insurance policy.
fraud	A clear and willful act of obtaining money or value under false pretenses. Insurance claim fraud is a criminal activity in which the claimant deliberately deceives the insurer about the circumstances of a loss.
frequency of loss	Indicates how often a loss occurs or is expected to occur.
geographic segmentation	A division of customers by location. This is the most widely used approach to segmentation. Companies target metropolitan or rural markets or regions with different climate, culture, and social characteristics.
good student discounts	Applied to personal auto policies for youthful drivers who have good scholastic records. Such drivers are expected to have lower loss involvement because they are more responsible in general and perhaps spend more time on school work and less time on the road than other youthful drivers.
graying	Refers to the overall aging of the population. The "baby boomers," who were born between 1946 and 1964, form a large percentage of the population. As this group ages, the average age of the population increases.
guarantee funds	A system to pay the claims of insolvent property and liability insurers. Generally, the money in a guarantee fund is provided by charges assessed against all insurers in the state.
hazard	Any condition that has the propensity to increase either the frequency or the severity of a potential loss.
Highway Loss Data Institute (HLDI)	The Highway Loss Data Institute (HLDI) is a nonprofit, public service organization. It is closely associated with and funded through the Insurance Institute for Highway Safety. HLDI gathers, compiles, and publishes data regarding insurance loss variations among different makes, models, and kinds of vehicles.
hold harmless agreement	The promise of one party to hold another harmless for any liability arising from an activity.
homogeneity	Similar characteristics among insureds in the same rating class. All insureds in rating classifications should have similar exposure characteristics. Homogeneity also describes the similarity among individuals in a market segment.
housekeeping	A term underwriters use to include more than keeping a clean house. This term includes maintenance, removal of debris, and safe conditions.
hurricane	A storm with winds that exceed speeds of seventy-four miles per hour.
implied permission	As used in the personal auto policy, liability coverage exists for a person who has reasonable belief of being entitled to use an insured auto. Permission might be explicit (the named insured tells his brother that the brother can borrow the car), or permission might be implied (the insured keeps the car keys on the table by the door with the understanding that a neighbor can take the keys and borrow the car whenever he needs it).
implied warranty	This type of warranty is understood rather than written. For example, for a watercraft to be covered by a yacht policy, a warranty of seaworthiness is implied (the insured watercraft must be in a seaworthy condition).

indemnify	To restore the party that has had a loss to the same financial position it held before the loss.
index system	See *diary, diary system*.
indirect loss	Loss of earnings or extra expenses taking place over a period of days, weeks, or months following a direct loss. Indirect losses increase with the passage of time.
inherent expectations	Customer anticipations about a business, industry, or product. Customers reasonably assume that certain services are provided by a business or industry because the services are elemental. A customer might have inherent expectations that a policy will be mailed within a reasonable period of time and that a claims representative will contact a claimant within a few days.
insurance	A system by which a risk is transferred by a person, business, or organization to an insurance company (insurer), which reimburses the insured for covered losses and provides for sharing the costs of losses among all insureds.
insurance company	See *insurer*.
Insurance Institute for Highway Safety (IIHS)	An independent, nonprofit, scientific, and educational organization. It is dedicated to reducing losses (deaths, injuries, and property damage) resulting from crashes.
insurance premium	A periodic payment by the insured to the insurance company in exchange for insurance coverage. A periodic payment is one that must be made at certain time intervals.
Insurance Regulatory Information System (IRIS)	An early warning system for the potential financial failure of an insurance company.
Insurance Services Office (ISO)	The largest insurance service office in the country, ISO performs a variety of services, such as developing statistical classification systems and collecting statistical data on insured claims from a large number of insurance companies, analyzing this information, and using it to develop cost data. Insurance companies that subscribe to ISO's services may use this loss-cost information in setting their own insurance rates.
insured	A person, business, or organization that is covered by an insurance policy.
insurer	Also known as an *insurance company*, an organization that sells insurance policies that protect insureds against financial hardship caused by financial loss.
intangible losses	Losses that cannot be appraised tangibly, for example, items with sentimental value.
intangible product	The opposite of a *tangible product*. When customers buy insurance products, they are buying promises that are intangible products.
intrafamily suit	A legal action that is initiated by one family member against another. For example, a woman sitting in the passenger seat of an auto who sues the driver (her husband) for injuries that she sustained as the result of an accident has brought an intrafamily suit.

invitee	A person who is on the insured's premises with permission (a guest or customer).
involuntary market	Also called *residual markets*, or *shared markets*, involuntary markets are sources of insurance formed by governmental bodies to provide insurance for those who could not obtain it otherwise.
knob and tube	An electrical wiring system characterized by glass insulation knobs nailed to roof and ceiling joists in the attic with wire strung between the knobs.
knot	A measurement of speed of watercraft. A knot equals 1.15 miles per hour.
lath and plaster	A wall covering method that was used before dry wall. Narrow boards (laths) were nailed to the wall supports with small spaces between the board. Wet plaster was smoothed over the boards to create a wall surface. Enough plaster oozed between the spaces between the boards to hold the plaster to the wall.
liability (legal concept)	As a legal concept, liability means that a person, organization, or group of people is legally responsible, or liable, for the injury or damage suffered by another person, organization, or group of people.
liability insurance	Covers accidental losses resulting from bodily injury or damage to someone else's property for which the insured is legally responsible (legally liable). If the loss is covered by the insurance policy, the payment is made directly to the party that suffered the loss.
licensee	A person who is on the insured's premises by mutual consent (such as police, a meter reader, or surveyors).
life-tenancy	The legal right to reside in a home for the remainder of an individual's life. Such an individual is referred to as a *life-tenant*.
litigation	The process of carrying on a lawsuit.
litigious	Prone to engaging in lawsuits. A person who is litigious might seek situations to bring a lawsuit in the hope of a positive financial outcome.
loadings	Additions made to insurance rates to allow for an insurer's administrative expenses.
local alarm	Creates a loud clamor that can be heard only at or near the premises.
loss	The happening or event for which insurance pays.
loss control	A risk management technique that reduces the frequency or severity of a loss.
loss costs	The expected losses relating to each exposure unit. An insurer can add its own loadings and modifications to establish its rates.
loss prevention	A loss control technique that seeks to lower the probable frequency of losses.
loss ratio	Indicates the percentage of premiums that are used to pay losses and loss expenses. To calculate a loss ratio, the dollars of loss and loss adjustment expenses are divided by the dollars of premium (usually measured for a year). Underwriters are frequently assigned loss ratio goals for the lines of business they underwrite.

loss reduction	A loss control technique that seeks to lower the severity of losses that occur.
mail surveys	Questionnaires distributed to a target or random audience.
market conduct examination	A review of an insurer's underwriting and rate-making practices conducted by the state insurance market conduct examiners.
market segmentation	Grouping customers with similar or related characteristics. These customers might be expected to buy a product or service that satisfies their similar needs.
market specialization	Targets a specific customer group for product and service development. Multiple lines of insurance products can then be targeted to that customer group.
market tier	A term that is used interchangeably with "market plan" or "market level." It describes the groupings of insureds into preferred, standard, and nonstandard categories for marketing purposes.
master	See *captain*.
maximizing behavior	Seeking a solution that offers the optimum or greatest payoff is maximizing behavior. This behavior is exhibited by an individual who seeks the alternative with the most favorable outcome.
modeling	A method of assisting an underwriter in the decision-making process by identifying hazards that would not be part of an ideal (or model) risk.
moral conduct	See *ethics*.
moral hazard	A condition that exists when a person might intentionally cause a loss or exaggerate a loss that has occurred.
morale hazard	A condition that exists when a person with insurance is not as careful as he or she would be if there were no insurance.
motor vehicle reports (MVR)	A state's official record of driving information, which usually contains traffic violation and accident information.
named nonowner's endorsement	Auto liability coverage for a person who does not own an auto is provided by named nonowner's endorsement added to a standard personal auto policy. Liability coverage is provided for any vehicle that the insured rents or borrows or for a company car. Liability coverage would apply in excess over any collectible coverage applying to the vehicle.
named perils	Coverage provided by an insurance policy is specified by a list of covered perils. Perils that do not appear on the list are not covered.
National Association of Insurance Commissioners (NAIC)	State insurance regulators belong to this organization, which coordinates insurance regulation among the states.
National Flood Insurance Program (NFIP)	Flood insurance, which may be sold by any licensed insurance agent, is available through this program developed by the federal government but often sold through private insurers.
Nationwide Marine Definition	An instrument that describes the kinds of risks and coverages that can be classified under state insurance laws as marine and inland marine insurance.

no-fault state	Offers automobile policyholders the right to recover financial losses from their own insurance, regardless of who caused the accident. This recovery is offered in the form of personal injury protection (PIP) coverage.
nonstandard auto market	This market is used for high-risk drivers whom insurers normally reject in a standard market.
nonwaiver agreement	A document designed by counsel specifically for a claim. The form requires the insured's signature. It is stronger than a reservation of rights letter but more difficult to execute.
numismatic property	This type of personal property includes money and collectible coins.
objective probability	The long-run relative frequency of an event based on the sum of an infinite number of observations and on the assumption of no change in the underlying conditions. In other words, it describes how often something will theoretically happen.
objective and task method	An insurer might use this method to set an advertising budget. This method develops communication budgets by defining specific objectives, determining the tasks to be performed, and estimating the costs of performing those tasks.
open competition	These laws, also called no-filing laws, do not require insurance department approval for an insurer to use rates developed.
other than collision (OTC)	This coverage is found in personal auto policies. It covers physical damage perils that are not otherwise excluded. The following list of perils is presented in the policy to clarify those perils not considered to be collision: missiles or falling objects; fire, explosion, or earthquake; theft, larceny, vandalism, malicious mischief, riot, civil commotion; windstorm, hail, water, or flood; contact with a bird or animal; breakage of glass.
pairs, sets, or parts	Items that increase in value because they are part of a group. The loss of part of the group greatly reduces the value of the items that remain. Consequently, losses are adjusted to take into consideration the economic loss of the whole group.
penetrating storm	A storm that enters a coastline at a right angle to the land.
percentage-of-sales method	An insurer might use this method to set an advertising budget. This method assumes that a certain amount of advertising creates a certain amount of sales. It limits communication expenses to a percentage of sales volume over a period of time (usually a year).
peril	A cause of property losses. Fire is one example of a peril.
permissive use	As used in the personal auto policy, permissive use describes permission granted to an individual to use an automobile. Permission might be either explicit (such as verbal or written permission) or implied (such as an understanding or reasonable belief).
personal articles floater (PAF)	Provides broad coverage for specified items such as jewelry, furs, silverware, and fine arts.
personal auto policy (PAP)	A specific standard auto policy designed to meet the auto insurance needs of a typical person or family.

personal auto voluntary markets	Many insurers have multiple personal auto programs, usually classified as preferred, standard, or nonstandard. Program definitions can differ greatly among insurers.
personal autos	Vehicles that are structurally created for individual and family use; personal autos include private passenger autos, vans, and trucks.
personal injury	A group of offenses specified within the umbrella policy language that includes bodily injury as well as many other offenses.
personal injury protection (PIP)	No-fault coverage that applies to auto-related injuries.
personal insurance	Insurance coverages purchased by individuals and families to cover non-business exposures. This term is often used interchangeably with "personal lines."
personal interview	A group of individual responses to a series of questions. This method is used to test customer receptivity to a new or modified product or service.
personal liability	The general (non-auto-related) liability exposures that accompany a person's nonbusiness activities.
personal property	Property other than *real property*.
philatelic property	This property includes collectible stamps.
physical damage coverage (auto)	Auto physical damage coverage, also known as "damage to your auto" coverage, insures against loss resulting from damage to an auto owned or operated by the insured, and it also provides coverage if the car is stolen.
pilot test	A trial of an advertisement or a product to a limited group or a limited geographic area in order to determine whether the desired results can be achieved.
planned urban development (PUD)	A preplanned community consisting usually of single and multifamily housing surrounding shops, restaurants, and offices. Motor vehicle use is restricted within a PUD; to get around within such a development, people normally walk or ride golf carts.
policy	A contract that states the rights and duties of the insurance company and the insured.
policy limits	Limits, also called limits of insurance, limits of liability, or policy limits, indicate how much insurance is provided. The limits in the policy set the maximum dollar amount the insurance company will pay.
policy provision	Any statement in an insurance policy.
portfolio	A group of policies with a common characteristic (such as geography, type of coverage, or producer). As a group, policies are analyzed for losses, change in size, and trends. A portfolio is also called a "book of business."
preferred auto market	The typical preferred program has lower rates than the other programs, coupled with stricter underwriting standards. Most insurers allow only one ticket (and no accidents) for such a program. Other requirements might involve type of car (no sports cars) or age of the drivers (all over twenty-five).

primary	When used with the umbrella policy, this term refers to the policies that provide the first level of coverage for a liability loss. The umbrella policy specifies the type and amount of coverage that must be provided by underlying policies.
primary data	In the marketing research process, primary data is information that is collected to answer specific questions about a current or future product.
primary insurance	As the term is used with personal umbrella insurance, primary insurance refers to the coverage provided by underlying policies. The umbrella policy stipulates the limits that must be provided by those policies.
primary rating factors	Many auto rating systems use these factors to differentiate the premium according to major classifications of driver characteristics. Secondary rating factors refine the premium for selected driver and use characteristics.
prior approval	A filing law that requires an insurer to file rates with the state insurance department and receive approval before the rates can be used.
private passenger autos	Vehicles that are individually or family-owned and used primarily for the transportation of people.
probable cost	The combination of the potential loss frequency and severity. It is an estimate of how often a loss is likely to occur and how severe the economic loss might be as a result.
producer	A common term used to refer to a member of the sales force in property and liability insurance. The term encompasses agents, brokers, solicitors, and customer service representatives who work directly with the customers.
product specialization	When used in insurance this term refers to tailoring an otherwise standard policy to meet the needs of a market segment.
proof set	A group of coins that are uncirculated (they have never been used as money). All coins in a proof set reflect the same mint year. The coins are valuable because they are in mint condition and because they are part of a set.
proprietary alarm	In the event of a break-in, a proprietary alarm notifies a security guard on the premises, who responds.
protection class	A number from 1 to 10 that signifies the level of protective services in an area. A 10 represents little or no fire protection or public service. A 1 represents the highest level of service.
protection and indemnity (P&I)	An old marine insurance term. It includes bodily injury and property damage liability.
proximate cause	That which in a natural and continuous sequence, unbroken by any intervening cause, produces injury or damage. Without proximate cause, the event or loss would not have occurred.
psychographic segmentation	A division of customers according to their lifestyles so that buyer behavior can be identified. It focuses on individual consumption patterns, according to the theory that people project a lifestyle through the products they consume.
purchasing group	A group of insurance buyers who purchase liability insurance together.

radiation shield	Protects combustible surfaces from the heat generated by a wood stove. The shield can be made of metal or a composite stoveboard material.
raking storm	A storm that "rakes" the coastline by alternately covering land and water. This type of storm is usually more intense than a penetrating storm.
rate	The price of insurance for each *unit of exposure*. The rate is multiplied by the number of exposure units to arrive at a premium.
rate filings	Documents submitted (or filed) with a state insurance department that contain the proposed rates and also, when necessary, the statistics on which the rates are based.
rate regulation	The control by state insurance regulators over the rates and classification and rating systems used by insurers.
rate rules	Describe the ways in which rates are applied and modified.
real property	Land, buildings, and other structures permanently attached to the land.
reinsurance (treaty)	See *treaty reinsurance*.
reinsurance recoverables	Amounts that are to be paid by reinsurers on losses and loss expenses that have already been paid to claimants by an insurer.
redlining	A practice underwriters once used of drawing a red line around an area on a map. Applicants within that area would be rejected solely on the basis of geographic location. This term has been extended to mean an exclusionary practice that judges an applicant on criteria that cannot be statistically substantiated. Redlining is a prohibited practice.
regulations	Federal, state, and local governments develop laws, but the details and enforcement of the laws are carried out in the form of regulations. These regulations are developed, altered, and enforced by regulatory agencies, such as a state's insurance commission.
remainderman	The person who will assume possession of the property at the death of the life-tenant.
reservation of rights	A general notice sent to an insured advising that the insurer is proceeding with a claims investigation. The notice advises the insured that this action does not create an admission of liability.
residual market	An applicant rejected by underwriters in the voluntary market might find insurance available through residual market programs such as auto insurance plans and FAIR plans. Some residual market programs have been formed by government bodies to provide insurance for those who could not otherwise obtain it. Also called *shared market*.
retention	This term has several meanings: 1. When used in reference to risk management, retention means self-insurance. An individual retains the loss exposure and pays for any losses from the individual's own funds. 2. This term can be synonymous with deductible. The insured will retain the first $100 to $1,000 of any loss, depending on the size of the deductible. Deductibles in personal insurance are almost always flat dollar amounts that apply to every loss.

retention (continued)	3. This term can also mean the percentage of policies that are renewed at an anniversary. The opposite of retention is attrition. A company might have a 90 percent retention rate for homeowners policies. This would mean that the attrition rate was 10 percent.
	4. Under an umbrella policy, this term acts like a deductible for any loss not covered by an underlying policy. The insured is responsible for the retention amount (usually $250 to $1,000). The umbrella policy insurer then stacks the coverage limit on top of the retention limit.
risk	This term has many meanings. In the API program, two applications of the word are used:
	1. The possibility of financial loss.
	2. The subject matter insured or being considered for insurance.
risk analysis	The process of identifying loss exposures and estimating the potential financial consequences of those losses.
risk averse	People uncomfortable in assuming the uncertainty and consequences of unknown outcomes.
risk-based capital	A model for developing the amount of capital an insurer must have available. It takes into consideration the insurer's assets (and their strength), the insurer's credit (including receivables and reinsurance recoverables), and the underwriting risks assumed by the insurer.
risk management	The application of techniques to eliminate, control, reduce, or finance loss exposures.
risk purchasing group	A group of insurance buyers who purchase liability insurance together.
risk retention group	A special type of group captive that provides limited insurance lines to business organizations that would otherwise have difficulty obtaining such insurance.
risk takers	People who have a higher degree of comfort with the unknown than those who are risk averse.
roll bar	A device to protect vehicle occupants from being crushed if a vehicle overturns. Often made of a heavy metal tube, it is attached to the vehicle frame and passes over the passenger compartment.
"R" value	Resistance to heat transfer. The higher the value, the better the resistance and insulation.
salvage title	The vehicle title applicable when a vehicle has sustained damage that exceeds its value.
schedule	A list of property items insured. Each item must be fully described in the policy and have an applicable limit of coverage per item.
scoring	A method of screening applications. Scoring is performed by a computer program that assigns a number grade to an application based on the information in the application.
screening	A process of categorizing applications to allow underwriters to concentrate only on those applicants that require a decision.

secondary data	In the marketing research process, secondary data is information that has already been collected for another purpose. Secondary data might be collected inside an insurance company (financial reports, loss histories, or policy records) or outside the organization (government reports, business or trade reports, or published reports).
semicompulsory insurance	Required by an organization other than a government regulatory group. For example, insurance required by a lending institution is semicompulsory.
separation	A risk management technique through which resources are divided to minimize the effect of a single event.
severity of loss	The dollar amount of damage that results or could result from a loss exposure.
shared market	See *involuntary market* and *residual market*.
smudging	See *agricultural smudging*.
special investigation unit	A group within an insurance company typically staffed by former law enforcement professionals who apply criminal investigation techniques to determine whether fraud has been committed. If fraud can be proven, the claim might be denied or referred for criminal prosecution.
spontaneous expectations	Occur during a transaction with a customer as a result of the situation or circumstance. These expectations are ideally acted on by the personal insurance specialist.
SR-22	The form number of the document that is attached to a personal auto policy. This form might be required by the department of transportation from an insurance company to confirm that required coverage is in force.
standard auto market	Risks that do not qualify for the preferred market are placed in the standard market. This market segment is composed of drivers falling just short of qualifying for preferred treatment, generally because of a prior claim record but also for other reasons, such as certain newly licensed drivers or youthful operators.
stated amount	A loss settlement option that might be applied to a personal auto policy for physical damage coverages. An appraisal is obtained for the vehicle, and the appraised value becomes the basis for rating. Maximum loss settlement is based on the lowest of (1) the stated amount, (2) the ACV, or (3) the amount to repair or replace.
stated-value policy	As the term is used in personal lines, this is a specialty policy that might be written for vehicles that have unusual valuation problems (such as antique autos, classic autos, or ATVs). Because these policies are not standard, each should be reviewed individually. Valuation might be based on an agreed value or a stated amount.
state-made rates	Calculated by the state under the direction of the insurance commissioner.
stoveboard	A shield made of twenty-four gauge or thicker steel plate that should be placed between the woodstove and the wall or floor.
subjective probability	An individual's personal estimate of the chance of loss.

subrogate, subrogation	When an insurer pays an insured for a loss, the insurer takes over the insured's right to collect damages from the other party responsible for the loss. The insurance company might subrogate against the party directly responsible for the loss.
sue and labor charges	Expenses incurred by the insured to take reasonable measures to prevent damage or injury.
surge protectors	Electrical breakers that are plugged into an outlet; electronic devices are then plugged into the surge protector outlets. Surge protectors guard computers, stereos, and other expensive electronic equipment from uneven electrical flow. These protectors are not a fail-safe guard against damage by lightning. A direct or nearby lightning strike generates too much voltage for a surge protector to be effective.
surplus lines	Any insurance for which there is no licensed insurer within the state. Coverage is written by a nonadmitted insurer. This is done through a surplus lines agent or broker who is licensed to provide this service.
suspense system	See *diary, diary system.*
tangible product	A product that can be seen, touched, and tested. In insurance, the tangible product is a legal contract represented by words on paper.
target marketing	A market segmentation approach that focuses on specific groups for marketing efforts.
telephone checks	A method of verifying information that an insurer has received on an application. An employee or a contractor hired by the insurer calls the applicant to verify statements made on the application. Questions might be worded differently to discover conflicting information.
telephone interviews	A popular way of collecting primary research data, especially when the research involves a random sample of the population, when the questions are few, and when face-to-face contact is not necessary or practical.
term	Policy period; the period during which a policy provides coverage.
termination	A policy cancellation during its term or a nonrenewal at the end of its term.
thimble	A double-walled pipe that allows a chimney pipe to pass through a combustible wall without heat contact.
third party	When this term is applied to an insurance contract, it means an entity who has certain rights under the terms of an insurance policy as a result of the insured's negligent acts covered by the policy.
tort	A wrongful act, other than a crime or a breach of contract, for which relief may be obtained in the form of damages or an injunction.
tort state	A state that provides for compensation to a victim of an auto accident through legal remedies.
tortfeasor	An individual who performed a wrongful act that might form the basis for legal action.
towing and labor coverage (auto)	Pays for road service or towing.

transfer	A risk management technique through which the financial responsibility for loss exposures is shifted from one party to another.
treaty reinsurance	An arrangement whereby a reinsurer agrees to automatically reinsure a portion of all the eligible insurance of the primary insurer. The treaty is a contract that defines the eligible insurance.
trespasser	A person who is on an insured's premises without permission.
umbrella policy	A liability insurance policy that takes over where basic liability policies end. Personal umbrella policies typically provide $1 million or more worth of coverage in addition to auto or homeowners policies.
unconsolidated soil	Soil that is made up of gravel and sand used to fill in low or wet land to create building sites.
underlying	Also synonymous with the term primary when used with the umbrella policy. This term refers to the policies that provide the first level of coverage for a liability loss. The umbrella policy specifies the type and amount of coverage that must be provided by underlying policies. The umbrella policy begins to pay only after the underlying policy has been exhausted (paid out).
underwriting	See *account underwriting*.
underwriting by exception	See *screening*.
underwriting guidelines	Also called "guides" or "underwriting policies," these are a set of parameters or limitations on the type of risks to be written. Guides are established by each insurance company for each line of business written.
Underwriters Laboratories (UL)	Tests and certifies electronic devices, alarm systems, and many other items for safety and accuracy of operation.
unfair discrimination	Involves applying different standards or methods of treatment for risks that have the same basic characteristics and loss potential. Insurers establish rates and underwriting guidelines based on "fair discrimination," which is the grouping of individuals with similar characteristics. Members of that group are then charged the same statistically supportable rate or are treated by the same underwriting guidelines.
unfiled	Classes not required to have form or rates filed with state regulators.
unibody	Literally means "one body." Supported by sheet metal, the body of the car acts as its frame. Many current models are constructed as unibodies. Some large passenger cars and full-size trucks still use a conventional frame (chassis) with a car body added on top of the frame.
uninsured motorists coverage	A coverage in personal or commercial auto policies that provides protection against bodily injury loss (also property damage in some states) when the insured is injured in an accident with a hit-and-run motorist or a motorist who has no insurance.
units of exposure	The standard units used in insurance rating (also called "exposure units" and "units"). For example, each $100 of insurance is the unit of exposure used to rate a homeowners policy.

use-and-file	A filing law that allows an insurer to use rates before they are filed with the state.
vehicle identification number (VIN)	A unique serial number assigned to each vehicle. The seventeen-digit number identifies the make, model year, body style, factory, and engine size of a vehicle. The VIN can also be used to identify the symbol used in rating physical damage coverages.
vicarious liability	Exists when one party is held liable for the actions of another. If an employee acts on the instructions of an employer, the employer might be held vicariously responsible for the employee's actions.
voluntary market	Applications accepted or rejected voluntarily (without regulatory constraint) by insurance companies are considered to be in the voluntary market.
warranty	A statement concerning the condition and use of a watercraft to be insured that is made for the purpose of permitting the underwriter to evaluate the risk. If the statement is found to be false, it could provide a basis for voiding the policy.
wreck removal	A coverage that provides funds to remove the remains of watercraft from the waterways after total loss.

Appendixes to This Text

Appendix 1-A
Enforcement of Compulsory
Auto Liability Insurance Laws *(Current as of November 1995)*

			State Compulsory Auto Insurance Laws			
State	**Insurance Required**	**Minimum Liability Limits**	**When Insured Must Have Proof of Insurance**			**Penalties for Noncompliance (First Offense)**
			Regis-tration	At/after accident	At all times	
AL	FR only	20/40/10	no	no	no	none
AK	BI/PD	50/100/25	no	no	no	registration suspension/revocation*
AZ	BI/PD	15/30/10	no	yes	yes	$250 fine
AR	BI/PD	25/50/15	yes	no	no	$250 fine, registration suspension, confiscation of plates*
CA	FR only	15/30/5	no	yes	yes	none
CO	BI/PD/PIP	25/50/15	no	yes	no	$100 fine
CT	BI/PD/UM/UIM	20/40/10	yes	yes	yes	license suspension/revocation, confiscation of plates*
DE	BI/PD/PIP	15/30/10	no	yes	yes	$150 fine, registration suspension, confiscation of plates*
DC	BI/PD/UM	25/50/10	yes	no	no	$100 fine or maximum 30 days in jail
FL	PD/PIP	10/20/10	yes	yes	yes	60-day license revocation, vehicle impoundment for subsequent offense*
GA	BI & PD	15/30/10	no	yes	yes	60-day license suspension
HI	BI/PD/PIP	25/10/25	no	yes	yes	$1,000 fine
ID	BI/PD	25/50/15	no	yes	yes	$75 fine*
IL	BI/PD/UM	24/40/15	no	yes	yes	60-day registration suspension*
IN	BI/PD	25/50/10	yes	no	no	*
IA	FR only	20/40/15	no	no	no	none
KS	BI/PD/PIP/UM	25/50/10	no	no	no	$100 fine*
KY	BI/PD/PIP	25/50/10	yes	yes	yes	$50 fine, up to 90 days in jail*
LA	BI/PD	10/20/10	yes	no	no	up to $500 fine, confiscation of plates*
ME	BI/PD/UM	20/40/10	no	yes	yes	$100-$500 fine, 30- day license and registration suspension
MD	BI/PD/PIP/UM	20/40/10	yes	no	no	$150 fine*
MA	BI/PD/PIP/UM	20/40/5	yes	no	no	$500 fine*
MI	BI/PD/PIP	20/40/10	yes	no	no	$200 fine*
MN	BI/PD/PIP/UM/UIM	30/60/10	no	yes	yes	license and/or registration revocation for 6 months*
MS	FR only	10/20/5	no	no	no	none
MO	BI/PD	25/50/10	no	yes	yes	license and registration revocation*
MT	BI/PD	25/50/10	no	yes	yes	$250 fine or not more than 10 days in jail*

State	Insurance Required	Minimum Liability Limits	When Insured Must Have Proof of Insurance			Penalties for Noncompliance (First Offense)
			Regis-tration	At/after accident	At all times	
NE	BI/PD	25/50/25	yes	yes	yes	*
NV	BI/PD	15/30/10	no	yes	yes	$100 fine*
NH	FR only	25/50/25	no	no	no	none
NJ	BI/PD/PIP/UM	15/30/5	no	yes	yes	$300 fine, community service, 1-year license suspension
NM	BI/PD	25/50/10	yes	no	no	$100 fine*
NY	BI/PD/PIP/UM	25/50/10	yes	yes	yes	$100 fine and/or jail*
NC	BI/PD	25/50/10	no	no	no	60-day registration suspension*
ND	BI/PD/PIP/UM	25/50/25	no	no	no	$150 fine, registration revocation, license suspension*
OH	FR only	12.5/25/7.5	no	yes	yes	90-day license suspension, $75 reinstatement fee
OK	BI/PD	10/20/10	yes	yes	yes	less than $500 fine, less than 6 months in jail*
OR	BI/PD/PIP/UM	25/50/10	no	yes	yes	license suspension and/or revocation*
PA	BI/PD/MED	15/30/5	no	yes	yes	license and registration suspension, confiscation of plates*
RI	BI/PD	25/50/25	no	no	no	$500 fine, confiscation of plates
SC	BI/PD/UM	15/30/5	yes	no	no	less than 30 days in jail, registration suspension*
SD	BI/PD/UM	25/50/25	no	yes	yes	1-year license suspension*
TN	FR only	25/50/10	no	no	no	none
TX	BI/PD	20/40/15	yes	yes	no	$75 fine, license and registration suspension*
UT	BI/PD/PIP	25/50/15	no	yes	yes	license and/or registration loss*
VT	BI/PD/UM/UIM	20/40/10	no	yes	yes	less than $100 fine*
VA	FR only	25/50/20	no	no	no	none
WA	BI/PD	25/50/10	no	no	no	less than $100 fine*
WV	BI/PD/UM	20/40/10	yes	yes	yes	90-day license suspension, registration revocation*
WI	FR only	25/50/10	no	no	no	none
WY	BI/PD	25/50/20	no	yes	yes	less than $750 fine, registration revocation*

FR—financial responsibility only. Insurance is not compulsory.

Compulsory Coverages:
- BI—bodily injury liability
- PD—property damage liability
- PIP—personal injury liability
- UM—uninsured motorist
- UIM—underinsured motorist

Minimum limits of liability: The first two numbers refer to bodily injury liability limits, and the third number refers to property damage liability limits. For example, 20/40/10 means coverage of up to $20,000 per person injured in an accident up to a limit of $40,000 for all injuries from that accident and $10,000 coverage for property damage.

* Penalties are provided for in the law but might not be mandatory for first offenses.

Source: Insurance Information Institute.

Indicators of Fraud

National Insurance Crime Bureau
10330 South Roberts Road
Palos Hills, Illinois 60465
708-430-2430

Indicators Of Application Fraud
Detection—The First Line Of Defense

Most applicants for insurance coverage are trustworthy, but some are dishonest. Therefore, it is appropriate for the agent to review all applications for possible fraud. Determining the "fraud potential factor" of any application is facilitated when the agent is familiar with various fraud indicators.

These indicators should help isolate those applications which merit closer scrutiny. No one indicator by itself is necessarily suspicious. Even the presence of several indicators, while suggestive of possible fraud, does not mean that a fraud is being committed. Indicators of possible fraud are "red flags" only, not actual evidence.

Suspicious applications may have to be accepted for lack of conclusive evidence of fraud; however, the underwriter should be made aware of the agent's suspicions, and subsequent referral to NICB for further review may be appropriate.

General Indicators of Application Fraud

- ☞ Unsolicited, new walk-in business, not referred by existing policyholder.
- ☞ Applicant walks into agent's office at noon or end of day when agent and staff may be rushed.
- ☞ Applicant neither works nor resides near the agency.
- ☞ Applicant's given address is inconsistent with employment/income.
- ☞ Applicant gives post office box as an address.
- ☞ Applicant has lived at current address less than six months.
- ☞ Applicant has no telephone number or provides a mobile/cellular phone number.
- ☞ Applicant cannot provide driver's license or other identification or has a temporary, recently issued, or out-of-state, driver's license.
- ☞ Applicant wants to pay premium in cash.
- ☞ Applicant pays minimum required amount of premium.
- ☞ Applicant suggests price is no object when applying for coverage.
- ☞ Applicant's income is not compatible with value of vehicle to be insured.
- ☞ Applicant is never available to meet in person and supplies all information by telephone.
- ☞ Applicant is unemployed or self-employed in transient occupation (e.g. roofing, asphalt).
- ☞ Applicant questions agent closely on claim handling procedures.
- ☞ Applicant is unusually familiar with insurance terms or procedures.
- ☞ Application is not signed in agent's view (e.g. mailed in).
- ☞ Applicant is reluctant to use mail.
- ☞ Applicant works through a third party.
- ☞ Applicant returns the completed application unsigned.
- ☞ Applicant has had driver's license for significant period, but not prior vehicle ownership and/or insurance.

Indicators Associated With Coverage

- ☞ Name of previous insurance carrier or proof of prior coverage cannot be provided.
- ☞ No prior insurance coverage is reported although applicant's age would suggest prior ownership of a vehicle and/or property.
- ☞ Significant break-in coverage is reported under prior coverage.
- ☞ Question about recent prior claims is left unanswered.
- ☞ Full coverage is requested for older vehicle.
- ☞ No existing damage is reported for older vehicle.
- ☞ Exceptionally high liability limits are requested for older vehicle inconsistent with applicant's employment, income or lifestyle.

National Insurance Crime Bureau
10330 South Roberts Road
Palos Hills, Illinois 60465
708-430-2430

Indicators Of Property Fraud
Detection—The First Line Of Defense

Most claims are legitimate, but many are inflated or fraudulent. Therefore, it is appropriate for the adjuster to review all claims for possible fraud. Determining the "fraud probability" of any claim is facilitated when the adjuster is familiar with various fraud indicators.

These indicators should help isolate those claims which merit closer scrutiny. No one indicator by itself is necessarily suspicious. Even the presence of several indicators, while suggestive of possible fraud, does not mean that a fraud has been committed. Indicators of possible fraud are not evidence that fraud has occurred.

All suspicious claims, though they may have to be paid for lack of conclusive evidence of fraud, should be referred to NICB. There is no limit to the number of cases you may refer. No claim is too small for referral.

General Indicators of Property Insurance Fraud

Note: Adjusters should familiarize themselves with the following general indicators of insurance fraud which may apply to more than one type of fraud scheme. After review of the general indicators, the adjuster can then refer to the more specific fraud categories which follow. The following categories of fraud are separated merely to facilitate your understanding of that type of fraud. However, multiple forms of fraud may appear in a single claim.

- Insured is overly pushy for a quick settlement.
- Insured is unusually knowledgeable regarding insurance terminology and the claims settlement process.
- Insured handles all business in person, thus avoiding the use of the mail.
- Insured is willing to accept an inordinately small settlement rather than document all claims losses.
- Insured contacts agent to verify coverage or extent of coverage just prior to loss date.
- Insured is recently separated or divorced.
- Suspiciously coincidental absence of insured or family at the time of the incident.
- Losses occur just after coverage takes effect, just before it ceases or just after it has been increased
- Losses are incompatible with insured's residence, occupation and/or income.
- Losses include a large amount of cash.
- Commercial losses that primarily involve seasonal inventory or equipment, and that occur at the end of the selling season, e.g. a ski inventory loss in the spring or a farm machinery loss in the fall.

General Indicators of Arson-for-Profit or Fire-Related Fraud

Note: While arson-for-profit is unquestionably the most vicious and costly economic assault on the property insurance industry, claims personnel should also be alert to fraud which occurs when an Insured takes criminal advantage of an accidental fire.

- Building and/or contents were up for sale at the time of the loss.
- Suspiciously coincidental absence of family pet at time of fire.

☞ Insured had a loss at the same site within the preceding year. The initial loss, though small, may have been a failed attempt to liquidate contents.

☞ Building and/or business was recently purchased.

☞ Commercial losses include old or non-saleable inventory or illegal chemicals/materials.

☞ Insured or insured's business is experiencing financial difficulties, e.g. bankruptcy, foreclosure.

☞ Fire site is claimed by multiple mortgagees or chattel mortgagees.

Indicators at the Fire Scene

☞ Building is in deteriorating condition and/or located in a deteriorating neighborhood.

☞ Fire scene investigation suggests that property/contents were heavily over-insured.

☞ Fire scene investigation reveals absence of remains of non-combustible items of scheduled property or items covered by floaters, e.g. coin or gun collections or jewelry.

☞ Fire scene investigation reveals absence of remains of expensive items used to justify an increase over normal 50% contents coverage, e.g. antiques, piano, or expensive stereo/video equipment.

☞ Fire scene investigation reveals absence of items of sentimental value: e.g. family Bible, family photos, trophies.

☞ Fire scene investigation reveals absence of remains of items normally found in a home or business. The following is a sample listing of such items, most of which will be identifiable at fire scenes except in total burns. Kitchen: major appliances, minor appliances, normal food supply in refrigerator and cabinets. Living Room: television/stereo equipment, record/tape collections, organ or piano, furniture (springs will remain). Bedroom: guns, jewelry, clothing and toys. Basement/Garage: tools, lawn mower, bicycles, sporting equipment, e.g. golf clubs (especially note if putter is missing from otherwise complete set). Business/Office: office equipment and furniture, normal inventory, business records (which are normally housed in metal filing cabinets and should survive most fires).

Indicators Associated With the Loss Incident

☞ Fire occurs at night, especially after 11 P.M.

☞ Commercial fire occurs on holiday, weekend or when business is closed.

☞ Fire department reports fire cause is incendiary, suspicious or unknown.

☞ Fire alarm and/or sprinkler system failed to work at the time of the loss.

Indicators of Burglary/Theft Fraud

☞ Losses include total contents of business/home including items of little or no value.

☞ Losses are questionable, e.g. home stereo stolen out of car, fur coat stolen on trip to Hawaii.

☞ Losses include numerous family heirlooms.

☞ Losses include numerous appraised items and/or items of scheduled property.

☞ Extensive commercial losses occur at site where few or no security measures are in effect.

☞ No police report or an over-the-counter report in situations where police would normally investigate.

Indicators Associated With the Claims Process

- ☞ Insured over-documents losses with a receipt for every loss and/or receipts for older items of property.

- ☞ Insured's loss inventory differs significantly from police department's crime report.

- ☞ Insured cannot provide receipts, cancelled checks or other proof of ownership for recently purchased items.

- ☞ Insured provides numerous receipts for inexpensive items, but no receipts for items of significant value.

- ☞ Insured provides receipt(s) with incorrect or no sales tax figures.

- ☞ Insured provides receipt(s) with no store logo (blank receipt). Loss inventory indicates unusually high number of recent purchases.

- ☞ Insured cannot recall place and/or date of purchase for newer items of significant value.

- ☞ Insured indicates distress over prospect of an examination under oath.

- ☞ Insured cannot provide bank or credit card records for recent purchases of significant value.

- ☞ Insured provides receipts/invoices from same supplier that are numbered in sequence.

- ☞ Insured provides receipts from same supplier with sequence numbers in reverse order of purchase date.

- ☞ Insured provides two different receipts with same handwriting or typeface.

- ☞ Insured provides single receipt with different handwriting or typefaces.

- ☞ Insured provides credit card receipts with incorrect or no approval code.

National Insurance Crime Bureau
10330 South Roberts Road
Palos Hills, Illinois 60465
708-430-2430

Indicators Of Casualty Fraud
Detection—The First Line Of Defense

General Indicators of Insurance Fraud

Note: Adjusters should familiarize themselves with the following general indicators of insurance fraud which may apply to more than one type of fraud scheme. After review of the general indicators, the adjuster can then refer to the more specific fraud categories which follow.

It should be noted that the following categories of fraud are separated merely to facilitate your understanding of that type of fraud. However, multiple forms of fraud may appear in a single claim. For example, in a slip and fall products liability claim, there may also be evidence of both medical and lost earnings fraud.

- ☞ Claimant or insured is excessively eager to accept blame for an accident, or is overly pushy or demanding of a quick, reduced settlement.
- ☞ Claimant or insured is unusually familiar with insurance terms and procedure, medical, or vehicle repair terminology.
- ☞ One or more claimants or insured list a post office box or hotel as address.
- ☞ All transactions were conducted in person; claimant avoids using the telephone or the mail.
- ☞ The kind of accident or type of vehicles involved are not typical of those seen on a regular basis.
- ☞ Claimant threatens to go to an attorney or physician if the claim is not quickly settled.
- ☞ Claimant is a transient or out-of-towner on vacation.

Indicators of Automobile Accident Schemes

- ☞ Either no police report or an over-the-counter report for an accident resulting in multiple injuries and/or extensive physical damage.
- ☞ Accident occurred shortly after one or more of the vehicles were purchased or registered, or after the addition of comprehensive and collision coverage to the policy.
- ☞ Insured has a history of accidents within a short period of time on one policy. Index returns indicate an active claim history.
- ☞ Insured has no record of prior insurance coverage although damaged vehicle was purchased much earlier than inception of policy and date of loss.
- ☞ Expensive, late model automobile was recently purchased with cash (no lienholder).
- ☞ Attorney's lien or representation letter is dated the day of the accident or soon after.

Indicators of Auto Physical Damage Fraud

- ☞ Serious accident with expensive physical damage claim but only minor, subjectively diagnosed injuries, with little or no medical treatment.
- ☞ Despite expensive damage claims, the claimant vehicle remains drivable. Often, there are no towing charges for removing vehicle from the scene of the accident.
- ☞ Claimant vehicle was struck by a rental vehicle soon after the rental had occurred.
- ☞ Claimant vehicle is not to be repaired locally, but driven or shipped out of state for repair.

- ☛ All vehicles in a reported accident are taken to the same body shop.
- ☛ Claimant vehicles are not readily available for independent appraisal.
- ☛ Reported accident occurred on private property near residence of those involved.

Indicators of Medical Fraud/Claim Inflation

- ☛ Three or more occupants in the claimant or "struck vehicle"; all of them report similar injuries.
- ☛ All injuries are subjectively diagnosed, such as headaches, muscle spasms, traumas, and others.
- ☛ Medical claims are extensive, but collision is minor with little physical damage to vehicles.
- ☛ All of the claimants submit medical bills from the same doctor or medical facility.
- ☛ Medical bills submitted are photocopies of originals.
- ☛ Summary medical bills are submitted without dates and descriptions of office visits and treatments, or treatment extends for a lengthy period without any interim bills.
- ☛ Vehicle driven by claimant is an old "clunker" with minimal coverage.
- ☛ Insured, even though legally liable for accident, is adamant that claimants were responsible for accident, indicating that the insured may have been "targeted" by the claimants.
- ☛ Claimants retain legal representation immediately after the accident is reported.
- ☛ Minor accident produces major medical costs, lost wages and unusually expensive demands for pain and suffering.
- ☛ Past experience demonstrates that the physician's bill and report, regardless of the varying accident circumstances, is always the same.
- ☛ Treatment prescribed for the various injuries resulting from differing accidents is always the same in terms of duration and type of therapy.
- ☛ Medical bills indicate routine treatment being provided on Sundays or holidays.

National Insurance Crime Bureau
10330 South Roberts Road
Palos Hills, Illinois 60465
708-430-2430

Indicators Of Vehicle Theft Fraud
Detection—The First Line Of Defense

Most claims are legitimate, but some are fraudulent. Therefore, it is appropriate for the adjuster to review all claims for possible fraud. Determining the "fraud probability" of any claim is facilitated when the adjuster is familiar with various fraud indicators.

These indicators should help isolate those claims which merit closer scrutiny. No one indicator by itself is necessarily suspicious. Even the presence of several indicators, while suggestive of possible fraud, does not mean that a fraud has been committed. Indicators of possible fraud are "red flags" only, not actual evidence.

Some claims, although suspicious, may have to be paid for lack of conclusive evidence of fraud; however, they should be referred to NICB for further review.

Indicators of Fraud Concerning the Insured

Insured:

- has lived at current address less than six months.
- has been with current employer less than six months.
- address is a post office box or mail drop.
- does not have a telephone.
- listed number is a mobile/cellular phone.
- is difficult to contact.
- frequently changes address and/or phone number.
- place of contact is a hotel, tavern, or other place which is neither his/her place of employment nor place of residence.
- handles all business in person, thus avoiding the use of the mail.
- is unemployed.
- claims to be self-employed but is vague about the business and actual responsibilities.
- has recent or current marital and/or financial problems.
- has a temporary, recently issued, or out-of-state driver's license.
- driver's license has recently been suspended.
- recently called to confirm and/or increase coverage.
- has an accumulation of parking tickets on vehicle.
- is unusually aggressive and pressures for quick settlement.
- offers inducement for quick settlement.
- is very knowledgeable of claims process and insurance terminology.
- income is not compatible with value of insured vehicle.
- claims expensive contents in vehicle at time of theft.
- is employed with another insurance company.
- wants a friend or relative to pick up settlement check.

☞ is behind in loan payments on vehicle and/or other financial obligations.

☞ avoids meetings with investigators and/or claim adjusters.

☞ cancels scheduled appointments with claim adjusters for statements and/or examination under oath.

☞ has a previous history of vehicle theft claims.

Indicators of Fraud Related to the Vehicle

Vehicle:

☞ was purchased for cash with no bill of sale or proof of ownership.

☞ is a new or late model with no lien holder.

☞ was very recently purchased.

☞ was not seen for an extended period of time prior to the reported theft.

☞ was purchased out of state.

☞ has a history of mechanical problems.

☞ is a "gas guzzler."

☞ is customized, classic, and/or antique.

☞ displayed "for sale" signs prior to theft.

☞ was recovered clinically/carefully stripped.

☞ is parked on street although garage is available.

☞ was recovered stripped, but insured wants to retain salvage, and repair appears to be impractical.

☞ is recovered by the insured or a friend.

☞ purchase price was exceptionally high or low.

☞ was recovered with old or recent damage and coverage was high deductible or no collision coverage.

☞ coverage is only on a binder.

☞ has an incorrect VIN (e.g., not originally manufactured, inconsistent with model).

☞ VIN is different than VIN appearing on the title

☞ VIN provided to police is incorrect.

☞ safety certification label is altered or missing.

☞ safety certification label displays different VIN than is displayed on vehicle.

☞ has theft and/or salvage history.

☞ is recovered with no ignition or steering lock damage.

☞ is recovered with seized engine or blown transmission.

☞ was previously involved in a major collision

☞ is late model with extremely high mileage (exceptions: taxi, police, utility vehicles).

☞ is older model with exceptionally low mileage (i.e., odometer rollover/rollback).

☞ is older or inexpensive model and insured indicates it was equipped with expensive accessories which cannot be substantiated with receipts

☞ is recovered stripped, burned, or has severe collision damage within a short duration of time after loss allegedly occurred.

☞ Leased vehicle with excessive mileage for which the insured would have been liable under the mileage limitation agreement.

Indicators of Fraud Related to Coverage

☞ Loss occurs within one month of issue or expiration of the policy.

☞ Loss occurs after cancellation notice was sent to insured.

☞ Insurance premium was paid in cash.

☞ Coverage obtained via walk-in business to agent.

☞ Coverage obtained from an agent not located in close proximity to insured's residence or work place.

☞ Coverage is for minimum liability with full comprehensive coverage on late model and/or expensive vehicle.

☞ Coverage was recently increased.

Indicators of Fraud Related to Reporting

☞ Police report has not been made by insured or has been delayed.

☞ No report or claim is made to insurance carrier within one week after theft.

☞ Neighbors, friends, and family are not aware of loss.

☞ License plate does not match vehicle and/or is not registered to insured.

☞ Title is junk, salvage, out-of-state, photocopied, or duplicated.

☞ Title history shows non-existent addresses.

☞ Repair bills are consecutively numbered or dates show work accomplished on weekends or holidays.

☞ An individual, rather than a bank or financial institution, is named as the lien holder.

Other General Indicators of Vehicle Theft Fraud

☞ Vehicle is towed to isolated yard at owner's request.

☞ Salvage yard or repair garage takes unusual interest in claim.

☞ Information concerning prior owner is unavailable.

☞ Prior owner cannot be located

☞ Vehicle is recovered totally burned after theft.

☞ Fire damage is inconsistent with loss description.

☞ VINs were removed prior to fire.

National Insurance Crime Bureau
10330 South Roberts Road
Palos Hills, Illinois 60465
708-430-2430

Indicators Of Catastrophe Fraud
Detection—The First Line Of Defense

All carriers need to maintain good faith when handling claims for catastrophe victims. However, massive disasters overload insurance claim personnel. Insurance personnel are under pressure to settle losses quickly to alleviate the hardship of insureds. Criminals recognize and exploit these crises.

Catastrophe related fraud and abuse primarily falls into three categories: insurance claim fraud, property repair fraud and fraud associated with claims and loss processes. Each category may involve bribery, kickbacks, misrepresentation, concealment, forgery and theft.

Even the presence of several indicators, while suggestive of possible fraud, does not mean that a fraud has been committed. Indicators are "red flags" only, not actual evidence. Suspicions raised by these "red flags" should be referred to the NICB for further review.

Indicators of Claim Related Fraud

Note: Catastrophe insurance claims fraud includes inflated and totally fabricated losses, intentionally caused damages, claims for pre-existing damage and backdated policies.

Insureds With Catastrophe Insurance Coverage (Earthquake, Flood, Hurricane, etc.)

- Insured declares extensive losses without physical evidence, photographs or documented receipts.
- Items claimed do not match claimant's life-style, decor, house, occupation or income.
- Lack of carpet indentation from alleged large furniture or appliances.
- Extensive commercial losses occur at site where few or no security measures are in effect.
- Insured is unusually knowledgeable regarding insurance terminology and the claims settlement process.
- Insured is overly pushy for quick settlement.
- Insured is willing to accept an inordinately small settlement rather than document all claims losses.
- On scene investigation reveals absence of remains of items claimed and normally found in a home or business. The following is a sample listing of such items: Kitchen—major and minor appliances; Living Room—television and/or stereo equipment, record/tape collections, organ or piano and furniture
- Investigation reveals absence of family photographs, heirlooms or items of sentimental value.

Insureds Without Catastrophe Insurance Coverage (Earthquake, Flood, Hurricane, etc.)
Theft
- Affected area was not evacuated.
- Lack of security in the area.
- No other homes were damaged or destroyed in the affected area.
- Name or address on receipt does not match insured name and/or address.
- Insured has no documentation or receipts (stolen, damaged or thrown out).
- Insured had all cash purchases.
- Insured claims items were new.
- Insured can't properly describe items as to function or features.

Fire/Flood Losses

☛ Insured property was not located in major damaged area

☛ Property was in poor condition prior to loss.

☛ No other homes or businesses were damaged or destroyed by fire or flood in the affected area.

Landlords

☛ Although the renter maintains a tenant policy, landlord claims tenant's contents.

Indicators of Property Repair Fraud

Note: Property repair fraud involves unethical, incompetent and dishonest building contractors, who employ a variety of illegal or question-able techniques. These include such activities as collecting for defective or unperformed service, damage inflation, insurance fraud conspiracy, bribery of insurance adjusters and kickbacks. Insureds may conspire with the repairer to cover their deductible, upgrade their property or repair pre-existing damage or defects.

Contractors/Providers

☛ Do not maintain a local office and/or have a local telephone number.

☛ Are not able to provide references.

☛ Want "cash" or payment up front.

☛ Have inadequate equipment to perform job.

☛ Arrive at loss site without being solicited.

☛ Offer below market prices . . . "too good to be true".

☛ Offer cash incentives to get the job.

☛ Estimate is very general . . . lump sum.

☛ Are not bonded or are underinsured, and are not licensed or are newly licensed.

Indicators Associated With the Claims Process

Note: Fraud related to the claims process includes people impersonating insureds and fraudulently collecting on their claims, forging and cashing claim payment drafts and using contractor damage repair estimates to collect for property damages never intended to be repaired.

☛ Insured unable to provide proof of identification and/or home ownership.

☛ Insured over-documents losses with a receipt for every item including older items of property.

☛ Insured cannot provide receipts, cancelled checks or other proof of ownership for recently pur-chased items (i.e. warranty information, user manuals).

☛ Insured provides numerous receipts for inexpensive items, but no receipts for items of signifi-cant value.

☛ Insured provides receipt(s) with incorrect or no sales tax figures.

☛ Insured provides receipt(s) with no store logo (blank receipt). Loss inventory indicates unusu-ally high number of recent purchases.

☛ Insured cannot recall place and/or date of purchase for newer items of significant value.

☛ Insured indicates distress over prospect of an examination under oath.

☛ Insured cannot provide bank or credit card records for recent purchases of significant value.

☛ Insured provides receipt/invoices from same supplier that are numbered in sequence.

☛ Insured provides receipts from same supplier with sequence numbers in reverse order of purchase date.

☛ Insured provides two different receipts with same handwriting or typeface.

☛ Insured provides single receipt with different handwriting or typeface.

☛ Insured provides credit card receipts with incorrect or no approval code.

☛ Insured claims the identical items under different policies or with a different insurance company.

State Insurance Department Phone Numbers and Addresses

State	Address	Phone
Alabama	35 S. Union St. #181 Montgomery AL 36130	(205) 269-2550
Alaska	P.O. Box D Juneau AK 99811	(907) 465-2515
Arizona	1030 N. 3rd St. Suite 1100 Phoenix AZ 85012	(602) 255-5400
Arkansas	400 University Tower Bldg. Little Rock AR 72204	(501) 371-1325
California	100 Van Ness Ave. San Francisco CA 94102	(800) 233-9045
Colorado	303 W. Colfax Ave. Suite 500 Denver CO 80204	(303) 620-4647
Connecticut	165 Capitol Ave. Hartford CT 06106	(203) 297-3800
Delaware	841 Silver Lake Blvd. Dover DE 19901	(302) 736-4251
District of Columbia	614 H. Street NW Suite 516 Washington DC 20001	(202) 727-7424
Florida	Plaza Level 11 Capitol Tallahassee FL 32399	(800) 342-2762
Georgia	2 Martin Luther King, Jr. Dr. Atlanta GA 30334	(404) 656-2056
Hawaii	P.O. Box 3614 Honolulu HI 96811	(808) 548-5450
Idaho	500 S. 10th St. Boise ID 83720	(208) 334-2250
Illinois	320 W. Washington St. Springfield IL 62767	(217) 782-4515

State	Address	Phone
Indiana	311 W. Washington St. Indianapolis IN 46204	(800) 622-4461
Iowa	Lucas State Bldg. 6th Floor Des Moines IA 50319	(515) 281-5705
Kansas	420 SW 9th St. Topeka KS 66612	(800) 432-2484
Kentucky	1229 W. Main St. Box 517 Frankfort KY 40602	(502) 564-3630
Louisiana	P.O. Box 94212 Baton Rouge LA 70804	(504) 342-5328
Maine	State House Station 34 Augusta ME 04333	(207) 582-8707
Maryland	501 St. Paul Pl. 7th Floor S. Baltimore MD 21202	(800) 492-7521
Massachusetts	280 Friend St. Boston MA 02114	(617) 727-7189
Michigan	P.O. Box 30220 Lansing MI 48909	(517) 373-9273
Minnesota	500 Metro Square Bldg., 5th Floor St. Paul MN 55101	(612) 296-2594
Mississippi	1804 Walter Sillers Bldg. Jackson MS 39201	(606) 359-3569
Missouri	301 W. High St. Jefferson City MO 65102	(314) 751-2451
Montana	126 N. Sanders Room 270 Helena MT 59620	(800) 332-6148
Nebraska	941 "O" St. Suite 400 Lincoln NE 68508	(402) 471-2201
Nevada	201 S. Fall St. Carson City NV 89710	(800) 992-0900
New Hampshire	169 Manchester St. Concord NH 03301	(800) 852-3416
New Jersey	20 W. State St. CN325 Trenton NJ 08625	(609) 292-5363
New Mexico	PERA Bldg. Room 248 Santa Fe NM 87504	(505) 827-4500
New York	160 W. Broadway New York NY 10013	(800) 342-3736

State	Address	Phone
North Carolina	Dobbs Bldg. Box 26387 Raleigh NC 27611	(919) 733-7343
North Dakota	600 Boulevard Ave. Bismarck ND 58505	(800) 247-0560
Ohio	2100 Stella Ct. Columbus OH 43266	(800) 282-4658
Oklahoma	P.O. Box 53408 Oklahoma City OK 73152	(800) 522-0071
Oregon	21 Labor & Industries Bldg. Salem OR 97310	(503) 378-4271
Pennsylvania	Strawberry Square, 13th Floor Harrisburg PA 17120	(717) 787-5173
Rhode Island	233 Richmond St. Providence RI 02903	(401) 277-2246
South Carolina	1612 Marion St. Columbia SC 29202	(803) 737-6117
South Dakota	910 E. Sioux Ave. Pierre SD 57501	(605) 773-3563
Tennessee	500 J. Robinson Pkwy. Nashville TN 37219	(800) 342-4029
Texas	1110 San Jacinto Blvd. Austin TX 78701	(512) 463-6501
Utah	P.O. Box 48503 Salt Lake City UT 84145	(801) 530-6400
Vermont	State Office Bldg. Montpelier VT 05602	(802) 828-3301
Virginia	700 Jefferson Bldg. Richmond VA 23209	(800) 552-7945
Washington	Insurance Bldg. AQ21 Olympia WA 98504	(360) 753-7301
West Virginia	2019 Washington St. E. Charleston WV 25305	(800) 642-9004
Wisconsin	P.O. Box 7873 Madison WI 53707	(800) 237-8517
Wyoming	122 W. 25th St. Cheyenne WY 82002	(307) 777-7401

Appendix 9-A

Comparison of Property Coverages on Standard Property Forms

Note: The following profiles provide an outline of the coverage provided by ISO policy forms. They can be used as a reference, and they provide an easy method for policy form comparison.

Only the actual policy forms contain complete coverage information. The actual policy form should be used to determine coverage wording.

Form #	Coverage and Limits	Additional Coverages	Property Items Covered/Limited/Excluded	Building Perils Covered	Contents Perils Covered	Buildings and Contents Exclusions
HO-1 Basic Form	A- Dwelling — Replacement cost B- Other Structures — 10% of A C- Personal Property — 50% of A D- Loss of Use — 10% of A	Debris removal–additional 5% available ($500 for trees that damage property) Reasonable repairs–included in limits Trees, shrubs, plants–limited perils (not including wind or hail) $500 per item and 5% coverage limit Fire department service charge–$500 Property removed–30 days Credit card, fund transfer card, forgery, counterfeit money–$500 Loss assessment–$1,000 Ordinance or law–10% of Coverage A	• Worldwide contents coverage • Limited contents: $ 200– money $1,000– documents $1,000– watercraft $1,000– trailers $1,000– jewelry (theft) $2,000– firearms (theft) $2,500– silverware (theft) $2,500– business property on premises $ 250– business property off premises $1,000– electronic equipment in vehicle • Excluded contents: –Items covered elsewhere –Animals –Motor vehicles –Aircraft –Property of tenants –Property in rented apartments –Rented property –Business data –Credit cards, ATM cards	Fire/lightning Windstorm/hail Explosion Riot Aircraft Vehicles Smoke Vandalism Theft Volcanic eruption	Fire/lightning Windstorm/hail Explosion Riot Aircraft Vehicles Smoke Vandalism Theft Volcanic eruption	Ordinance or law Earthquake Flood Power failure Neglect War Nuclear hazard Intentional loss

HO-1 notes:

- This is an extremely limited named-perils form. Many states no longer accept this form because of the limitations.
- Building values must be written to at least 80% of replacement cost coverage. If the coverage on the policy falls below 80%, building losses will be settled according to a "coinsurance" formula or actual cash value basis (whichever is higher).
- Contents losses are settled on an actual cash value basis.

Form #	Coverage and Limits		Additional Coverages	Property Items Covered/Limited/Excluded	Building Perils Covered	Contents Perils Covered	Buildings and Contents Exclusions
HO-2 Broad Form	A- Dwelling	Replacement cost	Debris removal—additional 5% available ($500 for trees that damage property)	• Worldwide contents coverage	Fire/lightning	Fire/lightning	Ordinance or law
	B- Other Structures	10% of A	Reasonable repairs—included in limits	• Limited contents:	Windstorm/hail	Windstorm/hail	Earthquake
	C- Personal Property	50% of A	Trees, shrubs, plants—limited perils (not including wind or hail) $500 per item and 5% coverage limit	$ 200— money	Explosion	Explosion	Flood
	D- Loss of Use	10% of A	Fire department service charge—$500	$1,000— documents	Riot	Riot	Power failure
			Property removed—30 days	$1,000— watercraft	Aircraft	Aircraft	Neglect
			Credit card, fund transfer card, forgery, counterfeit money—$500	$1,000— trailers	Vehicles	Vehicles	War
			Loss assessment—$1,000	$1,000— jewelry (theft)	Smoke	Smoke	Nuclear hazard
			Collapse—from limited perils excluding earthquake	$2,000— firearms (theft)	Vandalism	Vandalism	Intentional loss
			Glass or safety glazing—covers breakage	$2,500— silverware (theft)	Theft	Theft	
			Landlord furnishings—$2,500 at residence	$2,500— business property on premises	Falling objects	Falling objects	
			Ordinance or law—10% of Coverage A	$ 250— business property off premises	Weight of ice, snow, or sleet	Weight of ice, snow, or sleet	
				$1,000— electronic equipment in vehicle	Accidental discharge of water	Accidental discharge of water	
				• Excluded contents:	Sudden loss from water system	Sudden loss from water system	
				–Items covered elsewhere	Freezing	Freezing	
				–Animals	Power surge	Power surge	
				–Motor vehicles	Volcanic eruption	Volcanic eruption	
				–Aircraft			
				–Property of tenants			
				–Property in rented apartments			
				–Rented property			
				–Business data			
				–Credit cards, ATM cards			

HO-2 notes:

- This is a named-perils form. It provides a longer list of covered perils than the HO-1. More coverages are also provided under additional coverages.
- Building values must be written to at least 80% of replacement cost to receive replacement cost coverage. If the coverage on the policy falls below 80%, building losses will be settled according to a "coinsurance" formula or actual cash value basis (whichever is higher).
- Contents losses are settled on an actual cash value basis.

Form #	Coverage and Limits		Additional Coverages	Property Items Covered/Limited/Excluded	Building Perils Covered	Contents Perils Covered	Buildings and Contents Exclusions
HO-3 Special Form	A- Dwelling	Replacement cost	Debris removal—additional 5% available ($500 for trees that damage property)	• Worldwide contents coverage	"All-risks" except:	Fire/lightning	Ordinance or law
	B- Other Structures	10% of A	Reasonable repairs—included in limits	• Limited contents:	• Collapse	Windstorm/hail	Earthquake
	C- Personal Property	50% of A	Trees, shrubs, plants—limited perils (not including wind or hail) $500 per item and 5% coverage limit	$ 200— money	• Freezing of plumbing in vacant, unattended buildings	Explosion	Flood
	D- Loss of Use	20% of A		$1,000— documents	• Freezing of outdoor real property	Riot	Power failure
			Fire department service charge—$500	$1,000— watercraft	• Theft of construction materials	Aircraft	Neglect
			Property removed—30 days	$1,000— trailers	• Vandalism to buildings vacant for 30 days	Vehicles	War
			Credit card, fund transfer card, forgery, counterfeit money—$500	$1,000— jewelry (theft)	• Natural wearing and deterioration	Smoke	Nuclear hazard
			Loss assessment—$1,000	$2,000— firearms (theft)	• Damage by birds, vermin, rodents, insects, animals owned or kept by insured (water damage as a result of any of these exclusions *is* covered)	Vandalism	Intentional loss
			Collapse—from limited perils excluding earthquake	$2,500— silverware (theft)		Theft	Direct loss by:
			Glass or safety glazing—covers breakage	$2,500— business property on premises		Falling objects	• Weather conditions
			Landlord furnishings—$2,500 at residence	$ 250— business property off premises		Weight of ice, snow, or sleet	• Acts of a governmental body or group
			Ordinance or law—10% of Coverage A	$1,000— electronic equipment in vehicle		Accidental discharge of water	• Faulty planning, zoning, workmanship, materials, or maintenance
				• Excluded contents:		Sudden loss from water system	
				—Items covered elsewhere		Freezing	
				—Animals		Power surge	
				—Motor vehicles		Volcanic eruption	
				—Aircraft			
				—Property of tenants			
				—Property in rented rooms			
				—Rented property			
				—Business data			
				—Credit cards, ATM cards			

HO-3 notes:

- This is the most widely used of the homeowners forms. Mortgage companies often require this coverage (or the equivalent) for their collateral property.
- Building perils are increased to "all-risks." The contents continue to be named perils just like the HO-2.
- Building values must be written to at least 80% of replacement cost to receive replacement cost coverage. If the coverage on the policy falls below 80%, building losses will be settled according to a "coinsurance" formula or actual cash value basis (whichever is higher).
- Contents losses are settled on an actual cash value basis.

(Note: This HO-3 profile is repeated as Exhibit 9-1.)

Form #	Coverage and Limits	Additional Coverages	Property Items Covered/Limited/Excluded	Building Perils Covered	Contents Perils Covered	Buildings and Contents Exclusions

HO-4 Tenant	A- Dwelling — None
	B- Other Structures — None
	C- Personal Property — Actual cash value
	D- Loss of Use — 20% of C
		Debris removal—additional 5% available ($500 for trees that damage property)
		Reasonable repairs—included in limits
		Trees, shrubs, plants—limited perils (not including wind or hail): $500 per item and 5% coverage limit
		Fire department service charge—$500
		Property removed—30 days
		Credit card, fund transfer card, forgery, counterfeit money—$500
		Loss assessment—$1,000
		Collapse—from limited perils excluding earthquake
		Glass or safety glazing—covers breakage
		Building additions and alterations—10% of coverage C
		Ordinance or law—10% building additions and alterations limit
			• Worldwide contents coverage
			• Limited contents:
			  $ 200— money
			  $1,000— documents
			  $1,000— watercraft
			  $1,000— trailers
			  $1,000— jewelry (theft)
			  $2,000— firearms (theft)
			  $2,500— silverware (theft)
			  $2,500— business property on premises
			  $ 250— business property off premises
			  $1,000— electronic equipment in vehicle
			• Excluded contents:
			  –Items covered elsewhere
			  –Animals
			  –Motor vehicles
			  –Aircraft
			  –Property of tenants
			  –Property in rented apartments
			  –Rented property
			  –Business data
			  –Credit cards, ATM cards
				Not applicable under the HO-4	Fire/lightning
					Windstorm/hail
					Explosion
					Riot
					Aircraft
					Vehicles
					Smoke
					Vandalism
					Theft
					Falling objects
					Weight of ice, snow, or sleet
					Accidental discharge of water
					Sudden loss from water system
					Freezing
					Power surge
					Volcanic eruption
						Ordinance or law
						Earthquake
						Flood
						Power failure
						Neglect
						War
						Nuclear hazard
						Intentional loss

HO-4 notes:
- This form is designed for renters who need to insure contents, liability, and loss of use, but who do not own the building. This policy is often called a "renters" policy. It provides the same contents coverage as the HO-3, but the building coverages are excluded. Loss of use is based on 20% of the contents limit.
- Contents losses are settled on an actual cash value basis.

Form #	Coverage and Limits	Additional Coverages	Property Items Covered/Limited/Excluded	Building Perils Covered	Contents Perils Covered	Buildings and Contents Exclusions

HO-6 Unit-Owners Form	A- Dwelling $1,000
	B- Other Structures None
	C- Personal Property Actual cash value
	D- Loss of Use 40% of C
		Debris removal—additional 5% available ($500 for trees that damage property)
		Reasonable repairs—included in limits
		Trees, shrubs, plants—limited perils (not including wind or hail): $500 per item and 10% coverage limit C
		Fire department service charge—$500
		Property removed—30 days
		Credit card, fund transfer card, forgery, counterfeit money—$500
		Loss assessment—$1,000
		Collapse—from limited perils excluding earthquake
		Glass or safety glazing—covers breakage
		Ordinance or law—10% of Coverage A
			• Worldwide contents coverage
			• Limited contents:
			  $ 200— money
			  $1,000— documents
			  $1,000— watercraft
			  $1,000— trailers
			  $1,000— grave markers
			  $1,000— jewelry (theft)
			  $1,000— guns (theft)
			  $2,500— silverware (theft)
			  $2,500— business property on premises
			  $ 250— business property off premises
			  $1,000— electronic equipment in vehicle
			• Excluded contents:
			  — Items covered elsewhere
			  — Animals
			  — Motor vehicles
			  — Aircraft
			  — Property of tenants
			  — Property in rented apartments
			  — Rented property
			  — Business data
			  — Credit cards, ATM cards
				$1,000 worth of coverage is provided for fixtures in the condominium that become real property (additional coverage can be obtained):
				Fire/lightning
				Windstorm/hail
				Explosion
				Riot
				Aircraft
				Vehicles
				Smoke
				Vandalism
				Theft
				Falling objects
				Weight of ice, snow, or sleet
				Accidental discharge of water
				Sudden loss from water system
				Freezing
				Power surge
				Volcanic eruption
					Fire/lightning
					Windstorm/hail
					Explosion
					Riot
					Aircraft
					Vehicles
					Smoke
					Vandalism
					Theft
					Falling objects
					Weight of ice, snow, or sleet
					Accidental dis-charge of water
					Sudden loss from water system
					Freezing
					Power surge
					Volcanic eruption
						Ordinance or law
						Earthquake
						Flood
						Power failure
						Neglect
						War
						Nuclear hazard
						Intentional loss

HO-6 notes:

- This form is designed for condominium unit owners who have coverage needs similar to those of tenants. Condominium owners also "own" some property inside the unit they have purchased. What they own depends on the deed for the unit and the agreement by the building association they have joined. The property they "own" might be limited to the wall and floor coverings, or it might be as extensive as "everything within the weight-bearing walls." For this reason, the policy includes $1,000 for Coverage A items. This amount might be enough to cover a unit owner who only owns the floor and wall coverings. The Coverage A amount can be increased if the property owned inside the unit and the exposure are more extensive. Loss of use is based on 40% of the contents limit.

- The "loss assessment" coverage under the additional coverages is not unique, but it becomes important under this policy. A unit owner can be assessed for damage to the entire building that is not covered under the building association's policy. The loss must result from a peril covered by this policy in order for this coverage to be paid. The basic $1,000 can be increased by endorsement. This policy is also unique in that it can be endorsed to allow rental by a tenant.

- Contents losses and Coverage A items are settled on an actual cash value basis.

Form #	Coverage and Limits	Additional Coverages	Property Items Covered/Limited/Excluded	Building Perils Covered	Contents Perils Covered	Buildings and Contents Exclusions
HO-8 Modified Coverage Form	A- Dwelling — Market value (excluding land value) B- Other Structures — 10% of A C- Personal Property — 50% of A D- Loss of Use — 10% of A	Debris removal—included in coverage limits. ($500 for trees that damage property) Reasonable repairs—included in limits Trees, shrubs, plants—limited perils (not including wind or hail) $250 per item and 5% coverage limit Fire department service charge—$500 Property removed—30 days Credit card, fund transfer card, forgery, counterfeit money—$500 Loss assessment—$1,000 Glass or safety glazing—covers breakage	• Limit of 10% (or $1,000) of contents coverage is provided worldwide • Limited contents: $ 200— money $1,000— documents $1,000— watercraft $1,000— trailers $2,500— business property on premises $ 250— business property off premises $1,000— electronic equipment in vehicle • Excluded contents: – Items covered elsewhere – Animals – Motor vehicles – Aircraft – Property of tenants – Property in rented apartments – Rented property – Business data – Credit cards, ATM cards	Loss payments are limited to the cost of repairs using functionally equivalent materials and methods. If repairs are not or cannot be made, the policy pays the lesser of: 1. The limit of coverage 2. The market value at the time of loss 3. The cost of materials of like kind and quality Covered perils are: • Fire/lightning • Windstorm/hail • Explosion • Riot • Aircraft • Vehicles • Smoke • Vandalism • Theft (only on the residence premises) • Volcanic eruption	All losses are settled at the lesser of actual cash value or the cost to repair or replace. Covered perils are: Fire/lightning Windstorm/hail Explosion Riot Aircraft Vehicles Smoke Vandalism Theft (only on the residence premises) Volcanic eruption	Ordinance or law Earthquake Flood Power failure Neglect War Nuclear hazard Intentional loss

HO-8 notes:
- This is a homeowners policy with unique features regarding the value of the dwelling. There are no requirements that the dwelling be insured to a percentage of the replacement value. All building losses are settled on a replacement and repair basis. After a loss, the insured will get "functionally equivalent" material for repairs if it is cheaper. For example, instead of getting a hand-carved banister made of mahogany, an insured might get a pine banister. This makes the policy useful for older dwellings that might have a replacement cost that is higher than the market value. The features in the home might be unique, such as lath and plaster walls, slate roof, and carved banisters and moldings. Placing a replacement cost on the policy would not be practical or desirable.
- Building and contents perils are the same as the HO-1—very limited.
- Loss of use is limited to 10% of Coverage A.

Form #	Coverage and Limits	Additional Coverages	Property Items Covered/Limited/Excluded	Building Perils Covered	Contents Perils Covered	Buildings and Contents Exclusions
DP-1 Basic Form	All coverages are selected individually; premiums are based on coverage selection.	Other structures—up to 10% of A (does not increase coverage) Debris removal—included in limit of coverage Improvements, alterations, and additions—a tenant can use up to 10% of C (does not increase coverage) Worldwide coverage—up to 10% of C (does not increase coverage) Rental value—10% of A limited to 1/12 per month (does not increase coverage) Reasonable repairs—(does not increase coverage) Property removed—5 days' coverage	There is no worldwide coverage (other than that provided under additional coverages). • Excluded contents: – Money and documents – Animals – Aircraft – Vehicles – Boats other than rowboats and canoes	All losses are settled on an ACV basis. Covered perils are: • Fire/lightning • Explosion Extended coverage perils (optional) are: • Windstorm/hail • Explosion • Riot • Aircraft • Vehicles • Smoke • Vandalism or malicious mischief	Same perils and settlement as provided for buildings.	Ordinance or law Earthquake Flood Power failure Neglect War Nuclear hazard Losses to plants/trees

DP-1 notes:

- This dwelling property policy has the most limited coverage. Unlike the HO-1, it is widely written.
- Coverages are separated into "fire/lightning/explosion" and the optional "extended coverage perils." (The extended perils are easily remembered with the acronym WHARVES: windstorm, hail, aircraft, riot, vehicles, explosion, and smoke.) Vandalism or malicious mischief are other optional coverages that can be added. These limited perils are useful when there is an exposure or hazard that would make the risk unacceptable on another policy form. (For example, if the foundation is open, the pipes exposed to a freeze-loss might not be acceptable under another policy form, but the DP-1 does not cover this peril.)
- All losses are settled on an actual cash value basis.

Form #	Coverage and Limits	Additional Coverages	Property Items Covered/Limited/Excluded	Building Perils Covered	Contents Perils Covered	Buildings and Contents Exclusions

DP-2 Basic Form	All coverages are selected individually; premiums are based on coverage selection.	Other structures—up to 10% of A (additional coverage)
		
		Debris removal—included in limit of coverage
		
		Improvements, alterations, and additions—a tenant can use up to 10% of C (additional coverage)
		
		Worldwide coverage—up to 10% of C (does not increase coverage)
		
		Rental value—10% of A with no monthly limit (additional coverage)
		
		Reasonable repairs—(does not increase coverage)
		
		Property removed—30 days' coverage
		
		Lawns, plants, shrubs, and trees—5% of A up to $250 per item for limited perils (does not increase coverage)
			There is no worldwide coverage (other than that provided under additional coverages).
			
			• Excluded contents:
			  –Money and documents
			  –Animals
			  –Aircraft
			  –Vehicles
			
			• Boats other than rowboats and canoes
				Losses are settled on a replacement cost basis if coverage is carried to at least 80% of replacement.
				
				Covered perils are:
				• Fire/lightning
				• Windstorm/hail
				• Explosion
				• Riot
				• Aircraft
				• Vehicles
				• Smoke
				• Vandalism or malicious mischief
				• Breakage of glass
				• Damage by burglars (but not theft)
				• Falling objects
				• Weight of ice, snow, or sleet
				• Collapse
				• Water discharge
				• Freezing
				• Electrical surge
					Losses are settled on an ACV basis. Covered perils are:
					• Fire/lightning
					• Windstorm/hail
					• Explosion
					• Riot
					• Aircraft
					• Vehicles
					• Smoke
					• Vandalism or malicious mischief
					• Breakage of glass
					• Damage by burglars (but not theft)
					• Falling objects
					• Weight of ice, snow, or sleet
					• Collapse
					• Water discharge
					• Freezing
					• Electrical surge
						Ordinance or law
						Earthquake
						Flood
						Power failure
						Neglect
						War
						Nuclear hazard

DP-2 notes:

- Building and contents perils are written on a "named-perils" basis. The list of perils is broader than those provided under the DP-1.
- Building values must be written to at least 80% of replacement cost to receive replacement cost coverage. If the coverage on the policy falls below 80%, building losses will be settled according to a "coinsurance" formula or actual cash value basis (whichever is higher).
- Contents losses are settled on an actual cash value basis.
- The additional coverages have been expanded beyond the DP-1 form. They are percentages in addition to the coverage limits.

Form #	Coverage and Limits	Additional Coverages	Property Items Covered/Limited/Excluded	Building Perils Covered	Contents Perils Covered	Buildings and Contents Exclusions
DP-3 Special Form	All coverages are selected individually; premiums are based on coverage selection.	Other structures—up to 10% of A (additional coverage) Debris removal—included in limit of coverage Improvements, alterations, and additions—a tenant can use up to 10% of C (additional coverage) Worldwide coverage—up to 10% of C (does not increase coverage) Rental value—10% of A with no monthly limit (additional coverage) Reasonable repairs—(does not increase coverage) Property removed—30 days' coverage Lawns, plants, shrubs, and trees—5% of A, up to $250 per item for limited perils (does not increase coverage)	There is no worldwide coverage (other than that provided under additional coverages). • Excluded contents: –Money and documents –Animals –Aircraft –Vehicles • Boats other than rowboats and canoes	Losses are settled on a replacement cost basis if coverage is carried to at least 80% of replacement. "All-risks" are covered except: • Freezing of plumbing in vacant, unattended buildings • Freezing of outdoor real property • Theft to construction materials • Windstorm, hail, ice, snow, or sleet to radio/TV antennas • Vandalism to dwelling vacant over 30 days • Water seepage • Natural wearing and deterioration	Losses are settled on an ACV basis. Covered perils are: • Fire/lightning • Windstorm/hail • Explosion • Riot • Aircraft • Vehicles • Smoke • Vandalism or malicious mischief • Breakage of glass • Damage by burglars (but not theft) • Falling objects • Weight of ice, snow, or sleet • Collapse • Water discharge • Freezing • Electrical surge	Ordinance or law Earthquake Flood Power failure Neglect War Nuclear hazard

DP-3 notes:
- Building perils are written on an "all-risks" basis. The contents perils are written on a named perils basis.
- Building values must be written to at least 80% of replacement cost to receive replacement cost coverage. If the coverage on the policy falls below 80%, building losses will be settled according to a "coinsurance" formula or actual cash value basis (whichever is higher).
- Contents losses are settled on an actual cash value basis.
- The additional coverages are percentages in addition to the coverage limits.

Form #	Coverage and Limits	Additional Coverages	Property Items Covered/Limited/Excluded	Building Perils Covered	Contents Perils Covered	Buildings and Contents Exclusions
DP-8 Modified Form	All coverages are selected individually; premiums are based on coverage selection.	Other structures—up to 10% of A (does not increase coverage) Debris removal—included in limit of coverage Improvements, alterations, and additions—a tenant can use up to 10% of C (does not increase coverage) Worldwide coverage—up to 10% of C (does not increase coverage) Rental value—10% of A limited to 1/12 per month (does not increase coverage) Reasonable repairs—(does not increase coverage) Property removed—5 days' coverage	There is no worldwide coverage (other than that provided under additional coverages). • Excluded contents: —Money and documents —Animals —Aircraft —Vehicles —Boats other than rowboats and canoes	Loss payments are limited to the cost of repairs using functionally equivalent materials and methods. If repairs are not or cannot be made, the policy pays the least of: • The limit of coverage • The market value at the time of loss • Actual cash value Covered perils are: —Fire/lightning —Explosion —Windstorm/hail —Riot —Aircraft —Smoke —Vandalism or malicious mischief	All losses are settled on an ACV basis. Covered perils are: • Fire/lightning • Windstorm/hail • Explosion • Riot • Aircraft • Vehicles • Smoke • Vandalism or malicious mischief	Ordinance or law Earthquake Flood Power failure Neglect War Nuclear hazard

DP-8 notes:

• This dwelling policy is not filed for use in all states. It has unique features regarding the value of the dwelling. There are no requirements that the dwelling be insured to a percentage of the replacement value. All building losses are settled on a replacement and repair basis using modern materials if they are less expensive than obsolete or antique materials or methods. Loss settlement limitation makes the policy useful for older dwellings that may have a replacement cost that is higher than the market value. The features in the home might be unique, such as lath and plaster walls, a slate roof, and carved banisters and moldings. Placing a replacement cost on the policy would not be practical or desirable.

• Building and contents are limited perils, the same as for the DP-1.

Home Maintenance Checklist

Monthly Activity	Maintenance Tips
JAN FEB MAR APR MAY JUNE JULY AUG SEP OCT NOV DEC ❏ ❏ ❏ ❏ ❏ ❏ ❏ ❏ ❏ ❏ ❏ ❏ **Test automatic garage door opener.**	• Place a chair or wastebasket in the path of the closing door to make sure it functions properly. An automatic garage door opener should stop and reverse when it closes on a solid object (this is a safety feature to prevent injury to people or pets).
JAN FEB MAR APR MAY JUNE JULY AUG SEP OCT NOV DEC ❏ ❏ ❏ ❏ ❏ ❏ ❏ ❏ ❏ ❏ ❏ ❏ **Test GFCI outlets and circuit breakers.**	• Test by triggering the test button on the breakers. Ground fault circuit interruptors (GFCI) can be found on the kitchen or bathroom electrical outlets or in the main circuit breaker box. GFCI are used on outlets that might service appliances that require an electrical ground.
JAN FEB MAR APR MAY JUNE JULY AUG SEP OCT NOV DEC ❏ ❏ ❏ ❏ ❏ ❏ ❏ ❏ ❏ ❏ ❏ ❏ **Test smoke alarms.**	• Press the test buttons on smoke alarms to make sure they are functioning.
JAN FEB MAR APR MAY JUNE JULY AUG SEP OCT NOV DEC ❏ ❏ ❏ ❏ ❏ ❏ ❏ ❏ ❏ ❏ ❏ ❏ **Inspect hot water heater.**	• Check for rust stains or water on or around the hot water heater. This can indicate a leaking valve that requires replacement by a plumber. • Drain 1-2 gallons of water from the drain valve at the bottom of the water heater. Rust or debris will settle at the bottom of the tanks and on the lower heating element. This can shorten the life of the tank or the element. Draining the tank removes the sediments.

Monthly Activity	Maintenance Tips
JAN FEB MAR APR MAY JUNE JULY AUG SEP OCT NOV DEC ☐ ☐ ☐ ☐ ☐ ☐ ☐ ☐ ☐ ☐ ☐ ☐ **Clean frost-free refrigerator drain pan.**	• Remove the tray from the bottom of the refrigerator that collects the condensation. Empty it and wash it in soap and water before replacing. This stagnant water can breed bacteria. It is also a good idea to watch the water level in the tray; it normally evaporates as quickly as it accumulates. A tray that fills with water might indicate a refrigerator that requires adjustment.
JAN FEB MAR APR MAY JUNE JULY AUG SEP OCT NOV DEC ☐ ☐ ☐ ☐ ☐ ☐ ☐ ☐ ☐ ☐ ☐ ☐ **Inspect dishwasher for leaks.**	• Remove the access panel at the bottom of the front of the dishwasher and check underneath for any water. Any sign of water signals a problem that requires a plumber. • Check and clean the screen in the bottom interior for food particles that can decay and breed bacteria.
JAN FEB MAR APR MAY JUNE JULY AUG SEP OCT NOV DEC ☐ ☐ ☐ ☐ ☐ ☐ ☐ ☐ ☐ ☐ ☐ ☐ **Clean kitchen exhaust fan filters.**	• Remove the filters from exhaust fans and clean with soap and water or in the dishwasher. Filters can accumulate grease, decreasing their efficiency. Grease in a range hood and filter can accelerate a kitchen fire.
JAN FEB MAR APR MAY JUNE JULY AUG SEP OCT NOV DEC ☐ ☐ ☐ ☐ ☐ ☐ ☐ ☐ ☐ ☐ ☐ ☐ **Check garbage disposal for obstructions or clinging food particles.**	• Solid obstructions can jam or break the disposal. Follow the manufacturer's instructions for removing any objects. • Accumulated food particles can breed bacteria and cause odors (grind ice cubes to clean).
JAN FEB MAR APR MAY JUNE JULY AUG SEP OCT NOV DEC ☐ ☐ ☐ ☐ ☐ ☐ ☐ ☐ ☐ ☐ ☐ ☐ **Check heating system air filter.**	• Inspect the air filter for accumulated dust and dirt that make the heating unit work harder. A dust-filled filter will carry airborne bacteria back into the heating system and into the air. Replace the air filter if any dust accumulates.

Monthly Activity	Maintenance Tips
JAN FEB MAR APR MAY JUNE JULY AUG SEP OCT NOV DEC ❏ ❏ ❏ ❏ ❏ ❏ ❏ ❏ ❏ ❏ ❏ ❏ **Check sinks and drains.**	• Clean slow drains by plunging or with a plumber's snake (clogs can build until they become impassable; grease in the drain pipes can become more difficult to clear as time passes). • Pour water down unused drains, such as basement sump drains. This will maintain a level of water in the *trap* (the elbow-shaped joint) and stop sewer gasses from entering the house. • Inspect under all sinks for water or corrosion at the shut-off valves. Slow leaks can create mold and wood rot. Call a plumber to correct any problems.
JAN FEB MAR APR MAY JUNE JULY AUG SEP OCT NOV DEC ❏ ❏ ❏ ❏ ❏ ❏ ❏ ❏ ❏ ❏ ❏ ❏ **Check heating registers.**	• Look for soot streaks around any heat register that can be a signal of a problem with the heating system (requiring professional help).

Seasonal Activity	Maintenance Tips
❏ Spring ❏ Fall **Rake leaves and debris away from house and check foundation.**	• Prevent moisture and insects from direct contact with wood, which can cause decay and damage. • Note any cracks in the foundation or masonry. These are normal, but changes in the size of the cracks might indicate a more extensive problem that requires investigation for cause. • Check the interior foundation or basement walls for moisture or white residue on concrete blocks, which indicates water seepage. This could require waterproofing treatment.
❏ Spring ❏ Fall **Clean out gutters.**	• Remove debris from gutters, and clean the screens that lead to the downspouts. Accumulation can cause overflowing, moisture contact with wood, and decay. • Check the joints in the gutters for cracks.

Seasonal Activity	Maintenance Tips
❏ Spring ❏ Fall **Check roof penetrations for leaks.**	• Check around any items that penetrate the roof (chimney, vent pipes, or sky lights) for loose or broken shingles. • Check the interior ceiling and around roof penetrations for *witness lines* (water stains) that indicate leaks. Make repairs to stop any leaks that can lead to dry rot and structural damage.
❏ Fall **Check and repair caulk around exterior surfaces.**	• Check around windows and doors to make sure the caulking seals are secure. Remove and replace loose caulking.
❏ Spring **Clean mildewed areas of house exterior.**	• Remove dirt and mildew from exterior surfaces. Mildew can deteriorate paint and wood, leading to rot.
❏ Spring ❏ Fall **Clean gaps between deck boards.**	• Pressure wash the space between the surface boards to remove accumulated leaves and debris. This material can hold moisture against the wood leading to rot.
❏ Spring ❏ Fall **Clean area around air compressor.** **Wash or vacuum air compressor vents.**	• Remove the accumulated leaves and debris around the air compressor. Hand wash (do not use sprayer hose) or vacuum the vents to clear of debris. This activity allows the unit to work more efficiently.
❏ Spring ❏ Fall **Trim any shrubs around house.**	• Prune shrubs and trees away from the house and windows. Plants that are in contact with the exterior surface can promote insects and surface wear. Plants that obstruct windows create a shield that allows a thief to enter the home undetected.
❏ Spring ❏ Fall **Inspect weather stripping.**	• Check the weather stripping around the doors and windows for a proper seal. Replace any stripping that is hard or broken or that fails to seal.

Seasonal Activity	Maintenance Tips
❒ Spring ❒ Fall **Clean area between interior and exterior windows.**	• Clean the dirt and remove the debris from the space between the interior and exterior windows or screens. • Make sure the *weep holes* (small holes leading outside that drain off accumulated water and condensation) are clear.
❒ Spring ❒ Fall **Inspect furnace.**	• Look for rust (can indicate improper condensation draining). • Note any odd sounds or smells. • Test for proper draft at the furnace or water heater diverter (hold a small piece of tissue paper close to the exhaust to make sure air is flowing outward). • Examine flue for leaks, rust, and damage. • Seek professional maintenance for the furnace annually or if any of these unusual signs appear. Ask for specific maintenance or monitoring tips that are appropriate for your heating system.
❒ Spring ❒ Fall **Vacuum refrigerator coils.**	• Pull the refrigerator away from the wall and vacuum the dust from the condenser coils. Dust accumulations decrease the refrigerator's efficiency.
❒ Spring ❒ Fall **Drain and close exterior faucets in the fall. Open them in the spring.**	• Drain the water from the exterior faucets before cold weather to prevent freezing and damage to the pipes.
Annual Activity	**Maintenance Tips**
❒ **Clean and seal tile grout in bathrooms.**	• Clean the grout between bathroom tiles and seal to maintain the waterproofing. Silicone sealing is available that can be applied annually.
❒ **Inspect plumbing shutoff valves.**	• Check the shutoff valves for leaks or corrosion. The valves can be *exercised* (to prevent sticking).

Annual Activity	Maintenance Tips
❏ **Inspect toilets for rocking.**	• Check toilets for rocking indicating a loose seal. Flange bolts at the sides of the toilet can be gently tightened to improve the seal.
❏ **Exercise circuit breakers.**	• Exercise (open and close) circuit breakers to prevent sticking.
❏ **Vacuum smoke alarms.**	• Vacuum dust from smoke alarms to ensure proper operation. • Replace the batteries on alarms that are battery-powered.
❏ **Vacuum heating registers, vents, and radiators.**	• Vacuum heating vents and radiators to eliminate airborne dust and improve the airflow.
❏ **Inspect fireplace chimney for creosote.**	• Check for creosote accumulation in the chimney. It will appear as a shiny black coating on the interior walls of the chimney or liner. Any accumulation should be removed by a chimney sweep.

The maintenance tips suggested above are preventive. Stopping a problem when it is small can prevent more-extensive and costly repairs later.

For sources of home maintenance information, the following are recommended:

• A videotape demonstrating home maintenance is available by contacting:

    Project Guide: Preventive Home Maintenance
    Hometime
    4275 Norex Drive
    Chaska, Minnesota 55318

• Professional home inspections as well as pamphlets on home inspection and maintenance are available. Information can be obtained by contacting:

    American Society of Home Inspectors
    1735 North Lynn St. Suite 950
    Arlington, Virginia 22209-2022
    703-524-2008
    1-800-296-ASHI for publications

Major U.S. Hurricane Landfall

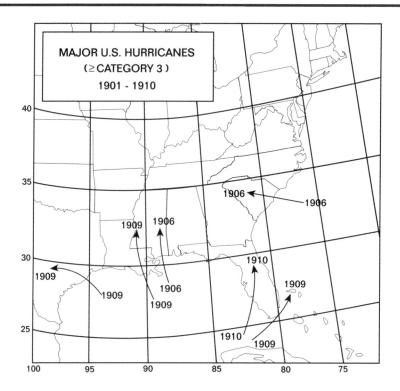

Figure 1. Major landfalling United States hurricanes (greater than or equal to a category 3) during the period 1901-1910.

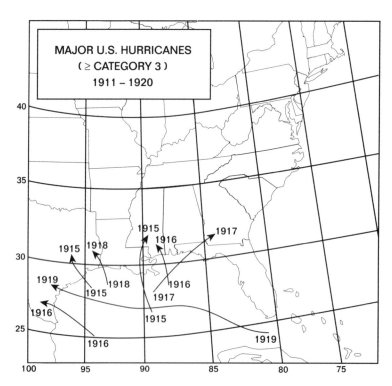

Figure 2. Major landfalling United States hurricanes (greater than or equal to a category 3) during the period 1911-1920.

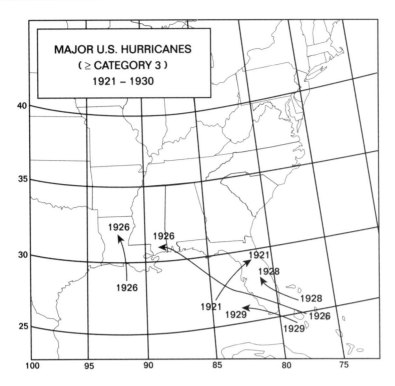

Figure 3. Major landfalling United States hurricanes (greater than or equal to a category 3) during the period 1921-1930.

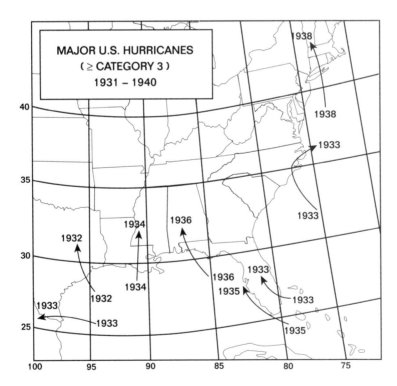

Figure 4. Major landfalling United States hurricanes (greater than or equal to a category 3) during the period 1931-1940.

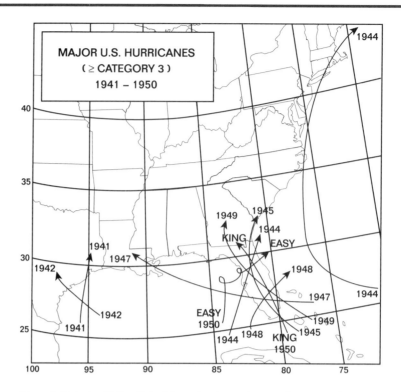

Figure 5. Major landfalling United States hurricanes (greater than or equal to a category 3) during the period 1941-1950.

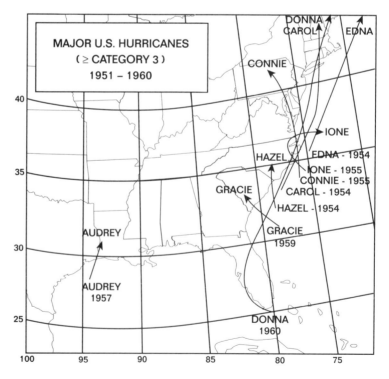

Figure 6. Major landfalling United States hurricanes (greater than or equal to a category 3) during the period 1951-1960.

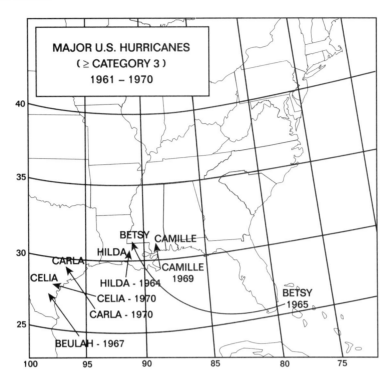

Figure 7. Major landfalling United States hurricanes (greater than or equal to a category 3) during the period 1961-1970.

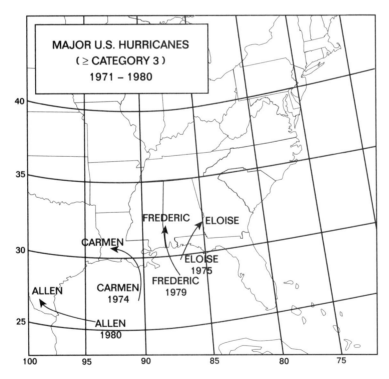

Figure 8. Major landfalling United States hurricanes (greater than or equal to a category 3) during the period 1971-1980.

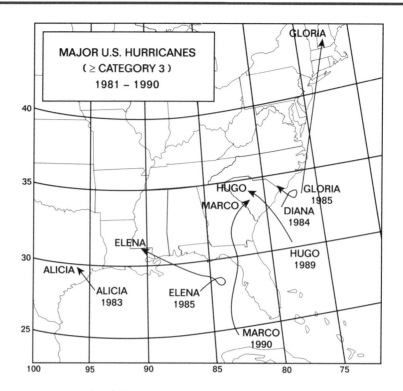

Figure 9. Major landfalling United States hurricanes (greater than or equal to a category 3) during the period 1981-1990.

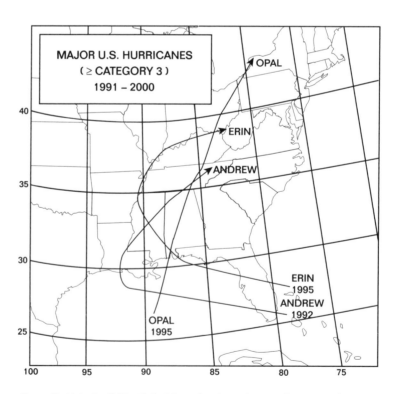

Figure 10. Major landfalling United States hurricanes (greater than or equal to a category 3) during the period 1991-2000.

Source: National Oceanic and Atmospheric Administration and the National Weather Service.

Appendix 10-A

Standard Homeowners Endorsements (ISO)

Form #	Form Name	What It Does and When To Write It	Underwriting Concerns
HO 00 15	Special Personal Property Coverage (HO 00 03 only)	Converts the perils on personal property to "all risks" coverage. This form is attached when a broad range of covered perils are desired for contents.	The perils provided on the contents of the home are broad. A positive loss history with an insured reduces the "risk" of this coverage extension.
HO 04 10	Additional Interest— Residence Premises	Names those who have an insurable interest (other than mortgagee) in the residence premises only. Parties named are notified if a policy is canceled or nonrenewed. This form is used whenever an additional interest needs to be identified.	This endorsement provides no coverage extension—it only provides cancellation or nonrenewal notification. The interest of the insurance companies should be determined. If there is additional ownership in the property, how does it affect the care and concern of the property by the occupant?
HO 04 11	Additional Limits of Liability for Coverages A, B, C, and D	This endorsement can be used with the HO-2 or HO-3 forms. If a loss occurs, the limits of liability will be amended to equal the current replacement of the dwelling	The endorsement requires the insured to agree to maintain insurance at full replacement cost. Determining the replacement cost of a residence is difficult. The insurer should establish a uniform method of determining and updating that value.
HO 04 12	Increased Limits on Business Property	Increases personal property (Coverage C) on business property located on the residence premises, and 10 percent of coverage is provided for business property off the premises. This form has limited usefulness, but it might be appropriate for a computer owned by the insured's business (at another location) that is kept at the insured's home to record the business data.	A stated amount of coverage is placed on business property on the residence premises. This doesn't apply to property stored or held for sale or business conducted on the residence premises. The underwriter should determine: • The nature of the business property • Any increase in hazards as a result of its presence at the home

Form #	Form Name	What It Does and When To Write It	Underwriting Concerns
HO 04 14	Special Computer Coverage	This form insures computers and related equipment for "all-risks" coverage for physical losses. This extension of perils is important for an insured with a valuable computer system. The insured should be advised that reconstruction of lost business data is not covered.	The perils of "dampness" and "extremes of temperature" are specifically excluded. Power failure is still excluded under SECTION I – EXCLUSIONS, but loss by power surge has not been excluded. For this reason and because of the possibility of lightning loss to computer components, a surge protector is an effective risk management option.
HO 04 16	Premises Alarm or Fire Protection System	Allows a premium credit for installation of smoke detectors, fire alarms, and burglar alarms. Insureds should be advised of the availability of the credit in exchange for their action in protecting the premises. This is a positive way for the insured and insurer to be partners in loss prevention.	The underwriter should evaluate the alarm system for eligibility of the credit. Credits are available for: • Central station burglary and/or fire alarm systems. • Alarm systems that alert the fire department or police department. • Fire and/or burglary local alarm system. The insured is agreeing to maintain the system and notify the company of any change to or deactivation of the system.
HO 04 18	Deferred Premium Payment	A form that is attached to the policy if the insured elects to pay the premium in installments.	None of strong significance.
HO 04 20	Specified Additional Amount of Insurance Coverage A	When this endorsement is attached to the policy, Coverage A is increased by either 25 percent or 50 percent (depending on the insured's preference) to provide full replacement cost of the building. Coverages B, C, and D are not affected.	The underwriting concerns for HO 04 11 also apply here.
HO 04 30	Theft Coverage Increase (Form HO 00 08)	Extends theft of personal property under the HO-8 on and off the premises. The insured should be warned about the theft limitation if the HO-8 is written. This is a very important coverage extension for an insured with valuable personal property.	The HO-8 contains a $1,000 limit for theft. This form increases that limit by a stated amount. The specialist must determine the reason for the placement of coverage on this form. Are any hazards increased because of the location of the property? Do any security problems place the home and contents at risk?

Form #	Form Name	What It Does and When To Write It	Underwriting Concerns
HO 04 35	Loss Assessment Coverage	Provides increased limits above the basic $1,000 for losses not covered by the condominium master policy. A condominium unit owner can be assessed for physical losses and liability that are not covered under the master policy that provides protection to the entire building structure and property. This can include the deductible, losses exceeding the coverage limits, and losses that are excluded. This endorsement can increase the basic $1,000 provided for property loss and liability losses up to a listed amount. Only those perils covered by the policy are covered under this assessment coverage.	All homeowners forms provide loss assessment, but it has the broadest application to the HO-6. Research into the master policy, total property values, exposures, and number of units is required to advise the insured of an adequate limit for this coverage and to determine the extent of the exposure. A condominium master policy that provides named perils coverage leaves the unit owners open to losses that they have to pay for under an assessment. This endorsement can also add assessment for additional units. This can be especially useful if the insured has purchased two units and removed walls to form one living space.
HO 04 36	Loss Assessment for Earthquake	Provides coverage for assessments made by the condominium association for earthquake losses that are not covered by the condominium master policy. This is an important coverage extension for any condominium unit owner in an earthquake-prone area. Coverage is subject to a deductible that is a percentage of the coverage limit provided by this endorsement.	This endorsement provides the peril of earthquake for condominium associations' assessments to unit owners. This peril is excluded under the HO 04 35. The same underwriting concerns apply.
HO 04 40	Structures Rented to Others—Residence Premises	Extends coverage to a structure on the residence premises rented to others. Other structures on the residence premises that are rented to others are excluded within the policy forms. This endorsement allows the buy-back of that coverage. Coverage limit is listed for each structure. Liability and medical payments are also extended to these units. This form is important for any insured who has converted an unattached garage into a rented apartment.	Underwriting applies as with any rental property: • What is the insured's experience with rentals? • Can any liability exposures result from the rental? (For example: The tenant has an aggressive dog. The landlord is listed in a suit when the dog bites a child, because the landlord knew of the presence of the dog and its nature.) • Could the tenant be exposed to any hazards on the premises?

Form #	Form Name	What It Does and When To Write It	Underwriting Concerns
HO 04 41	Additional Insured— Residence Premises	Extends coverage to others who maintain an insurable interest in the residence only. It provides protection for the financial interest in the dwelling, liability, and medical payments coverage.	The interest of the additional insured should be determined. If there is additional ownership in the property, how does it affect the care and concern of the property by the occupant?
HO 04 42	Permitted Incidental Occupancies— Residence Premises	Property of the permitted business is covered up to the Coverage C limits in the dwelling or any other structure on the residence premises. Liability and medical payments are extended for this business. This is an important extension for anyone who has business property in the home.	When a business is in the home: • What is the nature of the business? • Are additional hazards created by the business property (such as ignition sources or accelerants)? • Do the customers and employees have access to the entire dwelling, or only a restricted part? • Are customers involved in any activity that could result in injury as a result of the "necessary or incidental use of the premises"?
HO 04 44	Residence Premises— Three or Four Family Dwellings	Coverage is extended to the three- or four-family dwelling listed in the policy. This is an affordable way to extend liability and property coverage to a multifamily building in which the owner resides. This form can also be attached to an HO-4 to extend liability to an entire multifamily building.	If an insured owns a three- or four-family home and lives in one apartment, coverage can be added to the insured's HO-4 to extend liability to the entire building. The structure would be insured under a dwelling fire contract. This form can be attached to an HO-2 or HO-3 to extend both property and liability coverages if the state allows homeowners coverage on a three- or four-family residence.
HO 04 46	Inflation Guard Endorsement	Provides automatic annual increases for Coverage A, B, C, and D by a specified annual percentage rate that is prorated during the policy period. This is useful when inflation or building costs are increasing rapidly.	This is an option to maintain limits to keep pace with inflation and with the increased cost of building materials.
HO 04 48	Other Structures— Increased Limits	Increased limits of Coverage B (other structures) for a specified structure. The amount is in addition to the limit automatically provided. Items that become "real property" at the residence might have values in excess of the limit provided. These "other structures" are listed with additional limits under this form.	Each of these items should be reviewed along with the perils to which they are subject. For example, satellite receivers have special exposures from windstorm and lightning.

Form #	Form Name	What It Does and When To Write It	Underwriting Concerns
HO 04 49	Building Additions and Alterations— Other Residence	Covers additions and alterations made by the insured to a secondary residence rented by the insured. This form is useful when an insured has made improvements in a rental unit because of a special need or an insured is receiving a reduced rent in exchange for the improvements.	The nature and reason for these additions and alterations should be determined, as should the reason for insuring them against physical loss. For example: If an insured is disabled and installs ramps and rails in a rented dwelling, the insured will lose financially if the dwelling is destroyed and this investment must be made again in a new home. This is a clear insurable interest in these additions, even though the insured does not own the dwelling.
HO 04 50	Increased Limit on Personal Property in Other Residences	Increases coverage for personal property (above the 10 percent limit) at another residence. This form is especially useful for an insured with a second home or a child in school who is living in a dormitory.	The nature of the property and its location should be determined. If a significant amount of property is located at another residence, the location should be underwritten for security and hazards.
HO 04 51	Building Additions and Alterations— Increased Limits (Form HO 00 04)	The HO-4 allows up to 10 percent of the personal property coverage (Coverage C) for additions and alterations. This form allows additional coverage.	Refer to HO 04 49.
HO 04 52	Livestock Collision Coverage	Coverage up to the limits shown in the endorsement are provided for the death of animals caused by the collision or overturn of the vehicle in which they are being transported. Coverage is also provided if the animal is struck by a vehicle while on a public road.	Coverage applies to cattle, sheep, swine, goats, horses, mules, and donkeys. The specialist should identify the number and type of animals as well as the fencing used to keep them on the premises.
HO 04 53	Credit Card, Fund Transfer Card, Forgery and Counterfeit Money Coverage— Increased Limit	Increases the limit of coverage above the $500 provided under Additional Coverages. This would be important for an insured who carries many credit cards (more than 10) or who feels he or she has an increased exposure from forgery or counterfeit currency.	Public Law 91-508 limits cardholder's responsibility to $50 for a stolen credit card. Conceivably, a person carrying 10 cards would be adequately covered by the basic policy limits. The forgery and counterfeit currency exposures can run in excess of the $500 limit. Reasons for a request for an increase in coverage limit should be determined.

Form #	Form Name	What It Does and When To Write It	Underwriting Concerns
HO 04 54	Earthquake	Adds the peril of earthquake for property loss caused by earth movement, land shock, waves, or tremors. This is important for any property in an earthquake-prone area. Earthquake coverage provided by this endorsement does not apply to Coverage D or the Additional Coverages.	The exposure of the property and the concentration of property in an earthquake-prone region should be determined. A 5 percent deductible (not less than $250) applies. The deductible can be increased for a premium credit. This should be clearly communicated to the insured.
HO 04 56	Special Loss Settlement	This form can be added to the HO-1, HO-2, or HO-3. This form changes the standard 80 percent replacement cost provision. The cost provision is changed to 50-60 percent. This is a possible option for an insured who has a justifiable reason for not wanting to carry the full replacement cost value on a residence and does not want the reduced coverages provided by the HO-8.	Reasons for the change in loss adjustment and coverage limit basis should be determined.
HO 04 61	Scheduled Personal Property Endorsement	Provides "all-risks" coverage on specifically scheduled valuable items. Coverage is extremely broad, and the deductible is eliminated for these listed items. This is very important for an insured with substantial amounts of jewelry, furs, or silverware, especially single items of high value.	This personal articles floater is incorporated into the homeowners policy. All of the underwriting concerns and questions that apply to inland marine insurance also apply here.
HO 04 65	Coverage C Increased Special Limits of Liability	Allows increased amounts of coverage for the categories of personal property that have special limits in the policy. Perils are not increased. The deductible is not eliminated. This endorsement is useful when an insured has a number of small items that total in excess of the special limits, but the insured does not wish to list, appraise, and schedule the items individually.	Reasons for the increase and the nature of the items should be determined if the increase is substantial.
HO 04 66	Coverage C Increased Special Limits of Liability	This form is similar to HO 04 65 but is used with those policies to which the HO 00 05 and HO 17 31 have been attached.	Coverage has been extended to "misplacing or losing" an item of jewelry (up to $1,000 per item), firearms, or silverware. Concerns identified for the HO 04 65 apply here.

Form #	Form Name	What It Does and When To Write It	Underwriting Concerns
HO 04 77	Ordinance or Law Coverage	A loss caused by a peril insured against will be settled on the basis that a law or ordinance requires. This can be important for a home in a "historic" district or an area where zoning has been established since the residence was built.	This form can increase the cost of repairs in areas that have changes in zoning requirements or laws or homes in historic districts. If local code requires that a home be repaired or demolished after a covered peril, it might require replacing antique building fixtures.
HO 04 78	Multiple Company Insurance	When coverage is shared by two or more companies, this names the companies and the shares assumed.	If a dwelling had a high value, it was once common practice to "share" that limit with several companies and polices so that one insurer did not exceed an acceptable loss limit. With the use of reinsurance, this practice has decreased. The reason for any current sharing arrangement should be determined.
HO 04 80	Residence Rental Theft	Extends theft coverage while a portion of a residence usually occupied by the insured is occasionally rented in whole or in part to others or to a roomer or boarder. This is essential for insureds who occasionally rent their homes (for example, for a special event in a city such as the Olympics in Atlanta) or have roomers or boarders.	• Why is the house being rented? How long will the rental last? • What is the insured's experience in past rentals? • Does the renter have access to areas of the home?
HO 04 81	Actual Cash Value Loss Settlement	Indicates that losses to buildings are covered on an ACV basis, but not more than the amount required to repair or replace damaged property.	The underwriter should determine the reason for selection of the ACV settlement option. If the home is old with an ACV that is less than the replacement cost, this form might be appropriate. The insured should be fully informed of the loss settlement provisions.
HO 04 85	Fire Department Clause (Subscription Contract Services)	When a contract must be purchased from a local fire department, this form stipulates continuation of the agreement as a condition of the contract.	The form only states the existence of the service policy and the adjusted premium. It is advisable to establish a system to obtain the renewals of these policies or change the premium to reflect the higher protection class.

Form #	Form Name	What It Does and When To Write It	Underwriting Concerns
HO 04 90	Personal Property Replacement Cost	Provides replacement cost coverage for personal property up to the limit of liability for Coverage C. This form expands the coverage for contents to "replacement cost" and removes the depreciation for items lost because of a covered peril. However, the list of "property not eligible" for replacement is significant. The loss settlement is also limited. Advising an insured that the form provides "replacement cost" without additional explanation would be a mistake.	The least of the following will be paid in the event of a loss: • Replacement without depreciation • The cost to repair • The limit of liability • Special limits that apply • ACV until the item is replaced (if valued at more than $500)
HO 04 91	Coverage B-Off Premises—Forms HO-1, HO-2, HO-3	Covers structures that are owned by the insured but located away from the residence. The structure can only be used in connection with the residence premises. Examples of this form's use would include a garage or boathouse that is not located at the residence premises.	The circumstances and location of this building should be determined. Since the structure is away from the home, what is the use and security of the property? What exposures are added by the contents of the property?
HO 04 92	Specific Structures Away From the Residence Premises	Covers structures owned by the insured located away from the residence premises, but used in connection with the residence premises. Examples would include a garage or boathouse.	This structure can be specifically listed with a coverage limit, as long as it is not used as a dwelling or for a business. The location, security, and contents should be reviewed for a possible increase in hazards.
HO 04 93	Actual Cash Value Loss Settlement Roof Surfacing	This endorsement provides ACV for roof surfacing damaged by windstorm or hail. The insured assumes greater participation in a loss in exchange for a premium credit.	This is a coverage reduction from the replacement cost provided by many homeowners forms. This reduction should be clearly communicated to the insured.
HO 04 94	Windstorm or Hail Exclusion	Excludes coverage for losses caused by windstorm and hail. This form is allowed in some states that have windstorm plans. The insured receives a credit for the deletion of the coverage from the homeowners policy and purchase of a separate policy for these perils from the state association.	The exclusion from the homeowners policy does not include Coverage D-Loss of Use, which can provide payment for substantial losses. Attachment of this form does not eliminate all windstorm exposures.

Form #	Form Name	What It Does and When To Write It	Underwriting Concerns
HO 04 96	<u>No</u> Section II— Liability Coverage for Home Day Care Business <u>Limited</u> Section I— Property Coverages for Home Day Care Business	Liability and medical payments are excluded for those who provide day care as a business pursuit. Section I coverage is limited.	Liability and medical payments are excluded from home day-care enterprises at a residence when an insured receives compensation for the services. Exchange of day-care services and services provided to a relative are not considered compensation. This is an important exclusion that eliminates the exposure from an unknown day-care operation.
HO 04 97	Home Day Care Coverage Endorsement	Provides liability and medical payments for day care as a business pursuit. This form extends coverage to a day-care business in the home.	The number of persons receiving day care must be declared on this form. An annual aggregate limit is established for liability and medical payments that is equal to the limits of the coverages. If a day-care facility is insured under this endorsement, it should be underwritten as a business with attention to the possible injuries that a child can incur and the monetary results of those losses. From an advisory standpoint, the insured might want to consider the higher limits of liability offered under a commercial account.
HO 04 98	Refrigerated Property Coverage	Covers contents of a freezer or refrigerator on the premises from power failure or mechanical breakdown. This is a useful extension of coverage for an insured who has a substantial amount of frozen foods in the home. (For example, the insured shrimps, fishes, or hunts for family consumption; a family purchases and freezes meats from a wholesale market.)	A special deductible of $100 applies to losses covered by this form. An underwriter might want to ask what the insured has in refrigeration that is valued in excess of $100 and the total estimated value.
HO 04 99	Sinkhole Collapse	Insured for direct loss caused by sinkhole collapse.	The majority of sinkholes exist in areas where mines are present or areas where a stone base is underground with a water table that is below that rock layer. The likelihood of loss is low.

Form #	Form Name	What It Does and When To Write It	Underwriting Concerns
HO 05 30	Functional Replacement Cost Loss Settlement—Forms HO-2 and HO-3 Only	With this endorsement, building losses are settled for the amount it costs to repair or replace a damaged or destroyed building with less costly common construction materials and methods that are functionally equivalent to obsolete, antique or custom construction materials and methods used in the original construction of the building.	This could be a good option for a dwelling in a historical area that has a market value that is less than the replacement cost. The insured must be thoroughly advised that repairs to the dwelling might be made with modern materials (such as dry wall) rather than the original materials (such as lath and plaster).
HO 05 31	Modified Functional Replacement Cost Loss Settlement—Forms HO-2 and HO-3 Only	This endorsement is similar to HO 05 30; however, it states that functional repair or replacement will never be less than the ACV of the damaged property. This endorsement is used instead of HO 05 30 in 17 states (AZ, CA, FL, GA, ID, IA, LA, MN, MS, MO, NM, NY, OK, OR, PA, RI, and SC).	The underwriting considerations are the same as those stated for HO 05 30.
HO 17 31	Unit-Owners Coverage C Special Coverage—Form HO 00 06	Expands Coverage C perils in a condominium to "all-risks" coverage. See form HO 00 15.	This is a form similar to the HO 00 15 that is used on other policy forms. The same underwriting concerns regarding the broad nature of the contents coverage apply.
HO 17 32	Unit-Owners Coverage A Special Coverage—Form HO 00 06	Expands Coverage A perils to "all-risks" for a condominium. This form provides a much broader range of covered perils for the real property owned in a condominium unit.	The real property items attached to the condominium for which the insured is responsible are expanded to "all-risks" coverage. Care should be taken in advising the insured of the property limit of Coverage A. This is determined by the deed and the association agreement that stipulated the extent of ownership. If the insureds "own" a condo inside the weight-bearing walls, they have significantly more Coverage A exposure than an insured who "owns" the property inside the nonweight-bearing walls. This coverage is not available if the unit is rented.
HO 17 33	Unit-Owners Rental to Others	Extends coverage for a condominium while the unit is rented. This is a unique endorsement in that it allows the condominium to be "regularly rented" to others.	Theft coverage is excluded for a list of items (money, securities, and jewelry). Liability and medical payments are extended to the rental of this unit. Underwriting questions should follow those which would be asked for any rental exposure.

Form #	Form Name	What It Does and When To Write It	Underwriting Concerns
HO 23 92	Credit for Existing Insurance	Allows a credit for a homeowners policy that is in existence and will expire in the middle of the term of this policy. This form is generally used to ease the process of packaging coverages.	This form is useful when an insured is being rewritten from a standard homeowners policy to a package with home, auto, boat, umbrella, and so on. The policies do not usually expire at the same time. If the original homeowners policy is canceled midterm to be incorporated into the package, the funds available under escrow with a mortgagee might not be adequate to cover the new annual premium. A credit is granted for the existing homeowners policy. The package becomes excess until the original policy expires.
HO 24 13	Incidental Motorized Land Conveyances	Provides liability coverage to non-registered incidental motorized land conveyances having a maximum speed of 15 m.p.h. This form is used to extend liability to mopeds, motorized bicycles, and golf carts.	An underwriter might want to determine: • The presence of children in the household and their use of the vehicles • The extent to which the vehicles are lent to others or used by any children not in the immediate family • The insured's experience with this type of vehicle
HO 24 64	Snowmobile	Extends liability and medical payments coverage arising from use of a snowmobile. This form can be important if the insured owns a snowmobile or borrows one for use.	An underwriter might want to determine: • The presence of children in the household and their use of the vehicles • The extent to which the vehicles are lent to others or used by any children not in the immediate family • The insured's experience with this type of vehicle.
HO 24 70	Additional Residence Rented to Others— 1 to 4 families	Extends liability and medical payments to listed rental property. Liability coverage is extended to rental dwellings at other locations. This is usually an economical method of providing this coverage to a rental.	The locations should be reviewed for exposures to the tenants and liability exposures created by the tenants for which the insured (landlord) might be found negligent. (For example, the tenant keeps an old refrigerator in the yard. A neighbor child suffocates in the refrigerator. The landlord is listed in the suit for damages because he knew of the danger and did nothing to eliminate it.)

Form #	Form Name	What It Does and When To Write It	Underwriting Concerns
HO 24 71	Business Pursuits	Extends liability coverage to an insured arising from business activities declared on the endorsement. This is a limited coverage that might fill a gap for an individual who works for someone else and accidentally causes injury or property damage for which he or she would be held personally responsible.	Coverage is not provided for: • Professional liability • A business the insured owns or controls • Injury to a fellow employee If the insured is a teacher, many limitations apply.
HO 24 72	Incidental Farming Personal Liability	Extends liability for farming operations conducted at (or away from) the residence premises.	The name of the form indicates that farming is "incidental," but that type of work is not defined in the form. The underwriter might want to determine the extent and type of farming operation, the access of others onto the property, and the equipment used. Farming of any large extent might be covered more appropriately under a farmowners policy.
HO 24 73	Farm Personal Liability	Covers liability off the residence premises, operations, acreage, animals, and employees. This form extends liability to a scheduled list of exposures, including farm employees.	This coverage extension prompts investigation regarding the nature of the farming operation, types of employees (and their ages, experience, and tenure), the insured's experience in operating a farm, and loss experience.
HO 24 75	Watercraft	Extends liability and medical payment to watercraft and motors not automatically covered under the policy. The list of watercraft automatically covered by the liability section of the policy is limited. Coverage can be extended to other watercraft scheduled on this form.	Underwriting this form is like underwriting a watercraft policy: • What type of boat and motor are involved? • What is the ratio of horsepower to the length of the boat? • How is the boat used? (skiing?) • Where is the boat used? • Who uses the boat? • What is the insured's boating experience and loss history?
HO 24 82	Personal Injury	Expands liability to include libel, slander, defamation, and false arrest. These are important coverages in a litigious society. Even if an insured does not have a substantial exposure, this coverage can provide peace of mind.	Because of the nature of the additional coverages, an underwriter should determine the potential liability exposures for the insured and family. To what civic groups and volunteer organizations does the insured belong? Have there been any past losses? What were the circumstances?

Form #	Form Name	What It Does and When To Write It	Underwriting Concerns
HO 24 96	Exclusion of Farm Employees Illegally Employed	Liability and medical payments are excluded for those who are employed in violation of the law.	Such illegal employment might include underage children and illegal aliens if the insured had knowledge of the violation.
MH 04 01	Mobilehome Endorsement	Expands the definition of the property covered by the homeowners policy to include a mobilehome. Places a dollar limit on the "other structures" coverage.	This form alters the basic homeowners policy to encompass mobilehomes. It also provides $500 in additional coverages to remove a mobilehome endangered by a peril insured against.
MH 04 03	Transportation/Permission to Move	Extends protection to collision, sinking, and stranding for a mobilehome that is being moved.	Collision, upset, standing, and sinking perils are added while the mobilehome is being moved. The coverage period extends from 30 days of the date of the endorsement. The underwriter might want to determine that a professional moving company is being used.
MH 04 04	Mobilehome Lienholder's Single Interest	Provides coverage for the lienholder's interest while the mobilehome is transported or from loss caused by illegal conversion.	A listed lienholder's interest is automatically covered under the MH 04 01. If this form is requested to cover only the interest of the lienholder, the underwriter might want to question the purpose. Has the unit been repossessed? Has the owner abandoned the unit? What are the circumstances?

Summary of Underwriting for Personal Articles Floater Classes

Property Class	What Articles Are Covered by the PAF?	When Should Coverage Be Written?	How Should Value Be Determined?	What Are Typical Underwriting Questions?
All				1. Who is the individual being insured? 2. What is the property and exposure to loss? 3. Where is the exposure to loss? 4. Why should the underwriter accept the risk?
Jewelry	• Articles of personal adornment • Pens and pencils • Flasks and cigarette cases • Similar items composed in whole or in part of precious metals • Newly acquired jewelry is covered for 30 days, up to 25 percent of the schedule or $10,000, whichever is less	Jewelry should be scheduled when: • Any single item exceeds the homeowners policy • Jewelry of substantial value is subject to perils not covered by the homeowners policy	Appraisals are necessary and should be detailed, including the "Four C's" for any diamonds, a description of any colored gems, the weight and type of the metal, and a general description. An appraisal using GIA standards will be more consistent than appraisals using less formalized standards.	1. What is the insured's credit history? 2. What is the insured's loss history? 3. How does the jewelry value compare to the insured's salary or the value of the home?
Furs	• Furs, including imitation furs, rugs, and garments trimmed in fur or principally of fur • Newly acquired furs are covered for up to 25 percent of the schedule or $10,000, whichever is less	Furs should be scheduled when: • Furs are of a very high value • Furs are subject to perils not covered by the homeowners policy	No appraisal needed. The sales receipt is usually adequate.	1. Is there a high-value item? 2. Does the insured travel frequently? Does the insured carry furs while traveling?

Property Class	What Articles Are Covered by the PAF?	When Should Coverage Be Written?	How Should Value Be Determined?	What Are Typical Underwriting Questions?
Cameras	• Nonprofessional use equipment including cameras; projection machines; movable sound equipment pertaining to recording, projection, reproduction, and operation of motion pictures; home video cameras; and miscellaneous equipment • Blanket coverage can be written for up to 10 percent of the amount scheduled • Newly acquired cameras are covered for 30 days up to 25 percent of the schedule or $10,000, whichever is less	• Equipment with high values is exposed to losses not covered by the homeowners policy	• A receipt or list with manufacturer, model #, serial #, and description are usually adequate	1. Is there any professional use? 2. Is there any high-value equipment? 3. What has the insured's loss experience been?
Musical Instruments	• Nonprofessional use instruments (unless that warranty has been waived by the underwriter) • Musical instruments, sheet music, and equipment • Newly acquired musical instruments are covered for 30 days up to 25 percent of the schedule or $10,000, whichever is less.	Musical instruments should be scheduled when: • Instruments with high value are exposed to losses not covered under the homeowners policy	• A receipt with a description, manufacturer, and serial # are usually adequate	1. Is there any professional use? 2. Is there any high-value equipment? 3. Does the instrument remain at the residence, or is it taken to other locations frequently?
Silverware	• Silverware including silverplate and flatware • Coverage can be written on an individual or blanket basis	Silverware should be scheduled when: • Silverware has values totaling more than the $1,000 theft limitation under the homeowners policy	• Description of the pieces, manufacturer, type of items, and the pattern is usually adequate for smaller items • An appraisal on more valuable items	1. What is the total value of the silver? 2. Are there any large valuable pieces? 3. If there is a large collection, what is the security on the home?

Property Class	What Articles Are Covered by the PAF?	When Should Coverage Be Written?	How Should Value Be Determined?	What Are Typical Underwriting Questions?
Golfer's Equipment	• Golf clubs, golf clothing, golf equipment • Coverage can be written on a schedule or blanket basis	When an insured owns golf equipment of exceptionally high value	• A description of the items covered	1. What is the total value of the equipment? 2. Is the golfer a professional?
Fine Arts	• Private collections of paintings; etchings; pictures; tapestries; art glass; windows; works of art of rarity, historical value, or artistic merit • An additional 25 percent of the amount of insurance for scheduled items is provided newly acquired items for 90 days • Coverage can be added for breakage	Fine arts should be scheduled for: • Items exposed to perils that are not covered under the contents section of the homeowners policy • Valuable items that cannot easily be valued after a loss • Collectibles of value that are appreciating in value substantially	• Valuation is very important because coverage is provided on an agreed value basis • A professional appraisal is normally required on any items valued in excess of $1,000 • An appraisal would usually include: The artist Type of work Title or description Date or origin Distinguishing features Condition of the item	1. What probable perils is the item subject to? 2. Is this a rare or valuable item? 3. Can the value of the item be established? 4. Does the insured work as a dealer? (Could new store property be declared as a personal item covered under the schedule's 25 percent automatic coverage for newly acquired items?)
Postage Stamps and Coins	• Stamps in the custody or control of the insured, including similar collectibles, books, pages, and mountings • Coins include medals, paper money, bank notes, tokens, other numismatic property, albums, containers, frames, cards, display cabinets • Coverage is not intended for ingots or bullion	Stamps and coins should be scheduled for: • Insureds who have collections that exceed the limits provided under the homeowners policy for these items (usually $200)	• A list of the items with a description and indication of condition is usually sufficient.	1. What safeguards are taken at the residence? 2. What has the insured's loss experience been?

Glossary of Nautical Terms

Aboard	In or on the vessel; off the beam or side of the vessel.
Abreast	Opposite to or bearing 90° from ahead.
Aft	At, near, or toward the stern; between the stern and the amidship section of a vessel.
Ahead	Forward of the bow.
Alongside	Beside a pier or another vessel.
Amidship(s)	In the center of a vessel; halfway between stem and stern.
Anchor	An iron device shaped to grip the bottom and hold a vessel in place by the cable or line attached thereto.
Anchor light	White light visible all around the horizon; displayed by a ship at anchor.
Anchorage	Suitable place to anchor; a special place set aside for anchoring.
Astern	Signifying position, in the rear of or abaft the stern; as regards motion, the opposite of going ahead; backwards.
Athwart	At right angles to the center of the ship.
Auxiliary	An engine, other than the main propulsion unit, used to drive winches, pumps, generators, etc.
Backwash	Water thrown aft by the turning of the screw.
Ballast	Heavy weights such as iron, lead, stone, sand, or water, carried in the hold of a vessel to increase stability by lowering the center of gravity.
Beam	The maximum width of a vessel; the athwartship parts of the vessel's frame which supports the decks.
Bearing	The direction of any object expressed either in terms of degrees or compass points.
Berth	A vessel's place at anchor or at a dock.
Bight	Any part of a rope except the end; usually a loop in a rope.
Bilge	The curved part of a vessel's hull, where the sides and flat bottom meet inside the vessel.
Bilge water	Water accumulated in the bilge by seepage or leakage.

Bitts	A pair of vertical wooden or iron heads on board a vessel to which mooring or towing lines are made fast.
Blinker	A set of lights at the masthead or on the end of a yardarm connected to a telegraph key and used for sending flashing light signals, usually by International Morse Code.
Bollard	An upward wooden or iron post on a pier to which hawsers are secured.
Boom	A spar with special use, such as a cargo boom, the boom for a sail, etc.
Bow	The forward part of a vessel.
Bowline	A mooring or docking line leading from the bow of a vessel.
Bridge	The raised platform in the forward part of a vessel from which the vessel is navigated and controlled.
Broad on the bow	Bearing 45° from ahead; halfway between ahead and abeam.
Bulkhead	A partition separating compartments in a ship; corresponds to a wall in a building.
Buoy	A floating conical, cylindrical, or spar shaped object for marking channels, shoals, etc.
Cable	A chain or wire rope of great strength, used with an anchor or for towing.
Cable length	100 fathoms or 600 feet.
Chock	A heavy wooden or metal fitting secured on a deck or pier and having jaws through which lines or cables may be passed; a block or wedge of wood or other material used to secure cargo in the holds so that it will not work loose.
Cleat	A fitting of wood or metal with two horns used for securing lines.
Coaming	The raised framework about deck openings, hatches and cockpits of open boats.
Compass	An instrument for determining bearings and courses indicating magnetic or true north and the vessel's heading.
Cordage	A general term for line of all kinds.
Davits	A set of cranes or radical arms on the gunwale of the ship, from which the lifeboats are suspended.
Dead ahead	Directly ahead, as on an extension of the keel line of the vessel.
Dock	Water area adjacent to or alongside a pier, quay or wharf.
Draft	The depth of water from the waterline to the vessel's keel.
Drift	The leeway of a vessel or the amount of set of a tide or current.
Fathom	A nautical unit of measure equaling 6 feet.
Fore and aft	Parallel to the ship's center line.

Forecastle	The upper deck forward of the foremast, and the compartments immediately below this deck.
Forward	At, near, or toward the bow.
Foul	Jammed; not clear.
Freeboard	The distance from the waterline to the top of the weather deck on the side. Sometimes refers to the whole out-of-water section of a vessel's side.
Gear	The general term for spars, ropes, blocks, and other equipment.
Green water	A large body of solid water taken aboard.
Gunwale	The upper edge or rail of a vessel or a side of a boat.
Gypsy	The drum of a windlass or winch around which line or cable is turned.
Harbor master	The official in charge of the anchorage berths and harbor regulations of a port.
Hatch	A large opening in the deck of a vessel through which the cargo is hoisted in and out and access is had to the hold; also called hatchway.
Hawser	A heavy line 5 inches or more in circumference used for heavy work and towing.
Heave to	To bring the vessel's head or stern into the wind or sea and hold her there by the use of rudder and engines.
Heave the lead	To take soundings with a line and a lead.
Heaving line	A small line thrown to a vessel or pier for passing larger lines.
Heel	The lower end of a mast; to list over; a vessel turns on her heel when she turns in a short space.
Helm	The apparatus by which the ship is steered, including the rudder, tiller, and wheel.
Hold	The interior part of a vessel in which cargo is stowed.
Hull	The body of a vessel, not including its masting, rigging, etc.
Inboard	Toward the center line of the vessel.
Inland Rules	The rules enacted by Congress governing the navigation of the inland waters of the United States.
International Rule	The rules established by agreement between maritime nations governing navigation on the high seas.
Jury rig	A term applied to temporary structures, such as masts, rudders, etc., used in an emergency.
Kedge	A small anchor used to move a vessel. It is placed ahead or astern and the vessel is hauled up to it.

Keel	A longitudinal beam or plate in the extreme bottom of a vessel from which the ribs and floors start.
Lash	To tie or secure.
Lead line	A line secured to the lead and marked to be used in soundings.
Lee	Away from the direction of the wind.
Lighter	A small vessel used for loading and discharging vessels at anchor.
Line	A general term for a light rope.
List	Inclination of a vessel to one side or the other because of excess weight or shifted cargo.
Log	A record of the daily progress of a vessel and the events of a voyage; also a device for determining the speed of a vessel.
Logbook	A book containing the official record of a ship's activities together with observations of weather conditions.
Long blast	A whistle blast of at least 4 seconds duration.
Lubber line	A vertical black or white line marked on the inner surface of the compass bowl parallel with the keel and indicating the vessel's head.
Main deck	The highest complete deck extending from stem to stern and from side to side.
Masthead light	A white running light carried on the foremast or in the fore part of a steam vessel under way.
Mooring	Securing a vessel to a pier or buoy; anchoring; the place where the vessel is moored.
Offshore wind	A wind blowing off the land.
On the bow	The bearing of an object from 0° to 45° from ahead.
On the quarter	The bearing of an object from 135° to 180° from ahead.
Out of trim	A ship carrying a list or down by the head or stern.
Outboard	Toward the sides of a vessel; entirely outside the vessel.
Part	To break, as a break in a cable or rope.
Pay out	To let out cable or ease off on a line.
Pier	A construction work running at an angle with the shore line, providing landing places for vessels on both sides.
Port	The left side of the vessel facing forward; an opening in a vessel's side; a harbor.
Propeller	A device often called a screw, which rotates under the water in the stern of a vessel to propel her. A propeller has a hub and from two to four radial blades.

Quarter	The portion of a vessel's sides near the stern.
Quay	A cargo-discharging wharf which is parallel with the basin or harbor edge and has water on both sides.
Range	Two or more objects in line to indicate a preferred course to steer; distance in yards from a vessel to the target.
Range lights	Lights at or near a lighthouse, passage or channel, set in line to indicate the course of the channel.
Ribs	The frame of a vessel.
Ride	To lie at anchor.
Riding lights	Lights carried by a ship at anchor or moored.
Rigging	Fiber line or wire ropes securing masts, booms or sails.
Rudder	A flat vertical structure attached to the stern and connected with appropriate gear used to steer the vessel.
Rules of the Road	Regulations enacted to prevent collisions between vessels.
Salvage	To save a ship or cargo from danger; money paid for saving a ship or cargo.
Seaworthy	Capable of putting to sea and meeting usual sea conditions; it refers not only to the condition of the structure of the ship itself, but also means that it is properly laden, and provided with a competent master, a sufficient number of competent officers and seamen, and the requisite appurtenances and equipments, such as the ballast, cables and anchors, cordage and sails, food, water, fuel and lights, and other necessary or proper stores and implements for the voyage.
Secure	To make fast; safe; order given on completion of an operation.
Short blast	A whistle blast lasting about 1 second.
Slew	To yaw from side to side while at anchor or being towed.
Spar	A term applied to a pole serving as a mast, boom, gaff, bowsprit, etc. Spars are made of steel or wood.
Starboard	The right side of the vessel looking forward, indicated at night by a green light.
Stay	A rope of hemp or wire used to support a mast or spar in position.
Stern	The aft part of a vessel.
Stern line	A mooring line leading from the stern of a vessel.
Sternway	Movement of a vessel in the direction of the stern.
Stow	To put gear in its proper place.
Swell	Undulations of the sea having greater length than ordinary waves, usually caused by the wind of a distant storm.

Taut	Tight; without slack.
Tiller	A short piece of iron or wood fitting into the rudderhead, by which the rudder is turned.
Tow	To pull a vessel, barge, or other craft through the water by means of a line or cable; vessel or vessels being towed.
Trim	The difference in draft at the bow of a vessel from that at the stern.
Trough	The hollow between two waves; opposite of crest.
Ullage space	The unfilled part of a tank or container. Liquid at a certain level below this will roll around and affect the trim of the vessel.
Underway	Said of a vessel when not at anchor, not made fast to the shore, and not aground.
Veer	To pay out cable or line; to change the direction of a vessel in reference to the wind.
Waist	The middle part of a vessel, midway between the bow and the stern.
Warp	To move a vessel by line or by anchor.
Waterline	The line printed on the side of a vessel at the water's edge to indicate a proper trim.
Wharf	Installation for loading or discharging vessels; particularly a platform of timber, stone, or concrete against which vessels may be secured to load or discharge.
Winch	A hoisting engine secured to the deck used to haul lines or wire rope by turns around a horizontally turning drum.
Windward	In the direction from which the wind is blowing.
Yard	A spar attached at its center point to a mast running athwartship; used as a support for signal halyards or signal lights.
Yaw	To steer badly, zigzagging back and forth across an intended course.

Federal Requirements and Safety Tips for Recreational Boats

Boating
Safety
Hotline

U.S. Department
of Transportation

**United States
Coast Guard**

- Information on
  boating safety recalls.

- To report possible
  defects in boats.

- To comment on U.S.C.G.
  boarding procedures.

800-368-5647

Call Toll Free
for Information

- For answers to boating
  safety questions.

- For boating safety
  literature.

Produced by the U.S. Coast Guard Boating Education Branch 3/1/92

Equipment Requirements

The Coast Guard sets minimum safety standards for vessels and associated equipment. To meet these standards some of the equipment must be Coast Guard approved. "Coast Guard Approved Equipment" has been determined to be in compliance with USCG specifications and regulations relating to performance, construction, or materials.

Personal Flotation Devices (PFDs)

PFDs must be Coast Guard Approved, in good and serviceable condition, and of appropriate size for the intended user. Wearable PFDs must be readily accessible, meaning you must be able to put them on in a reasonable amount of time in an emergency (vessel sinking, on fire, etc.). They should not be stowed in plastic bags, in locked or closed compartments or have other gear stowed on top of them. *Throwable devices must be immediately available for use.* Though not required, a PFD should be worn at all times when the vessel is underway. A wearable PFD may save your life, but only if you wear it.

Boats less than 16 feet in length (including canoes and kayaks of any length) must be equipped with one Type I, II, III, IV, or V PFD for each person aboard.

Boats 16 feet and longer must be equipped with one Type I, II, III, or V PFD for each person aboard PLUS one Type IV.

Type V PFDs have use restrictions marked on them which must be observed.

If a type V PFD is to be counted toward minimum carriage requirements, it must be worn.

Federal law does not require PFDs on racing shells, rowing skulls, and racing kayaks; State laws vary.

For the Courtesy Marine Examination (CME) boats under 16 feet must be equipped with a minimum of 2 PFDs. Boats 16 feet and over must have a minimum of 2 wearable and one throwable PFD.

Remember, PFDs will keep you from sinking, but not necessarily from drowning. Extra time should be taken in selecting a properly sized PFD to insure a safe fit. Testing your PFD in shallow water or guarded swimming pool is a good and reassuring practice.

Types of PFD

A TYPE I PFD, or OFF-SHORE LIFE JACKET provides the most buoyancy. It is effective for all waters, especially open, rough, or remote waters where rescue may be delayed. It is designed to turn most unconscious wearers in the water to a face-up position. The Type I comes in two sizes. The adult size provides at least 22 pounds buoyancy, the child size, 11 pounds, minimum.

Off-shore Life Jacket

A TYPE II PFD, or NEAR-SHORE BUOYANT VEST is intended for calm inland water or where there is a good chance of quick rescue. This type will turn **some** unconscious wearers to a face-up position in the water. The turning action is not as pronounced and it will not turn as many persons to a face-up position under the same conditions as a Type I. An adult size device provides at least 15½ pounds buoyancy, a medium child size provides 11 pounds. Infant and small child sizes each provide at least 7 pounds buoyancy.

Near-shore Buoyant Vest
(See drawing on top of next page.)

Near-shore Buoyant Vest

A TYPE III PFD, or FLOTATION AID is good for calm, inland water, or where there is a good chance of quick rescue. It is designed so wearers can place themselves in a face-up position in the water. The wearers may have to tilt their heads back to avoid turning face-down in the water. The Type III has the same minimum buoyancy as a Type II PFD. It comes in many types, colors, and sizes and is generally the most comfortable type for continuous wear. Float coats, fishing vests, and vests designed with features suitable for various sports activities are examples of this type PFD.

Flotation Aid

A TYPE IV PFD, or THROWABLE DEVICE is intended for calm, inland water with heavy boat traffic, where help is always present. It is designed to be thrown to a person in the water and grasped and held by the user until rescued. It is not designed to be worn. Type IV devices include buoyant cushions, ring buoys, and horseshoe buoys.

Throwable Device

A TYPE V PFD, or SPECIAL USE DEVICE is intended for specific activities and may be carried instead of another PFD *only if used according to the approval condition on the label.* Some Type V devices provide significant hypothermia protection. Varieties include deck suits, work vests, board sailing vests, and Hybrid PFDs.

A TYPE V HYBRID INFLATABLE PFD is the least bulky of all PFD types. It contains a small amount of inherent buoyancy, and an inflatable chamber. Its performance is equal to a Type I, II, or III PFD (as noted on the PFD label) when inflated. *Hybrid PFDs must be worn when underway to be acceptable.*

Inflated Hybrid PFD

Water Skiing and PFDs

A water skier is considered on board the vessel and a PFD is required for the purposes of compliance with the PFD carriage requirements. It is advisable and recommended for a skier to wear a PFD designed to withstand the impact of hitting the water at high speed. "Impact Class" marking on the label refers to PFD strength, not personal protection. Some State laws require skiers to wear a PFD.

Visual Distress Signals

All vessels, used on coastal waters, the Great Lakes, territorial seas, and those waters connected directly to them, up to a point where a body of water is less than two miles wide, must be equipped with U.S.C.G. Approved visual distress signals. Vessels owned in the United States operating on the high seas must be equipped with U.S.C.G. Approved visual distress signals. The following vessels are not required to carry day signals but must carry night signals when operating from sunset to sunrise:

- Recreational boats less than 16 feet in length.
- Boats participating in organized events such as races, regattas, or marine parades.
- Open sailboats less than 26 feet in length not equipped with propulsion machinery.
- Manually propelled boats.

Pyrotechnic Devices

Pyrotechnic Visual Distress Signals must be Coast Guard Approved, in serviceable condition, and readily accessible. They are marked with a date showing the service life, which must not have expired. Launchers manufactured before January 1, 1981, intended for use with approved signals, are not required to be Coast Guard Approved. If pyrotechnic devices are selected, a minimum of three are required. That is, three signals for day use and three signals for night. Some pyrotechnic signals meet both day and night use requirements. Pyrotechnic devices should be stored in a cool, dry location. A watertight container painted red or orange and prominently marked "DISTRESS SIGNALS" is recommended.

U.S.C.G. Approved Pyrotechnic Visual Distress Signals and associated devices include:

- Pyrotechnic red flares, hand-held or aerial.
- Pyrotechnic orange smoke, hand-held or floating.
- Launchers for aerial red meteors or parachute flares.

Non-Pyrotechnic Devices

Non-Pyrotechnic Visual Distress Signals must be in serviceable condition, readily accessible, and certified by the manufacturer as complying with USCG requirements. They include:

- Orange distress flag.
- Electric distress light.

The distress flag is a day signal only. It must be at least 3 × 3 feet with a black square and ball on an orange background. It is most distinctive when attached and waved on a paddle, boathook, or flown from a mast.

The electric distress light is accepted for night use only and must automatically flash the international SOS distress signal (...— — —...)

Under Inland Navigation Rules, a high intensity white light flashing at regular intervals from 50-70 times per minute is considered a distress signal.

Regulations prohibit display of visual distress signals on the water under any circumstances except when assistance is required to prevent immediate or potential danger to persons on board a vessel.

All distress signals have distinct advantages and disadvantages. No single device is ideal under all conditions or suitable for all purposes. Pyrotechnics are universally recognized as excellent distress signals. However, there is potential for injury and property damage if not properly handled. These devices produce a very hot flame and the residue can cause burns and ignite flammable material.

Pistol launched and hand-held parachute flares and meteors have many characteristics of a firearm and must be handled with caution. In some states they are considered a firearm and prohibited from use.

The following illustrates the variety and combination of devices which can be carried in order to meet the requirements:

- Three hand-held red flares (day and night).
- One hand-held red flare and two parachute flares (day and night).
- One hand-held orange smoke signal, two floating orange smoke signals (day) and one electric distress light (night only).

Red Flare
(hand held/day and night)

Parachute Flare
(day and night)

Orange Smoke Signal
(hand held/day only)

Floating Orange Smoke Signal
(day only)

Red Meteor
(day and night)

Orange Flag
(day only)

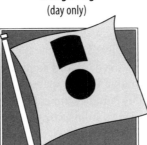

Arm Signals

Electric Distress Signals
(night only)

All boaters should be able to signal for help. For the CME, boaters must have current dated U.S.C.G. Approved day and night signals for all boats operating on coastal and open bodies of water. The Auxiliary also requires some method of emergency signals for inland water. This may be a signal flag for day and a flashlight for night.

Fire Extinguishers

Coast Guard Approved fire extinguishers are required on certain boats. Extinguishers are classified by a letter and number symbol. The letter indicates the type fire the unit is designed to extinguish (Type B for example are designed to extinguish flammable liquids such as gasoline, oil and grease fires). The number indicates the relative size of the extinguisher (minimum extinguishing agent weight).

Coast Guard Approved extinguishers are hand-portable, either B-I or B-II classification and have a specific marine type mounting bracket. It is recommended the extinguishers be mounted in a readily accessible position.

	Foam	Dry CO_2	Chemical	Halon
Classes	(Gals)	(LBS)	(LBS)	(LBS)
B-I	1.25	4	2	2.5
B-II	2.5	15	10	10

Fire extinguishers are required if any one or more of the following conditions exist:

- Inboard engines.
- Closed compartments and compartments under seats where portable fuel tanks may be stored.
- Double bottoms not sealed to the hull or which are not completely filled with flotation materials.
- Closed living spaces.
- Closed stowage compartments in which combustible or flammable materials are stored.
- Permanently installed fuel tanks. Fuel tanks secured so they cannot be moved in case of fire or other emergency are considered permanently installed. There are no gallon capacity limits to determine if a fuel tank is portable. If the weight of a fuel tank is such that persons on board cannot move it, the Coast Guard considers it permanently installed.

Inspect extinguishers monthly to make sure that:

- Seals & tamper indicators are not broken or missing.

- Pressure gauges or indicators read in the operable range. (Note: CO_2 extinguishers do not have gauges.)
- There is no obvious physical damage, corrosion, leakage or clogged nozzles.

Minimum number of hand portable fire extinguishers required:

Vessel Length	No Fixed System	With Approved Fixed Systems
Less than 26'	1 B-I	0
26' to less than 40'	2 B-I or 1 B-II	1 B-I
40' to 65'	3 B-I or 1 B-II and 1 B-I	2 B-I or 1 B-II

Coast Guard Approved extinguishers are identified by the following marking on the label:

"Marine Type USCG Approved,
Size..., type:::, 162.028/.../", etc.

Fire Extinguishers

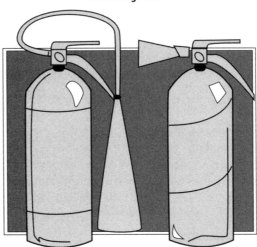

Weigh extinguishers annually to assure that the minimum weight is as stated on the extinguisher label.

For the CME, Halon units to be counted toward the minimum requirements must be inspected and tagged by a recognized authority within 6 months of the examination. The pressure gauge is not an accurate indicator that Halon extinguishers are full. The units should be checked regularly.

All portable extinguishers must be mounted in a readily accessible position. The Auxiliary requires at least 1 B-I handheld fire extinguisher on all motorboats and sailboats (without motors) 16 feet or longer.

Ventilation

All vessels built after April 25, 1940 which use gasoline for electrical generation, mechanical power or propulsion are required to be equipped with a ventilation system.

A natural ventilation system consists of at least two ventilator ducts, fitted with cowls or their equivalent:

- A minimum of one exhaust duct installed so as to extend from the open atmosphere to the lower portion of the bilge; and

- A minimum of one intake duct installed so as to extend to a point at least midway to the bilge or at least below the level of the carburetor air intake.

A powered ventilation system consists of one or more exhaust blowers. Each intake duct for an exhaust blower should be in the lower one-third of the compartment and above the normal accumulation of bilge water.

Between April 25, 1940 and July 31, 1978, the regulations covering ventilation systems applied to the owner/operator. *If your boat was built between April 25, 1940 and July 31, 1978, a natural ventilation system is required for all engine and fuel tank compartments, and other spaces to which explosive or flammable gases and vapors for these compartments may flow, except compartments which are open to the atmosphere.* There was no requirement for a powered ventilation system; however, some boats were equipped with a blower.

The Coast Guard Ventilation Standard, a manufacturer requirement, applies to all boats built on or after August 1, 1980. Some builders began manufacturing boats in compliance with the Ventilation Standard as early as August 1978. If your boat was built on or after August 1, 1978 it might have been equipped with either (1) a natural ventilation system, or (2) both a natural ventilation system and a powered ventilation system. If your boat bears a label containing the words, "This boat complies with U.S. Coast Guard safety standards," etc., you can assume that the design of your boat's ventilation system meets applicable regulations.

Boats built after August 1, 1980 which comply with the Coast Guard Ventilation Standard must display at each ignition switch, a label which contains the following information:

Warning

- Gasoline vapors can explode. Before starting engine operate blower for at least 4 minutes and check engine compartment bilge for gasoline vapors.

All owners are responsible for keeping their boats' ventilation systems in operating condition. This means making sure openings are free of obstructions, ducts are not blocked or torn, blowers are operating properly and worn out components are replaced with equivalent marine type equipment.

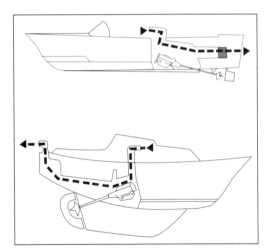

For the CME, all blower motors installed in exhaust ducts must be in working condition regardless of the date of manufacture.

Backfire Flame Control

Gasoline engines installed in a vessel after April 25, 1940, except outboard motors, must be equipped with an acceptable means of backfire flame control. The device must be suitably attached to the air intake with a flametight connection and is required to be Coast Guard Approved or comply with SAE J-1928 or UL 1111 standards and marked accordingly.

Flame Arrester

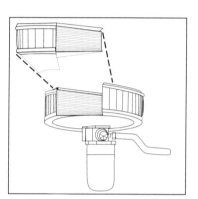

Sound Producing Devices

The navigation rules require sound signals to be made under certain circumstances. Meeting, crossing and overtaking situations described in the Navigation Rules section are examples of when sound signals are required. Recreational vessels are also required to sound fog signals during periods of reduced visibility. Therefore, you must have some means of making an efficient sound signal, although regulations do not specifically require vessels less than 12 meters to carry a whistle, horn or bell. *Vessels 12 meters or more in length are required to carry on board a power whistle or power horn and a bell.*

Signaling Devices

For the CME, the Auxiliary requires some type of horn or whistle capable of a 4 second blast audible for 1/2 mile for all boats. (Athletic whistles are not acceptable on boats over 12 meters.)

Blank Watercraft Survey

Date: _____

Pursuant to the request of _____, the Undersigned Surveyor did, on _____ 1996, hold a Condition and Valuation Survey for insurance purposes on the Motor Yacht _____, as she lay afloat moored behind the residence at _____.

NAME	**OFFICIAL NUMBER**

DIMENSIONS   **TONNAGES**

Length–   Gross–

Breadth–   Net–

Depth–

OWNERS   **DOCUMENTED SERVICE**

DATE AND PLACE OF CONSTRUCTION   **DATE LAST DRYDOCKED**

CAPACITIES   **INTENDED SERVICE**

Fuel oil—

Fresh water—

GENERAL DESCRIPTION

CONSTRUCTION

NAVIGATION/COMMUNICATION EQUIPMENT

MAIN ENGINE CONTROL AND MONITORING

STEERING SYSTEM

GALLEY/ACCOMMODATION/MISCELLANEOUS EQUIPMENT

SANITARY FACILITIES/FRESH WATER SYSTEM

MAIN ENGINE

ELECTRICAL SYSTEM

FUEL SYSTEM

BILGE PUMPING SYSTEM

GROUND TACKLE AND FITTINGS

FIREFIGHTING EQUIPMENT

LIFE-SAVING EQUIPMENT

RISK

SURVEYOR'S NOTES

GENERAL CONDITION

ESTIMATED VALUES

Fair Market—$

Replacement—$

RECOMMENDATIONS

As far as may be ascertained from a general examination of the subject vessel, without removals, opening up to expose parts ordinarily
concealed and taking drillings to ascertain thickness of structural
members, testing for tightness or opening up the machinery, it is
the opinion of the Undersigned that the hull, machinery and equipment of the subject vessel appear to be in satisfactory condition
for operation as well as for proposed intended service, subject to
completion of or compliance with the recommendations made by the
Attending Surveyor.

Further, no determination of inherent structural integrity or stability has been made and no opinion is expressed in this respect.

This report is made, signed and submitted without prejudice to whom
it may concern.

Respectfully,

_____

Enclosures: Photographs

Appendix 11-D

Completed Watercraft Survey—Sample

13 June 1996

Pursuant to the request of Joe Underwriter, the Undersigned Surveyor did, on 12 June 1996, hold a Condition and Valuation Survey for insurance purposes on the Motor Yacht "SS Institute," as she lay afloat moored behind the residence at 720 Providence Road, Malvern, PA.

NAME	OFFICIAL NUMBER
SS Institute	6442100

DIMENSIONS	TONNAGES
Length—45.6'	Gross—16
Breadth—13.0'	Net—11
Depth—4.5'	

OWNERS	DOCUMENTED SERVICE
Maria Sanchez	Pleasure
720 Providence Rd.	
Malvern, PA	

DATE AND PLACE OF CONSTRUCTION	DATE LAST DRYDOCKED
1947	May 1995
Susan, VA	

CAPACITIES	INTENDED SERVICE
Fuel oil—200 gallons	Bays and Rivers
Fresh water—50 gallons	

GENERAL DESCRIPTION

The vessel is a wooden former oyster watch boat, converted to a motor yacht, with a rake stem, straight sides, and a round stern. It is powered by a single diesel engine driving a marine reduction reverse gear turning a single shaft and propeller. The vessel has a deck-raised forecastle cabin and step up raised pilothouse, with engine room aft of the pilothouse. Below the main deck are marine sanitary facilities and the galley.

CONSTRUCTION

The vessel is a Chesapeake Bay style oyster watch boat, with Carvel 1 1/2" yellow pine side shell planks and 2 1/2" yellow pine transverse bottom shell planks. Side shell frames are 3 1/2" x 4" yellow pine. The decks are 2 1/2" x 2 1/2" fir planks.

NAVIGATION/COMMUNICATION EQUIPMENT

(1) Furuno, Model 1721 Radar.

(1) Icom, IC-M55 VHF FM Radio.

(1) Landmark Depth Sounder, Model MK272.

(1) 4", Dirigo Magnetic Compass.

(1) Sony, AM/FM Radio/Tape Player, with four Bose, Model 151, Speakers.

(1) 6" bell.

(1) Double trumpet air horn.

(1) Perko, 6" searchlight.

Complete set of navigation lights and anchor light.

MAIN ENGINE CONTROL AND MONITORING

(1) Morse throttle and clutch controls.

(1) Engine monitoring panel with engine oil pressure, engine water temperature, and clutch oil pressure gauges, and battery ampere meter.

(1) Push button engine start switch and manual push shutdown cable.

STEERING SYSTEM

(1) Spoked wood steering wheel. Steering is mechanical rope and pulley system from the pilothouse to the steering quadrant.

(1) Captain's chair and mate's bench at the helm.

GALLEY/ACCOMMODATION/MISCELLANEOUS EQUIPMENT

(1) 5" turbine ventilation fan provides ventilation to the forward cabin.

GALLEY/ACCOMMODATION/MISCELLANEOUS EQUIPMENT (continued)

(2) Bunks located aft end of the pilothouse.

(1) 2″ ship's clock located in the pilothouse.

(1) 2″ barometer located in the pilothouse.

(1) Quasar microwave oven in the galley.

The main salon has bench seats on the port and starboard sides. An inclined ladder provides access to the main deck.

A vinyl canopy with stainless steel stanchions and supports is installed from forward of the pilothouse, for the breadth of the vessel and aft to the stern.

A wooden table with folding leaves is mounted on the centerline on the aft deck. Deck lounge chairs are provided on the aft deck.

SANITARY FACILITIES/FRESH WATER SYSTEM

A marine toilet is located in the forecastle with a sink and mirror.

A 50-gallon fresh water tank is filled from the top of the tank, and water pressure is provided by a Par, Model 36970-1000, electric motor driven pump.

MAIN ENGINE

A single General Motors, Model 6-71, diesel engine is fitted with a General Motors, 2.0:1 ratio reduction reverse gear, which drives a 1 3/4″ stainless steel shaft and 28″ x 24″ four blade bronze propeller. Engine is electric start and fresh water heat exchanger cooled.

ELECTRICAL SYSTEM

(2) 12 volt D.C. batteries provide starting power for the main engine.

(1) 55 amp alternator is belt driven off the main engine.

(1) Dayton, 6 volt automatic battery charger.

(1) Buell, electric motor driven air compressor, with air receiver tank, relief valve, and gauge.

ELECTRICAL SYSTEM (Continued)

A 12 volt DC electrical system is protected by circuit breakers, and a 120 volt AC shore power system is protected by circuit breakers.

FUEL SYSTEM

(1) Port and starboard 100-gallon steel fuel tanks, which are ventilated and filled from the main deck. The tanks have 3/8" copper fuel lines with shut-off valves at the tanks and flexible hoses to the primary fuel filters and secondary filters on the engine.

The engine/fuel tank space below the main deck is vented with intake and outlet cowl type vents on the port and starboard sides of the main deck.

BILGE PUMPING SYSTEM

A single belt driven Jabsco, 1 1/2" bilge pump is located in the engine room.

A 10-gallon-per-minute hand bilge pump provides back up.

GROUND TACKLE AND FITTINGS

(1) 35 lb. stockless anchor rigged with 3/8" riding chain and 200' of 5/8" nylon anchor rope.

(1) Port and starboard 4" x 4" single wood bitt with steel pin on the bow and stern with chocks on the bulwarks rail.

FIREFIGHTING EQUIPMENT

(2) BI dry chemical fire extinguishers.

(1) BII dry chemical fire extinguisher.

LIFE-SAVING EQUIPMENT

(10) Type I, U.S. Coast Guard Approved life preservers with retro-reflective tape.

LIFE-SAVING EQUIPMENT (Continued)

(16) Type II, U.S. Coast Guard Approved buoyant vests.

(1) Type IV, U.S. Coast Guard Approved buoyant cushion.

(2) Type IV, 24" ring buoys.

(1) Orion, distress signal kit, with very signal pistol, three red signal flares, and three hand-held red and one hand-held orange smoke flares.

(1) Medical Sea Pak, first-aid kit.

RISK

Satisfactory, upon completion of recommendations, proper care, maintenance, and prudent operation.

SURVEYOR'S NOTES

1.) The vessel was recently hauled out of the water at SEPTA Railway and painted. The vessel is hauled out every year for cleaning, painting, maintenance, and repairs.

2.) The vessel has been undergoing, for the past three years, an extensive maintenance and restoration project. The decks were repaired, sealed, and treated. The addition of more ventilation ducts at the aft end of the lazarette has improved the overall condition within the hull. The areas under the aft deck have been cleaned and treated. The deck edge covering board on each side was being removed in stages to permit inspection, repairs, and maintenance to the heads of the frames and ends of the deck beams.

3.) The vessel's overall appearance and general condition have improved significantly since the survey conducted in May 1991.

GENERAL CONDITION

The vessel is in very good condition considering her age. The housekeeping, preservation, and maintenance have been excellent. The engine compartment is clean and free of oil and debris. There are no electrical jury rigs. The owner has an ongoing maintenance and repair program for full restoration of the vessel.

ESTIMATED VALUES

Fair Market—$35,000.00

Replacement—$150,000.00 based on a fiberglass hull of comparable size.

RECOMMENDATIONS

1.) Provide and install lagging over the exhaust pipe aft of the manifold.

2.) Install suitable chocks to hold the starting batteries in place.

As far as may be ascertained from a general examination of the subject vessel, without removals, opening up to expose parts ordinarily concealed and taking drillings to ascertain thickness of structural members, testing for tightness or opening up the machinery, it is the opinion of the Undersigned that the hull, machinery and equipment of the subject vessel appear to be in satisfactory condition for operation as well as for proposed intended service, subject to completion of or compliance with the recommendations made by the Attending Surveyor.

Further, no determination of inherent structural integrity or stability has been made and no opinion is expressed in this respect.

This report is made, signed and submitted without prejudice to whom it may concern.

Respectfully,

Happy Surveyors, Inc.

Enclosures: Photographs

Appendix 12-A

Sample Miscellaneous Vehicle Applications

Motor Home and Truck Camper Insurance Policy

Named
Insured _____

Phone
Number _____

| Last | First | Middle |

Residence
Address _____

| Street | City | County | State | Zip |

Where
Garaged? Same as Above ☐   Other _____

Mortgagee _____

| Name | Address |

DESCRIPTION OF VEHICLE

YEAR	LENGTH	HORSEPOWER	MAKE	MODEL	SERIAL NO.	PURCHASE PRICE	DATE PURCH'D	NEW ☐ USED ☐

CAMPER BODY	YEAR	MAKE	MODEL	IDENTIFICATION NO.	CHASSIS MOUNTED ☐ SLIDE-IN ☐	% USE	PURCHASE PRICE	DATE PURCHASED

COVERAGES

BODILY INJURY AND PROPERTY DAMAGE LIABILITY

Limits: (check box) $15/30/10 ☐ | $25/50/15 ☐ | $50/100/25 ☐ | $100/300/50 ☐

MEDICAL PAYMENTS

Limits: (check box) $500 ☐ | $750 ☐ | $1,000 ☐ | $2,000 ☐

UNINSURED MOTORISTS COVERAGE, LIMITS $10,000/20,000 (See detailed explanation on reverse)

    Required by law to be included with liability policies, unless rejected in writing. If desired, include additional premium of $

    If NOT desired, sign rejection below.

    I have read and understand the explanation of uninsured motorists coverage and I hereby specifically reject the coverage.

_____   _____

          Date   Signature of Insured

PHYSICAL DAMAGE COVERAGES

Coverage	Deductible	Purchase Price or Actual Cash Value
Comprehensive	$ 25	$ _____
Collision	$ 50	$ _____
	$100	$ _____
	$250	$ _____

PERSONAL EFFECTS COVERAGE

                              ACV
                              Limit

    Broad form (Excludes Theft) $ _____ (Min. Prem. $5.00)

    Comprehensive form (Includes Theft) $ _____ (Min. Prem. $7.50)

RENTAL ENDORSEMENT SURCHARGE If insured unit will occasionally be rented to others, add surcharge of 50% of all above premiums except uninsured motorists and personal effects.

Check intended use of vehicle: Private Pleasure ☐, Occasional Rental (not commercial) ☐

DRIVERS NAMES:	% USE	OCCUPATION	BIRTH DATE	SEX	MARRIED YES	MARRIED NO	DRIVERS LICENSE NO.	YEARS LICENSED

Driving records past 3 years for all drivers (Explain all YES answers below)

Accidents? ☐ YES ☐ NO   Violations? ☐ YES ☐ NO

License suspensions? ☐ YES ☐ NO   Insurance Cancellations? ☐ YES ☐ NO

SR 22 required? ☐ YES ☐ NO   Case Number _____

DRIVING RECORD EXPLANATIONS AND SURCHARGES
(Please give driver name with explanation on reverse side)

AGENT'S ACC'T # _____   Agent's Name _____   TOTAL PREMIUM _____

I hereby declare to the best of my knowledge and belief that all of the statements contained in this application are true and that these statements are offered as an inducement to the company to issue the policy for which I am applying.

Signature of Applicant _____

Motorcycle Insurance Application

APPLICANT (NAME INSURED)		PLEASE PRINT		OCCUPATION & EMPLOYER		
(LAST NAME)	(FIRST NAME)		(MIDDLE INITIAL)			

STREET ADDRESS	CITY	COUNTY	ZIP CODE	POLICY TERM	EFFECTIVE DATE		
				❏ 12 Months	MO.	DAY	YEAR
				❏ 6 Months			

DESCRIPTION OF MOTORCYCLE			SERIAL NUMBER	DISPLACEMENT IN CC'S	PURCHASE PRICE INCLUCING STANDARD FACTORY EQUIPMENT OR ACTUAL CASH VALUE ON USED CYCLE	DATE PURCHASED			
YEAR	MAKE	MODEL				MO.	DAY	YEAR	❏ NEW ❏ USED

Loss Payee Name
Address
City & State _____ Zip _____

DEALER FROM WHOM CYCLE WAS PURCHASED
Name
Address

DRIVER INFORMATION Complete for principal operator and any other driver

NAME OF PERSON EXACTLY AS SHOWN ON LICENSE	AGE	BIRTH DATE	MARITAL STATUS	ANY CHARGEABLE MOTORCYCLE ACCIDENTS OR INSURANCE CLAIMS PAST 12 MOS.	HAVE YOU BEEN PRINCIPAL OPERATOR OF A MOTORCYCLE	OPERATOR'S LICENSE NO.
Principal Operator				❏ YES ❏ NO	UNDER 1 YEAR ❏ OVER 1 YEAR ❏	
Other Operators of this motorcycle						
				❏ YES ❏ NO	UNDER 1 YEAR ❏ OVER 1 YEAR ❏	
				❏ YES ❏ NO	UNDER 1 YEAR ❏ OVER 1 YEAR ❏	

When motorcycle has other than standard Factory Equipment, list below Custom Parts or Accessories you wish covered in the package policy and add 15% of their value (round to nearest dollar) in the appropriate section of the premium column.

ITEM	VALUE
_____	$ _____
_____	$ _____
_____	$ _____
_____	$ _____
	$ _____
Total Value	$ _____
	$ _____ × .15

Custom Parts
and Accessories
Premium $ _____

Indicate here the coverages desired.

COVERAGES DESIRED	PREMIUMS
❏ LIABILITY ONLY .... $ _____	
❏ PACKAGE POLICY—New & Current Year Models .... $ _____	
Used Models .... $ _____	

ADDITIONAL COVERAGES AVAILABLE

❏ Custom Parts & Accessories .... $ _____	
❏ SR 22 Filing.. $ _____	
❏ Extended Forks—Add 50% surcharge to each coverage written .... $ _____	
❏ Total of Applicable Discounts .... % $ _____	
TOTAL PREMIUM $ _____	

❏ A.M.
❏ P.M.

DATE & TIME OF APPLICATION: _____ , 19 _____

PRODUCER _____

AGENT LICENSE NO._____ No coverage bound until application received and accepted by General Agent.

I hereby apply to Company for a policy of insurance as set forth above on the basis of the statements contained herein. I agree that such policy shall be null and void if such information is false, or misleading, or would materially affect acceptance of the risk by Company.

PREVIOUS INSURANCE CARRIER

DATE   SIGNATURE OF APPLICANT (NAME INSURED) X

As part of our underwriting procedure, a routine inquiry may be made which will provide applicable information concerning character, general reputation, personal characteristics and mode of living. Upon written request, additional information as to the nature and scope of the report, if one is made, will be provided.

Off-the-road Vehicles (Unlicensed)
Insurance Application

EFFECTIVE DATE _____ 19 _____

(POLICY PERIOD: 12 months from 12:01 AM on above date)

APPLICANT'S NAME	BIRTH DATE	PRODUCER'S NAME
ADDRESS	Producer No.	ADDRESS
CITY, STATE	Prior Policy No.	CITY, STATE

DESCRIPTION OF VEHICLE(S)

PLEASE CHECK TYPE OF VEHICLE TO BE INSURED: ❏ MINI BIKE   ❏ GOLF CART   ❏ TRAIL BIKE
❏ ALL TERRAIN VEHICLE   ❏ OTHER _____

	YEAR	MANUFACTURER & MODEL	SERIAL NO.	H.P.	MO. & YR. PURCHASED	COST
Vehicle 1						$
Equipment (itemize)						$
Vehicle 2						$
Equipment (itemize)						$
Trailer						$

LIENHOLDER: NAME _____   ADDRESS _____

UNDERWRITING INFORMATION:

- Is vehicle(s) to be rented, leased or used for racing?   ❏ No   ❏ Yes, Explain _____
- Is any operator physically impaired?   ❏ No   ❏ Yes, Explain _____
- Any accidents or violations in last three (3) years?   ❏ No   ❏ Yes, Explain _____
- Names and ages of other operators _____

PROGRAMS   ❏ ANNUAL POLICY   ❏ 6 MONTH LAY-UP   ❏ 4 MONTH LAY-UP   ❏ OTHER _____

Policy is written for a full one year with Liability and Collision suspended from _____ to _____ (where applicable)

COVERAGES	LIMITS OF LIABILITY		PREMIUMS
PACKAGE PROGRAM			
PHYSICAL DAMAGE	Actual cash value including equipment less $50 deductible		
VEHICLE 1	$		$
VEHICLE 2	$		$
LIABILITY	$,000 per occurrence		INCLUDED
PHYSICAL DAMAGE—TRAILER	Actual cash value including equipment less $50 deductible		$
LIABILITY ONLY	$,000 per occurrence	VEHICLE 1	$
		VEHICLE 2	$
OPTIONAL COVERAGES		VEHICLE 1	$
		VEHICLE 2	$
		VEHICLE 1	$
		VEHICLE 2	$
ENDORSEMENTS		TOTAL	$
		Less Multi-Unit Discount *(5% of Total to nearest dollar)*	$
		TOTAL PREMIUM	$

Snowmobile Insurance Application

DATE OF APPLICATION _____

APPLICANT'S NAME	Birth Date	Producer No.	PRODUCER'S NAME
ADDRESS (STREET)		Prior Policy No.	ADDRESS
CITY, STATE AND ZIP CODE			CITY, STATE AND ZIP CODE

POLICY EFFECTIVE DATE: _____ 19 _____ (POLICY IN FORCE FOR 12 FULL MONTHS WITH COVERAGE IN EFFECT AS SHOWN BELOW)

❒ PROGRAM I
- LIABILITY — In effect from September 1 to June 1
- COLLISION

❒ PROGRAM II
- COMPREHENSIVE — Full term (*Includes Fire & Theft*)
- LIABILITY — In effect from September 15 to May 15
- COLLISION

❒ PROGRAM III
- COMPREHENSIVE — Full term (*Includes Fire & Theft*)
- LIABILITY — In effect from October 15 to April 15
- COLLISION

❒ PROGRAM IV
- COMPREHENSIVE — Full term (*Includes Fire & Theft*)
- LIABILITY COVERAGES ONLY
  - ❒ 9 months—Coverage suspended from June 1 to September 1
  - ❒ 8 months—Coverage suspended from May 15 to September 15
  - ❒ 6 months—Coverage suspended from April 15 to October 15

LIENHOLDER: _____

ADDRESS: _____

	COVERAGES	LIMITS OF LIABILITY		PREMIUM	
SECTION I	PHYSICAL DAMAGE (*ALL RISK*)—ACTUAL CASH VALUE INCLUDING EQUIPMENT LESS $50 DEDUCTIBLE				
	VEHICLE 1	$		$	
	VEHICLE 2	$		$	
	TRAILER(S)	$		$	

	COVERAGES	LIMITS OF LIABILITY		PREMIUM	
SECTION II	LIABILITY—SINGLE LIMIT COVERAGE	$,000. per occurrence		Vehicle 1	$
				Vehicle 2	$
*optional UMC	UNINSURED MOTORIST COVERAGE—(*FAMILY PROTECTION*)	$,000. per person $,000. per accident		Vehicle 1	$
				Vehicle 2	$
	*Follow the Uninsured Motorist Coverage Insurance Statutes of the applicant's state of residence.			TOTAL	$

ENDORSEMENTS	Less Multi-Unit Discount (5 % of Total to nearest dollar)	$
	TOTAL POLICY PREMIUM	$

DESCRIPTION OF VEHICLE(S)

	Year	Manufacturer & Model	Serial No.	H.P.	Month & Year Purchased	Cost
Vehicle 1					/	$
Equipment (*itemize*)						$
Vehicle 2					/	$
Equipment (*itemize*)						$
Trailer 1					/	$
Trailer 2					/	$

UNDERWRITING INFORMATION

1. Is vehicle(s) to be rented, leased or used for racing? ❒ No ❒ Yes, Explain _____
2. Is any operator physically impaired? ❒ No ❒ Yes, Explain _____
3. Any accidents or violations in last three (3) years? ❒ No ❒ Yes, Explain _____